THE CON

A New and S

'The F

Li Fu Chen, Chinese scholar, engineer and politician,
lives in Taiwan

THE CONFUCIAN WAY

A New and Systematic Study of

'The Four Books'

Li Fu Chen

Translated from the Chinese by
Shih Shun Liu

Foreword by Joseph Needham

KPI

LONDON AND NEW YORK

First published in 1986 by KPI Ltd
This edition published in 1987 by KPI Ltd,
11 New Fetter Lane, London EC4P 4EE

Distributed by
Routledge & Kegan Paul, Associated Book Publishers (UK) Ltd
11 New Fetter Lane, London EC4P 4EE

Methuen Inc, Routledge & Kegan Paul
29 West 35th Street, New York, NY10001, USA

Printed in Great Britain by
T. J. Press (Padstow) Ltd,
Padstow, Cornwall

ISBN 0-7103-0250-9 (paperback)
ISBN 0-7103-01715 (cased)

This edition is dedicated
with many thanks to
Mr. Henry H. H. Yong and
Colonel Mark P. Hsu, CAF
(retired) who helped to
bring this book
to the west.

Foreword

It is a great pleasure and honour for me to be asked to contribute a foreword for the British edition of Ch'en Li-Fu's "The Confucian Way", for it is indeed an excellent exposition of those doctrines which have served the Chinese people so well for two thousand five hundred years. When in 1942, as a comparatively young man, I became Scientific Counsellor at the British Embassy in Chungking, Dr. Ch'en Li-Fu was no less than Minister of Education in the Chinese government. He befriended me most kindly, and in due course gave me sets of the Dynastic Histories of the two Han dynasties (*Ch'ien Han Shu* and *Hou Han Shu*) printed in Szechuan with large characters; and these we have used ever since in the East Asian History of Science Library in Cambridge.

There can be no doubt that one of the most enlightening of experiences for anyone brought up in the tradition of Israel, Christianity and Islam, a tradition which accepts the idea of a transcendent creator God, is to spend some years among a people who have never needed this conception, and nevertheless have got on no worse than others over the centuries. Master K'ung said that Heaven (*T'ien*) would justify his words, and the Taoists, headed by Lao Tzu, spoke of the *Tao*, the Order of Nature, running through all things; so that in both these ways of looking at the world, God was impersonal and immanent. It is very salutary for any Westerner or Middle Easterner to realise that his or her own tradition of interpreting the universe is not the only one which all peoples have adopted, and such a realisation has an extremely liberating effect.

Perhaps Confucius (Master K'ung) was greatest as an educationalist, for he averred that every young man who could profit from education ought to have it, irrespective of rank or birth. This conviction he never gave up, even though he lived in a feudal age, surrounded by arbitrary princes who could have had him tortured to death with as little compunction a man might crush a fly. It was not his only grand subversive doctrine either, for in the "rectification of names" (*chêng ming*) he insisted that a spade should be called a spade, no matter how powerful were the influences which wanted it called a shovel. I remember also from my early years in China meeting another friend Lo Chung-Shu, who told me that his two given names, *Chung*, loyalty and conscientiousness, and *Shu*, forgiveness and understanding, summed up all the essence of Confucianism. But I must not trespass too far on the subjects so clearly expounded in this book.

There was another reason why I was fortunate in the timing of my first stay in China. The Chinese were being very hard-pressed by the imperialist-fascist enemy, and had no time to worry about what a foreigner was doing—thus I was able to bend my steps into many a deserted temple. In that way I learnt how extremely numinous the Confucian Temples (*Wên Miao*) could be, with the ancient trees in the courtyard, the semi-circular pond and the library building; while in the main hall there was never any image, only an altar with candles and a great inscription above which said "The perfumed throne of the Sage, the Teacher of Ten Thousand Generations" (*K'ung Tzu, Wan Shih chih Hsiang Wei*). The only clergy were the local officials, who came once a year to celebrate the sage's birthday; and indeed it was his belief in education which made him for two millennia the patron saint of the bureaucratic mandarinate. Whether or not you call Confucianism a religion depends on your definition of the word; if, as I would maintain, this is primarily concerned with the "sense of the holy", then Master K'ung certainly founded a religion.

I reckon that I have always been much more sympathetic to socialism than Ch'en Li-Fu. But how to get "socialism with a human face"? This is what, like George Orwell, I have always wanted, and I have all my life been essentially a Christian Socialist. Some indications of Master K'ung's sociology can be obtained from pp.412 ff. of the present book, but it is not much use trying to trace back such modern conceptions into the sayings of ancient people. Of course, his exalted doctrines were *de facto* compatible with gross exploitation and class oppression for many centuries, but that is not an argument against them as such today. Nowhere on earth has there ever been a truly just and enlightened society; it is the goal we are always working towards, and the ideas of Master K'ung, together with those of all the great prophets, priests, sages and saints of every generation give us light upon the way.

Lastly, one may ask whether Confucianism helped or hindered the development of the sciences and the technologies in China. The answer must be both. On the one hand, it helped because of its rationalism and its thoroughgoing scepticism; on the other it deprecated too much study of non-human, non-social, Nature. Yet one of the phrases from the Confucian books, ''the investigation of things is the beginning of wisdom'' (*chih chih tsai ko wu*) reverberated down through the ages, becoming the signal and watchword of all Chinese scientists and naturalists down to our own times. Confucianism did not flee the world, as Buddhism wanted to do, and its insights were not, like the Tao, essentially mystical and inscrutable; the only trouble was that its doctrines were essentially those of personal cultivation and social organisation, not outward-looking towards Nature as such. The Taoists felt in their bones that until we knew more about non-human Nature, human society could not be perfectly arranged or governed; and they may well have been right, but all the same Confucion doctrines deserve our warmest homage. Hence my homage to this present book, and its learned author.

Joseph Needham
Cambridge

Preface

When I was a schoolboy, my teacher once had me write on "The Way to Enrich the Country." I based my composition on the seventh of the "nine standard rules for the government of the empire and its states," set down in the *Doctrine of the Mean*. And so I enlarged on the principle that "by encouraging the enterprise of all classes of artisans, his (the ruler's) resources for expenditure are rendered ample." The essay brought high praise from my teacher. But little did I realize that the idea I had in mind at that time would become the controlling factor in my life's ambition—which to this day has remained unfulfilled.

Shortly after the successful Chinese Revolution in 1911, my uncle, Ying-shih, who was one of the Founding Fathers of the Republic of China, decided to move our family to Shanghai. While there I attended the Nanyang College of Railroad Engineering and Mining. During summer vacations, through a Y. M. C. A. program, I was able to visit a number of factories. These visits strengthened my early belief that the road to the country's enrichment did indeed lie in industrial development. Naturally, I was deeply impressed by the farsightedness of Confucius.

Later I entered the School of Mining at the Peiyang University in Tientsin. After graduation I came to the United States to attend the University of Pittsburgh, where I chose for my master's thesis: "The Application of Mechanical and Electrical Devices to the Coal Mines of China." I joined John L. Lewis' United Mine Workers and worked for more than a year in coal mines of the Pittsburgh-Scranton region.

Before I returned to China, I read and admired Dr. Sun Yatsen's "Project for National Reconstruction." I especially agreed wholeheartedly with his "Industrial Plan." This accounted for my decision to join the Kuomintang at its main branch in San Francisco.

After I set foot once more in my native land, I decided to accept the invitation of Mr. Ch'ien Hsin-chih of the Chung-hsing Coal Mining Company to serve as one of his engineers. However, at about the same time, I received an unexpected telegram from President Chiang Kai-shek of the Whampoa Military Academy.

He asked me to go to Canton immediately. On my arrival he strongly urged me to become a secretary of the academy. I felt obliged to accept his offer, even though it meant giving up my original plan of embarking on an engineering career. So instead of becoming a working engineer, I became an official of a military institution. Later, during the Northern Expedition I was transferred to the party. When the war of resistance against Japan broke out, I was transferred once again to a new field of activity; this time it was the political sphere.

All these things happened more or less against my will. Since I had no opportunity to work in engineering, my specialty, I did not have a keen interest in my work; consequently, I had little success in it.

By the time I first undertook party work, the purge had started. Of prime importance, of course, was the theoretical struggle taking place. Like many other party leaders, I started making propaganda speeches on the "Three Principles of the People" by Dr. Sun Yatsen. But as I talked with young students in one interview after another, I began to realize that the underlying cause for the infiltration of fallacious theories was a drastic loss of national self-confidence. With this discovery, I determined to put all the emphasis at my command on the original culture of our country. As I proceeded along this line, I realized that the unique feature of our culture was the discovery of the principles of human existence—those principles which enabled millions of people to form one single family and maintain a glorious history through more than 5,000 years.

Arrayed against these concepts were the theories of Communism— alien in origin and directly opposed to our traditional thinking. They took hatred as their starting point and used cruelty and falsehood as means to their ends. They relied on violence, advocated struggle, emphasized the material and sought to destroy the fabric of humanity. They were diametrically opposed to the principles of Confucianism, whose starting point was benevolence and love. Confucian thought took sincerity as the basis of self-cultivation; it stressed morality and advocated the love of peace, good faith, justice, honesty and virtue, along with the Doctrine of the Mean.

In all my speeches I strove to get this message across to my audiences, which totaled more than 100,000 in a single year. I tried to awaken a national consciousness in my listeners. And with some success, for more than 10,000 young Communists were won over to our side. With their past errors forgiven, they were given a chance to re-orient themselves.

I was so encouraged that I collected some of my addresses in a book and published them under the title *Vitalism* (Vol. 1). My central points were: (1) that life is composed of both spirit and matter, (2) that stress on either idealism or materialism alone would tip the scale out of balance, (3) that this one-sidedness was evident in Chinese culture, which had always tended to belittle materialism.

I also attempted to make clear that Dr. Sun Yatsen had carried on the Chinese philosophical tradition. His teachings were physiological in nature and therefore quite different from the pathology of Marxism. The Communists' concepts groaned when there was no sickness; they derived from self-deception as well as the deception of others, and were thus unsound.

Due to the pressure of my work, I could not find time to finish the book, and the second volume was never published. Later, however, I wrote *A Philosyphy of Life*, which followed the same line of thought.

No sooner was this book published than it gained a very wide circulation. This strongly confirmed my belief in the importance of national self-confidence. As time went on, the struggle between our party and the Communists became more acute both in theory and in action. As my elder brother, Kuo-fu, and I assumed leadership in party affairs, we became prime targets of the Communists. They called us all kinds of names—so-called "C.C." elements, diehards, reactionaries. They even charged us with being members of one of the Big Four families.

The name-calling was simple slander, totally without foundation. Yet so often and in so many places were these falsehoods repeated that many persons tended to believe them. For our part, we knew that since we were fighting for truth, opposition was inevitable. We determined not to yield, or even bend. After all, our aim was nothing less than to work out our national salvation; of this we were certain. With a clear conscience we refused to fear; nothing was going to deter us from our course.

At the beginning of the war of resistance against Japan, I was Acting Dean of the Central Institute of Politics. Later I became Minister of Education. In the past, institutions of higher learning had been situated mostly in coastal cities. Once these cities were occupied, however, the institutions had to be moved westward. The exodus was a mammoth task. The number of refugee faculty members and students totaled more than 100,000, and immediate relief was required by them. Since I received my appointment at this time of distress, I had to do my utmost to feed, clothe and otherwise take care of this ill-fated lot. A difficult, challenging, and in many ways a rewarding task.

But when it came to the content of our education, I could not help feeling that our system had not yet veered from the sphere-of-influence pattern common in what was formerly a sub-colony. Here the English, and there the German, system was adopted; other schools differed according to the nationality of those in charge, or according to the customs of foreign countries in which key officials had studied.

As for curriculum content, it was generally split off from the political and economic requirements of the country. Some institutions did not even have Chinese textbooks.

Agricultural schools are a case in point. More than 90 per-cent of our population is agricultural, and water conservation is as important to farming as systems of communication are to industry and commerce. Yet the Nanking Vocational School for River and Marine Engineering, the only one of its kind in China, had been discontinued. Studies in such areas as fertilizer, seeds, plant diseases and insect pests scarcely figured in the agricultural curriculum. And there was not a single school which specialized in the study and improvement of silk, tea, porcelain, *tung* oil and bristles, our export staples. The same was true of industrial products required for clothing, food, lodging and transportation.

Thus, to a great degree the poverty and weakness of the country were conditions of our own making.

As for discussion of the way a man should conduct himself, it was practically non-existent, mostly because it was regarded as inconsequential. While the Bible was held in high regard, our own classics could be burned as trash. I was apprehensive about this situation, for I believed this: To seek the enrichment and the strengthening of the country, it was vitally important to match up the content of its education with the country's requirements. In line with this idea, I brought forward a wartime educational program containing nine principles and seventeen items which was adopted by the People's Political Council and put into effect.

With reference to moral uplift, a separate training program was issued. It stressed "self-confidence and faith in the Way, self-government and the administration of government affairs, self-support and the support of others, self-defense and national defense." The goal was to form men who would have the ability to administer, educate, support and defend. At the same time, in line with the government's instructions, "propriety, righteousness, incorruptibility and the sense of shame" were held up as ideals to be shared by all schools. The program was designed to impress on students the importance of self-cultivation and a regard for humanity, with a view to the perfection of virtue and the completion of wisdom.

In addition, despite a shortage of funds, steps were taken to encourage academic research, acquire larger supplies of scientific instruments and equipment, procure exchange professors from abroad, and send students to other countries for higher studies.

However, my specialty was mining engineering, not educational administration. Education is a long-term undertaking. It demands adequate, timely preparations and the pursuit of its objectives with the greatest sincerity. Without these two requisites, how could we hope to "adjust the great invariable relations of mankind and establish the great fundamental virtues of humanity"? Since I could not decline the trust reposed in me, I had to review in depth those classics which in my youth I had studied but not thoroughly comprehended. Like a miner I had to dig for what was needed, in this instance, cultural treasures. Once I unearthed them, I could to the best of my ability pass them on to the younger generation. This I determined to do, in an effort to contribute toward the betterment of all mankind.

Therefore I took the opportunity afforded by my regular inspections to speak on our cultural heritage at the various schools. In these talks, my aim was to use the scientific method to explain the way of human conduct taught by the *Four Books*. Invariably the response of my audiences was very enthusiastic; I was deeply touched and inspired. After several years of lecturing and studying, I decided to rearrange the *Four Books* into a systematic work in order to provide students with the essential principles for human conduct in one compact volume.

Our old teaching method took advantage of youngsters' abilty to memorize. We had them learn by rote in their early years, feeling that later when their power of understanding was developed, they would recall and think over what they had acquired. The philosopher Chu Hsi of the Sung dynasty put it this way: "He (the student) will suddenly find himself possessed of a wide and far-reaching penetration. Then the qualities of things, whether external or internal, the subtle or the coarse, will all be apprehended, and the mind, in its entire substance and its relations to things, will be perfectly intelligent." But the complexity of the present-day school curriculum made this teaching method inappropriate.

Dr. Sun Yatsen taught the rising generation to rescue the essential moral wisdom and ability of our people by the scientific method and forge ahead to catch up with the material science of the West. His idea was to take what was best from other cultures to remedy our shortcomings, and at the same time contribute our own merits toward the improvement of mankind; thus we could advance with the peoples of the world while meeting the requirements of the times and gaining an equal footing with the other nations.

I plucked up my courage and in the spring of 1929 I started to dig, collect, sift and—in the language of mining engineering—smelt and cast. After three years of sustained effort I finished the first draft of the present work, whose aim was to prove the one connecting principle of the Confucian Way. This occurred at the time the new Constitution was adopted. Then I was again transferred to party work and had to leave my educational post. Later I served as Vice President of the Legislative Yuan (Council). During this interval I had to suspend the revision and reorganization of the first draft.

Soon the mainland was lost to the Communists, and the Government moved to Taiwan. A reexamination of the roots of the trouble brought the realization that faulty economic and financial policies had had an adverse influence on the operation of the war; also, the conduct of party affairs was not blameless. After taking part in the Government's preparations for reorganization, I relinquished all my positions in both the party and the government and came to the United States to brood over past errors and make further studies.

Another decade has gone by. I have long been anxious about the future of mankind, but with my own eyes I have seen international intrigue at its worst, unbridled human desire seeking selfish gain. The rise of nuclear weapons had added complications. Ambitious aggressors became so blinded that they saw in it their great opportuniey. We even heard—and how can we forget it?— the daring and unabashed threat of one national leader to bury the people of another country. Under these circumstances, indeed, we cannot shut our eyes to the possible rapid onrush of the end of the world. The painful and costly lessons learned from the last two world wars seem to have been totally lost on us.

Since her victorious emergence from both global conflicts, the United States has risen to a position of world leadership unique in history. She has reaped many benefits from her superior strength and fabulous wealth, but there have been disadvantages too. The ebb in social behavior and outright misbehavior have reached alarming proportions. The rise in crime, especially juvenile delinquency, has justly caused serious concern. If no timely effort is made to do some soul-searching, moral cultivation and appeal to conscience, then the great disaster will come to pass—not from without, but from within.

In contrast, Chinese youths in America are noted for their law-abiding nature. Their conduct has turned people's thoughts to the beneficial influence of Chinese culture, which in turn has evoked the increasing attention recently paid to the study of Chinese and the different branches of Chinese learning.

Not too long ago, *Time* magazine published my photograph on the cover of one of its issues, with Confucius' portrait and a rural scene in the background. As a result, some of my American friends, thinking that I must have made a deep study of Confucianism, came with great sincerity to visit me and put questions to me. This strengthened my belief that the clarification and spread of Chinese culture was an urgent, vital task. It confirmed in me the idea that if the present work could be published and translated into English, it could perhaps supply the answers to some of the questions asked of me.

However, as I had to earn my living, I could not find sufficient leisure for the task. Fortunately or unfortunately, a couple of years ago a forest fire destroyed the larger part of my farmhouse in New Jersey, and I had to suspend my work there. Thus later I found the time. Burying myself for more than a year in the huge undertaking, I was pleased to be able to finish it and see it in print at long last.

This work incorporates the whole of the *Four Books.* The rearrangement of the contents of these classics according to the eight subdivisions of the *Great Learning* is designed to make us realize how they are connected from beginning to end and how there is not even one sentence which goes beyond the scope of the said eight headings. This alone demonstrates the minuteness with which Confucius carried out the enlargement of the Way and the illustration of virtue. Was it an exaggeration to say of Confucius, as was done years ago, that "his virtue was coequal to heaven and earth, and his Way penetrated all times"?

It is obvious that one connected principle runs through all the *Four Books,* and that what they teach is the Way of enlargment and durability, based on the common existence and evolution of mankind. I have often said that the weal or woe of the human race depends on the good or evil of the human heart. Licentious thought can drive one mad, while benign thoughts can contribute to the making of a saint. Because of one man's selfishness, millions of human lives may be sacrificed, as evidenced by two global wars.

Therefore the fundamental remedy lies in a painstaking effort to cultivate morality, beginning with the sincerity of thoughts and right molding of hearts. There must be a definite understanding that:

*Nature should be guided into the correct channels rather than be let loose;

*Desire should be restrained, and not be permitted to turn into license;

*Wealth is a mere branch of the life-tree, while virtue is the root;

*Force should come last and virtue first;

*Fillial piety is the foremost of all virtues;

*Sensuality is the source of all evils;

*Sincerity is the primary basis for the establishment of virtue;

*The Mean is the proper Way of dealing with the world;

*The search for benevolence is the prerequisite of human conduct;

*Vigorous action is the immutable principle for success;

*Loyalty and reciprocity are the foundation of satisfactory dealings between men;

*Mutual confidence and righteousness should govern relations between nations.

All this has prominently figured in the teachings of Confucius. It is what not only the people of our country urgently need today, but also what the whole of mankind should seek with all humility. Though I am not an accomplished scholar, I am second to none in my wish for the salvation of not only my own country, but the whole world. As long as I live, I shall never relax my efforts to this end. That is why I have had this book published. I shall be most happy if this attempt is capable of provoking similar studies worthier than mine.

The main concern of this book has been to present in a systematic manner the original Confucian classics in order to clear the way for a fresh start in their study. While it has been deemed necessary to rearrange the texts according to the eight headings contained in the *Great Learning,* which is one of the *Four Books,* any material produced by the recent scholarship of subsequent writers and not emanating from the original works has been omitted. This has been done because such material would be both irreleveant to the purpose I had in mind and confusing to the reader.

To Dr. Shih Shun Liu my warm thanks are due, not only for the translation of this work into English, in the course of which he has made signal contributions to the improvement of the monumental rendering by James Legge, but also for his extensive assistance and meticulous care in the verification of the original Chinese version of this book.

Li Fu Chen

Translator's Note

This volume in the original is the work of a Chinese scholar. His deep-rooted background in the classics is unequaled by any man of like attainments in his entire native land. For Li Fu Chen is more than a scholar. He was a prominent political figure in the Republic of China for many years. Indeed, it is amazing that in his busy life he has found time to use his Western scientific training to fashion this first really systematic study of the Confucian Way as embodied in the *Four Books*.

He has adopted the logical method—original with him—of basing his thorough analysis on the eight well-known sub-divisions of the *Great Learning*, one of the *Four Books*. He has used these sub-divisions, the skeleton of the work, as his chapter headings. Further, he has in the body of the book used appropriate quotations from the original classics to clarify each of his commentaries. The result is the production of such an *opus magnum* that I deem it a signal honor to have been entrusted with the task of its translation.

In setting forth his commentaries, the author has made reference to all the contents of the *Four Books*. The basic text I have used for the English version of these books is the monumental *Chinese Classics* by James Legge. Despite its rather antiquated language and occasional inaccuracies, Legge's work is still considered the standard translation of the *Four Books*.

Before dealing with the merits of relevant portions of Legge and other volumes, I propose to set down here a number of basic terms which consistently run through the Confucian classics. These terms, worked out by various scholarly translators, I have carefully sifted and finally adopted. I present here the transliterations of the original Chinese words or phrases and set beside them their English equivalents as found in various renditions which have preceded mine:

Ch'êng 誠　　Sincerity; honesty; truthfulness; being one's true self.

Chiao 教　　Instruction; teaching; culture.

Chih 智　　Wisdom; knowledge.

Chün-Tzŭ 君子 Superior man; princely man; the Lord's man; ruler;
　　　　　　　sovereign; perfect gentleman; man of worth; man

of perfect virtue; the moral man; the truly moral man.

Chung 忠	(1) Loyalty; faithfulness; conscientiousness.
中	(2) Equilibrium; center; our central self; our true central self.
Chung Yung 中庸	The Doctrine of the Mean; Golden Mean; the universal moral order.
Hsiao 孝	Filial piety; filial.
Hsiao-jên 小人	The mean man; the common man; small man; lesser man; bad man; vulgar man; unworthy man; man in low position.
Hsin 信	Truthfulness; faithfulness; good faith; keeping of promises; fidelity; sincerity.
Hsing 性	Nature; human nature; personal character.
Jên 仁	Benevolence; benevolent action; perfect virtue; goodness; moral sense; humanity; human-heartedness; love; kindness; charity.
Li 禮	Propriety; ceremony; ritual; moral and religious institutions; the laws and usages of social life; code of proper conduct; rules of social conduct.
Ming 命	Fate; destiny; decree of Heaven.
Shu 恕	Reciprocity; consideration; sympathy; altruism.
Tao 道	The Way; the moral law; truth; principle.
Têh 德	Virtue; moral qualities; man's character.
T'i 悌	Fraternal submission; fraternal love.
Yi 義	Righteousness; sense of justice.
Yung 勇	(1) Fortitude; valor; courage; energy.
庸	(2) The constant; the ordinary; the unchanging.

In the text which forms the body of this book, the following meanings have been adopted for the terms given above:

Ch'êng	Sincerity.
Chiao	Instruction; teaching.
Chih	Wisdom.
Chün-tzŭ	The superior man; the man of virtue or perfect virtue; the ruler (sovereign, prince).
Chung	(1) Faithfulness; loyalty.
	(2) Equilibrium.
Chung Yung	The Doctrine of the Mean.
Hsiao	Filial piety; filial.

Hsiao-jên	The mean man; the common man; the man in low position.
Hsin	Truthfulness; good faith; fidelity; sincerity.
Hsing	Nature.
Jên	Benevolence; perfect virtue.
Li	Propriety; rules of propriety.
Ming	Destiny.
Shu	Reciprocity.
Tao	The Way
Têh	Virtue.
T'i	Fraternal love; fraternal submission.
Yi	Righteousness.
Yung	(1) Courage.
	(2) The constant.

Perhaps a word of explanation is in order about the character *jên*. Its usual rendition as "benevolence" is, of course, too narrow in scope; it also fails to convey the sense of "virtue" or "perfect virtue" with which the word was often endowed by Confucius and his school. Nevertheless, so long as we bear in mind its wide scope in our understanding of the word, we may not be far wrong in continuing to translate it as "benvolence," as has traditionally been done.

From the above listing it can be seen that a great many scholars tried their hand at translating the *Four Books,* either in part or in whole. Out of the large mass of such renderings, I have chosen those of James Legge as being still authoritative enough to be used with some confidence. A close second is perhaps Soothill, another of the former English missionaries in China, who has, however, only translated the *Analects.* One of the most original translations of the *Doctrine of the Mean* is doubtless that by a distinguished Chinese scholar, Ku Hungming, who has in many instances followed in the footsteps of Legge. I have plenty of evidence to prove my observation, but suffice it to quote the following:

Ku	**Legge**
Let a man really proceed in this manner, and, though dull, he will surely become intelligent; though weak, he will surely become strong.	Let a man proceed in this way, and, though dull, he will surely become intelligent; though weak, he will surely become strong.

In this connection, we might consider an opinion of Lin
Yutang, whose admiration for Ku Hung aing, like that of all of
us, is unparalleled, and whose *Wisdom of Confucius* incorporates
in extenso with great justification almost the whole of Ku's
translation.   Lin had this to say in a footnote on page 113: "I
cannot help paying tribute to Ku Hungming for rendering this
passage with such beauty. The surprising thing is that it is almost
verbally faithful to the orignal."   In fact, however, the rendering
of the passage referred to is almost identical with that by James
Legge, and as will be seen from the following, only a few words
have been changed by Ku.

Ku	Legge
For God in giving life to all created things is surely bountiful to them according to their qualities. Hence the tree that is full of life he fosters and sustains, while that which is ready to fall he cuts off and destroys.	Thus it is that Heaven, in the production of things, is sure to be bountiful to them, according to their qualities. Hence the tree that is flourishing, it nourishes, while that which is ready to fall, it overthrows.

This shows how much more, in all fairness, Legge, rather than
Ku, deserved Lin Yutang's praise in this particular instance, and
how my own conclusion regarding the usefulness of Legge's work
has some justification.

However, despite his profound knowledge of the Chinese classics
and the painstaking researches he did—doubtless with the invaluable
and unforgettable assistance rendered to him by the Chiness scholar
Wang T'ao 王韜 —Legge was not without his mistakes. I have
pointed out the more serious of these in appropriate footnotes, and
I shall content myself with calling attention here to just a few of
the most glaring errors.

(1) The word *yi* 義 has various meanings, one of which
is "meaning" or significance." Yet Legge has shown definite evidence
that he only understood the word as meaning "righteousness." For
example, in the following passage: "I venture to ask what
principle of righteousness is involved in a scholar's not going to
see the princes," the words "what principle of righteousness is
involved" actually mean "what it means"[1] Also, in the passage
"The principle of righteousness was the same in all the cases,"

what was meant is "The meaning was the same in all the cases."[2]

(2) The words k'ung k'ung 空空 denote "sincerely" instead of "emptiness," as the characters ordinarily may signify. So, in the following instance, "...if a mean person, who appears quite emptylike, ask anything of me, I set it forth from one and to the other, and exhaust it," should have been rendered as "...if an uneducated person asks anything of me with sincerity, I set it forth..."[3]

(3) The word 多 usually means "much" or "many" but in some cases it may also mean "to make or think much of." Hence, "Does the superior man think much of such variety of ability?"[4]

I have attempted to revise Legge's renderings in these and other respects, with a view to making them more intelligible. I may not have done as much as Ku Hungming did in his rendition of the *Doctrine of the Mean*, but I sincerely believe I have made a a number of meaningful changes. If the result is found to be fairly satisfactory and the revised rendition serves a useful purpose, I shall be most happy. With Ku's remarkable command of English, he has truly put to shame many English and American scholars, whose expertise in Chinese often places them at a distinct disadvantage. Nonetheless, I believe that he has rather overdone in many instances, and so I have not followed him uniformly.

Moreover, he was by no means free of error. To cite a few examples:

"In considering how to regulate his personal conduct and character, it is necessary for him to do his duties toward those nearly related to him."[5] The original sense of the words translated as "those nearly related to him" was actually "his parents."[6]

In the passage "If the people in inferior positions do not have confidence in those above them, government of the people is an impossibility,"[7] the meaning is twisted, since it is the importance of gaining the confidence of those above that is stressed here.[8]

In the passage appearing on page 107, two sentences: "He stands erect in the middle and does not incline to either side" and "How firm he is in his strength!" have been omitted.[9] Whether this has been due to an oversight in transcription, I have no way of telling.

In alphabetical order I cite below but a few of the mistakes made by some of the other translators:

Chai, Ch'u and Winburg, *The Humanist Way in Ancient China:*

(1) The rendering of the name of the philosopher Tsêng, which Should be "Shên," as "Ts'ang" (p. 19). The correct pronunciation of this character is so well-known that the introduction of another sound seems hardly conceivable, although the word has some other pronunciations in other contexts.

In this connection, I may add that while in the body of the text Legge has translated the word as "Shên," he made the pronunciation optional by indicating in brackets "or Ts'an" in Chapter V of Volume I of his work, p. 117. This may have been due to the influence of his many years in Hong Kong, since I have been informed that in some parts of Kwangtung Province the word is quite exceptionally pronounced "Ts'an." But we can infer his preference from his use of "Shĕn" throughout the body of his text.

(2) The rendering of "the Duke of Shêh" as "the Duke of Yeh" (pp. 40, 44).

(3) In the passage "Were I to be given a few more years, I would give fifty to the study of the Yi" (p.44), the actual meaning is "If some years were added to my life, I would study the *Book of Changes* after fifty,..."[10]

(4) In "A man who is boastful in words will be indolent in action" (p. 39), the translation has fallen short of the true sense of the original, which is: "He who speaks without modesty will find it difficult to make his words good."[11]

(5) In "You are not equal to him. I commend you for realizing that you are not equal to him,"[12] the mistranslation of one word, *yü*, 與 which means "to approve or commend" rather than the usual conjunction "and," has resulted in Chai's mistaken version of "Not equal to him, you *and* I are indeed not equal to him" (p. 83).

E. R. Hughes, *The Great Learning and the Mean-in-Action*:

One of the most ridiculous mistakes in rendition was made by Hughes in this passage: "There has never been a true monarch of this kind who became widely known as 'a highly reputable parasite'" (p. 138). Let me give Legge's correct verson first: "Never has there been a ruler, who did not realize this description, that obtained an early renown throughout the world."[13] The cause of this mistake made by Hughes was the word *tsao*, 蚤 which, while it may mean "a flea," is just another form of the more common word 早 and means exactly the same thing, "early." It is amusing how Hughes, taking the word to mean "a flea," twisted the first part of the sentence to suit the "reputable parasite" his imagination had conjured up.

Lin Yutang, *Wisdom of Confucius*:

(1) Like Chai, he pronounced the name of the philosopher Tsêng, "Ts'an" (p. ix) and "the Duke of Shêh," "Duke Yeh" (p. 160).

(2) In "I may perhaps compare myself to my old friend Laop'eng," (p. 163) Lao P'êng, according to the philosopher Chu's annotation, was a *ta-fu*, a Great Official, of the Shang dynasty. The reign of this dynasty started in 1766 B. C. and ended in 1123 B. C., while Confucius was not born untill 551 B. C. It is hardly conceivable that the Shang official could have been the Master's "old friend." Besides, nowhere in the original are the words "old friend" to be found."[14]

(3) In "I have sometimes talked with Hui for a whole day, and he just sits still there like a fool" (pp. 173-174), the words "just sits still there" do not convey the original meaning of "he does not make any objection to anything I say."[15]

Ezra Pound, *Coufucian Analects*:

(1) "When Tzŭ-lu had heard of anything he couldn't practice he was only worried about having heard it" (p. 21). The real meaning of the original was as rendered by Legge: "When Tzŭ-lu heard anything, if he had not yet succeeded in carrying it into practice, he was only afraid lest he should hear something else."[16]

(2) "If many years were added to me, I would give fifty to the study of the *Book of Changes...*" (p. 31). I suspect that this was where the Chais got their erroneous version.

(3) "For me there is one thing that flows through, holds things together, germinates" (p. 73). It is curious how this passage was distorted and how unintelligible the last word is.[17]

(4) "If a mean contrivance functions there must be something in it worth attention, but carry it far; 'ware mud. That's why the proper man doesn't use it" (p. 93). The word "mud" is a misrepresentation of the original *ni*, 泥, which ordinarily means "mud," but which in this connection should be read differently

to mean "obstruction."[18]

(5) "Like a dog by spent camp-fire, remembering, studying and not satiate..." (p. 28). This is also a ludicrous rendering of the passage "silently committing knowledge to memory; learning without satiety..."[19]

(6) "When a man don't say, 'What's it like, what's it like?' I don't (bother to) compare him to anything, and that's that (*aliter*: I don't know when he'll end up)" (p. 75). Compare this with the correct version and also the altogether different language of James Legge: "When a man is not in the habit of saying—'What shall I think of this? What shall I think this?' I can indeed do nothing with him!"[20]

Arthur Waley, *The Analects of Confucius:*

(1) The same mistake was made by Waley as by some of the others: "Give me a few more years, so that I may have spent a whole fifty years in study..." (p. 126). He even outdid them by omitting the mention of the *Book of Changes.*

(2) "As far as taking trouble goes, I do not think I compare badly with other people" (p. 212). The correct version by Legge is "In letters I am perhaps equal to other men..."[21]

(3) "Do not be too ready to speak of it, lest the doing of it should prove to be beyond your powers" (p. 186). The original statement was much more positive than what Waley made out of it. (See (4) on page xvi above)

I have sought to reduce the length of the above discussion to the very minimum so as not to render this Note too tedious. All in all, it shows, I think, how difficult the job of translation is. I am more than grateful for the opportunity to ferret out some of the many mistakes that have been made and to corret them. If this arouses interest in improving translations of the *Four Books* to the extent that a critical study is made of my humble effort, I shall welcome it more than anyone else.

In the transliteration of Chinese words the familliar Giles-Wade system has been adopted throughout.

At the end of the book will be found a Glossary and a Bibliography containing most of the translations that have been made of the *Four Books.*

Shih Shun Liu

Footnotes for Translator's Notes

1. *W rks of Mencius*, Bk. III, Pt. II, Ch. VII; Bk. V, Pt. II, Ch. VII. *Vide infra.* pp 323, 419
2. *Works of Mencius*, Bk. V Pt. I, Ch. VI. *Vide infra*, p. 532.
3. *Analects*, Bk. IX, Ch. VII. *Vide infra*, p. 363.
4. *Analects*, Bk. IX, Ch. VI. *Vide infra*, p. 20.
5. Lin, *op. cit.*, p. 117.
6. *Doctrine of the Mean*, Ch. XX.
7. *Ibid.* Lin, *op. cit.*, p. 121.
8. *Doctrine of the Mean*, Ch. XX. *Vide infra*, p. 508.
9. *Doctrine of the Mean*, Ch. X.
10. *Analects*, Bk. VII, Ch. XI, *Vide infra*, p. 67.
11. *Analects*, Bk. XIV, Ch. XXI. *Vide infra*, p. 46.
12. *Analects*, Bk. V, Ch. VIII. *Vide infra*, p. 52.
13. *Doctrine of the Mean*, Ch. XXIX. *Vide infra*, p. 41.
14. *Analects*, Bk. VII, Ch. I. *Vide infra*, p. 23.
15. *Analects*, Bk. II, Ch. IX. *Vide infra*, p. 126.
16. *Analects*, Bk. V, Ch. XIII. *Vide infra*, p. 47.
17. *Analects*, Bk. XV, Ch. II. *Vide infra*, p. 27.
18. *Analects*, Bk. XJX, Ch. IV. *Vide infra*, p. 26.
19. *Analects*, Bk. VII, Ch. II. *Vide infra*, p. 27.
20. *Analects*, Bk. XV, Ch. XV. *Vide infra*, p. 35.
21. *Analects*, Bk. VII, Ch. XXXII. *Vide infra*, p. 45.

CONTENTS

CHAPTER I

Introduction

Confucius was exalted as the Ancient Sage and Ancient Teacher in the Han dynasty (206 B. C. - 219 A. D.), when great strides were made in the development of schools. During later dynasties — the T'ang (618 - 905), Sung (960 - 1276), Ming (1277 - 1643), and Ch'ing (1644 - 1911) — he was acclaimed first as Most Accomplished, then Highest Sage and Ancient Teacher. So he has been revered through more than twenty centuries.

The culmination of the academic thought of the ages, Confucius' philosophy has become the very heart of Chinese culture. Although countless dynasties have changed hands, the reverence paid to him has never waned. We might point to this as a proof that truth is everlasting.

In the Sung and Ch'ing dynasties four other great scholars — Yen Hui, Tsêng Shên, Tzǔ-ssǔ and Mencius — were highly regarded; in fact, they were assigned special niches in the Temple of Confucius right next to his shrine.

Of all the disciples of Confucius, Yen Hui was the wisest and most studious. He also had the deepest knowledge of the Confucian Way.

Tsêng Shên, also a disciple of the great Master, was the author of the *Great Learning*, a unique record of Confucius' teachings.

Tzǔ-ssǔ, a grandson of Confucius and disciple of Tsêng Shên, wrote the *Doctrine of the Mean*. This work was described by Ch'eng Yi, a great neo-Confucianist in the Sung dynasty, as the "law of the heart" handed down by the Confucian school.

Mencius was taught by Tzǔ-ssǔ and left his *Works* in seven books. His basic thinking derived from Confucius, and he was a successor to the Confucian tradition, which he developed with great distinction. He said:

> The influence of a sovereign sage terminates in the fifth generation. The influence of a mere sage does the same. Although I could not be a disciple of Confucius himself, I have been given the benefits of his teachings by others who are.[1]

These four men not only knew and practiced the Confucian Way, they also could and did transmit it to later generations. And for this, their great achievement, they have been revered by the Chinese people to the present day.

Confucius edited the *Book of Songs* and the *Book of History*, compiled the *Book of Rites* and the *Book of Music*, annotated the *Book of Changes*, and wrote the *Spring and Autumn Annals*. These were called the "Six Classics," and as early as the Han dynasty they were singled out by scholars as the "Six Arts."

It is true that the "Six Arts" referred to in Chou Li (*Rituals of Chou*) consisted of rites, music, archery, charioteering, writing and numbers. However, in general the arts dealt (1) with practice and the classics and (2) with theory set down in writing; their function was the clarification of connected principles. Confucius was merely being humble when he said he was "a transmitter and not a maker, believing in and loving ancient studies."

> The Master said, "Tz'ǔ, do you think that I am one who learns many things and keeps them in memory?"
> Tzǔ-kung said, "Yes. Is it not so?"
> "No," was the answer, "I am guided by a connected principle."[2]
> The Master said, "Shên, my Way is all based on a connected principle."[3]

In its chapter on "Interpretation of the Classics," the *Record of Rites* states: "When one enters a country, its teachings can be ascertained. When the people are gentle and honest, they show the teachings of the *Book of Songs*. When they are thorough and farsighted, they show the teachings of the *Book of History*. When they are profound and good, they show the teachings of the *Book of Music*. When they are pure, quiet and subtle, they show the teachings of the *Book of Changes*. When they are polite, frugal, grave and respectful, they show the teachings of the *Book of Rites*. When they put their words together and compare events and deeds, they show the teachings of the *Spring and Autumn Annals*." Thus it can be seen that the teachings of the six classics constitute the knowledge required for the advancement of virtue and the perfection of wisdom by scholars.

The *Book of Filial Piety* delves into the revelation of the heaven-aspiring heart. As it is said in the "Chronicle of Literature and Art," contained in the *History of the Han Dynasty:* "Filial Piety is the rule of Heaven, the (sense of) righteousness of Earth and the (basis of the) people's conduct. Pointing up the essence, it is therefore entitled the *Book of Filial Piety*." A later scholar also made this observation: "Confucius set his mind on the *Spring and Autumn Annals* and acted in accordance with the *Book of Filial Piety*." In short, both works elucidate the origin of human nature and are concerned with the existence and continuity of mankind. Perhaps it was this that moved Confucius to write them despite the fact that he did not regard himself as a "maker."

Prior to the Sung dynasty, the *Great Learning* and the *Doctrine of the Mean* had formed part of the *Record of Rites*. Even though they had been circulated separately as a mark of respect and distinction, at this time they had not yet been combined with the *Conucian Analects* and the *Works of Mencius* to form the *Four Books*.

According to the "Chronicle of Literature and Art" in the *History of the Han Dynasty*, the *Analects* recorded question-and-answer exchanges between the Master on the one hand and his contemporaries and disciples on the other; it also presented interviews between these disciples, with comments from the Master. In those days the disciples kept their own records, and it was only after the death of the Master that they began to compile and edit these varying records; hence, the title *Analects*.

The *Works of Mencius* was at first included in the writings of the various schools of philosophy. Following in the footsteps of the two Ch'êngs—Ch'êng Hao (1032 - 1085) and Ch'êng Yi (1033 - 1107), two great philosophers in the Sung dynasty—Chu Hsi (1130 - 1200), another great neo-Confucianist, compiled the *Four Books*, known as the *Books of the Four Masters*. Included were the *Great Learning*, the *Doctrine of the Mean*, the *Confucian*

Analects and the *Works of Mencius*. From that time on, this collection became known throughout the country as the *Four Books*.

In the Yüan dynasty, during the reign of Emperor Jên-tsung (1312 - 1320), when the State examination was resumed, the *Four Books* were the basic texts from which examination questions were drawn. Under the system adopted at the beginning of the Ming dynasty, the *Book of Changes*, the *Book of History*, the *Book of Songs*, the *Record of Rites* and the *Spring and Autumn Annals* were grouped together as the *Five Classics*. At the same time the *Great Learning*, the *Doctrine of the Mean*, the *Analects* and the *Works of Mencius* were combined as the *Four Books*. This explains how the two sets of books became two separate collections of works. Then, as the *Four Books* were adopted in the Ch'ing dynasty as the basic sources of examination questions, they came to be the most widely studied of the popular readers.

Later, with the introduction of Western culture and the establishment of modern schools, only sections of the *Four Books* and the *Five Classics* were used in Chinese literature courses. But another course, "Cultivation of the Person," was included in the curriculum. The essentials of both courses were drawn from the *Four Books*. After the May 4th Movement of 1919, Confucianism was severely criticized and the course on the "Cultivation of the Person" was abolished.

In the West, the schools concentrate on the students' intellectual and physical training during week-days; then on weekends the students receive their spiritual education at church. When our country adopted the Western system, it went only halfway. We had no churches to attend on weekends. This was bad enough. But to make matters worse, we also discarded our own system of moral education as if it were trash. So it is no accident that (1) our national morality has been declining for some time now and (2) our advancement in scientific knowledge has been given a similar, serious setback.

Down through the ages, Confucius has been reverenced as our Highest Sage and Ancient Teacher because his teachings are so profound, subtle and all-embracing. They contain both the principles of mankind's existence and the means of applying them. And these principles can and should be observed by all men because they are easy to learn and easy to practice in all matters, great or small. For more than 2,000 years these credentials of Confucianism were never disputed. Then came the May 4th Movement, and Confucianism was subjected to harsh criticism

Why? There must be a reason for this change. Could it be that the thinking of Confucius is not suited to the modern age? Is it because language used by him is too ancient to be intelligible? Is it because his philosophy is unsystematic and incompatible with the scientific method? All these questions deserve a thorough investigation and accurate answers.

We could take ideas from the *Four Books* out of context and dub one or two sentences here and there as outmoded thought, denying their fundamental value and charging them with backwardness. But then we ourselves would fall far short of the scientific method. Indeed, in that case there would be no valid ground for us to criticize the ancients for not being farsighted enough to think of their descendants more° than 2,500 years later.

The *Four Books* have been valued because of their contributions to the teaching and cultivation of men. This is a task which, as the Chinese are accustomed to saying, takes as long as a century, and for this very reason it is an extermely difficult one. All knowledge is aimed at human existence and evolution, and any branch of knowledge which complies with this principle should have sufficient value to survive. As to whether the language of the books is that of the present age and whether the presentation is systematic and scientific, these are minor quesions of detail which should not be permitted to affect the main principle.

One of the *Four Books,* the *Great Learning,* has given in great detail the aims of human existence and the steps and methods that should be adopted for their achievement. Dr. Sun Yatsen has regarded this book as "China's political philosophy," and as "the most systematic study, which has never been conceived by political philosophers of any other country, nor ever stated by them, and which is a treasure possessed by China alone." The philosopher Ch'êng Yi was right when he said that this book was "the gate by which first learners enter into virtue."

Since the book was flawed by errors and omissions, the philosopher Ch'êng compiled a new version of it as the standard text. Later the philosopher Chu Hsi, on the basis of this text, divided the *Great Learning* into a chapter of classical text and ten chapters of commentary. At the outset Chu Hsi quotes Ch'êng:

> Master Ch'êng said, "The *Great Learning* is a book by the
> Confucian School and forms the gate by which first learners enter
> into virtue. That we can now perceive the order in which the
> ancients pursued their learning is solely owing to the preservation
> of this work, the *Analects* and *Works of Mencius* coming after it.
> Learners must commence their course with this, and then it may
> be hoped they will be kept from error."[4]

Everything in the world has first its essence, then its utility.
According to an immutable law, whatever is endowed with a
substantial essence has great utility. The same holds true of human
conduct. In order to substantiate his essence, a man must first of all
perfect himself; next, in order to increase the utility of things, it
is important for him to perfect them. To "illustrate illustrious
virtue" is to perfect oneself, proceeding from the investigation of
things through the extension of knowledge, the sincerity of thought
and the rectification of the heart to the cultivation of the person.
To "renovate the people" is to perfect things, proceeding from the
cultivation of the person through the regulation of the family, the
good government of the state and the pacificaton of the world.

Both processes should advance toward the objective of the
highest good, which is the real meaning of "resting in the highest
excellence." If man can achieve wisdom by making use of what
he takes from the universe and achieve virtue by returning it to
the world (for the well-being of mankind), he will be acting in
the spirit of "sharing the world community" with all others.
Therefore, in the *Great Learning* it is said:

> What the *Great Learning* teaches is—to illustrate illustrious
> virtue; to renovate the people; and to rest in the highest excellence.
> The point where to rest being known, the object of pursuit is then
> determined; and that being determined, a calm unperturbedness
> may be attained to. To that calmness there will succeed a tranquil
> repose. In that repose there may be careful deliberation, and that
> deliberation will be followed by the attainment of the desired end.
>
> Things have their root and their branches. Affairs have their
> end and their beginnning. To know what is first and what is last
> will lead near to what is taught in the *Great Learning*.
>
> The ancients, who wished to illustrate illustrious virtue
> throughout the world, first ordered well their own States. Wishing

to order well their States, they first regulated their families. Wishing to regulate their families, they first cultivated their persons. Wishing to cultivate their persons, they first rectified their hearts. Wishing to rectify their hearts, they first sought to be sincere in their thoughts. Wishing to be sincere in their thoughts, they first extended to the utmost their knowledge. Such extension of knowledge lay in the investigation of things.

Things being investigated, knowledge becomes complete. Knowledge being complete, one's thoughts are sincere. One's thoughts being sincere, one's heart is then rectified. One's heart being rectified, one's person is cultivated. One's person being cultivated, one's family is regulated. One's family being regulated, one's State is rightly governed. One's State being rightly governed, the whole world is pacified.

From the Son of Heaven to the masses of the people, all must consider the cultivation of the person the root of everything besides.

It cannot be, when the root is neglected, that what should spring from it will be well ordered. It never has been the case that what was of great importance has been slightly cared for, and, at the same time, that what was of slight importance has been greatly cared for.

"The preceding chapter of classical text is in the words of Confucius handed down by the philosopher Tsêng. The ten chapters of explanation which follow contain the views of Tsêng and were recorded by his disciples. In the old copies of the work there appeared considerable confusion in these, from the disarrangement of the tablets. But now, availing myself of the decisions of the philosopher Ch'êng, and having examined anew the classical text, I have arranged it in order, as follows:"[5]

This statement is basic: "From the Son of Heaven to the masses of the people, all must consider the cultivation of the person the root of everything besides." It follows that all men—be they gentle or simple, young or old—must cultivate their persons, and the cultivation of the person is the root of everything else. "It cannot be, when the root is neglected, that what should spring from it will be well ordered." We can thus see how important this tenet is.

The way to cultivate the person is to be fond of learning so as to gain wisdom, to practice with vigor so as to achieve benevolence and to possess the feeling of shame so as to have courage. Of the three, benevolence is the most important, and so it is said that wisdom is to know benevolence; and courage, to practice it. All three in turn originate from sincerity. Hence:

> The Master said, "To be fond of learning is akin to wisdom.
> To practice with vigor is akin to benevolence. To possess the feeling
> of shame is akin to courage."[3]
> Wisdom, benevolence, and courage—these three are the virtues
> universally binding. It is by the same means that the duties
> (mentioned before) are carried into practice.[7]

What is meant by "the same means"? It is sincerity. But in
their development sincerity and wisdom have a causal relationship.
The greater the sincerity, the greater is the intelligence; and the
greater the intelligence, the greater is the sincerity.

> But given the sincerity, and there shall be the intelligence;
> given the intelligence, and there shall be the sincerity.[8]

If a man can make good use of his instinct (nature) to seek
wisdom and enrich his life, if he can employ the wisdom he has
obtained from his education (instruction) to strengthen his
sincerity, and if he can guide his nature so well as to achieve the
result of "to live and let live" (the Way), then the aims of human
existence can be fulfilled. Hence:

> When we have intelligence resulting from sincerity, this
> condition is to be ascribed to nature; when we have sincerity
> resulting from intelligence, this condition is to be ascribed to
> instruction.[9]
> What Heaven has conferred is called nature; an accordance with
> this nature is called the Way; the cultivation of this Way is called
> instruction.[10]

Owing to the uninterrupted development of wisdom and the
definite achievement of sincerity, man can proceed from the
cultivation and perfection of his nature. He can, in accordance
with his nature, advance on the high road (Way) to the common
existence and common evolution of mankind. At the same time
he will be regulating his family, contributing to the well-ordering
of the State, and pacify the world. This is called the quest for
benevolence. Only when this quest is followed by the achievement
of benevolence can it be said that education (instruction) has
played its role successfully.

When thoughts are sincere, faith is established. When faith is
established, strength is created. The application of strength,

however, must be correctly directed. When the direction is correct, good is accomplished; conversely, when the direction is not correct, evil is the result. The distinction between good and evil depends on wisdom. When man comes into contact with other men or things, desire is created and situations arise.

The solution to these situations depends on the wisdom of both sides. When two forces meet, they merge and their combined force frequently veers in a direction completely different from the direction of either one of the original forces. It is imperative that adjustments be made at all times, so that harmony may reign and hearts may be rectified. What is gratifying to both sides—and practiced by them—must evolve from these adjustments, and these stand for the Mean. This is how the principles of loyalty, reciprocity and observance of rules of conduct have come into being. It is also how the first foundations of morality were laid.

Negatively, we have the principles of "not doing unto others what we would not have them do unto us" and of "requiring in others only the good qualities one is possessed of oneself." Positively, we have the principles of "seeking to establish and enlarge others when wishing to establish and enlarge oneself" and of "regarding someone else's skill as one's own." In this way oneself and others are taken care of, and others are treated as oneself. This is the understanding of the two extremities and the utilization of the Mean. How great the utility of the Mean is!

The *Doctrine of the Mean* is our precious national heritage. It embodies the moral tradition received by Confucius from antiquity; also, this same tradition was extensively developed by him. Sincerity in this context means the sincerity of thoughts; and the Mean, the rectification of hearts. Both are prerequisites for the cultivation of the person. With the cultivation of the person comes the fullness of the essence, and with fullness of essence comes the wide extent of utility. To regulate the family, to contribute to the well ordering of the state, to pacify the world— these are but steps in the development of utility and they are means used to point up its efficacy.

So, the *Great Learning* is like a perfect blueprint, a detailed construction program for the building of an edifice. The *Doctrine of the Mean* is similar to a project, complete with all the needed specifications for the foundations of the house; and the *Analects* and the *Works of Mencius* are like good materials—bricks, tile, cement, timber, hardware, etc.—for the construction of the house. A beautiful mansion, however, cannot be built until each of these materials is placed in the spot assigned to it; in other words, the materials must be rearranged, classified and then used by one or more energetic architects.

To carry this figure of speech still further, we can say that with these materials a person can build an imposing and magnificent mansion (a sage, a truly wise person); or a tall, spacious and comfortable house (a superior man); or an ordinary residence (a good and constant man). The result depends on the nature of the architect and the choices he makes.

In the *Analects* and the *Works of Mencius* there are references to (1) propriety as a door and righteousness as a path, (2) benevolence as a habitation, (3) virtue as an ornament, (4) the great Way as a wall, and (5) propriety and rites as the circle, square and marking-line of a great artisan. For example:

(1) "Now, righteousness is the way, and propriety is the door."[11]

(2) "Benevolence is the tranquil habitation of man."[12]

(3) "Wealth adorns a house, and virtue adorns the person."[13]

(4) "The wall of my master is several fathoms high. If one does not find the door and enter by it, he cannot see the ancestral temple with its beauties, nor all the officials in their rich array. But I may assume that they are few who find the door."[14]

(5) "A master workman, in teaching others, uses the compass and square, and his pupils do the same."[15] "A great artificer does not, for the sake of a stupid workman, alter or do away with the marking-line."[16]

This indicates how appropriately we can compare the cultivation of man to the construction of a house. Through the ages men have classified and rearranged the "building materials" and assigned them to their proper places, but never have they constructed the complete edifice.

Chên Têh-hsiu, a scholar in the Sung dynasty, in his book on *Ta-hsüeh Yen-i* ("Study of the *Great Learning*"), expressed similar views. But regrettably his work was for the exclusive perusal of the Emperor; it was very narrow in scope and did not include all of the *Four Books*. As a result, it does not answer the purpose we have in mind.

What is urgently needed today is to build a house with all

the materials contained in the *Four Books* according to the directions of the blueprint. The construction will contain detailed explanations of the blueprint, but without relying on the *Five Classics* except when absolutely necessary. The goal is to show everyone how to lay the foundation of the house, how to construct the walls, how to erect the scaffolding, how to put a roof over it, how to handle the interior decoration, even how to build the road. The ultimate aim is to make construction of the house easy—as easily learned and as easily practiced as plain old common sense. Then let everyone become an architect and help others do likewise.

In this way the cultivation of the person will be achieved. And herein lies my motive for writing this book. This chapter is the outline. Now to flesh out the points made.

Footnotes for Chapter I

1. *Works of Mencius*, Bk. IV, Pt. II, Ch. XXII.
2. *Analects*, Bk. XV, Ch. II.
3. *Ibid.*, Bk. IV, Ch. XV.
4. *Great Learning*, Text.
5. *Ibid.*
6. *Doctrine of the Mean*, Ch. XX.
7. *Ibid.*
8. *Ibid.*, Ch. XXI.
9. *Ibid.*
10. *Ibid.*, Ch. 1.
11. *Works of Mencius*, Bk. V, Pt. II, Ch. VII.
12. *Ibid.*, Bk. IV, Pt. I, Ch. X.
13. *Great Learning*, Commentary, Ch. VI.
14. *Analects*, Bk. XIX, Ch. XXIII.
15. *Works of Mencius*, Bk. VI, Pt. I, Ch. XX.
16. *Ibid.* Bk. VII, Pt. I, Ch. XLI.

CHAPTER II

The Investigation of Things

A. A Preliminary Word

The life span of the myriad things in the universe differs widely. Since human beings have a higher degree of intelligence than all other living things, they have a right to use these other things as materials for their own livelihood. These materials—comprising an inexhaustible, broad mass of living things—vary in size, quantity, quality, strength and appearance. The large and the small, the many and the few, the fine and the coarse, the strong and the feeble, the beautiful and the ugly—all parade before the eyes of mankind in a variegated array.

In their uninterrupted quest for existence, human beings must have uninterrupted contacts with these countless things. As a result, endless events—perhaps affairs is a better word—take place. Those who can understand, analyze and judge affairs and things are considered wise; and those who cannot are judged ignorant. Those who can utilize, deal with, control affairs and things are considered clever: and those who cannot are called stupid. The wise and clever excel and win, while the ignorant and stupid are destined for inferiority and defeat. It is with this yardstick that the progress or backwardness of the world's nationalities is measured.

How can mankind become wise and clever? In the *Great Learning* it is said: "Things being investigated, knowledge became complete." Again, "Such extension of knowledge lay in the investigation of things." Man's knowledge has as its object the investigation of all things and affairs in the universe. From what is seen by the eye, heard by the ear, smelled by the nose, tasted by the tongue and touched by the body, man perceived differing colors, sounds, odors, flavors, qualities and quantities. Those with little wisdom may find it difficult to distinguish and verify these different senses in detail. However, close scrutiny will tell us that they all are indeed sources of human knowledge.

Moreover, the more the materials collected from the external world, the more extended will be the scope of knowledge. But we need not here delve into the complexity or variety of things; rather what we should be concerned with is whether our cognition is real. Be it large or small, fine or coarse, strong or feeble, beautiful or ugly, everything is useful. However, when and where it can be put to proper use depends on its suitability to the time and space involved. So, before the application of anything takes place, its weight, thickness, depth, urgency, distance and timing must be carefully gauged. This is necessary to bring it—and for that matter, every affair—into accord with the time and space for proper utilization. Consequently, when mankind's knowledge is complete, everything can be put to use, every affair (event) can succeed, and there will be in the universe few things that are wasted and few affairs that fail.

The ancients made a number of different interpretations of the "investigation of things," and there was a long controversy over it. In the Sung and Ming dynasties neo-Confucianists were divided into two schools of thought on this point. The first was the school of the two Ch'êngs and Chu Hsi, who defined "investigation" as "perfection," meaning that the principles of affairs and things should be exhausted until nothing was left unknown. Let us quote this passage from the *Great Learning*:

> This is called knowing the root.
> This is called the perfecting of knowledge.
> "The above fifth chapter of the commentary explained the meaning of 'investigating things and carrying knowledge to the utmost extent,' but it is now lost. I have ventured to take the views of the scholar Ch'êng to supply it, as follows: The meaning of the expression 'The perfecting of knowledge depends on the

investigation of things' is this: If we wish to carry our knowledge to the utmost, we must investigate the principles of all things we come into contact with, for the intelligent mind of man is certainly formed to know, and there is not a single thing in which its principles do not inhere. But so long as all principles are not investigated, man's knowledge is incomplete. On this account, the Learning for Adults, at the outset of its lessons, instructs the learner, in regard to all things in the world, to proceed from what knowledge he has of their principles, and pursue his investigation of them, till he reaches the extreme point. After exerting himself in this way for a long time, he will suddenly find himself possessed of a wide and far-reaching penetration. Then, the qualities of all things, whether external or internal, the subtle or the coarse, will all be apprehended, and the mind, in its entire substance and its relations to things, will be perfectly intelligent. This is called the investigation of things. This is called the perfection of knowledge."[1]

According to the other school, led by Wang Shou-jên (1472 - 1529), the word "investigation" meant "rectification" and only the removal of the selfishness of human desire could bring divine justice. But in the *Great Learning* the "investigation of things" deals with sustained effort; it does not depend solely on abstract comprehension and appreciation. Furthermore, the life of mankind cannot be separated from affairs, and if human desire were excluded it would be tantamount to the denial of human life. For this reason a number of scholars doubt the validity of Wang's theory.

On the other hand, when it comes to the investigation of the principles of things to the point of perfection, the interpretation of the first school is consistent with the spirit of scientific research. Still, if the investigation were confined to the complicated details of things and if their application to daily routines were neglected, we might not be able to reach the entire substance of things.

Therefore, in our view, the investigation of things consists of observation, distinction, analysis, measurement and comparison. The nature of things is essentially very complex; likewise, the classification of events is exceedingly varied. If we do not make a detailed distinction and analysis of all affairs and things and emphasize their comparison and application, it is impossible to see the attributes of things and the cause and effect of affairs; also, we cannot then obtain real knowledge and penetrating judgmet to benefit human life in a practical manner.

We should, therefore, resort first to deduction to understand clearly the real individual nature of all affairs and things (exhaustion of the nature of things). Next we should lay down the common principles relating to all affairs and things. Then we should proceed to induction and, on the basis of the common principles derived from our examination, infer the real individual nature of all affairs and things. After this clear analysis and integrated study of affairs and things, we can proceed to compare their sequence and degree of difficulty in the light of the time and space involved, to determine the urgency of action and speed of movement. Then, no matter how many affairs and things there are, we can get to know their advantages and disadvantages, their prospects for success and failure, and by making a skillful application of them ensure satisfaction.

To achieve symmetry in the eight steps mentioned in the *Great Learning*, the first step is not given as "investigation of affairs and things," but simply as "investigation of things." This is because the reference to "things" necessarily includes "affairs." To make the picture complete, the following passage spells out both affairs and things:

> Things have their root and their branches. Affairs have their end and their beginning. To know what is first and what is last will lead near to what is taught in the *Great Learning*.[2]
>
> It cannot be, when the root is neglected, that what should spring from it will be well ordered. It never has been the case that what was of great importance has been slightly cared for, and, at the same time, that what was of slight importance has been greatly cared for.[3]

It can thus be seen that affairs and things are interrelated. So far as its integral being is concerned, everything has its root and also its branches. As far as its totality is concerned, every affair has its beginning and its end. So, when we speak of affairs and things, we cannot be separated from their beginning and end or their root and branches. The beginning and the root must come first, and the end and the branches must follow. The order of their sequence cannot be altered. In order not to upset this sequence, we must clearly recognize the respective periods in which the beginning and the end occur.

In the *Book of Chuang-tzŭ* it is said: "Action, which is simple at the beginning, grows big toward the end." All affairs and things start out to be very simple, but prudence at the beginning makes for their success at the end. What the *Great Learning* referred to as "great" or "slight care" meant the same thing as "strong" or "light emphasis." As the beginning and the end must not be reversed, so also must strong and light emphasis not be reversed. When the root is stressed, complete success throughout the branches can be assured; and when the beginning is emphasized, complete success to the end can be assured. When the root is well ordered, so also are the branches, and when the root is disorderly, so also are the branches. In no case can the latter be well ordered when the former is disorderly. This is the rational conclusion obtained from the process of deduction.

For example, legislation is initiated not in the expectation that people will violate the law, but in the hope that they will not violate it. So, virtue is the root and law merely one of the branches. The two should never be reversed.

> The Master said, "in hearing litigations, I am like anyone else. What is necessary is to cause the people to have no litigation." So, those who cannot present the facts cannot finish what they say and will have a great awe for public opinion. This is called knowing the root.[4]

That the "investigation of things" means the observation, distinction, analysis, measurement and comparison of affairs and things can be seen in the first chapter of the *Great Learning*. This chapter uses the contrasting words "roots" and "branches," "beginning" and "end," "well ordered" and "disorderly," "great care" and "slight care." The last chapter is filled with words meaning "measurement" and "comparison"; it also frequently refers to the causes and effects of what is measured and compared. For example:

> ...by gaining the people, the state is gained, and by losing the people, the state is lost[5]

> Hence, the accumulation of wealth is the way to scatter the people; and the letting it be scattered among them is the way to collect the people. And hence, the ruler's words going forth contrary to right will come back to him in the same way, and wealth, gotten by improper ways, will take its departure by the same.[6]

> Thus we see that the sovereign has a Great Way to pursue.

He must show loyalty and faithfulness to attain it, and by pride and extravagance he will lose it.[7]

All such contrasting words as "gain" and "lose," "accumulation" and "scattering," "going forth" and "coming back" divide the actions of mankind in a general way. Either the effects are guaged from the causes, or vice versa. The interpretation or disposition of all affairs and things according to the law governing cause and effect can not only avoid reversals and mistakes; it can ensure the success of life.

Those whose knowledge is immature frequently know only one side of affairs and things; they overlook the othe side. "Knowledge of life and not of death; knowledge of gain and not of loss," as mentioned in the *Book of Changes,* is due to lack of adequate knowledge. At times persons with inadequate knowledge may see both sides of affairs and things, but they fail to see which is the root and which the branch, which should be slightly cared for and which greatly cared for. Further, they do not perceive how a gain can be made and how a loss is sure to be sustained. They do not see because they do not know; they lack the knowledge. As a result, the root is taken for the branch, what should be lightly stressed is strongly emphasized, what is not urgent is regarded as compelling, what should be greatly cared for is only slightly heeded.

These acts, the products of mistaken judgment, are bound to lead to failure. We must realize that the foundation of human life is built on complete and accurate knowledge. To obtain complete and accurate knowledge, it is imperative to devote strenuous effort to observation, distinction, analysis, measurement and comparison. There must be not only the cognition of both sides of affairs and things, but the ability to deal with changes and shifts on both sides. This is what the *Doctrine of the Mean* meant by "seeking to carry it out to its breadth and greatness, so as to omit none of the more exquisite and minute points which it embraces, and to raise it to its greatest height and brilliancy, so as to pursue the course of the mean."[8]

Here is what the *Doctrine of the Mean* teaches regarding the perfection of "investigation":

To this attainment there are requisite the extensive study of what is good, accurate inquiry about it, careful reflection on it, the clear discrimination of it and the earnest practice of it.

The superior man may not engage in studying, but once he does, he does not relax until he can understand all that he studies. He may not make an inquiry, but once he does, he does not relax until he knows everything about which he inquires. He may not reflect, but once he does, he does not relax until he apprehends everything on which he reflects. He may not discriminate, but once he does, he does not relax until he is clear in his discrimination. He may not practice, but once he does, he does not relax until he is earnest in his practice. If another man succeeds by one effort, he will use a hundred efforts. If another man succeeds by ten efforts, he will use a thousand.

Let a man proceed in this way, and, though dull, he will surely become intelligent; though weak, he will surely become strong.[9]

This work of "investigation" has its own method and proce-dure. We want the material of our knowledge to be rich, and so there must be extensive study. We want the pursuit of our knowledge to be precise, and so there must be accurate inquiry. We want the examination of our knowledge to be thorough, and so there must be careful reflection. We want the judgment of our knowledge to be strict, and so there must be clear discrimination. With the completion of these four stages of investigation knowledge is obtained and action is bound to follow.

But knowledge-induced action may not be enough. So, to offset the possibility that action may not be effective, practice must be added as the last stage in the process. And the practice must be earnest. Where there is study, it must aim at the ability to understand. Where there is inquiry, it must aim at knowledge. Where there is reflection, it must aim at apprehension. Where there is discrimination, it must aim at clarity.

In other words, study, inquiry, reflection, discrimination and practice all must be intensively carried through to the end. They must not be interrupted, they must not be altered because of a change of circumstances, and they must not cease until the destination is reached. Only then can there be hope for success.

To make a hundred efforts against someone else's single try, and one thousand attempts against someone else's ten, calls for dedication so strong that it far exceeds the efforts of other persons.

The change from dullness to intelligence and from weakness to strength shows how great an effect can be achieved by the thrust of intensive, dedicated effort. However, even if we succeed in reaching this stage we should not be conceited.

Although the process of investigation has been divided into five stages, these do not necessarily follow one another; rather, they call for simultaneous action. It is true that study, inquiry, reflection and discrimination belong to the general field of knowledge, while practice is in a class of its own; however, knowledge and practice are not opposed to each other, nor do they differ in their importance. Actually, the scope of practice and knowledge is the same. We do not seek knowledge for the sake of knowledge; we seek knowledge for the sake of practice. This does not mean that when we seek knowledge, practice comes to a standstill. And it does not mean that when we engage in practice, knowledge is neglected. The truth of the matter is that we seek knowledge while we engage in practice—and the more extended our practice, the greater becomes our knowledge. There is no reason to say our quest for knowledge does not belong to the field of practice. The mutual relationship between knowledge and practice is very intimate. Though human life is many-sided, we can sum it up as the intermingling of knowledge and practice.

The following detailed discussion of study, inquiry, reflection, discrimination and practice as outlined in the *Doctrine of the Mean* is presented here because of the significance of these points to coming generations in their investigation of things.

B. Extensive Study

What is extensive study? It is the widespread collection of the material of knowledge. "The scope of knowledge is very wide," Dr. Sun Yatsen said. "It extends to the whole universe." Again, "As we exist in the world, we must make our knowledge advance with the increase of affairs and things." In other words, all affairs (events) and things of the universe are the material of knowledge. And since this material is increasing every day, we must step up our efforts to collect it. Otherwise, out collection will not be "extensive."

Confucius was the first man to make an "extensive study."

A man of the village of Ta-hsiang said, "Great indeed is the philosopher K'ung! His learning is extensive, and yet he does not render his name famous by any particular thing."

The Master heard the observation and said to his disciples, "What shall I practice? Shall I practice charioteering, or shall I practice archery? I will practice charioteering."[10]

In the village of Ta-hsiang it was felt that a man could become well known only by practicing one art. But the men of extensive learning could not be confined to one skill or one art.

A high official asked Tzŭ-kung, saying, "May we not say that your Master is a sage? How various his ability is!"

Tzŭ-kung said, "Certainly Heaven has endowed him unlimitedly to be a great sage. And, moreover, his ability is various."

The Master heard of the conversation and said, "Does the high official know me? When I was young, my condition was low, and therefore I acquired my ability in many things, but they were mean matters. Does the superior man think much of such variety of ability? No, he does not."

Lao said, "The Master said, 'Having no official employment, I acquired many arts.' "[11]

The variety of Confucius' ability and attainments was a proof of his extensive learning. Because of them he preferred not to restrict himself. So he frequently practiced the skill he had acquired.

The Master said, "Is it not pleasant to learn with a constant perseverance and application?"[12]

Since the scope of knowledge is so wide, we can perceive how unlimited learning is. For this reason, we can only diligently observe the phenomena of the universe, read as many books as possible and gain cognition and appreciation of the persons and things we come into contact with day by day. As for what has already been acquired, we should not forget it; indeed, we must constantly review it in a quest to learn something new from old knowledge. Thus, the more we seek, the more extensive the field becomes, and the more extensive the field, the greater subtlety our knowledge attains.

The Master said, "Learn as if you could not reach your object, and were always fearing also lest you should lose it."[13]

Tzŭ-hsia said, "He, who from day to day recognizes what he has not yet, and from month to month does not forget what he has attained to, may be said indeed to love to learn."[14]

The Master said, "If a man reviews what he has learned so as to acquire new knowledge, he may be a teacher of others."[15]

1. The Observation of the Phenomena of the Universe with a View to the Understanding of the Laws of the Natural World.

The heaven now before us is only this bright shining spot; but when viewed in its inexhaustible extent, the sun, moon, stars and constellations of the zodiac are suspended in it, and all things are overspread by it. The earth before us is but a handful of soil, but when regarded in its breadth and thickness, it sustains the Hua Mountain without feeling its weight, contains the rivers and seas without their leaking away, and holds myriad things. The mountain now before us appears only a stone; but when contemplated in all the vastness of its size, we see how the grass and trees are produced on it, birds and beasts dwell on it and precious things which men treasure up are found on it. The water now before us appears but a ladleful; yet extending our view to its unfathomable depths, the largest tortoises, iguanas, iguanodons, dragons, fishes and turtles are produced in them, articles of value and sources of wealth abound in them.

It is said in the the Book of Songs, "The ordinances of Heaven, how unceasingly profound they are!" The meaning is that it is thus that Heaven is Heaven. And again, "How illustrious it was, the purity of the virtue of King Wên!" indicating that it was thus that King Wên was what he was. His purity likewise is unceasing.[16]

It was from observation that knowledge was acquired about the brightness and vastness of the sky, the expanse and depth of the earth, the stupendous size and boundless wealth of mountains and the unfathomable depths and rich resources of the sea. All this was apparent from an examination of merely the static features of our environment.

From the dynamic side of these same things it was learned that there is such a thing as a moving force and power in the universe. For otherwise there would be no explanation for such things as the incessant motion of the heavenly bodies and the endless onward flow of the rivers. Thus, from the way the word "sincerity" is used in the following quotations, certain cognitions and inferences have been deduced. First, the quotations:

> Sincerity is the Way of Heaven.[17]
> Hence to entire sincerity there belongs ceaselessness. Not ceasing, it continues long. Continuing long, it evidences itself. Evidencing itself, it reaches far. Reaching far, it becomes large and substantial. Large and substantial, it becomes high and brilliant.[18]

Now, the Chinese equivalent of the word "universe" contains two charactors, *yü* and *chou*. Acourding to one ancient authority, Huai-nan-tzŭ, "*yü* means what is above, what is below and the four directions; anc *chou* means ancient and modern times." What is above, what is below and the four directions constitute the three dimensions of space; ancient and modern times constitute the fourth dimension, time. It is only with motion, uninterrupted motion, that space and time can be produced. Therefore, the universe is the same as time and space, which take their eternal effect from a kind of dynamism, called "sincerity."

> The Master, standing by a stream, said, "It passes on just like this, not ceasing day and night!"[19]
> The disciple Hsü said, "Chung-ni often praised water, saying, 'O water! O water!' What did he find in water to praise?"
> Mencius replied, "There is a spring of water; how it gushes out! It rests not day nor night. It fills up every hole, and then advances, flowing on to the four seas. Such is water having a spring! It was this which he found in it to praise. But suppose that the water has no spring.—In the seventh and eighth months when the rain falls abundantly, the channels in the fields are all filled, but their being dried up again may be expected in a short time. So, a superior man is ashamed of a reputation beyond his merits."[20]

Though the incessant flow of water is attributable to the gravitation of the earth's core it is also due to a kind of dynamism which gives man many associations of ideas. The source or spring from which water flows can be compared to the existence of an origin for the moral system—viz., sincerity which is unceasing.

Knowledge about both the always balanced motion of the earth and the heavens, and the constant growth of all things led to this thought:

This equilibrium is the great root from which grow all the human actings in the world, and this harmony is the universal path which they all should pursue. Let the states of equilibrium and harmony exist in perfection, and a happy order will prevail throughout heaven and earth, and all things will be nourished and flourish.[21]

In the universe there are so many celestial bodies which move without collision or friction that they must be subject to regulation (equilibrium), with proper arrangements made for them (harmony). Otherwise they could not all keep to their positions, follow their set orbits, proceed without incident and carry on their endless cycles. Hence, "equilibrium" and "harmony" are the highest principles governing the production, continued existence and happiness of all things, and they represent a state of complete perfection for them.

2. The Study of Books with a View to Learning What the Ancients and Moderns Have Already Known.

Truth has no time limit. While the truth about things can be ascertained from the laboratory, the truth about men must be learned from experiments in daily social living. The experiences of preceding generations have been recorded in books. By reading them we can enjoy the fruits of the authors' labors—and avoid their pitfalls—without wasting time and effort. Therefore the thoughtful reading of books is the most important part of "extensive study."

This is why it has been said that "the use of ancient history as a mirror can provide knowledge of the rise and fall of dynasties" and that "to be stupid and self-confident, to be lowly and act at one's own arbitrary will, to live in the modern age and go against the ancient ways—this is to bring disaster upon oneself."

> The Master said, "A transmitter and not a maker, believing in and loving ancient studies, I venture to compare myself with our Lao P'êng."[22]
> The Master said, "I am not one who was born in the possession of knowledge; I am one who is fond of antiquity, and earnest in seeking it there."[23]
> Tzŭ-chang asked whether the affairs of ten ages after could be

known. Confucius said, "The Yin dynasty followed the regulations of the Hsia: wherein it detracted from or added to them may be known. The Chou dynasty has followed the regulations of the Yin: wherein it has detracted from or added to them may be known. Some other may follow the Chou, but though it should be at the distance of a hundred ages, its affairs may be known."[24]

It almost goes without saying that the serious student is never satisfied with partial knowledge. He continually strives to push back the frontiers of intellectual discovery. And the more deeply he delves into the wisdom of the past, the greater need there is for adjustment and recapitulation, the more important it is that he give special attention to key points of his findings. Otherwise no matter how much material his research yields, it will not attain the significance it could and should. On this point ancient sages have given important directions.

> The Master said, "The superior man, extensively studying all learning and keeping himself under the restraint of the rules of propriety, may thus likewise not overstep what is right."[25]
> Mencius said, "In learning extensively and discussing minutely what is learned, the object of the superior man is that he may be able to go back and set forth in brief what is essential."[26]

"Learning" refers to the material of knowledge; "propriety," to the principles of affairs and things. In gathering material, a person must try to be universal, "extensively studying all learning." In examining principles, he must strive to be concise, "keeping... under the restraint of the rules of propriety."

"Discussing minutely what is learned" means "analysis," and "to go back and set forth in brief what is essential" translates to "induction." While analysis aims at the principles of affairs and things, induction seeks their essence. With these two tools, a man can regulate his words and actions in such a way that they are always proper. At the same time he can keep things from conflicting with their utility and prevent affairs from contravening reason. Hence he "may thus likewise not overstep what is right."

Although the Chou dynasty was on the decline in its Spring and Autumn period (722 - 481 B.C.), the teachings and achievements of Kings Wên and Wu along with the institutions and traditions of their great dynasty were not yet forgotten or lost.

The wise could remember their essentials, and even the stupid and unworthy could recall some of them. We learn that the knowledge of Confucius was derived from his transmission of ancient learning. Despite the fact that he had no constant teacher, we can see the origin of his education.

> Kung-sun Ch'ao of Wei asked Tzŭ-kung, saying, "From whom did Chung-ni get his learning?"
>
> Tsŭ-kung replied, "The doctrines of Wên and Wu have not yet fallen to the ground. They are to be found among men. Worthy men remember their greater principles, and the unworthy remember the smaller. Thus, all possess the doctrines of Wên and Wu. Where could our Master go that he should not have an opportunity of learning them? And yet what necessity was there for his having a regular teacher?"[27]

Important as reading is—and the above excerpt indicates this—not all the material contained in books can be believed. Some of it may be biased, it may represent falsehood as truth, or make much of unimportant coincidences. To merit belief, material from books must be based on substantial evidence: "no credence without proof."

> Mencius said, "It would be better to be without books than to give entire credit to them. In the 'Completion of the War,' I select two or three passages only, which I believe. The benevolent man has no enemy under heaven. When the prince the most benevolent was engaged against him who was the most opposite, how could the blood of the people have flowed till it floated the pestles of the mortars?"[28]
>
> The Master said, "I could describe the ceremonies of the Hsia dynasty, but Ch'i cannot sufficiently attest my words. I could describe the ceremonies of the Yin dynasty, but Sung cannot sufficiently attest my words. (They cannot do so) because of the insufficiency of their records and wise men. If those were sufficient, I could adduce them in support of my words."[29]

In studying, teachers are needed for guidance and friends for assistance. Therefore respect of teachers and the formation of friendships are indispensable to the achievement of "extensive knowledge." By sincere effort a student can win many friends, teachers as well as others.

The Master said, "When three of us walk along, one or both of the others surely serve as my teachers. I will select their good qualities and follow them, their bad qualities and avoid them."[30]

The philosopher Tsêng said, "The superior man on grounds of culture meets with his friends, and by their friendship helps his virtue."[31]

3. Attention to Affairs and Things Encountered Daily and Attainment of New Knowledge and Positive Proofs from Action.

Extensive knowledge is not gained solely by observation and reading, however. Contact with men and things is also a vital factor.

When the villagers were going through their ceremonies to drive away pestilential influences, he (Confucius) put on his court robes and stood on the eastern steps.[32]

When Confucius was in office in Lu, the people struggled together for the game taken in hunting, and he also did the same.[33]

No doubt one of the reasons Confucius took part in the two events described above was to get a first-hand glimpse of the customs and character of the people.

When the Master went to Wei, Jan Yu acted as driver of his carriage. The Master said, "How numerous the people are!"[34]

As soon as Confucius entered the state of Wei, he was impressed by both the large throngs and their economic prosperity. This shows not only how observant the Master was, but what importance he attached to social problems.

The Master said, "See what a man does. Mark his motives. Examine in what things he rests. How can a man conceal his character? How can a man conceal his character?"[35]

A man's actions indicate how he thinks, his motives show the course he pursues, and his recreational preferences disclose his habits. All these things can be used as criteria to judge the will and actions of men with whom one comes into contact.

Tzŭ-hsia said, "Even in small skills there is something worth seeing; but if carried further, they may meet with obstruction. Therefore, the superior man does not practice them."[36]

The "small skills" mentioned above refer to the miscellaneous crafts of various schools. Though some inventions and discoveries are rational, they are of no great value if they are coarse rather than subtle, and partial rather than complete. These minor skills, though within the limits of knowledge, may well be worth observing; but Tzŭ-hsia fears that if these skills are widely copied, only minor fields of knowledge will be encouraged. Therefore it is necessary to see things from a higher plane.

> The Master said, "There may be those who act without knowing why. I do not do so. Hearing much and selecting what is good and following it, seeing much and keeping it in memory—this is only second to full knowledge."[37]

Hearing and seeing can provide material for the memory, but it may not be knowledge necessarily, hence, "second to full knowledge." When thinking and analysis are added to memory, however, then hearing and seeing also may become sources of knowledge. The implied fear is this: that things heard and seen will not be recorded in the mind—so nothing will have actually been heard or seen.

> The Master said, "To tell, as we go along, what we have heard on the way, is to cast away our virtue."[38]

When one tells whatever is heard at random, it is an irresponsible act, the "casting away of virtue."

> The Master said, "Tz'ŭ, do you think that I am one who learns many things and keeps them in memory?"
> Tzŭ-kung replied, "Yes. Is it not so?"
> "No," was the answer. "I am guided by a connected principle."[39]
> The Master said, "Silently committing knowledge to memory, learning without satiety, and instructing others without being wearied: What if I can do all these things?"[40]

Committing knowledge to memory is a way to collect the material of knowledge. It also implies the consistent cognition of the material collected and the formation of indepenent judgment on it.

The greatness of Confucius lay in his wide knowledge of past learning and his ability to transmit it to later generations. What he committed to memory and comprehended was the moral system handed down by our ancient sages. He silently recorded in his mind what he heard and saw, and from this tremendous mass of knowledge he selected the quintessence, studied it and classified it for transmission to others. This knowledge was not original with him; nevertheless he did not selfishly keep it to himself; hence, "What if I can do all these things?" This observation also shows his great modesty.

> Mencius said, "Confucius ascended the eastern mountain, and Lu appeared to him small. He ascended the T'ai mountain, and all beneath the heavens appeared to him small. So, he who has contemplated the sea finds it difficult to think anything of other waters, and he who has wandered in the gate of the sage finds it difficult to think anything of the words of others. There is an art in the contemplation of water.—It is necessary to look at it as foaming in waves. The sun and moon being possessed of brilliancy, their light admitted even through an orifice illuminates. Flowing water is a thing which does not proceed till it has filled the hollows in its course. The student who has set his mind on the Way does not advance to it but by completing one lesson after another."[41]

The theme of this discussion is the unlimited nature of learning. The more a man learns, the more he realizes his inadequacies; and the higher and deeper his knowledge, the more he realizes how shallow he is. It is therefore imperative to make a gradual advancement without any let-up. Those who regard their knowledge as extensive are merely exposing their shallowness.

C. Accurate Inquiry

What is accurate inquiry? It is the investigation of the material of knowledge in order to perfect knowledge already possessed. There are three motives for inquiry: (1) to discover what is unknown; (2) to dispel doubts about something which is known; and (3) to unearth details in an effort to complete knowledge already known.

Inquiry and study complement one another. Without inquiry, study cannot result in clear understanding or correct cognition.

In the Confucian school, inquiries were made into many things, among them "benevolence," "filial piety," "government" and "scholars." Confucius answered these literally searching questions according to differences in an individual's personality and environment, with the result that the inquirers reaped the tremendous benefit of rectifying their thought and action while increasing their fund of knowledge.

Moreover, inquiry is by no means easy, for its object is first to obtain clear explanations, and then to accept and apply them. If the urgency and complexity of the problem are not examined so that the inquiry can be made with discernment, the result of the whole effort may turn out to be empty and futile. Actually, the inquirer must limit the scope of his quest. While being always aware of the key points involved in the problem, he must really zero in on it to come up with an effective solution. Said Tzŭ-hsia, "...to inquire pertinently and think closely..." The word "pertinently" indicates that inquiry should not be confused, empty or mistaken; in other words, it indicates "accurate inquiry."

> Tzŭ-chang having asked how virtue was to be exalted and delusions to be discovered, the Master said, "Hold your faithfulness and sincerity as first principles, and be moving continually to what is right—this is the way to exalt one's virtue. You love a man and wish him to live; you hate him and wish him to die. Having wished him to live, you also wish him to die. This is a case of delusion."[42]
>
> Fan Ch'ih, rambling with the Master under the rain altars, said, "I venture to ask how to exalt virtue, to correct cherished evils, and to discover delusions."
>
> The Master said, "Truly a good question! If doing what is to be done is made the first business, and success a secondary consideration—is not this the way to exalt virtue? To assail one's own wickedness and not assail that of others—is not this the way to correct cherished evil? For a single day's anger to disregard one's own life and involve that of his parents—is not this a case of delusion?"[43]

More can be gleaned from the above quotes than the obvious fact that Confucius gave different answers to the same questions. Note, for example, that he very definitely regarded the inquiries as most pertinent. He even praised Fan Ch'ih for having raised a "good question." The inference is that whoever can come up with a worthwhile query doubtless possesses a certain degree of desired acumen; on the other hand, those who fail to raise questions are less perceptive. Also, since Fan Ch'ih kept to the essential points, Confucius gave him a simple answer to each question. Here are more examples of "accurate inquiry";

> Tzǔ-chang asked, "What must a scholar be, who may be said to be distinguished?"
> The Master said, "What is it you call being distinguished?"
> Tzǔ-chang replid, "It is to be heard of through the State, to be heard of throughout his clan."
> The Master said, "This is notoriety, not distinction. Now the man of distinction is solid and straightforward and loves righteousness. He examines people's words and looks at their countenances. He is anxious to humble himself to others. Such a man will be distinguished in the country; he will be distinguished in his clan. As to the man of notoriety, he assumes the appearance of virtue, but his actions are opposed to it, and he rests in this character without any doubts about himself. Such a man will be heard of in the country; he will be heard of in the clan."[44]

Mistaking "notoriety" for "distinction," Tzǔ-chang put a question which was inconsistent with its original intention. Confucius first corrected his mistake, then explained to him the difference between "notoriety" and "distinction." The latter is soundness, politeness and the ability to conduct oneself with humility; "notoriety," on the other hand, is pretension with a view to winning empty renown. Although Tzǔ-chang had not been a good inquirer, he did learn the difference between notoriety and distinction—thereby receiving the benefit of his inquiry nevertheless.

Persons who wish to perfect their knowledge must not be conceited or self-deceiving. The self-deceptionists regard themselves as arbitrarily in the know, when in reality they are not. The conceited frequently are content with what they have acquired. They have no desire for further progress and so rest calmly in their state of vulgarity, ignorance and inferiority. This points to the reason why the serious inquirer must be humble at heart. As widely learned as Confucius was, he even once asked Lao-tzǔ about the rules of propriety. Lao-tzŭ was at one time a Chou dynasty archivist in charge of the classics and books of past centuries; naturally, he was familiar with ancient rites and institutions. This is but one instance which shows that Confucius never passed up an opportunity to make an inquiry.

The Master, when he entered the grand temple, asked about everything. Someone said, "Who will say that the son of the man of Tsou knows the rules of propriety? He has entered the grand temple and asks about everything." The Master heard the remark and said, "This is a rule of propriety."[45]

The grand temple was the Temple of the Duke of Chou in the state of Lu. The rites and vessels of the temple were mostly concerned with our ancient culture. Although Confucius was well versed in the knowledge of all these things, yet he asked about everything. He did it to deepen his study, to learn even more. An intellectually alert person seizes every opportunity to increase his knowledge.

The Master said, "Was not Shun a great intellect? Shun had a natural curiosity of mind and he loved to inquire into ordinary conversation. He ignored the bad in others and broadcast the good. Taking two extreme counsels, he held the mean between them and applied it in his dealings with the people. Was it by this that he was Shun?"[46]

It is interesting to note here that Confucius, himself an intellectual giant, called Shun a great intellect—and the first reason he gave was that Shun loved to ask questions.

The philosopher Tsêng said, "Gifted with ability and yet putting questions to those who were not so; possessed of much and yet putting questions to those possessed of little; having, as though he had not; full, and yet counting himself as empty; offended against, and yet entering into no altercation: formerly I had a friend who pursued this style of conduct."[47]

No one in this world is omniscient or omnipotent, nor is anyone ignorant of everything or unable to do anything. Confucius once said of himself, "I am not even as good as an old farmer," and again, "I am not even as good as an old gardener." Since knowledge is unlimited, who but an expert can master any one scientific subject? Besides, even the wise cannot avoid occasional mistakes, and even the stupid can score a point once in a while. When he who has much knowledge puts questions to him who has little, the questioner is bound to end up with even more knowledge. Likewise, when he who is possessed of much queries him who is possessed of little, the former's wisdom is bound to be greater. So, as it is said in the *Book of Changes*, "Humility benefits."

Only by regarding possession as not possessing can one be free from self-deception; only by regarding fullness as emptiness can one be free of conceit; and only by not quarreling when offended can one rid himself of arbitrariness and learn to accept others' opinions. All these concepts are secrets for the advancement of virtue and pursuit of knowledge.

The friend referred to by the philosopher Tsêng was, according to some, Yen Yüan. Of all the disciples of Confucius, Yen Yüan was the fondest of learning, and although he "never contradicted" Confucius by asking naïve questions, he more than the others liked to make inquiries of his inferiors. Learning and inquiry are one and the same thing. Those who are fond of learning never tire of asking questions.

> Tzŭ-kung asked, saying, "On what ground did K'ung Wên get that title of Wên?" The Master said, "He was clever and fond of learning, and he was not ashamed to ask questions of his inferiors... On these grounds he has been styled Wên."[8]

Here again we find high esteem for a questioning seeker after knowledge. K'ung Yü, a worthy official of Wei, canonized as Wên, liked to ask questions because he was fond of learning. The perfection of learning is always due to diligence. But the importance of putting questions to one's inferiors lies not so much in the increase of knowledge as in the elimination of pride and self-importance. The proud, ashamed of questioning subordinates, fail to realize what a tremendous loss they sustain in the acquisition of true knowledge.

> The disciple Kung-tu said, "When Kêng of T'êng made his appearance in your school, it seemed proper that a polite consideration should be paid to him, and you did not answer him. Why was that?"

Mencius replied, "I do not answer him who questions me presuming on his nobility, nor him who presumes on his talents, nor him who presumes on his age, nor him who presumes on his services performed to the State, nor him who presumes on old acquaintance. Two of those things were chargeable on Kêng of T'êng."[49]

Kêng, a younger brother of the prince of T'êng, was one of Mencius' disciples. Now, while Mencius was happy to teach others, he often refused to answer Kêng's questions. The reason was that Kêng regarded himself as a member of the aristocracy who had preformed meritorious services to the state. He was conceited and lacked sincerity in putting his questions to his master. Mencius' refusal to answer Kêng also was a method of teaching. He used it to show his disciples that Kêng should not have diluted his quest for knowledge by presuming on anything.

Accurate inquiry can be compared to the extraction of mineral reserves. It is essential for those who seek the treasures of wisdom from others to assume an attitude of humility and sincerity.

D. Careful Reflection

What is careful reflection? It is deliberation on the material of knowledge in order to master it completely. In the realm of knowledge we must associate what we know with what we remember, and deliberate on their mutual relationships. Only thus can conceptions be formed, and without conceptions the material of knowledge becomes diffuse and useless. Said Mencius: "Without thinking, the eyes and ears are hidden from things." Reflection is all-important; seeing and hearing are not enough. In fact, we might say that if one does not think, then the more extensive the material of knowledge is, the more will wisdom be thwarted. As Mencius also has stated: "The mind thinks. With thinking something is gained, but without thinking nothing is gained."[50]

So the mind is definitely complementary to the eyes and ears. If there is careful thinking, "even with the height of heaven and the distance of the stars, once their reasons are sought, what is accessible only in a thousand years can be reached sitting down."

On the other hand, if a man does not think, the contact his eyes and ears make with affairs and things results in nothing but fluctuating shadows. Reflection, then, is required not only in learning but even in daily speech and action. This is why

> The Master said, "The superior man has nine things which are subjects with him of thoughtful consideration. In regard to the use of his eyes, he is anxious to see clearly. In regard to the use of his ears, he is anxious to hear distinctly. In regard to his countenance, he is anxious that it should be benign. In regard to his demeanor, he is anxious that it should be respectful. In regard to his speech, he is anxious that it should be sincere. In regard to his doing of business, he is anxious that it should be reverently careful. In regard to what he doubts about, he is anxious to question others. When he is angry, he thinks of the difficulties (his anger may involve him in), and when he sees gains to be got, he thinks of righteousness."[51]

Mencius concluded that "with thinking something is gained, but without thinking nothing is gained." The great political achievements of the Duke of Chou, for example, were attributed by Mencius to the Duke's constant reflection.

> Mencius said, "Yü hated the pleasant wine and loved good words. T'ang held fast the Mean and employed worthy men without regard to their qualifications. King Wên looked on the people as he would on a man who was wounded, and he looked towards the Way as if he could not see it. King Wu did not forget the distant. The Duke of Chou desired to unite in himself the virtues of those kings, those founders of the three dynasties, that he might display in his practice the four things which they did. If he saw anything in them not suited to his time, he looked up and thought about it, from daytime into the night, and when he was fortunate enough to master the difficulty, he sat waiting for the morning."[52]

Yü, T'ang, Wên and Wu were the founders of the three dynasties of Hsia, Shang and Chou, and each of them possessed distinctive virtues. The Duke of Chou, anxious to acquire the merits of all four of his great predecessors, probed the reasons for their achievements and examined the methods they used to improve the situation prevailing in their eras. "He looked up and thought about it" indicates the depth of the Duke's deliberation. Thinking "from daytime into the night" notes his diligence. After this stint of careful reflection, "he sat waiting for the

morning" to put what he learned into execution. It all shows
how much importance ancient sages attached to moral endeavor
and how hard they worked at it.

> The Master said, "hard it is to deal with him, who will stuff
> himself with food the whole day, without applying his mind to
> anything good! Are there not gamesters and chessplayers? To be
> one of these would still be better than doing nothing at all."[53]

A man's failure to realize his intellectual potential can be
due largely to indolence. To avoid this pitfall, Confucius taught
others to use their minds. Without mental exertion, stagnation
sets in, a condition which blocks attempts to improve knowledge.
Although gambling and chessplaying are trifles, they can open up
and stimulate one's intelligence. This approach, used here by
Confucius, emphasizes the importance of using one's mind. On
one occasion Mencius compared the mind to a mountain path and
noted what would happen to it if it fell into disuse.

> Mencius said to the disciple Kao, "There are footpaths along
> the hills; if suddely they are used, they become roads; and if shortly
> afterward they are not used, the wild grass fills up your mind."[54]

Although Confucius, like all good teachers, was skillful in
guiding his disciples, he thought himself incapable of inducing
those who did not apply their minds to make progress.

> The Master said, "When a man is not in the habit of saying,
> 'What shall I think of this?' I can indeed do nothing with him!"[55]

Mencius, too, thought that a teacher could only show a
student the method, and the student had to take it from there.
A teacher, he felt, could not instill mental perseverance in his
student, nor could he increase subtlety of thought: these depended
on the student himself.

> Mencius said, "A carpenter or a carriage-maker may give a
> man the circle and square, but cannot make him skillful in the
> use of them."[56]

Tzŭ-hsia was one of the disciples of Confucius who was fond
of learning. Here is his view regarding learning and thinking:
"There are learning extensively and having a firm and sincere

aim; inquiring pertinently and reflecting from what is near at hand—virtue is in such a course."[57]

The three things—extensive learning, pertinent inquiry and reflection—are consistent with the process of searching for knowledge. "Inquiring pertinently" refers to asking only relevant questions, while "reflecting from what is near at hand" touches on deliberating over material already gathered before engaging in thought. These are key elements in the process; hence "earnest practice is near virtue." Tzŭ-hsia is stressing that simultaneous attention should be given to thinking and learning. We cannot afford nonapplication of our minds on the one hand, just as we should not venture into the vague and the obscure on the other.

The object of all thinking should be the increase of the material of knowledge. To attain this goal, according to Confucius, study and diligent reflection are "musts."

> The Master said, "I have been the whole day without eating, and the whole night without sleeping—occupied with thinking. It was of no use. The better plan is to learn..[58]
> The Master said, "Learning without thinking is labor lost; thought without learning is perilous."[59]

These statements clearly underline the close relationship between thinking and learning. "Labor lost" means, of course, that nothing is gained. Being in a "perilous" state involves bewilderment, the lack of peace of mind. In neither case can any benefit be received. Only through coordination of thinking and learning can the results of deliberations be true and correct.

> The Master said, "I do not open up the truth to one who is not eager to get knowledge, nor help out anyone who is not anxious to explain himself. When I have presented one corner of a subject to anyone, and he cannot from it learn the other three, I do not repeat my lesson."[60]

Teaching consists mainly of guidance, and no teacher can exhaust the presentation of knowledge. So long as a student can think deeply and with perseverance, he should be able to extend his knowledge of "one corner of a subject" to that of its other three corners: to penetrate without impediment all sides of any question. Hence,

"How the flowers of the aspen-plum flutter and turn! Do I not think of you? But your house is distant." The Master said, "It is the want of thought about it. How can it be. distant?"[31]

It is only when a man is eager to obtain knowledge that his mind can be opened to the truth, and it is only when he is anxious to explain himself that he can be helped. The teacher can do no more than assist a student and push him forward. As it is said in the "Record of Scholarship": "If even after explanation understanding does not result, it is justified to leave the matter where it is." Where deep, steady thought was lacking, even Confucius would not continue his instruction. From this we can see Confucius' method of teaching.

Yet, important as it is, thinking should not be excessive. An inordinate amount of thinking borders on timidity. To think twice is enough; it is unnecessary to think thrice.

Chi Wên thought thrice and then acted. When the Master was informed of it, he said, "Twice may do."[32]

E. Clear Discrimination

What is clear discrimination? It is the classification of the material of knowledge in order to render it as clear as possible. (Discrimination, as used in the context of this chapter, and indeed in the whole of this book, means the act of distinguishing from other things by observing differences; discernment.) In the universe there are many types of affairs and things; their nature is highly complex. They are like or unlike one another, positive or negative, true or false, good or evil, right or wrong. Their reality can be ascertained and their purposes understood only after a deep and clear analysis. So, it is stated in the *Book of Changes*, "Things are grouped together because of their similarity and divided because of their variety." First by grouping together and then by dividing, any amount of the material of knowledge could and should be analyzed and classified. Only in this way can correct conclusions be deduced. Although this may be a painstaking and subtle process, it is absolutely indispensable.

> The Master said, "I hate the manner in which purple takes away the luster of vermillion. I hate the way in which the songs of Chêng confound the music of the Ya. I hate those who with their sharp mouths overthrow their countries."[63]

The above quotation from the *Analects* cites only a few examples of almost innumerable affairs and things—the true and the false, the good and the evil, which confuse each other. Confucius, as quoted by Mencius in the statements below, was even more detailed.

> Confucius said, "I hate a semblance which is not the reality. I hate the darnel, lest it be confounded with the rice. I hate glib-tonguedness, lest it be confounded with righteousness. I hate sharpness of tongue, lest it be confounded with sincerity. I hate the music of Chêng, lest it be confounded with the true music. I hate the purple, lest it be confounded with vermillion. I hate your good careful men of the villages, lest they be confounded with the truly virtuous. The superior man seeks simply to bring back the unchanging standard, and, that being correct, the masses are roused to virtue. When they are so aroused, forthwith perversities and glossed wickedness disappear."[64]

When there are clearly discernible differences in the nature and condition of affairs and things, they are of course easily marked out. The affairs and things most difficult to distinguish are those which are similar in their nature and condition and whose appearances and substances do not coincide. In such instances an effort must be made to discriminate between their advantages and disadvantages, their right and wrong. For example, purple and vermillion are both thick colors, and the music of Chêng and that of Ya are both very beautiful. But vermillion is an orthodox, and purple merely a subsidiary color. Likewise the music of the Ya is orthodox, and that of Chêng, lusty. Superficially the two colors and styles of music are similar, but in substance they are different in respect to their orthodoxy.

Again, rice and darnel are both herbs. Both grow in the fields. But rice is a cereal and darnel a mere weed which can harm rice. "Glib-tonguedness" is eloquence gone wrong; the position taken with it, while seemingly reasonable, is not really so. A sharp tongue may be persuasive, but it is insincere. Therefore, if its argument is accepted, it may destroy a family or ruin a nation, for as a rule only well-balanced, carefully weighed words can be constructive. The "good careful men of the villages," though gentlemen to all outward appearances, aim only at enhancing their reputation. If their speech and actions are scrutinized, more often than not they will be found both lacking and confounding virtue.

> The Master said, "He who puts on an appearance of stern firmness, while inwardly he is weak, is like one of the small, mean people—yea, is he not like the thief who breaks through, or climbs over, a wall?"[65]
> The Master said, "Your good, careful people of the villages are the thieves of virtue."[66]

These examples single out people and things that are seemingly the same while actually different: They confound orthodoxy with heterodoxy, and truth with falsehood. Although there are numerous similar cases in the universe, we need not be confused if we possess a sharp power of discrimination.

> Tzŭ-chang asked what constituted intelligence. The Master said, "He, with whom neither slander that gradually soaks into the mind nor statements that startle like a wound in the flesh are successful, may be called intelligent indeed. Yea, he, with whom neither soaking slander nor startling statements are successful, may be called far-seeing."[67]

When the sinister nature of "soaking slander" and "startling statements" is not detected and the facts are not known, one can easily be deluded by them. Therefore it is necessary to exercise clear discrimination to prevent unsavory results before they can be produced. In short, it is only when rumors and unfounded statements are nipped in the bud that there can be intelligence and far-sightedness.

Good and evil, right and wrong, truth and falsehood, analogy and difference—these are the distinguishing marks of affairs and things. Since unfounded judgments make for mistakes, effective evidence is important. Such evidence should determine whether affairs and things are good, right, true or similar. Even though Confucius devoted himself to learning all his life, he never felt he should draw conclusions lightheartedly. A confidence born of conceit was not in him. This is why he said: "When you know a thing, to hold that you know it; and when you do not know a thing, to allow that you do not know it—this is knowledge." He used the word "knowledge" here as an all-embracing concept which included deep understanding and clear judgment. Only when there is definite insight can one pass judgment.

> The Master said, "I could describe the ceremonies of the Hsia dynasty, but Ch'i cannot sufficiently attest my words. I could describe the ceremonies of the Yin dynasty, but Sung cannot sufficiently attest my words. (They cannot do so) because of the insufficiency of their records and wise men. If those were sufficient, I could adduce them in support of my words."[33]

Ch'i descended from the Hsia dynasty, and Sung from the Yin dynasty. Although Confucius could have described the ceremonies of Hsia and Yin, he did not wish to do so because he believed there was a lack of ancient records and wise men. The full proof was missing and therefore he felt he could not draw any definite conclusions on those ceremonies as a whole with what documents were available. He felt this way despite the probable accuracy of inferences from the legacies of the Chou dynasty, which could well have applied to as many as one hundred succeeding generations. The attitude of the sage toward the pursuit of knowledge was indeed cautious.

> Mencius said, "It would be better to be without books than to give entire credit to them. In the 'Completion of the War,' I select two or three passages only, which I believe. The benevolent man has no enemy under heaven. When the prince the most benevolent was engaged against him who was the most opposite, how could the blood of the people have flowed till it floated the pestles of the mortars?"[69]

Thus, Mencius took the position that with regard to any book there must be clear discrimination—and no room for indiscriminate credulity—hence what he said above. For another example there is the story of the attack of King Wu on Chou.

> He who attains to the Kingly Way in the empire, having those three important things, shall be able to effect that there shall be few errors under his government.

However excellent may have been the regulations of those of former times, they cannot be attested. Not being attested, they cannot command credence, and not being credited, the people would not follow them. However excellent might be the regulations made by one in an inferior situation, he is not in a position to be honored. Unhonored, he cannot command credence, and not being credited, the people would not follow his rules.

Therefore the institutions of the Ruler are rooted in his own character and conduct, and sufficient attestation of them is given by the masses of the people. He examines them by comparison with those of the three kings and finds them without mistake. He sets them up before heaven and earth and finds nothing in them contrary to their mode of operation. He presents himself with them before spiritual beings and no doubts about them arise. He is prepared to wait for the rise of a sage a hundred ages after and has no misgivings.

His presenting himself with his institutions before spiritual beings without any doubts arising about them shows that he knows Heaven. His being prepared, without any misgivings, to wait for the rise of a sage a hundred ages after shows that he knows men.

Such being the case, the movements of such a ruler, illustrating his institutions, constitute an example to the world for ages. His acts are for ages a law to the world. His words are for ages a lesson to the world. Those who are far from him look up to him; and those who are near him are never wearied with him.

It is said in the Book of Songs, "Not disliked there, not tired of here, from day to day and night to night, will they perpetuate their praise." Never has there been a ruler, who did not realize this description, that obtained an early renown throughout the world.[70]

Before a system can be established, there must be a sound, well-founded theory. If a system were based on empty speculation, not only would it not be respected by the people, but those who govern would not be able to command obedience. It follows that a system is good only (1) when it is believed by the ruler himself and by others, (2) when it is proved by the past and is feasible for the future, and (3) when it is consistent with both human nature and divine justice.

In making his investigations and transmitting ancient traditions, Confucius always based his conclusions on widely collected manifestations. "Evidencing itself, it (sincerity) reaches far.

Reaching far, it becomes large and substantial. Large and substantial, it becomes high and brilliant."[71] Only by "evidencing itself" can sincerity become high and brilliant.

Dr. Sun Yatsen said: "Anything which obeys divine justice is consistent with human nature, follows the tide of the world and meets the requirements of mankind, and which those who are first informed and who first comprehend decide to put into practice, can never fail." This observation has the same subtle significance as the above quotation from the *Doctrine of the Mean.*

Distinctions based on superficialities cannot be called clear discrimination.

> The disciple Kao said, "The music of Yü was better than that of King Wên." Mencius observed, "On what ground do you say so?" and the other replied, "Because at the pivot the knob of Yü's bells is nearly worn through."
>
> Mencius said, "How can that be a sufficient proof? Are the ruts at the gate of a city made by a single two-horsed chariot?"[72]

Conclusions regarding men based merely on the temporary likes and dislikes, praises and slanders of the crowd also cannot qualify as clear discrimination.

> The Master said, "When the multitude hates a man, it is necessary to examine into the case."[73]
>
> Mencius said, "There are cases of praise which could not be expected, and of reproach when the parties have been seeking to be perfect."[74]

If something should be done but no one is sought out to do it, mistakes may occur. This cannot be called clear discrimination.

> Shên T'ung, on his own impulse, asked Mencius, saying, "May Yen be smitten?" Mencius replied, "It may. Tzŭ-k'uai had no right to give Yen to another man, and Tzŭ-chih had no right to receive Yen from Tzŭ-k'uai. Suppose there were an official here, with whom you, Sir, were pleased and that, without informing the king, you were privately to give to him your salary and rank; and suppose that this official, also without the king's orders, were privately to receive them from you:—would such a transaction be allowable? And where is the difference between the case of Yen and this?"
>
> The people of Ch'i smote Yen. Someone asked Mencius, saying, "Is it really the case that you advised Ch'i to smite Yen?" He

replied, "No. Shên T'ung asked me whether Yen might be smitten, and I answered him, 'It may.' They accordingly went and smote it. If he had asked me—'Who may smite it?' I would have answered him, 'He who is the minister of Heaven may smite it.' Suppose the case of a murderer, and that one asks me—'May this man be put to death?' I will answer him—'He may.' If he asks me—'Who may put him to death?' I will answer him—'The chief criminal judge may put him to death.' But now with one Yen to smite another Yen:—how should I have advised this?"[75]

Therefore, clear discrimination must come only after many-sided observation, analysis, measurement and comparison. Only from these exercises can correct conclusions be deduced. This involves, of course, painstaking effort.

F. Earnest practice

What is earnest practice? It is the practical application of the material of knowledge so as to make it effective. After the four stages of study, inquiry, reflection and discrimination have been diligently pursued, the acquisition of knowledge is largely completed. The next step is to apply this knowledge, to prove its correctness, to seek further knowledge from its application and to strengthen belief in it. Though knowledge and application are two distinct stages in the process of learning, they cannot be locked into water-tight compartments; rather, they should push each other forward progressively.

Knowledge without application plunges human life into a void. If we do not apply what we learn from the four basics-- extensive study, accurate inquiry, careful reflection and clear discrimination—we can hardly be certain that our hard-won knowledge is feasible. It is only in application that the distance between theory and practice can be bridged. For there are some things that can be learned only from experience—and not from books or observation alone.

The upshot of this is that true insight and sound judgment can be assured only by the person's simultaneously acquiring knowledge and applying it. This predetermined mode of action is essential. Only with this method can the process of investigation begin. Actually, earnest practice is not different from scientific experimentation, which seeks evidence from application along with an increase of knowledge from the evidence thus obtained.

Ku T'ing-lin (1613 - 1681), a great Ming scholar, developed the theory of "simplicity" to counter the emptiness of certain scholars in the Han and Sung dynasties. The method he put forward emphasized creation, extensive proof and practical application. A study of his ideas shows they were a continuation of principles upheld by our ancient sages—and consistent with the spirit of scientific experimentation today!

Realizing that a deep-rooted shortcoming of the Chinese people was failure to apply their knowledge, Dr. Sun Yatsen advocated the theory that "knowledge is difficult, while application is easy." In order to encourage "energetic practice," President Chiang Kai-shek also espoused the "philosophy of energetie practice" and added a new dimension to the meaning of the "principle of action."

No matter how perfect doctrines or plans may be, if they are confined to discussion and never tested, they will become empty, vague and sterile. Their advocates may pride themselves on their knowledge, but the fact of the matter is: they do not possess the knowledge they think they have because a test of true knowledge is the ability to use it. This brings us to another point. Knowledge whose depth is inadequate causes hesitation in applying it, which in turn submerges affairs and things in stagnation and waste. And here lies the reason for our country's scientific backwardness, lack of political progress and our national impotence.

> The Master said, "Though a man may be able to recite the three hundred odes, yet if, when entrusted with a governmental charge, he knows not how to act, or, if, when sent to any quarter on a mission, he cannot give his replies unassisted, notwithstanding the extent of his learning, of what practical use is it?"[76]

This explains how the value of learning lies in its application and not in the quantity of "knowledge" acquired.

> The Master said, "A youth, when at home, should be filial, and, abroad, respectful to his elders. He should be earnest and

truthful. He should overflow in love to all and cultivate the friendship of the good. When he has time and opportunity, after the performance of these things, he should employ them in polite studies."[77]

The Master said, "In letters I am perhaps equal to other men, but the character of the superior man, carrying out in his conduct what he professes, is what I have not yet attained to."[78]

To Confucius, a man's conduct and action were more important than his accomplishments in arts and letters. His attitude is indicated by the statement: "When he has the opportunity...he should employ them in polite studies." Then again, the very first chapter of the *Analects* opens with the query: "Is it not pleasant to learn with a constant perseverance and application?" To learn is to seek knowledge; to learn with application is to familiarize oneself with the materials of knowledge by using them. By seeking knowledge and by practicing it at the same time, by translating knowledge into action and by proving action with knowledge—this is the way to achieve immeasurable personal benefit and happiness.

Confucius' words to the effect that he had not attained the character of the superior man are, of course, the self-appraisal of a modest man. However, the reason he gives when he depicts the superior man as "carrying out in his conduct what he professes" indicates the type of life-style he feels his students should strive to develop.

To sum up, having obtained knowledge, we should put it into practice; at the same time we should seek to increase our knowledge, for knowledge is vital to substantiate the force of action. Study, inquiry, reflection and discrimination are stages in the build-up of latent power, while earnest practice goes a step further and develops personal dynamism. Without the build-up there can be no development. So the five stages complete the process of investigation of things, an investigation which is severely crippled if even one of the stages is bypassed.

The reverse of earnest practice is empty talk, and this is indeed the arch-enemy of mankind. Confucius realized this when he spoke the following words of wisdom:

Tzŭ-kung asked what constituted the superior man. The Master said, "He acts before he speaks, and afterwards speaks according to his actions."[79]

The Master said, "The superior man wishes to be slow in his speech and quick in his conduct."[80]

The Master said, "The superior man is modest in his speech, but exceeds in his actions."[81]

The Master said, "The reason why the ancients did not readily give utterance to their words was that they feared lest their actions should not come up to them."[82]

The Master said, "He who speaks without modesty will find it difficult to make his words good."[83]

Those who have really absorbed the art of earnest practice are generally men of few words; they voice their thoughts cautiously. Even those persons who are adept at speaking and acting rank below them. This underlines the utmost importance of personal application while, conversely, it singles out empty talk as extremely undesirable. "Words must have regard for action, and action for words." When a man's ability is inadequate for action, he should prefer not to talk about it. If his words are mere talk, they will indicate nothing but his inadequacy or total lack of ability. If they constitute unabashed bragging, it becomes an even worse disgrace.

Tsai Yü being once asleep during the daytime, the Master said, "Rotten wood cannot be carved; a wall of dirty earth will not receive the trowel. This Yü!—what is the use of my reproving him?"

The Master said, "At first, my way with men was to hear their words and give them credit for their conduct. Now my way is to hear their words and look at their conduct. It is from Yü that I have learned to make the change."[84]

If a man's action is not sincere and earnest, it is bound to tend toward boastfulness and decadence. In Tsai Yü's case, Confucius compared him to "rotten wood" and "a wall of dirty earth." Although it was not the sage's intention to belittle others, yet it was regrettable that there were a number of pretentious persons whose actions did not comply with their words. This meant it was necessary to observe their conduct to assess their true attitudes. It did not take minute observation to conclude that Tsai Yü's action lacked earnestness, and the Master set him down accordingly.

When Tzŭ-lu heard anything, if he had not yet succeeded in carrying it into practice, he was only afraid lest he should hear something else.[85]

Tzŭ-lu asked whether he should immediately carry into practice what he heard. The Master said, "Your father and elder brothers are still living; why should you act on that principle of immediately carrying into practice what you hear?" Jan Yu asked the same, whether he should immediatedly carry into practice what he heard, and the Master answered, "Immediately carry into practice what you hear." Kung-hsi Hua said, "Yu asked whether he should carry immediately into practice what he heard, and you said, "Your father and elder brothers are still living." Ch'iu asked whether he should immediately carry into practice what he heard, and you said, "Carry it immediatly into practice." I, Ch'ih, am perplexed and venture to ask you for an explanation." The Master said, "Ch'iu is retiring and slow; therefore I urged him forward. Yu has more than his own share of energy; therefore I kept him back."[86]

Among the disciples of Confucius, Tzŭ-lu was impetuous and excessively forward. Therefore the Master advised him to be cautious. Jan Ch'iu, on the other hand, was prudent and very retiring; so Confucius advised him to be more forward. This shows how the sage varied his method of teaching earnest practice in accordance with the natural inclinations of his disciples. How difficult practice is!

Practice may involve blind and misdirected action. The guilty here fail to see both the reason for their action and the correct method to use to gain their ends. Their prolonged practice then yields no results, and time as well as energy is wasted. In other instances those who initiate their practice lack the strong will to see it through; they may not have duly assessed the value of its success. Their trial may be accidental more than anything else, and after a time they try to get out from under it somewhat. They may have had the courage of their convictions for a time, but due to their lack of persistence, the inevitable result more often than not is that "the greater the initial progress, the quicker the retrogression."

These failures in the last analysis can be ascribed to lack of learning and self-cultivation. Without a clear comprehension of his objective, a man is apt to be ignorant of the reason for his action as well as the right method for carrying it out; consequently, no results can be expected. Moreover, without concentration of will, one cannot act with thoroughness.

Dr. Sun Yatsen stated: "By forming a consciousness out of knowledge, producing a system from the consciousness, preparing a plan on the basis of the system and devoting one's effort according to the plan, one can expect immediate success." These are the necessary stages in the knowledge-to-practice process. Only when we direct our effort according to a system or plan can we be free from misdirected or blind action and hope for success on schedule.

All his life Dr. Sun Yatsen was single-minded in all his actions. He prepared his plans beforehand and carried them out with unswerving determination. In him the real significance of earnest practice was exemplified.

In short, practice is the true evidence of knowledge. Without going down the path of practice, knowledge cannot be proved correct. Practice is the last stage in the quest for knowledge, following study, inquiry, reflection and discrimination. Therefore, "the extension of knowledge lies in the investigation of things" and "things being investigated, knowledge becomes complete."

Footnotes for Chapter II

1. *Great Learning*, Com., Ch. V.
2. *Ibid.*, Text.
3. *Ibid. Vide Supra*, p. 7.
4. *Great Learning*, Com., Ch. IV
5. *Ibid.*, Ch. X.
6. *Ibid.*,
7. *Ibid.*,
8. *Doctrine of the Mean*, Ch. XXVII.
9. *Ibid.*, Ch. XX. Legge's original translation shows some misunderstanding here.
10. *Analects*, Bk. IX, Ch. II.
11. *Ibid.*, Bk. IX, Ch. VI. The rendering "He is about a sage" was a misinterpretation. The word *to* means "to think much of" instead of "have" or "need."
12. *Ibid.*, Bk. I, Ch. I
13. *Ibid.*, Bk. VIII, Ch. XVII.
14. *Ibid.*, Bk. XIX, Ch. V.
15. *Ibid.*, Bk. II, Ch. XI.
16. *Doctrine of the Mean*, Ch. XXVI. *Hua* is the name of a mountain, but *yüeh* is the word for "mountain" itself, and so the two words together should be translated as "the Hua Mountain." Legge mistook them for the names of

two mountains.

17. *Ibid.*, Ch. XX.

18. *Ibid.*. Ch. XXVI.

19. *Analects*, Bk. IX, Ch. XVI.

20. *Works of Mencius*, Bk. IV, Pt. II, Ch. XVIII.

21. *Doctrine of the Mean*, Ch. I.

22. *Analects*, Bk. VII, Ch. I. According to accepted usage, Lao P'êng was the name of a high official in the Shang dynasty. Legge's rendering, "our old P'ang," was an error. A worse mistake was made by Lin Yutang, *vide supra*, page vii.

23. *Ibid.*, Ch. XIX.

24. *Ibid.*, Bk. II, Ch. XXIII.

25. *Ibid.*. Bk. VI, Ch. XXV.

26. *Works of Mencius*, Bk. IV, Pt. II, Ch. XV.

27. *Analects*, Bk. XIX, Ch. XXII.

28. *Works of Mencius*, Bk. VII, Pt. II, Ch. III.

29. *Analects*, Bk. III, Ch. IX.

30. *Ibid.*. Bk. VII, Ch. XXI.

31. *Ibid.*. Bk. XII, Ch. XXIV.

32. *Ibid.*, Bk. X, Ch. X.

33. *Works of Mencius*, Bk. V, Pt. II, Ch. IV.

34. *Analects*, Bk. XIII, Ch. IX.

35. *Ibid.*, Bk. II, Ch. X.

36. *Ibid.*, Bk. XIX, Ch. IV.

37. *Ibid.*, Bk. VII, Ch. XXVII.

38. *Ibid.*, Bk. XVII, Ch. XIV.

39. *Ibid.*, Bk. XV, Ch. II. *Vide supra*, p. 2.

40. *Analects*, Bk. VII, Ch. II.

41. *Works of Menci.us*, Bk. VII, Pt. I, Ch. XXIV.

42. *Analects*, Bk. XII, Ch. X.

43. *Ibid.*, Ch. XXI.

44. *Ibid.*. Ch. XX.

45. *Ibid.*, Bk. III, Ch. XV.

46. *Doctrine of the Mean*, Ch. VI.

47. *Analects*, Bk. VIII, Ch. V.

48. *Ibid.*. Bk. V, Ch. XIV.

49. *Works of Mencius*. Bk. VII, Pt. I, Ch. XLIII.

50. *Ibid.*, Bk. VI, Pt. I, Ch. XV.

51. *Analects*, Bk. XVI, Ch. X.

52. *Works of Mencius*, Bk. IV, Pt. II, Ch. XX.

53. *Analects*, Bk. XVII, Ch. XXII.

54. *Works of Mencius*. Bk. VII, Pt. II, Ch. XXI.

55. *Analects*, Bk. XV, Ch. XV.

56. *Works of Mencius*, Bk. VII, Pt. II, Ch. V.

57. *Analects*, Bk. XIX, Ch. VI.

58. *Ibid.*, Bk. XV, Ch. XXX.

59. *Ibid.*. Bk. II, Ch. XV.

60. *Ibid.*. Bk. VII, Ch. VIII.

61. *Ibid.*, Bk. IX, Ch. XXX.
62. *Ibid.*, Bk. V, Ch. XIX.
63. *Ibid.*, Bk. XVII, Ch. XVIII.
64. *Works of Mencius*, Bk. VII, Pt. II, Ch. XXXVII.
65. *Analects*, Bk. XVII, Ch. XII.
66. *Ibid.*, Ch. XIII.
67. *Ibid.*, Bk. XII, Ch. VI.
68. *Ibid.* Bk. III, Ch. IX. *Vide supra*, p. 40.
69. *Works of Mencius*, Bk. VII, Pt. II, Ch. III. *Vide supra*, p. 40.
70. *Doctrine of the Mean*, Ch. XXIX
71. *Ibid*, Ch. XXV.
72. *Works of Meucins*, Bk. VII, Pt. II, Ch. XXII.
73. *Analects*, Bk. XV, Ch. XXVII.
74. *Works of Mencius*, Bk. IV, Pt. I, Ch. XXI.
75. *Ibid.*, Bk. II, Pt. II, Ch. VIII.
76. *Analects*, Bk. XIII, Ch. V.
77. *Ibid.*, Bk. I, Ch. VI.
78. *Ibid.*, Bk. VII, Ch. XXXII.
79. *Ibid.*, Bk. II, Ch. XIII.
80. *Ibid.*, Bk. IV, Ch. XXIV.
81. *Ibid.*, Bk. XIV, Ch. XXIX
82. *Ibid.*, Bk. IV, Ch. XXII.
83. *Ibid.*, Bk. XIV, Ch. XXI.
84. *Ibid.*, Bk. V, Ch. IX.
85. *Ibid.*, Ch. XIII.
86. *Ibid.*, Bk. XI, Ch. XXI.

CHAPTER III

The Extension of Knowledge

A. A Preliminary Word

The wisdom obtained from the entire process of extensive study, accurate inquiry, careful reflection, clear discrimination and earnest practice changes with time. This is "what is learned with study" or "what is learned with painstaking effort." Another part of our knowledge comes naturally; it is acquired without learning and without deliberation. Quite simply, this knowledge is "what one is born with." For example, a newborn baby knows naturally how to take the milk that sustains it; when it grows up, knowledge of sex to a great extent is naturally acquired. So the three sources of knowledge are birth, study and painstaking effort.

As to the volume of knowledge, this depends on the degree of a person's natural endowments and his ability to absorb and discriminate (discern). When the former is high and the latter strong, a man is wise. When the former is low and the latter weak, he is less than wise, if not stupid. Differences between the two can be substantial. To use a Chinese idiom, "some persons may know ten and others two when they hear about one," while still others may know nothing at all after hearing anything. (The ten-two-one statement has to do with elements of pertinent knowledge which a person can draw from his background, education and experience to throw light on the subject being discussed.)

Perhaps not one in ten thousand persons can belong to the first category, for a "genius" is indeed a rare and prized specimen of mankind.

> Some are born with knowledge. Others acquire it with study, and still others with painstaking effort. After the knowledge is acquired, it comes to the same thing.[1]
>
> The Master said, "Those who are born with the possession of knowldge are the highest class of men. Those who acquire knowledge with study are the next. Those who do so with painstaking effort are another class next to these. Those who do not make a painstaking effort to acquire knowledge are the lowest of the people.[2]

Of Confucius' three thousand disciples, only one, Yen Yüan, would "know ten after hearing about one." Even Confucius himself admitted his inferiority to this "genius." The Master said, "I am not one who was born in the possession of knowledge; I am one who is fond of antiquity, and earnest in seeking it there."[3] Tzŭ-kung confessed that he "knew only two after hearing about one."

> The Master said to Tzŭ-kung, "Which do you consider superior, yourself or Hui?
>
> Tzŭ-kung replied, "How dare I compare myself with Hui? Hui hears one point and knows ten about a subject; I hear one point and know a second.
>
> The Master said, "You are not equal to him. I commend you for realizing that you are not equal to him."[4]

The knowledge with which a man is born can be called a gift of nature; it does not come from human effort. On the other hand, the knowledge acquired through study and effort is attributable to learning and experience; it evolves from practice, which is of course subject to individual control. Some engage in this practice with a natural ease, some with vigorous effort, others with a desire for its advantages. The difference lies in a person's initiative, the strength or weakness of it. But when success is achieved, "it comes to the same thing":

> Some practice them (duties of universal obligation) with a natural ease; some from a desire for their advantages; and some by strenuous effort. But the achievement being made. it comes to the same thing.[5]

Man's wisdom, then, is the sum-total of these three kinds of practice. Frequently men who have a low degree of natural endowment more than make up for it with their fondness for learning and the earnestness with which they engage in practice. Sometimes they even accomplish more than those who have a high degree of natural talent coupled with apathy toward learning and refusal to engage in earnest practice. Hence, "after the knowledge is acquired, it comes to the same thing," and "the achievement being made, it comes to the same thing."

Whether knowledge is acquired through study or painstaking effort, this is clear: all the stages in the investigation of things must be traversed. Also, there must be constant application leading toward perfection in learning and self-cultivation.

> In the *Book of songs*, it is said, "Look at the banks of the Ch'i, with the green bamboos so luxuriant: Here is our elegant and accomplished prince: As we cut and then file; as we chisel and then grind; so has he cultivated himself. How grave he is and dignified! How majestic and distinguished! Our elegant and accomplished prince never can be forgotten." That expression, "as we cut and then file," indicates the work of learning. "As we chisel and then grind" indicates that of self-culture. "How grave he is and dignified!" indicates the feeling of cautious reverence. "How majestic and distinguished!" indicates an awe-inspiring deportment. "Our elegant and accomplished prince never can be forgotten," indicates how, when virtue is complete and excellence extreme, the people cannot forget him.[6]

In mankind's search for the reasons for its existence and evolution, learning takes place everywhere at all times. This is why continuous progress is made in the realm of human wisdom. If ever the thrust for progress is halted, retrogression will begin; hence the proverb: "Learning, like upstream navigation, moves backward when no progress is made." Stupidity and brilliance, weakness and strength are relative terms, and the following method is the only certain way of achieving brilliance and strength:

> The superior man may not engage in studying, but once he does, he does not relax until he can understand all that he studies. He may not make an inquiry, but once he does, he does not relax until he knows everything about which he inquires. He may not reflect, but once he does, he does not relax until he apprehends

everything on which he reflects. He may not discriminate, but once he does, he does not relax until he is clear in his discrimination. He may not practice, but once he does, he does not relax until he is earnest in his practice.

If another man succeeds by one effort, he will use a hundred efforts. If another man succeeds by ten efforts, he will use a thousand.

Let a man proceed in this way, and, though dull, he will surely become intelligent; though weak, he will surely become strong.[7]

In examining the above excerpt from the *Doctrine of the Mean,* we can say that not to "relax" means to continue unceasingly with all stages in the investigation of things. The reason for devoting a hundred efforts in place of one, and a thousand in place of ten by others, is to increase one's knowledge to supplement what one is born with, so that the dull may become intelligent and the weak strong. This is what is meant by "human effort can overcome nature," and in one who is physically and mentally healthy this is of course subject to one's own control.

With clarification of "knowledge becoming complete after the investigation of things," we can proceed to examine the importance of the following categories of knowledge: (1) knowledge of heaven, (2) knowledge of destiny, (3) knowledge of nature, (4) illustration of the Way, (5) illustration of virtue, (6) illustration of instruction, (7) knowledge of men, and (8) knowledge of things.

B. Knowledge of Heaven

Man is a social being. All his life he lives in close contact with other human beings. As soon as he is born, he needs parental care. And through the years he lives with his parents, brothers and sisters; he learns from his teachers and enjoys his friends; he marries and earns his livelihood by working with others; in society he serves and governs others, even as they serve and govern him. He cannot isolate himself from all other persons for as much as a single day. Therefore, since his life is essentially social, a man must come to know his fellow men. Especially, he must know how to live with them.

Now, part of a man's knowledge of other men is derived from

observation of the universe. To put it another way: the object of a knowledge of heaven is knowledge of men. "In order to know men, he (the superior man) may not dispense with a knowledge of Heaven."[8]

Section B of Chapter II touched on the dynamic and static phenomena of the universe with a view to gaining some understanding of the laws of the natural world.[9] The preliminary conclusion is embodied in the following;

The Way of Heaven and Earth may be completely declared in one sentence: They are witout any doubleness, and so they produce things in a manner that is unfathomable.

The Way of Heaven and Earth is large and substantial, high and brilliant, far-reaching and long-enduring.[10]

Large and substantial; this is how it (sincerity) contains all things. High and brilliant; this is how it overspreads all things. Reaching far and continuing long; this is how it perfects all things.[11]

Since man is a vital part of the universe and the most intelligent of all living things, it follows that man's virtue should be compatible with the universe, his environment. This is especially so since it is clear that the Way of Heaven and Earth is altruistic, unceasing and shows its greatness by being large and substantial, high and brilliant, far-reaching and long-enduring. Therefore it is said:

So large and substantial, the individual possessing it (sincerity) is the co-equal of Earth. So high and brilliant, it makes him the co-equal of Heaven. So far-reaching and long-continuing, it makes him infinite. Such being its nature, without any display, it becomes manifested; without any movement, it produces changes; and without any effort, it accomplishes its ends.[12]

Chung-ni handed down the doctrines of Yao and Shun and adopted the traditions of Wên and Wu. He showed them to harmonize with the laws of heaven above and to conform to the movements of water and land below.

He may be compared to heaven and earth in their supporting and containing, their overshadowing and curtaining all things. He may be compared to the four seasons in their alternating progress, and to the sun and moon in their successive shining.

All things are nourished together without their injuring one another. The operations of nature take their course without conflict or confusion. The smaller energies are like river currents: the greater energies are seen in mighty transformations. It is this which makes heaven and earth so great.[13]

"Supporting and containing" and "overshadowing and curtaining" all things refer to the all-embracing and impartial nature of heaven and earth. This in turn accounts for the simultaneous "nourishment" of all things "without their injuring one another" and the concomitant "course" of natural operations "without conflict or confusion." For it is only with largeness that all things can be contained, and it is only with durability that all things can be perfected. This way of largeness and durability is what should be sought by all mankind in order to achieve the objects of common existence and evolution.

The movement of heaven is ceaseless. To support this movement, there must be a great and inexhaustible dynamism. And this dynamism is called "sincerity." That is why it is said: "Sincerity is the Way of Heaven."[14]

It is the destiny of man, endowed with this dynamism, to emulate the example of heaven and earth in containing all things, to choose what is good and hold fast to it, to strengthen himself continually and strive for wisdom.

> The attainment of sincerity is the way of men. He who possesses sincerity is he who, without any effort, hits what is right and apprehends, without the exercise of thought; he is the sage who naturally and easily embodies the right way. He who attains to sincerity is he who chooses what is good and firmly holds fast to it.[15]

The four seasons come and go, one following the other as night follows day, as each night the moon moves across a sky which the brilliant sun has left. In this orderly movement, the heavens and the earth show forth their balanced strength. As a result:

> This equilibrium is the great root from which grow all the human actings in the world, and this harmony is the universal path which they all should pursue. Let the states of equilibrium and harmony exist in perfection, and a happy order will prevail throughout heaven and earth, and all things will be nourished and flourish.[16]

Equilibrium and harmony—these are the forces sustaining the common existence of mankind. If a man can understand this and integrate himself with these forces, he will know

While there are no stirrings of pleasure, anger, sorrow or joy, the mind may be said to be in the state of equilibrium. When these feelings have been stirred, and they act in their due degree, there ensues what may be called the state of harmony.[17]

As a man lives and works with others, he cannot help but show his feelings—pleasure, anger, sorrow, joy. But for all men to live peacefully with one another it is essential that feelings are expressed "in their due degree," which means that they do not incline to either side; hence, "Being withont inclination to either side is called *'chung'* (equilibrium)." When both sides are satisfied, peace and harmony are produced. This is basic theory when it comes to the maintenance of peace.

When the component parts of a given nation—the people of China—strive ceaselessly to (1) strengthen themselves, (2) maintain equilibrihm and harmony, and (3) perpetually pursue the objectives of "largeness" and "durability"—then this nation is bound to become more and more flourishing (with 600 million persons in one family). Its history and culture will stretch through endless ages (more than 5,000 years of direct succes.ion). The teachings of Confucius have indeed laid a brilliant and enduring philosophical foundation for the Chinese nation.

The *Book of Changes*, an exhaustive work on natural phenomena and laws, combines into one the Ways of Heaven and men. Heaven surrounds and towers above the earth, and its controlling deity is called God. At one time in Chinese history, the authority of Heaven on earth was called the "Son of Heaven," much the same as Christ is regarded as the Son of God in the West. The "Son of Heaven" was conceded the right to rule over the country, and those rulers who could forsake evil for good were thought fit to "sacrifice to God."

Mencius said, "If the lady Hsi had been covered with something unclean, all people would have stopped their noses in passing her. But though a person may be ugly, if he purifies his heart, fasts and bathes, he may sacrifice to God."[18]

Confucius was born when the Chou dynasty was on the decline. Concerned about the moral degeneration of the era, he traveled through the various States and preached the Way to the ruling feudal lords. Actually, he hoped that one or more of them would accept his services and support him in his efforts to carry out his moral mission. However, though he served as Prime Minister of the State of Lu and saw the operation of good government there after three months, regrettably he could not remain in office for long.

For fourteen more years Confucius traveled and preached. In this time he won the respect of many rulers, but none drew him into their governments in an official capacity, and he was disappointed ultimately in what he felt was the failure of his historic mission. After his return to Lu, he edited the *Book of Songs* and the *Book of History*, compiled the *Book of Rites* and the *Book of Music*, annotated the *Book of Changes*, and wrote the *Spring and Autumn Annals*.

Confucius' original work, the *Spring and Autumn Annals*, was a presentation of the facts of history designed to drive home the distinction between right and wrong and to teach the then reigning rulers how to uplift the moral plane of the times. Although Confucius was never a Son of Heaven, he did transmit the Way of Heaven, which was a function of the Son of Heaven. According to Mencius:

> ...the world fell into decay and principles faded away. Perverse statements and oppressive deeds waxed rife. There were instances of ministers who murdered their sovereigns and of sons who murdered their fathers. Confucius was afraid and wrote the *Spring and Autumn Annals*. What this work contained are matters proper to the Son of Heaven. On this account Confucius said, "Yes! It is the *Spring and Autumn Annals* that will make men know me, and it is the *Spring and Autumn Annals* that will make men condemn me."[19]
>
> Confucius completed the *Spring and Autumn Annals* and rebellious ministers and villainous sons were struck with terror.[20]

Spring is the season of growth, while autumn is a time of grim destruction. The two are diametrically opposed. Although the *Spring and Autumn Annals* was an historical work, its subtle criticisms were meant to convey commendation and condemnation where merited. The juxtaposition of the words spring and autumn in the title was used by Confucius to help his readers look at the future through the mirror of the past. He felt they then could better distinguish between right and wrong, between allegiance and disaffection.

"In the *Book of Songs* are three hundred pieces, but the design of them all may be embraced in one phrase—'Having no depraved thoughts.'" It is evident that the *Book of Songs* can rectify the human heart. Confucius extended the *Book of Songs* with his *Spring and Autumn Annals* which, again, put the accent on the rectification of the human heart. "When those (royal) odes ceased to be made," said Mencius, "then the *Spring and Autumn Annals* was produced."

> Mencius said, "The traces of sovereign rule were extinguished, and the royal odes ceased to be made. When those odes ceased to be made, the *Spring and Autumn Annals* was produced. The Ch'êng of Chin, the T'ao-Wu of Ch'u and the *Spring and Autumn Annals* of Lu were books of the same character. The subject of the latter was the affairs of Duke Huan of Ch'i and Duke Wen of Chin, and its style was the historical.. Confucius said, 'Its righteous decisions I ventured to make.'"[21]

Whenever the affairs of man are discussed, the word "Heaven" signifies environment. But the force of environment is composed of innumerable factors, and their influence can only be felt. So, any unknown power which controls the affairs of man is called "Heaven." Said Mencius: "...that which is done without man's doing is from Heaven."[22] He gave the following examples·

> ...and by the passage of the "T'ai Chia"—When Heaven sends down calamities, it is still possible to escape from them; when we occasion the calamities ourselves, it is not possible to live any longer.[23]
>
> Duke P'ing of Lu was about to leave his palace, when his favorite, one Tsang Ts'ang, made a request to him, saying, "On other days, when you have gone out, you have given instructions to the officials as to where you were going. But now, the horses have been put to the carriage, and the officials do not yet know where you are going. I venture to ask." The duke said, "I am going to see Mencius." "How is this?" said the other. "That you demean yourself, prince, in paying the honor of the first visit to a common man is, I suppose, because you think he is a worthy man. From such men the rules of ceremonial proprieties and right emanate. But on the occasion of Mencius' second mourning, his observances exceeded those of the former. Do not go to see him, prince." The duke said. "I will not."

The official Yüeh-chêng entered the court and had an audience. He said, "Prince, why have you not gone to see Mêng K'o?" The duke said, "Someone told me that, on the occasion of Mencius' second mourning, his observances exceeded those of the former. It is on that account that I have not gone to see him." "How is this!" answered Yüeh-chêng. "By what you call 'exceeding' you mean, I suppose, that, on the first occasion, he used the rites appropriate to a scholar, and, on the second, those appropriate to a great official; that he first used three tripods and afterwards five tripods." The duke said, "No; I refer to the greater excellence of the coffin, the shell, the grave-clothes and the shroud." Yüeh-chêng said, "That cannot be called 'exceeding.' This was the difference between being poor and being rich."

After this, Yüeh-chêng saw Mencius and said to him, "I told the prince about you, and he was consequently coming to see you, when one of his favorites, named Tsang Ts'ang, stopped him and therefore he did not come as he had intended." Mencius said, "A man's advancement is effected, it may be, by others, and the stopping him is, it may be, from the efforts of others. But to advance a man or to stop his advance is really beyond the power of other men. My not finding in the prince of Lu a ruler who would confide in me and put my counsels into practice, is from Heaven. How could the scion of the Tsang family cause me not to find the ruler that would suit me?"[1]

In these passages the word "Heaven" refers to the influence of environment. The same word conveys the same meaning in such expressions as "turning back Heaven with human strength," "There is no way of turning back Heaven," and "Human effort can overcome Heaven."

Wan Chang said, "Was it the case that Yao gave the throne to Shun?" Mencius said, "No. The Son of Heaven cannot give the throne to another."

"But who gave Shun the throne that he had?" "Heaven gave it to him," was the answer.

"Heaven gave it to him," said Wan Chang. "Does it mean that Heaven conferred its appointment on him with specific injunctions?"

Mencius said, "No, Heaven does not speak. It simply showed its will by his personal conduct and his conduct of affairs."

"It showed its will by his personal conduct and his conduct of affairs," said Wan Chang. "How was this?" Mencius' answer was, "The Son of Heaven may present a man to Heaven, but he cannot make Heaven give that man the throne. A prince can present a man to the Son of Heaven, but he cannot cause the Son of Heaven to make that man a prince. A great official can present a man to his prince, but he cannot cause the prince to make that man a great official. Yao presented Shun to Heaven, and Heaven accepted him. He presented him to the people, and the people accepted him. Therefore I say, 'Heaven does not speak. It simply indicated its will by his personal conduct and his conduct of affairs.' "

Wan Chang said, "I presume to ask how it was that Yao presented Shun to Heaven, and Heaven accepted him; and that he exhibited him to the people, and the people accepted him."

Mencius replied, "He caused him to preside over the sacrifices, and all the spirits were well pleased with them. He caused him to preside over the conduct of affairs, and affairs were well administered, so that the people reposed under him;—thus the people accepted him. Therefore I said, 'The Son of Heaven cannot give the throne to another.'

"Shun assisted Yao in the government for twenty-eight years;—this was more than man could have done, and was from Heaven. After the death of Yao, when the three years' mourning was completed, Shun withdrew from the son of Yao to the south of South River. The princes of the empire, however, repairing to court, went, not to the son of Yao, but to Shun. Litigants went, not to the son of Yao, but to Shun. Singers sang, not of the son of Yao, but of Shun. Therefore I said, 'Heaven gave him the throne.'

"It was after these things that he went to the Middle Kingdom and occupied the seat of the Son of Heaven. If he had earlier taken up residence in the palace of Yao and brought pressure to bear on the son of Yao, it would have been an act of usurpation, and not the gift of Heaven.

"This sentiment is expressed in the words of the 'Great Declaration,"—'Heaven sees as the people see; Heaven hears as the people hear.' "[25]

Tzŭ-hsia said..."There is the following saying which I have heard: 'Death and life have their determined destiny; riches and honors depend upon Heaven.' "[26]

Therefore the institutions of the ruler are rooted in his own character and conduct, and sufficient attestation of them is given by the masses of the people. He examines them by comparison with those of the three kings and finds them without mistake. He sets them up before heaven and earth and finds nothing in them contrary to their mode of operation. He presents himself with them before spiritual beings and no doubts about them arise. He is prepared to wait for the rise of a sage a hundred ages after and has no misgivings.

His presenting himself with his institutions before spiritual beings without any doubts arising about them shows that he knows Heaven. His being preparped, without any misgivings, to wait for the rise of a sage a hundred ages after shows that he knows men.[27]

The word "Heaven in all the above passages refers to the unknown power which controls the affairs of men.

When we suffer a sudden pain we frequently cry out, "Heavens!" When we encounter danger and are unafraid, we believe in Heaven. When we are unhappy and unwilling to speak, we use Heaven as an example. Here are some illustrations:

> The Master said, "Alas! There is no one that knows me."
> Tzŭ-kung said, "What do you mean by thus saying—that no one knows you?"
> The Master replied, "I do not murmur against Heaven. I do not grumble against men. My studies lie low, and my penetration rises high. But there is Heaven that knows me!"[28]
> The Master said, "Heaven produced the virtue that is in me. Huan-t'ui—what can he do to me?"[29]
> The Master said, "I would prefer not speaking."
> Tzŭ-kung said, "If you, Master, do not speak, what shall we, your disciples, have to record?"
> The Master said, "Does Heaven speak? The four seasons pursue their courses, and all things are continually being produced, but does Heaven say anything?"[30]

It is difficult to trace the origin of mankind—and of everything else, for that matter. However, as all things are produced from the natural world, they are often referred to as heaven-born. Following are some examples:

> Mencius said, "It is said in the *Book of Songs,* 'Heaven, in producing mankind,/Gave them their various faculties and relations with their specific laws./These are the invariable rules of nature for all to hold,/And all love this admirable virtue."[31]
> The Master said, "...Thus it is that Heaven, in the production of things, is sure to be bountiful to them, according to their qualities. Hence the tree that is flourishing, it nourishes, while that which is ready to fall, it overthrows."
> In the *Book of Songs* it is said, "The admirable, amiable prince displayed conspicuously his excelling virtue. He was suited to rule his people. Therefore, he received from Heaven the emoluments

of dignity. It protected him, blessed him and decreed him the throne; sending him from Heaven these favors repeatedly."

We may say therefore that he who has great virtue will be sure to receive the appointment of Heaven.[32]

Mencius said, "...Heaven's plan in the production of mankind is this: that they who are first informed should instruct those who are later in being informed, and they who first apprehend the way should instruct those who are slower in doing so. I am the one of Heaven's people who has first apprehended; I will take this way and instruct this people in it. If I do not, who will do so?"[33]

To sum up, what we recognize as heaven is high and brilliant, large and all-embracing, impartial and unselfish, sincere and transforming, steadily moving and ceaseless, strong, enduring, well-balanced and harmonious, continuously reproductive, and endowed with an overwhelming force. For this reason it can do the impossible. If man can be aware of his environmect at all times and act in accordance with divine justice, he can be the "co-equal of Heaven." This means he can "merge with Heaven and Earth above and below," "participate in the transforming and nurturing operations of Heaven and Earth" and "collaborate with Heaven and Earth." The knowledge of Heaven is the knowledge of the virtues enjoined upon men, to which they can seek to be equal.

Since it is up to men to be co-equals of Heaven, it follows that the position of men is very high, even sacred. This leads men to cultivate self-respect, to avoid offending against Heaven and, when necessary, to pray for Heaven's pardon.

Wang-sun Chia asked, saying, "What is the meaning of the saying, 'It is better to pay court to the furnace than to the southwest corner of the house?'"

The Master said, "Not so. He who offends against Heaven has none to whom he can pray."[34]

C. Knowledge of Destiny

Destiny frequently is regarded as akin to superstition. As a matter of fact, however, destiny denotes quite simply the "trend" of things, or to put it another way, the effect which can be deduced from the cause.

A close look at the word "destiny" may help us understand it. For it forms part of the Chinese equivalent of the word "revolution," which when literally translated means "riddance of destiny." According to Sun Yatsen, "Anything which obeys divine justice is consistent with human nature, follows the tide of the world and meets the requirements of mankind, and which those who are first informed and who first apprehend decide to put into practice, can never fail."

He was talking here, of course, about revolution. And with him we can see that if the politically inspired actions and activities of any government are inconsistent with divine justice, human nature, the tide of the world and the requirements of mankind—if they cause the people misery—then the nation is ripe for revolution. And impending revolt will become a reality when revolutionary leaders—those who are first informed and who first apprehend—take over and mobilize the strength of the masses to reverse the downward trend of the country and bring it back to its former glory. In short, with human effort, evil effects produced by evil causes can be removed.

Needless to say, this is totally scientific and in no way superstitious. Confucius even regarded the knowledge of destiny as a requisite condition for all superior men.

> The Master said, "Without knowing destiny, it is impossible to be a superior man. Without knowing the rules of propriety, it is impossible for the character to be established. Without knowing the force of words, it is impossible to know men."[35]

Since the superior man has an uncommonly high degree of wisdom and virtue, he should be able to figure out what effect will follow from a given cause and thereby know the proper trend to follow.

> In the "Declaration to K'ang" it is said, "The decree may not always rest on us; that is, goodness obtains the decree, and the want of goodness loses it."[36]

This means the trend of public opinion, the people's will may change at any time; more, that those who obey divine justice and comply with human nature can receive the decree, while those who do not can lose it.

> Confucius said, "There are three things of which the superior man stands in awe. He stands in awe of the ordinances of Heaven.

He stands in awe of great men. He stands in awe of the words of sages. The mean man does not know the ordinances of Heaven, and consequently does not stand in awe of them. He is disrespectful to great men. He makes sport of the words of sages."[37]

Confucius is implying that the superior man can understand and forecast environment (Heaven) and the trend (destiny), for that is why he fears and respects great men, sages and the ordinances of Heaven. The mean man, on the contrary, is something else again.

So, the superior man is quiet and calm, waiting for his destiny, while the mean man walks in dangerous paths expecting the uncertain chances of luck.[38]

Mencius said, "Yao and Shun were what they were by nature; T'ang and Wu were so by returning to natural virtue.

"When all the movements in the countenance and every turn of the body are exactly what is proper, that shows the extreme degree of the complete virtue. Weeping for the dead should be from real sorrow, and not because of the living. The regular path of virtue is to be pursued without any bend, and not with a view to emolument. The words should all be necessarily sincere, not with any desire to do what is right.

"The superior man performs the rule of right and thereby waits simply for his destiny."[39]

This means that the superior man, remaining in an environment in which things change, acts according to the rules of virtue and silently observes the trend (waits for his destiny) in order to cope with the situation. The mean man, on the other hand, does not understand the trend. He looks for lucky occurrences and runs risks. On the basis of these principles Mencius predicted that P'ên-ch'êng Kua was bound to be put to death. And his prophesy was fulfilled—because P'en-ch'êng was a man of little ability; he had not learned the great doctrines of the superior man while walking his dangerous paths.

P'ên-ch'êng Kua having obtained an official position in Ch'i, Mencius said, "He is a dead man, that P'ên-ch'êng Kua!" P'ên-ch'êng Kau having been put to death, the disciples asked, saying, "How did you know, Master, that he would meet with death?" Mencius replied, "He was a man, who had a little ability but had not learned the great doctrines of the superior man. He was just qualified to bring death upon himself, but for nothing more."[40]

Whether the Way could be put into practice depended on certain conditions and the trend of the situation. It could not be influenced one way or the other by the effort of one man. Neither could it be changed by the killing of one man. So, Confucius said, "What can Kung-po Liao do where destiny is concerned?"

> Kung-po Liao, having slandered Tzǔ-lu to Chi-sun, Tzǔ-lu informed Confucius of it, saying "Our Master is certainly being led astray by Kung-po Liao, but I have still power enough left to kill Liao and expose his corpse in public."
> The Master said, "If the Way is to prevail, it is destiny. If it is to fall to the ground, it is destiny. What can Kung-po Liao do where destiny is concerned?"[41]

The trend is not formed overnight. The factors involved may be extremely complex and not easily foreseen, or they may be simple and easily predictable.

Of the former, Mencius said: "That which happens without man's causing is destiny."[42] Here is an example:

> Po-niu being ill, the Master went to make an inquiry. He took hold of his hand through the window and said, "It is killing him. It is destiny, alas! That such a man should have such a sickness! That such a man should have such a sickness."[43]

As far as the simple factors are concerned, they are easily predictable. Take the case of old people who have no children; we know they will suffer. Also, to use Mencius' example, a man who stands under a tottering wall invites death; it is not something a wise person would do:

> Mencius said, "Destiny is involved in everything. A man should receive submissively what is normal destiny.
> "Therefore he who has the knowledge of destiny will not stand beneath a precipitous wall.
> "Death sustained in the full practice of the Way is normal destiny.
> "Death under handcuffs and fetters is not normal destiny."[44]

This means that although there are many different changes in a man's lifetime, from infancy through old age and death, the general trend of his life is the same. Hence the statement: "Life and death are pre-ordained by destiny." On the other hand, suicide or death due to the commission of a crime are thought of as "not in accordance with normal destiny," not predestined.

The *Book of Changes* is different from other classics because it deals, not with the normal occurrences of our environment, but with the changing rules derived from the myriad changes taking place in the universe. It simplifies and clarifies the changes. As a result, these rules have become immutable laws. It is by understanding the changes and their trend that man can meet those changes in a state of equilibrium, without excesses or inadequacies. The principles of the *Doctrine of the Mean* were derived from this understanding.

The utility of the *Book of Changes* is due to the fact that its origin lies in astronomy. The very word which stands for "changes" in Chinese is composed of the characters "sun" and "moon." Many variables of the sun, moon and four seasons can be foretold by referring to the *Book of Changes*. The usefulness of the volume is extensive, for all persons who work in sciences that deal with these changes—medicine and the military, for instance—will find it helpful, perhaps essential. Later generations have disparaged this book, regarding it as merely a study of fortune-telling, but they have failed to see that its essence and great utility lie in the fact that it does indeed present the "knowledge of Heaven's decree and exhaustion of human effort."

> The Master said, "If some years were added to my life, and I could study the *Book of Changes* after fifty, then I might come to be without great faults."[45]

It is said that when Confucius annotated the *Book of Changes* he was already an old man, a fact which underlines the depth and inscrutability of this classic. According to the Master, he had gained the knowledge of Heaven's decree by the time he had reached his fiftieth year. Here he was approaching the sunset of his life, and still he was expressing the hope that a few more years would be given him to study the classic. He felt that with added study he could gain from it even more sound views on the laws of nature and society, and at the same time learn to avoid great faults. Indeed, he could well see that the *Book of Changes* would give him the knowledge of Heaven and destiny.

> The subjects of which the Master seldom spoke were profit, destiny and benevolence.[46]

Why did Confucius rarely delve into these three ideas? The reason is simple. Confucius never spoke of personal interest, let alone profit and its future trend. In the *Book of Changes* it is said "profit is the harmony of righteousness" and "to profit things can result in the harmony of righteousness." The superior man regarded profit as righteousness, and so the latter was always mentioned when the former was discussed, for only when men and things were profited could there be righteousness. On the other hand, the mean man, concerned only with profit, did not have any conception of righteousness. While Confucius could not always avoid the subject of profit—there were many instances where it was dealt with in the *Book of Changes*—its meaning was so subtle to him that he seldom mentioned it when discoursing with his disciples.

Since destiny was another extremely subtle subject, Confucius seldom talked about it. This is what lay behind Tzŭ-kung's comment: "It is impossible to hear our Master's views on nature and the Heavenly Way."

The *Analects* took up the subject of benevolence many times, yet Confucius is said to have discussed it rarely. The reason, probably, is that he did not presume to have the quality of benevolence, nor did he lightly concede it to others.

In regard to Heaven and destiny, Mencius offered the following interpretations:

> Mencius said, "He who has exhausted all his mental constitution knows his nature. Knowing his nature, he knows Heaven.
>
> "To preserve one's mental constitution and nourish one's nature is the way to serve Heaven.
>
> "When neither a premature death nor long life causes a man any double-mindedness, but he waits in the cultivation of his personal character for whatever issue; this is the way in which he establishes his destiny."[47]

This means that, although the destiny of Heaven cannot be known, a man should spend himself throughout his life in the pursuit of self-cultivation as year after year he awaits his destiny. To "wait for" one's destiny is not to contend with it. But self-cultivation is something which one can achieve by sheer dint of exhaustive effort—and the achievement cannot be swept away by destiny. In this lies the vital importance of a knowledge of destiny.

Now that we have explored the meanings of "Heaven" and "destiny," we can approach the question: What does the combination of the two concepts signify? Briefly, the answer goes like this: Some persons have ability without learning; some have knowledge without deliberation. There may be differences in the extent of ability and knowldge, but there is no exception to the possession of either. Mencius called them "intuitive ability" and "intuitive knowledge." Confucius described people possessing them as born with knowledge. In popular parlance the words most used to depict them are "instinct" and "human nature."

The only way to trace the origin of instinct is to plumb the history of mankind's evolution. This is impossible through human effort, of course; so "instinct" is referred to as "Heaven's decree." And this is consistent with the scientific spirit envisaged in the statement: "When you know a thing, to hold that you know it; and when you do not know a thing, to allow that you do not know it—this is knowledge."

D. Knowledge of Nature

Everything in the universe has its instinct, by virtue of which it is in existence. This instinct is called nature; it comes with life itself and acquires its faculty without teaching. Hence, "what Heaven has conferred is called nature."[48]

Since instinct is nature, it is one of the dynamisms in the universe. Again, since each thing in the universe has its nature, each also has its own dynamism. Also, dynamism exists in spite of everything else, which, nonetheless, must depend on dynamism for existence. Phenomenally, movement and static exist by turns, but the static of matter retains its inherent dynamism, which can free the static and resume the movement. So, in essence, dynamism has its absolute existence and is what man is endowed with by Heaven.

The cognition of all humanistic essence must come from that of natural essence. Things come to life when they are endowed with the motive force of the universe. From the standpoint of the cognition of natural essence, this force is called "dynamism;"

and from the standpoint of the cognition of humanistic essence, it is called "sincerity." By possessing this dynamism, man shows forth the principle of existence. Hence, "When we have intelligence resulting from sincerity, this condition is to be ascribed to nature."[49]

All living things, not only man, possess this instinct. The philosopher Kao once sought the advice of Mencius on the definition of "nature" as "life" itself. Mencius said he regarded this definition as too general, although he did not see anything basically wrong in it. To Mencius' way of thinking, the fact that the definition made no distinction between mankind and the animal kingdom could lead to undesirable consequences.

> The philosopher Kao said, "Life is what we call nature."
> Mencius asked him, "Do you say that by nature you mean life, just as you say that white is white?"
> "Yes, I do," was the reply.
> Mencius added, "Is the whiteness of a white feather like that of white snow, and the whiteness of white snow like that of white jade?"
> Kao again said, "Yes."
> "Very well," pursued Mencius. "Is the nature of a dog like the nature of an ox, and the nature of a man?"[50]

In fact and as a definition, however, the philosopher Kao's statement was not mistaken.

For living things to attain the object of their existence—to exist in the present and to continue in existenue in the future—they must develop their instinct. To maintain life, their absolute minimum requirement is sufficient food, and for the continuation of life the minimum is the sex act. As the philosopher Kao stated: "Food and sex are part and parcel of nature."[51]

It is said, "Food and sex are the great desires of man." But if man were to develop only his instinct for food and sex, what would be the difference between him and an animal? Also, how could he call himself the most intelligent of all living things? Of course the difference lies in the fact that man brightens and enlarges his life by knowing and pursuing benevolence and righteousness. Therefore, the pursuit of benevolence along with the search for food and sex comprise man's three basic instincts.

Mencius said, "That whereby a man differs from the lower animals is but small. The mass of people cast it away, while superior men perserve it.

"Shun clearly understood the multitude of things and closely observed the relations of humanity. He walked along the path of benevolence and righteousness; he did not need to pursue benevolence and righteousness."[52]

Propriety is the expression of benevolence and righteousness in everyday life. When a choice must be made between propriety on the one hand and food and sex on the other, propriety should take precedence.

A man of Jen asked the disciple Wu-lu, saying, "Is an observance of the rules of propriety in regard to eating, or the eating the more important?"

The answer was, "The observance of the rules of propriety is the more important."

"Is the gratifying of the appetite of sex, or the doing so only according to the rules of propriety, the more important?" The answer again was, "The observance of the rules of propriety in the matter is the more important."

The man pursued, "If the result of eating only according to the rules of propriety will be death by starvation, while by disregarding those rules we may get food, must they still be observed in such a case? If according to the rule that he shall go in person to meet his wife a man cannot be married, while by disregarding that rule he may get married, must he still observe the rule in such a case?"

Wu-lu was unable to reply to these questions, and the next day he went to Tsou and told them to Mencius. Mencius said, "What difficulty is there in answering these questions?

"If you do not adjust them at their lower extremities, but only put their tops on a level, a piece of wood an inch square may be made to be higher than the pointed peak of a high building.

"Gold is heavier than feathers; but does that saying have reference, on the other hand, to a single clasp of gold, and, on the other, to a wagon-load of feathers?

"If you take a case where the eating is of the utmost importance and the observing the rules of propriety is of little importance, and compare the things together, why should the eating not be more important? So, taking the case where the gratifying the appetite of sex is of the utmost importance and the observing the rules of propriety is of little importance, why should the gratifying the appetite not be more important?

"Go and answer him thus, 'If, by twisting your elder brother's arm and snatching from him what he is eating, you can get food for yourself, while if you do not do so, you will not get anything to eat, will you so twist his arm? If, by getting over your eastern neighbor's wall and dragging away his virgin daughter, you can get a wife, while, if you do not do so, you will not be able to get a wife, will you so drag her away?"[53]

Why are benevolence and righteousness a part of man's instinct? A man cannot be isolated from his fellow beings. In his first years of life, he lives with his parents and relies upon them. As he matures, again he is constantly with people; in fact, it is essential that he associate with others for he is in need of mutual love and mutual aid. Therefore, benevolence—love which comes from the heart—and righteousness—love which is expressed in action—should be an essential part of man's instinct. Mencius called them intuitive ability and intuitive knowledge, the high nobility of Heaven, the tranquil habitation and straight path, and the four beginnings.

Mencius said, "The ability possessed by men without having been acquired by learning is intuitive ability, and the knowledge possessed by them without the exercise of thought is their intuitive knowledge.

"Children carried in the arms all know to love their parents, and when they are grown a little, they all know to respect their elder brothers.

"Filial affection for parents is the working of benevolence. Respect for elders is the working of righteousness. There is no other reason for those feelings:—they extend to all under heaven."[54]

Mencius said, "There is a nobility of Heaven, and there is a nobility of man. Benevolence, righteousness, loyalty and faithfulness, with unwearied joy in goodness; these constitute the nobility of Heaven. To be a *kung,* a *ch'ing* or a *ta-fu;* this constitutes the nobility of man.

"The men of antiquity cultivated their nobility of Heaven, and the nobility of man came to them in its train.

"The men of the present day cultivate their nobility of Heaven in order to seek for the nobility of man, and when they have obtained that, they throw away the other;—their delusion is extreme. The issue is simply this, that they must lose that nobility of man as well."[55]

Mencius said, "Benevolence is the tranquil habitation of man, and righteousness is his straight path."[56]

"The feeling of commiseration is the beginning of benevolence. The feeling of shame and dislike is the beginning of righteousness. The feeling of modesty and concession is the beginning of propriety. The feeling of right and wrong is the beginning of wisdom."[57]

Since benevolence and righteousness are part of man's inherent nature, their expression is always natural, never forced or affected. Mencius emphasized this when he refuted a point raised by the philosopher Kao in this exchange:

The philosopher Kao said, "Man's nature is like the *ch'i*-willow, and righteousness is like a cup or a bowl. The fashioning of benevolence and righteousness out of man's nature is like the making of cups and bowls from the *ch'i*-willow."

Mencius replied, "Can you, leaving untouched the nature of the willow, make with it cups and bowls? You must do violence and injury to the willow before you can make cups and bowls with it. If you must do violence and injury to the willow in order to make cups and bowls with it, do you mean that you will likewise do violence and injury to humanity in order to fashion from it benevolence and righteousness? What your words are bound to do is to lead all men on to make havoc of benevolence and righteousness."[58]

Indeed, Confucius and Mencius went even a step further by regarding benevolence as something indispensable to man. Consider the following statements:

Benevolence is the characteristic element of humanity.[59]

Mencius said, "benevolence is the distinguishing characteristic of man. As embodied in man's conduct, it is called the Way."[60]

Confucius spoke of benevolence, but Mencius spoke of benevolence and righteousness (which is benevolence seen in practice). Actually, both sages had the same thing in mind, and both regarded it as an instinct for existence. However, the importance of benevolence and righteousness is far greater than the importance of one's own life. The lack of food and sex can cause only the failure to maintain and perpetuate one's own life. But the absence of benevolence and righteousness can result in the extinction of all mankind. Therefore, when a choice must be made between the observance of benevolence and righteousness and the preservation of one's own life, the latter should be sacrificed to make possible the former.

The Master said, "The determined scholar and the man of virtue will not seek to live at the expense of injuring their virtue. They will even sacrifice their lives to preserve their virtue complete."[61]

Jan Yu said, "Is our Master for the ruler of Wei?" Tzŭ-kung said, "Oh! I will ask him."

He went in accordingly, and said, "What sort of men were Po-i and Shu-ch'i?" "They were ancient worthies," said the Master. "Did they have any repinings?" "They sought to act virtuously, and they succeeded in doing so. What was there for them to repine about?"

On this, Tzŭ-kung went out and said, "Out Master is not for him."[62]

Mencius said, "I like fish, and I also like bear's paws. If I cannot have the two together, I will let the fish go and take the bear's paws. So, I like life, and I also like righteousness. If I cannot keep the two together, I will let life go and choose righteousness.

"I like life indeed, but there is that which I like more than life, and therefore, I will not seek to possess it by any improper ways. I dislike death indeed, but there is that which I dislike more than death, and therefore there are occasions when I will not avoid danger.

"If among the things which man likes there were nothing which he liked more than life, why should he not use every means by which he could preserve it? If among the things which man dislikes there were nothing which he disliked more than death, why should he not do everything by which he could avoid danger?

"There are cases when man by a certain course might preserve life, and they do not employ it; when by certain things they might avoid danger, and they will not do them.

"Therefore, men have that which they like more than life, and that which they dislike more than death. They are not worthy men only who have this mental nature. All men have it; what belongs to such worthy men is simply that they do not lose it.

"Here are a small basket of rice and a platter of soup, and the case is one in which the getting of them will preserve life and the want of them will be death; if they are offered with an insulting voice, even a tramp will not receive them, or if you first tread upon them, even a beggar will not stoop to take them.

"And yet a man will accept ten thousand *chung* without any consideration of propriety or righteousness. What can the ten thousand *chung* add to him? When he takes them, is it not that he may obtain beautiful mansions, that he may secure the services of a wife and concubines, or that the poor and needy of his acquaintance may be helped by him?

"In the former case the offered bounty was not received, though it would have saved from death, and now the emolument is taken for the sake of beautiful mansions. The bounty that would have preserved from death was not received, and the emolument is taken to get the services of a wife and concubines. The bounty that would have saved from death was not received, and the emolument is taken that one's poor and needy acquaintances may be helped by him. Was it then not possible likewise to decline this? This is a case of what is called—'Losing the proper nature of one's mind.'"[33]

To sum up and build on what we have learned, our reason tells us: (1) Benevolence and righteousness are in the inherent nature of man, by which he attains the objective of common existence and common evolution. (2) In normal times man will readily love and help others. (3) In case of necessity, he will even sacrifice his life for the existence and well-being of the multitude. (4) Therefore this inherent nature must doubtless be good.

In this way the theoretical basis for the goodness of human nature is established. Here is the pertinent statement of Mencius on this question:

The philosopher Kao said, "Man's nature is like water whirling round in a corner. Open a passage for it to the east, and it will flow to the east; open a passage for it to the west, and it will flow to the west. Man's a nature is indifferent to good and evil, just as the water is indifferent to the east and west."

Mencius replied, "Water indeed will flow indifferently to the east or west, but will it flow indifferently up or down? The tendency of man's nature to good is like the tendency of water to flow downwards. There are none but have this tendency to good, just as all water flows downwards.

"Now by striking water and causing it to leap up, you may make it go over your forehead, and by damming and leading it, you may force it up a hill;—but are such movements according to the nature of water? It is the force applied which causes them.

When men are made to do what is not good, their nature is dealt with in this way."[64]

Is it possible for environment to exert any influence on this instinct of man? According to Confucius and Mencius, the answer is yes. But if inherent nature is preserved, nurtured, directed and exhausted, then benevolence and righteousness can still be maintained and practiced.

The Master said, "By nature, men are nearly alike; by practice, they get to be wide apart."[65]

The Master said, "Man is born for uprightness. If a man loses his uprightness and yet lives, his escape from death is the effect of mere good fortune."[66]

The disciple Kung-tu said, "The philosopher Kao says, 'Man's nature is neither good nor bad.'

"Some say, 'Man's nature may be made to practice good, and it may be made to practice evil, and accordingly under Wên and Wu the people loved what was good, while under Yu and Li they loved what was cruel.'

"Some said, 'The nature of some is good, and the nature of others is bad. Hence it was that under such a sovereign as Yao there yet appeared Hsiang; that with such a father as Ku-sou there yet appeared Shun; and that with Chou for their sovereign and the son of their elder brother besides, there were found Ch'i, the viscount of Wei, and the prince Pi-kan.'

And now you say, 'The nature is good.' Then are all those wrong?"

Mencius said, "For the feelings proper to it, it is constituted for the practice of what is good. This is what I mean in saying that the nature is good.

"If men do what is not good, it cannot be blamed on their ability.

"The feeling of commiseration belongs to all men; so does that of shame and dislike; and that of reverence and respect; and that of right and wrong. The feeling of commiseration implies the principle of benevolence; that of shame and dislike, the principle of righteousness; that of reverence and respect, the principle of propriety; and that of right and wrong, the principle of knowledge. Benevolence, righteousness, propriety and knowledge are not infused into us from without. We are inherently furnished with them, but only we do not think about them. Hence it is said, 'Seek and you will find them. Neglect and you will lose them.' Men differ from one another in regard to them; some as much again as others, some five times as much and some to an incalculable extent: it is because they cannot carry out fully their ability.

"It is said in the *Book of Songs*,

> 'Heaven in producing mankind,
> Gave them their various faculties and relations with their specific laws.
> These are the invariable rules of nature for all to hold,
> And all love this admirable virtue.'

"Confucius said, 'The maker of this ode knew indeed the Way!' We may thus see that every faculty and relation must have its law, and since there are invariable rules for all to hold, they consequently love this admirable virtue."[37]

Mencius said, "In good years the children of the people are most of them good, while in bad years the most of them abandon themselves to evil. It is not owing to any difference in the ability with which Heaven has endowed them that they are thus different. The abandonment is owing to their minds being ensnared and drowned by hunger and cold.

"There now is barley—Let it be sown and covered up; the ground being the same, and the time of sowing likewise the same, it grows rapidly up, and when the full time is come it is all found to be ripe. Although there may be inequalities of produce, that is owing to the difference of the soil, as rich or poor, to the unequal nourishment afforded by the rains and dews and to the different ways in which man has performed his labor.

"Thus all things which are the same in kind are like to one another. Why should we doubt solely in regared to man? The sage and we are the same in kind.

"So, the scholar Lung said, 'Even if a man makes hempen sandals without knowing the size of people's feet, yet I know that he will not make them like baskets.' Sandals are all like one another, because all men's feet are like one another.

"And so also it is with the ear. In the matter of sounds, the whole people hope to hear music made by Shih-k'uang; that is, the ears of all men are like one another.

"And so it is also with the eye. In the case of Tzŭ-tu, there is no man but would recognize that he was handsome. Anyone who would not recognize the good looks of Tzŭ-tu must have no eyes.

"Therefore I say, men's mouths agree in having the same relishes; their ears agree in enjoying the same sounds; their eyes agree in recognizing the same beauty: shall their minds alone have nothing in common? What is it that they have in common? It is, I say, reason and righteousness. The sages only apprehended before me that which my mind has in common with other men. Therefore reason and righteousness are agreeable to my mind, just as the meat of grass- and grain-fed animals is agreeable to my mouth."[68]

To sum up, the desire for food and sex are in the nature of man, and the fulfillment of these desires is sought with a view to individual existence. Benevolence and righteousness also are in the nature of man. But they are also virtues whose perfection is sought with a view to the common existence of mankind.

The knowledge of things for personal or private ends is easily gained. However, the knowledge of things for public ends and for others is gained only with difficulty. Confucius often got very emotional when he spoke of these things.

The Master said, "I have not seen one who loves virtue as he loves beauty."[69]

The Master said, "Is it not all over? I have not seen one who loves virtue as he loves beauty."[70]

The Master said, "Yu, those who know virtue are few."[71]

In the course of the uninterrupted reproduction of mankind, the things that are required for the maintenance and perpetuation of life may not be sufficiently produced or evenly distributed. Thus economic problems arise.

The question of how to develop and guide the instinct of man toward the proper fulfillment of the object of common existence—without excesses or inadequacies (the Golden Mean)—gives rise to moral problems. The *development of instinct*, with a view to reaching the state of widening and bettering life so as to assist the transforming and nourishing functions of Heaven, is called the fulfillment of nature. The *control of instinct* in order to prevent interference with the existence of others is called the suppression of nature. *Conformity with instinct*, to make it consistent with the objective of common existence, is called accordance with nature. The ultimate objective of all three of these concepts is the increase of material and spiritual production and an even distribution of the products. Hence, "The accordance with nature is the Way."[72] Again,

It is said in the *Book of Songs*,
"Heaven in producing mankind,

Gave them their various faculties and relations with their specific laws.

These are the invariable rules of nature for all to hold, And all love this admirable virtue."

Confucius said, "The maker of this ode knew indeed the Way!" We may thus see that every faculty and relation must have its law, and since there are invariable rules for all to hold, they consequently love this admirable virtue.[73]

The evolution of the history of mankind can be divided into three periods: (1) the period of struggle between men and animals, (2) the period of struggle between men and men, and (3) the period of struggle between men and the natural world for the well-being of humanity.

The first period is long past (except in a few uncivilized areas), and the second should soon be concluded. So, we can say we are entering the third period. However, because morality has not been able to make the same rapid progress as science, we are still hovering around the second stage and are in danger of falling backward. Moreover, the brutal nature inherited from the first period has been extended, thanks to the progress of science. As a result, the future of mankind gives cause for grave concern.

During the start of the second period, the mutual strife and massacre of mankind were aimed at the quest for food (*Lebensraum*) and sex. It is indeed a paradox that food and sex, conditions for the maintenance of human existence, turned out to be the main reasons for strife and massacre. This vital problem must be solved. The following solutions are suggested.

1. The sharpest possible reduction of the individual desire for food and sex must be achieved so that the cause of mutual strife and massacre will be removed. This is the goal set up by all religious leaders. Missionaries are an example. They avoid "wordly" entanglements, adopt vegetarian diets, dispense with marriage, advocate loving and helping others, practice self-denial, exhort good conduct, inhibit killing, curb avarice and counsel a healthy attitude if not outright avoidance of sex. The object here is to play down and contain man's desire for food and sex, while striving to attain unlimited fulfillment of the nature of benevolence and righteousness. Only in this way can goodness be continued, nature fulfilled, virtue achieved and the Way cultivated.

2. Men must see the vital importance of benevolence and righteousness, and act accordingly. This means they must cultivate the Way and learn how to establish meaningful relations among themselves, so as to limit the scope of sex. "A scholar, whose mind is set on the Way and who is ashamed of bad clothes and bad food, is not fit to be discoursed with" and "having repose in poverty and delight in the Way" is the duty of the scholar. These exhortations look toward the reduction of the requirements for food. Whenever a choice must be made between the preservation of one's life and the observance of benevolence and righteousness, the latter should be preferred so that (1) no disgrace is brought on one's ancestors, (2) virtue is practiced wherever it is sought, and (3) there is accordance with one's nature to achieve the Way and the fulfillment of one's nature to illustrate virtue.

This theory was adopted by Confucius and philosophers and educators in general. More, they set personal examples for others to emulate.

Both of these measures, the passive and the positive, have the same aims—to solve the problem of the common existence of mankind, to be in accordance with one's own nature, and to fulfill the desire of one's nature to bring about the well-being of the multitude. As to the strife among different religions, this is indeed the most stupid action of mankind because thereby the true significance of religion is lost.

"Nature" is frequently paired with "destiny" to denote "life." How can we distinguish between the two? As stated above, nature is the instinct with which a man is endowed by Heaven for his existence, while destiny is a trend in the course of his life. Those who can control their instinct (attain accordance with nature) have the trend toward good, and those who cannot tend toward evil. Sweet tastes, beautiful colors, pleasant sounds, fragrant odors and ease and rest are all for a person's enjoyment, but they all come from without. Although he wishes to enjoy these things, the superior man will not seek them from the outside; rather, he prefers to keep to his customary mode of life, be it one of affluence or poverty. Benevolence, righteousness, propriety and knowledge—they are all for others; they are what one already possesses. Success in attaining them depends on sincerity and and earnest practice. Therefore, Mencius said in regard to nature, "these things are natural, but there is a destiny connected with them," and in regard to destiny, "these are destiny, but they involve nature." Only the superior man can know destiny and fulfill nature, thus clearly perceiving the subtlety existing in each.

> Mencius said, "For the mouth to desire sweet tastes, the eye to desire beautiful colors, the ear to desire pleasant sounds, the nose to desire pleasant odors and the four limbs to desire ease and rest —these things are natural. But there is destiny connected with them, and the superior man does not say of his pursuit of them, 'It is my nature.'
>
> "The exercise of love between father and son, the observance of righteousness between sovereign and minister, the rules of ceremony between guest and host, the display of knowledge by the worthy man and the fulfillment of the Heavenly Way by the sage:—these are destiny, but they involve our nature. The superior man does not say, in reference to them, 'It is destiny.'"[14]

Although the philosopher Kao knew that the desire for both food and sex is in a man's nature, he regarded benevolence as internal and righteousness as external. The disciple Mêng-chi also doubted the internal nature of righteousness. Mencius resolved the doubts of both men by taking as part of nature both benevolence and righteousness without any distinction whatsoever.

> The philosopher Kao said, "Food and sex are nature. Benevolence is internal and not external; righteousness is external and not internal."
>
> Mencius asked him, "What is your ground for saying that benevolence is internal and righteousness external?"
>
> He replied, "There is a man older than I, and I give honor to him. It is not that there is first in me a principle of such reverence to age. It is just as when there is a white man and I consider him white;—according as he is so externally to me. On this account I say that righteousness is external."
>
> Mencius said, "There is no difference between our pronouncing a white horse to be white and our pronouncing a white man to be white. But is there no difference between the regard with which we acknowledge the age of an old horse and that with which we regared the age of an old man? And what is it which is called righteousness?—the fact of a man's being old? or the fact of our giving honor to his age?"
>
> Kao said, "There is my younger brother:—I love him. But the younger brother of a man of Ch'in I do not love: that is, the

feeling is determined by myself, and therefore I say that benevolence is internal. On the other hand, I give honor to an old man of Ch'u, and I also give honor to an old man of my own people: that is, the feeling is determined by the age, and therefore I say that righteousness is external."

Mencius answered him, "Our enjoyment of meat roasted by a man of Ch'in does not differ from our enjoyment of meat roasted by ourselves. Thus, what you insist on takes place also in the case of such things, and will you say likewise that our enjoyment of a roast is external?"[75]

The disciple Mêng-chi asked Kung-tu, saying, "On what ground is it said that righteousness is internal?"

Kung-tu replied, "We therein act out of our feeling of respect, and therefore it is said to be internal."

The other objected, "Suppose the case of a villager older than my elder brother by one year, to which of them would I show the greater respect?"

"To your brother," was th reply.

"But for which of them should I first pour out wine at a feast?"

"For the villager."

Mêng-chi argued, "Now your feeling of reverence rests on the one, and now the honor due to his age is rendered to the other;—this is certainly determined by what is without, and does not proceed from within."

Kung-tu was unable to reply and told the conversation to Mencius. Mencius said, "You should ask him, 'Which do you respect most,—your uncle or your younger brother?' He will answer, 'My uncle.' Ask him again, 'If your younger brother is personating a dead ancestor, to which do you show the greater respect,—to him or to your uncle?' He will say, 'To my younger brother.' You can go on, 'But where is the respect due, as you said, to your uncle?' He will reply to this, 'I show the respect to my younger brother, because of the position which he occupies,' and you can likewise say, 'So my respect to the villager is because of the position which he occupies. Ordinarily my respect is rendered to my elder brother; for a brief moment, on occasion, it is rendered to the villager.'

Mêng-chi heard this and observed, "When respect is due to my uncle, I respect him; the thing is certainly determined by what is without and does not proceed from within."

Kung-tu replied, "In winter we drink hot soup, and in summer cold water; and so, on your principle, eating and drinking also depend on what is external."[76]

E. Illustration of the Way

As each man develops his natural instinct (nature), trouble may—and often does—arise. This is partly due to unequal production and distribution. For when a man lays hold of what he feels is required by him for the satisfaction of his desire for existence, he may—and often does—take what others feel they require for their existence. This can lead to strife, massacre and indeed wholesale destruction (such as future nuclear holocaust). And this is what Confucius meant when he said, in reply to Tzŭ-chang's question on the exaltation of virtue and discovery of delusions: "Having wished him (a man) to live, you also wish him to die. This is a case af delusion."

To solve this problem, it is necessary to analyze it from these four positions:

(1) To seek one's own existence through the death of others. This is impossible. Even if it were possible, it would be entirely meaningless for one to live when all others have died.

(2) To seek the existence of others through one's own death. This can occur, but only in cases of extreme necessity—when a person sacrifices his life for the observance of benevolence and righteousness: when a man desires something more than his own life, or despises something more than death.

(3) To live and let live. This is the most rational solution for both sides. It is in full compliance with benevolence. Also, it is interesting to note that the Chinese character *jên* (benevolence) is composed of the characters *jên* (man or men) and *erh* (two).

(4) To die when others also die. In this case mankind would no longer exist, and basically no question would arise.

"To live and let live," then, is the most rational answer to the question. In fact, it is the sole solution. Therefore, every man should strive to make it his very own life-style. Hence it is said that the Way is the road to the common existence and evolution of mankind. Each man should conform his inherent nature to it with a view to fulfiilling the object of common existence. "The accordance with nature is the Way."[77]

As a man cannot totally withdraw from the rest of mankind for even an instant, so can he not leave the Way.

Mencius said, "Benevolence is the distinguishing characteristic of humanity. As embodied in man's conduct, it is called the Way."[78]

The Way may not be left for an instant. If it could be left, it would not be the Way. On this account the superior man does not wait till he sees things to be cautious, nor till he hears things to be apprehensive.

There is nothing more visible than what is concealed, and nothing more manifest than what is minute. Therefore the superior man is watchful over himself when he is alone."[79]

Since the Way is manifestly intertwined with our daily actions, it is part and parcel of our life. It would be a mistake to regard the Way as something profoundly exalted and inaccessible.

Mencius said, "The Way lies in what is near, and men seek for it in what is remote. The work lies in what is easy, and men seek for it in what is difficult. If each man would love his parents and respect his elders, the whole world would enjoy peace.[80]

I am a man, as anyone else is a man. Therefore I should not do to others what I do not wish to have done to myself. We can call this loyalty and reciprocity; when attained, these virtues can bring us close to the Way.

The Master said, "The Way is not far from man. When men seek the Way by going far away from man, this course cannot be considered the Way.

"In the *Book of Songs* it is said, 'In hewing an ax-handle, the pattern is not far off.' We grasp one ax-handle to hew the other; and yet, if we look askance from one to the other, we may consider them as apart. Therefore the superior man governs men, according to their nature, with what is proper to them, and as soon as they change what is wrong, he stops.

"Loyalty and reciprcoity are not far away from the Way. What you do not like when done to yourself, do not do to others.

"In the Way of the superior man there are four things, to not one of which have I as yet attained—To serve my father, as I would require my son to serve me; to this I have not attained. To serve my prince, as I would require my minister to serve me; to this I have not attained. To serve my elder brother, as I would require my younger brother to serve me; to this I have not attained. To be the first to behave to a friend, as I would require him to behave to me; to this I have not attained. Earnest in practicing the ordinary virtues and careful in making ordinary utterances, if, in his practice, he has anything defective, the superior man dares not but exert himslf; and if, in his words, he has left anything unsaid, he dares not exhaust them. Thus his words have respect to his actions, and his actions have respect to his words. How can the superior man help being prudent?"[31]

"How the flowers of the aspen-plum flutter and turn! Do I not think of you? But your house is distant."

The Master said, "It is the want of thought about it. How is it distant?"[32]

The master said, "Who can go out but by the door? How is it that men will not walk according to these ways?[33]

Mencius replied, "The Way is like a great road. What difficulty is there to know it? The trouble is that men will not seek it. Do go home and search for it, and you will have an abundance of teachers."[34]

Since the Way is the road taken by everyone, it must be before our eyes and easy to know and practice. In doubtful cases, the things one should or should not do can be determined by putting oneself in the other person's position. This is what is called the "rule of conduct according to example."

What a man dislikes in his superiors, let him not display in the treatment of his inferiors; what he dislikes in his inferiors, let him not display in the service of his superiors: what he hates in those who are before him, let him not therewith percede those who are behind him; what he hates in those who are behind him, let him not therewith follow those who are before him; what he hates to receive on the right, let him not bestow on the left; what he hates to receive on the left, let him not bestow on the right;—this is what is called the rule of conduct according to example.[85]

In short, wherever a benefit accrues, one should first think of others and then of oneself. If this is done, there will be nothing incompatible with the Way. On the other hand, if a person cares only about himself, the Way is obstructed. It is only when both sides are taken into consideration that a man can go through the Way without hindrance. Recalling once again that the two Chinese charactors jên (man or men) and erh (two) combine to make the character jên (benevolence), we can say that the spiritual way between two men should always be kept clear of encumbrances, for the Way is based on benevolence and benevolence cannot be far from man. The Master said, "Is benevolence a thing remote? I with to be benevolent and lo! benevolence is at hand."[86]

Therefore, whether or not there is benevolence determines whether the Way does or does not prevail. When the Way prevails in the world, one should assume the responsibility for carrying it out. Conversely, when the Way does not prevail in the world, one should sacrifice even one's life for it, because the importance of the Way is greater than the importance of one's life.

> Mencius said, "When the Way prevails in the world, a person should be subordinated to it. When the Way does not prevail in the world, a person should be sacrificed for it. I have not heard of the sacrifice of one's Way for someone else's."[87]

Relations between men are very complex, for there are distinctions between the public and the private, between the elder and the younger, between the superior and the inferior. Within the family there are parents and children, elder and younger brothers and sisters, hushbands and wives. In society there are rulers and ministers as well as friends. Although these sets of relations commonly exist between man and man, there are differences in intimacy and formality. Basically these relations of humanity can be reduced to five duties of universal obligation and three virtues universally binding. Herein lies the theoretical and practical significance of "morality," whose Chinese equivalent is composed of two characters representing precisely the above-mentioned duties and virtues which are identified in the *Doctrine of the Mean:*

> The duties of universal obligation are five and the virtues wherewith they are practiced are three. The duties are those between sovereign and minister, between father and son, between husband and wife, between elder brother and younger, and those belonging to the intercourse of friends. Wisdom, benevolence and courage, these three are the virtues universally binding. And there is only one means by which they carry out the duties into practice.[88]

What is the order of precedence, if any, in practicing the five duties? It is from the intimate to the less intimate, from the near to the remote, and from men to things. If one starts from filial piety and fraternal love, the root will be established and the Way opened wide.

> The philosopher Yu said, "They are few who, being filial and fraternal, are fond of offending against their superiors. There have been none, who, not liking to offend against their superiors, have been fond of stirring up confusion.
>
> "The superior man bends his attention to the root. That being established, the Way grows up. Filial piety and fraternal submission—are they not the root of benevolence?"[89]
>
> The Way is cultivated by cherishing benevolence. Benevolence is the distinguishing element of humanity, and the highest expression of it is in being affectionate to those nearly related to one. Righteousness is the accordance of actions with what is right, and the highest expression of it is in honoring the worthy.[90]
>
> Mencius said, "In regard to other living things than men, the superior man is kind and not benevolent. In regard to the people, he is benevolent but not loving to them. He is loving to his relatives and benevolent to the people. He is benevolent to the people and kind to living things other than men."[91]

To sum up, the Way is the spiritual high road to the common existence and evolution of mankind. All men who walk this road, conforming to their instinct for existence (accordance with nature), will make it an integral part of their daily life (the Way is not far from man). But the road is frequently in need of repair in order to keep it open and unhindered. That is why education (cultivation of the Way) is required.

There are a great many roads and they differ in size, but essentially they can be reduced to five super highways (relations between sovereign and minister, between father and son, between elder and younger brothers, between husband and wife, between friend and friend). The object of taking these roads and keeping them repaired is the love of men. (The superior man, in learning the Way, loves men; the Way is cultivated by cherishing benevolence.) Therefore the focal point of the Way is benevolence. Where there is benevolence, there is the Way; where there is no benevolence, the Way is lost.

The root of benevolence lies in filial piety and fraternal love. When extended beyond love for relatives it becomes benevolence to all people. And when extended still further, it takes the form of kindness to all living things.

Therefore benevolence is what sustains human existence. It is the foundation of morality and prerequisite for human conduct. When benevolence is present, the Way prevails, mankind exists. This is the reason why the importance of the Way is greater than that of even human life itself. Hence it is said, "The Way may not be left for an instant. If it could be left, it would not be the Way."

F. Illustration of Virtue

The Way is the high road. Virtue is choosing and taking that road. So it is said that when the Way is taken and the result is reaped in the mind, it is called virtue. The Way awaits man and his decision to take it. As Confucius said, "A man can enlarge the Way; the Way does not enlarge the man."[92]

Since virtue is adoption of the Way, it is easy to see why the illustration of great virtue is of prime importance in human life. Indeed, it is the first of the three principles of the *Great Learning*.

> What the *Great Learning* teaches is to illustrate illustrious virtue; to renovate the people; and to rest in the highest excellence.[93]
>
> In the "Announcement to K'ang" it is said, "He was able to make his virtue illustrious."
>
> In the T'ai Chia" it is said, "He contemplated and studied the illustrious decrees of Heaven."
>
> In the "Canon of the Emperor (Yao)" it is said, "He was able to make illustrious his lofty virtue."
>
> These passages all show how those sovereigns made themselves illustrious.[94]

Since the Way is rooted in benevolence, virtue also naturally rests on benevolence. Although wisdom, benevolence and courage are all universally binding virtues, wisdom aims at the knowledge of benevolence and courage in its practice.

Wisdom sweeps away doubt about benevolence, and courage casts out fear in the practice of benevolence. A man with benevolence can act to the limit of his potential without anxiety. As the Master said in the *Analects* (Book IX, Ch. XXVIII): "The wise are free from perplexities; the benevolent from anxiety; and the courageous from fear."

Then too the virtuous are never isolated from their fellow men: "The Master said, 'Virtue is not left to stand alone. He who practices it will have neighbors.' "[95]

In his daily life, a man should srtive to make all his thoughts and actions conform to virtue. Since virtue is not as abstract as the Way—there is a path to follow—it obviously is more concrete. However, when it comes to practical problems, a man must decide which action is not only harmless but also the most rational and beneficial to others. A sense of proportion is required. And the regulation of this sense of proportion is "propriety." The adoption of rational, natural and pleasing action is "music." When the action which should be taken and the action which should not be taken are clearly defined, it is "law."

Propriety and music are the concrete expressions of virtue. Law, in turn, is the concrete expression of propriety and music. Despite the complexity of human affairs, the process from the Way to virtue, propriety (and music) and law can be easily understood. Some persons may contend that the law eliminates the need for propriety and virtue. Not so, for if this were true it would result in the loss of the Way, the oblivion of the root.

> The Master said, "Set your mind on the Way. Hold fast to virtue. Adhere to benevolence. Seek relaxation and enjoyment from the arts."[96]

This means that the Way is the root and the arts are merely branches. Whether instruction is given through the arts or government, it is a mistake to put the heavy emphasis on law rather than morality.

The Way, after all, is the origin of virtue. At the same time benevolence is its foundation, and righteousness is the practice of benevolence, from which springs courage ("Carry out righteousness courageously whenever it is seen"). Wisdom is knowing benevolence and righteousness without departing from them, while propriety and music regulate them in order to bring about a state of equilibrium and harmony. All these things contribute toward bringing about the common existence of mankind. Mencius has made the clearest exposition of them:

> Mencius said, "The reality of benevolence is the service of one's parents. The reality of righteousness is obedience to one's

elder brothers. The reality of wisdom is knowing those two things and not departing from them. The reality of propriety is ordering and adorning those two things. The reality of music is taking delight in those two things. When there is delight, pleasure is produced. With the production of this pleasure, how can they cease to grow? When they cannot cease to grow, then unconsciously the feet begin to dance and the hands to move."[97]

Mencius is saying that while the practice of benevolence and righteousness toward others is the first obligation of man, it cannot be done without making distinctions as to intimacy and importance. The ability to make these distinctions depends on wisdom. At the same time, the well-ordered and harmonious practice of these two virtues depends on propriety and music.

> Benevolence is the distinguishing element of humanity, and the highest expression of it is in being affectionate to those closely related to one. Righteousness is the accordance of actions with what is right, and the highest expression of it is in honoring the worthy. The degree of love for relatives and honor for the worthy is the basis for the principle of propriety,[98]
>
> The philosopher Yu said, "In practing the rules of propriety, the sense of harmony is to be prized. In the Way prescribed by the ancient kings, this is an attribute of excellence, and in all things, great or small, we follow it.
>
> "Yet it is not to be observed in all cases. If one, knowing that harmony should be prized, manifests it, without regulating it with propriety, this likewise is not to be done."[99]

The above passages show how propriety is produced and how it takes effect.

Propriety pertains to the regulation of reason and action. Its manifestation is solemn and orderly, like the attitude of an austere father. Music has to do with the harmonization of feeling and thinking. Its manifestation is gracious and harmonious, like the attitude of a kind mother. The combination of the two virtues produces children with strong reasoning power and rich feeling. When large groups are instructed in these two virtues, the desired result is a people with orderly action and agreeable sentiment. Hence it is said, "Propriety regulates the multitude and music harmonizes it." The two are mutually complementary, like the wheels of a carriage—if either wheel is missing the carriage cannot move. Therefore, whenever there is an important ceremony, it is accompanied by grand music, and while the movements of an army are wholly regulated by propriety, they are entirely directed by music (harmonization of feeling and thinking).

Solemnity is required in any method of education. But this may produce a feeling of fear and passivity in those who are taught. Solemenity must be regulated by an attitude of grace, which produces affection and spontaneity. Flexibility then is the goal in teaching; indeed, it is the highest possible form that education can take. For flexibility leads a teacher to the stage where he is "gentle but strict, strong but not violent, polite but at ease."

> The Master said, "They who know the truth are not equal to those who are fond of it, and they who are fond of it are not equal to those who delight in it."[100]

Fondness for the truth is a step toward taking sheer delight in reasoning and knowing the truth. The fondness, however, stands between the knowledge and the delight. Men may never tire of an opera but they feel that seeing a play twice is excessive, because an opera has music while a play has only the spoken word. When a man's feelings are aroused, when he is delighted by something, he is not likely to tire of it even when it is repeated many times. Hence the statements: "Seek relaxation and enjoyment from the arts," and "The reality of music is taking delight in those two things. When there is delight, pleasure is produced. With the production of pleasure, how can they cease to grow? When they cannot cease to grow, then unconsciously the feet begin to dance and the hands to move." It can be seen then that the arts can advance virtue to the highest stage; their importance is evident.

When a person knows benevolence and righteousness, when he is fond of them and takes delight in them, then nature and virtue are combined into a unified whole:

> The fulfillment of our being is perfect virtue, The fulfillment of the nature of things is knowledge. These are the powers or faculties of our being. They combine the inner or subjective and outer or objective use of the power of the mind. Therefore, with sincerity everything done is right.[101]

Only then can nature be led to its highest stage. Here he who possesses sincerity and "without an effort hits what is right and apprehends without the exercise of thought—he is the sage who naturally and easily embodies the right Way." This is the achievement of the sage, the acquisition of the Way.

Ancient education stressed the six arts—rites, music, archery, charioteering, writing and numbers. Modern education consists of moral, mental and physical advancement. Rites and music approximated our moral education; archery and charioteering, our physical education; and writing and numbers, our mental education. Subsequently, social and aesthetic education were added to make up our five forms of education. As a matter of fact, however, by regulating and harmonizing the people, rites and music serve the purposes of social education with complete satisfaction. Also, with well-regulated, orderly rites and natural, lively music, we have all the aesthetics that we may desire. So the addition of the two new forms of education seems superfluous.

Although propriety and music originate from virtue, they contain both natural elements ("substance") and man-made elements ("polish"). The proportion between the two marks the distinction between barbarism and civilization.

> The Master said, "Where substance is in excess of polish, we have rusticity; where polish is in excess of substance, we have the manners of a clerk."[102]

From this we can see that since rites and music contain man-made elements, they are national, local and historical. Each nation has its rites and music, but each is not far different from the others in this respect. We can also see that the word "civilization" is a general term denoting all the inventions made by man, and that the word "culture" is a general term denoting those inventions which have an influence on life.

History is the record of human affairs, and we cannot of course expect it to be completely unbiased and objective truth. Law is the concrete expression of rites and music. It is bound to contain a large number of man-made elements and is very much subject to national, local and historical influences. Each country has its own constitution, the basic law of the land. Since they cannot depart radically from the fundamental principles of morality, however, the constitutions of the various nations are more or less similar to each other. Therefore if mankind (1) can really understand the true significance of morality, (2) has confidence in "sharing the world community" with all peoples, and (3) adopts concrete action to make the Way prevail—then the ideal of a world of Great Harmony can be attained with little difficulty.

Natural elements are plain and unaffected, while man-made elements are pretentious and artificial. Since propriety seeks to be in a state of equilibrium in order to meet the requirements of both oneself and the other party concerned, it contains both "substance" and "polish." But if a choice must be made, according to Confucius, "substance" should be preferred to "polish" because it is nearer to truth.

> The Master said, "The men of former times, in matters of ceremonies and music, were rustics, it is said, while the men of these latter times, in ceremonies and music, are accomplished gentlemen.
>
> "If I have occasion to make an application, I follow the men of former times."[103]
>
> Tzŭ-hsia asked, saying, "What is the meaning of the passage: 'The pretty dimples of her artful smile! The well-defined black and white of her eye! The plain ground for the colors'?"
>
> The Master said, "The business of laying on the colors follows (the preparation of) the plain ground."
>
> Said Tzŭ-hsia, "Ceremonies then are a subsequent thing?"
>
> The Master said, "It is Shang who can bring out my meaning. Now I can begin to talk about the odes with him."[104]

This means there must be a plain background on a canvas before a work of art can be painted on it. Since propriety is that which regulates, there must be "substance" before "polish" can be added. The suggestion of Tzŭ-hsia served as a lead to bring out Confucius' meaning. The Master, realizing this, regarded him as thoughtful enough to engage in a mutual discussion about the odes. A similar idea is contained in the reply of Confucius to a question by Lin Fang:

> Lin Fang asked what was the first thing to be attended to in ceremonies.
>
> The Master said, "A great question indeed! In festive cermonies it is better to be sparing than extravagant. In the cermonies of

mourning it is better that there be a deep sorrow than a minute attention to observance."[105]

In short, "in practicing the rules of propriety the sense of harmony is to be prized." It is most important that "polish" should not damage "substance." Extravagance and strict observance put stress on external appearances and easily lead to excesses. This is inconsistent with the original intent of propriety. The great exercise of propriety lies in its regulation and equilibrium.

The Master said, "Respectfulness, without the rules of propriety, becomes laborious bustle; carefulness, without the rules of propriety, becomes timidity; boldness, without the rules of propriety, becomes insubordination; straightforwardness, without the rules of propriety, becomes rudeness.

"When those who are in high stations perform well all their duties to their relations, the people are aroused to virtue. When old friends are not neglected by them, the people are preserved from meanness."[106]

Respectfulness, carefulness, boldness and straightforwardness are all excellent virtues, but if they are practiced excessively they unexpectedly become laborious bustle, timidity, insubordination and rudeness. Only by regulating them with the rules of propriety can they be appropriate and attain perfection. Here are a few more examples:

1. Not to deceive.

The Master being very ill, Tzŭ-lu wished the disciples to act as ministers to him.

During a remission of his illness, he said, "Long has the conduct of Yu been deceitful! By pretending to have ministers when I have them not, whom do I cheat? Do I cheat Heaven?

"Moreover, than that I should die in the hands of ministers, is it not better that I should die in the hands of you, my disciples? And though I may not get a great burial, shall I die upon the road?"[107]

2. Not to exceed one's limits.

The officer Kung-hang having on hand the funeral of one of his sons, the Master of the Right went to condole with him. When this noble entered the door, some went forward and spoke with him, and after he took his seat some went to his place and spoke with him.

Mencius did not speak with him, so that he was displeased and said, "All the gentlemen have spoken with me. There is only Mencius who does not speak to me, thereby slighting me."

Mencius, having heard of this remark, said, "According to the prescribed rules, in the court, individuals may not go out of their places to speak with one another, nor may they pass from their ranks to bow to one another. I was wishing to observe this rule, and Tzŭ-ao understands that I was slighting him—is not this strange?"[108]

3. To stress the spiritual instead of the material.

Tzŭ-kung wished to do away with the offering of a sheep connected with the inauguration of the first day of each month.

The Master said, "Tz'ŭ, you love the sheep; I love the ceremony."[109]

4. Not to lose propriety because of preference.

When Yen Yüan died, Yen Lu begged the carriage of the Master to sell and get an outer shell for his son's coffin.

The Master said, "Everyone calls his son his son, whether he has talents or has not talents. There was Li; when he died, he had a coffin but no outer shell. I would not walk on foot to get a shell for him, because, having followed in the rear of the great officials, it was not proper that I should walk on foot."[110]

5. Not to have a great burial against propriety.

When Yen Yüan died, the disciples wished to give him a great burial, and the Master said, "You may not do so."

The disciples did bury him in great style.

The Master said, "Hui behaved towards me as his father. I have not been able to treat him as my son. The fault is not mine; it belongs to you, O disciples."[111]

6. Not to violate custom.

The Master, when he entered the grand temple, asked about everything. Someone said, "Who will say that the son of the man of Tsou knows the rules of propriety? He has entered the grand temple and asks about everything." The Master heard the remark and said, "This is a rule of propriety."[112]

7. To avoid extravagance.

"In festive ceremonies, it is better to be sparing than extravagant."[113]

8. Not to trifle with the great sacrifice.

The Master said, "At the great sacrifice, after the pouring out of the libation, I have no wish to look on."[114]

Just as propriety and music are like the two wheels of a carriage, each indispensable, so also are the *Record of Music* and the *Record of Rites*. In compiling the two books, Confucius prepared the teaching material for moral education. His work attached the same importance to music as he in his discourses did to propriety. In the *Record of Music* it is said, "When music has its way, principles are clear, ears and eyes effective, blood and spirit peaceful, customs transformed and all the world tranquil." A high accolade indeed for music.

As to the manifestation of political and educational conditions in propriety and music, consider this quotation from the *Works of Mencius:*

Mencius said, "...Tzǔ-kung said, 'By viewing the ceremonial ordinances of a prince, we know the character of his government. By hearing his music, we know the character of his virtue.' "[115]

Confucius acted on his convictions about music. Once he even left the court of the ruler of Lu when that high dignitary was carried away by a group of women musicians presented to him by the people of Ch'i.

The people of Ch'i sent to Lu a present of female musicians, which Chi Huan received, and for three days no court was held. Confucius took his departure.[116]

Because "the music of Chêng was sensual," Confucius could not tolerate it. The Master, however, was a great lover of music and had a profound understanding of it. This is evidenced by the following examples:

When the Master was in Ch'i, he heard the Shao, and for three months did not know the taste of meat. "I did not think," he said, "that music could have been made so excellent as this."[117]

The Master said, "When the Music-Master Chih first entered on his office, he made Kuan Chü the concluding chapter of his music. How magnificent it was and how it filled the ears!"[118]

The Master, instructing the Grand Music-Master of Lu, said, "How to play music may be known. At the commencement of the piece, all the parts should sound together. As it proceeds, they should be in harmony, while severally distinct and flowing without break, and thus on to the conclusion."[119]

The Master said of the Shao that it was perfectly beautiful and also perfectly good. He said of the Wu that it was perfectly beautiful but not perfectly good.[120]

The Master said, "I returned from Wei to Lu, and then music was reformed, and the pieces in the Royal songs and Praise songs all found their proper places."[121]

The grand Music-Master, Chih, went to Ch'i. Kan, the master of the band at the second meal, went to Ch'u. Liao, the band-master at the third meal, went to Ts'ai. Ch'üeh, the band-master at the fourth meal, went to Ch'in. Fang-shu, the drum-master, went to the north of the river. Wu, the master of the hand-drum, withdrew to the Han. Yang, the assistant music-master, and Hsiang, master of the musical stone, withdrew to an island in the sea.[122]

Following are two more of Confucius' discussions of music with his disciples:

The Master, having come to Wu-ch'êng, heard there the sound of stringed instruments and singing. Well-pleased and smiling, he said, "Why use an ox-knife to kill a fowl?"

Tzŭ-yu replied, "Formerly, Master, I heard you say, 'When the man of high station learns the Way, he loves men; when the man of low station learns the Way, he is easily ruled.!"

The Master said, "My disciples, Yen's words are right. What I said was only in sport."[123]

The Master said, "What has the lute of Yu to do in my door?" The other disciples began not to respect Tzŭ-lu. The Master said, "Yu has ascended to the hall, though he has not yet passed into the inner apartments."[124]

To Confucius the adoption of the rules of propriety and music was a task of great magnitude. In fact, he felt it was the responsibilty of the Son of Heaven. The occupation of the throne alone without virtue was not sufficient, nor was virtue alone sufficient without the occupation of the throne. Hence it is said, "It (the Way) waits for the proper man, and then it is taken," and "Without perfect virtue, the perfect Way cannot become a fact."[125]

> The Master said, "Let a man who is ignorant be fond of using his own judgment; let a man without rank be fond of assuming a directing power to himself; let a man who is living in the present age go back to the ways of antiquity;...on the persons of all who act thus calamities will be sure to come."
>
> To no one but the Son of Heaven does it belong to discuss ceremonies, to fix the measures, and to determine the written characters.
>
> Now, over the entire world, carriages have all wheels of the same size; all writing is with the same characters; and for conduct there are the same principles.
>
> One may occupy the throne, but if he has not the proper virtue, he may not dare to make ceremonies or music. One may have the virtue, but if he does not occupy the throne, he may not presume to make ceremonies or music.
>
> The Master said, "I may describe the ceremonies of the Hsia dynasty, but Ch'i cannot sufficiently attest my words. I have learned the ceremonies of the Yin dynasty, and in Sung they still continue. I have learned the ceremonies of Chou, which are now used, and I follow Chou."[126]

Virtue is what enlarges the Way, and ceremonies and music are what illustrate virtue. Just as the Way and virtue tend toward benevolence, so also do ceremonies and music. Both lay stress on the spirit and not on form.

> The Master said, "It is according to the rules of propriety,' they say...'It is according to the rules of propriety,' they say. Are gems and silk all that is meant by propriety? 'It is music,' they say...'It is music,' they say. Are bells and drums all that is meant by music?"[127]

Whatever action is pursued, of course, depends on the person. A man who is not benevolent loses virtue, and in such a case there are no ceremonies to speak of, nor music either.

> The Master said, "If a man be without benevolence, what has he to do with propriety? If a man be without benevolence, what has he to do with music?"[128]

To sum up, propriety and music are manifested in our daily life. As far as the individual is concerned, they indicate the compliance of his vision, hearing, speech and action with the rules of conduct. Or to put it another way, they show his balance of "polish" and "substance," the repose of his heart in benevolence, how well he practices righteousness. As far as a group is concerned, "propriety regulates the multitude, and music harmonizes it" so that there is perfect order, cooperation and unity in a closely-knit organization. As far as a country is concerned, "by viewing the ceremonial ordinances of a prince, we know the character of his government, and by hearing his music, we know the character of his virtue."

When propriety and music are in a state of growth, the law is administered properly; the people are happy and seek to do good. To the substance of the Way, propriety and music add polish, just as a road after being constructed with gravel and cement is overlaid with asphalt, which presents a smooth and level surface to facilitate passage.

In the very first chapter of the *Doctrine of the Mean* we find the statement: "The cultivation of the Way is called instruction."[129] Since wisdom, benevolence and courage are the three virtues universally binding, we should see that they are taught properly. So let us take a long look at each of these virtues.

1. Wisdom

In Chapter II on "The Investigation of Things" the method and procedure for the extension of knowledge were discussed in detail. At the beginning of this chapter, the point was made that the extension of knowledge includes the knowledge of Heaven, destiny and nature, the illustration of the Way, virtue and instruction, and the knowledge of men and things. The goal of all these individual pursuits is the attainment of wisdom. It follows that the more fond one is of learning, the nearer he is to wisdom. As Confucius stated: "To be fond of learning is to be akin to wisdom."[130]

However, wisdom cannot be attained merely by being fond of learning, which really is only the application of strength. Wisdom depends on skill as well as strength. To attain it, man must have the ability to distinguish between right and wrong, the true and the false. A thorough grasp of essentials is vitally necessary.

Mencius said, "...As a comparison for wisdom, we may liken it to skill, and as a comparison of sageness we may liken it to strength, as in the case of shooting at a mark a hundred paces distant. That you reach it is owing to your strength, but that you hit the mark is not owing to your strength."[131]

The principal aim of shooting is to hit the bullseye, not merely to reach the target. Wisdom likewise is expected in order to hit the bullseye. To quote Confucius again, "In archery it is not going through the leather which is the principal thing—because people's strength is not equal. This was the old way."[132]

The greater the wisdom, the stronger the power of discrimination. The stronger the power of discrimination, the more all words and actions will be regulated—and, needless to say, the more consistent they will be with the Way, virtue, benevolence and righteousness. What is consistent with the Way is "right," and what is not is "wrong." As Mencius said, "The feeling of right and wrong is the beginning of wisdom."[133] And again, "A man cannot be a man without the feeling of right and wrong..."[134]

True, human nature is fond of good and dislikes evil. But due to the complexity of affairs and things in the universe, the distinction between right and wrong, good and evil, orthodox and heterodox, true and false, advantageous and disadvantageous can be definitely made only through the processes of extensive study, accurate inquiry, careful reflection, clear discrimination and earnest practice. Sometimes it is impossible to make the distinction because of doubts. Men who can distinguish between right and wrong are said to be intelligent, while those who cannot are said to be perplexed. According to Confucius, "The wise are free from perplexities."[135]

In another part of the *Analects*, Confucius said, "At forty, I had no doubts."[136] It is interesting to note that even with his great wisdom, Confucius felt that it was not until he was forty years old that he could—without doubts—distinguish between right and wrong. This indicates how boundless the field of learning actually is.

The power of discrimination frequently is limited by environment. But man easily overlooks the limitations on his knowledge.

The Master said, "Men all say, 'We are wise;' but being driven forward and taken in a net, a trap or a pitfall, they know not how to escape. Men all say, "We are wise;' but happening to choose the course of the Mean, they are not able to keep it for a round month."[137]

In addition to learning how to make the distinction between right and wrong, a study should be made of the roots and branches of things, also the beginning and end of affairs. The aim of such a study would be to isolate the more important and urgent among them so that they can be dealt with properly. We can call this the knowledge of the important.

Mencius said, "The wise embrace all knowledge, but they should deal with what is of the greatest urgency. The benevolent embrace all in their love, but what they consider of the greatest urgency is to cultivate an affection for the worthy. Even the wisdom of Yao and Shun did not extend to everything, but they attended urgently to what was important. Their benevolence did not show itself in acts of kindness to every man, but they urgently cultivated an affection for the worthy.

"Not to be able to keep the three years' mourning, and to be very particular about that of three months or that of five months; to eat immoderately and swill down the soup, and at the same time to inquire about the precept not to tear the meat with the teeth—such things show what I call an ignorance of what is most important."[138]

Fan Ch'ih asked what constituted wisdom. The Master said, "To give oneself earnestly to the duties due to man, and, while respecting spiritual beings, to keep aloof from them, may be called wisdom." He asked about perfect virtue. The Master said, "The man of virtue makes the difficulty to be overcome his first consideration, and success only a subsequent consideration. This may be called perfect virtue."[139]

Here the affairs of the people are shown to be realistic and important, while spiritual beings are considered obscure and unimportant. It would be unwise to reverse the order as to their relative urgency.

Though we should try to extend our knowledge, we should at the same time "omtt none of the more exquisite and minute points."[140] As stated above, even the wisdom of Yao and Shum did not evtend to everything. Those who profess to have clear vision often do not possess true wisdom. Men of great wisdom must come to a sure knowledge of the branches by studying the root, discern the less important by ascertaining the more important. They must apply their minds to the remote and their strength to the near and more accessible. They must emphasize whatever deserves it, adopting a proper order of sequence. They should use their wisdom to the utmost to bring about the Way, illustrate virtue and practice benevolence. Then they will have attained wisdom.

> Tzŭ-hsia said, "Mechanics dwell in their shops in order to accomplish their works. The superior man learns in order to reach to the utmost of the Way."[141]

What is generally called wisdom applies only to the minor skill of an individual. Men of truly great wisdom, however, determine the equations and principles relating to affairs and things and then act in strict accordance with their nature. Not only do they accomplish something worthwhile—they accomplish it easily. What Yü did in harnessing the waters was merely to comply with their nature by dredging the rivers and leading them to the sea. In like manner, in astronomy we can accurately determine the calendars of the next thousand years by simply surveying the course of the stars.

> Mencius said, "Whoever in the world speaks about nature should merely follow what is already in existence, which is based on natural tendency.
> "What we dislike in the wise is their boring out their conclusions. If they would only act as Yü did when he conveyed away the waters there would be nothing to dislike in their wisdom. The manner in which Yü conveyed away the waters was by doing what gave him no trouble. If your wise men would also do that which gave them no trouble, their wisdom would also be great.
> "There is heaven so high; there are the stars so distant. If we seek the natural tendency of what is already in existence, we may, by sitting in our places, go back to the solstice of a thousand years ago."[142]
> Po Kuei said, "My management of the waters is superior to that of Yü."
> Mencius replied, "You are wrong, Sir. Yü's regulation of the waters was according to the laws of water. He therefore made the four seas their receptacle, while you make the neighboring States their receptacle. Water flowing out of its channels is called an

inundation, which is detested by a benevolent man. You are wrong, my good Sir.'[143]

Wisdom can take different forms. Mencius regarded Yü as an exemplary figure of great intelligence for the way in which he used the laws of water. In the following quotation Confucius called Shun a man of great intellect for using his mind in quite a different way:

> The Master said, "Was not Shun a great intellect? Shun had a natural curiosity of mind and he loved to inquire into ordinary conversation. He ignored the bad in others and broadcast the good. Taking two extreme counsels, he held the mean between them and applied it in his dealings with the people. Was it by this that he was Shun?"[144]

To question others with interest is to seek wisdom diligently, to study their words is to exercise good judgment, to conceal what is bad and display what is good is to make a careful distinction between good and evil, to grasp the two extremes and employ the Mean shows an understanding of the principles of equilibrium and harmony. Therefore the man of great wisdom must "honor his virtuous nature and maintain constant inquiry and study, seeking to carry it out to its breadth and greatness, so as to omit none of the more exquisite and minute points which it embraces, and to raise it to the greatest height and brilliancy, so as to pursue the course of the Mean."[145] By ending up with benevolence, a man enlarges his wisdom.

2. Benevolence

In the preceding section of this chapter on "Illustration of the Way," Mencius was quoted as saying: "Benevolence is the distinguishing element of humanity. As embodied in man's conduct, it is called the Way. In this section on "Illustration of Virtue" we quoted from the *Doctrine of the Mean:* "Wisdom, benevolence and courage, these three are the virtues universally binding." It follows that the realization of benevolence is the realization of morality; more, that whether or not a man is benevolent determines whether or not he is a man. How important this is!

The Way is not far from man, nor is virtue kept away from

him. Just so, benevolence is never far from him, and he should not avoid it for even one moment.

> The Master said, "Is benevolence a thing remote? I wish to be benevolent, and lo! benevolence is at hand."[146]
>
> The Master said, "...If a superior man abandons benevolence, how can he achieve his good name?
>
> "The superior man does not, even for the space of a single meal, act contrary to benevolence. In moments of haste he cleaves to it. In seasons of danger he cleaves to it."[147]

Therefore benevolence is the core of human living. Whatever is within the purview of collective existence and evolution can be placed within the limits of benevolence. It is the cardinal virtue, the one which controls all acts of morality from self-perfection to the perfection of things, from the cultivation of the person to the pacification of the world. For this reason it is extremely difficult to give a simple, hard and fast definition of benevolence. Whenever Confucius was asked about it by his disciples, he never gave the selfsame answer. Consider these examples:

> Yen Yüan asked about benevolence. The Master said, "To subdue oneself and return to propriety is benevolence. If a man can for one day subdue himself and return to propriety, all under heaven will ascribe benevolence to him. Is the practice of benevolence from a man himself or is it from others?"
>
> Yen Yüan said, "I beg to ask the steps of that process."
>
> The Master replied, "Look not at what is contrary to propriety; listen not to what is contrary to propriety, speak not what is contrary to propriety; make no movement which is contrary to propriety."
>
> Yen Yüan then said, "Though I am deficient in intelligence and vigor, I will make it my business to practice this lesson."[148]
>
> Chung-kung asked about benevolence. The Master said, "It is, when you go abroad, to behave to everyone as if you were receiving a great guest; to employ the people as if you were assisting at a great sacrifice; not to do to others as you would not wish done to yourself; to have no murmuring against you in the country and none in the family."
>
> Chung-kung said, "Though I am deficient in intelligence and vigor, I will make it my business to practice this lesson."[149]
>
> Ssŭ-ma Niu asked about benevolence. The Master said, "The man of benevolence is cautious and slow in his speech."
>
> "Cautious and slow in his speech!" said Niu;—"Is this what is

meant by benevolence?"

The Master said, "When a man feels the difficulty of doing a thing, can he be other than cautious and slow in speaking of it?"[150]

Fan Ch'ih asked about benevolence. The Master said, "It is to love all men."[151]

Fan Ch'ih asked about benevolence. The Master said, "It is, in retirement, to be sedately grave; in the management of business, to be reverently attentive; in intercourse with others, to be strictly sincere. Though a man go among the barbarians, these qualities may not be neglected."[152]

Tzŭ-kung asked about the practice of benevolence. The Master said, "The mechanic, who wishes to do his work well, must first sharpen his tools. When you are living in any State, take service with the worthy among its great officials and make friends of the benevolent among its scholars."[153]

Tzŭ-chang asked Confucius about benevolence. Confucius said, "To be able to practice five things everywhere under heaven constitutes benevolence." He begged to ask what they were and was told, "Politeness, generosity, truthfulness, expedition and kindness. If you are polite, you will not be treated with disrespect. If you are generous, you will win all. If you are truthful, people will repose trust in you. If you are expeditious, you will accomplish much. If you are kind, this will enable you to employ the services of others."[154]

In answering each of the questions his disciples asked him about benevolence, Confucius as a rule dealt with only one aspect of the virtue and his advice varied according to the natural endowment and academic background of the inquirer. To Yen Yüan, however, who was the most gifted and studious of his disciples, Confucius postulated the full import of benevolence. For this reason the Master's discourses with Yen Yüan on benevolence present his most important thought on this virtue.

The "subduing of oneself" is self-discipline. The "return to propriety" is the preservation and cultivation of inherent nature. Efforts not to speak, look, listen or make a move contrary to propriety embody both the positive and negative points noted above. When translated into practice, they gradually will disclose the essence of benevolence for the people of the whole world to see. (For a more detailed study of this point, see the section on "Self-Control" in Chapter VI, "The Cultivation of the Person."[155]

No sooner had Yen Yüan heard Confucius' analysis of benevolence than he declared, "I will make it my business to practice this lesson." How quick Yen was to comprehend the words of the Master, and how determined to improve himself! However, he succeeded in not acting contrary to benevolence for only three consecutive months; but even at that he was far ahead of his fellow students.

> The Master said, "Such was Hui that for three months there would be nothing in his mind contrary to benevolence. The others may attain to this on some days or in some months, but nothing more."[156]

When his disciples queried Confucius on who or what was benevolent, the Master made the following replies:

> Mêng Wu asked whether Tzǔ-lu was benevolent. The Master said, "I do not know."
> He asked again, when the Master replied, "In a State of a thousand chariots, Yu might be employed to manage the military levies, but I do not know whether he is benevolent."
> "And what do you say of Ch'iu"? The Master riplied, "In a city of a thousand families or a clan of a hundred chariots, Ch'iu might be employed as the chief executive, but I do not know whether he is benevolent."
> "What do you say of Ch'ih?" The Master replied, "With his sash girt and standing in a court, Ch'ih might be employed to converse with the visitors and guests, but I do not know whether he is benevolent."[157]
> Someone said, "Yung is truly benevolent, but he is not ready with his tongue."
> The Master said, "What is the good of being ready with the tongue? They who encounter men with smartness of speech for the most part procure themselves hatred. I know not whether he is truly benevolent, but why should he show readiness of the tongue?"[158]
> "When the love of superiority, boasting, resentments and covetousness are repressed, this may be deemed benevolence."
> The Master said, "This may be regarded as the achievement of what is difficult. But I do not know that it is to be deemed benevolence."[159]

In the following quotations both Tzǔ-yu and the philosopher Tsêng regarded Tzǔ-chang as not benevolent:

Tzŭ-yu said, "My friend Chang can do things which are hard to do, but yet he is not benevolent."[160]

The philosopher Tsêng said, "How imposing the manner of Chang is! It is difficult along with him to practice benevolence:"[161]

We can conclude from these excerpts that Tzŭ-lu, Jan Yu, Kung-hsi Hua, Chung-kung, Yüan Hsien and Tzŭ-chang were not counted among the benevolent. Besides this group of Confucian disciples, Minister Tzŭ-wên of Ch'u, Ch'ên Wên of Ch'i and Kuan Chung of Lu were all men of great renown and respected by their contemporaries, but not one of these either was thought to be benevolent by Confucius.

Tzŭ-chang asked, saying, "Minister Tzŭ-wên thrice took office and manifested no joy in his countenance. Thrice he retired from office and manifested no displeasure. He made it a point to inform the new minister of the way in which he had conducted the government;—what do you say of him?"

The Master replied, "He was loyal."

"Was he benevolent?"

"I do not know. How can he be pronounced benevolent?"

Tzŭ-chang proceeded, "When the official Ts'ui killed the prince of Ch'i, Ch'ên Wên, though he was the owner of forty horses, abandoned them and left the country. Coming to another State, he said, 'They are here like our great official Ts'ui,' and left it. He came to a second State, and with the same observation left it also;—what do you say of him?"

The Master replied, "He was pure."

"Was he benevolent?"

"I do not know. How can he be pronounced benevolent?"[162]

Tzŭ-kung said, "Possibly was Kuan Chung not wanting in benevolence? When Duke Huan caused his brother Chiu to be killed, Kuan Chung was not able to die with him. Moreover, he became Prime Minister to Duke Huan."

The Master said, "Kuan Chung served as Prime Minister to Duke Huan, made him leader of all the princes and united and rectified the whole empire. Down to the present day, the people enjoy the gifts which he conferred. But for Kuan Chung, we should now be wearing our hair unbound and the lappets of our coats buttoning on the left side.

Will you require from him the small fidelity of common men and common women, who would commit suicide in a stream or ditch, no one knowing anything about them?"[163]

Tzŭ-lu said, "Duke Huan caused his brother Chiu to be killed, when Chao Hu died with his master, but Kuan Chung did not die. May not I say that Kuan Chung was wanting in benevolence?"

The Master said, "Duke Huan assembled all the princes together, and that not with weapons of war and chariots:—it was all through the influence of Kuan Chung. It was his benevolence! It was his benevolence!"[164]

Kuan Chung deserved great credit for establishing internal peace, repelling external aggression and keeping China from being conquered by barbarians. Yet Confucius merely said of him that there was none whose benevolence was like his; he still refused, deftly, to recognize in him the full application of benevolence. The essence of benevolence is extremely subtle; at the same time its utility has great scope. Benevolence is such a lofty quality that it has all but become one with the highest attributes of heaven and earth. It cannot be lightly ascribed to any man.

However, we must not make the mistake of regarding benevolence as unattainable. Mencius said, "Benevolence is man's mind";[165] "The feeling of commiseration implies the principle of benevolence",[166] "The feeling of commiseration is the beginning of benevolence";[167] "He who is devoid of the feeling of commiseration is not a man";[168] and "The feeling of commiseration is shared by all men."[169]

Therefore it is clear that benevolence is inborn. It is in a man's mind and does not have to be sought from outside. What it needs is only its retention and cultivation, and this should not prove to be excessively difficult.

Mencius said, "That whereby man differs from the lower animals is but small. The mass of people cast it away, while superior men preserve it.

"Shun clearly understood the multitude of things and closely observed the relations of humanity. He walked along the path of benevolence and righteousness; he did not need to pursue benevolence and righteousness."[170]

The Master said, "Those who are without becevolence cannot abide long either in a condition of poverty and hardship or in a condition of enjoyment. The benevolent rest in benevolence; the wise are benefited by benevolence."[171]

The object of benevolence is man. Therefore, Shun had to understand clearly a number of things, and he had to observe closely the relationships between men. Walking along the path of benevolence is resting in benevolence. Also, those who pursue benevolence are benefited by it. In both cases the mind is involved. Without benevolence, superficially a man cannot long endure poverty and lowliness without complaint, nor long enjoy wealth and power without pride; more profoundly, a man bereft of benevolence degenerates into a lower animal. For this reason, in the teachings of both Confucius and Mencius the central thought is basically "benevolence." And they constantly strove to inculcate their followers with this virtue.

> The Master said, "Is benevolence a thing remote? I wish to be benevolent, and lo! benevolence is at hand."[172]
>
> The Master said, "If the will be set on benevolence, there will be no practice of wickedness."[173]
>
> The Master said, "I have not seen a person who loved benevolence or one who hated what was not benevolent. He who loved benevolence would esteem it as above everything else. He who hated what is not benevolent would practice benevolence in such a way that he would not allow anything that is not benevolent to approach his person.
>
> "Is anyone for one day able to apply his strength to benevolence? I have not seen the case in which his strength would be insufficient.
>
> "Should there possibly be any such case, I have not seen it."[174]
>
> The Master said, "Benevolence is more to man than either water or fire. I have seen men die from treading on water and fire, but I have never seen a man die from treading the course of benevolence."[175]

From these excerpts we can draw the following conclusion: Benevolence is the great sense of sympathy and inexhaustible love. It begins with intimacy with relatives and progresses to love of people and kindness to things. It starts with the feeling of commiseration and pity and extends from what cannot be borne to what can be borne, to the treatment of others like oneself, altruism and unselfishness, love and assistance to others, the exaltation of propriety and the pursuit of righteousness. In case of necessity it even enjoins the sacrifice of one's life for the sake of the greater self. This is the consummation of benevolence, being co-equal with Heaven.

The philosopher Yu said, "...The superior man bends his attention to the root. That being established, the Way grows up. Filial piety and fraternal submission—are they not the root of benevolence?"[176]

Mencius said, "...The feeling of commiseration is shared by all men"[177].

Mencius said, "All men have some things which they cannot bear; extend that feeling to what they can bear, and benevolence will be the result...If a man can give full development to the feeling which makes him shrink from injuring others, his benevolence will be more than can be called into practice.[178]

A benevolent man bears the important burden of universal love ("Benevolence is the burden which he considers it is his to sustain—is it not heavy?"). He bears it as a life-long responsibility ("Only with death does his course stop—is it not long?"). Although he must attend to the relatively unimportant and short-term activities of his daily life, he must continually be aware of the important things and long-term goals. He should subdue himself. This self-discipline is vital, for it will enable him to (1) assume heavy responsibility, (2) return to propriety in order to free himself from blame, and (3) cultivate and create a reservoir of inexhaustible love. His aim, of course, is self-perfection (cultivation of the person) and the perfection of others and things (regulation of the family, good government in the nation and pacification of the world).

His attitude should be grave. He must be broadminded and possess vigorous endurance. Also, he must avoid empty talk; rather, his words must show his faithfulness and sincerity. He must be convinced that practice is important, and his acts must be earnest and respectful. Although he can be imposed upon, he cannot be fooled. He is a prey to neither anxiety nor fear. He has the magnanimity to strengthen and help others when he wishes to be supported and helped himself; likewise, he will enlarge others (further their spiritual and intellectual capacities) when he wishes to be enlarged himself.

He has the courage to make the supreme sacrifice of himself for the sake of the Way ("A man of benevolence must have courage."). Combined with this he possesses endurance that is unbending (A scholar must be broadminded and have vigorous endurance). He stresses morality and does not attach importance to his own life. In line with this, he is fond of good and hates evil. Due to his ability to practice benevolence and righteousness, he never brings disgrace on his birthright.

The philophere Tsêng said, "A scholar may not be without breadth of mind and vigorous endurance. His burden is heavy and his course is long.

"Benevolence is the burden which he considers it is his to sustain; is it not heavy? Only with death does his course stop; is it not long?"[179]

Tzŭ-hsia said, "There are learning extensively and having a firm and sincere aim, inquiring pertinently and reflecting from what is near at hand: virtue is such a course."[180]

The Master said , "To subdue oneself and return to propriety is benevolence."[181]

The Master said, "The firm, the enduring, the simple and the modest are near to benevolence."[182]

The Master said, "Fine words and an insinuating appearance are seldom associated with benevolence."[183]

Tsai Wo asked, saying, "A benevolent man, though it be told him,—'There is a man in the well,' will go in after him, I suppose." Confucius said, "Why should he do so? A superior man may be made to go to the well, but he cannot be made to go down into it. He may be imposed upon, but he cannot be befooled."[184]

The Master said, "...the benevolent are free from anxiety..."[185]

Tzŭ-kung said, "Suppose the case of a man extensively conferring benefits on the people and able to assist all, what would you say of him? Might he be called benevolent?"

The Master said, "How can he be called benevolent merely? It must be a sage who can do this. Even Yao and Shun wished they could have accomplished it.

"Now the man of benevolence, wishing to be established himself seeks also to establish others; wishing to be enlarged himself, he seeks also to enlarge others.

"To be able to take example from what is near at hand may be called the method of benevolence."[186]

The Master said, "It is only the benevolent man who can love or who can hate others."[187]

The Master said, "The determind scholar and the man of benevolence will not seek to live at the expense of injuring their benevolence. They will even sacrifice their lives to preserve · their benevolence complete."[188]

How do the benevolent compare with the wise?

The Master said, "The wise find pleasure in water; the

benevolent find pleasure in hills. The wise are active; the benevolent are tranquil. The wise are joyful; the benevolent are long-lived."[189]

Confucius' comparison in this last quotation is based on the merits of both wisdom and benevolence and what they emphasize. It does not bring out the total role of the two. The wise, unobstructed in their movement, are as active as flowing water; with no perplexities, they are always joyful. The benevolent, free from vacillation, are as tranquil as the hills; with no anxieties, they are long-lived. But the wisest and most benevolent men, with perfect virtue, are both active and tranquil, joyful and long-lived.

Those who lack benevolence, on the other hand, have lost their inherent nature. They have no sympathy, are cruel, impolite, and have a *Schadenfreude* over others' calamities.

> Mencius said, "How is it possible to speak with those princes who are not benevolent? Their perils they count safety, their calamities they count profitable, and they have pleasure in the things by which they perish. If it were possible to talk with them who so violate benevolence, how could we have such destruction of States and ruin of families?"[190]
>
> The Master said, "High station filled without indulgent generosity; ceremonies performed without reverence; mourning conducted without sorrow;—wherewith should I contemplate such ways?"[191]

As water prevails over fire, benevolence can ultimately prevail over the lack of it, for benevolence is the condition for the common existence of mankind and is upheld by all. The person with only superficial benevolence is like the man who pours a cup of water on a flaming wagon-load of firewood and then says in self-defense that water cannot put out a fire. This is self-deception as well as deception of others. Since truth is eternal, we should not lose our confidence.

> Mencius said, "Benevolence prevails over the lack of it, just as water prevails over fire. Those, however, who nowadays practice benevolence do it as if with one cup of water they could save a whole wagon-load of firewood which was on fire, and when the flames were not extinguished, were to say that water cannot prevail over fire. This conduct, moreover, greatly encourages those

who are not benevolent. The final result will only be destruction."[192]

3. Courage

Strictly interpreted, courage involves the use of energy. Those men of strong will who can make full use of their energy have abundant spirit and sound bodies. Without this spirit they would not be able to apply their mental energy, and without sound bodies they would not be able to apply their physical energy.

The Master said, "The courageous are free from fear."[193] Because they lack fear the courageous have great endurance. They can forge ahead without obstruction and can overcome their difficulties and assume their responsibilities. On the other hand, if they were decadent and dispirited, this would indicate a lack of strength and they would timidly retreat from challenges.

However, although courage involves great energy, this energy is vigor and not violence. If courage were misunderstood to be an indication of violent struggle, it would mean a clash with the interests of others, the destruction of the social order, the commission of crimes and the outbreak of disturbances; all lead to disastrous results.

The Master said, "The man who is fond of daring and is dissatisfied with poverty will proceed to insubordination. So will the man who is not benevolent, when you carry your dislike of him to an extreme."[194]

Tzŭ-lu said, "Does the superior man esteem valor?" The Master said, "The superior man holds righteousness to be of highest importance. A man in a superior position, having valor without righteousness, will be guilty of insubordination; one of the lower people, having valor without righteousness, will commit robbery."[195]

The Master said, "For a man to sacrifice to a spirit which does not belong to him is flattery. To see what is right and not to do it is want of courage."[196]

Tzŭ-kung said, "Has the superior man his hatreds also?" The Master said, "He has his hatreds. He hates those who proclaim the evil of others. He hates the man who, being in a low position, slanders his superiors. He hates those who have valor merely and are unobservant of propriety. He hates those who are forward and determined and, at the same time, of contracted understanding."

The Master then inquired, "Tz'ŭ, have you also your hatreds?" Tzŭ-kung replied, "I hate those who pry out matters and ascribe the knowledge to their wisdom. I hate those who are only immodest and think that they are valorous. I hate those who make known secrets and think that they are straightforward."[197]

These four quotations explain the real meaning of courage. It is important that courage be accompanied by benevolence and propriety. Courage without modesty and propriety is a kind of violence which was hated not only by Confucius but also by Tzŭ-kung. Of all Confucius' disciples, Tzŭ-lu was the fondest of courage as well as righteousness; however, regrettably, his courage was mostly physical. For this reason Confucius surmised that he would meet a violent death.

> The Master said, "With my Way not prevailing, I will get upon a raft and float about on the sea. He that will accompany me will be Yu, I dare say." Tzŭ-lu, hearing this, was glad, upon which the Master said, "Yu is fonder of daring than I am. But I have not yet found the material for the raft."[198]
> The disciple Min was standing by his side looking bland and precise; Tzŭ-lu, looking bold and soldierly; Jan Yu and Tzŭ-kung, with a free and straightforward manner. The Master was pleased. (He said,) "Yu there!—it seems that he will not die a natural death."[199]

Tzŭ-lu, proud of his courage, regarded himself as indispensable to the army. Confucius, however, preferred men well-versed in strategy to those who were merely unafraid of death. He frequently drove home this point in conversations with Tzŭ-lu and urged him to strive for the courage of the superior man.

> The Master said to Yen Yüan, "When called to office, to undertake its duties; when not so called, to lie retired;—it is only I and you who have attained to this."
> Tzŭ-lu said, "If you had the conduct of the armies of a great State, whom would you have to act with you?"
> The Master said, "I would not have to act with me, who will unarmed attack a tiger or cross a river without a boat, dying without any regret. My associate must be the man who proceeds to action full of solicitude, who is fond of adjusting his plans and then carries them into execution."[200]

Confucius singled out the various types of strength possessed by the people residing in various regions of the country. He said the strength of the North was near to stubbornness; the people were willing to meet death without regret. The strength of the South, he said, was close to reciprocity; the people there did not avenge unreasonable conduct. However, the strength of the superior man had nothing to do with physical bravery; rather, it set great store on righteousness. The superior man was independent and fearless. He did not associate with all types of persons indiscriminately, nor did he incline to eithir side; he was unchanging and unbending. He manifested the solidity of his inherent strength, and he could not be swayed by any external force.

Tzŭ-lu asked about strength. The Master said, "Do you mean the strength of the South, the strength of the North or the strength which you should cultivate yourself?

"To show magnanimity and gentleness in teaching others, and not to avenge unreasonable conduct:—this is the strength of the South, and the superior man makes it his study. To lie under arms and meet death without regret:—this is the strength of the North, and the forceful make it their study. Therefore the superior man cultivates a friendly harmony and does not show the weakness of indiscriminate association. How firm he is in his strength! He stands erect in the middle and does not incline to either side. How firm he is in his strength! When the Way prevails in the country, he does not change from what he was in retirement. When the Way no longer prevails, he maintains his course to death without changing. How firm he is in his strength!"[201]

Mencius distinguished between much and little courage. When a man died without justification, this was not courage; in fact, it was contrary to courage.

King Hsüan of Ch'i asked, saying, "Is there any way to regulate the intercourse with neighboring countries? Mencius replied, "There is. But it is only a perfectly virtuous prince who can, with a great country, serve a small one, as, for instance, T'ang served Ko and King Wên served the K'un barbarians. And it is only a wise prince who can, with a small country, serve a great one, as, for instance, King T'ai served the Hsün-yu and Kou-chien served Wu.

"He who, with a great State, serves a small one, delights in Heaven. He who, with a small State, serves a large one, stands in awe of Heaven. He who delights in Heaven can preserve the whole empire, and he who stands in awe of Heaven can preserve his own country.

"It is said in the *Book of Songs*, 'I fear the Majesty of Heaven and thus I can protect my country.' "

The King said, "What a great saying! But I have an infirmity;—I love valor."

"I beg Your Majesty," was the reply, "not to love small valor. If a man brandishes his sword, looks fiercely and says, 'How dare he withstand me?'—this is the valor of a common man, who can be the opponent only of a single individual. I beg Your Majesty to greaten it.

"It is said in the *Book of Songs*,

The king blazed with anger
And he marshaled his hosts,
To stop the march to Chü,
To consolidate the prosperity of Chou,
To meet the expectations of the nation.

"This was the valor of King Wên. King Wên, in one blast of his anger, gave repose to all the people of the empire.

"In the *Book of History* it is said, 'Heaven, having produced the inferior people, made for them rulers and teachers, with the purpose that they should be assisting to God, and therefore distinguished them throughout the four quarters of the land. Whoever are offenders and whoever are innocent, here am I to deal with them. How dare any under heaven give indulgence to their refractory wills?' There was one man pursuing a violent and disorderly course in the empire, and King Wu was ashamed of it. This was the valor of King Wu. He also, by one display of his anger, gave repose to all the people of the empire.

"Let now Your Majesty also, in one burst of anger, give repose to all the people of the empire. The people are only afraid that Your Majesty does not love valor."[202]

Mencius said, "...When it appears proper to sacrifice one's life, and afterwards not proper, to sacrifice it is contrary to bravery."[203]

"To give repose to all the people of the empire" is great benevolence, and it is only when there is great benevolence that there can be great courage. Here is how Mencius explained the rise and cultivation of great courage by means of an unperturbed mind and nourishment of the vast, flowing passion-nature:

Kung-sun Ch'ou asked Mencius, saying, "Master, if you were to be appointed a high noble and the prime minister of Ch'i, so as to make your Way prevail, it would be nothing strange for you to raise the ruler to the headship of all the princes or even to the imperial dignity. In such a position would your mind be perturbed or not?" Mencius replied, "No. At forty I attained to an unperturbed mind."

Ch'ou said, "If so, my Master, you are far beyond Mêng Pên." "This is not difficult," said Mencius. "The scholar Kao had attained to an unperturbed mind at an earlier period of life than I did."

Ch'ou asked, "Is there any way to an unperturbed mind?" The answer was, "Yes."

"Pei-kung Yu had this way of nourishing his valor:—He did not flinch from any strokes at his body. He did not turn his eyes from any thrusts at them. He considered that the slightest push from anyone was the same as if he were beaten before the crowds in the market-place, and that what he would not receive from a common man in his loose large garments of coarse cloth, neither should he receive from a prince of ten thousand chariots. He viewed stabbing a prince of ten thousand chariots just as stabbing a fellow dressed in coarse cloth. He feared not any of all the princes. A bad word addressed to him he always returned.

"Mêng Shih-shêh had this way of nourishing his valor:—He said, 'I look upon not conquering and conquering in the same way. To measure the enemy and then advance; to calculate the chances of victory and then engage:—this is to stand in awe of the opposing force. How can I be certain of conquering? I can only rise superior to all fear.'

Mêng Shih-shêh resembled the philosopher Tsêng. Pei-kung Yu resembled Tzǔ-hsia. I do not know to the valor of which of the two the superiority should be ascribed, but yet Mêng Shih-shêh attended to what was of the greater importance.

"Formerly the philosopher Tsêng said to Tzǔ-hsiang, 'Do you love valor? I heard an account of great valor from the Master. It speaks thus:—If, on self-examination, I find that I am not upright, shall I not be in fear even of a poor man in his loose garments of coarse cloth? If, on self-examination, I find that I am upright, I will go forward against thousands and tens of thousands.'

"Yet, what Mêng Shih-shêh maintained, being merely his physical energy, was after all inferior to what the philosopher Tsêng maintained, which was indeed of the most importance."

Kung-sun Ch'ou said, "May I venture to ask an explanation from you, Master, of how you maintain an unperturbed mind and how the philosopher Kao does the same?" Mencius answered, "Kao says, 'What is not attained in words is not to be sought for in the mind; what produces dissatisfaction in the mind is not to be helped by passion-effort.' This last,—when there is unrest in the mind, not to seek relief from passion-effort, may be conceded. But not to seek in the mind for what is not attained in words cannot be conceded. The will is the leader of the passion-nature. The passon-nature pervades and animates the body. The will is first and chief, and the passion-nature is subordinate to it. Therefore I say,—Maintain firm the will, and do no violence to the passion-nature."

Ch'ou observed, "Since you say—'The will is chief and the passion-nature is subordinate,' how do you also say, 'Maintain firm the will, and do no violence to the passion-nature'?" Mencius replied, "When it is the will alone which is active, it moves the passion-nature. When it is the passion-nature alone which is active, it moves the will. For instance, now, in the case of a man falling or running, that is from the passion-nature, and yet it moves the mind."

"I venture to ask," said Ch'ou again, "wherein you, Master, surpass." Mencius told him, "I understand words. I am skillful in nourishing my vast, flowing passion-nature."

Ch'ou pursued, "I venture to ask what you mean by your vast, flowing passion-nature!" The reply was, "It is difficult to describe.

"This is the passion-nature:—It is exceedingly great and exceedingly strong. Being nourished by rectitude and sustaining no injury, it fills up all between heaven and earth.

"This is the passion-nature:—It is the mate and assistant of righteousness and the Way. Without it there is a serious inadequacy.

"It is produced by the accumulation of righteous deeds; it is not to be obtained by incidental acts of righteousness. If the mind does not feel complacency in the conduct, the nature becomes seriously inadequate. I therefore said, 'Kao has never understood righteousness, because he makes it something external.'

"There must be the constant practice of this righteousness, but without anticipating the results. Let not the mind forget its work, but let there be no assisting the growth of the nature. Let us not be like the man of Sung. There was a man of Sung, who was grieved that his growing rice was not longer, and so he pulled it up. Having done this, he returned home, looking very stupid, and said to his people, 'I am tired today. I have been helping the rice to grow long.' His son ran to look at it, and found the rice all withered. There are few in the world, who do not deal with their passion-nature, as if they were assisting the rice to grow long. Some indeed consider it of no benefit to them and let it alone:— they do not weed their rice. What they do is not only of no benefit to the nature, but it also injures it."[204]

From the foregoing it can be seen that great courage is produced by the accumulation of righteous deeds practiced for the sake of benevolence. Therefore the benevolent man must have courage. As for those who have courage but no benevolence or propriety, they are unruly ruffians who can in no way be described as brave men; they are devoid of virtue.

> The Master said, "The virtuous will be sure to speak correctly, but those whose speech is good may not always be virtuous. Benevolent men are sure to be courageous, but those who are courageous may not always be benevolent men."[205]

Men who have wisdom, benevolence and courage possess illustrious virtue. When they regulate these qualities in equilibrium, they have the knowledge of propriety. How to reach this stage depends on sincerity—the motive power of life. Hence it is said, "And there is only one means by which they (men) carry the duties (of universal obligation) into practice." What is this one means? It is sincerity. Hence it is also said, "Their knowledge being complete, their thoughts are sincere."[206]

G. Illustration of Instruction

The object of instruction, stripped down, is the cultivation of the Way. Since the Way is the high road to the common existence and evolution of mankind, everyone should travel it at all times. The raw material for the construction of this high road is "benevolence." Hence, "The Way is cultivated by benevolence."[207]

The prevalence of the Way is then, simply, benevolence cultivating the Way. Without benevolence, the Way is bound to be destroyed and ultimately it will not prevail. Wherever it is said in the *Four Books* that the Way does or does not prevail, it means benevolence is present or absent.

> Mencius said, "...Confucius said, 'There are but two Ways to be pursued, that of benevolence and that of its absence.' "[208]

Though instruction must vary according to differences in human intelligence, the basic courses to be followed are invariable. In a word, the Way is the root and the arts are branches.

> The Master said, "Set your mind on the Way. Hold fast to virtue. Adhere to benevolence. Seek relaxation and enjoyment from the arts."[209]

According to Confucius, four principles were basic to the conduct of education. "There were four things which the Master taught—letters, ethics, loyalty and faithfulness"[210]

Instruction begins with youth, and so home education is the starting point, the foundation of education. Without a firm foundation nothing can be built. Now, benevolence is the basis of education, and filial piety and fraternal love are the basis of benevolence. It follows that filial piety and fraternal love also are the core of home education. It is a moot question whether Confucius himself wrote the *Book of Filial Piety*, but the discussion of filial piety and fraternal love is diffused throughout the *Analects,* and the disciples laid great emphasis on these virtues.

> The Master said, "A youth, when at home, should be filial, and, abroad, respectful to his elders. He should be earnest and truthful. He should overflow in love to all and cultivate the friendship of the good. When he has time and opportunity, after the performance of these things, he should employ them in polite studies."[211]

> The philosopher Yu said, "They are few who, being filial and fraternal, are fond of offending against their superiors. There have been none who, not liking to offend against their superiors, have been fond of stirring up confusion.

> "The superior man bends his attention to the root. That being established, the Way grows up.

> "Filial piety and fraternal submission—are they not the root of all benevolent actions?"[212]

The story of growth tells of progression from the small to the large, from the near to the remote, from the root to the branches. In like manner, instruction in benevolence must start with the love of one's family and relatives, and progress to kindness (benevolence) to other persons, and finally extend to kindness toward all other living things.

> Mencius said, "In regard to other living things than men, the superior man is kind and not benevolent. In regard to the people, he is benevolent but not loving to them. He is loving to his relatives and benevolent to the people. He is benevolent to the people and kind to living things other than men."[213]

It is interesting to note that the Chinese expression for "religion" is composed of two characters, *tsung* and *chiao,* meaning "the origin of education." All religions teach men to cultivate the Way: (1) to have universal love, (2) to be loving to their relatives, (3) to subdue themselves and uphold propriety, and (4) to sacrifice themselves for the sake of the greater self (consummation of benevolence). By and large there is no exception anywhere in the world to teaching "cultivation of the Way with benevolence."

The teaching on love for one's relatives is discussed later in Chapter VII, "The Regulation of the Family." Here let us note that the education of men must start with their daily life. They must be taught to observe the rules of conduct (propriety). This education must proceed from the shallow to the deep and take its examples from the near, which is the method of teaching benevolence.

> Tzŭ-kung said, "...Now the man of benevolence, wishing to be established himself, seeks also to establish others; wishing to be enlarged himself, seeks also to enlarge others.
> "To be able to judge of others by what is nigh in ourselves; this may be called the art of benevolence."[214]

In their discussion of teaching, Tzŭ-hsia and Tzŭ-yu differed in emphasis, but both attached great importance to the teaching method.

> Tzŭ-yu said, "The disciples and followers of Tzŭ-hsia, in sprinkling and sweeping the ground, in answering and replying, in advancing and receding, are sufficiently accomplished. But these are only the branches of learning, and they are left ignorant of what is essential. How can they be acknowledged as sufficiently taught?"
> Tzŭ-hsia heard of the remark and said, "Alas! Yen Yu is wrong. According to the Way of the superior man in teaching, what departments are there which he considers of prime importance to be transmitted first? What are there which he considers of secondary importance and allows himself to be idle about? But as in the case of plants, which are assorted according to their classes, so learning should be differentiated. How can the Way of a superior man be indiscriminately taught? Is it not the sage alone whe can unite in one the beginning and consummation of learning?"[215]

The *Book of Songs* gives vent to the will, the *Book of History* records events, the *Book of Rites* gives guidance for conduct, the *Book of Music* shows harmony, the *Book of Changes* deals with *yin* and *yang*, and the *Spring and Autumn Annals* distinguishes between right and wrong. They all contain important teaching materials. But the first three are more intimately connected with daily life, and so Confucius frequently discussed them with his disciples. He also ordered his son to study them, saying: "If you do not learn the Book of Songs, you will not be fit to converse with" and "If you do not learn the Rules of Propriety, your character cannot be established."

In editing the *Book of Songs* and the *Book of History*, compiling the *Book of Rites* and the *Book of Music*, annotating the *Book of Changes* and writing the *Spring and Autumn Annals*, Confucius aimed also at the selection and preparation of teaching materials.

> The Master's frequent themes of discourse were the *Book of Songs*, the *Book of History* and the maintenance of the Rules of Propriety. On all these he frequently discoursed."[216]
>
> Ch'ên K'ang asked Po-yü, saying, "Have you heard any lessons from your father different from what we have all heard?"
>
> Po-yü replied, "No. He was standing alone once, when I passed below the hall with hasty steps, and said to me, 'Have you studied the *Book of Songs?*' On my replying 'Not yet,' he added, 'If you do not study the *Bonk of Songs,* you will not be fit to converse with.' I retired and studied the *Book of Songs.*
>
> "Another day, he was in the same way standing alone, when I passed by below the hall, and said to me, 'Have you studied the Rules of Propriety?' On my replying, 'Not yet,' he added, 'If you do not study the Rules of Propriety, your character cannot be established.' I then retired and studied the Rules of Propriety.
>
> "I have only heard these two things from him."
>
> Ch'ên K'ang retired, and, quite delighted, said, "I asked one thing, and I have got three things. I have heard about the *Book of Songs.* I have heard about the Rules of Propriety. I have also heard that the superior man maintains a distant reserve towards his son."[217]
>
> Tzŭ-kung said, "The Master's personal displays of his principles and ordinary descriptions of them may be heard. His discourses about man's nature and the Way of Heaven cannot be heard."[218]

This last point takes note of the fact that Confucius seldom spoke of nature and the Way cf Heaven because they were comparatively abstract.

In the preceding section on the "Illustration of Virtue" the importance of the *Book of Rites* and the *Book of Music* were discussed. Propriety and music are the concrete expressions of virtue. As such they are visible in human conduct. Popularly known as the "compass and square" (rules of conduct), they are the first things to be taught. In fact, the instruction on the six arts also started with propriety and music.

> Mencius said, "Yi, in teaching men to shoot, made it a rule to draw the bow to the full, and his pupils also did the same.
> "A master-workman, in teaching others, uses the compass and square, and his pupils do the same."[119]

Teaching with the compass and square can only achieve average results; nothing better can be expected. It cannot instill skill because skill has to do with individual intelligence.

> Mencius said, "A carpenter or a carriage-maker may give a man the circle and square, but cannot make him skillful in the use of them."[120]

The rules of conduct cannot accommodate men, who must try to comply with them. This is so because before propriety all men are equal.

> Kung-sun Ch'ou said, "Lofty is your Way and admirable, but to learn it may well be likened to ascending the heavens,—something which cannot be reached. Why not adapt your teaching so as to cause learners to consider it attainable and so daily exert themselves?"
> Mencius said, "A great artificer does not, for the sake of a stupid workman, alter or do away with the marking-line. Yi did not, for the sake of a stupid archer, change his rule for drawing the bow.
> "The superior man draws the bow, but does not discharge the arrow, seeming to see it leap to the mark; and he there stands exactly in the middle of the path. Those who are able follow him."[221]

The technique of instruction should be adjusted to the ability of those being taught. In general five ways of teaching were outlined:

> Mencius said, "There are five ways in which the superior man effects his teaching.
> "There are some on whom his influence descends like the seasonable rain.

"There are some whose vritue he perfects.

"There are some the development of whose talent he assists.

"There are some whose inquiries he answers.

"There are some who privately learn from him and cultivate themselves.

"These five ways are the methods in which the superior man effects his teaching."[222]

Those who did not go far enough were prodded to press forward, while those who went too far too fast were restrained. The aim was to make certain that what the students learned could be of practical value and what they did was appropriate.

Tzŭ-lu asked whether he should immediately carry into practice what he heard. The Master said, "Your father and elder brothers are still living; why should you act on that principle of immediately carrying into practice what you hear?"

Jan Yu asked the same, whether he should immediately carry into practice what he heard, and the Master answered, "Immediately carry into practice what you hear."

Kung-hsi Hua said, "Yu asked whether he should immediately carry into practice what he heard, and you said, 'Your father and elder brothers are still living.' Ch'iu asked whether he should immediately carry into practice what he heard, and you said, 'Carry it immediately into practice.' I, Ch'ih, am perplexed and venture to ask you for an explanation."

The Master said, "Ch'iu is retiring and slow; therefore I urged him forward. Yu has more than his own share of energy; therefore I kept him back."[223]

Since love of men is the basic condition for human conduct, the teaching of others to be good (fidelity) is included in the love of men. "The teaching others what is good is called 'the exercise of fidelity.' "[224]

Those who are first informed should instruct those who come later, and those who first apprehend the Way should instruct those who are slower to grasp it. This is one of man's responsibilities. For example, water flows downward from high places till it finds its level; electricity is transmitted from high to low voltage till a balance is struck; when heat and cold are mixed, the former helps warm the latter till the same temperature is reached. It is the way of Heaven to be altruistic and collaborate with others in the performance of good. When those who first apprehend the Way instruct those who are slower in learning it, they practice the Way of Heaven and accelerate the progress of mankind.

> Mencius said, "Yi Yin said, 'Heaven's plan in the production of mankind is this: that they who are first informed should instruct those who are later in being informed, and they who first apprehend the Way should instruct those who are slower to do so. I am one of Heaven's people who have first apprehended; I will take this Way and instruct this people in it.'
>
> "He thought that among all the people of the world, even the private men and women, if there were any who did not enjoy such benefits as Yao and Shun conferred, it was as if he himself pushed them into a ditch. He took upon himself the heavy charge of the world in this way,..."[225]

Moreover, instruction is the cultivation of the Way. And it entails a responsibility for those who are slower so that through them the Way of Heaven is transmitted and enlarged. Only man has this ability to teach cultivation of the Way. For it is man who takes the road; the road does not force man to take it. As Confucius said, "A man can enlarge the Way; the Way does not enlarge the man."[226]

If everyone can instruct untiringly those who are slower than they in apprehending the Way, the inevitable result will be uninterrupted continuity and development of our national culture.

However, the teacher and his pupil edify each other. It is especially important for the teacher to be sincere in his instruction. He should hide nothing from his pupil. Confucius put it this way: "Do you think, my disciples, that I have any concealments? I conceal nothing from you. There is nothing which I do that is not shown to you, my disciples—that is my way."[227]

It devolves on the knowledge-seeking pupil to take more delight in the Way than in life itself. Confucius maintained, "If a man hears the Way in the morning, he may die in the evening without regret."[228]

However, if a pupil adheres to pre-conceived, irrelevant presumptions as he comes to seek knowledge, he cannot be sincere. No attention should be paid to him.

> The disciple Kung-tu said, "When Kêng of T'êng made his appearance in your school, it seemed proper that a polite consideration

should be paid to him, and yet you did not answer him. Why was that?"

Mencius replied, "I do not answer him who questions me presuming on his nobility, nor him who presumes on his talents, nor him who presumes on his age, nor him who presumes on services performed to the State, nor him who presumes on old acquaintance. Two of those things were chargeable on Kêng."[229]

When pupils display a sincere desire to receive instruction, their efforts should be welcomed wholeheartedly and without discriminating among the pupils. There should be no class distinction in education. To quote Confucius, "I have never refused instruction to anyone bringing his bundle of dried meat or upwards;[230] and again, "In teaching there should be no distinction of classes."[231]

Even if the prospective pupil had some defects before, he should be excused and accepted.

When Mencius went to T'eng, he was lodged in the upper palace. A sandal in the process of making had been placed there in a window, and when the keeper of the place came to look for it, he could not find it.

On this someone asked Mencius, "Can it be that your followers have hidden it?" Mencius replied, "Do you think that they came here to pilfer the sandal?" The man said, "I apprehend not."

Mencius said, "When I set up my school, I do not go back to inquire into the past, and I do not reject those who come to me. If they come with the mind to learn, I receive them without any more ado."[232]

To repeat, it is vitally necessary that teacher and pupil show mutual sincerity, even as they edify each other. If a pupil seeks knowledge without ever asking questions, something is lacking; the teacher will find his work uninteresting, and even more important, neither he nor his pupil will receive the benefit of mutual enlightenment. Of course, there are exceptions. Yen Hui, "knowing ten after hearing one," had few questions. Confucius realized this and so did not withhold praise of his wisdom and worthiness.

The Master said, "After I have talked with Hui for a whole day, he does not make any objection to anything I say—as if he were stupid. After he retires, I examine his conduct and find him able to illustrate my teachings. Hui! He is not stupid."[233]

The Master said, "Hui gives me no assistance. There is nothing that I say in which he does not delight."[234]

There are many methods of teaching. One is refusal to teach, for this, too, can stimulate the incentive to learn. Consider these examples:

Mencius said, "There are many arts in teaching. If out of contempt I refuse to teach a man, I am only thereby still teaching him.[235]

Ju Pei wished to see Confucius, but Confucius declined, on the ground of being sick, to see him. When the bearer of this message went out at the door, (the Master) took his lute and sang to it, in order that Pei might hear him.[236]

In short, since teaching is the cultivation of the Way, it should be done correctly. And this includes choosing the right curriculum. Otherwise more harm than good will result. "The study of strange doctrines," Confucius said, "is injurious indeed!"[237] However, if teaching were confined to the arts and neglected morality, it could result in the sacrifice of life.

Nan-kung Kua, submitting an inquiry to Confucius, said, "Yi was skillful at archery and Ao could move a boat along upon the land, but neither of them seems to have died a natural death. Yü and Chi personally wrought at the toils of husbandry, and they became posessors of the empire." The Master made no reply; but when Nan-kung Kua went out, he said, "A superior man indeed is this! An esteemer of virtue indeed is this![238]

P'eng Mêng learned archery of Yi. When he had acquired all the art of Yi, he thought that in all the empire only Yi was superior to himself, and so he slew him. Mencius said, "In this case Yi also was to blame. Kung-ming Yi indeed said, 'It would appear as if he were not to be blamed,' but he thereby only meant that his blame was slight. How can he be held without any blame?

"The people of Chêng sent Tzŭ-cho Ju to make an attack on Wei, which sent Yü-kung Ssŭ to pursue him. Tzŭ-cho Ju said, 'Today I feel unwell, so that I cannot hold my bow. I am a dead man!' At the same time he asked his driver, 'Who is it that is pursuing me?' The driver said, 'It is Yü-kung Ssŭ,' on which he exclaimed, 'I shall live.' The driver said, 'Yü-kung Ssŭ is the best archer of Wei. What do you mean by saying that you will live?'

Ju replied, 'Yü-kung Ssŭ learned archery from Yin-kung T'o, who in turn learned it from me. Now Yin-kung T'o is an upright man, and the friends of his selection must be upright also.' When Yü-kung Ssŭ came up, he said, 'Master, why are you not holding your bow?' Ju answered, 'Today I am feeling unwell and cannot hold my bow.' On this Ssŭ said, 'I learned archery from Yin-kung T'o, who in turn learned it from you. I cannot bear to injure you with your own art. The business of today, however, is the prince's business, which I dare not neglect.' He then took his arrows, knocked off their steel points against the carriage-wheel, discharged four of them and returned."[239]

This further proves how true it is that "virtue is the root and the arts are the branches." Today educators stress the arts and forget virtue. If this course is pursued to its logical conclusion and there is no awakening from the delusion involved, then indeed we are in trouble. For nuclear energy, which could prove to be a blessing, might ultimately turn out to be a disaster for mankind. Wisdom is to know benevolence, and courage is to practice it. Only when there is benevolence can the Way be cultivated, and only when the Way is cultivated can instruction be perfected.

The cultivation of the Way is rightly called instruction.

H.   Knowledge of Men

"In order to know men, he (the superior man or sovereign) may not dispense with the knowledge of Heaven,"[240] and so the object of the knowledge of Heaven is the knowledge of men. "Without knowing destiny it is impossible to be a superior man,"[241] and so the object of the knowledge of destiny is the knowledge of how to behave. The object of the knowledge of nature is to be in accord with it and to fulfill it, to understand the way of existing together with others. The object of the illustration of the Way and the illustration of virtue is to establish and enlarge oneself and others; also, not to do unto others what one would not have others do unto oneself. The object of the illustration of instructson is to know how to teach others and how to be taught.

Thus the extension of knowledge is in every respect connected with the conduct of men. How important indeed men are! When Fan Ch'ih asked about wisdom, Confucius answered, "It is to know all men."[242]

When a person does not know himself, it is due to his lack of knowledge of men. On the other hand, when he does not know others, it is due to his own lack of knowledge of men and the fault lies in himself. As Confucius said, "I will not be afflicted at men's not knowing me; I will be afflicted that I do not know men."[243]

In seeking to know men, the first essential is observation. What can least easily be concealed are the eyes. A man's eyes invariably disclose whether or not all is right within his mind. The ears too are important. By listening to what a man says, a person can usually find out what kind of man he is.

> Mencius said, "Of all the parts of a man's body there is none more excellent than the pupil of the eye. The pupil cannot be used to hide a man's weakness. If within the breast all be correct, the pupil is bright. If within the breast all be not correct, the pupil is dull.
> "Listen to a man's words and look at the pupil of his eye. How can a man conceal his character."[244]

Even if a man attempts to hide his wickedness, "what truly is within will be manifested without." As a result, the more he tries to conceal, the more he reveals.

> There is no evil to which the mean man, dwelling retired, will not proceed, but when he sees a superior man, he instantly tries to disguise himself, concealing his evil and displaying what is good. The other beholds him, as if he saw his lungs and liver; of what use is his disguise? This is an instance of the saying: "What truly is within will be manifested without." Therefore the superior man must be watchful over himself when he is alone.[245]
> Tzŭ-hsia said, "The mean man is sure to gloss his faults."[246]

It is not easy to observe men. Superficially there is no great difference between them. Even Yao, Shun and Confucius at first sight seemed no different from other men.

> Ch'u said to Mencius, "Master, the King sent persons to spy out whether you were really different from other men." Mencius said, "How should I be different from other men? Yao and Shun were just the same as other men."[247]

It would be even more delusive to consider oneself the same as another person because of some similar physical characteristic such as height. Here is how Mencius handled this pitfall:

Chiao of Ts'ao asked Mencius, saying, "It is said, 'All men may be Yaos and Shuns;'—is it true?" Mencius replied, "It is."

Chiao went on, "I have heard that King Wên was ten cubits high and T'ang nine. Now I am nine cubits four inches in height. But I can do nothing but eat my millet. What am I to do to realize that saying?"

Mencius answered him, "What has this—the question of size—to do with the matter? It all lies simply in acting as such. Here is a man whose strengh was not equal to lift a duckling; he was then a man of no strength. But today he says, 'I can lift 3,000 catties' weight,' and he is a man of strength. And so, he who can lift the weight which Wu Huo lifted is just another Wu Huo. Why should a man make a want of ability the subject of his grief? It is only that he will not do the thing.

"To walk solwly, keeping behind his elders, is to perform the part of a younger brother. To walk quickly and precede his elders is to violate the duty of a younger brother. Now, is it what a man cannot do—to walk slowly? It is what he does not do. The way of Yao and Shun was simply that of filial piety and fraternal submission.

"Wear the clothes of Yao, repeat the words of Yao and perform the acts of Yao, and you will just be a Yao. And, if you wear the clothes of Chieh, repeat the words of Chieh and perform the acts of Chieh, you will just be a Chieh."

Chiao said, "I shall be having an interview with the prince of Tsou, and can ask him to let me have a house to lodge in. I wish to remain here and enter your school for instruction."

Mencius replied, "The Way is like a high road. It is not difficult to know it. The trouble is only that men will not seek it. Do you go home and search for it, and you will have an abundance of teachers."[248]

In observing men we can find out much from their eyes, true. But it is much more important that we pay attention to their attitude and determine as far as we can what they may do in the future. Confucius stressed this point repeatedly, using it as a guide to adapt his instruction to the ability of each of his disciples.

The disciple Min was standing by his side, looking bland and precise; Tzŭ-lu, looking bold and soldierly; Jan Yu and Tzŭ-kung, with a free and straightforward manner. The Master was pleased. (He said,) "Yu there! It seems that he will not die a natural death."[249]

Next, attention should be paid to language, for without the knowledge of words it is impossible to know men.

The Master said, "Without knowing destiny it is impossible to be a superior man. Without knowing the rules of propriety it is impossible for the character to be established. Without knowing the force of words it is impossible to know men."[250]

Words, when they truly show loyalty and sincerity, are the badge of superior men. When words are fashioned into flattery and lack sincerity, however, they brand a man as a despicable person.

In answering a question of Kung-sun Ch'ou, Mencius prided himself on knowing the force of words; he even taught the disciple four secrets to distinguishing words. He also defined "good words" and the "good Way."

Kung-sun Ch'ou asked Mencius, saying, "...I venture to ask wherein you, Master, surpass. Mencius told him, "I understand words..."

Ch'ou pursued, "I venture to ask what you mean by your saying that you understand words." Mencius replied, "When words are one-sided, I know how the mind of the speaker is clouded over. When words are extravagant, I know how the mind is fallen and sunk. When words are all-depraved, I know how the mind has departed from principle. When words are evasive, I know how the mind is at its wit's end. These evils growing in the mind do injury to government and, displayed in the government, are hurtful to the conduct of affairs. When a sage shall again rise, he will certainly follow my words."[251]

Mencius said, "Words which are simple, while their meaning is far-reaching, are good words. The Way, which, as held, is compendious, while its application is extensive, is the good Way. The words of the superior man do not go below the girdle, but the Way is contained in them.

"The principle which the superior man holds is that of personal cultivation, but the empire is thereby pacified.

"The disease of men is this: that they neglect their own fields and go to weed the field of others, and that what they require from others is great, while what they lay upon themselves is light."[252]

However, one cannot get to know men by observing only their words and behavior; some men are mean internally while superior externally. It is important, therefore, to observe keenly, yes, but to exercise great prudence too. Confucius put it in the form of a question: "If, because a man's discourse appears solid

and sincere, we allow him to be a good man, is he really a
superior man? Or is his gravity only in appearance."[253]

Abstention from artful words and sophism is a sign of sincerity
and solidity. But this alone does not necessarily mark a man as
benevolent. In fact, men who use fine words are often detestable,
especially when they confuse truth with falsehood and make a
mockery of virtue.

> The Master said, "Fine words and an insinuating appearance
> are seldom associated with benevolence."[254]
> The Master said, "Specious words confound virtue. Want of
> forbearance in small matters confounds great plans."[255]
> Someone said, "Yung is truly benevolent, but he is not ready
> with his tongue. They who encounter men with smartness of
> speech for the most part procure themselves hatred. I know not
> whether he is truly benevolent, but why should he show readiness
> of the tongue?"[256]
> Tzŭ-lu got Tzŭ-kao appointed governor of Pi.
> The Master said, "You are injuring a man's son."
> Tzŭ-lu said, "There are (there) people to rule, and there are
> the altars of the spirits of the land and grain. Why must one read
> books before one can be considered to have learned?"
> The Master said, "It is on this account that I hate your
> glib-tongued people."[257]

Those who talk big frequently cannot do anything practical
because they are not sincere to begin with. They are inherently
empty, for "without sincerity there can be nothing." Confucius
put it this way: "He who speaks without modesty will find it
difficult to make his words good."[258]

According to Confucius, a man's ability and wisdom could
easily be seen, but it would take a fairly long period of on-the-
spot observation to judge the solidity of his virtue. Such
observation would be especially accurate if the observer shared
adversity with him.

> The Master said, "Of those who were with me in Ch'ên and
> Ts'ai, there are none to be found in my school.
> "Distinguished for their virtuous principles and practice, there
> were Yen Yüan, Min Tzŭ-ch'ien, Jan Po-niu and Chung-kung; for
> their ability in speech, Tsai Wo and Tzŭ-kung; for their
> administrative talents, Jan Yu and Chi Lu; for their literary
> acquirements, Tzŭ-yu and Tzŭ-hsia."[259]

Ch'ai is simple. Shên is dull. Shih is specious. Yu is coarse.[260]

Tzŭ-kung asked, "What do you say of me, Tz'ŭ?" The Master said, "You are a utensil." "What utensil?" "A gemmed sacrificial utensil."[261]

Mêng Wu asked whether Tzŭ-lu was benevolent. The Master said, "I do not know."

He asked again, when the Master replied, "In a State of a hundred chariots, Yu might be employed to manage the military levies, but I do not know whether he is benevolent."

"And what do you say of Ch'iu?" The Master replied, "In a city of a thousand families or a hundred chariots, Ch'iu might be employed as governor, but I do not know whether he is benevolent."

"What do you say of Ch'ih?" The Master replied, "With his sash girt and standing in a court, Ch'ih might be employed to converse with the visitors and guests, but I do not know whether he is benevolent."[262]

Though it is not easy to detect from direct observation whether a man is benevolent, it can be indirectly learned from his faults. As Confucius said: "The faults of men are characteristic of the class to which they belong. By observing a man's faults, it may be known whether he is benevolent."[263]

Because of Tsai Yü's sleeping in the daytime, Confucius changed his method of observing men; he decided judgment should be based not on words only, but on words plus actions.

Tsai Yü being once asleep during the daytime, the Master said, "Rotten wood cannot be carved; a wall of dirty earth will not receive the trowel. This Yü'!—what is the use of my reproving him?"

The Master said, "At first, my way with men was to hear their words and give them credit for their conduct. Now my way is to hear their words and look at their conduct. It is from Yü that I have learned to make this change."[264]

Inconsistency between speech and action is untruthfulness, deceit. No one wishes to associate with men who lie habitually and, naturally, they are avoided by everyone.

The Master said, "I do not know how a man without truthfulness is to get on. How can a large carriage be made to go without cross-bar for yoking the oxen to, or a small carriage without the arrangement for yoking the horses?"[265]

Indeed, for purposes of observation, conduct is more important than words. But in observing a man's conduct, the main point is to find out his motives. Where does his mind rest? To quote Confucius: "See what a man does. Mark his motives. Examine in what things he rests. How can a man conceal his character? How con a man conceal his character?"[266]

Those who can gain the favor of the neighborhood are not necessarily good, and vice versa. We might say that only those who are liked by all the good men of the area and disliked by all the despicable men are really good persons. Also, popular likes and dislikes are sometimes caused by emotional outbursts and do not necessarily represent the truth with regard to right and wrong.

> Tzǔ-kung asked, saying, "What do you say of a man who is loved by all the people of his neighborhood?" The Master replied, "We may not for that accord our approval of him." "And what do you say of him who is hated by all the people of his neighborhood?" The Master said, "We may not for that conclude that he is bad. It is better than either of these cases that the good in the neighborhood love him and the bad hate him."[267]

No man is free from fault. If a man is considered bad whenever he has a fault, this judgment is frequently inaccurate. Any man who follows the rules of conduct and can function in any environment is not necessarily a useless man. Confucius chose one of the former type as his son-in-law and one of the latter as his nephew-in-law. So it was said that there are "few men in the world who love and at the same time know the bad qualities of the object of their love, or who hate and yet know the excellence of the object of their hatred."[268] Confucius was one of the few.

> The Master said of Kung-yeh Ch'ang that he might be wived; although he was put in bonds, he had not been guilty of any crime. Accordingly, he gave him his own daughter to wife.
> Of Nan Jung he said that if the country were well-governed he would not be out of office, and if the country were ill-governed he would escape purnishment and death. He gave him the daughter of his own elder brother to wife.[269]

Those who lose their inherent nature are really incurable. They are "numb." Confucius spoke of these men feelingly as persons whom he did not understand: "Ardent and yet not upright; stupid and yet not honest; untalented and yet not sincere —such persons I do not understand."[270]

So what do we learn from the observation of persons—from their faces, their eyes, their comrades, their faults? Quite simply we learn whether (1) their hearts are rectified, (2) their thoughts are sincere, (3) their words are faithful and (4) their acts are earnest and respectful. When these criteria are used to judge good and evil, they may not insure absolute accuracy, but they will not lead one far astray. For basically it is only by understanding the immutable truths that men can come to know other men. In the *Doctrine of the Mean* we find these words: "His (the superior man's) being prepared, without any misgivings, to wait for the rise of a sage a hundred ages after, shows that he knows men."[271]

Men can be divided into sages, worthy men, good men, great men, superior men and mean men. Without going into all these classes, let us confine ourselves to the differences between superior and mean men. To know these differences will give us the knowledge of men that we seek.

In ancient times the expression *Chün-tzu* had two connotations: those worthy men who were in responsible positions and cultivated gentlemen. For example:

> It is said in the Book of Songs, "In silence is the offering presented and the spirit approached to; there is not the slightest contention." Therefore the superior man does not use rewards, and the people are stimulated to virtue. He does not show anger, and the people are awed more than by hatchets and battle-axes.[272]
>
> The philosopher Tsêng said, "The superior man, in his thoughts, does not go out of his place.[273]
>
> Tzŭ-hsia said, "The superior man, having obtained their confidence, may then impose labors on his people. If he has not gained their confidence, they will think that he is oppressing them. Having obtained the confidence of his prince, he may then remonstrate with him. If he has not gained his confidence, the prince will think that he is vilifying him."[274]

In the above passages the expression "superior man" denotes a man who was in a responsible position. Now, the phrase *hsiao-*

jen also had two meanings: little people without knowledge and unvirtuous degenerates. For example:

The Master said, "He who puts on an appearence of stern firmness, while inwardly he is weak, is like one of the small, mean people; yea, is he not like the thief who breaks through, or climbs over, a wall?"[275]

The Master, having come to Wu-ch'êng, heard there the sound of stringed instruments and singing.

Well pleased and smiling, he said, "Why use an ox-knife to kill a fowl?"

Tzŭ-yu replied, "Formerly, Master, I heard you say, 'When the man of high station is well instructed, he loves men; when the man of low station is well instructed, he is easily ruled.' "

The Master said, "My disciples, Yen's words are right. What I said was only in sport."[276]

In the *Book of Songs* it is said, "Ah! the former kings are not forgotten." Future princes deem worthy what they deemed worthy and love what they loved. The common people delight in what delighted them, and are benefited by their beneficial arrangements. It is on this account that the former kings, after they have quit the world, are not forgotten."[277]

Confucius replied, "...The relation between superiors and inferiors is like that between the wind and the grass. The grass must bend, when the wind blows across it."[278]

Mencius said, "...Thus, the men of station of Shang took baskets full of black and yellow silks to meet the men of station of Chou, and the lower classes of the one met those of the other with baskets of rice and vessels of congee. (King Wu) saved the people from the midst of fire and water, seizing only their oppressor and destroying him."[279]

In contrast to *hsiao-jen* and *chün-tzu*, the meaning of a "scholar after the style of the superior man" and one "after that of the mean man" is not very clear even now. Yet Confucius once told Tzŭ-hsia, "Do you be a scholar after the style of the superior man and not after that of the mean man."[280]

According to the neo-Confucianists of the Sung dynasty, "scholars after the style of the superior men are for themselves, while those after the style of mean men are for others." But this is not a satisfactory interpretation unless it is applied to ancient times. For then scholars pursued a special learning and belonged to a special profession. Their task was to study rites, literature, vessels and mathematics, from which they were to survey politics, the relationships between humanity and morality. These were the scholars after the style of superior men. On the other hand, those scholars who only committed to memory rites, literature, vessels and mathematics and who assisted in the details of social etiquette and sacrificial rites in dynastic temples were scholars after the style of mean men.

Though Tzǔ-hsia was well versed in literature, his disciples and followers were described by Tzǔ-yu as merely accomplished in the minor details of sprinkling and sweeping the ground, answering and replying and receding. This confirms the judgment that Tzǔ-hsia, while familiar with the externals of propriety, did not necessarily possess a thorough knowledge of its essence. For this reason Confucius took occasion to advise him to "be a scholar after the style of the superior man and not after that of the mean man."

Perhaps this is a more appropriate interpretation: Scholars after the style of superior men are worthy men who recognize the essence of propriety; those after the style of mean men are unworthy men who see only the minor details of propriety. In other instances where superior and mean men are contrasted in the *Four Books*, the former generally denote cultivated gentlemen and the latter, degenerates who are lacking in virtue. The contrast underlines the importance of making the proper choice, of improving ourselves and striving to be superior men.

From the following eighteen passages we can see the main distinctions between superior and mean men.

...Thus it is that the superior man is quiet and calm, waiting for his destiny, while the mean man walks in dangerous paths, expecting the uncertain chances of luck.[261]

...Just so, it is the way of the superior man to prefer the concealment of his virtue, while it daily becomes more illustrious, and it is the way of the mean man to seek notoriety, while he daily goes more and more to ruin.[262]

Chung-ni said, "The superior man embodies the course of the Mean; the mean man acts contrary to the course of the Mean.

"The superior man's embodying the course of the Mean is because he is a superior man, and so always maintains the Mean. The mean man's acting contrary to the course of the Mean is because he is a mean man and has no caution."[263]

The Master said, "The progress of the superior man is upwards; the progress of the mean man is downwards.[234]

The Master said, "The mind of the superior man is conversant with righteousness; the mind of the mean man is conversant with gain.[285]

The Master said, "The superior man is satisfied and composed: the mean man is always full of distress.[256]

The Master said, "The superior man is catholic and no partisan; the mean man is a partisan and not catholic.[257]

The Master said, "The superior man thinks of virtue; the small man thinks of comfort. The superior man thinks of the sanctions of law; the small man thinks of favors which he may receive."[253]

The Master said, "The superior man helps others accomplish what is favorable, and not what is unfavorable, to them. The small man does the opposite of this."[239]

The Master said, "The superior man is affable, but not adulatory; the mean man is adulatory, but not affable.[290]

The Master said, "The superior man has a dignified ease without pride. The mean man has pride without a dignified ease.[291]

The Master said, "The superior man is easy to serve and difficult to please. If you try to please him without complying with the Way, he will not be pleased. But in his employment of men, he uses them according to their capacity. The mean man is difficult to serve and easy to please. If you try to please him though without complying with the Way, he may be pleased. But in his employment of men, he wishes them to be equal to everything."[292]

The Master said, "Superior men, and yet not always benevolent, there have been, alas! But there never has been a mean man and at the same time benveolent."[293]

Duke Ling of Wei asked Confucius about tactics. Confucius replied, "I have heard all about sacrificial vessels, but I have not learned military matters." On this, he took his departure the next day.

When he was in Ch'ên, their provisions were exhausted, and his followers became so ill that they were unable to rise.

Tzŭ-lu, with evident dissatisfaction, said, "Has the superior man likewise to endure want?" The Master said, "The superior man may indeed have to endure want but the mean man, when he is in want, gives way to unbridled license.[294]

The Master said, "What the superior man seeks is in himself. What the mean man seeks is in others."[295]

The Master said, "The superior man cannot be known in little matters, but he may be entrusted with great concerns. The small man may not be entrusted with great concerns, but he may be known in little matters."[296]

Confucius said, "There are three things of which the superior man stands in awe. He stands in awe of the ordinances of Heaven. He stands in awe of great men. He stands in awe of the words of sages.

The mean man does not know the ordinances of Heaven, and consequently does not stand in awe of them. He is disrespectful to great men. He makes sport of the words of sages."[297]

Mencius said, "...Now, righteousness is the road, and propriety is the door, but it is only the superior man who can follow this road and go in and out by this door. It is said in the *Book of Songs:*

'The way to Chou is level like a whetstone
And straight as an arrow.
The officials tread it
And the lower people see it.' "[298]

The criteria used in the above passages to distinguish between superior and mean men include will, faith, mental approach, personal cultivation, attitude, deportment and insight. All this has to do with the fulfillment of human nature, which is quite consistent with scientific analysis. The employment of such criteria in seeking to obtain the knowledge of men cannot be far wrong, although it may not always be completely accurate.

I. Knowledge of Things

We discussed in detail, in Chapter II, how affairs and things are investigated in order to achieve the knowledge of Heaven, of destiny and of men. But because we live with other men, affairs arise and a host of things are encountered at all times. This makes it very important to understand the most appropriate way of dealing with affairs and things. Of utmost urgency is to know which of them should come first and to distinguish between the root and the branches. Hence it is said, "Things have their root and their branches."[299]

In our country, China, special importance has been attached to the observation of the root and the branches as part of learning. For this reason the *Four Books* have always referred to the root in important instances. The following passages, for example, are relevant:

The superior man bends his attention to the root. That being established, the Way naturally grows up. Filial piety and fraternal submission! Are they not the root of all benevolent actions?[300]

The root of the empire is in the State, that of the State in the family and that of the family in the person.[301]

From the Son of Heaven to the mass of the people, all must consider the cultivation of the person the root of everything besides.[302]

There are many services, but the service of parents is the root of all others. There are many charges, but the charge of oneself is the root of all others.[303]

Virtue is the root; wealth the result.[304]

It is only the individual possessed of the most entire sincerity that can exist under heaven, who can adjust the great invariable relations of mankind, establish the great fundamental virtues of humanity...[305]

In teaching men how to behave, the essence of virtuous conduct is to remember the root always. For when the root is well-ordered, what springs from it also will be well-ordered. Conversely, when the root is in disorder, it is difficult for what springs from it to be well-ordered.

Let us now take from the conclusions drawn by the ancients from their experiences the following thirty sets of contrasting words and expressions, and explain each of them as an aid to attaining the knowledge of affairs and things.

1. Root and Branches

The root and its branches are opposites, although they are related to each other. The distinction between the two is the same as that between beginning and end. From the standpoint of the integral nature of things, we can belittle neither the root nor the branches. But in the last analysis the root is the more important of the two.

Virtue is the root; wealth the result.

If he makes the root his secondary object and the result his primary, he will only contend with his people and teach them rapine.

Hence, the accumulation of wealth is the way to scatter the people; and the letting it be scattered among them is the way to collect the people. And hence the ruler's words going forth contrary to right will come back to him in the same way; and wealth, gotten by improper ways, will take their departure by the same.[306]

Only with virtue can the common existence of mankind be rendered possible; only when there is this common existence can man live in peace; only when he lives in peace can he take delight in his business; only when he takes delight in his business can manpower and land resources be fully devoted to production; and only when there is abundant production can there by sufficient wealth. Hence,

> On this account, the ruler will first take pains about his own virtue. Possessing virtue will give him the people. Possessing the people will give him the territory. Possessing the territory will give him its wealth. Possessing the wealth, he will have resources for expenditure.[307]

When a ruler exalts virtue, his people will rally around him wholeheartedly. When his subjects cultivate virtue, there will be love and unity. When the people have wealth, the country is bound to be rich. On the other hand, if the people's welfare is neglected and sole attention is paid to the collection of wealth, there may be temporary abundance but the people's faith will be lost. By reversing the order of the root and the branches this way, a ruler invites his own ruin.

Tzŭ-yu and Tzŭ-hsia had the following debate concerning the teaching on the root and the branches:

> Tzŭ-yu said, "The disciples and followers of Tzŭ-hsia, sprinkling and sweeping the ground, in answering and replying, in advancing and receding, are sufficiently accomplished. But these are only the branches of learning, and they are left ignorant of what is essential. How can they be acknowledged as sufficiently taught?
>
> Tzŭ-yu heard of the remark and said, "Alas! Yen Yu is wrong. According to the Way of the superior man in teaching, what departments are there which he considers of prime importance to be transmitted first? What are there which he considers of secondary importance and allows himself to be idle about? But as in the case of plants, which are assorted according to their classes, so learning should be differentiated. How can the Way of a superior man be indiscriminately taught? Is it only the sage who can unite in one the beginning and consummation of learning.?"[308]

In this instance Tzŭ-hsia used a different method of teaching. He proceeded from the branches to the root. As stated by Tzŭ-yu, sprinking and sweeping, etc., are merely the branches of learning. The rectification of the heart and the cultivation of the person are the concerns of the Great Learning. While Tzŭ-yu derided Tzŭ-hsia's disciples for neglecting the root and pursuing the branches, nevertheless it is true that differences in natural endowment call for diverse methods of teaching. As aptly stated by Tzŭ-hsia, these differences are the same as those between different classes of plants; some are large and others small. Individuals with great talent may be taught the root only, which they themselves can extend to the branches. However, those with little talent must pay attention first to the branches and then work back to the root. Only a sage can unite and put together the root and the branches, the beginning and the end. The method of teaching must be varied to suit the endowments of the learner.

2. Great and Small

"Great" and "small" are contrasting words, but they can be rationally defined as follows:

> ...Thus it is that, were the superior man to speak of his Way in all its greatness, nothing in the world would be found able to embrace it, and were he to speak of it in its minuteness, nothing in the world would be found able to split it.[309]

What cannot be embraced by anything must be the greatest of all, and what cannot be split must be the smallest (in nuclear physics the atom can be split because it is not yet the smallest).

While usually it is easy to discern how big or how small a thing is, there is an added dimension in judging affairs. The requirements and influence of an affair must be examined to determine its greatness or smallness. Sometimes something great must be done in a small way, and vice versa. It depends on our judgment.

> The Master said, "Specious words confound virtue. Want of forbearance in small matters confounds great plans."[310]

To speak specious words is to confound truth with falsehood. To lack forbearance in small matters is to injure the great with the small; it is the courage of a small man who cannot be entrusted with a great undertaking.

Tzŭ-hsia said, "When a person does not transgress the boundary line in the great virtues, he may pass and repass it in the small virtues"[311]

Great and small virtues correspond to the main principles of conduct and the minor details. The latter should not be disregarded, but the former by all means should be adhered to faithfully.

Tzŭ-hsia, being Governor of Chü-fu, asked about government. The Master said, "Do not be desirous to have things done quickly; do not look at small advantages. Desire to have things done quickly prevents their being done thoroughly. Looking at small advantages prevents great affairs from being accomplished."[312]

The "want of forbearance in small matters," stated in the first of the three preceding passages, refers to the failure to weigh matters carefully and gain time. The result, more often than not, is the miscarriage of great plans. In the last passage, the tendency to "look at small advantages" refers to the failure to consider advantages and disadvantages, gains and losses. This often keeps important matters from being successfully accomplished.

Therefore, on the one hand we must weigh the greater or lesser importance of all matters, and on the other hand we must understand the mutual influence of the two kinds of matters. Moreover, some things can be consummated quickly, while others take time. Accelerating what cannot be accelerated invites failures.

The Master said, "The superior man cannot be known in little matters; but he may be entrusted with great concerns. The small man cannot be entrusted with great concerns; but he may be known in small matters."[313]

To be "entrusted with great concerns" means that what is embraced is large in size and/or importance. To be "known in little matters" means that what is demonstrated is of lesser significance. With his wide intelligence the superior man can exhaust his talent only when he is "entrusted with great concerns." With his more restricted intellectual capacity the small man will not exceed the bounds of his potential only when he is "known in little matters." A reversal of the proper relationship between the two is irrational.

The disciple Kung-tu said, "All are equally men, but some are great men and some are little men; how is this?" Mencius replied, "Those who follow that part of themselves which is great are great men; those who follow that part of themselves which is little are little men."

Kung-tu pursued, "All are equally men, but some follow that part of themselves which is great, and some follow that part which is little; how is this?" Mencius answered, "The senses of hearing and seeing do not think and are obscured by external things. When one thing comes into contact with another, as a matter of course it leads it away. To the mind belongs the office of thinking. By thinking, it gets the right view of things; by neglecting to think, it fails to do this. These things—the senses and the mind—are what Heaven has given to us. Let a man first stand fast in the supremacy of the nobler part of his constitution, and the inferior part will not be able to take it from him. It is simply this which makes the great man."[314]

Mencius said, "...Some parts of the body are noble and some ignoble; some great and some small. The great must not be injured for the small, nor the noble for the ignoble. He who nourishes the little belonging to him is a little man, and he who nourishes the great is a great man."[315]

Mencius said, "The great man is he who does not lose his child's heart."[316]

Mencius said, "Acts of propriety which are not really proper and acts of righteousness which are not really righteous, the great man does not do."[317]

Mencius said, "The great man does not think beforehand of his words that they may be sincere, nor of his actions that they may be resolute; he simply speaks and does what is right."[318]

As affairs and things are divided into great and small, so too are men. The principle is of course that the great should be stressed over the small. The great and noble must not be injured by deferring to the small and ignoble. But if we stand firmly by the nobler part of our constitution, we can also look after the inferior part. Here the nobler part is our greater self anddenotes the soul; the inferior part is our smaller self and denotes the body. He who nourishes the nobler part is a great man, wise and omniscient, with the organ of thinking playing its proper role. He who nourishes the small part is a little man, avaricious and lustful, with the organs of seeing and hearing playing disproportionate roles.

It should be apparent that the great part may be made noble, and the small part ignoble. To regard the body as supremely important is to treat the ignoble as the noble. To regard the soul as unimportant is to treat the noble as the ignoble. This shows a lack of understanding of the real difference between the great and small parts. The reversal of the noble and the ignoble can lead only to injury of the small by the great.

3. Light and Heavy

The lightness and heaviness of things is determined by comparing them. So, Mencius said, "By weighing, we know what things are light and what heavy. By measuring, we know what things are long and what short."[319] While the exact weights and measurements of things can easily be obtained by using the standards applicable to them, the determination of the greater or lesser importance of affairs is not a simple matter; it must be done by applying the mind. For this reason the inability of the disciple Wu-lu to answer questions put to him by a man Jên gave rise to a subtle debate on the part of Mencius.

A man of Jên asked the disciple Wu-lu, saying, "Is an observance of the rules of propriety in regard to eating, or the eating, the more important?" The answer was, "The observance of the rules of propriety is the more important."

"Is the gratifying the appetite of sex, or the doing so only according to the rules of propriety, the more important?" The answer again was, "The observance of the rules of propriety in the matter is the more important."

The man pursued, "If the result of eating only according to the rules of propriety will be death by starvation, while by disregarding those rules we may get food, must they still be observed in such a case? If according to the rule that he shall go in person to meet his wife a man cannot get married, while by disregarding that rule he may get married, must he still observe the rule in such a case?"

Wu-lu was unable to reply to these questions, and the next day he went to Tsou and told them to Mencius. Mencius said, "What difficulty is there in answering these inquiries?

"If you do not adjust them at their lower extremities, but only put their tops on a level, a piece of wood an inch square may be made to be higher than the pointed peak of a high building.

"Gold is heavier than feathers; but does that saying have reference, on the one hand, to a single clasp of gold and, on the other, to a wagonload of feathers?

"If you take a case where the eating is of the utmost importance and the observing the rules of propriety is of little importance, and compare the things together, why should the eating not be more important? So, taking the case where the gratifying the appetite of sex is of the utmost importance and the observing the rules of propriety is of little importance, why should the gratifying the appetite not be more important?

"Go and answer him thus, 'If, by twisting your elder brother's arm and snatching from him what he is eating, you can get food for yourself, while, if you do not do so, you will not get anything to eat, will you so twist his arm? If by getting over your neighbor's wall and dragging away his virgin daughter, you can get a wife, while, if you do not do so, you will not be able to get a wife, will you so drag her away?' "[320]

This debate shows that nothing is absolutely important or unimportant. Because of their relationship with the continuation of human life, food and sex cannot be said to be unimportant. However, the rules of propriety may at times prove to be less important than food and sex. Compared to starvation, eating according to the rules of propriety is a comparatively minor matter. Similarly, according to Mencius, obtaining a wife is important, while meeting one's wife in person is a comparatively minor matter. These examples show the lesser importance of propriety when compared with food and sex.

On the other hand, to go without food is a small matter when compared to twisting an elder brother's arm to obtain food. Similarly, to get no wife is a small matter, while scaling a neighbor's wall and abducting his daughter is a serious matter. These examples show the lesser importance of food and sex when compared with propriety.

The upshot of this is obvious: The importance of things is not inflexible, and to secure the Mean or equilibrium they must be considered from every pertinent angle at all times and in all places. While gold is heavier than feathers, a wagonload of feathers obviously outweighs a single clasp of gold. Only after judging all the aspects of the case can a completely accurate knowledge of things be obtained.

4. New and Old

The age of things new and old is determined by comparing the order of their production or the length of time they have been in use. What is new today becomes old tomorrow. What is new when compared with one thing may be old when compared with another. Moreover, the renovation of something old is a common occurrence. Hence it is said in the *Great Learning:*

> On the bathtub of T'ang the following words were engraved: "If you can one day renovate yourself, do so from day to day. Yea, let there be daily renovation."
>
> In the "Announcement to K'ang" it is said, "To stir up the new people."
>
> In the *Book of Songs* it is said, "Although Chou was an ancient State, the ordinance which alighted on it was new."
>
> Therefore the superior man in everything uses his utmost endeavors.[321]

This indicates how far our ancient sages would go to renovate their old rule and bring about good government. After a long period of growth and application, everything becomes old. But we can always make progress and introduce reform by constantly renovating and renewing institutions like the government. The revolutions led by Kings T'ang and Wu were basically steps in the renewal process. Furthermore, "daily" progress in self-renovation was both urged and expected. Thus the old was to give way to the new.

It took a long time for the Chou dynasty to establish itself, but through the uninterrupted reforms introduced by Kings Wên, Wu, Ch'êng and K'ang the country obtained a new lease on life. In speaking of renewal, what holds for the country is also true of individuals. It is said that "the superior man in everything uses his utmost endeavors". Only with effort by all of us can we hope to overtake the times and free ourselves from backwardness. That is why the *Great Learning* sets down "the people's renovation" as one of its main principles.

5. Different and Identical

> Mencius said, "...There now is barley. Let it be sown and covered up; the ground being the same, and the time of sowing

likewise the same, it grows rapidly up, and when the full time is come, it is all found to be ripe. Although there may be inequalities of produce, that is owing to the difference of the soil, as rich or poor, to the unequal nourishment afforded by the rains and dews, and to the different ways in which man has performed his business in reference to it.

"Thus all things which are the same in kind are like to one another; why should we doubt in regard to man, as if he were a solitary exception to this? The sage and we are the same in kind.

"In accordance with this the scholar Lung said, "If a man makes hempen sandals without knowing the size of people's feet, yet I know that he will not make them like baskets.' Sandals are all like one another, because all men's feet are like one another."[322]

In this passage Mencius compared human nature to barley. He implied that just as the seeds of barley are the same, human nature is always good. Although the sowing is done at the same time and in the same place, the degree of the crop's richness depends on the soil, rains, dews and human effort. And so differences result. Similarly, though the sage and common people are the same in kind, yet due to differences in the method of cultivation and environment, the sage turns out to be different from the common people. However, since basically all human beings are alike, they all can strive to become sages and worthy men. Mencius made this point in encouraging those who came after him.

Strictly speaking, neither things nor men can all be the same in this world. With human factors as they are, it is not only impossible but also unnecessary to try to make all men identical. The highest ideal is to create a "world of harmony" in which all the people share the same community. The greatest mistake the Communists make is trying to force all men into the same mold. Their actions are against human nature.

6. Pure and Impure

Purity and impurity are also the result of comparison. But when there is a difference in essence, the effect will also differ. It is a matter of course for the pure to gather with the pure and for the impure to get together with the impure. However, people do not usually pay attention to this fact.

Mencius said, "There was a boy singing,

'When the water of Ts'ang-lang is clear,
It does to wash the strings of my cap;
When the water of the Ts'ang-lang is muddy,
It does to wash my feet.'

"Confucius said, 'Hear what he sings, my children. When clear, then he will wash his cap-strings; and when muddy, he will wash his feet with it. This different application is brought by the water on itself.' "[323]

After listening to the singing of the boy, Confucius made a comment which showed his profound insight. To him the purity and impurity of the water signified the noble and ignoble character of man. When a man has self-respect, he has the respect of others. When a man is unworthy, he is despised by others. Therefore the superior man carefully sees to it that he is not downgraded, for if he is, the hatred of all is concentrated on him. In ascribing its use to the quality of the water itself, Confucius conveyed a significant meaning, which served as a warning to future generations.

7. Polish and Substance

In olden times human life was so primitive that there was little distinction between civilization and barbarism. As mankind progressed, increasing emphasis was put on the external appearances of things; at the same time their substance was more and more neglected. This transformation coincided with constant changes in human institutions. In the Confucian *Analects* there are brief discussions of this development.

The Master said, "Where substance is in excess of polish, we have rusticity; where polish is in excess of substance, we have the manners of a clerk. When polish and substance are equally blended, we then have the man of virtue."[324]

Substance is that which has not been touched by the human hand; it maintains its original form. Polish is that which has been brought about by human effort; it assumes a man-made form. As long as the natural prevailed over the man-made form, mankind remained in its prehistoric barbaric state. It was only when man-made form began to prevail that mankind entered its age of recorded history. When an undue excess of polish came with the years, however, the tendency toward pretension and falsehood inevitably came with it. So the ideal condition was thought to be one in which human effort and nature were evenly blended. This was the standard for adjusting human nature. Toward the end of the Spring and Autumn period, for instance, polish was so much in evidence that it gave the impression of excessive reform.

> Chi Tzŭ-ch'êng said, "In a superior man it is only the substance which is wanted; why should we seek for polish?"
>
> Tzŭ-kung said, "Alas! Your words, Sir, show you to be a superior man, but four horses cannot overtake the tongue.
>
> "Polish is as substance; substance is as polish. The hide of a tiger or leopard stripped of its hair is like the hide of a dog or goat stripped of its hair."[325]

Chi Tzŭ-ch'êng, concerned with the reform required by his time, pleaded for substance in place of polish. To Tzŭ-kung it was regrettable that Chi Tzŭ-ch'êng had erred (and that once the words were out of his mouth they could not be overtaken, not even by four horses). In Tzŭ-kung's view, mankind had advanced so far toward civilization that it was impossible to return to the plain living of former times. He cited the example of the four animal hides and concluded that substance and polish should be equally blended so that there would be neither excess nor inadequacy.

8. Gain and Loss

Without gains there can be no losses. Human gains and losses are no mere accidents. Greater gains and losses concern a State or the world, while lesser gains and losses concern a family or an individual. While gains and losses are irregular, their occurrence depends on a person's effort and the conditions under which he exerts that effort.

> In the *Book of Songs* it is said, "Before the sovereigns of the Yin dynasty had lost the hearts of the people, they could be co-equal with God. Take warning from the house of Yin. The great decree is not easily conferred." This shows that, by gaining the people, the kingdom is gained, and, by losing the people, the kingdom is lost.[326]

With the people behind him, the Son of Heaven could be co-equal with Heaven. On the other hand, when the people lost confidence in their leader, the throne was rejected and the country ruined. Profiting from the example of the Yin dynasty, the Chou dynasty coupled the gaining of the country to the winning of the people. The lesson is obvious: The preservation of a country lies first of all in winning the hearts of the people—and this principle holds true always.

> In the "Announcement of K'ang," it is said, "The decree indeed may not always rest on us," that is, goodness obtains the decree, and the want of goodness loses it.[327]

The decree in this passage is synonmous with the "great decree" in the previous quotation. Goodness obtained it and lack of goodness lost it. Goodness or the lack of it was the cause, and the gain or loss of the decree was the effect. The law of cause and effect can never be violated with impunity.

> Mencius said, "Chieh and Chou's losing the throne arose from their losing the people, and to lose the people means to lose their hearts. There is a way to get the empire: get the people, and the empire is got. There is a way to get the people: get their hearts, and the people are got. There is a way to get their hearts: it is simply to collect for them what they like and not to lay on them what they dislike."[328]

Here again the same lesson is driven home—he who gains the people's hearts is sure to win the empire; to love what the people love and to hate what they hate is the secret of winning their approval. This theory was upheld by both the *Great Learning* and Mencius.

> The Master said, "There are those mean creatures! Is it possible along with them to serve one's ruler?
>
> "While they have not got their aims, their anxiety is how to get them. When they have got them, their anxiety is lest they should lose them.
>
> "When they are anxious lest such things should be lost, there is nothing to which they will not proceed."[329]

The "mean creatures" are those men whose over-riding quest for profit drives them to stop at nothing in order to secure their own benefits. Their self-interest so constantly haunts them that they cannot be expected to be loyal to their work or their country.

The Master said, "When a man's wisdom is sufficient to attain, and his virtue is not sufficient to enable him to hold whatever he may have gained, he will lose again.

"When his wisdom is sufficient to attain, and he has virtue enough to hold fast, if he cannot govern with dignity, the people will not respect him.

"When his wisdom is sufficient to attain, and he has virtue enough to hold fast; when he governs also with dignity; yet if he tries to move the people contrary to the rules of propriety—full excellence is not reached."[330]

It takes wisdom to attain something worthwhile, but it takes virtue to hold it.   This is so because where there is virtue, what has been obtained is shared by all concerned and not enjoyed by one person only; thus all are unwilling to lose it and all will do everything possible to hold it.   This established principle has a name: the Great Way.   In the *Great Learning* we read: "Thus we see that the sovereign has a great Way to pursue.   He must show loyalty and faithfulness to attain it, and by pride and extravagance he will lose it."[331]

If we understand these principles, we shall know how to do our duty and dispense with our anxiety about the gain or loss of anything.

9. Existence and Extinction

There is a difference between gain and loss on the one hand, and existence and extinction on the other.   In the latter case the distinction is between the things that still exist and those which do not.   In gain and loss, the distinction lies in things still in existence and those which have merely changed hands.   Therefore we should give our attention not only to our own gains and losses, but also to the existence and extinction of things, for when a thing is lost it can still be regained, but when it is extinct it can no longer exist.

Mencius said, "They who accord with Heaven are preserved, and they who rebel against Heaven perish."[332]   There is nothing more momentous than the fate of a nation.   It is to nations that the distinction between "existence and extinction" applies.   The will of Heaven is the will of the people, which in turn is the basis of the requirements of environment and time.   The nation which meets these requirements survives, and the nation which goes against them inevitably becomes extinct. This is an immutable law.

> Duke Ai asked about government.
> The Master said, "The government of Kings Wên and Wu is displayed in the records—the tablets of wood and bamboo. Let there be the men and the government will flourish; but without the men, their government ceases."[333]

The prince of Lu was a descendant of the Duke of Chou, and so the political heritage of Kings Wên and Wu was well-preserved in that State. But while the records were there, the governmental system could have ceased to operate in the absence of its application and reform by the proper men. Hence, "Let there be the men and the government will flourish; but without the men, their government ceases," and "the administration of government lies in getting proper men."[334]

10. Subtraction and Addition

Though addition and subtraction bring about a change in the condition or quantity of things, they may still be preserved in part at least, and each addition or subtraction is not without its significance. On the one hand, such additions and subtractions are intended to meet the requirements of the moment. But the aim also is to secure the greatest advantage and the least disadvantage. So we are concerned here not only with addition and subtraction, but also with advantage and disadvantage.

> Tzŭ-chang asked whether the affairs of ten ages after could be known.
> The Master said, "The Yin dynasty followed the regulations of the Hsia: wherein it subtracted from or added to them may be known. The Chou dynasty has followed the regulations of the Yin: wherein it has subtracted from or added to them may be known. Some other may follow the Chou, but though it should be at the distance of a hundred ages, its affairs may be known."[335]

Tzŭ-chang wished to know about the future, but Confucius spoke of the past. This is because nothing could have been produced from the void; there must have been a foundation of things in their original state which in time came to be recognized by the people at large. Every creation or reform must build on this foundation by introducing additions or subtracions and forming a new condition or effect. This process of change is especially evident in the history of a country's institutions. The additions or subtractions made in one age not only can indicate the changes effected—they can also help us speculate on the future. That is why Confucius said that the affairs of even a hundred ages hence could be known.

> Confucius said, "There are three friendships which are advantageous and three which are injurious. Friendship with the upright; friendship with the sincere; and friendship with the man of much observation: these are advantageous. Friendship with the man of specious airs; friendship with the insinuatingly soft; and friendship with the glib-tongued: these are injurious."
>
> Confucius said, "There are three things men find enjoyment in, which are advantageous, and three things they find enjoyment in, which are injurious. To find enjoyment in the discriminating study of ceremonies and music; to find enjoyment in speaking of the goodness of others; to find enjoyment in having many worthy friends: these are advantageous. To find enjoyment in extravagant pleasures; to find enjoyment in idleness and sauntering; to find enjoyment in the pleasures of feasting: these are injurious."[336]

The above passages concern advantage and disadvantage or injury. Friendships and pleasures are indispensable conditions for human life. It is of course imperative for each person to choose the advantageous and shun the injurious.

11. Difficult and Easy

The ease or difficulty with which something is done depends on judgments based on a person's experience and observation. But these judgments differ according to environment, time and the opposites involved. Nothing should be left undone because it is easy, nor should it be belittled and avoided because it is difficult. Whatever is beneficial to mankind must be done despite its difficulty. Hence it is said, "Earnest action is akin to benevolence."[337]

According to Confucius, "To be poor without murmuring is difficult. To be rich without being proud is easy."[338] Here difficulty and ease are related to the contrasting conditions of poverty and wealth. It is not the hardest thing in the world to keep oneself from murmuring constant criticisms, but it is certainly much more difficult to be poor without complaining against Heaven and blaming others than it is to be rich without giving way to pride; this, despite the fact that the rich have a constant tendency to feel proud of their wealth. Even though there is no definite rule regarding difficulty and ease, Confucius' observation nevertheless embodies a great truth.

> The Master said, "The superior man is easy to serve and difficult to please. If you try to please him without complying with the Way, he will not be pleased. But in his employment of men, he uses them according to their capacity. The mean man is difficult to serve and easy to please. If you try to please him, though without complying with the Way, he may be pleased. But in his employment of men, he wishes them to be equal to everything."[339]

The superior man, a just person, regards as his duty what is consistent with righteousness. This is the reason he is hard to please but easy to serve. But the mean man, ever eager for personal gain, appears happy after reaping some benefit; he will complain and blame others whenever he sustains a loss. For this reason he is easy to please but difficult to serve.

12. Thick and Thin

Just how thick or thin objects are is of course easily measured. Here the words refer to the importance of men and things, whether it is great or slight. The *Great Learning* states: "It never has been the case that what was of great importance has been slightly cared for and, at the same time, that what was of slight importance has been greatly cared for."[340] In other words, man should stress the root and pay less heed to the branches. If the root is not emphasized, naturally much less attention is given to the branches. A popular saying has it: "One should censure oneself strongly and others lightly." In contrasting the relative importance of oneself and others in receiving the blame for anything, this saying shows the significance of self-examination.

> Mencius said, "He who stops short, where stopping is acknowledged to be not allowable, will stop short in everything. He who behaves shabbily to those whom he ought to treat well,

will behave shabbily to all.

"He who advances with precipitation will retire with speed."[341]

There must be a proper balance between cordial and indifferent treatment. He who treats indifferently someone who should be cordially treated cannot be expected to treat cordially someone who may be treated indifferently. As a result, he will always be indifferent in his treatment of others.

He who stops short when he is not permitted to do so tends to neglect what he should do. If this goes on long enough, he is bound to lapse into the state of doing nothing whatever.

13. Glory and Disgrace

Glory and disgrace are opposite and contrary terms. In human life, contrary results are due to contrary causes. There is a common saying that when you sow beans you reap beans, and when you sow melons you reap melons. By ascertaining the causes, you can foresee the results.

> Mencius said, "benevolence brings glory to a prince, and the opposite of it brings disgrace. For the princes of the present day to hate disgrace and yet to live complacently doing what is not benevolent is like hating moisture and yet living in a low situation."[342]

It is human nature to love glory and hate disgrace. But only those who love and help others can have glory, and those who cannot do so are disgraced. To hate disgrace but not to be benevolent is to create an evil cause, and it is then impossible to avoid evil results. If a man hates moisture, how can he avoid it by choosing to live in a low place?

14. Poverty and Prosperity

Poverty implies obscurity; and prosperity, prominence. Mencius said, "What belongs by his nature to the superior man cannot be increased by the largeness of his sphere of action, nor diminished by his dwelling in poverty and retirement."[343] What he meant was that the distinction between poverty and prosperity applied only to others. So far as it concerned oneself, even when there was prosperity, it would not necessarily benefit others.

Mencius said to Sung Kou-chien, "Are you fond, Sir, of traveling to the different courts? I will tell you about such traveling.

"If others acknowledge you, be perfectly satisfied. If no one does so, be the same."

Kou-chien said, "What is to be done to secure this perfect satisfaction?" Mencius replied, "Honor virute and delight in righteousness, and so you may always be perfectly satisfied.

"Therefore a scholar, though poor, does not let go his righteousness; though prosperous, he does not leave his Way.

"Poor and not letting righteousness go; it is thus that the scholar holds possession of himself. Prosperous and not leaving his Way; it is thus that the people's expectations of him are not disappointed.

"When the men of antiquity realized their wishes, benefits were conferred by them on the people. If they did not realize their wishes, they cultivated their personal character and became illustrious in the world. If poor, they attended to their own virtue in solitude; if advanced to dignity, they made the whole world virtuous as well."[344]

The realization of one's wishes is prosperity or prominence; for instance, when one occupies a superior position, enjoying the prerogative of administering the government and practicing benevolence. The failure to realize one's wishes is poverty; for instance, when one remains in a low station, assuming the responsibility for cultivating oneself and bringing tranquillity to others. Our ambition should be to make the whole world virtuous. But if the environment prevents us from fulfilling this ambition, we should at least cultivate ourselves, honor virtue and delight in righteousness so that we can feel at ease wherever we may be.

15. Nobility and Lowliness

Nobility and lowliness are not fixed conditions. Those who have become noble may revert to lowliness; those who are lowly at first may become noble; those who are more lowly than some may become nobler than others. The distinction between nobility and lowliness frequently changes with time. Only absolute nobility is eternally unchangeable.

Mencius said, "To desire to be honored is the common mind of men. And all men have in themselves that which is truly

honorable. Only they do not think of it. The honor which men
confer is not honor in essence. Those who Chao Mêng ennobles
he can make mean again:"[345]

To "have in oneself that which is truly honorable" is to have
"benevolence, righteousness, loyalty and faithfulness, and delight
in goodness untiringly"—these constitute the nobility of Heaven.
The "honor which men confer" denotes high positions of government;
this constitutes the nobility of men. The nobility of Heaven is
that with which men are endowed by nature; but they do not
truly regard it as honorable. On the other hand, the nobility of
men is that which men confer—but which men can also take
away. So it may or may not be honorable, and the authority to
confer it is exercised by others. Unlike the nobility of Heaven,
it is not absolutely honorable nor externally irremovable. The
common saying, "To ask nothing from others is honorable," is
truly undeniable.

16. Poverty and Wealth

Although poverty and wealth are contrasting words, their
standards are not absolute. Normally he whose income is not
sufficient to support his family is poor, and only he who has a
considerable surplus can be called wealthy. But he who along
with his surplus also has a fondness for benevolence and propriety
is truly wealthy. At the other end of the scale, he who though
poor is happy and does not lose his righteousness is not injured
by his poverty.

> Tzŭ-kung said, "What do you pronounce concerning the poor
> man who yet does not flatter and the rich man who is not proud?"
> The Master replied, "They will do; but they are not equal to him
> who, though poor, is yet cheerful, and to him who, though rich,
> loves the rules of propriety."
> Tzŭ-kung said, "It is said in the *Book of Songs,* 'As you cut
> and then file, as you carve and then polish.' The meaning is the
> same, I apprehend, as that which you have just expressed."
> The Master said, "With one like Tz'ŭ, I can begin to talk
> about the odes. I told him past, and he knew what is to follow
> in future."[346]

The treatment of virtue as the root and wealth as a branch

was the greatest discovery made by Confucius. It has now become the center of Oriental culture and the foundation of the faith of scholars in their repose in poverty and delight in the Way. Hence it was said, "Riches and honors are what men desire. If it cannot be done in the proper way, they should not be held. Poverty and meanness are what men dislike. If it cannot be done in the proper way, they should not be avoided. If a superior man abandons benevolence, how can he fulfill the requirements of that name?"[347] If a man is poor but happy, he delights in the Way, is at peace, and naturally no longer flatters. If a man is rich but fond of propriety, he rests in benevolence, practices righteousness, and naturally is no longer proud. This is what is meant by the observation: "Let a man first stand fast in the supremacy of the nobler part of his constitution, and the inferior part will not be able to take it from him."[348]

However, if excessive importance were attached to repose in poverty, if the necessity for educating the people to promote their well-being were neglected, it would be detrimental to the national economy and cause the economic ruin of the country concerned. This would be an unfortunate misinterpretation of the Way of Confucius.

17. Praise and Reproach

If a man is earnest in his self-cultivation, he need not feel ill at ease because of praise or reproach. Confucius put it this way: "Is he not a superior man who feels no discomposure though men may take no note of him?"[349] Also, "I will not be concerned at men's not knowing me; I will be concerned at my own want of ability."[350] And "The superior man is distressed by his want of ability. He is not distressed by men's not knowing him."[351]

The point is that learning and morality are aimeds at self-cultivation, not at seeking fame. Moreover, neither adds to one's personal achievement nor detracts from it. He who is unduly happy when he is praised and angry when he is reproached cannot deserve to be called a superior man.

> Mencius said, "There are cases of praise which could not be expected, and of reproach when the parties have been seeking to be perfect."[352]

Unexpected praise is not always merited; it is not something that should send a person into ecstasies. Excessive reproach, fault-finding, can be helpful and supply an impetus to self-improvement.

> The Master said, "In my dealings with men, whose evil do I blame and whose goodness do I praise? If I do sometimes praise a person, I must have tried him out. This people are the same as those who were taught to practice righteousness in the three dynasties."[353]

To "blame" meant to exaggerate one's fault beyond the truth, and to "praise" meant to exalt one's goodness in excess of the fact. Confucius never praised or blamed anyone lightly because, although time changes many things, the criteria of right and wrong remain unaltered and personal criticism is not in order. Confucius felt that whenever he praised anyone, the praise had to be clearly justified by the facts so that the party concerned could receive the intended encouragement. It was his gracious way of treating others to show his approval of the slightest good performed by them.

18. Life and Death

Life and death are important events in human existence. But wherever there is life, death cannot be avoided. Mencius said, "There is that which I like more than life...there is that which I dislike more than death..."[354] Obviously, the love of life and the dislike of death are shared by all men. But life and death are stages in the process of physiological change and therefore they should be in accordance with nature.

So, Tzŭ-hsia said, "Death and life have their determined destiny; riches and honors depend upon Heaven."[355] Confucius also said, "You love a man and wish him to live; you hate him and wish him to die. Having wished him to live, you also wish him to die. This is a case of delusion."[356] It is so because a man's life and death cannot follow his own or someone else's likes and dislikes. We can only abide by the principle of physiology and seek the improvement, extension and prolongation of our lives.

Mencius made two weighty pronouncements on this question

which are worthy of our attention:

Mencius said, "He who has exhausted all his mental constitution knows his nature. Knowing his nature, he knows Heaven.

"To preserve one's mental constitution and nourish one's nature is the way to serve Heaven.

"When neither a premature death nor long life causes a man any double-mindedness, but he waits in the cultivation of his personal character for whatever issue; this is the way in which he establishes his destiny."[357]

Mencius said, "Destiny is involved in everything. A man should receive submissively what is normal destiny.

"Therefore he who knows his destiny will not stand beneath a precipitous wall.

"Death sustained in the full practice of the Way is normal destiny.

"Death under handcuffs and fetters is not normal destiny.[358]

The "exhaustion of mental constitution" leads to the knowledge of nature, which in turn leads to the "knowledge of Heaven." Hence it was said, "Knowing his nature, he knows Heaven." The preservation of mental constitution is the nourishment of nature, and vice versa. Since nature is endowed by Heaven, the preservation of mental constitution and nourishment of nature are for the service of Heaven, hence "the way to serve Heaven."

This is the true meaning of human life. No matter whether it is a long or short life, a man must exhaust the knowledge and ability with which he is endowed by nature, hence the "cultivation of personal character to wait for whatever issue." Although he may die in this process, his death is normal destiny.

On the other hand, if a man were subjected to the injuries and oppression imposed by selfish desire—handcuffs and fetters—and lose his life, this would not be, personally, a worthy death.

Therefore, although we need not be afraid of death, we should not go out of our way—stand beneath a precipitous wall—to encounter the possibility of a violent death. The "exhaustion of one's Way" is the exhaustion of the Way to cultivate the person, to preserve the mental constitution and to nourish nature. Thus, by observing the rules of propriety and practicing righteousness, we hope to be worthy of our ancestors, hence the "normal destiny."

Chi Lu asked about serving the spirits of the dead. The Master said, "While you are not able to serve men, how can you serve their spirits?" Chi Lu added, "I venture to ask about death." He was answered, "While you do not know life, how can you know about death?"[359]

Life is realistic, while spirits are based only on mystic hearsay. "Death" is the beginning of the human body's dissolution, while "life" is the continuation of human activity. Since the attention of Confucianists focused on the practical problems of human life, Confucsus did not answer Tzŭ-lu's inquiry directly. Rather he implied that Tzŭ-lu should concern himself more with the grasp of realism and strive for the betterment of humnn life.

19. Likes and Dislikes

These two words are expressions of emotion. If they are not tempered by reason they can lead to dangerous results or at least frequently be unconsciously erroneous.

The Master said, "When the multitude hates a man, it is necessary to examine into the case. When the multitude likes a man, it is necessary to examine into the case."[360]

Tzŭ-kung asked, saying, "What do you say of a man who is loved by all the people of his neighborhood?" The Master replied, "We may not for that accord our approval of him." "And what do you say of him who is hated by all the people of his neighborhood?" The Master said, "We may not for that conclude that he is bad. It is better than either of these cases that the good in the neighborhood love him and the bad hate him."[361]

Human nature is often swayed by prejudice or tends to take the line of least resistance. In addition, the masses are inclined to be emotional. So, even if a man is loved or hated by all the area, his neighbors' attitude may or may not be valid. A careful investigation should be made, and the man should be loved or despised only when the facts justify it.

According to Confucius, "It is only the benevolent man who can love or who can hate others."[362] Now, in the collective life of mankind, good and evil must be sorted out before a fair judgment can be passed. If this is done, the people can be inspired to do good and dissuaded from doing evil. Only in this way can society continue to progress. Since the benevolent have the common existence of mankind at heart, they can encourage their fellow men to do good and admonish them against evil. However, if a man is concerned only with his own selfish interest, he will not necessarily love good men and hate the evil ones.

> In the *Book of Songs* it is said, "How much to be rejoiced in are these princes, the parents of the people!" When a prince loves what the people love and hates what the people hate, then is he what is called the parent of the people.[363]
>
> To love those whom men hate and to hate those whom men love; this is to outrage the natural feeling of men. Calamities cannot fail to come down on him who does so.[364]

Likes and dislikes must be in accordance with justice. If they are confused and reversed, they become prejudices. They then conflict with the common existence of mankind and invite calamities. This applies especially to nations, as well as to individuals.

20. Upright and Crooked

Those who are sincere and act according to reason are upright, and those who are insincere and act against reason are crooked (perverse, deceitful). The two are irreconcilable. If we cannot distinguish between them, we not only fail to know men but we can easily distort the facts and become irrational ourselves.

> Fan Ch'ih asked about benevolence. The Master said, "It is to love all men." He asked about wisdom. The Master said, "It is to know all men."
>
> Fan Ch'ih did not immediately understand these answers.
>
> The Master said, "Employ the upright and put aside the crooked; in this way the crooked can be made to be upright."
>
> Fan Ch'ih retired, and seeing Tzŭ-hsia, he said to him, "A little while ago, I had an interview with our Master and asked him about wisdom. He said, 'Employ the upright and put aside the crooked; in this way the crooked can be made to be upright.' What did he mean?"
>
> Tzŭ-hsia said, "Truly rich is his saying! Shun, being in possession of the empire, selected from among all the people and employed Kao-yao, on which those who were devoid of virtue became virtuous, as if the unvirtuous had gone far away. T'ang,

being in possession of the empire, selected from among all the people and employed Yi Yin, and those who were devoid of virtue became virtuous, as if the unvirtuous had gone far away."[355]

Confucius' answer to Fan Ch'ih was simple but its wide implications brought the exclamation from Tzŭ-hsia, "Truly rich is his saying!" Knowledge of men, indeed, is not easy to acquire. For one thing, the word "knowledge" implies the distinction between uprightness and the lack of it, between submissiveness and rebellion. This distinction leads to the selection of the proper personnel. In the case of Shun and T'ang they chose upright men, which in turn caused those who were not benevolent to improve themselves.

> Duke Ai asked, saying, "What should be done in order to secure the submission of the people?" Confucius replied, "Advance the upright and set aside the crooked, then the people will submit. Advance the crooked and set aside the upright, then the people will not submit."[366]

It is human nature to be fond of the upright and to hate the perverse. If evil men are selected over the upright, it will not set right with the multitude, and the people are bound to react unfavorably.

> Hui of Liu-hsia, being chief criminal judge, was thrice dismissed from his office. Someone said to him, "Is it not yet time for you, Sir, to leave?" He replied, "Serving men in an upright way, where shall I go and not experience such a thrice-repeated dismissal? If I choose to serve men in a crooked way, what necessity is there for me to leave the country of my parents?"[367]

In times of disorder very few can distinguish between uprightness and the lack of it, between submissiveness and rebellion. Hui of Liu-hsia acted according to the principles of right, yet he was repeatedly cast aside. Despite the dismissals, however, he refused to leave his fatherland or to change his behavior to keep his position. This is why Mencius called him the "accommodating" sage.

21. Retirement and Acceptance of Office

Work and human ambition being what they are, there is no doubt that a man should exercise the greatest care in choosing his profession. Mencius said, "Men must be decided on what they will not do, and then they are able to act with vigor on what they ought to do,"[368] and "Let a man not do what he should not do, and let him not desire what he should not desire—this is all he has to do."[369] Retirement and acceptance of an office involve what a man should or should not do. He accepts an office if it is in compliance with the conditions of propriety and retires from it if it is not. The proper choice is made after careful consideration.

> The disciple Ch'ên said, "What were the principles on which superior men of old took office?" Mencius replied, "There were three cases in which they accepted office and three in which they left it.
>
> "If received with the utmost respect and all polite observances, and told that their words would be carried into practice, then they took office. Afterwards, although there might be no remission in the polite demeanor of the prince, if their words were not carried into practice, they would leave him.
>
> "The second case was that in which, though the prince could not be expected at once to carry their words into practice, yet being received by him with the utmost respect, they took office with him. But afterwards, if there was a remission in his polite demeanor, they would leave him.
>
> "The last case was that in which the superior man, who had nothing to eat, either morning or evening, was so famished that he could not move out of his door. If the prince, on hearing of his state, said, 'I have first of all failed to adopt his Way and also to follow his words, and I am ashamed to subject him to starvation in my country.' The relief offered in such a case might be accepted, but not beyond what was sufficient to avert death."[370]

Briefly stated, Mencius' conditions for accepting office were (1) action according to the candidate's words, (2) his polite reception, and (3) rescue from an impossible situation without disgrace. When these conditions are not fulfilled, the office-holder should retire. Putting himself in the position of the ancients, Mencius adopted a cautious attitude to the acceptance or rejection of office.

22. High and Low

The ancients frequently described space as containing six

confluences—up and down, right and left, front and back. The *Great Learning* states, "What a man dislikes in his superiors, let him not display in the treatment of his inferiors; what he dislikes in his inferiors, let him not display in the service of his superiors; what he hates in those who are before him, let him not therewith precede those who are behind him; what he hates in those who are behind him, let him not therewith follow those who are before him; what he hates to receive on the right, let him not bestow on the left; what he hates to receive on the left, let him not bestow on the right—this is what is called 'The principle with which, as with a measuring-square, to regulate one's conduct.' "[371]

The "measuring square" here signifies the role of intelligence. Without it a man may see only what is above and miss what is below; he will see only what is before and miss what is behind, see only what is on the left and miss what is on the right. What is above and below, before and behind, left and right, are opposites. There can be nothing below, behind or on the right without something above, before, or on the left. We must understand the total and mutual relationship between these opposites before we can take hold of the two extremes and make use of the Mean.

> In a high situation, he (the superior man) does not domineer over his inferiors. In a low situation, he does not court the favors of his superiors. He rectifies himself and seeks for nothing from others, so that he has no dissatisfactions. He does not murmur against Heaven, nor grumble against men.[372]

It is easy for a superior to treat his inferiors with contempt; it is easy for an inferior to curry favor with his superiors. For this reason they should guard against, respectively, pride and flattery. Men should not alter their proper conduct according to the positions held by them. When the nobility of Heaven is stressed in place of the nobility of man, when a man seeks only from himself and does not grumble against another, when he understands the necessity for avoiding what he dislikes in his superiors' treatment of their inferiors and in his inferiors' service of their superiors, then there will be neither pride nor flattery.

23. Far and Near

When speaking of "far and near," we begin with what is near

and extend to what is far. Confucius said, "What is near is to serve your father, and what is far is to serve your sovereign." Mencius noted that "King Wu did not slight the near and did not forget the distant." Both what is far and what is near are equally important. The near should not be neglected, nor the far forgotten. To plan what is far from what is near is the secret of success.

> The Duke of Shêh asked about government.
> The Master said, "Good government obtains when those who are near are made happy and those who are far off are attracted."[373]

Good government sees to it that the people—each person .in his proper place—live in peace and enjoy their work. If this is accomplished, the news of it will get around and persons from far-off nations will come to see how such an ideal situation was achieved. The point is that without first planning what is near, what is far away cannot be reached. And this applies to both government and education. Hence it was said, "Words which are simple, while their meaning is far-reaching, are good words."[374]

Both time and space are marked by nearness and distance. As far as time is concerned, several things must be taken into consideration: (1) the close connection between the various stages of human affairs emphasize that long term and short term are merely the two ends of a period of time; (2) long term and short term are related and influence each other; (3) therefore the farsighted refuse to confine their planning to the short term and neglect the long term. But as they pay attention to the long term, they cannot neglect the short term. Confucius once said: "If a man takes no thought about what is distant, he will find sorrow near at hand."[375]

24. Morning and Evening

Morning and evening enclose a short span of time. But human activity never ceases. By paying close attention even to this short interval, a person can gain time by making use of each instant. Confucius put it this way: "If a man hears the Way in the morning, he may die in the evening without regret."[376]

The Way is the truth, which is not easily heard. Once the truth is learned, however, a man can die peacefully, without regret. This underlines the tremendous value of truth. A man should rather sacrifice his life for truth than vice versa. For the sacrifice here is for benevolence and righteousness, for the Way.

25. Deep and Shallow

Depth and shallowness also are opposed to one another. What is shallow in one instance may be deep in another. It is commonly said, "The ancients admonished against deep words in cases of shallow friendship." The depth of words depends on the closeness of friendly ties; both excess and inadequacy are improper. Since depth and shallowness are standards for all speech and conduct, we must guage and compare them carefully at all times.

> The Master was playing one day on a musical stone in Wei, when a man, carrying a straw basket, passed the door of the house where Confucius was, and said, "His heart is full who so beats the musical stone!"
> After a while he added, "How contemptible is the narrow obstinancy those sounds display! When one is taken no notice of, one has simply at once to give over one's wish for public employment. 'Deep water must be crossed with the clothes on; shallow water may be crossed with the clothes held up.'"
> The Master said, "How determined he is in his purpose! But I cannot blame him."[377]

The man carrying the straw basket derided Confucius for not forgetting the world even though he could not secure employment It seemed to the man that the Master had lost his sense of balance between depth and shallowness. Confucius could only sigh and comment that if he could be as unconcerned about the world as his critic, he would have nothing to say; but that at times one cannot help being somewhat shallow.

26. In and Out

When a man is at home, he is "in." When he goes into the city or capital, he is "out." Hence, "A youth, when at home, should be filial and, abroad, respectful to his elders,"[378] and "Abroad, to serve the high ministers and nobles; at home, to serve one's father and elder brothers."[379] Also, when a man is within his own country, he is "in"; and when he goes abroad, he is "out."

Mencius said, "...If a prince has not about his court families attached to the laws and worthy counselors, and abroad there are no hostile states or other external calamities, his country will generally come to ruin.

"From these things we see how life springs from sorrow and calamity and death from ease and pleasure."[380]

Strong neighbors who menace a nation's existence are one side of a coin that can help purchase a thriving country; the other side is a sufficient number of upright men who can maintain the country's laws. Without these two—upright men and threatening neighbors—those men who are in and out of the government may easily lapse into a false sense of security and a life of pleasure. And this state of affairs will inevitably lead to ruin. Therefore pleasure seems to benefit life, but actually can, on occasion, bring death; and impending calamity, which seems to threaten death, can in a way actually benefit life. The rise and fall of a nation as well as the success and failure of an individual hinge on these considerations.

27. Ancient and Modern

Time can be divided into past, present and future. The present is modern; and the past, ancient. But time flies, and soon what is modern now will become ancient. Therefore it is necessary to hold fast to the present and at the same time examine the past, for the past and the present are links between the preceding period and a future era. In the continued growth of human life, there can be no present without the past. The responsibility of modern men is to move forward from the past and pave the way for the future.

Confucius lived during the decline of the Chou dynasty, when the good systems of the past had almost all been destroyed. Social morality was at a low ebb and the life of the common man was difficult. That is why he frequently said that modern times could not compare with the past. Here are two such passages:

The Master said, "In ancient times, men learned with a view to their own improvement. Nowadays men learn with a view to the approbation of others."[381]
The Master said, "Anciently, men had three failings, which now perhaps are not to be found.

"However, the high-mindedness of antiquity showed itself in a disregard of small things; the high-mindedness of the pressent day shows itself in wild license. The stern dignity of antiquity showed itself in grave reserve; the stern dignity of the present day shows itself in quarrelsome perverseness. The stupidity of antiquity showed itself in straightforwardness; the stupidity of the present day shows itself in sheer deceit."[382]

Though the merits of the past should be preserved and developed, it is a gross mistake to say that the past necessarily surpassed the present. The *Great Learning*, for instance, adopted as its principle the "people's renovation" and advised "renovation from day to day" and "daily renovation." It is quite evident that the present was expected to surpass the past, that the future was expected to surpass the present. The merits and shortcomings of each period should always be clearly distinguished, and there must be no bias about them. We can increase our self-confidence by noting the merits of the past. We also can spur ourselves to make meaningful progress by anticipating greater merits in the future. But if we decide things arbitrarily and make great display of wisdom while disregarding environment and trends, we will be doomed to failure and even invite disaster.

The Master said, "Let a man who is ignorant be fond of using his own judgment; let a man without rank be fond of assuming a directing power to himself; let a man who is living in the present age go back to the ways of antiquity;—on the persons of all who act thus calamaties will be sure to come."[383]

28. First and Last

Everything progresses with time. So, some things come first and some last. The *Great Learning* said, "To know what is first and what is last will lead near to the Way."[384] If we can determine the order of sequence for everything, if we do not advance what should come later or put off what is urgent, then we can proceed properly without creating confusion.

Confucius once said, "A minister, in serving his prince, reverently discharges his duties and makes his emolument a secondary consideration."[385] In discharging his duties first and then thinking about his reward, an official shows loyalty to his country. But if he reverses the order, he is putting selfish interest before the well-being of the public. In the *Analects* we read, "The stable being burned down, when he was at court, on his return, the Master said, 'Has any man been hurt?' He did not ask about the horse."[386] If Confucius had inquired first about the horse, he would have gone against human nature. Again,

> Fan Ch'ih...asked about benevolence. The Master said, "The man of benevolence makes the difficulty to be overcome his first business and success only a subsequent consideration; this may be benevolence."[387]

Read heavy responsibility for "difficulty" in the above passage, and rich reward for "success." By giving the discharge of his responsibility priority over his anticipated reward, a man shows his sincerity in helping others. He can be called benevolent.

29. Regular Rule and Exigency

Ordinarily we observe the regular rule, but in exceptional cases we take emergency measures. If we resort to the emergency measures all the time, however, we show our lack of confidence in choosing the path of goodness and holding fast to it. We then are insincere.

> Shun-yü K'un said, "Is it the rule that males and females shall not allow their hands to touch in giving or receiving anything?" Mencius replied, "It is the rule." K'un said, "If a man's sister-in-law be drowning, shall he rescue her with his hand?" Mencius said, "He who would not so rescue the drowning woman is a wolf. For males and females not to allow their hands to touch in giving and receiving is the general rule; when a sister-in-law is drowning, to rescue her with the hand is a peculiar exigency."
> K'un said, "The whole world is drowning. Why is it that you do not rescue it?"
> Mencius answered, "A drowning world must be rescued with the Way, as a drowning sister-in-law has to be rescued with the hand. Do you wish me to rescue the world with my hand?[388]

The custom of not touching hands was rooted in the large-scale family system in which many relatives, both men and women, lived under the same roof. To avoid friction between brothers due to intimacy between in-laws, one of the established rules of behavior forbade the touching of hands when giving or receiving anything. But this rule, like so many others, can and should be swept aside in a dire emergency, like the drowning described. If a brother-in-law abides by the rule and does not rescue his drowning sister-in-law, he is thought to lack courage as he behaves like a lower animal: for saving a life is more important than observing a rule of conduct. The point is that it is necessary to weigh everything carefully to determine whether the cicumstances demand strict observance of the regular rule or whether emergency measures should be taken. This is the Way of sages and worthy men.

30. Righteousness and Gain

The word "righteousness" originally meant what is proper in human conduct. With the passing of time, however, the word took on a new significance, until today it conveys the meaning of both "a proper act" and "a magnanimous sacrifice." It is said that at a time when the nation is supreme, everyone is called on to sacrifice the small self (self-sacrifie) to preserve the greater self (the nation).

The ancients had nothing against gain. In the "Plan of Kao Yao" it is said, "With upright virtue and gainful use, living is enriched and harmonized." In the "Declaration of (the Duke of) Ch'in we find this passage: "Is it not a gain to be able to protect my sons, grandsons and black-haired people?" In the *Book of Changes* it is stated, "Only Ch'ien (denoting Heaven) can benefit the world with good gain." In Confucius' notes to this book he wrote, "There should be change throughout, so as to exhaust the gain," and "Things are supplied for use and vessels made so as to confer gain on the world."

In all these instances the word "gain" denoted the happiness of the majority of people. But after the Eastern Chou dynasty, human depravity became more widespread and the Way declined. The word "gain" took on a new meaning—private or selfish interest—which overshadowed the original meaning of public interest. With this development, people vied with one another in enriching themselves and seeking their private ends. It broke ground for what may be described as the custom of plunder and robbery. In response, worthy men underscored the necessity for "righteousness" as distinguished from selfish or petty gain.

The Commentary of Tso on the *Spring and Autumn Annals* makes reference to this remark of Tzŭ-fan of Ch'u: "Righteousness builds gain." Chao Shuai of Chin made the same point: "Virtue and righteousness are the foundations of gain." In both cases the idea was to accent public over private interest as the basis of gain. Only acts of righteousess, it was emphasized, could make for universal gain and happiness—and this in itself was a pointed commentary on the downward trend of the time. The words of Mêng Hsien recorded in the *Great Learning* were especially profound and exhaustive.

> The official Mêng Hsien said, "He who keeps horses and a carriage does not look after fowls and pigs. The family which keeps its stores of ice does not rear cattle or sheep. So, the house which possesses a hundred chariots should not keep a minister to look out for imposts that he may lay them on the people. Than to have such a minister, it were better for that house to have one who should rob it of its revenues." This is in accordance with the saying: "In a state, pecuniary gain is not to be considered to be prosperity, but its prosperity will be found in righteousness."
>
> When he who presides over a State makes his revenues his chief business, it must have started with mean men who are capable in this respect. When such men are employed in the administration of a State, calamities and injuries will befall it together, and, though good men may take their place, they will not be able to remedy the evil. This illustrates again the saying, "In a state, gain is not to be considered prosperity, but its prosperity will be found in righteousness."[389]

In the government of a State, officials must focus their attention on the interests of the people as a whole, especially on their key long-term interests. If an eye is kept only on their immediate and minor interests, if stress is laid only on the interests of the minority, if attention is confined to the accumulation of wealth without encouraging production, then the hearts of the people will be lost—even though there may be temporary gain. This is what the mean man does. It is harmful and can never be beneficial to a country. As Confucius said, "If only minor gain is seen, nothing great can be accomplished." Furthermore, he was the first one to point to the difference between righteousness and gain as the distinction between superior and mean men. To quote him: "The mind of the superior man is conversant with righteousness; the mind of the mean man is conversant with gain."[390]

The distinction between righteousness and gain corresponds to the difference between public and private interest. The superior man is public-spirited and acts according to benevolence, whereas the mean man practices exactly the opposite. This was the basis for the central theory of virtue as the root and wealth as a branch. For righteousness, public interest and virtue are all opposed, respectvely, by gain, private interest and wealth. As one rises, the other declines, and vice versa. This is inevitable. In the very first chapter of his works, Mencius answered the question of King Hui of Liang on the difference between righteousness and gain, showing how important the question was at the time. The central faith of Mencius throughout his life was in the Kingly Way or Way of Right, which had to be based on benevolence and righteousness. It is the Way for personal living just as it is for good government.

> Mencius went to see King Hui of Liang. The king said, "Venerable Sir, since you have not counted it far to come here, a distance of a thoussnd *li*, may I presume that you are provided with counsels to profit my kingdom?"

> Mencius replied, "Why must Your Majesty use that word 'profit'? It will suffice to have benevolence and righteousness.

> If Your Majesty says, 'What is to be done to profit my kingdom?' the great officials will say, 'What is to be done to profit our families?' and the inferior officials and the common people will say, 'What is to be done to profit our persons?' Superiors and inferiors will try to snatch this profit one from the other, and the kingdom will be endangered. In the kingdom of ten thousand chariots, the murderer of his prince must be the chief of a family of a hundred chariots. To have a thousand in ten thousand. and a hundred in a thousand, cannot be said not to be a large allotment, but if righteousness be put last and profit be put first, they will not be satisfied without snatching all.

> "There never has been a benevolent man who neglected his parents. There never has been a righteous man who made his sovereign an after consideration.

> "Let Your Majesty say, 'Benevolence and righteousnes' only. Why must you use that word—'profit'?"[391]

King Hui of Liang was formerly Marquis Ying of Wei. After usurping the title of king, he welcomed Mencius to his court with humble words and the offer of high rewards. But the first thing he mentioned was profit, showing the importance attached to it by the princes of the Warring States period. Mencius dealt him a serious blow by replying: "Why must Your Majesty use that word 'profit'? It will suffice to have benevolence and righteousness." He ended by saying, "Let your Majesty also say, 'Benevolence and righteousness' only. Why must you use that word—'profit'?"

Throughout his life Mencius staunchly believed that benevolence and righteousness alone meant profit, and there was no profit apart from benevolence and righteousness. For, to him, profit in the material sense, was the main cause of strife and slaughter, and those who sought peace and order for their country had to remove the causes of disorder first. This was indeed surpassingly keen judgment.

The following words spoken by Mencius to Sung K'êng also can be classed as immortal:

Sung K'êng being about to go to Ch'u, Mencius met him in Shih-ch'iu.

"Master, where are you going?" asked Mencius.

K'êng replied, "I have heard that Ch'in and Ch'u are fighting together, and I am going to see the King of Ch'u and persuade him to cease hostilities. If he shall not be pleased with my advice, I shall go to see the King of Ch'in and persuade him in the same way. Of the two kings I shall surely find that I can succeed with one of them."

Mencius said, "I will not venture to ask about the particulars, but I should like to hear the scope of your plan. What course will you take to try to persuade them?" K'êng answered, "I will tell them how unprofitable their course is to them." "Master," said Mencius, "your aim is great, but your argument is not good.

"If you, starting from the point of profit, offer your persuasive counsels to the Kings of Ch'in and Ch'u, and if those kings are pleased with the consideration of profit so as to stop the movements of their armies, then all belonging to those armies will rejoice in the cessation of war, and find their pleasure in the pursuit of profit. Ministers will serve their sovereign for the profit of which they cherish the thought; sons will serve their fathers and younger brothers will serve their elder brothers from the same consideration —and the issue will be that, abandoning benevolence and righteousness, sovereign and minister, father and son, elder brother and younger, will carry on all their intercourse with this thought of profit cherished in their breast. But never has there been such a state of society without ruin being the result of it.

"If you, starting from the ground of benevolence and righteousness, offer your counsels to the Kings of Ch'in and Ch'u so as to stop the operations of their armies, then all belonging to those armies will rejoice in the stopping from war and find their pleasure in benevolence and righteousness. Ministers will serve their sovereign, cherishing the principles of benevolence and righteousness; sons will serve their fathers and younger brothers will serve their elder brothers in the same way—and so, sovereign and minister, father and son, elder brother and younger, abandoning the thought of profit, will cherish the principles of benevolence and righteousness and carry on all their intercourse upon them. Never has there been such a state of society, without the State where it prevailed rising to the Kingly Way. Why must you use that word 'profit'?"[392]

It seemed sensible to Sung K'êng to persuade Ch'in and Ch'u to stop their war on the grounds of mutual profit. Mencius, however, felt that even if this line of argument succeeded, the basically erroneous conceptions of the two kings would still not be corrected. He thought the only proper course to adopt was to persuade them to seek benevolence and righteousness. Mencius deeply believed the crux of order or disorder lay in the human heart. Therefore it was especially urgent to rectify the thinking of the rulers. So, without paying heed to the current trend of thought, Mencius took his strong stand in pleading what he regarded as a just cause, perhaps the only cause that could save an aggravating situation. His attitude was certainly that of a great statesman and educator.

To sum up, profit represents personal interest, while righteousness takes into account the interest of all concerned. It is easy to take care of personal interest, and so just about everyone seeks his own gain; when this fails, strife results. On the other hand, it is difficult to take care of the public interest, and so almost everyone overlooks it and cares little about public gain or loss. If each man can uphold righteousness for the sake of others, the profit he is entitled to is also included.

What is the use of seeking private interest ceaselessly, and where is the necessity for strife? While profit is contained in righteousness, complaint and not righteousness is necessarily contained in the misconception of "profit." We cannot forget that complaint will beget blame and hatred for others, even forcible seizure from others. As Confucius said, "He who acts with a constant view to his own advantage will be much murmured against."[393]

The above examples point to things which men frequently encounter in the course of their lives. If they can distinguish between the root and branches of things, between their beginning and end, and arrange correct priorites to meet the changing social environment, they may hope to avoid serious blunder. Thus the effect of the investigation of things will be perceived and the success of the extension of knowledge will be achieved. Hence, "it is near to the Way," and "The superior man engages in learning to achieve the Way."

Footnotes for Chapter III

1. *Doctrine of the Mean*, Ch. XX.
5. *Analects*, Bk. XVI, Ch. IX.
2. *Ibid.*, Bk. VII, Ch. XIX.
4. *Ibid.*, Bk. V, Ch. VIII.
5. *Doctrine of the Mean*, Ch. XX.
6. *Great Learning*, Com., Ch. III.
7. *Doctrine of uhe Mean*, Ch. XX. *Vide supra*. p. 18.
8. *Doctrine of the Mean*, Ch. XX.
9. *Vide supra*, p. 21.
10. *Doctrine of the Mean*, Ch. XXVI.
11. *Ibid.*
12. *Ibid.*
13. *Ibid.*, Ch. XXX.
14. Ibid., Ch. XX.
15. *Ibid.*
16. *Ibid.*, Ch. I. *Vide supra*, p. 23.
17. *Doctrine of the Mean*, Ch. I.
18. *Works of Mencius*, Bk. IV, Pt. II, Ch. XXV.
19. *Ibid*, Bk. III, Pt. II, Ch. IX.
20. *Ibid.*
21. *Ibid.*, Bk. IV, Pt. II, Ch. XXI.
22. *Ibid.*, Bk. V, Pt. I, Ch. VI.
23. *Ibid.*, Bk. II, Pt. I, Ch. IV; Bk. IV, Pt. I, Ch. VIII.
24. *Ibid.*, Bk. I, Pt. II, Ch. XVI.
25. *Ibid,*, Bk. V, Pt. I, Ch. V.
26. *Analects*, Bk. XII, Ch. V.
27. *Doctrine of the Mean*, Ch: XXIX. *Vide supra*, p. 41.
28. *Analects*, Bk. XIV, Ch. XXXVII.

29. *Ibid.*, Bk. VII, Ch. XXII.
30. *Ibid.*, Bk. XVII, Ch. XIX.
31. *Works of Mencius*, Bk. VI, Pt. I, Ch. VI.
32. *Doctrine of the Mean*, Ch. XVII.
33. *Works of Mencius*, Bk. V, Pt. I, Ch. VII.
34. *Analects*, Bk. III, Ch. XIII.
35. *Analects*, Bk. XX, Ch. III.
36. *Great Learning*, Com., Ch. X.
37. *Analects*, Bk. XVI, Ch. VIII.
38. *Doctrine of the Mean*. Ch. XIV. *Vide infra*, p. 288.
39. *Works of Mencius*, Bk. VII, Pt. II, Ch. XXXIII.
40. *Ibid.*, Ch. XXIX.
41. *Analects*. Bk. XIV, Ch. XXXVIII.
42. *Works of Mencius*, Bk. V, Pt. I, Ch. VI.
43. *Analects*, Bk. VI, Ch. VIII.
44. *Works of Mencius*, Bk. VII, Pt. I, Ch. II.
45. *Analects*, Bk. VII, Ch. XVI.
46. *Ibid.*, Bk. IX, Ch. I.
47. *Works of Mencius* Bk. VII, Pt. I, Ch. I.
48. *Doctrine of the Mean*. Ch. I. *Vide supra*, p. 8.
49. *Ibid.*. Ch. XXI.
50. *Works of Mencius*. Bk. VI, Pt. I, Ch. III.
51. *Ibid.*, Ch. IV.
52. *Ibid.*, Bk. IV, Pt. II, Ch. XIX.
53. *Ibid.*, Bk. VI, Pt. II, Ch. I.
54. *Ibid.*, Bk. VII, Pt. I, Ch. XV.
55. *Ibid.*, Bk. VII, Pt. I, Ch. XVI.
56. *Ibid.*, Bk. IV, Pt. I, Ch. X.
57. *Ibid.*, Bk. II, Pt. I, Ch. VI.
58. *Ibid.*, Bk. VI, Pt. I, Ch.
59. *Doctrine of the Mean*, Ch. XX.
60. *Works of Mencius*, Bk. VII, Pt. II, Ch. XVI.
61. *Analects*, Bk. XV, Ch. VIII.
62. *Ibid.*. Bk. VII, Ch. XIV.
63. *Works of Mencius*, Bk. VI, Pt. I, Ch. X.
64. *Ibid.*, Ch. II.
65. *Analects*, Bk. XVII, Ch. II.
66. *Ibid.*. Bk. VI, Ch. XVII.
67. *Works of Mencius*. Bk. IV, Pt. I, Ch. VI. *Vide supra*, p. 62.
68. *Works of Mencius*, Bk. VI, Pt. I, Ch. VII.
69. *Analects*. Bk. IX, Ch. XVII.
70. *Ibid.*. Bk. XV, Ch. XII.
71. *Ibid.*, Ch. III.
72. *Doctrine of the Mean*, Ch. I.
73. *Works of Mencius*, Bk. VI, Pt. I, Ch. VI. *Vide supra*, pp. 62, 78. 81.
74. *Works of Mencius*, Bk. VII, Pt. II, Ch. XXIV.
75. *Ibid.*, Bk. VI, Pt. I, Ch. IV.
76. *Ibid.*, Ch. V.
77. *Doctrine of the Mean*, Ch. I. *Vide supra*, p. 8.

78. *Works of Mencius,* Bk. VII, Pt. II, Ch. XVI.
79. *Doctrine of the Mean,* Ch. I.
80. *Works of Mencius,* Bk. IV, Pt. I, Ch. XI.
81. *Doctrine of the Mean,* Ch. XIII.
82. *Analects,* Bk. IX, Ch. XXX. *Vide supra,* p. 37.
83. *Analects,* Bk. VI, Ch. XV.
84. *Works of Mencius,* Bk. VI, Pt. II, Ch. II.
85. *Great Learning,* Com., Ch. X.
86. *Analects,* Bk. VII, Ch. XXIX.
87. *Works of Mencius,* Bk. VII, Pt. I, Ch. XLII.
88. *Doctrine of the Mean,* Ch. XX.
89. *Analects,* Bk. I, Ch. II.
90. *Doctrine of the Mean,* Ch. XX.
91. *Works of Mencius,* Bk. VII, Pt. II, Ch. XLV
92. *Analects,* Bk. XV, Ch. XXVIII.
93. *Great Learning,* Text. *Vide supra,* p. 6.
94. *Great Learning,* Com. Ch. I.
95. *Analects,* Bk. IV, Ch. XXV.
96. *Ibid.,* Bk. VII, Ch. VI.
97. *Works of Mencius,* Bk. IV, Pt. I, Ch. XXVII.
98. *Doctrine of the Mean,* Ch. XX. *Vide supra,* p. 87.
99. *Analects,* Bk. I, Ch. XII.
100. *Ibid.,* Bk. VI, Ch. XVIII.
101. *Doctrine of the Mean,* Ch. XXV.
102. *Analects,* Bk. VI, Ch. XVI.
103. *Ibid.,* Bk. XI, Ch. I.
104. *Ibid.,* Bk. III, Ch. VIII.
105. *Ibid.,* Ch. IV.
106. *Ibid.,* Bk. VIII, Ch. II.
107. *Ibid.,* Bk. IX, Ch. XI.
108. *Works of Mencius,* Bk. IV, Pt. II, Ch. XXVII.
109. *Analects,* Bk. III, Ch. XVII.
110. *Ibid.,* Bk. XI, Ch. VII.
111. *Ibid.,* Ch. X.
112. *Ibid.,* Bk. III, Ch. XV. *Vide supra,* p. 34.
113. *Analects,* Bk. III, Ch. IV.
114. *Ibid.,* Ch. X.
115. *Works of Mencius,* Bk. II, Pt. I, Ch. II.
116. *Analects,* Bk. XVIII, Ch. IV.
117. *Ibid.,* Bk. VII, Ch. XIII.
118. *Ibid.,* Bk. VIII, Ch. XV.
119. *Ibid.,* Bk. III, Ch. XXIII.
120. *Ibid.,* Ch. XXV.
121. *Ibid.,* Bk. IX, Ch. XIV.
122. *Ibid.,* Bk. XVIII, Ch. IX.
123. *Ibid.,* Bk. XVII, Ch. IV.
124. *Ibid.,* Bk. XI, Ch. XIV.
125. *Doctrine of the Mean,* Ch. XXVII.
126. *Ibid.,* Ch. XXVIII.

127. *Analects.* Bk. XVII, Ch. XI.
128. *Ibid.* Bk. III, Ch. III.
129. *Doctrine of the Mean.* Ch. I.
130. *Ibid.,* Ch. XX.
131. *Works of Mencius.* Bk. V, Pt. II, Ch. II.
132. *Analects.* Bk. III, Ch. XVI.
133. *Works of Mencius.* Bk. II, Pt. I, Ch. VI.
134. *Ibid.*
135. *Analects.* Bk. IX, Ch. XVI.
136. *Ibid.,* Bk. II, Ch. IV.
137. *Doctrine of the Mean.* Ch. VII.
138. *Works of Mencius.* Bk. VII, Pt. Ch. XLVI.
139. *Analects,* Bk. VI, Ch. XX.
140. *Doctrine of the Mean,* Ch. XXVII.
141. *Analects.* Bk. XIX, Ch. VII.
142. *Works of Mencius,* Bk. IV, Pt. II, Ch. XXVI,
143. *Ibid.,* Bk. VI, Pt. II, Ch. XI.
144. *Doctrine of the Mean,* Ch. VI. *Vide supra,* p. 31.
145. *Doctrine of the Mean.* Ch. XXVII.
146. *Analects,* Bk. VII; Ch. XXIX. *Vide Supra,* p. 86.
147. *Analects,* BK. IV, Ch. V.
148. *Ibid.,* Bk. XII, Ch. I,
149. *Ibid.,* Ch. II.
150. *Ibid.,* Ch. III.
151. *Ibid.,* Ch. XXII.
152. *Ibid.,* Bk. XIII, Ch. XIX.
153. *Ibid.,* Bk. XV, Ch. IX.
154. *Ibid.,* Bk. XVII, Ch. VI·
155. *Vide infra,* p. 289.
156. *Analects,* Bk. VI, Ch. V.
157. *Ibid.,* Bk. V, Ch. VII.
158. *Ibid.,* Ch. IV.
159. *Ibid.,* Bk. XIV, Ch. II.
160. *Ibid.,* Bk. XIX, Ch. XV.
161. *Ibid.,* Ch. XVI.
162. *Ibid.,* Bk. V, Ch. XVIII.
163. *Ibid.,* Bk. XIV, Ch. XVIII.
164. *Ibid.,* Ch. XVII.
165. *Works of Mencius,* Bk. VI, Pt. I, Ch. XI.
166. *Ibid.,* Ch. VI.
167. *Ibid.,* Bk. II, Pt. I, Ch. VI.
168. *Ibid.,*
169. *Ibid.,* Bk. VI, Pt. I, Ch. VI.
170. *Ibid.,* Bk. IV, Pt. II, Ch. XIX. *Vide supra,* p. 71.
171. *Analects,* Bk. IV, Ch. II.
172. *Ibid.,* Bk. VII, Ch. XXIX. *Vide supra,* pp. 86, 109.
173. *Analects,* Bk. IV, Ch. IV.
174. *Ibid.,* Ch. VI.
175. *Ibid.,* Bk. XV, Ch. XXXIV.

176. *Ibid.*, Bk. I, Ch. II.
177. *Works of Mencius*, Bk. VI, Pt. I, Ch. VI.
178. *Ibid.*, Bk. VII, Pt. II, Ch. XXXI.
179. *Analects*, Bk. VIII, Ch. VII.
180. *Ibid.*, Bk. XIX. Ch. VI. *Vide supra*, p. 36.
181. *Analects*, Bk. XII, Ch. I.
182. *Ibid.*, Bk. XIII, Ch. XXVII.
183. *Ibid.* Bk. I, Ch. III.
184. *Ibid.*, Bk. VI, Ch. XXIV.
185. *Ibid.*, Bk. IX, Ch. XXVIII.
186. *Ibid.*, Bk. VI, Ch. XXVIII.
187. *Ibid.*, Bk. IV, Ch. III.
188. *Ibid.*, Bk. XV, Ch. VIII. *Vide supra*, p. 74.
189. *Analects*, Bk. VI, Ch. XXI.
190. *Works of Mencius*, Bk. IV, Pt. I, Ch. VIII.
191. *Analects*, Bk. III, Ch. XXVI.
192. *Works of Mencius*, Bk. VI, Pt. I, Ch. XVIII.
193. *Analects*, Bk. IX, Ch. XXVIII.
194. *Ibid.*, Bk. VIII, Ch. X.
195. *Ibid.*, Bk. XVII, Ch. XXIII.
196. *Ibid.*, Bk. II, Ch. XXIV.
197. *Ibid.*, Bk. XVII, Ch. XXIV.
198. *Ibid.*, Bk. V, Ch. VI.
199. *Ibid.*, Bk. XI, Ch. XII.
200. *Ibid.*, Bk. VII, Ch. X.
201. *Doctrine of the Mean*, Ch. X.
202. *Works of Mencius*, Bk. I, Pt. II, Ch. III.
203. *Ibid.*, Bk. IV, Pt. II, Ch. XXIII.
204. *Ibid.*, Bk. II, Pt. I, Ch. II.
205. *Analects*, Bk. XIV, Ch. V.
206. *Great Learning*, Text. *Vide supra*, p. 7.
207. *Doctrine of the Mean*, Ch. XX.
208. *Works of Mencius*, Bk. IV, Pt. I, Ch. II.
209. *Analects*, Bk. VII, Ch. VI. *Vide supra*, p. 89.
210. *Analects*, Bk. VII, Ch. XXIV.
211. *Ibid.*, Bk. I, Ch. VI.
212. *Ibid.*, Ch. II.
213. *Works of Mencius*, Bk. VII, Pt. II. Ch. LXV. *Vide supra*, p. 87.
214. *Analects*, Bk. VI, Ch. XXVIII. *Vide supra*, p. 121.
215. *Analects* Bk. XIX, Ch. XII.
216. *Ibid.*, Bk. VII, Ch. XVII.
217. *Ibid.*, Bk. XVI, Ch. XIII.
218. *Ibid.*, Bk. V, Ch. XII.
219. *Works of Mencius*, Bk. VI, Pt. I, Ch. XX.
220. *Ibid.*, Bk. VII, Pt. II, Ch. V.
221. *Ibid.*, Pt. I, Ch. XLI.
222. *Ibid.*, Ch. XL.
223. *Analects*, Bk. XI, Ch. XXI. *Vide supra*, p. 47.
224. *Works of Mencius*, Bk. III, Pt. I, Ch. IV.

225. *Ibid.,* Bk. V, Pt. II, Ch. I.
226. *Analects,* Bk. XV, Ch. XXVIII.
227. *Ibid.,* Bk. VII, Ch. XXIII.
228. *Ibid.,* Bk. IV, Ch. VII.
229. *Works of Mencius,* Bk. VII, Pt. I, Ch. XLIII. *Vide supra,* p. 32.
230. *Analects,* Bk. VII, Ch. VII.
231. *Ibid.,* Bk. XV, Ch. XXXVIII.
232. *Works of Mencius,* Bk. VII, Pt. II, Ch. XXX.
233. *Analects,* Bk. II, Ch. IX.
234. *Ibid.,* Bk. XI, Ch. III.
235. *Works of Mencius,* Bk. VI, Pt. II, Ch. XVI.
236. *Analects,* Bk. XVII, Ch. XX.
237. *Ibid.,* Bk. II, Ch. XVI.
238. *Ibid.,* Bk. XIV, Ch. VI.
239. *Works of Mencius,* Bk. IV, Pt. II, Ch. XXIV.
240. *Doctrine of the Mean,* Ch. XX.
241. *Analects,* Bk. XX, Ch. III.
242. *Ibid.,* Bk. XII, Ch. XXII.
243. *Ibid.,* Bk. I, Ch. XVI.
244. *Works of Mencius,* Bk. IV, Pt. I, Ch. XV.
245. *Great Learning.* Com., Ch. VI.
246. *Analects,* Bk. XIX, Ch. VIII.
247. *Works of Mencius,* Bk. IV, Pt. II, Ch. XXXII.
248. *Ibid.,* Bk. VI, Pt. II, Ch. II.
249. *Analects,* Bk. XI, Ch. XII. *Vide supra.* p. 114.
250. *Analects,* Bk. XX, Ch. III. *Vide supra,* pp. 64, 131.
251. *Works of Mencius,* Bk. II, Pt. I, Ch. II.
252. *Ibid.,* Bk. VII, Pt. II, Ch. XXXII.
253. *Analects,* Bk. XI, Ch. XX.
254. *Ibid.,* Bk. I, Ch. III. *Vide supra,* p. 111.
255. *Analects,* Bk. XV, Ch. XXVI.
256. *Ibid.,* Bk. V, Ch. IV. *Vide supra,* p. 106.
257. *Analects,* Bk. XI, Ch. XXIV.
258. *Ibid.,* Bk. XIV, Ch. XXI. *Vide supra.* p. 46.
259. *Analects,* Bk. XI, Ch. II.
260. *Ibid.,* Ch. XVIII.
261. *Ibid.,* Bk. V, Ch. III.
262. *Ibid.,* Ch. VII. *Vide supra,* p. 106.
263. *Analects,* Bk. IV, Ch. VII.
264. *Ibid.,* Bk. V, Ch. IX. *Vide supra.* p. 46.
265. *Analects,* Bk. II, Ch. XXII.
266. *Ibid.,* Ch. X. *Vide supra,* p. 29.
267. *Analects,* Bk. XIII, Ch. XXIV.
268. *Great Learning,* Com., Ch. VIII.
269. *Analects,* Bk. V, Ch. I.
270. *Ibid.,* Bk. VIII, Ch. XVI.
271. *Doctrine of the Mean,* Ch. XXIX.
272. *Analects,* Bk. XIX, Ch. X.
273. *Ibid.,* Bk. XIV, Ch. XXVIII.

274. *Ibid.*, Bk. XIX, Ch. X.
275. *Ibid.*, Bk. XVII, Ch. XII. *Vide supra*, p. 39.
276. *Analects*, Bk. XVII, Ch. IV. *Vide supra*, p. 97.
277. *Great Learning*, Com., Ch. III.
278. *Analects*, Bk. XII, Ch. XIX.
279. *Works of Mencius*, Bk. III, Pt. II, Ch. V.
280. *Analects*, Bk. VI, Ch. XI.
281. *Doctrine of the Mean*, Ch. XIV. *Vide supra*, p. 65.
282. *Doctrine of the Mean*, Ch. XXXIII.
283. *Ibid.*, Ch. II.
284. *Analects*, Bk. XIV, Ch. XXIV.
285. *Ibid.*, Bk. IV, Ch. XVI.
286. *Ibid.*, Bk. VII, Ch. XXXVI.
287. *Ibid.*, Bk. II, Ch. XIV.
288. *Ibid.*, Bk. IV, Ch. XI.
289. *Ibid.*, Bk. XII, Ch. XVI.
290. *Ibid.*, Bk. XIII, Ch. XXIII.
291. *Ibid.*, Ch. XXVI.
292. *Ibid.*, Ch. XXV·
293. *Ibid.*, Bk. XIV, Ch. VII.
294. *Ibid.*, Ch. XV, Ch. I.
295. *Ibid.*, Ch. XX.
296. *Ibid.*, Ch. XXXIII.
297. *Ibid.*, Bk. XVI, Ch. VIII.
298. *Works of Mencius*, Bk. V, Pt. II. Ch. VII.
299. *Great Learning*, Text.
300. *Analects*, Bk. I, Ch. II.
301. *Works of Mencius*, Bk. IV, Pt. I, Ch. V.
302. *Great Learning*, Text.
303. *Works of Mencius*, Bk. IV, Pt. I, Ch. XIX.
304. *Great Learning*, Com., Ch. X.
305. *Doctrine of the Mean*, Ch. XXXII.
306. *Great Learning*, Com., Ch. X. *Vide supra*, p. 18.
307. *Great Learning*, Com., Ch. X.
308. *Analects*, Bk. XIX, Ch. XII. *Vide supra*, p. 121.
309. *Doctrine of the Mean*, Ch. XII.
310. *Analects*, Bk. XV, Ch. XXVI. *Vide supra*, p. 132.
311. *Analects*, Bk. XIX, Ch. XI.
312. *Ibid.*, Bk. XIII, Ch. XVII.
313. *Ibid.*, Bk. XV, Ch. XXXIII.
314. *Works of Mencius*, Bk. VI, Pt. I, Ch. XV.
315. *Ibid.*, Ch. XIV.
316. *Ibid.*, Bk. IV, Pt. II, Ch. XII.
317. *Ibid.*, Ch. VI.
318. *Ibid.*, Ch. XI.
319. *Ibid.*, Bk. I, Pt. I, Ch. VII.
320. *Ibid.*, Bk. VI, Pt. II, Ch. I. *Vide supra*, p. 71.
321. *Great Learning*, Com., Ch. II.
322. *Works of Mencius*, Bk. VI, Pt. I, Ch. VII.

323, *Ibid.,* Bk. IV, Pt. I, Ch. VIII.

324. *Analects,* Bk. VI, Ch. XVI. *Vide supra,* p. 92.

325. *Analects,* Bk. XII, Ch. XIII.

326. *Great Learning,* Com., Ch. X.

327. *Ibid. Vide supra,* p. 64.

328. *Works of Mencius,* Bk. IV, Pt. I, Ch. IX.

329. *Analects,* Bk. XVII, Ch. XV.

330. *Ibid.,* Bk. XV, Ch. XXXII.

331. *Great Learning,* Com., Ch. X. *Vide Supra,* p. 17.

332. *Works of Mencius,* Bk. IV, Pt. I, Ch. VII.

333. *Doctrine of the Mean.* Ch. XX.

334. *Ibid.*

335. *Analects,* Bk. II, Ch. XXIII.

336. *Ibid.,* Bk. XVI, Ch. IV and V.

337. *Doctrine of the Mean,* Ch. XX.

338. *Analects,* Bk. XIV, Ch. XI.

339. *Ibid.,* Bk. XIII, Ch. XXV. *Vide supra,* p. 138.

340. *Great Learning,* Text.

341. *Works of Mencius,* Bk. VII, Pt. I, Ch. XLIV.

342. *Ibid.,* Bk. II, Pt. I, Ch. IV.

343. *Ibid.,* Bk. VII, Pt. I. Ch. XXI.

344. *Ibid.,* Ch. IX.

345. *Ibid.,* Bk. VI, Pt. I, Ch. XVII.

346. *Analects,* Bk. I, Ch. XV.

347. *Ibid.,* Bk. IV, Ch. V.

348. *Works of Mencius,* Bk. VI, Pt. I, Ch. XV.

349. *Analects,* Bk. I, Ch. I.

350. *Ibid.,* Bk. XIV, Ch. XXXI.

351. *Ibid.,* Bk. XV, Ch. VV.

352. *Works of Mencius,* Bk. IV, Pt. I, Ch. XXI. *Vide supra,* p. 42.

353. *Analects,* Bk. XV, Ch. XXIV.

354. *Works of Mencius,* Bk. VI, Pt. I, Ch. X

355. *Analects,* Bk. XII, Ch. V.

356. *Ibid.,* Bk. XII, Ch. X.

357. *Works of Mencius,* Bk. VII, Pt. I, Ch. I. *Vide supra,* p. 68.

358. *Works of Mencius,* Bk. VII, Pt. I, Ch. II. *Vide supra,* p. 66.

359. *Analects,* Bk. XI, Ch. XI.

360. *Ibid.,* Bk. XV, Ch. XXVII. *Vide supra,* p. 42.

361. *Analects,* Bk. XIII, Ch. XXIV. *Vide supra,* p.. 134.

362. *Analects,* Bk. IV, Ch. III. *Vide supra,* p. 125.

363. *Great Learning,* Com., Ch. X.

364. *Ibid.*

365. *Analects,* Bk. XII, Ch. XXII.

366. *Ibid.,* Bk. I, Ch. XIX.

367. *Ibid.,* Bk. XVIII, Ch. II.

368. *Works of Mencius,* Bk. IV, Pt. II, Ch. VIII.

369. *Ibid.,* Bk. VII, Pt. I, Ch. XVII.

370. *Ibid.,* Bk. VI, Pt. II, Ch. XIV.

371. *Great Learning,* Com., Ch. X.

372. *Doctrine of the Mean*, Ch. XIV.
373. *Analects*. Bk. XIII, Ch. XVI.
374. *Works of Mencius*, Bk. VII, Pt. II, Ch. XXXI.
375. *Analects*, Bk. XV, Ch. XI.
376. *Ibid.*, Bk. IV, Ch. VIII. *Vide supra*, p. 131.
377. *Analects*, Bk. XIV, Ch. XLII.
378. *Ibid.*, Bk. I, Ch. VI.
379. *Ibid.*, Bk. IX, Ch. XV.
380. *Works of Mencius*, Bk. VI, Pt. II, Ch. XV.
381. *Analects*, Bk. XIV, Ch. XXV.
382. *Ibid.*, Bk. XVII. Ch. XVI.
383. *Doctrine of the Mean*, Ch. XXVIII.
384. *Great Learning*. Text.
385. *Analects*, Bk. XV, Ch. XXXVII.
386. *Ibid.*, Bk. X, Ch. XII.
387. *Ibid.*, Bk. VI, Ch. XX.
388. *Works of Mencius*. Bk. IV, Pt. I, Ch. XVII.
389. *Great Learning*, Com., Ch. X.
390. *Analects*, Bk. IV, Ch. XVI. *Vide supra*, p. 138.
391. *Works of Mencius*, Bk. I, Pt. I, Ch. I.
392. *Ibid.*, Bk. VI. Pt. II, Ch. IV.
393. *Analects*, Bk. IV, Ch. XII.

CHAPTER IV

The Sincerity of Thoughts

Learning and morality, for the most part, are mutually complementary. Learning consists of the knowledge of different fields. It branches out from one origin into myriad ramifications, and so the further one goes, the more complex it becomes. Morality, on the other hand, is the realization of common existence. It reduces itself from myriad ramifications to one common origin, and so the further one goes, the simpler it becomes. This is what Lao-tzŭ meant when he said, "Learning increases as it is pursued, and the Way narrows as it is traveled."

According to the previous sections on the "Illustration of the Way" and the "Illustration of Virtue," the Way can be reduced to five duties of universal obligation and virtue to three universally binding virtues. These in turn can be reduced to the one word, "sincerity." Also, by the "one means" the Way is carried into practice. In the same way Western morality pays the highest respect to God. Therefore "sincerity" is the source of morality, and God is the symbol of the highest respect paid to it.

> The Master said, "...Sincerity is the Way of Heaven, The attainment of sincerity is the Way of men."[1]

Men depend on sincerity for the rectification of their hearts and the cultivation of their persons. And the family, the State and the world depend, respectively, on sincerity for their regulation, government and pacification.

> The Master said, "...All who have the government of the empire and State to attend to have nine standard rules to follow; viz., the cultivation of their persons; the honoring of worthy men; affection towards their relatives; respect towards the great ministers; kind and considerate treatment of the whole body of officials; dealing with the mass of people as children; encouraging the resort of all classes of artisans; indulgent treatment of men from a distance; and the kindly cherishing of the princes of the States...All who have the governments of the empire and State to attend to have the above nine standard rules. It is by the same means that they are carried into practice."[2]

The government of King Wên of the Chou dynasty was regarded as the model of all governments because of the purity of its conduct. By "purity" here the ancients meant incorruptibility and sincerity.

> It is said in the *Book of Songs*, "The ordinances of Heaven, how unceasingly profound they are!" The meaning is that it is thus that Heaven is Heaven. And again, "How illustrious it was, the purity of the virtue of King Wên!" indicating that it was thus that King Wên was what he was. His purity likewise is unceasing.[3]

It is true there is no end to learning. However, learning cannot ultimately be separated from practical application. Morality too derives its value from practice, for it is aimed at the common existence of mankind. But the point is that there must be a driving force, be it application or practice; also, a definite goal must be set. In learning the objective is "sincerity of thoughts"; in morality it is the "knowledge of where to rest."

In the chapter on "The Investigation of Things" we observed that sincerity is the dynamism of the universe. With this dynamism man has initiative and can exist; he has the needed power for life. Therefore "the attainment of sincerity is the Way of men."

So, with this ability to exist, man has life. But in its advancement life cannot be bereft of a goal. And the selection of the objective of man's life is the setting of the will, which is the knowledge of where to rest. When the objective is set, and only then, can a man concentrate his strength so that he will achieve preliminary success and make progress toward the goal. *The Great Learning* puts it this way:

The point where to rest being known, the object of pursuit is then determined; and that being determined, a calm unperturbedness may be attained to. To that calmness will succeed a tranquil repose. In that repose there may be careful deliberation, and that deliberation will be followed by the attainment of the desired end.[4]

In both learning and morality a man must go through this process from the "knowledge of where to rest" to the "attainment of the desired end." He must (1) "illustrate illustrious virtue" himself, (2) attempt to make people in general renovate themselves every day and from day to day, and (3) advance toward the objective of the highest excellence ("to rest in the highest excellence"). Thus will he grasp and attain the real significance and value of human life. This is called the Way of the *Great Learning*. To quote from that work: "What the *Great Learning* teaches is—to illustrate illustrious virtue; to renovate the people; and to rest in the highest excellence."[5]

To "rest", means to hold to the definite objective perpetually and without deviation. This is the setting of the will. As there is no swerving from the goal, so there are rest, calmness, repose, careful deliberation, and finally the attainment of the desired end. All human accomplishments in high scholarship and morality are derived from the determination to be perpetually unswerving.

In the *Book of Songs* it is said, "The imperial capital of a thousand *li* is where the people rest."

In the *Book of Songs*, it is said, "The twittering yellow bird rests on a corner of the mound." The Master said, "When it rests, it knows where to rest. Is it possible that a man should not be equal to this bird?"

In the *Book of Songs* it is said, "Profound was King Wên. With how bright and unceasing a feeling of reverence he regarded his resting-place!" As a sovereign, he rested in benevolence. As a minister, he rested in reverence. As a son, he rested in filial piety. As a father, he rested in kindness. In communication with his subjects, he rested in good faith.[6]

In the above passage, we see how the people love their national territory and therefore choose to make their homes there, just as the yellow bird knows how to pick a corner of the mound for its nest. The aim of both the people and the yellow bird is to select the best place for residence. This selection is much like the perfect moral course; it must be steadfastly adhered to once it has been chosen. If there is vacillation and constant change, the final resting place will never be reached. This is why the *Great Learning*, after referring to "resting in perfect excellence," continued: "The point where to rest being known, the object of pursuit is then determined." In other words, we must first posssess a deep understanding before we can have earnest faith and conduct.

Moreover, the wording of the *Great Learning* is not "may be determined," but "is determined." A great deal of discretion was exercised in adopting this precise phraseology, because while "may be determined" denotes merely a temporary determination, "is determined" denotes a permanent and firm decision. Because the decision is permanent and firm, the state of perfect excellence can be reached and there is no shying away from it

But what is perfect excellence in human virtue? The answer is five-fold: (1) No perfect excellence of a ruler can compare with benevolence; (2) no perfect excellence of a minister can compare with reverence; (3) no perfect excellence of a son can compare with filial piety; (4) no perfect excellence of a father can compare with kindness; (5) no perfect excellence of a friend can compare with faithfulness. These are the basic requisites of collective human existence. We should regard them—benevolence, reverence, filial piety, kindness and faithfulness—as perfect excellence. More, we should choose them and steadfastly adhere to them all of our lives, and we should never deviate from them as we progress to the summit. This is the fruit of our "knowledge of where to rest" and the reward of our efforts to attain the "sincerity of Thoughts." Hence, "He who attains to sincerity is he who chooses what is good and holds fast to it."[7]

True, the acquisition of knowledge depends on the whole process of investigation of things and real judgment in the extension of knowledge. But the ability to engage in this investigation and extension, to know where to rest and attain intelligence, must first of all depend on the wisdom with which man is naturally endowed; i. e., nature. Consider:

> When we have intelligence resulting from sincerity, this condition is to be ascribed to nature.[8]

Man, by using the wisdom with which he is naturally endowed, coupled with his own effort, can reach real judgment and produce faith through study or through arduous struggle. In the *Doctrine of the Mean* we read, "When we have sincerity resulting from intelligence, this condition is to be ascribed to instruction."[9]

This is what the philosopher Chu of the Sung dynasty meant when he said: "...the learning for adults, at the outset of its lessons, instructs the learner, in regard to all things in the world, to proceed from what knowledge he has of their principles and pursue his investigation of them till he reaches the extreme point. After exerting himself in this way for a long time, he will suddenly find himself possessed of a wide and far-reaching penetration. Then, the qualitites of all things, whether external or internal, the subtle or the coarse, will all be apprehended, and the mind, in its entire substance and its relation to things, will be perfectly intelligent."[10]

For man to "reach the extreme point" he must give his nature its full development, and this must proceed from the most complete sincerity. ("Only he who is possessed of the most complete sincerity...can fulfill his own nature."[11]) There must be the most complete sincerity before "a wide and far-reaching penetration" can be "suddenly" possessed. Such is intelligence, and such also is true knowledge. "Whenever mankind studies the principles of a thing," Dr. Sun Yatsen has said, "thinking is first produced. When thinking is penetrated, faith comes. Faith gives rise to strength, with which the principles can be consolidated and well-established." Only what is consolidated and well-established is true knowledge (intelligence).

The greater the sincerity, the greater the intelligence; also, the greater the intelligence, the greater the sincerity. It is like a rolling snowball—the more it is rolled, the larger it becomes. Hence, "...given the sincerity, and there shall be the intelligence; given the intellignce, and there shall be the sincerity."[12]

A man can appreciate Heaven's Way and practice it only (1) by showing the most complete sincerity and fully understanding the principles of his own existence and (2) by extending this to the comprehension of the principles of the common existence of mankind as well as all living things. Once he can appreciate Heaven's Way and practice it, a man can assist the transforming and nourishing powers of Heaven and Earth.

It is only he who is possessed of the most complete sincerity that can exist under heaven, who can fulfill his own nature. Able to fulfill his own nature, he can do the same to the nature of other men. Able to fulfill the nature of other men, he can fulfill the natures of animals and things. Able to fulfill the natures of creatures and things, he can assist the transforming and nourishing powers of Heaven and Earth. Able to assist the transforming and nourishing powers of Heaven and Earth, he may with Heaven and Earth form a ternion.[13]

Modern theology and philosophy teach man to fulfill his own nature. Modern sociology and the humanities teach him to fulfill the nature of others. Modern natural and applied sciences teach him to fulfill the natures of things. As to assistance in the transforming and nourishing powers of Heaven and Earth, this can be included in the modern biological sciences.

The extension of knowledge discussed in a previous chapter is the acquisition of intelligence from sincerity; therefore it has to depend on instruction. The knowledge of Heaven is for the sake of following the example of Heaven, being coequal with Heaven and prevailing over Heaven. The knowledge of destiny is for the sake of setting up destiny, waiting for destiny and changing destiny (revolution). The knowledge of nature is for the sake of cultivating nature, complying with nature and fulfilling nature. The illustration of the Way is for the sake of practicing the Way, enlarging the Way and cultivating the Way. The illustration of virtue is for the sake of resting in benevolence, taking the road of righteousness and upholding propriety. The knowledge of men is for the sake of distinguishing between good and evil. The knowledge of things is for the sake of distinguishing between right and wrong.

From the above it can be seen that wherever there is knowledge, wherever there is intelligence, there is always an object, directed at (1) the perfection of oneself and of things, (2) the cultivation of oneself to tranquillize others, (3) the selection of the good, holding to it and practicing it, and (4) the detection of evil, forsaking it and avoiding it.

Selecting the good and holding to it is the same as so concentrating on goodness that a person cannot bear to abandon it. It is another way of saying "faith," and so the "attainment of sincerity" is the same as faith. "He who attains to sincerity is he who chooses what is good and holds fast to it."[14]

He who has faith, he who chooses the good and holds fast to it, is unchangeable. Conversely, he who cannot be persuaded to have faith is unchangeable. The former has the highest wisdom, and the latter the greatest stupidity; however, their immutability is the same. Confucius put it this way: "There are only the wise of the highest class and the stupid of the lowest class who cannot be changed."[15]

But what about the man who chooses the good but cannot hold fast to it? When he is said to exist, in fact he does not; and when he is said not to exist, he does seem to do so. Even if such a man obtains something (virtue), he cannot extend it; even if he occasionally believes in something (the Way), he cannot adhere to it steadfastly. So, he cannot be said to know the Way or have virtue.

> Tzŭ-chang said, "When a man holds fast to virtue without seeking to enlarge it and believes in the Way without earnestness, what account can be made of his existence or non-existence?"[16]

Ordinary men proceed from intelligence to sincerity in most instances, and so they must rely on instruction. With his particularly high intelligence, the sage proceeds from sincerity to intelligence in most instances, and so he apprehends what is right without effort.

> The Master said, "...He who possesses sincerity hits what is right without an effort and apprehends without thinking; he is the sage who embodies the Way with calm and ease."[17]

This means that the sage, or the man with the most complete sincerity, can combine the Ways of Heaven and men into one. He can make things agree internally and externally. He can act properly, whether dynamically or statically, whether to the left or to the right. He can cultivate true nature and express true feelings without falsehood. This is called the satisfaction of the design of bodily organization.

> Mencius said, "The bodily organs with their functions belong to our Heaven-conferred nature. But a man must be a sage before he can satisfy the design of his bodily organization."[18]

So much for clarifying the essentials of sincerity. Now the question arises: What is the most complete sincerity? To answer this question, let us refer to the principles of physics.

Since sincerity is dynamism, it is like dynamism expressed in waves, such as light waves, sound waves, electric waves and power waves. Light waves can be concentrated on a single point, the focus, which is of course the brightest point. The focus represents "intelligence" in the statement, "Given the sincerity, and there will be the intelligence." When sound waves concentrated on one point are changed into electric waves, they can be broadcast over tremendous distances. Therefore the most complete sincerity can become as great as it is and reach as far as it does, from "endurance out of ceaselessness" to "boundless perpetuity."

When accumulated electric waves penetrate throught the minutest electric current, they produce heat. This corresponds to what is called "warm sincerity." When they are applied to the dissolution of matter, the process is called electrolysis, which accounts for the saying, "Only the most complete sincerity in the world can bring about change." When power waves are concentrated on a single point, they can move other things; they possess irresistible strength and can break anything, no matter how strong. Hence it is said, "Never has there been one possessed of the most complete sincerity who did not move others. Never has there been one who had not sincerity who was able to move others." Again, "Wherever pure sincerity reaches, even gold and stone can be opened."

Thus it can be seen that the "sincerity of thoughts" is the concentration of dynamism. Ordinary men have to make an effort to bring about this concentration, and only a sage can "hit what is right without an effort." What is popularly known as faith and the concentration of the will has the same meaning.

The purpose of religion is faith, and the reason for education is the cultivation of sincerity. The goal of both is to increase inherent strength to perfect oneself and things. So, the spirit of a man with the most complete sincerity is concentrated, his heart is rectified, and the pupils of his eyes are bright. At one glance one knows him to be true and warmhearted. His words are those of faithfulness, sincerity, straightforwardness, and his acts are earnest, respectful, determined. Hence is is said, "What is truly within will be manifested without."[19]

Straightforwardness is a manifestation of sincerity. There is not a child who is not straightforward. As he grows older, however, and as he can distinguish between advantage and disadvantage, the degree of his straightforwardness gradually diminishes. But straightforwardness is a virtue worth retaining, and straightforward friends are beneficial friends. Confucius said, "There are three friendships which are advantageous...friendship with the upright (straightforward); friendship with the sincere; and friendship with the man of much observation."[20]

To Confucius, human beings were by nature straightforward, and he praised the historian Yü for his straightforwardness.

> The Master said, "Man is born for uprightness. If a man loses his uprightness and yet lives, his escape from death is the effect of mere good fortune."[21]
> The Master said, "Truly straightforward was the historiographer Yü. When good government prevailed in his State, he was like an arrow. When bad government prevailed, he was like an arrow."[22]

But straightforwardness can often be a cause of offense to others; at times it can even endanger one's life. Only the enlightened can practice it with peace of mind and with no misgivings. Hui of Liu-hsia was an example.

> Hui of Liu-hsia, being chief criminal judge, was thrice dismissed from his office. Someone said to him, "Is it not yet time for you, Sir, to leave office?" He replied, "Serving men in an upright way, where shall I go and not experience such a thrice-repeated dismissal? If I chose to serve men in a crooked way, what necessity is there for me to leave the country of my parents?"[23]

In contrast, there is the story about Wei-shêng Kao, a warmhearted man. When someone asked him for some vinegar, he provided it after getting it from a neighbor. Some persons regarded him as straightforward, but not Confucius. The Master regarded him as neither sincere nor straightforward because he abused someone else's generosity: "The Master said, 'Who says of Wei-shêng Kao that he is straightforward? One begged some vinegar of him, and he begged it of a neighbor and gave it to the man.'"[24]

The man who proudly calls himself straightforward is prone

to blame or abuse others to show his own courage. He goes beyond the scope of straightforwardness, for he is more eager to impress others with his straightforwardness than his sincerity. Straightforwardness cannot exceed the rules of propriety; when it does, it is rudeness and the exposure of secrets.

> The Master said, "...straightforwardness without the rules of propriety becomes rudeness."[25]
>
> Tzŭ-kung said, "Has the superior man his hatreds also?" The Master said, "He has his hatreds..."
>
> The Master then inquired, "Tz'u, have you also your hatreds?" Tzŭ-kung replied, "...I hate those who make known secrets and think that they are straightforward."[26]

Sincerity can illustrate the Way and complete the full development of nature. So, the establishment of sincerity can lead to the revelation of the heart and the fulfillment of nature. For this reason, sincerity is the source of morality, the power of life, the origin of faith and the foundation of the common existence of mankind. Let us now compare references to sincerity in the *Doctrine of the Mean* with references to God in the Christian Bible.

1. "Sincerity is the Way of Heaven." We read in the *Doctrine of the Mean*, "The attainment of sincerity is the Way of men." This corresponds to the Christian belief that God is in heaven, that God (Christ) is the Way. The implied exhortation is clear: Men should copy the example of Heaven (God, or the God-man Christ); they can appreciate Heaven's Way and should practice it.

The preceding chapter explains in detail what Heaven and the Way are. Thus "sincerity" is the dynamism with unceasing vitality in the universe from which all things derive their life. ("Sincerity is the fulfillment of oneself.") Without dynamism there is nothing ("Without sincerity there would be nothing.") For this reason, sincerity is the controller of all things, their creator (God). Sincerity can rule over everything (God is King), control everything and judge everything (God is the Judge). Sincerity, then, is what is referred to as "God" or "Heavenly Father" in the Old and New Testaments. Thus sincerity is God in the abstract, and God is the concrete form and personification of sincerity.

Sincerity is the fulfillment of oneself, and its Way is that by which man must direct himself.

Sincerity is the end and beginning of things; without sincerity there would be nothing. On this account the superior man regards the attainment of sincerity as the most excellent thing.[27]

2. "Sincerity is the end and beginning of things." In other words, the process of life—from accumulation and formation to dissolution—is controlled by sincerity; in the Christian context, this is expressed in the belief that God is life. The process from a thing's existence to non-existence on this earth is called the process of its life. The birth and destruction of things, the life and death of men, the beginning and end of affairs, the existence and extinction of nations—all can be described by this process, whose seven stages are stated in this passage:

Next to the above is he who cultivates to the utmost the minute parts of goodness in him. From those he can attain to the possession of sincerity. This sincerity becomes apparent. From being apparent, it becomes manifest. From being manifest, it becomes brilliant. Brilliant, it affects others. Affecting others, they are changed by it. Changed by it, they are transformed. It is only he who is possessed of the most complete sincerity that can exist under heaven, who can transform.[28]

The progression from existence to non-existence is a process of the transformation of dynamism and the accumulation and diffusion of matter. Dynamism manifested in a state of equilibrium is what man calls matter. Dynamism manifested in a state of free fluctuation is what man calls spirit. Thus matter and spirit are the two essential factors for the formation of life; neither is dispensable. The rise and decline of either depends on the proportion of time and space involved.

Now, the universe itself is another name for the combination of time and space. The two Chinese characters which make up the equivalent of "universe" are *yü* ann *chou*. According to an ancient definition, "Up, down and the four directions are called *yü* and ancient and modern times *chou*.[29] Up, down and the four directions, of course, constitute three-dimensional space; ancient and modern times, the fourth dimension, time. Our Chinese ancients were far ahead of Einstein in making this discovery. Hence it is said, that (1) matter and spirit are the essence of ending in equilibrium and harmony; (2) time and space are the utility of life, ending in proper conduct; and (3) with the coordination of its essence and utility, life is brought to fruition, enlarged and prolonged, ending in the Mean. These are the principles of life.

3. As we noted above, sincerity is faith (in Christian belief, God is faith). It corresponds to the selection of the good and holding fast to it to the point of being unable to bear abandoning it (God is good).

> The Master said, "...He who attains to sincerity is he who chooses what is good and firmly holds fast to it."[30]
> The Master said, "...There is a way to the attainment of sincerity in one's self; if a man does not understand what is good, he will not attain sincerity in himself."[31]
> Mencius said, "If a superior man does not have faith, how shall he take a firm hold of things?"[32]

4. Sincerity is intelligence (God is wisdom), and so "given the sincerity, and there will be the intelligence (God is light). "He who has the most complete sincerity can have prescience," like a spirit (God is spirit).

> It is characteristic of the most entire sincerity to be able to fore-know. When a nation is about to flourish, there are sure to be happy omens; and when it is about to perish, there are sure to be unlucky omens. Such things are seen in the milfoil and tortoise and affect the movements of the four limbs. When calamity or happiness is about to come, the good shall certainly be foreknown by him, and the evil also. Therefore the individual possessed of the most complete sincerity is like a spirit.[33]

5. Sincerity is love (God is love; God is kind). It perfects oneself and things. It is benevolence and wisdom. Therefore it shows universal love and all-out protection (God is refuge) by treating people as brothers and sisters, and things as companions.

> Sincerity is not only the fulfillment of our own being; it is that by which we also fulfill the nature of things. The fulfillment of our being is perfect virtue. The fulfillment of the nature of things is knowledge. These are the powers or faculties of our being. They combine the inner or subjective and outer or objective use of the power of the mind. Therefore, with sincerity, everything done is right.[34]

Mencius said, "All things are already complete in us.

"There is no greater delight than to be conscious of sincerity on self-examination.

"If one acts with a vigorous effort at the law of reciprocity. one cannot be closer to the search for benevolence."[35]

6. Sincerity is strength (God is strength), and so it can move without cessation. It can be determined without fear and can destroy anything, however strong. It is popularly said, "Wherever pure sincerity reaches, even gold and stone can be opened."

Hence the most complete sincerity does not cease. Not ceasing, it continues long.[36]

"Never has there been one possessed of complete sincerity who did not move others. Never has there been one who had not sincerity who was able to move others."[37]

Points 4, 5 and 6 above dealt with the three virtues universally binding—wisdom, benevolence and courage. Clearly the power for carrying them into practice is sincerity.

7. Sincerity can reveal truth (God is truth). The words "true" and "truly" used in the vernacular indicate the genuine absence of falsehood. So, sincerity is the source of truth and the justice (God is righteousness) and mutual confidence indispensable to the existence of man with man.

What is meant by "making the thoughts sincere" is the allowing no self-deception, as when we hate a bad smell and as when we love what is beautiful. This is called self-enjoyment. Therefore the superior man must be watchful over himself when he is alone.[38]

8. Sincerity can become great (God is great), and so it can help adjust the great invariable relations of mankind and establish the great fundamental virtues of mankind.

It is only the individual possessed of the most entire sincerity that can exist under heaven, who can adjust the great invariable relations of mankind and establish the great fundamental virtues of mankind, and know the transforming and nourishing operations of Heaven and Earth; shall this individual have anything beyond his sincerity to depend on?

His benevolence is genuine. His depth is like an abyss. His vastness is like Heaven. Who can have this knowledge except one who is possessed of true wisdom, a sage's knowledge and the comprehension of Heavenly virtue?[39]

9. As sincerity can give nature its full development (God is almighty), it can give the nature of all things its full development. In this way it assists the transforming and nourishing powers of Heaven and Earth, since there is nothing it cannot do.

> It is only he who is possessed of the most complete sincerity that can exist under heaven, who can fulfill his own nature. Able to fulfill his own nature, he can do the same to the natures of other men. Able to fulfill the natures of other men, he can fulfill the natures of animals and things. Able to fulfill the natures of creatures and things, he can assist the transforming and nourishing powers of Heaven and Earth. Able to assist the transforming and nourishing powers of Heaven and Earth, he may with Heaven and Earth form a ternion.[40]

10. Sincerity can transform (God is power), and so man can be moved by it. He also takes delight in being assimilated by it. This accounts for the sayings: "The greater energies are seen in mighty transformations;" There is transformation where the superior man passes;" and "A sage is one who is great and who can transform." All these point to the inconceivably great strength of sincerity, which "without any display...becomes manifest; without any movement...produces changes; and without any effort...accomplishes its end."[41] As we read in the *Doctrine of the Mean*: "...It is only he who is possessed of the most complete sincereity that can exist under heaven, who can transform."[42]

In the foregoing ten points we have attempted to clarify and distill the detailed and exhaustive study of sincerity made in the *Doctrine of the Mean*. Likewise, in the Christian Bible we can find similar clarifications of the conception of God. We can see that the teachings of both Confucius and Jesus Christ agree in that they make clear the real meaning of human life; both base it on the common existence of mankind. Truth is no different, whether it emanates from the Orient or from the Occident. The purposes and principles are the same wherever men translate into practice their comprehension of the Way of Heaven.

The only differences are in point of time and space. Confucius was born 550 years before Christ, and the peoples of the two areas concerned observed different customs and functioned on different levels of knowledge.   This accounts for Confucius adopting the educational formula, and Christ the religious, for the elucidation of their respective truths.   All in all, the principles upheld by both sages are fundamentally the same.   For religion is the cultivation of the Way, the illustration of virtue and the foundation of instruction.   Since both Confucius and Christ aimed at the cultivation of the Way, there is no distinction between them despite their geographical difference.   Hence it is said in the *Doctrine of the Mean,* "The cultivation of the Way is called instruction."[43]

Auguste Comte, the French philosopher, divied the development of human knowledge into three stages—religious, metaphysical and testimonial.   This accords with the above observation.

The sincerity of thoughts is the premise of the rectification of hearts and the foundation of self-cultivation.   It is required by any religion and it is indispensable to anyone who cultivates the Way.   The attitude taken by Confucius toward the Way was: "All things are nourished together without their injuring one another, and the Ways are pursued together without any collision among them."[44]

In Confucius' system of philosophy there was absolutely no room for bigotry.   This is why the Chinese people find it easier than many others to accept truths, why they possess more widely the ideals of common humanity, why they seek to be like others in the main and yet tolerate minor differences with them.   This is indeed the Way that is consistent with divine justice and human nature.   For unconscious obedience to bias takes place when ignorance is taken for knowledge and pressure is brought to bear on others to follow blindly.

Sincerity is the source of morality, and intelligence the penetration of learning.   When the two are complementary to each other, there is no limit to advancement.   If there is only intelligence without sincerity, it is not true intelligence; and if there is only sincerity without intelligence, it is not true sincerity either.   Only true knowledge and penetrating judgment can produce faith and strength.   Hence, "Their knowledge being complete, their thoughts are sincere."[45]

Following are references to the Bible from which the above-mentioned characteristics of God have been taken. God is:

Almighty	Gen. 17: 1; 28: 3; 35: 11; Psa. 91: 1; Job 36: 5; Psa. 91: 1.
Creator	Gen. 1:1, 2, 7; John 1: 3; Isa. 40: 26, 28; 65: 17; Col. 1: 16; Eph. 2: 10.
Father	John 4: 23; 5: 30, 36; 17: 25; Matt. 6: 8, 9; Luke 23: 46.
Faithful	Psa. 119: 86, 90; 1 Peter 4: 19; 11 Thes. 3: 3; 1 Cor. 1: 9.
Good	John 10: 11; Psa. 23: 6; 31: 19; 34: 8; 33: 5; 52: 1; 104: 23; Psa. 107: 1.
Judge	Psa. 50: 6; Acts 17: 31; 11 Cor. 5: 10.
King	Psa. 50: 6; John 19: 14; 1 Tim. 6: 15; Rev. 17: 14.
Life	John 3: 16; 4: 14; 6: 40; 14: 6; 1 John 5: 11.
Light	John 1: 9; 8: 12; Matt. 5: 14; 1 John 1: 5; Isa. 60: 20; Psa. 27: 1; 119: 105.
Love	John 3: 16; 13: 34, 35; Matt. 5: 44; 22: 38; Mark 12: 30; 1 John 4: 7, 8; Rm. 8: 35-39; 1 Peter 4: 8; 1 Cor. 13: 3, 7, 13.
Power	Matt. 19: 26; 28: 18; Luke 1: 37; Col. 2: 10; Psa. 62: 11; 11 Sam. 22: 23.
Refuge	Deut. 33: 27; Psa. 46: 1, 7; 57: 1; 62: 7.
Righteousness	Matt. 25: 46; Psa. 1: 6; 37: 17; 11: 7; Prov. 12: 28; 14: 34.
Savior	Matt. 1: 21; Luke 2: 11; Acts 5: 31; 13: 23; Eph. 5: 23; John 4: 42; 1 John 4: 14; 1 Tim. 1: 15; 11 Tim. 1: 10; 11 Peter 1: 1, 11; 2: 20; 3: 2, 18.
Spirit	John 4: 23, 24; 3: 5, 6; Acts 5: 32; Gen. 1: 2; 1 Cor. 6: 19; 1 Thes. 4: 8.
Strength	Psa. 46: 1; 73: 26; 11 Sam. 22: 33.
Truth	Psa. 110: 142, 151, 160; 100: 5; 1 King 17: 24; John 6: 32; 14: 6; John 16: 13; 17: 17; 18: 37; 1: 17.
Way	John 14: 6; Isa. 53: 8, 9.
Wisdom	Col. 2: 3; Rm. 11: 33; Prov. 1: 7; 3: 7, 9, 10; Jan. 3: 13-17.

Footnotes for Chapter IV

1. *Doctrine of the Mean*, Ch. XX.
2. *Ibid.*
3. *Ibid.*, Ch. XXVI.
4. *Great Learning*, Text.
5. *Ibid.*, *Vide supra*, p. 6.
6. *Great Learning*, Com., Ch. III.
7. *Doctrine of the Mean*, Ch. XX.
8. *Ibid.*, Ch. XXI. *Vide supra*, p. 8.
9. *Doctrine of the Mean*, Ch. XXI.
10. Quoted from the philosopher Chu.
11. *Ibid.*, Ch. XXII. *Vide supra*, p. 8.
12. *Doctrine af the Mean*, Ch. XXI.
13. *Ibid.*, Ch. XXII.
14. *Ibid.*, Ch. XX.
15. *Analects*, Bk. XVII, Ch. III.
16. *Ibid.*, Bk. XIX. Ch. II.
17. *Doctrine of the Mean*, Ch. XX.
18. *Works of Mencius*, Bk. VII, Pt. I, Ch. XXXVIII.
19. *Great Learning* Com., Ch. VI.
20. *Analects*, Bk. XVI, Ch. IV.
21. *Ibid.*, Bk. VI, Ch. XVII. *Vide supra*, p. 76.
22. *Analects*, Bk. XV, Ch. VI.
23. *Ibid.*, Bk. XVIII, Ch. II. *Vide supra*, p. 164.
24. *Analects*, Bk. V, Ch. XXIII.
25. *Ibid.*, Bk. VIII, Ch. II.
26. *Ibid.*, Bk. XVII, Ch. XXIV. *Vide supra*, p. 113.
27. *Doctrine of the Mean*, Ch. XXV.
28. *Ibid.*, Ch. XXIII.
29. *Vide supra*, p. 22.
30. *Doctrine of the Mean*. Ch. XX. *Vide supra*, pp. 191-2.
31. *Doctrine of the Mean*, Ch. XX.
32. *Works of Mencius*, Bk. VI, Pt. II, Ch. XII.
33. *Doctrine of the Mean*, Ch. XXIV.
34. *Ibid.*, Ch. XXV. *Vide supra*, p. 91.
35. *Works of Mencius*, Bk. VII, Pt. I, Ch. IV.
36. *Doctrine of the Mean*, Ch. XXVI.
37. *Works of Mencius*, Bk. IV, Pt. I, Ch. XIII.
38. *Great Learning*, Com., Ch. VI.
39. *Doctrine of the Mean*, Ch. XXXII.
40. *Ibid.*, Ch. XXII. *Vide supra*, p. 191.
41. *Doctrine of the Mean*, Ch. XXVI.
42. *Ibid.*, Ch. XXIII.
43. *Ibid.*, Ch. I.
44. *Ibid.*, Ch. XXX.
45. *Great Learning*, Text.

CHAPTER V

The Rectification of Hearts

Once thoughts have become sincere, the three virtues universally binding—wisdom, benevolence and courage—establish their foundation. At the same time, so much vitality is generated that it flows ceaselessly and transforms deeply. When static, it can recognize the great and see the distant; when in motion, it can determine the direction and act in its due degree.

All things in the universe are constantly moving. When two or more forces encounter one another, they have the inevitable tendency to be influenced by their opposites to a certain extent; this, whether they are rising or declining. The encounter inevitably changes their original direction, and this change may cause the original objective (rest) to be missed. Therefore, adjustments must be made as time goes on. For example, in a ship the helm provides the means by which the ship's direction is constantly adjusted. Man's helm is his heart. Since man's inherent strength is fully developed by the sincerity of his thoughts, his external strength, too, is controlled by this development. But if the heart has a definite direction, it still can return to normal even if an external force exerts a temporary influence. This underlines the importance of the rectification of hearts.

Since man is an animal endowed with emotions, he cannot be free from feelings of pleasure, anger, sorrow or joy. When these emotions are not stirred, a state of equilibrium exists. When they are stirred and act in their due degree, a state of harmony exists.

> While there are no stirrings of pleasure, anger, sorrow, or joy, the mind may be said to be in the state of equilibrium. When those feelings have been stirred and they act in their due degree, there ensues what may be called the state of harmony. This equilibrium is the great root from which grow all the human actings in the world, and this harmony is the universal path which they all should pursue. Let the states of equilibrium and harmony exist in perfection, and a happy order will prevail and all things will be nourished and flourish.

In the first chapter which is given above,

> Tzŭ-ssŭ states the views which had been handed down to him, as the basis of his discourse. First, it shows clearly how the Way is to be traced to its origin in Heaven and is unchangeable, while the subatance of it is provided in ourselves and may not be departed from. Next, it speaks of the importance of preserving and nourishing this and of exercising a watchful self-scrutiny with reference to it. Finally, ti speaks of the meritorious achievements and transforming influence of sages and spiritual men in their highest extent. The wish of Tzŭ-ssŭ was that hereby the learner should direct his thoughts inwards, and by searching in himself, there find these truths, so that he might put aside all outward temptations appealing to his selfishness and fill up the measure of the goodness which is natural to him. This chapter is what the writer Yang called "The sum of the whole work." In the ten chapters which follow, Tzŭ-ssŭ quotes the words of the Master to complete the meaning of this.[1]

Only the sage who is possessed of the most complete sincerity and who can give nature its full development can make his feelings act in their due degree after they have been stirred (practice it with natural ease). Ordinary men will have to make adjustments at all times (practice it from a desire for their advantages or by strenuous effort), in order to return to the state of rectification.

> The Master said, "...He who possesses sincerity hits what is right without effort and apprehends without thinking;...he is the sage who embodies the Way with calm and ease."[2]

The direction of the heart can be swayed by the incitement of feelings. These conditions have been given:

What is meant by "The cultivation of the person depends on the rectifying of the mind" may be thus illustrated: If a man be under the influence of passion, he will be incorrect in his conduct. He will be the same, if he is under the influence of terror, or under the influence of fond regard, or under that of sorrow and distress.

When the mind is not present, we look and do not see; we listen and do not hear; we eat and do not know the taste of what we eat.

This is what is meant by saying that the cultivation of the person depends on the rectifying of the mind.[3]

Feelings of passion, terror, fond regard, sorrow and distress are unavoidable in a person's ordinary daily routine—and the influences they produce are very substantial. Passion makes the mind wild. Terror stupefies it. Fond regard deludes it. Sorrow and distress can break it. Wildness and delusion have the effect of expanding the mind, while stupefaction and breakdown have the effect of contraction. Both types of result are psychologically abnormal and can cause a person to lose his initiative and state of rectification.

What is meant by "The regulation of one's family depends on the cultivation of his person" is this: Men are partial where they feel affection and love: partial where they despise and dislike; partial where they stand in awe and reverence; partial where they feel sorrow and compassion; partial where they are arrogant and rude. Thus it is that there are few men in the world, who love and at the same time know the bad qualities of the object of their love, or who hate and yet know the excellences of the object of their hatred.

Hence it is said, in the common adage, "A man does not know the wickedness of his son; he does not know the richness of his growing rice."

This is what is meant by saying that if the person be not cultivated, a man cannont regulate his family.[4]

Love, dislike, sorrow, reverence and arrogance are commonly felt by all men and frequently have an influence on their psychological condition. Most persons can only see what is good in those whom they love and revere or with whom they commiserate; they can only see what is ugly and evil in those whom they hate and despise. This is distorted psychology, and it gives rise to bias for it is generally due to failure to keep to the Mean. The result:

truth is confused, facts are distorted, incorrect judgments are made, improper conduct is pursued—unwittingly one is plunged into the error of unfairness. Hence, "there are few men in the world, who love and at the same time know the bad qualities of their love, or who hate and yet know the excellences of the object of their hatred."

The above-mentioned mistakes can be corrected if the mind regains some measure of self-control, if a person puts himself in the position of others so that he will not do to them what he would not want them to do to himself. This is the Way of faithfulness and reciprocity.

The mind's loss of its proper direction can be ascribed to desire and feeling. This is the case, for instance, when a hungry and thirsty man does not get the proper taste from what he eats and drinks.

> Mencius said, "The hungry think any food sweet, and the thirsty think the same of any drink, and thus they do not get the right taste of what they eat and drink. The hunger and thirst, in fact, injure their palate. And is it only the mouth and belly which are injured by hunger and thirst? Men's minds are also injured by them.
>
> "If a man can prevent the evils of hunger and thirst from being any evils to his mind, he need not have any sorrow about not being equal to other men."[5]

Even if reason can control feeling and restrain desire, reason itself has to be regulated, so that it can act in its due degree. In his answer to a question put to him by King Hsüan of Ch'i, Mencius said,

> "...By weighing, we know what things are light and what heavy. By measuring it, we know what things are long and short. The relations of all things may be thus determined, and it is of the greatest importance to estimate the motions of the mind. I beg Your Majesty to measure it."[6]

We weigh and measure things to determine their proper weights and measurements, to make certain that there is neither too much nor too little. In the cultivation of the mind this is of utmost importance, although difficult to accomplish.

The Master said, "There are some with whom we may study in common, but we shall find them unable to go along with us to the Way. Perhaps we may go on with them to the Way, but we shall find them unable to get established in it along with us. Or if we may get so established along with them, we shall find them unable to weigh the occurring events along with us."[7]

Desire, we have noted, can cause the mind to lose its proper direction. It follows then that the best way to nourish the mind is to reduce desires. With the reduction of desires, the temptation of external forces is decreased while the control of internal forces is increased. A popular saying points out, "When there is no desire, there is uprightness." Where there is uprightness, the temptations of external forces can be controlled.

Mencius said, "To nourish the mind there is nothing better than to make desires few. Here is a man whose desires are few: in some things he may not be able to keep his heart, but they will be few. Here is a man whose desires are many; in some things he may be able to keep his heart, but they will be few."[8]

The Master said, "I have not seen an upright man." Someone replied, "There is Shên Ch'ang." "Ch'ang," said the Master, "is under the influence of his desires; how can he be pronounced upright?"[9]

Men have little difficulty in learning how to protect external things. They know fairly well how to nourish their persons. But they seem to overlook easily how to nourish their minds. Mencius has discussed this subject very extensively.

Mencius said, "anybody who wishes to cultivate the *t'ung* or the *tzŭ*, which may be grasped with one or both hands, knows by what means to nourish them. In the case of their own persons, men do not know by what means to nourish them. Is it to be supposed that their regard for their own persons is inferior to their regard for a *t'ung* or *tzŭ*? Their want of reflection is extreme."[10]

Mencius said, "There is no part of himself which a man does not love, and as he loves all, so he must nourish all. There is not an inch of skin which he does not love, and so there is not an inch of skin which he will not nourish. For examining whether his way of nourishing is good or not, what other rule is there but this, that he determines by reflecting on himself where it should be applied?

"Some parts of the body are noble, and some ignoble; some great, some small. The great must not be injured for the small, nor the noble for the ignoble. He who nourishes the little belonging to him is a little man, and he who nourishes the great is a great man.

"Here is a plantation-keeper, who neglects his *wu* and *chia* and cultivates his sour jujube trees; he is a poor plantation-keeper.

"He who nourishes one of his fingers, neglecting his shoulders or his back, without knowing that he is doing so, is a man who resembles a confused person who cannot attend to his sickness.

"A man who only eats and drinks is counted mean by others; because he nourishes what is little to the neglect of the great.

"If a man, fond of his eating and drinking, were not to neglect what is of more importance, how should his mouth and belly be considered as no more than an inch of skin?"[11]

Mencius said, "Here is a man whose fourth finger is bent and cannot be stretched out straight. It is not painful, nor does it incommode his business, and yet if there be anyone who can make it straiget, he will not think the way from Ch'in to Ch'u far to go to him; because his finger is not like the finger of other people.

"When a man's finger is not like those of other people, he knows to feel dissatisfied, but if his mind is not like that of other people, he does not know to feel dissatisfaction. This is called ignorance of the relative importance of things."[12]

Mencius said, "The trees of the Niu mountain were once beautiful. Being situated, however, in the borders of a large State, they were hewn down with axes and bills; and could they retain their beauty? Still through the activity of the vegetative life day and night and the nourishing influence of the rain and dew, they were not without buds and sprouts springing forth, but then came the cattle and goats and browsed upon them. To these things is owing the bare and stripped appearance of the mountain, and when people now see it, they think it was never finely wooded. But is this the nature of the mountain?

"And so also of what properly belongs to man; shall it be said that the mind of any man was without benevolence and righteousness? The way in which a man loses his proper goodness of mind is like the way in which the trees are denuded by axes and bills. Hewn down day after day, can it—the mind—retain its beauty? But there is a development of its life day and night, and in the calm air of the morning, just between night and day, the mind feels in a degree those desires and aversions which are proper to humanity, but the feeling is not strong, and it is fettered and destroyed by what takes place during the day. This fettering takes place again and again, the restorative influence of the night is not sufficient to preserve the proper goodness of the mind; and when this proves insufficient for that purpose, the nature becomes not much different from that of the irrational animals, and when people now see it, they think that it never had those powers which I assert. But does this condition represent the feelings proper to humanity?

"Therefore, if it receives its proper nourishment, there is nothing which will not grow. If it loses its proper nourishment, there is nothing which will not decay.

"Confucius said, 'Hold it fast, and it remains with you. Let it go, and you lose it. Its outgoing and incoming cannot be defined as to time and place.' Is this not said only of the mind?"[13]

Just as the reduction of desires is the negative method of nourishing the mind, so the practice of benevolence only is the positive method. With the successful reduction of his desires, man can be said to have achieved only his self-completion. But in a man's dealings with another man, feeling and desire come from both sides, and so it takes adjustments on both sides at all times to satisfy each man's requirements. Therefore the practice of benevolence is better than the mere reduction of desires.

Man's trouble lies in a lack of strength to control his mind, which is permitted to run riot until a mishap befalls it. It is like an unmanaged ship or car; the one invites shipwreck, the other careens off a precipice. And after the catastrophe, it is too late to find a remedy.

Mencius said, "Benevolence is man's mind, and righteousness is man's path.

"How lamentable it is to neglect the path and not pursue it, to lose his mind and not know to seek it again!

"When man's fowls and dogs are lost, they know to seek for them again, but they lose their mind and do not know to seek for it.

"The great end of learning is nothing else but to seek for the lost mind."[14]

This means that the method of learning is to hold (seek for) the mind and to place it under one's own control rather than under the control of others. Only the ability to resist external temptations and pressures without being moved by them can be called the achievement of rectification. Mencius had a great deal to say about the "unperturbed mind." Consider this passage:

Kung-sun Ch'ou asked Mencius, saying, "Master, if you were

to be appointed a high noble and the prime minister of Ch'i, so as to be able to carry your Way into practice, though if you should thereupon raise the ruler to the headship of all the other princes and even to imperial dignity, it would not be wondered at. In such a position would your mind be perturbed or not?" Mencius replied, "No. At forty I attained to an unperturbed mind."

Ch'ou said, "Since it is so with you, my Master, you are far beyond Mêng Pen." "It is not difficult," said Mencius. "The scholar Kao had attained to an unperturbed mind at an earlier period of life than I did."

Ch'ou asked, "Is there any way to an unperturbed mind?" The answer was "Yes."

"Pei-kung Yu had this way of nourishing his courage: He did not flinch from any thrusts at them. He considered that the slightest push from anyone was the same as if he were beaten before the crowds in the market-place, and that what he would not receive from a common man in his loose large garments of coarse cloth, neither would he receive from a prince of ten thousand chariots. He viewed stabbing a prince of ten thousand chariots just as stabbing a fellow dressed in coarse cloth. He feared not any of all the princes. A bad word addressed to him he always returned.

"Mêng Shih-shêh had this way of nourishsng his courage: He said, 'I look upon not conquering and conquering in the same way. To measure the enemy and then advance; to calculate the chances of victory and then engage: this is to stand in awe of the opposing force. How can I make certain of conquering? I can only rise superior to all fear.'

"Mêng Shih-shêh resembled the philosopher Tsêng. Pei-kung Yu resembled Tzŭ-hsia. I do not know to the courage of which of the two the superiority should be ascribed, but yet Mêng Shih-shêh attended to what was of the greater importance.

"Formerly the philosopher Tsêng said to Tzŭ-hsiang, 'Do you love courage? I heard an account of great courage from the Master. It speaks thus: 'If, on self-examination, I find that I am not upright, shall I not be in fear even of a poor man in his loose garments of coarse cloth? If, on self-examination, I find that I am upright, I will go forward against thousands and tens of thousands'.

"Yet, what Mêng Shih-shêh maintained, being merely his physical strength, was after all inferior to what the philosopher Tsêng maintained, which was indeed of the greatest importance."

Kung-sun Ch'ou said, "May I venture to ask an explanation from you, Master, of how you maintain an unperturbed mind and how the philosopher Kao does the same?" Mencius answered, "Kao says, 'What is not attained in words is not to be sought for in the mind; what produces dissatisfaction in the mind is not to be helped by passion-effort.' This last,—when there is unrest in the mind, not to seek for relief from passion-effort, may be conceded. But not to seek in the mind for what is not attained in words cannot be conceded. The will is the leader of the passion-effort. The passion-nature pervades and animates the body. The will is first and chief, and the passion-nature is subordinate to it. Therefore I say, maintain firm the will and do no violence to the passion-nature."

Ch'ou observed, "Since you say, 'The will is chief and the passion-nature is subordinate,' how do you also say, 'Maintain firm the will and do no violence to the passion-nature'?" Mencius replied, "When it is the will alone which is active, it moves the passion-nature. When it is the passion-nature alone which is active, it moves the will. For instance, now, in the case of a man falling or running, that is from the passion-nature, and yet it moves the mind."

"I venture to ask," said Ch'ou again, "wherein you, Master, surpass Kao." Mencius told him, "I understand words. I am skillful in nourishing my vast, flowing passion-nature."

Ch'ou pursued, "I venture to ask what you mean by your vast, flowing passion-nature." The reply was, "It is difficult to describe it.

"This is the passion-nature: It is exceedingly great and exceedingly strong. Being nourished by rectitude and sustaining no injury, it fills up all between heaven and earth.

"This is the passion-nature: It is the mate and assistant of righteousness and the Way. Without it there is a serious inadequacy.

"It is produced by the accumulation of righteous deeds; it is not to be obtained by incidental acts of righteousness. If the mind does not feel complacency in the conduct, the nature becomes seriously inadequate. I therefore said, 'Kao has never understood righteousess, because he makes it something external.'

"There must be the constant practice of this righteousness, but without the object of nourishing the passion-nature. Let not the mind forget its work, but let there be no assisting the growth of that nature. Let us not be like the man of Sung. There was a man of Sung, who was grieved that his growing rice was not longer, and so he pulled it up. Having done this, he returned home, looking very stupid, and said to his people, 'I am tired today, I have been helping the rice to grow long.' His son ran to look at it, and found the rice all withered. There are few in the world today, who do not deal with their passion-nature as if they were assisting the rice to grow long. Some indeed consider it of no benefit to them and let it alone; they do not weed their rice. They who assist it to grow long pull out their rice. What they do is not only of no benefit to the nature, but it also injures it."

Kung-sun Ch'ou further asked, "...What do you mean by saying that you understand words?" Mencius replied, "When words are one-sided, I know how the mind of the speaker is clouded over. When words are extravagant, I know how the mind is fallen and sunk. When words are all-depraved, I know how the mind has departed from principle. When words are evasive, I know how the mind is at its wit's end. These evils, growing in the mind, do injury to government, and, displayed in the government, are hurtful to the conduct of affairs. When a sage shall again arise, he will certainly follow my words."

On this Ch'ou observed, "Tsai Wo and Tzŭ-kung were eloquent. Jan Niu, the disciple Min and Yen Yüan could speak skillfully about virtuous conduct. Confucius united the qualities of the disciples in himself, but still he said, "In the matter of speeches I am not competent.' Then, Master, have you attained to be a sage?"

Mencius said, "Oh, what words are these? Formerly Tzŭ-kung asked Confucius, saying, 'Master, are you a sage?' Confucius answered him, 'A sage is what I cannot rise to. I learn without satiety and teach without being tired.' Tzŭ-kung said, 'To learn without satiety is wisdom, and to teach without being tired is benevolence. Benevolent and wise, Master, you are a sage.' Even Confucius would not regard himself as a sage. What words were these?"

Ch'ou said, "Formerly I once heard this: Tzŭ-hsia, Tzŭ-yu and Tzŭ-chang had each one part of the sage. Jan Niu, the disciple Min and Yen Yüan had all the parts, but in small proportions. I venture to ask, with which of these are you pleased to rank yourself?"

Mencius replied, "Let us drop speaking about these, if you please."

Ch'ou then asked, "What do you say of Po-i and Yi Yin?" "Their Ways were different from mine," said Mencius. "Not to serve a prince whom he did not esteem, nor command a people whom he did not approve; in a time of good government, to take office, and on the occurrence of confusion, to retire; this was Po-i. To say, 'Whom may I not serve as my ruler? Whom may I not command as my people?' In a time of good government, to take office, and when disorder prevailed, also to take office; this was Yi Yin. When it was proper to go into office, then to go into it; when it was proper to keep retired from office, then to keep retired from it; when it was proper to continue in it long, then to continue in it long; when it was proper to withdraw from it quickly, then to withdraw quickly; this was Confucius. These were all sages of antiquity, and I have not attained to do what they did. But what I wish to do is to learn to be like Confucius."

Ch'ou said, "Comparing Po-i and Yi Yin with Confucius, are they to be placed in the same rank?" Mencius replied, "No. Since there were living men until now, there never was another Confucius."

Ch'ou said, "Then, did they have any points of agreement with him?" The reply was, "Yes. If they had been sovereign over a hundred *li* of territory, they would all of them have brought all the princes to attend in their court and have obtained the throne. And none of them, in order to obtain the throne, would have committed one act of unrighteousness or put to death one innocent person. In those things they would have agreed with him."

Ch'ou said, "I venture to ask wherein he differed from them." Mencius replied, "Tsai Wo, Tzŭ-kung and Yu Jo had wisdom sufficient to know the sage. Even had they been low in wisdom, they would not have demeaned themselves to flatter their favorite.

"Now Tsai Wo said, 'According to my view of our Master, he was far superior to Yao and Shun.'

"Tzŭ-kung said, 'By viewing the ceremonial ordinances of a prince, we know the character of his government. By hearing his music, we know the character of his virtue. After the lapse of a hundred years I can arrange, according to their merits, the kings of a hundred ages; not one of them can escape me. From the birth of mankind till now, there has never been another like our Master.'

"Yu Jo said, 'Is it only among men that it is so? There is the unicorn among quadrudeds, the phoenix among birds, the T'ai mountain among mounds and ant-hills, and rivers and seas among rain-pools. Though different in degree, they are the same in kind. So the sages among mankind are also the same in kind. But they stand out from their fellows and rise above the level, and from the birth of mankind till now, there never has been one so glorious as Confucius.' "[15]

To have the unperturbed mind and nourish the vast, flowing passion-nature which Mencius discusses above, it is necessary to coordinate righteousness with the Way. Otherwise the passion-nature will become inadequate and rectification will be lost. Only by copying the conduct of the sage and nourishing the vast, flowing passion-nature can man deal with all extraordinary conditions and possess an unperturbed mind.

Mencius said, "...to be above the power of riches and honors to make dissipated, of poverty and mean condition to make swerve from principle, and of prowess and force to make bend—these charateristics constitue the great man."[16]

This means that a man with faith is bound to have strength and a rectified mind. Only with a rectified mind can he preserve his integrity and keep himself from being dissipated, from deserting principle, from being bent. And only then can he be called a great man.

Since the mind of man is like a helm, it is always in motion and continually needs adjustment, so that when it deals with things it is not in excess nor does it fall short; and this is the state of equilibrium. "Being without inclination to either side is called *chung* (equilibrium)."[17]

Equilibrium can achieve (1) a rectified mind so far as an individual is concerned, (2) faithfulness and reciprocity so far as others are concerned, and (3) rational results so far as things are concerned. Hence, "This equilibrium is the great root from which grow all the human actings in the world."[18] Again, "By *chung* (equilibrium) is denoted the correct course to be pursued by all under heaven."[19]

The concept of equilibrium had an early introduction in Chinese history. More than 1700 years before Confucius lived, Yao handed down to Shun the secret of "sincerely holding fast the due Mean." Shun handed down to Emperor Yü this secret: "The mundane mind being perilous and the moral mind being delicate, by subtlety and by singleness hold fast to the due Mean sincerely." Yü took the advice, but the culmination came with Confucius, who added the concept of *yung* (admission of no change) to that of *chung* (equilibrium). The word *yung* denotes a principle which is ordinarily and perpetually applicable to the greatest majority.

In his brief introduction to the *Doctrine of the Mean*, the philosopher Chu Hsi said:

My Master, the philosopher Ch'êng, says: "Being without inclination to either side is called *chung;* admitting of no change is called *yung.* By *chung* is denoted the correct course to be pursued by all under heaven; by *yung* is denoted the fixed principle regulating all under heaven. This word contains the law of the mind, which was handed down from one to another, in the Confucian school, till Tzŭ-ssŭ, fearing lest in the course of time errors should arise about it, committed it to writing and delivered it to Mencius. The Book first speaks of one principle; it next spreads this out, and embraces all things; finally, it returns and gathers them all up under the one principle. Unroll it, and it fills the universe; roll it up, and it retires and lies hidden in mysteriousness. The relish of it is inexhaustible. The whole of it is solid learning. When the skillful reader has explored it with delight till he has apprehended it, he may carry it into practice all his life, and will find that it cannot be exhausted."

Following is the preface of the philosopher Chu Hsi to the *Loctrine of the Mean:*

Why was the *Doctrine of the Mean* written? It was written, because Tzŭ-ssŭ was concerned that moral learning might fail to be handed down. For from the earliest times of ancient sages and saints, who succeeded to the supreme reign of Heaven, moral traditions had their origins. As recorded in the classics, Yao conferred on Shun the ordinance, "Sincerely hold fast the due Mean." Shun modified it and conferred it on Yü, saying "The mundane mind being perilous and the moral mind being delicate, by subtlety and by singleness, hold fast the due Mean sincerely." The brief message of Yao was comprehensive and exhaustive enough. By adding a few more remarks, Shun showed that only by heeding them could Yao's message hope to be implemented.

I have expressed the view before that in its soul and consciousness the mind is the same in all instances, but that the difference between the mundane and the moral mind has probably arisen from the difference between the self-centered form and the rectified nature, thus producing different feelings, one being perilous and ill at ease and the other delicate and difficult to discern. But all men have this form, and even the wisest cannot be without the mundane mind; all men have this nature, and even the most ignorant cannot be without the moral mind. The two exist together, and if they are not properly controlled, the perilous will become more perilous and the delicate more delicate, and fair-minded divine justice cannot ultimately prevail over selfish human desire. By subtlety the two are examined and are not mixed; by singleness the rectification of the mind is preserved and not deviated from. By engaging in this work without interruption, one can certainly make the moral mind always the main factor in the body, to which the mundane mind will at all times yield its obedience. Thus the perilous will become safe and the delicate manifest, and whether dynamic or static, in speech or in action, there will naturally be no excess or inadequacy.

Yao, Shun and Yü were great sages of the world, and the transmission of their throne was a great event. Yet, in bringing to pass a great event of the world, the great sages of the world had merely the above-mentioned counsel to hand down. It can be seen that the principles governing the world could not exceed the limits of that counsel.

From then on, sages followed one another in rapid succession. T'ang, Wên and Wu as rulers and Kao-yao, Yi Yin, Fu Yüeh and the Dukes of Chou and Chao as ministers—they all succeeded in the same way to the moral tradition. As to our Master, Confucius, although he did not hold the position fo which he was entitled, yet, as the heir to bygone ages and the forerunner of rising generations of scholars, his service far exceeded that of Yao or Shun. However, at the time, of those who had the knowledge, Yen Yüan and Tsêng Shên were the only disciples to whom the transmission of the orthodox principles was made, and the latter in turn handed them down to Tzŭ-ssŭ, the Master's grandson, who was in point of time far away from the sage and who witnessed the beginning of heterodoxy.

Apprehending that the greater the lapse of time, the more easily the true principles would be lost, Tzŭ-ssŭ traced back to the ideas handed down by Yao and Shun, collated them with the words heard from his father and teacher, and wrote this book as a legacy to subsequent scholars. So deep was his apprehension that his observations were pertinent, and so far-reaching were his misgivings that his statements were detailed.

His references to the heavenly ordinance and accordance with nature had to do with the moral mind, those to the choice of the good and holding fast to it had to do with subtlety and singleness, and those to the Mean of the superior man at all times had to do with holding fast to the due Mean. Though more than a thousand years had intervened, the later words were so strikingly the same as the earlier that they agreed completely. Never before had selections and outlines taken from books of ancient sages showed the hidden meanings in an equally clear and exhaustive manner.

Thenceforth, the book was handed down to Mencius, who could elucidate it and carry on the traditions of ancient sages. But when he died, no further transmission was made. While the Confucian Way could not go beyond what the words and language conveyed, heterodoxy made its incursions day by day and month by month until the Taoists and Buddhists appeared and preached seemingly rational principles, which greatly confused the truth.

However, it is fortunate that this book was kept intact. With the emergence of our masters, the brothers Ch'êng, who did their research and continued the learning, which had been interrupted for a thousand years. This gave them the basis for refuting the fallacies of the Taoist and Buddhist schools, which seemed right but were wrong. Herein lies the great credit due to Tzŭ-ssŭ, but without the Ch'êng masters his words would not have been employed to elucidate his mind. It is regrettable that their views have not been handed down, and the material edited by the scholar Shih has emanated from the notes of their disciples. Though the general principles are clear, the subtler part has not been clarified. As to the views expressed by the disciples themselves, though they are tolerably detailed and contain many new discoveries, they run at times counter to those of their teachers and are influenced by Taoism and Buddhism.

In my early years, I had occasion to read the above, but I had my doubts. After some years of quiet study I seem to have gained a comprehension of the essentials. On that basis I gathered together the views of the various schools and sought to balance them. As a result, I divided the book into chapters for the reference of future scholars. At the same time, one or two fellow-workers have gone into the book of the scholar Shih once more, omitting those of its parts which are tautological and confusing, and summarizing it, with an appendix containing a record of the debates that had taken place with regard to the selections and omissions made and giving a number of the questions that were posed.

With all this done, the purposes of this book have been clarified and analyzed, its ramifications linked up, a balance struck between its excessive detail and over-simplification, its major and minor points brought out, and the similarities and differences, advantages and disadvantages of the various views on it fully examined with the greatest interest. Although I have not ventured to discuss the transmission of the moral tradition freely, those who have just begun to learn may have something to gain here. If so, it may mean some help to the advancement of learning.

Chu Hsi
from Hsin-an

Third Moon, 16th Year of
Shun-hsi (1189)

Before beginning a quest for equilibrium, a knowledge of the two extremes is essential. For the Mean can be used only when the extremes are known; the Mean cannot exist independently.

The Master said, "Was Shun not a great intellect? Shun had a natural curiosity of mind and he loved to inquire into ordinary conversation. He ignored the bad in others and broadcast the good. Taking two extreme counsels, he held the mean between them and applied it in his dealings with the people. Was it by this that he was Shun?"[20]

Therefore the superior man honors his virtuous nature and maintains constant inquiry and study, seeking to carry it out to its breadth and greatness, so as to omit none of the more exquisite and minute points which it embraces, and to raise it to its greatest height and brilliancy, so as to pursue the course of the Mean.[21]

While the Mean appears to be simple, it is difficult to practice. There must be sufficient wisdom first, to know the two extremes and, secondly, to determine the Mean. In the last analysis, the extension of knowledge is required. Moreover, since the two extremes of an affair are constantly changing, they are not as easily detected as the extremes of a thing. But if no allowance is made for exigency, holding the Mean is like holding one extreme.

Mencius said, "The principle of the philosopher Yang was 'Each one for himself.' Though he might have benefited the whole world by plucking out a single hair, he would not have done it.

"The philosopher Mo loved all equally. If by rubbing smooth his whole body from the crown to the heel he could have benefited the world, he would have done it.

"Tzŭ-mo holds a medium between these. By holding that medium, he is nearer the right. But by holding it without leaving room for the exigency of circumstances, it becomes like their holding their one point.

"The reason why I hate that holding to one point is the injury it does to the Way. It takes up one point and disregards a hundred others."[22]

Therefore, to secure the Mean, it is necessary (1) to seek one's own enlightenment, (2) to have complete knowledge, sincere thoughts and faith, (3) to be able to reach sound judgments, and (4) to pay constant attention to the environment and general trends. In this way the state of equilibrium can be attained. It is interesting to note that although Confucius strongly advocated the Mean, he could not refrain from complaining occasionally:

The Master said, "Is the Mean not perfect? For a long time few have been able to practice it."[23]

The Master said, "I know how it is that the Way does not prevail: The knowing go beyond it, and the stupid do not come up to it. I know how it is that the Way is not understood: The worthy men go beyond it, and the worthless do not come up to it.

"There is nobody but eats and drinks. But they are few who can distinguish flavors."[24]

The Master said, "Is the Mean not perfect as a virtue? For a long time few have had it."[25]

The Master said, "Alas! How the Way does not prevail!"[26]

The Master said, "The empire and its States may be perfetcly ruled; dignitaries and emoluments may be declined; naked weapons may be borne; but the Mean cannot be attained to."[27]

It is easy to advocate either extreme, but is indeed difficult to hold to the Mean. Whenever the Mean could not be attained, Confucius could only select the well-meaning men among those who inclined to either extreme and direct them toward the Way. However, he could never compromise with those who pretended to be superior men, such as the careful men of the villages. These men confused the true with the false. They were really thieves of virtue. Mencius delved deeply into this matter.

The Master said, "Since I cannot get men pursuing the due medium, to whom I might communicate my instructions, I must find the ardent and the cautiously-decided. The ardent will advance; the cautiously-decided will keep themselves from what is wrong."[28]

Wan Chang asked, saying, "Confucius, when he was in Ch'ên, sad, "Why should I not return? The scholars of my school are amibitious but hasty. They are for advancing and seizing their object, but cannot forget their early ways.' Why did Confucius, when he was in Ch'ên, think of the ambitious scholars of Lu?"

Mencius replied, "Confucius, not getting men pursuing the true medium, to whom he might communicate his instructions, determined to take the ardent and the cautiously-decided. The ardent would advance to seize their object: the cautiously-decided would keep themselves from the certain things. Could we say that Confucius did not wish to get men pursuing the true medium? Being unable to assure himself of finding such, he therefore thought of the next class."

"I venture to ask what sort of men they were who couid be styled 'the ambitious'?"

"Such," replied Mencius, "as Ch'in Chang, Tsêng Hsi and Mu P'i, were those whom Confucius styled 'ambitious.' "

"Why were they styled 'ambitious'?"

The reply was, "Their aim led them to talk magniloquently, saying, 'The ancients! The ancients!' But when we examine their actions, we find that they cannot conceal their boasts.

"When he found that he could not get such as were thus ambitious, he wanted to get scholars who would consider anything impure as beneath them. Those were the cautiously-decided, a class next to the former."

Chang pursued his questioning, "Confucius said, 'They are only your good careful people of the villages at whom I feel no indignation, when they pass my door without entering my house. Your good careful people of the villages are the thieves of virtue.' What sort of people were they who could be styled 'your good careful people of the villages'?"

Mencius replied, "They are those who say, 'Why are they so magniloquent?' Their words have not respect to their actions, and their actions have not respect to their words, but they say, '*The ancients! The ancients!*' Why do they act so peculiarly and are so cold and distant? Born in this age, we should be of this age, to be good is all that is needed. Keeping others in the dark, they seek to flatter them, such are your good careful people of the villages."

Wan Chang said, "Their whole village styles those men good and careful. In all their conduct they are so. How was it that Confucius considered them the thieves of virtue?"

Mencius replied, "If you would blame them, you find nothing to allege. If you would criticize them, you have nothing to criticize. They agree with the current customs. They consent with an impure age. Their principles have a semblance of right-heartedness and truth. Their conduct has a semblance of disinterestedness and purity. All men are pleased with them, and they think themselves right, so that it is impossible to proceed with them to the principles of Yao and Shun. On this account they are called 'the thieves of virtue.'

"Confucius said, 'I hate a semblance which is not the reality. I hate the darnel, lest it be confounded with the rice. I hate glib-tonguedness, lest it be confounded with righteousness. I hate sharpness of tongue, lest it be confounded with sincerity. I hate the music of Chêng, lest it be confounded with the true music. I hate the purple, lest it be confounded with vermillion. I hate your good careful men of the villages, lest they be confounded with the truly virtuous.'

"The superior man seeks simply to bring back the unchanging standard and, that being correct, the masses are roused to virtue.

When they are so aroused, forthwith perversities and glossed wickedness disappear."[29]

Mencius, upholding the Mean, was critical of excesses and inadequacies. Following are some examples:

1. With regard to taking and giving, life and death.

Mencius said, "When it appears proper to take a thing, and afterwaros not proper, to take it is contrary to moderation. When it appears proper to give a thing, and afterwards not proper, to give it is contrary to kindness. When it appears proper to sacrifice one's life, and afterwards not proper, to sacrifice it is contrary to bravery."[30]

2. With regard to acceptance of office and retirement.

Mencius said, "Po-i would not serve a prince whom he did not approve, nor associate with a friend whom he did not esteem. He would not stand in a bad prince's court, nor speak with a bad man. To stand in a bad prince's court or to speak with a bad man would have been to him the same as to sit with his court robes and court cap amid mire and ashes. Pursuing the examination of his dislike of evil, we find that he thought it necessary, if he happened to be standing with a villager whose cap was not rightly adjusted, to leave him with a high air, as if he were going to be defiled. Therefore, although some of the princes made application to him with very proper messages, he would not accept their appointments. He would not accept their appointments, counting it inconsistent with his purity to go to them.

"Hui of Liu-hsia was not ashamed to serve an impure prince, nor did he think it low to be an inferior official. When advanced to employment, he did not compromise his rectitude, but made it a point to abide by his Way. When neglected and left without office, he did not murmur. When straitened by poverty, he did not grieve. Accordingly he said, 'You are you and I am I. Although you stand by my side with breast and arms bare, or with your body naked, how can you defile me?' Therefore, self-possessed, he companied with men indifferently, at the same time not losing himself. When he wished to leave, if pressed to remain in office, he would remain. He would remain in office, when pressed to do so, not counting it required by his purity to go away."

Mencius said, "Po-i was narrow-minded, and Hui of Liu-hsia was wanting in respect. The superior man will not take the course of either narrow-mindedness or lack of respect."[31]

Mencius said, "The principle of the philosopher Yang was—'Each one for himself.' Though he might have benefited the whole world by plucking out a single hair, he would not have done it.

"The philosopher Mo loved all equally. If by rubbing smoothly his whole body from the crown to the heel he could have benefited the whole world, he would have done it.

"Tzŭ-mo holds a medium between them. By holding that medium, he is nearer the right. But by holding it without leaving room for the exigency of circumstances, he becomes like their holding their one point.

"The reason why I hate that holding to one point is the injury it does to the Way. It takes up one point and disregards a hundred others."[32]

Of all the disciples of Confucius, Yen Hui was the only one who could choose the Mean and hold to it without wavering. Others, like Tzŭ-chang and Tzŭ-hsia, either went to excess or fell short.

The Master said, "This was the manner of Hui: he made choice of the Mean, and whenever he got hold of one thing that was good, he embraced it with all his might and never lost it."[33]

Tzŭ-kung asked which of the two, Shih or Shang, was the superior. The Master said, "Shih goes beyond the due mean, and Shang does not come up to it.

"Then," said Tzŭ-kung, "the superiority is with Shih, I suppose." The Master said, "To go beyond is as wrong as to fall short."[34]

In seeking to rectify his mind, Confucius himself chose the Mean and held to it. In line with this attitude, all psychological conditions injurious to the Mean—preconception, arbitrariness, obstinacy, egoism—were carefully avoided by him.

There were four things from which the Master refrained. He had no foregone conclusions, no arbitrary pre-determinations, no obstinacy and no egoism."[35]

The Way of the Mean is the proper Way. It should not be abandoned at the halfway point, even though it is equally difficult to know it and to practice it. We should observe the Mean without seeking renown, without resorting to unusual acts to please the public. The superior man follows the Mean without drawing attention to his behavior.

The Master said, "To live in obscurity and yet resort to strange practices, in order to be mentioned and known to subsequent generations; this is what I do not do.

"Nor can I do as the superior man who tries to proceed according to the Way, but who abandons it halfway.

"The real superior man accords with the course of the Mean. Though he takes himself away from the world and is unknown, he has no regrets. It is only the sage who is capable of this."[36]

Tzŭ-hsia said, "Even in small skills there is something worth seeing; but if carried further they may meet obstruction. Therefore the superior man does not practice them."[37]

So far as individuals are concerned, the Mean can be explained from the viewpoints of both the dynamic and the static states. When the mind is static, there are no stirrings of pleasure, anger, sorrow and joy; there is no inclination to either side, and equilibrium obtains. When the mind is dynamic, the feelings are stirred to the right pitch; and the result is harmony and fairness between oneself and others, or among these others. There is no excess or inadequacy because all is correctly controlled. And this is called harmony. The principles of faithfulness and reciprocity and the rules of human conduct are all based on the Mean. The foundation of propriety is equilibrium, and its utility is harmony.

In short, in the dealings of man with man, progress and the proper Way can be attained only when there is satisfaction on both sides. If there is inclination to either side, the result is unevenness, disharmony and failure to reach the Mean. Therefore the rectification of the mind depends entirely on (1) the accurate abservation of the two extremes, (2) the appropriate adjustment of feelings, and (3) the elimination of preconceptions. These three points, in turn, rely on a firm grasp of the Mean at all times.

How did our ancestors discover this great principle? How did they make it a precious teaching bearing on the foundation of our country? Indeed, how did they make it the central thought of our nation, and even name our country after it (the Middle Kingdom)? Actually, they did it only after keen observation of (1) the principles that should govern human relationships and (2) the accumulation of their rich experiences. Generation after generation of our sages found that the universe is always moving and changing. They discovered the rules that govern this motion and change. They saw the "essence" and "utility" of the universe. And they continued their process of observation and comprehension until one of them wrote the great classic, the *Book of Changes*.

This immortal work described how the essence consisted of the change of the illimitable or infinite to the absolute and how the utility involved the change of the absolute to the two powers or manners, thence to the four emblems or phenomena, thence to the eight trigrams, and thence further to the sixty-four double trigrams. The progress of change from the *Ch'ien* trigram (denoting Heaven) to the *Wei-chi* double trigram (denoting an unaccomplished state) was an extremely complex one and contained the stages through which human life itself evolved. The meaning was so deep that even a man as wise and learned as Confucius had to wait till he was fifty to devote himself to the study of this great classic. On one occasion he even expressed the devout wish that his life might be extended a few years so he could continue that study. As to his annotation of the *Book of Changes*, it must have been done toward the end of his life.

At last, from the principles governing the motion and change of the natural world he deduced the rules for the conduct of the daily routine of mankind. These rules were embodied in *Chung Yung* (the *Doctrine of the Mean*), which eventually became the law of the mind handed down by the Confucian school. This work enables us not only to "know the ordinances (trends) of Heaven (environment), but to know how to give its full development to human nature and give their full development to the natures of other living things and oneself."

Since the *Doctrine of the Mean* originated from the *Book of Changes*, the essential points resulting from a combined study of the two works are given here:

(1) All things in the universe have their material existence and energy. Owing to differences in time and space, these things move and change; and so there is the necessity for understanding time and space. The reason for the motion and change lies in the existence of dynamism. This dynamism is called "sincerity." (See Chapter IV, "The Sincerity of Thoughts," for details.)

(2) All things in the universe have life because of the

mating of matter and spirit. Although the length of life varies, there is no exception to motion and change in life at all times The phenomenon of life is represented by many ripples in a surging wave. The rise and fall, growth and decline, existence and extinction of each life are ascribable to the relationship of cause and effect. By sincerity each life is formed, manifested, illustrated, moved, changed and transformed. Though it is a long process from the formation of life to its dissolution, and though it cannot be expected to exist forever, yet by means of adjustment (equilibrium) the more or less prolonged existence of life can be maintained.

(3) When seen from the side, a wave forms a sine curve; when seen from the front, it forms a circle. After it advances to the extreme point, it goes in the opposite direction. From the point of view of space, this is still advancing; but from the point of view of phenomena, it is retreating.

(4) Any two contrary phenomena, which are originally opposed, must have common existence and have an effect on their mutual rise and decline. Therefore, it is necessary to ascertain the real situation of both sides in order to find out which is the point of excess, which is the point of inadequacy, which should rise and which should decline. Also, reasons for their behavior must be learned before the proper choice can be made and evenness and perfection achieved. The adoption of a neutral attitude toward right and error, good and evil is no different from the extension of assistance to the evil-doer and cannot be called equilibrium.

(5) As all things are nourished, the universe is filled with innumerable moving waves. Their mutual friction cannot be avoided, and to secure their common existence, the work of adjustment at all times is indispensable. The adjustment is called *chung* or "equilibrium."

(6) Everything which, after adjustment, can be applied to the largest number of people and meet the longest-term requirements, must be very ordinary and nonstimulating. This is called *yung* or "harmony."

Comment on Point 1: The Chinese believe that "sincerity is the Way of Heaven" and that "the attainment of sincerity is the Way of men." To them the Way of Heaven and Earth is altruistic and unselfish; more, it is completely sincere and unceasing, large and substantial, high and brilliant, benevolent and nourishing to all things. Mankind is Heaven and Earth in miniature. Its virtue should naturally be co-equal with Heaven and Earth, giving its nature full development and making possible accordance with Heaven and Earth in order to assist them in their transforming and nourishing operations. The power behind the Way of Heaven and Earth is "sincerty."

Comment on Point 2: The Chinese generally attach no importance to theories which give merely temporary satisfaction. They believe principles which can bring about the extension and prolongation of life are worthy of reverence and respect. Only what can "extend" life is big enough to contain things, and only what can "prolong" life gives enough time for the completion of things. As for individuals, the ideal personality is "being large and substantial enough to be the co-equal of Earth, high and brilliant enough to be the co-equal of Heaven, and long-lasting enough to be infinite." So far as families are concerned, husbands and wives expect "to remain married until the couples' heads are white;" they hope to have "five generations living at the same time," and to "multiply and continue as the gourds." As for their native land, they expect to "enjoy enduring peace and tranquillity" and "thousands of years" of peaceful reign.

Due to their knowledge of "long-lasting" existence and the stress they place on it, the Chinese can never endorse the use of force and wealth to maintain political control. For though reliance on force and wealth can assure temporary success, the results thus achieved can never last. Only the Kingly Way, the Way of Right backed by the "practice of benevolence with virtue" can replace the Way of Might supported by the "abuse of benevolence with force." Only the gifts of "charity with virtue" in place of pride and extravagance ("relying on wealth") can preserve enduring wealth and power; only with these gifts can a people reach the state of extended and lasting life. The ability of China to accumulate 600 million people (extended life) and maintain a cultural tradition of more than 5,000 years (lasting life) may be due to this cognition.

Comment on Point 3: The Chinese are never fond of going to extremes. They know full well that continued flight to the east ends up in the west. Just so, they understand that going to the extreme marks the beginning of moving backward. This is why it is absolutely impossible for the philosophies of either "materialism" or "idealism" to take hold in China—both incline to one side and lose sight of the whole. Human life can exist only when both the mind and matter are complete.

Consequently, the Chinese frequently admonish the people of the world with such warnings as, "Things must turn around when they go to the extreme," and "The extremes of pleasure produce sorrow." On the other hand, they often encourage the people of the world with such prophecies as, "Extreme misery leads to happiness," and "Sorrowful soldiers are sure to win."

This is true not only in philosophy, but also in litereature, art and music. Chinese art does not attach any importance to exact resemblance, but unlike abstract impressionism it does not rule out likeness completely. A few strokes portraying the spirit are considered masterpieces. Chinese music emphasized quiet harmony without paying close attention to stimulation. This also is a principle derived from the above-mentioned cognition.

Comment on Point 4: When there are two opposite or contrary things involved, the Chinese can frequently look at both sides. They make it a point to examine carefully the root and the branches of things as well as their order of sequence. For example, others and oneself are opposed, but when one thinks of himself he should think of others, too. Such consideration produces the principles of faithfulness and reciprocity in addition to rules of conduct applicable to both sides. "Do not do unto others what you would not have them do unto you"…"The ruler must himself be possessed of the good qualities, and then he may require them in the people"…"The man of benevolence, wishing to be established himself, seeks to establish others; wishing to be enlarged, he seeks also to enlarge others" (thus treating others like himself). All these theories are products of the above-mentioned cognition.

All this mainfests the significance of "benevolence." To repeat, the Chinese character for benevolence, *Jên,* is composed of two parts, *Jên* and *erh.* The former, meaning "men," and the latter "two," indicate the love between man and man and the foundation of the common existence of mankind.

Let us take the relationship between the old and the young

as another example. The Chinese speak of kindness to the young on the one hand, and filial piety from the young on the other. Naturally kindness is easier to practice than filial piety. Precisely because the latter is more difficult, it is more highly prized; and because it is more highly prized, it is taught with special emphasis. Filial piety is love with reverence. It is pure love, eternal love. Therefore it is the foundation of "benevolence." Because of the existence of this dual conception in Chinese culture, selfish individualism, the doctrine of self-centered material enjoyment, has not been able to develop to any great degree in China.

The observation of the root and the branches also is part of the special learning of China. It too has arisen from Point 4. "Things have their root and their branches. Affairs have their end and their beginning. To know what is first and what is last will lead near to the Way." The root and the branches, the end and the beginning, the first and the last are all opposites. Both sides must be taken into account to determine which should come first and which last, which is important and which unimportant. When this has been done, the two extremes can be determined and the Mean can be put to use.

Comment on Point 5: The Chinese were the first to discover the spiritual center of gravity, and this is as important as the material center of gravity discovered by Westerners. The center of gravity is the most stable point at which the forces from all directions are centralized and balanced. In other words, it is the center which is not inclined to one side or the other. This is what the philosopher Ch'êng meant by saying in his statement quoted in the introduction to the *Doctrine of the Mean:* "Being without inclination to either side is called *chung.*" Whoever can control the central point is bound to be fair and rational. He can exist together with others in "harmony" and treat them with "equality." Therefore the Mean is also the basis of peace.

Comment on Point 6: The Chinese regard as harmful those things which are excessively stimulating. To them it is the plain things, the things that are in no way unusual, that can last. Water is colorless and tasteless. Rice and bread are both plain and rather tasteless. But this drink and this food are taken by us all our lives, and we do not tire of them. On the other hand, both tobacco and alcohol are stimulating; yet the Chinese do not go to such excesses as Westerners in their smoking and drinking of alcoholic beverages. What we have said holds true not only in matters of food and drink, but also in the theories of political economy. In the view of the Chinese, all significant systems—those which can last—are bound to be measures which are easy and human. A society which needs constant stimulation is unwholesome. This is the precious lesson which the Chinese have learned from their cognition of "harmony."

It is hoped that these words have clarified the importance of the *Doctrine of the Mean* and its application to the rectification of the mind. However, the principle of the Mean is concealed as well as far-reaching. It seems shallow but is actually deep. It seems small but is actually great, subtle at the beginning but manifest ultimately, noiseless and tasteless, plain but not tiring, simple yet polished, gentle yet orderly. It knows that what is distant starts from what is near. It knows the origin of the wind and knows that what is minute is bound to be manifested. With it one can enter into virtue.

> The Way which the superior man pursues is far-reaching and yet concealed.
>
> Common men and women, however ignorant, may know it; yet in its utmost reaches, there is that which even the sage does not know. Common men and women, however unworthy, can carry it into practice; yet in its utmost reaches, there is that which even the sage is not able to carry into practice. Great as heaven and earth are, men still find some things in them with which to be dissatisfied. Thus it is that were the superior man to speak of his Way in all its greatness, nothing in the world would be found able to embrace it, and were he to speak of it in all its minuteness, nothing in the world would be found able to split it.
>
> It is said in the *Book of Songs,* "The hawk flies up to heaven; the fishes leap in the deep." This expresses how this Way reaches up and down.
>
> The Way of the superior man begins with the relations between husband and wife; but at its utmost it reaches as far as heaven and earth.[38]
>
> It is said in the *Book of Songs,* "When an embroidered robe is worn, a plain, single garment is put on over it," intimating a dislike to the display of the elegance of the former. Just so, the Way of the superior man seems concealed, but it daily becomes more illustrious; and the Way of the mean man seems to seek

notoriety, but he daily goes more to ruin. The Way of the superior man is plain but not tiring, simple but polished, gentle but orderly. It knows the distant and the near, the main principles and the details, the minute and the manifest. Such a man can enter into virtue.

It is said in the Book of Songs, "A concealed and unseen object can become manifest." Therefore the superior man is satisfied if, after examining his heart, he finds nothing wrong there and has nothing to be ashamed of. But where the superior man cannot be equaled—does it not lie in what cannot be seen by others?

It is said in the *Book of Songs*, "When you are seen in your room, perhaps you can feel unashamed even toward the northwestern corner of the house." Therefore the superior man, even when he is not moving, has a feeling of reverence, and while he speaks not, he has the feeling of truthfulness.

It is said in the *Book of Songs*, "In silence is the offering presented and the spirit approached; there is not the slightest contention." Therefore the superior man does not use rewards, and the people are stimulated to virtue. He does not show anger, and the people are awed more than by hatchets and battle-axes.

It is said in the *Book of Songs*, "What needs no display is virtue. All the princes imitate it." Therefore, with the superior man sincere and reverential, peace is brought to the whole world.

It is said in the *Book of Songs*, "I yearn for illustrious virtue, without making a great display of it in sounds and appearances." The Master said, "Among the appliances to transform the people, sounds and appearances are but trivial influences. It is said in another ode, 'His virtue is light as hair.' Still, a hair will admit of comparison as to its size. 'The doings of the supreme Heaven have neither sound nor smell.' That is perfect virtue."

The above is the thirty-third chapter. Tzŭ-ssŭ, having carried his descriptions to the extremest point in the preceding chapters, turns back in this and examines the·source of his subject; and from the work of the junior learner in cultivating himself and exercising prudence when he is alone, he carries out his description and does not cease till he brings peace to the world by sincerity and reverence. He further eulogizes its mysteriousness, till he speaks of it at last as without sound or smell. He here takes up the sum of his whole work and speaks of it in a compendious manner. Most deep and earnest was he in thus going again over his ground, admonishing and instructing men: shall the learner not do his utmost in the study of the Work?[30]

Our understanding of the above essentials tells us that the *Doctrine of the Mean* has elucidated the highest principles of "sincerity" and "equillibrium." It not only enables us to comprehend that the sincerity of thoughts and rectification of hearts are prerequisites for the cultivation of the person; it also lays the foundation for the extended and prolonged life of mankind. The principle of the Mean, therefore, can also be called the principle of humanitarianism. The culture produced by this great principle is humanitarian culture. Who can deny that from this culture an unlimited and inexhaustible spirit of humanities and history can be developed?

Footnotes for Chapter V

1. *Doctrine of the Mean*, Ch. I.
2. *Ibid.*, Ch. XX. *Vide supra*, p. 192.
3. *Great Learning*, Com., Ch. VII.
4. *Ibid.*, Ch. VIII.
5. *Works of Mencius*, Bk. VII. Pt. I, Ch. XXVII.
6. *Ibid.*, Bk. I, Pt. I, Ch. VII.
7. *Analects*, Bk. IX, Ch. XXIX.
8. *Works of Mencius*, Bk. VII, Pt. II, Ch. XXXV.
9. *Analects*, Bk. V, Ch. X.
10. *Works of Mencius*, Bk. VI, Pt. I, Ch. XIII.
11. *Ibid.*, Ch. XIV.
12. *Ibid.*, Ch. XII.
13. *Ibid.*, Ch. VIII.
14. *Ibid.*, Ch. XI.
15. *Ibid.*, Bk. II, Pt. I, Ch. II. Vida supra, pp. 116-118, 131
16. *Works of Mencius*, Bk. III, Pt. II, Ch. II.
17. *Doctrine of the Mean*, the philosopher C'hêng's statement.
18. *Ibid.*, Ch. I.
19, *Ibid.*, the philosopher C'hêng's statement.
20. *Ibid.*, Ch. VI. *Vide supra*, pp. 31, 103
21. *Doctrine of the Mean*, Ch. XXVII.
22. *Works of Mencius*, Bk. VII, Pt. I, Ch. XXVI.
23. *Doctrine of the Mean*, Ch. III.
24. *Ibid.*, Ch. IV.
25. *Analects*, Bk. VI, Ch. XXV.
26. *Doctrine of the Mean*, Ch. V.
27. *Ibid.*, Ch. IX.
28. *Analects*, Bk. XIII, Ch. XXI.
29. *Works of Mencius*, Bk. VII, Pt. II, Ch. XXXVII.
30. *Ibid.*, Bk. IV, Pt. II, Ch. XXIII.
31. *Ibid.*, Bk. II, Pt. I, Ch. IX.
32. *Ibid.*, Bk. VII, Pt. I, Ch. XXVI. *Vide supra*. p. 218.
33. *Doctrine of the Mean*, Ch. VIII.

34. *Analects*, Bk. XI, Ch. XV.
35. *Ibid.*, Bk. IX, Ch. IV.
36. *Doctrine of the Mean*, Ch. XI.
37. *Analects*, Bk. XIX, Ch. IV. *Vide supra*, p. 30.
38. *Doctrine of the Mean*, Ch. XII.
39. *Ibid.*, Ch. XXXIII.

CHAPTER VI

The Cultivation of the Person

A. General Principles

Now that the true significance of morality has been clarified, the meaning of human life should be clear. The driving force for one's motion is provided by sincere thoughts, and the direction of one's motion is determined by the rectification of the heart. Thereafter, all speech and action will depend on virtue and will follow propriety. The common existence and evolution of mankind will then be maintained for an unlimited length of time.

However, all things in the universe are constantly changing. Living in the midst of such a universe, a man can hold the Mean to meet these changes, but such changes, by their very motion, will create friction. After continued motion, damages are certain to be sustained. Like a machine, these are in need of lubrication from time to time, as well as cleaning, repair, adjustment and upkeep. Thus, the old parts can be kept in good working order, and the new ones will last longer. Efficiency remains undiminished, and the machine continues to work without trouble.

This is true of all things, and man is no exception. Such is the true significance of the cultivation of the person. So it is that all men—young or old, high or low, rich or poor, noble or not—must cultivate their persons. Cultivation of the person is especially important for one who wished to be a superior man or a ruler of the people.

> From the Son of Heaven to the people, all must consider the cultivation of the person the root of everything besides.[1]
>
> "Hence the superior man may not neglect the cultivation of his character. Wishing to cultivate his character, he may not neglect to serve his parents. In order to serve his parents, he may not neglect to acquire a knowledge of men."[2]
>
> "...Knowing how to cultivate his own character, he knows how to govern other men. Knowing how to govern other men, he knows how to govern the empire with its States."[3]

On what principle should the cultivation of the person be based? What steps should be taken to achieve it? The answer is: "The cultivation of the person is through the Way."[4]

In other words, the cultivation of the person should be based on the principle of common existence. Since that principle is the Way, its application cannot be removed from virtue; i. e. wisdom, benevolence and courage. However, since human knowledge is always advancing, new wisdom cannot be acquired if there is no fondness for learning; the result is bound to be backwardness. If we see others making progress and we are not shamed by this, we can never catch up to the others even if we one day realize what we have failed to do. If we speak empty words and do not act vigorously, or if we lack the courage to act righteously, we will have suffered a great loss.

Thus it is essential in the cultivation of the person to begin with a fondness for learning, vigorous action and a feeling of shame, which qualities are respectively near to wisdom, benevolence and courage.

> The Master said, "To be fond of learning is to be akin to wisdom. To practice with vigor is to be akin to benevolence. To possess the feeling of shame is to be akin to courage.
>
> "He who knows these three things knows how to cultivate his own character. Knowing how to cultivate his own character, he knows how to govern other men. Knowing how to govern other men, he knows how to govern the empire with its States."[5]

1. Fondness for Learning

Fondness for learning is not wisdom, but is only akin to it.

Without this quality, however, one can never acquire wisdom. On this point Confucius and Tzŭ-hsia observed:

> The Master said, "The superior man does not seek to gratify his appetite for food, nor to have ease in his residence; he is quick in action but careful in speech; he frequents the company of men of principle that he may be rectified—such a person may be said indeed to love to learn."[3]
>
> The Master said, "Learn as if you could not reach your object and were always fearing also lest you should lose it."[7]
>
> The Master said, "Is it not pleasant to learn with a constant perseverance and application?"[3]
>
> Tzŭ-hsia said, "He who from day to day recognizes what he has not yet, and from month to month does not forget what he has attained to, may be said indeed to love to learn."[9]

They meant that in learning one must be devoted to the accumulation of knowledge without a moment's relaxation, that one must feel as if one's object is unattainable, and that one must review what he has already learned as a path to new knowledge. One must also be assiduous at all times and must, if necessary, sacrifice food and sleep for the sake of study. This is fondness for learning.

Confucius confessed that all his life he never felt satiated with learning nor did he ever tire of teaching. He decided to devote himself to learning at age 15. He even intended to continue studying the *Book of Changes* to be free from fault.

> The Master said, "At fifteen, I had my mind bent on learning. At thirty, I stood firm. At forty, I had no doubts. At fifty, I knew the decrees of Heaven. At sixty, my ear was an obedient organ for the reception of truth. At seventy, I could follow what my heart desired without transgressing what was right."[10]
>
> The Master said, "If some years were added to my life and I could study the *Book of Changes* after fifty, then I might come to be without great faults."[11]

Only rudimentary knowledge is acquired before the age of fifteen It is a time for elementary education. If we examine the curriculum of today's elementary and secondary schools, we find that it is little more than common sense. Only when one enters college are more profound studies pursued. In this early period, Confucius decided to devote himself to learning and personal cultivation. At thirty he was able to stand on his own feet. A decade later, he had comprehended the principles relating to everything and no longer had any doubts. At fifty he understood the subtleties of the relationship between the universe and human life. At sixty he was able to reach the objectives he pursued without thinking, without effort. At seventy he "could follow what his heart desired without transgressing what was right."

From the example of Confucius' planning and achievements at the various stages of his life, we find that in learning and in the cultivation of the person we must proceed step by step. We must possess the spirit of untiring effort from childhood to old age.

> "Confucius said, 'A sage is what I cannot rise to. I learn without satiety and teach without being tired.' Tzŭ-kung said, 'You learn without satiety; that shows your wisdom. You teach without being tired; that shows your benevolence. Benevolent and wise, Master, you are a sage.' "[12]
>
> The Master said, "I am not one who was born in the possession of knowledge. I am one who is fond of antiquity and earnest in seeking it there."[13]
>
> The Master said, "In a hamlet of ten families, there must be one faithful and sincere as I am, but not so fond of learning."[14]
>
> The Master said, "A transmitter and not a maker, believing in and loving ancient studies, I venture to compare myself with our Lao P'eng."[15]

In ancient times, education was the function of historians. Lao P'eng is said to have been a historian and writer in the Shang dynasty, noted for his profound scholarship. Confucius, who was fond of antiquity, sought diligently to obtain new judgments by studying old learning. Thus, he advises us to acquire new knowledge from the study of the old.

Though he confined himself to a restatement of old laws, customs and institutious, Confucius was in fact creative because he was a "transmitter." This great sage not only carried on earlier traditions, but opened up new roads to knowledge. He organized and clarified the material he studied, developing his own theories from these sources. Though he was a very humble man, when he spoke of the fondness for learning, Confucius did not hesitate to say that in a village of ten families there might be a man as faithful and sincere as he was, but no one so fond of learning. His object here was to encourage a fondness for learning.

> The Duke of Shêh asked Tzŭ-lu about Confucius, and Tzŭ-lu did not answer him.
>
> The Master said, "Why did you not say to him, 'He is simply a man, who in his eager pursuit (of knowledge) forgets his food, who in the joy of its attainment forgets his sorrows, and who does not perceive that old age is coming on?'"[16]

Confucius meant that learning is a lifelong pursuit. He became so fond of it himself, he never tired of it. This development involved several distinct stages: recognizing the importance of learning, acquiring a fondness for it and enjoying it.

Of all his disciples, Yen Hui was the only one Confucius regarded as really fond of learning. Unfortunately, he was short-lived. Yen Hui possessed great intelligence—he was capable of "knowing ten when he heard just one" point—so it was no surprise to find that, with his fondness for learning, he was the first to see the Way.

> Duke Ai asked which of the disciples loved to learn. Confucius replied to him, "There was Yen Hui; he loved to learn. He did not transfer his anger; he did not repeat a fault. Unfortunately, he was short-lived and he died; and now there is not such another. I have not yet heard of anyone who loves to learn as he did."[17]
>
> Chi K'ang asked which of the disciples loved to learn. Confucius replied to him, "There was Yen Hui; he loved to learn. Unfortunately he was short-lived and he died. Now there is no one who loves to learn as he did."[18]
>
> The Master said, "Never flagging when I set forth anything to him; ah! that is Hui!"[19]
>
> The Master said of Yen Yüan. "Alas!" I saw his constant advance. I never saw him stop in his progress."[20]
>
> The Master said, "After I have talked with Hui for a whole day, he does not make any objection to anything I say—as if he were stupid. After he retires, I examine his condut and find him able to illustrate my teachings. Hui!—he is not stupid."[21]

Confucius was deeply sorrowed by the early death of Yen Hui. Confucius had the highest hopes that this disciple would teach others the Way, and his death was a great blow.

> When Yen Yüan died, the Master said, "Alas! Heaven is destroying me! Heaven is destroying me!"[22]

> When Yen Yüan died, the Master bewailed him exceedingly, and the disciples who were with him said, "Master, your grief is excessive."
>
> "Is it excessive?" said he. "If I am not to mourn bitterly for this man, for whom should I mourn?"[23]

If one concentrated on general studies and ignored specialization, the result would be unsatisfactory. On the other hand, if one's efforts were spasmodic or half-completed, one would be unable to learn.

> Mencius said, "It is not to be wondered at that the king is not wise! Suppose the case of the most easily growing thing in the world—if you let it have one day's genial heat and then expose it for ten days to cold, it will not be able to grow. It is but seldom that I have an audience of the king, and when I retire, there come all those who act upon him like the cold. Though I succeed in bringing out some buds of goodness, of what avail is it?
>
> "Now chess-playing is but a small art, but without his whole mind being given, and his will bent to it, a man cannot succeed in it. Chess Ch'iu is the best chess-player in all the kingdom. Suppse that he is teaching two men to play. The one gives to the subject his whole mind and bends to it all his will, doing nothing but listening to Chess Ch'iu. The other, although he seems to be listening to him, has his whole mind running on a swan which he thinks is approaching, and wishes to bend his bow, adjust the string to the arrow and shoot it. Although he is learning along with the other, he does not come up to him. Why?—because his intelligence is not equal? Not so."[24]
>
> The Master said, "It is not easy to find a man who has learned for three years without giving consideration to his emoluments."[25]

Confucius explained to Tzŭ-lu that fondness for learning is close to wisdom because it can remove the six obstacles to and deficiencies in virtuous conduct.

> The Master said, "Yu, have you heard the six words to which are attached six becloudings?" Yu replied, "I have not."
>
> "Sit down, and I will tell them to you. There is the love of being benevolent without the love of learning; the beclouding here leads to a foolish simplicity. There is the love of wisdom without the love of learning; the beclouding here leads to dissipation of mind. There is the love of truthfulness without the love of learning; the beclouding here leads to an injurious disregard of consequences. There is the love of straightforwardness without the love of learning; the beclouding here leads to rudeness. There is the love

of courage without the love of learning; the beclouding here leads to trouble. There is the love of firmness without the love of learning; the beclouding here leads to extravagant conduct."[26]

In view of Tzŭ-lu's courage in doing what was right, Confucius was disturbed that he might have acted hastily and opened the door to evil consequences and mistakes. So he enumerated the virtues—benevolence, wisdom, faithfulness, straightforwardness, courage and firmness—and explained that their cutlivation depended on learning. This is so because there is sincerity only where there is intelligence. In the *Doctrine of the Mean* it is said that the superior man "honors his virtuous nature and maintains constant inquiry and study." Important as virtuous nature is, one must constantly inquire and study to determine the rules of conduct. Only then can all things be compatible with equilibrium and be near to wisdom. This is why everyone should be fond of learning.

2. Vigorus Conduct

Vigorous conduct by itself is not benevolence, but is very near to it. What is vigorous conduct?

In the section on "Earnest Conduct" in the chapter on "The Investigation of Things," it is explained that the importance of conduct depends on experimentation with knowledge as a means to true wisdom. Here the significance of vigorous conduct lies in the application of knowledge already acquired to the promotion of human welfare. In other words, it means the translation of benevolence into action. One must not merely pay lip service to it. Neither empty words nor fine words constitute benevolence. It is only by vigorous conduct that benevolence can be manifested.

> The Master said, "Fine words and an insinuating appearance are seldom associated with benevolence."[27]
> The same passage was repeated in Book XVII of the *Analects*.[28]
> The Master said, "The firm, the enduring, the simple and the modest are near to benevolence."[29]
> Tzŭ-hsia said, "There are learning extensively and having a firm and sincere aim; inquiring pertinently and reflecting from what is near at hand—virtue is in such a course."[30]

The actions viewed in this passage all involve vigorous conduct, especially the last two points, which deal with the practical and the easily understood. Hence, it is also said, "To be able to take examples from what is near at hand may be called the method of benevolence."[31]

Learning aims at practical application. If one possessed extensive knowledge and could neither classify nor apply it, it would be like a library with thousands of unclassified and uncatalogued books. Such a library would be worthless, because it would be impossible to find a book one was seeking. A man possessing such impractical knowledge would be of no help to himself or to anyone else. A man who possessed less knowledge but who acted vigorously would be far more preferred.

> Tzŭ-hsia said, "If a man withdraws his mind from the love of beauty and applies it as sincerely to the love of the virtuous; if, in serving his parents, he can exert his utmost strength; if, in serving his prince, he can devote his life; if, in his intercourse with his friends, his words are sincere—although men say that he has not learned, I will certainly say that he has."[32]

If one possesses learning and does not apply it, he remains ignorant and has nothing akin to wisdom.

> The Master said, "Tsang Wên-Chung built a house to keep a large tortoise. On the capitals of its pillars he had hills carved, and on the small pillars above the beams he had duckweed painted—of what sort was his wisdom?"[33]

Only rarely did Confucius refer to persons from ages past as benevolent men. The three he mentions here all showed the same spirit, although in different ways, while living under the rule of despots. They demonstrated their vigorous conduct and were regarded by Confucius as benevolent men.

> The Viscount of Wei withdrew from the court. The Viscount of Chi became a slave of Chou. Pi-kan remonstrated with him and died.
>
> Confucius said, "The Yin dynasty possessed three men of benevolence."[34]

The basic aim of learning is to practice the Way, to love men and substantiate the ability to love, not to ornament oneself.

> Tzŭ-hsia said, "Mechanics dwell in their shops in order to accomplish their works. The superior man learns in order to reach

to the utmost of the Way."[35]

When the man of high station learns the Way, he loves men: when the man of low station learns the Way, he is easily ruled.[36]

The Master said, "In ancient times men learned with a view to their own improvement. Nowadays men learn with a view to the approbation of others."[37]

This is why Mencius stressed the importance of righteousness in addition to benevolence. He compared benevolence to a peaceful house and righteousness to a straight path, claiming righteousness was the application of benevolence. Thus Han Yü, a great scholar in the T'ang dynasty, said, "Conduct which is proper is called righteousness."

> Mencius said, "...Benevolence is the tranquil habitation of man, and righteousness is his straight path."[39]

Mencius believed that benevolence which cannot be carried into practice is as useless as unripe grain.

> Mencius said, "Of all the seeds the best are the five kinds of grain, yet if they are not ripe, they are not equal to lower grades of grain. So, the value of benevolence depends entirely on its being brought to maturity."[39]

Mencius used easily understood examples to explain the positive and negative sides of the principles of benevolence and righteousness. He regarded the extension of refraining from injuring others as the love of men or benevolence. Likewise, he regarded the extension of refraining from robbing others as an aid to men or righteousness. Both benevolence and righteousness are principles of human conduct. Their achievement depends upon vigorous conduct, not mere lip service.

> Mencius said, "All men have some things which they cannot bear; extend that feeling to what they can bear, and benevolence will be the result. All men have some things which they will not do; extend that feeling to the things which they do, and righteousness will be the result.
>
> "If a man can give full development to the feeling which makes him shrink from injuring others, his benevolence will be more than can be called into practice. If he can give full development to the feeling which refuses to break through, or jump over a wall, his righteousness will be more than can be called into practice.

"If he can give full development to the real feeling of dislike with which he receives the salutation, 'Thou,' 'Thou,' he will act righteously in all places and circumstances.

"When a scholar speaks what he ought not to speak, by guile of speech seeking to gain some end; and when he does not speak what he ought to speak, by guile of silence seeking to gain some end; both these cases are of a piece with breaking through a neighbor's wall."[40]

Since righteousness is the practice of benevolence and only vigorous conduct can be akin to benevolence, the knowledge of righteousness is the knowledge of vigorous conduct.

In the *Doctrine of the Mean*, it is written: "Righteousness is the accordance of actions with what is right."[41] This is the simplest and most correct definition of righteousness. It agrees with Han Yü's saying: "Conduct which is proper is called righteousness."

In their collective lives, all the actions of men are either proper or improper. It is proper to do what should be done. It is improper to do what should not be done. Whatever is proper is in accord with truth and consistent with time and space. Before we speak any word or perform any act, we should determine whether our words and acts are in agreemnt with the requirements of time and space or whether they are opposed to the nature of things. We must consider these things carefully, especially when great principles are at stake. Something that should be done must be done. We should not shirk our responsibility, no matter what danger faces us. Something that should not be done must not be done, no matter what the temptation may be.

The sages, worthy men and outstanding personages in our history have always followed these principles, never deviating even in the slightest degree.

The Master said, "The superior man in everything considers righteousness to be the substance. He performs it according to the rules of propriety. He brings it forth in humility. He completes it with sincerity. This is indeed a superior man."[42]

"Substance," here, means "essence." In everything, we must distinguish between what should and what should not be done. When we have determined what to do, we should act vigorously according to the rules of conduct, proceeding step by step to the consummation of the action. Confucius believed righteousness to be the basis of all actions. As Mencius said, "Righteousness is the way";[43] "righteousness is man's path";[44] "righteousness is his straight path";[45] and "one's path should be righteousness."[46] Mencius also regarded righteousness as the path along which human actions must pass. It is the foundation. If this foundation is not laid, that which is built upon it cannot be solid. Once the wrong road is taken, the rest of the journey will lead in the wrong direction.

In one of the passages previously quoted, Mencius said, "All men have some things which they will not do; extend that feeling to the things which they do, and righteousness will be the result."[47] On another occasion he also said, "Men must be decided on what they will not do, and then they are able to act with vigor in what they ought to do."[48] If we wish to know what we should do, we should first determine what we should not do. If we refuse to do what we should not do, we shall do only what we should do. This is the essential point of Mencius' teaching on the practice of righteousness. If we do not have enough faith to concentrate on what should be done, we will accomplish little in our lifetimes.

To act and not to act, though apparently contrary, are actually complementary. They are respectively the positive and negative sides of righteousness. To do what should be done is righteousness. To avoid what should not be done is also righteousness. If one decides to avoid corruption, he should maintain incorruptibility. If one decides to avoid evil, he should persist in doing good. To act is positive and not to act is negative, but both lead to the same path and both are examples of vigorous conduct, which is near to benevolence.

Hence, Mencius said, "If he (a man) can give full development to the feeling which refuses to break through, or jump over, a wall, his righteousness will be more than can be called into practice. If he can give full development to the real feeling of dislike with which he receives the salutation, 'Thou, Thou,' he will act righteously in all places and circumstances."

Mencius said, "...to take what one has not a right to is contrary to righteousness."[49]

Mencius said, "...The feeling of shame and dislike is the beginning of righteousness."[30]

Breaking through or jumping over a wall is an act of theft or robbery, and accepting the salutation, "Thou, Thou," is an act of meanness. We must dislike such acts and be ashamed of them. Since man has the sense of dislike and shame, he should not steal or obtain what is not due him. If this feeling is extended, it should be so broadened that whoever does not steal will even give generous alms to others. Likewise, whoever does not disgrace himself will have self-respect. In such ways will righteousness and uprightness pervade the universe and be admired everywhere.

The love of men is benevolence. So is the perfection of oneself. As the *Doctrine of the Mean* tells us, "Fulfillment of our being is perfect virtue."[51] When this is reflected in conduct, it is righteousness. Hence, we have the "choice of righteousness" advocated by Mencius and the "fulfillment of benevolence" taught by Confucius. Both are acts of courage and the culmination of vigorous conduct.

Mencius said, "I like fish, and I also like the bear's paws. If I cannot have the two together, I will let the fish go and take the bear's paws. So, I like life, and I also like righteousness. If I cannot keep the two together, I will let life go and choose righteousness.

"I like life indeed, but there is that which I like more than life, and therefore I will not seek to possess it by any improper ways. I dislike death indeed, but there is that which I dislike more than death, and therefore there are occasions when I will not avoid danger.

"If among the things which man likes there were nothing he liked more than life, why should he not use every means by which he could preserve it? If among the things which man disliked there were nothing which he disliked more than death, why should he not do everything by which he could avoid danger?

"There are cases when men by a certain course might preserve life, and they do not employ it; when by certain things they might avoid danger, and they will not do them.

"Therefore men have that which they like more than life and that which they dislike more than death. They are not worthy men only who have this mental nature. All men have it; what belongs to such worthy men is simply that they do not lose it.

"Here are a small basket of rice and a platter of soup, and the case is one in which the getting of them will preserve life and the want of them will be death; if they are offered with an insulting voice, even a tramper will not receive them, or if you first tread upon them, even a beggar will not stoop to take them.

"And yet a man will accept ten thousand *chung* without any consideration of propriety or righteousness. What can the ten thousand *chung* add to him? When he takes them, is it not that he may obtain beautiful mansions, that he may secure the services of a wife and concubines, or that the poor and needy of his acquaintance may be helped by him?

"In the former case the offered bounty was not received, though it would have saved from death, and now the emolument is taken for the sake of beautiful mansions. The bounty that would have preserved from death was not received, and the emolument is taken to get the services of a wife and concubines. The bounty that would have saved from death was not received, and the emolument is taken that one's poor and needy acquaintances may be helped by him. Was it then not possible likewise to decline this? This is a case of what is called 'losing the proper nature of one's mind.'"[52]

How noble and edifying this passage from Mencius is! No one dislikes life, nor is there anyone who likes death. However, the culmination of righteousness often results in the sacrifice of one's life. When a choice is demanded between one's life and righteousness, we must make the proper choice. The life of the small self must be sacrificed for the righteousness of the greater self.

However, one is often misled by the dislike of death. Then, one acts without righteousness. In such cases, we forget that righteousness is more to be desired than life, and that unrighteousness should be more disliked than death.

We must make the strictest determination in such cases. If we strove only to protect our lives in all cases, without regretting the loss of our feelings of shame, dislike, modesty, concession, right and wrong, we would be like the lower animals. So it has been said, "Vigorous conduct is near to benevolence," and only the culmination of vigorous conduct can manifest the "fulfillment of benevolence after seeking for it."

3. Knowledge of Shame

The knowledge of shame cannot be regarded as courage, but only akin to courage. How can a man be said to know shame? The difference between human beings and the lower animals is simply that human beings know shame and animals do not. Shame is a driving force for the progress of mankind. Only when there is knowledge of shame can there be vigorous effort. Only when there is vigorous effort can there be accomplishment. All civilizations of mankind start from the knowledge of shame. If his sense of shame were lost, man would become degenerate, numb, listless, licentious and mean. In short, he would be no different from the lower animals. Thus, the sage, in giving instruction, had to teach people to know shame. Only then could there be a morality and culture to speak of.

> The Master said, "If the people are led by laws and uniformity sought to be given them by punishment, they will try to avoid the punishment, but have no sence of shame.
> "If they are led by virtue and uniformity sought to be given them by the rules of propriety, they will have the sense of shame and moreover can progress till they are perfect."[53]

The greatest effect of government and law can be no more than the freedom of people from crime. Only through instruction can people be constantly reminded of the sense of shame. Only then will they become conscious of themselves and uplift themselves until they are perfect.

The sense of shame has a dual effect. Negatively, it enables people to realize their mistakes and shortcomings. Positively, shame causes them to seek to act correctly. Negatively, people must be aware of their inferiority, and, positively, they must be aware of their superiority. Self-reliance and self-exertion would be of no help if people made no effort to stand out among their peers.

> Mencius said, "The sense of shame is of great importance to a man.
> "Those who form contrivances and versatile schemes distinguished for their artfulness do not allow their sense of shame to come into action.
> "When one does not feel the sense of shame when one cannot compare with others, how can one ever compare with others in anything?"[54]

The Master said, "The leaving virtue without proper cultivation; the not thoroughly discussing what is learned; not being able to move towards righteousness of which a knowledge is gained; and not being able to change what is not good—these are the things which occasion me solicitude."[55]

This means that the sense of shame has a very important bearing on human life. Only when one feels this sense of shame, realizing that his accomplishments cannot compare with those of others, will he make an effort to equal or surpass others. The manifestation of this shame is no less than courage. There is no sense of shame in a man who is an opportunist and a schemer. Such a man is insincere and false, and he will not try to correct his mistakes when they are known. Confucius was concerned about this.

> Mencius said, "A man may not be without shame. When one is ashamed of having been without shame, he will afterwards not have occasion to be ashamed."[56]

Because of the important relationship between shame and human life, Mencius reminded us that man can never be without it. If we can feel ashamed of being without shame, we can always be free from feeling ashamed at all.

> Hsien asked what was shameful. The Master said, "When good government prevails in a State, to be thinking only of salary; and when bad government prevails, to be thinking, in the same way, only of salary—this is shameful."[57]

Hsien, who was also known as Yüan Ssŭ, was noted for his incorruptible character. Naturally, he was very loyal to the State. However, the knowledge of shame must be applied positively, not negatively. When there is good government, a man must make whatever contribution he can. When there is bad government, one must make every effort to change it. Hsien, in his incorruptibility, tended toward passivity. Confucius answered his inquiry, saying that any thought of salary without an attempt to make a positive contribution is shameful.

> The Master said, "With sincere faith he (a man) unites the love of learning: holding firm to death, he is perfecting the Way.
> "Such a person will not enter a tottering State, nor dwell in a disorganized one. When the Way prevails in the empire, he will show himself: when it does not, he will keep concealed.
> "When the Way prevails in a country, poverty and a mean

condition are things to be ashamed of. When it does not prevail, riches and honors are things to be ashamed of."[58]

While it is shameful to seek wealth and power without making any effort to reform an ill-governed country, it is even more shameful to be satisfied with poverty and poor conditions in a well-governed country. If a man refuses to live in his State when it is near collapse or thoroughly disorganized, he must live in a foreign country. One's appearance or concealment in a country, depending whether the Way prevails or not, affects the empire as a whole. For the peace and tranquillity of one's homeland, one should, except under extraordinary circumstances, serve one's country as best he can. Confucius praised such men. He admired men who were loyal, sincere and earnest. He admired men who combined sincere faith with a love of learning, standing firm even unto death in search of the perfection of the Way.

> The Master said, "Fine words, an insinuating appearance and excessive respect; Tso Ch'iu-ming was ashamed of them. I also am ashamed of them. To conceal resentment against a person and appear friendly with him; Tso Ch'iuming was ashamed of such conduct. I also am ashamed of it."[59]
>
> The Master said, "Without the specious speech of the litanist T'o and the beauty of the prince Chao of Sung, it is difficult to escape in the present age."[60]
>
> The Master said, "The superior man is modest in his speech, but exceeds in his actions."[61]

If we consider excessive words shameful, then our words must match our actions. Likewise our actions must match our words, and we must "translate our words into action first." Only then can we deserve to be called sincere.

To teach men to possess shame is no more than to motivate them to develop their inherent sense of shame. It is difficult to enumerate all the things which should occasion shame, but if we constantly search our memories, we will be able to do so. We must realize that the sense of shame has a close relationship with knowledge, will and faith. Thus, men differ in their sense of shame just as they do in their degrees of intelligence and desire. While the uneducated consider attention to minor virtues shameful, scholars of strong will and benevolent men do not agree.

The Master said, "A scholar whose mind is set on the Way and who is ashamed of bad clothes and bad food is not fit to be discoursed with."[32]

The Master said, "Dressed himself in a tattered robe quilted with hemp, yet standing by the side of men dressed in furs and not ashamed—ah! it is Yu who is equal to this!

"He injured none, he covets nothing; what can he do but what is good?"

Tzŭ-lu kept continually repeating these words of the ode, when Confucius said, "This is but one way, but those things are by no means sufficient to constitute (perfect) excellence."[63]

Common people regard coarse clothes and poor food as shameful. However, scholars of strong will are ashamed only of their failure to cultivate the person and to practice the Way. They neither consider wealth and position a source of pride nor do they think poverty and low station a source of shame. Though shabbily dressed, Tzŭ-lu was not affected when standing alongside someone dressed in furs. He regarded the minor details of food and clothing as inconsequential. Confucius, however, did not believe this to be in full compliance with the saying quoted from the *Book of Songs*,

Thus, we should feel "unashamed before Heaven above and men below."[64] Only then can we consider ourselves to possess the sense of shame and courage.

B. Objectives

When a man is fond of learning, engages in vigorous conduct and knows shame, he possesses the three basic conditions for the cultivation of his person. What then are the objectives of the cultivation of the person?

The first objective is the "completion of self," or, the building of oneself into a man of perfect personality. The second objective is "the completion of things," which is the extension of the perfect personality to his common existence with others, and includes the increase of human well-being, the regulation of the family, proper government of the State and world peace.

Everything in the world has its essence and its utility. That which has great essence must have great usefulness. The completion of the self has as its first concern the enlargement of essence with a view to increased usefulness.

The man of perfect personality is a sage. Next we have the superior man, the good man and the constant man. Constancy, however, is the prerequisite of the first three categories of man.

> The Master said, "A sage it is not mine to see; if I see a superior man, I am satisfied."
> The Master said, "A good man it is not mine to see: if I see a man possessed of constancy, I am satisfied.
> "Having not and yet affecting to have, empty and yet affecting to be full, straitened and yet affecting to be at ease—it is difficult with such characteristics to have constancy."[55]

It is commonly said that "to aim at the medium, emulate the highest." Thus, even if one is willing to be but a superior man, he should attempt to become a sage. The level of personality and character one can attain depends upon the effort one makes.

> The disciple Kung-tu said, "All are equally men, but some are great men and some are little men; how is this?" Mencius replied, "Those who follow that part of themselves which is great are great men; those who follow that part of themselves which is little are little men."
> Kung-tu pursued, "All are equally men, but some follow that part of themselves which is great and some follow that part which is little; how is this?" Mencius replied, "The senses of hearing and seeing do not think and are obscured by external things. When one thing comes into contact with another, as a matter of course it leads it away. To the mind belongs the office of thinking. By thinking, it gets the right view of things; by neglecting to think, it fails to do this. These things—the senses and the mind—are what Heaven has given to us. Let a man first stand fast in the supremacy of the nobler part of his constitution, and the inferior part will not be able to take it from him. It is simply this which makes the great man."[66]

1 The Sage

> Mencius said, "The compass and square produce perfect circles and squares. By the sages, the human relations are perfectly exhibited."[57]

Clearly, the compass and the square are the standards for producing circles and squares. In the same manner, the sage is the standard upon which the human personality should be modeled.

The sage possesses profound learning and is of lofty character. "His movements for ages point the way for the world. His acts are for ages a law to the world. His words are for ages an example to the world. Those who are far from him look up to him; and those who are near him are never wearied with him."[68] Thus he can be the teacher of all succeeding generations.

> Mencius said, "A sage is the teacher of a hundred generations. This is true of Po-i and Hui of Liu-hsia. Therefore when men now hear the character of Po-i, the corrupt become pure and the weak acquire determination. When they hear the character of Hui of Liu-hsia, the mean become generous and the niggardly become liberal. They exerted themselves a hundred generations ago, and after a hundred generations those who hear of them are aroused. Could such be the case if they had not been sages? And how much more did they affect those who were personally under their inspiring influence?"[69]

The influence of the sage—in making the corrupt pure, the weak determined, the mean generous, and the niggardly liberal— has been eternal and boundless, without limits of time and space. Hence:

> Mencius said, "...When this great man exercises a transforming influence, he is what is called a sage."[70]
> How great the Way of the Sage is! Like the overflowing water, it sends forth and nourishes all things and rises up to the height of heaven.
> All-complete is its greatness! It embraces the three hundred rules of ceremony and the three thousand rules of demeanor. It waits for the proper man, and then it is practiced.
> Hence it is said, "Without perfect virtue, the perfect Way cannot be crystallized."

Therefore the superior man honors his virtuous nature and maintains constant inquiry and study, seeking to carry it out to its breadth and greatness, so as to omit none of the more exquisite and minute points which it embraces and to raise it to its greatest height and brilliancy, so as to pursue the course of the Mean. He reviews his old knowledge and thus continually acquires new. He exerts an honest, generous earnestness in the esteem and practice of propriety.

Thus, when occupying a high situation he is not proud, and in a low situation he is not insubordinate. When the country is well-governed, he is sure to make it proper with his words; and when it is ill-governed, he is sure to be tolerated by his silence. Is not this what we find in the *Book of Songs*, "Intelligent is he and prudent, and so preserves his person"?[71]

Mencius, after studying the characteristics of the ancient sage, divided them into four categories: pure, accommodating, responsible and timeous.

Mencius said, "Po-i would not allow his eyes to look on a bad sight nor his ears to listen to a bad sound. He would not serve a prince whom he did not approve nor command a people whom he did not esteem. In a time of good government he took office, and on the occurrence of confusion he retired. He could not bear to dwell either in a court from which a lawless government emanated, or among lawless people. He considered his being in the same place with a villager, as if he were to sit amid mud coals with his court robes and court cap. In the time of Chou he dwelt on the shores of the North sea, waiting for the purification of the empire. Therefore when men now hear the character of Po-i, the corrupt become pure and the weak acquire determination.

"Yi-Yin said, 'Where is the prince that I cannot serve? Where are the people that I cannot command?' In a time of good government he took office, and when confusion prevailed he also took office. He said, 'Heaven's plan in the production of mankind is this: that they who are first informed should instruct those who are later in being informed, and they who first apprehend the Way should instruct those who are slower in doing so. I am one of Heaven's people who has first apprehended: I will take this Way and instruct this people in it.' He thought that among all the people of the empire, even the common men and women, if there were any who did not share in the enjoyment of such benefits as Yao and Shun conferred, it was as if he himself pushed them into a ditch: for he took upon himself the heavy charge of the empire.

"Hui of Liu-hsia was not ashamed to serve an impure prince nor did he think it low to be an inferior official. When advanced to employment, he did not conceal his virtue, but made it a point to carry out his principles. When dismissed and left without office, he did not murmur. When straitened by poverty, he did not grieve. When thrown into the company of village people he was quite at ease and could not bear to leave them. He had a saying, 'You are you and I am I. Although you stand by my side with breast and arms bare, or with your body naked, how can you defile me?' Therefore when men hear the character of Hui of Liu-hsia, the mean become generous and the niggardly become liberal.

"When Confucius was leaving Ch'i he strained off with his hand the water in which his rice was being rinsed, took the rice and went away. When he left Lu, he said, 'I will set out by-and-by:'—it was right he should leave the country of his parents in this way. When it was proper to go away quickly, he did so; when it was proper to remain longer, he did so; when it was proper to keep in retirement, he did so; and when it was proper to go into office, he did so—this was Confucius."

Mencius said, "Po-i among the sages was the pure one: Yi Yin was the most responsible one; Hui of Liu-hsia was the most accommodating one; and Confucius was the timeous one.

"In Confucius we have the culmination of the great attainments of sagehood. This culmination is like a complete concert in which the large bell proclaims the commencement of the music and the ringing stone proclaims its close. The metal sound commences the blended harmony of all the instruments, and the winding up with the stone terminates that blended harmony. The commencing that harmony is the work of wisdom. The terminating it is the work of sageness.

"As a comparison for wisdom, we may liken it to skill, and as a comparison for sageness, we may liken it to strength; as in the case of shooting at a mark a hundred paces beyond. That you reach it is owing to your strength, but that you hit the mark is not owing to your strength."[72]

To be a pure, accommodating and responsible sage is unattainable for ordinary men. Embodying all the characteristics of a sage, Confucius was the paragon among sages. He deserved to be the teacher of generations to come. He was called "timeous," meaning that without subjecting himself to the limits of time, he represented the highest possible type of human personality. Yet, he was humble enough to say, "As to sageness, I am incapable of it," and "As to sageness and benevolence, how can I deserve them?"

The *Doctrine of the Mean* defines the highest sage thus:

It is only the highest sage in the world that can show himself quick in apprehension, clear in discernment, of far-reaching intelligence and all-embracing knowledge, fitted to rule the people; magnanimous, wholehearted, benign and mild, fitted to exercise forbearance; energetic, firm and enduring, fitted to maintain a firm hold; self-adjusted, grave, never swerving from the Mean and correct, fitted to command reverence; minutely observant and searching, fitted to excercise discrimination.

All-embracing is he and vast, deep and active as a fountain, sending forth in their due season his virtues.

All-embracing and vast, he is like heaven. Deep and active as a fountain, he is like the abyss. He is seen, and the people all reverence him; he speaks, and the people all believe him; he acts, and the people all are pleased with him.

Therefore his fame overspreads the Middle Kingdom and extends to all barbarous tribes. Wherever ships and carriages reach; wherever the strength of man penetrates; wherever the heavens overshadow and the earth sustains; wherever the sun and moon shine; wherever frosts and dews fall:—all who have blood and breath unfeignedly honor and love him. Hence it is said, "He is the equal of Heaven."[73]

The highest sage must have the ability and knowledge to deal with others. He must possess great magnanimity, strong faith, a strict demeanor and profound learning. Only when these qualities are attained can one's personality be called perfect. It is toward the attainment of these objectives that the man who wishes to cultivate his person must aim.

Sageness and worthiness have been identified as synonymous, but they are not the same. The connotation of worthiness includes the abundance of talent and wisdom. Often, this meaning is present in the comparative degree. This comparison is also apparent when worthiness is contrasted with unworthiness.

Tzŭ-kung replied, "The doctrines of Wĕn and Wu have not yet fallen to the ground. They are to be found among men. Worthy men remember their greater principles, while the unworthy remember the smaller. Thus all possess the doctrines of Wĕn and Wu. Where could our Master go that he did not have an opportunity of learning them, and what necessity was there for his having a regular teacher?"[74]

Certain institutions of the Chou dynasty were profound and important, while others were shallow and unimportant. The talented and wise know which to attend to, while others do not. Thus, worthiness and unworthiness are relative rather than absolute.

Tzŭ-kung was in the habit of criticizing others. The Master said, "Is Tz'ŭ truly worthy? As to me, I have no leisure for this."[75]

While Tzŭ-kung felt qualified to criticize others, Confucius doubted his superiority to those whom he criticized. And that is why he commented on Tzŭ-kung as he did.

> The Master said, "He who does not anticipate attempts to deceive him, nor think beforehand of his not being believed, and yet apprehends these things readily (when they occur)—is he not a worthy man?"[76]

Deceit and falsehood are common in human society, but we must not prejudge others. As long as we have clear consciences, we can take adequate precautions that we will not be deceived afterwards. Is this not better than to prejudge?

It is apparent that the original meaning of "worthiness" is comparative, meaning "better" or "superior." Mencius made special reference to "wisdom" when he mentioned "worthy men." Thus it is evident that worthy men are wise men whose talents and intelligence surpass those of the average man.

> Mencius said, "Anciently, worthy men by means of their own enlightenment made others enlightened. Nowadays, it is tried, while they are themselves in darkness, and by means of that darkness, to make others enlightened."[77]

Thus the worthy can enlighten others only through their own enlightenment. If one is in darkness, he can hardly enlighten others, much as a blind man cannot serve as a guide.

> The Master said, "Some worthy men retire from the world.
> "Some retire from particular States.
> "Some retire because of disrespectful looks.
> "Some retire because of contradictory language."[78]

Different kinds of worthy men carry out their retirement in varying degrees, taking great care that they might preserve themselves. Unlike the unworthy, they are not influenced by the consideration of gain in any of the instances just mentioned.

> Kung-sun Ch'ou said, "Yi Yin said, 'I cannot be near and see him so disobedient to reason,' and therewith he banished T'ai-chia to T'ung. The people were much pleased. When T'ai-chia became virtuous, he brought him back, and the people were again much pleased.
> "When worthies are ministers, may they indeed banish their sovereigns in this way when they are not virtuous?"

Mencius replied, "If they have the same purpose as Yi Yin, they may. If they have not the same purpose, it would be usurpation."[79]

T'ai-chia was the son of T'ang. He was regarded as unworthy because after succeeding to the throne, he did not follow the traditions of his great father. Yi Yin, a worthy man and loyal minister with great talent and wisdom, banished T'ai-chia to make him repent. He reinstated him after T'ai-chia corrected his previous conduct. Though Yi Yin's actions in these two instances were diametrically opposed, both were motivated by his sense of justice and loyalty. In this respect he complied with the wishes of the people. Thus, Yi Yin succeeded in consolidating the reign of the Shang dynasty.

2. The Superior Man

The expression "superior man" has a widely varied significance. It cannot be reduced to a hard and fast definition. It may help us to understand the various connnotations of this expression if we consider all the passages from the *Four Books* which deal with it. As for the difference between the superior man and the mean man, this has been discussed in the section on "Knowledge of Men" in Chapter III.

> The Master said, "The superior man does not seek to gratify his appetite for food, nor have ease in his residence; he is quick in his action but careful in his speech; he frequents the company of men of principle that he may be rectified—such a person may be said indeed to love to learn."[80]
>
> The Master said, "The object of the superior man is the Way. Food is not his object. There is plowing; even in that there is sometimes want. So with learning; emolument may be found in it. The superior man is anxious lest he should not obtain the Way; he is not anxious lest poverty should come upon him."[81]

Thus, the superior man sees the Way as important and gives little thought to food. He studies hard in seeking for the Way, and he does not feel disturbed about his poverty.

> The Master said, "...Is he not a superior man, who feels no discomposure though men may take no note of him?"[82]
>
> The Master said, "The superior man is distressed by his want of ability. He is not distressed by man's not knowing him."[83]

The Master said, "The superior man dislikes the thought of his name not being mentioned after his death."[81]

The superior man should seek to examine himself. While he is not distressed with not being known in his lifetime, he is distressed by not being known after his death.

The Master said, "...In the Way of the superior man there are four things, to not one of them have I as yet attained. To serve my father as I would require my son to serve me: to this I have not attained; to serve my prince as I would require my minister to serve me: to this I have not attained; to serve my elder brother as I would require my younger brother to serve me: to this I have not attained; to be first to behave to a friend as I would require him to behave to me: to this I have not attained. Earnest in practicing the ordinary virtues and careful in making ordinary utterances, if, in his practice, he has anything defective, the superior man dares not but exert himself; and if, in his words, he has left anything unsaid, he dares not exhaust them. Thus his words have respect to his actions, and his actions have respect to his words. How can the superior man help being prudent?"[85]

The philosopher Yu said, "...The superior man bends his attention to the root. That being established, the Way grows up. Filial piety and fraternal submission—are they not the root of benevolence?"[86]

This makes clear that the superior man, being careful in speech and action, takes filial piety, fraternal love, loyalty and faithfulness as the foundations of his conduct.

The Master said, "If the superior man is not grave, he will not call forth any veneration and his learning will not be solid.

"Hold loyalty and faithfulness as first principles.

"Have no friends not equal to yourself.

"When you have faults, do not fear to rectify them."[37]

Tzŭ-kung said, "The faults of the superior man are like the eclipses of the sun and moon. He has his faults, and all men see them; he changes again, and all men look up to him."[38]

The Master said, "Where substance prevails over polish, we have rusticity; where polish is in excess of substance, we have the manners of a clerk. When substance and appearance are equally blended, we then have a superior man."[39]

Before he can become a man of propriety, the superior man must combine natural and man-made grace.

"The Master said, 'The superior man is not a utensil."[90] Thus, the superior man is well-rounded and not confined to any one field.

The Master said, "The superior man is modest in his speech, but exceeds in his actions."[91]

The Master said, "The superior man wishes to be slow in his speech and quick in his conduct."[92]

The superior man must be consistent in his words and actions. Ashamed of allowing his words to exceed his actions, he would rather act before he speaks.

The Master said, "The superior man, in the world, does not set his mind either for anything or against anything; what is right he will follow."[93]

The Master said, "The superior man in everything considers righteousness to be the substance. He performs it according to the rules of propriety. He brings it forth in humility. He completes it with sincerity. This is indeed a superior man."[94]

The superior man is never arbitrary and neither disregards nor denies anything. He considers what is proper in each instance, doing what should be done and avoiding what should not. He follows the rules of reason, striving to be earnest and sincere and working to achieve his end.

The Master said, "The superior man is faithful in principle, but does not show firmness on minor details."[95]

Mencius said, "If a superior man does not have faith, how shall he take a firm hold of things?"[96]

The superior man, then, is not obstinate, but he should remain firm and adhere steadfastly to principle.

The Master said, "The superior man is dignified, but does not wrangle. He is sociable, but not a partisan."[97]

The Master said, "The superior man has no contentions. If it be said he cannot avoid them, shall this be in archery? But he bows complaisantly to his competitors; thus he ascends the hall, descends and imposses on the loser the forfeit of drinking, In his contention, he is still the superior man."[98]

Thus, while the superior man maintains his dignity, he has no quarrel with others. While he is sociable, he shows no partiality to those of whom he is fond. Even in an archery contest, in which there must be a winner, he follows the rules of propriety from beginning to end. Bowing complaisantly to his competitors, he goes up to the hall and then descends, imposing on the loser the forfeit of drinking. These are the rules of the game. They are in compliance with "fair play" and "sportsmanship" in the modern sense.

> The Master said, "The superior man does not promote a man simply on account of his words, nor does he put aside good words because of the man."[99]

So it is, that in his dealings with men, the superior man does not believe everything told to him. Neither does he lightly disregard the words of others. He reaches his decision only after careful consideration because the character of a man cannot always be determined by his words. Thus, Confucius said, "The virtuous man will be sure to speak correctly, but those whose speech is good may not always be virtuous."[100]

> The Master said, "...If a superior man abandons benevolence, how can he achieve his good name? The superior man does not, even for the space of a single meal, act contrary to benevolence. In moments of haste, he cleaves to it. In seasons of danger, he cleaves to it."[101]
>
> The Master said, "The Way of the superior man is threefold, but I am not equal to it. Benevolent, he is free from anxieties; wise, he is free from perplexities; courageous, he is free from fear." Tzŭ-kung said, "The Master was speaking of himself here."[102]
>
> Ssŭ-ma Niu asked about the superior man. The Master said, "The superior man has neither anxiety nor fear."
>
> "Being without anxiety or fear," said Niu, "does this constitute what we call the superior man?"
>
> The Master said, "When internal examination discovers nothing to be sorry for, what is there to be anxious about, what is there to fear?"[103]

The superior man gains freedom from anxiety, perplexity and fear by cultivating the virtues of wisdom, benevolence and courage.

> Confucius said, "There are three things which the superior man guards against. In youth, when the physical powers are not yet settled, he guards against lust. When he enters manhood and the physical powers are full of vigor, he guards against

quarrelsomeness. When he is old and the animal powers are decayed, he guards against covetousness."[104]

Thus, the superior man, from youth through manhood to old age, must guard against certain things.

Tzŭ-hsia said, "The superior man undergoes three changes. Looked at from a distance, he appears stern; when approached, he is mild; when he is heard to speak, his language is firm and decided."[105]

The superior man maintains an attitude of mildness and firmness at the same time. This was the attitude assumed by Confucius when he was described to be "mild and yet dignified, majestic and yet not fierce; respectful and yet easy."[106]

Confucius said, "The superior man has nine things which are sujects with him of thoughtful consideration. In regard to the use of his eyes, he is anxious to see clearly. In regard to the use of his ears, he is anxious to hear distinctly. In regard to his countenance, he is anxious that it should be benign. In regard to his demeanor, he is anxious that it should be respectful. In regard to his speech, he is anxious that it should be sincere. In regard to his doing of business, he is anxious that it should be reverently careful. In regard to what he doubts about, he is anxious to question others. When he is angry, he thinks of the difficulties (his anger may involve him in). When he sees gain to be got, he thinks of righteousness."[107]

In all his dealings, the superior man must consider carefully what he must do. He must do so without relaxation and without compromise so that he might achieve the state of perfection.

Mencius said, "The superior man has three things in which he delights, but to be ruler over the empire is not one of them.

"That his father and mother are both alive and that the condition of his brothers affords no cause for anxiety; this is one delight.

"That, when looking up, he has no occasion for shame before Heaven and, below, he has no occasion to blush before men; this is a second delight.

"That he can get from the whole empire the most talented individuals and educate them; this is the third delight.

"The superior man has three things in which he delights, but to be ruler over the empire is not one of them."[108]

Mencius said, "Wide territory and a numerous people are desired by the superior man, but what he delights in is not here.

"To stand in the center of the empire and tranquillize the people within the four seas; the superior man delights in this, but the highest enjoyment of his nature is not here.

"What belongs by his nature to the superior man cannot be increased by the extensive prevalence of the Way nor diminished by his dwelling in poverty and retirement; because it is determinately apportioned to him by Heaven.

"What belongs by his nature to the superior man are benevolence, righteousness, propriety and wisdom. These are rooted in his heart; their growth and manifestation are a mild harmony appearing in the countenance, a rich fullness in the back and the character imparted to the four limbs. Those limbs understand to arrange themselves, without being told."[109]

Thus, the superior man delights in the perfection of himself and of other things, as well as the preservation of his inherent virtues, rather than enjoying the admiration of external wealth and honors. Should he reach the stage where he is satisfied with the profundity of the cultivation he has attained, he can be happy beyond description, be he rich or poor.

Mencius said, "...Wherever the superior man passes through, transformation follows. What exists in his mind is supernatural. It flows above and beneath with Heaven and Earth. Who can say that it is only of small benefit to the world?"[110]

The spiritual accomplishments of the superior man reach the highest stage. Since his influence flows together with that of Heaven and Earth, his virtue can be said to be equal to theirs, and he can be called a sage.

From this analysis, it is clear that the superior man is simply seeking to fulfill the conditions required of a sage when he attempts to be qualified to rule the people, exercise forbearance, maintain a firm hold on the situation, command respect and act with discrimination. When a person strives to be a superior man, he does not necessarily become a sage, but by developing himself into a man of perfect character, he can bring peace to mankind and perfection to all things. In a word, the key is self-cultivation.

Tzŭ-lu asked what constituted the superior man. The Master said, "The cultivation of himself in reverential carefulness." "And is this all?" said Tzu-lu. "He cultivates himself so as to give rest to others," was the reply. "And is this all?" again asked Tzŭ-lu. The Master said, "He cultivates himself so as to give rest to all the people—even Yao and Shun could have deplored their deficiency in this respect."[111]

The distinction between the superior man and the mean man, as described in the chapter on "The Extension of Knowledge," and the qualities which should be possessed by the superior man, as discussed in this chapter, explain how a person can completely fulfill the requirements necessary to attain the character of a superior man. When Tzŭ-lu posed his question regarding the "complete" or perfect man, Confucius answered him by giving several examples.

> Tzŭ-lu asked what constituted a complete man. The Master said, "Suppose a man with the wisdom of Tsang Wu-chung, the freedom from covetousness of Kung-ch'o, the bravery of Chuang of Pien and the varied talents of Jan Ch'iu; add to these the accomplishments of the rules of propriety and music—such a person might be reckoned a complete man.
>
> He then added, "But what is the necessity for a complete man of the present day to have all these things? The man, who in the view of gain thinks of righteousness; who in the view of danger is prepared to give up his life; and who does not forget an old agreement however far back it extends—such a person may be reckoned a complete man."[112]

From this we can see that Confucius had lowered his qualifications for the superior man of his time. Yet we can conclude that those who possess the qualities of wisdom, benevolence, righteousness, courage, faithfulness, literary and artistic talent, propriety and music are men of character.

3. The Good Man

Good is the antithesis of evil. True, a good man is unwilling to do evil, and not only is he opposed to doing evil, but he promotes the performance of good. He may, however, lack the strength to achieve the most far-reaching accomplishment so as to reach sagehood; nevertheless, he may yet turn out to be a good man in society.

Tzŭ-chang asked what were the characteristics of the good man. The Master said, "He does not tread in the footsteps of his predecessors, nor can he thereby enter the chamber of the sage."[113]

Mencius once referred to the degree in which the good man differs from the sage.

Hao-shêng Pu-hai asked, saying, "What sort of man is Yüeh-chêng?" Mencius replied, "He is a good man, a truthful man."

"What do you mean by 'a good man, a truthful man'?"

The reply was, "A man who commands our liking is what is called a good man. He whose goodness is part of himself is called an honest man. He whose goodness has been filled up is what is called a beautiful man. He whose completed goodness is brightly displayed is what is called a great man. When this great man exercises a transforming influence, he is what is called a sage. When the sage is beyond our knowledge, he is what is called a spirit-man.

"Yüeh-chêng is between the two first categories and below the four last."[114]

Mencius clearly defined goodness, honesty, beauty, greatness, sageness and "the state of the spirit-man." From his definitions, we learn that the "good" man only commands the "liking" of others and cannot compare with the sage. The sage is not only "great"; he exercises a "transforming influence." Though he is indispensable to society, the good man cannot hope for great achievements. So, if he is entrusted with the govenment of a country, he can teach his people to be patriotic and resist external aggression only after a period of seven years. He can transform the violently evil and abolish capital punishment only after a century.

The Master said, "Let a good man teach the people seven years, and they may then likewise be employed in war."[115]

The Master said, "It is said, 'If good men were to govern a country in succession for a hundred years, they would be able to transform the violenly bad and dispense with capital punishment.' True indeed is this statement."[116]

Thus, mere goodness is not sufficient for good government. For good government can be accomplished only after lengthy effort.

4. The Constant Man

What is so important about constancy? The answer can be

found in one of the passages quoted in the chapter on "The Investigation of Things." The crux of this passage is: "If another man succeeds by one effort, he will use a hundred effort. If another man succeeds by ten efforts, he will use a thousand. Let a man proceed in this way, and, though dull, he will surely become intelligent; though weak, he will surely become strong." For either a hundred or a thousand efforts, constancy is indispensable. By being constant, a dull person can become intelligent and a weak person strong. Strenuous effort enables a person to achieve the same wisdom and success as another person who has received such gifts from nature. This is the value of constancy.

> The Master said, "The people of the South have a saying: 'A man without constancy cannot be either a wizard or a doctor.' Good!
> "'Inconstant in his virtue, he will be visited with disgrace.'"
> The Master said, "This arises simply from not attending to the prognostication."[117]

The wizard prays for patients, and the doctor treats them. Though it is not impossible to acquire either specialty, one can achieve no success with them without constancy and concentration. Confucius, after reading the last quotation from the *Book of Changes*, deplored the lack of constancy among men. He thought that this occurred because men failed to heed the warning offered in the quotation. Possessing constancy, he never tired of learning or teaching others. This was the secret of his success. It is pointed out in the popular saying, "Constancy is the root of success."

> The Master said, "The prosecution of learning may be compared to what may happen in raising a mound. If only one basket of earth is needed to complete the work, and I stop, the stopping is my own work. It may be compared to throwing down the earth on the level ground. Though but one basketful is thrown at a time, the advancing with it is my own going forward"[118]

A shovelful of earth isn't a great deal, but many make a mountain. On the other hand, lacking one shovelful, all previous effort may be in vain. Confucius used this comparison to teach the importance of constancy. So did Mencius.

Mencius said, "A man with definite aims to be accomplished may be compared to one digging a well. To dig the well to a depth of seventy-two cubits and stop without reaching the spring, is after all throwing away the well."[119]

Though one referred to building a mountain and the other to digging a well, both Confucius and Mencius meant the same thing. In both instances, the waste of effort was equally deplored. The comparisons are simple, but their implications are profound.

Confucius thought himself fortunate whenever he could see the practice of constancy. He said, "Having not and yet affecting to have, empty and yet affecting to be full, straitened and yet affecting to be at ease—it is difficult with such characteristics to have constancy."[120]

Thus, it is evident that inconstancy is a universal malady. The contributing factor is the failure to seek the satisfactory and full attainment of success in one's work or learning, stopping halfway and pretending to "have," to "be full," or to "be at ease" when the contrary is the case. One's attention may also be diverted by other work or learning. The result of this is deficiency and emptiness. Everyone, therefore, must guard against inconstancy.

It has been wisely said, "...to entire sincerity there belongs ceaselessness. Not ceasing, it continues long. Continuing long, it evidences itself. Evidencing itself, it reaches far...Reaching far and continuing long—this is how it perfects all things."[121] Indeed, constancy is an indispensable condition for all: the sage, the superior man, and the good man.

C. Methods

The foregoing analysis not only provides us with the standards of human character; it also shows us that the cultivation of the human person may be carried out according to these standards. The methods for achieving this follow.

1. Setting of the Will

"Things stand when there is preparation, without which they come to naught." This is equally true of human life. Only when an object and an ideal exist can the direction and action to be taken be determined, so as to advance gradually toward final success. Hence, it is said, "Those who have the will are destined to succeed."

The Chinese character for "will" is composed of two parts which denote the destination of the mind. Additionally, to know where to rest amounts to making up one's mind or setting one's will.

> The point where to rest being known, the object of pursuit is then determind: and, that being determined, a calm unperturbedness may be attained to. To that clamness will succeed a tranquil repose. In that repose there may be careful deleberation, and that deliberation will be followed by the attainment of the desired end.[122]

Where there is will, there is farsightedness and great expectation. In the event of difficulties and obstacles, every effort is certain to be made to overcome them, thereby generating bravery and endurance and removing anxiety.

> The Master said, "If a man takes no thought about what is distant, he will find sorrow near at hand."[123]

Human life being limited, those who attained the age of one hundred were regarded as national celebrities. Even those who lived to seventy were regarded as rare. With the progress of medical science, life expectancy has been extended, but the golden age for one's achievements is still limited. Therefore, men cannot afford to go through life's journey without planning. The plans made and the success achieved by Confucius can be summarized as follows:

> The Master said, "At fifteen, I had my mind bent on learning.
> "At thirty, I stood firm.
> "At forty, I had no doubts.
> "At fifty, I knew the decrees of Heaven.
> "At sixty, my ear was an obedient organ for the reception of truth.
> "At seventy, I could follow what my heart desired, without transgressing what was right."[124]

Thus, we see that before thirty the Master lay the foundation for his learning. After thirty, he used his knowledge, free from doubt, to build his career, especially his knowledge of the decrees of Heaven. After sixty, acquiring the obedience of his ear to truth and the fulfillment of his heart's desire, he perfected his character, finding satisfaction and happiness everywhere as a result of his practice of the Mean.

As a rule, each generation should surpass the preceding one. So it is said that youth should be regarded with awe. As far as the lifetime of any individual is concerned, the golden age is between the fortieth and fiftieth years. If, during this period, no success is achieved, there is usually little hope for such a man during the remainder of his life. As a familiar Chinese proverb so aptly puts it: "Lack of effort in youth brings grief in old age."

> The Master said, "When a man at forty is the object of dislike, his whole life is at an end."[125]
> The Master said, "A youth is to be regarded with awe. How do you know that his future will not be equal to our present? If he reaches the age of forty or fifty and has not made himself known, then indeed he will not be worth being regarded with awe."[126]

The *Book of Songs* expressed the will of men. For this reason, it can encourage men to forge ahead and remove improper thought. Since the character of the book looks toward the cultivation of human virtue, Confucius took every opportunity to persuade his disciples to make a serious study of it. Confucius even edited the book himself so as to hand it down in good form to later generations.

> The Master said, "My children, why do you not study the *Book of Songs*?
> "The Odes serve to stimulate the mind.
> "They may be used as guides for the observation of political institutions.
> "They teach the art of sociability.
> "They show how to regulate feelings of resentment.
> "From them you learn the more immediate duty of serving one's father and the remoter one of serving one's prince.
> "From them we become largely acquainted with the names of birds, beasts and plants."[127]
> The Master said, "It is by the Odes that the mind is aroused.
> "It is by the Rules of Propriety that the character is established.

"It is from Music that the finish is received."[128]

The Master said to Po-yü, "Do you give yourself to the Chou-nan and the Chao-nan? Is the man who has not studied the Chou-nan and the Chao-nan not like one who stands with his face right against a wall?"[129]

The Master said, "The meaning of the three hundred pieces in the *Book of Songs* may be embraced in one sentence: 'Having no depraved thoughts.' "[130]

The Master said, "The Kuan-sui is expressive of enjoyment without being licentious and of grief without being hurtfully excessive."[131]

Mencius said, "The will is the leader of the passion-nature. The passion-nature pervades and animates the body."[132] As the leader of the passion-nature, the will leads the body as a general commands an army. As the spirit which pervades and animates the body, the passion-nature represents the troops which form the army. Without the general an army cannot be controlled, and without the troops an army cannot fight.

Confucius went even further in placing the will of the individual in a stronger position than the commander of an army. In his view the commander may be taken prisoner by an enemy, but the will of an individual can never be captured by anybody; hence, the importance of setting the will.

The Master said, "The commander of the forces of a large State may be carried off, but the will of even a common man cannot be taken from him."[133]

When in the company of his disciples, Confucius allowed them to state their wills. He wished to see all the people in the world in their proper places, that is, "in regard to the aged, to give them rest; in regard to friends, to show them sincerity; in regard to the young, to treat them tenderly." What an admirable ambition this was!

Yen Yüan and Chi Lu being by his side, the Master said to them, "Come, let each of you tell his wishes."

Tzŭ-lu said, "I should like, having chariots and horses and light fur dresses, share them with my friends, and though they should spoil them, I would not be displeased."

Yen Yüan said, "I should not boast of my excellence, nor make a display of my meritorious deeds."

Tzŭ-lu then said, "I should like, sir, to hear your wishes." The Master said, "They are, in regard to the aged, to give them rest; in regard to friends, to show them sincerity; in regard to the young, to treat them tenderly."[134]

With regard to the wishes expressed by Tzŭ-lu, Jan Yu, Tsêng-Hsi and Kung-hsi Hua, Confucius especially endorsed those of Tsêng Hsi because he was contented and aimed at the distant future.

Tzŭ-lu, Tsêng Hsi, Jan Yu and Kung-hsi Hua were sitting by the Master. He said to them, "Though I am older than you, do not think of that. From day to day you are saying, 'We are not known.' If you were known, what would you like to do?"

Tzŭ-lu hastily and lightly replied, "Suppose the case of a State of one thousand chariots; let it be straitened between other large States; let it be suffering from invading armies; and to this let it be added a famine. If I were entrusted with the government of it, in three years' time I could make the people bold and cognizant of the rules of righteous conduct." The Master smiled at him.

Turning to Jan Yu, he said, "Ch'iu, what are your wishes?" Ch'iu replied, "Suppose a State of sixty or seventy li square or one of fifty or sixty, I could make plenty to abound among the people after governing them for three years. As to teaching them the principles of propriety and music, I must wait for the rise of a superior man to do that."

"What are your wishes, Ch'ih," said the Master next to Kung-hsi Hua. Ch'ih replied, "I do not say that my ability extends to these things, but I shall wish to learn them. At the services of the ancestral temple and at the meetings of the princes, dressed in the dark square-made robe and the black linen cap, to act as a small assistant."

Last of all, the Master asked Tsêng-Hsi, "Tien, what are your wishes?" Tien, pausing as he was playing on his lute, while it was yet twanging, laid the instrument aside and rose. "My wishes," he said, "are different from the cherished purposes of these three gentlemen." "What harm is there in that?" said the Master; "do you also, as well as they, speak out your wishes." Tien then said, "In this, the last month of spring, with the dress of the season all complete, along with five or six young men who have assumed the cap and six or seven boys, I would wash in the Yi, enjoy the breeze among the rain altars and return home singing." The Master heaved a sigh and said, "I give my approval to him."

The three others having gone out, Tsêng Hsi remained behind

and said, "What do you think of the words of these three friends?" The Master said, "They simply told each one their wishes.

Hsi pursued, "Master, why did you smile at Yu?"

He was answered, "The management of a State demands the rules of propriety. His words were not humble; therefore I smiled at him."

Hsi again said, "But was it not a ·State which Ch'iu proposed for himself?" The reply was, "Yes; did you ever see a territory of sixty or seventy *li* or one of fifty or sixty, which was not a State?"

Once more Hsi inquired, "And was it not a State which Ch'ih proposed for himself?" The Master again replied, "Yes; who but princes have to do with ancestral temples and meetings? If Ch'ih were to be a small assistant in these ceremonies, who could be a great one?".[135]

Thus, the setting of the will is the first important lesson in human life.

2. Love of Goodness

Mencius gave this definition of "goodness" when he said, "A man who commands our liking is what is called a good man." Therefore, anything which fulfills the requirements of the common existence of mankind must be good. The distinction between good and evil can always be made when there is fair-mindedness.

"Unwearied joy in goodness" was regarded by Mencius as "a nobility of Heaven." He also observed that "he who rises at cock-crowing and addresses himself earnestly to doing good is a disciple of Shun." Only by being fond of goodness can one aspire to continuing advancement and accept the criticism and advice of others. Herein lies the difference between the sage and the ordinary man.

Mencius said, "There is a nobility of Heaven, and there is a nobility of man. Benevolence, righteousness, loyalty and thruthfulness, with unwearied joy in goodness—these constitute the nobility of Heaven. To be a *kung*, a *ch'ing* or a *ta-fu*—this constitutes the nobility of man."[136]

Mencius said, "He who rises at cock-crowing and addresses himself earnestly to doing is a disciple of Shun. He who rises at cock-crowing and addresses himself earnestly to the pursuit of gain is a disciple of Chih. If you want to know what separates Shun from Chih, it is simply this—the interval between the thought of gain and the thought of goodness."[137]

No other lovers of goodness in ancient times can serve as examples to succeeding generations as can Shun and Yü. Shun derived goodness from others, and Yü bowed whenever he heard good words.

> Mencius said, "When Shun was living amid the deep retired mountains, dwelling with the trees and rocks and wandering among the deer and swine, the difference between him and the rude inhabitants of those remote hills appeared very small. But when he heard a single good word or saw a single good action, he was like a stream or a river bursting its banks and flowing out in an irresistable flood."[138]
>
> Mencius said, "When anyone told Tzŭ-lu that he had a fault, he rejoiced.
>
> "When Yü heard good words, he bowed to the speaker.
>
> "The great Shun had a still greater delight in what was good. He regarded virtue as the common property of himself and others, giving up his own way to follow that of others and delighting to learn from others to practice what was good.
>
> "From the time when he plowed and sowed, exercised the plotter's art and was a fisherman, to the time when he became emperor, he was continually learning from others.
>
> "To take example from others to practice virtue is to help them in the same practice. Therefore there is no attribute of the superior man greater than his helping men to practice virtue."[139]

The State of Ch'u was able to become a strong and prosperous power because it knew how to treasure goodness. In the *Book of Ch'u* it is said: "Nothing is valued in the State of Ch'u except the practice of goodness."[140]

Mencius often pleaded with reigning princes to be fond of goodness, believing that it was the beginning of kingly government and a prerequisite for the enlistment of worthy and talented men.

> The Prince of Lu wanting to commit the administration of his government to the disciple Yüeh-chêng, Mencius said, "When I heard of it, I was so glad that I could not sleep."
>
> Kung-sun Ch'ou asked, "Is Yüeh-chêng a man of vigor?" and was answered, "No." "Is he wise in council?" "No." "Is he possessed of much information?" "No."
>
> "What then made you so glad that you could not sleep?"
>
> "He is a man who loves what is good."
>
> "Is the love of what is good sufficient?"

"The love of what is good is more than a sufficient qualification for the government of the empire; how much more is it so for the State of Lu?

"If a minister loves what is good, all within the four seas will count 1,000 *li* but a short distance, and will come and lay their good thoughts before him.

"If he does not love what is good, men will say, 'How self-conceited he looks! He is saying to himself, I know it.' The language and looks of that self-conceit will keep men off at a distance of 1,000 *li*. When good men stop 1,000 *li* off, calumniators, flatterers and sycophants will make their appearance. When a minister lives among calumniators, flatterers and sycophants, though he may wish the State to be well governed, is it possible?"[141]

From this we can see that the love or dislike of goodness can determine not only the future of an individual but the destiny of a country as well.

3. Self-Requirement

The success or failure of anything has its causes. When one does not possess the necessary conditions, one can make the greatest mistake by hoping to achieve success through sheer luck, which is inconsistent with scientific principles. If after one's own failure, one hopes for the success of others, it is simply admitting one's own inferiority and is tantamount to seeking help from others. A familiar Chinese proverb says, "It is difficult to ascend to the sky, but it is even more so to seek the help of others." A wise man does not rely on others for his entire lifetime, nor does he place all his hopes upon them.

On this account, the ruler must himself be possessed of the good qualities, and then he may require them in the people. He must not have the bad qualities in himself, and then he may require that they shall not be in the people. Never has there been a man, who, not having reference to his own character and wishes in dealing with others, was able effectively to instruct them.[142]

To require of oneself is to hope that one can possess good qualities. Only when one possesses these good qualities can he enjoy the confidence of others.

"He whose goodness is part of himself is called an honest man."[143]

If a man has real ability, others are bound to recognize it. What a man fears is that he does not have ability worthy of being known. When he has ability, he need not concern himself with his lack of advancement; what he ought to be concerned with is his lack of ability.

> The Master said, "A man should say, I am not concerned that I have no place, I am concerned how I may fit myself for one. I am not concerned that I am not known, I seek to be worthy to be known."[144]
>
> The Master said, "I will not be concerned at men's not knowing me; I will be concerned at my own want of ability."[145]

Realizing that the scholars of his time acquired learning for the sake of seeking fame, distinction and riches, rather than in an attempt to cultivate their morality and increase their knowledge, Confucius voiced his regrets.

> The Master said, "In ancient times, men learned with a view to their own improvement. Nowadays, men learn with a view to the approbation of others."[146]

Confucius was a man of profound learning and superb ability, devoted to the practice of the Way. Though the State of Lu became a well-governed country only three months after he became its Minister of Justice, he did not remain in office till the end, but traveled through the various states for fourteen years. After the failure of his mission, he returned to Lu to write and thereby teach succeeding generations (i). Because of the existence in name only (ii) of the superior systems of propriety handed down from ancient times (iii), the recurring retirement of worthy scholars (iv), the lack of good government (v) and the decay of morality (vi), he deeply deplored the steady decline of the Way and his inability to make it prevail (vii).

> (i) When the Master was in Ch'ên, he said, "Let me return! Let me return! The little children of my school are ambitious but inexperienced. They are accomplished and can write, but they do not know how to restrain and shape themselves."[147]
>
> (ii) The Master said, "Chou had the advantage of viewing the two past dynasties. How complete and elegant its regulations are! I follow Chou."[148]
>
> (iii) The Master said, "A cornered vessel without corners—a strange cornered vessel! A strange cornered vessel!"[149]

(iv) The Master said, "Seven men have already retired."[150]

(v) The Master said, "The governments of Lu and Wei are brothers.!"[151]

(vi) The Master said, "Even in my early days I could see that a historiographer would leave a blank in his text (when in doubt), and that he who had a horse would lend him to another to ride. Now, alas, nothing of this kind happens.!"[152]

(vii) The Master said, "The phoenix does not come, nor does the picture emerge from the river (ancient signs of propitious government); it is all over with me!"[153]

At the time, some expressed regrets about Confucius' actions, while others ridiculed him and still others misunderstood him. The Master, however, was completely at ease, adopting the attitude of "not murmuring against Heaven" and "not grumbling against men." Even when most agonized, he simply sighed, "Can it be that only Heaven knows me?"

The border-warden of Yi requested to be introduced to the Master, saying, "When superior men come to this, I have never been denied the privilege of seeing them." The followers of the sage introduced him, and when he came out of the interview, he said, "My friends, why are you distressed by your master's loss of office? The empire has long been without the Way; Heaven is going to use your master as a bel with its wooden tongue."[154]

The madman of Ch'u, Chieh-yü, passed by Confucius, singing and saying, "O Phoenix! O Phoenix! How is your virtue degenerated? As to the past, reproof is useless; but the future may still be provided against. Give up your vain pursuit. Give up your vain pursuit. Peril awaits those who now engage in affairs of government."

Confucius alighted and wished to converse with him, but Chieh-yü hastened away, so that he could not talk with him.[155]

The Master was playing one day on a musical stone in Wei, when a man, carrying a straw basket, passed the door of the house where Confucius was, and said, "His heart is full who so beats the musical stone."

After a while he added, "How contemptible is the narrow obstinacy those sounds display! When one is taken no notice of, one has simply at once to give over one's wish for public employment. 'Deep water must be crossed with the clothes on; shallow water may be crossed with the clothes held up.' "

The Master said, "How determined he is in his purpose! But I cannot blame him."[156]

Tzŭ-lu happening to pass the night in Shih-men, the gate-keeper said to him, "Whom do you come from?" Tzŭ-lu said, "From Mr. K'ung" "It is he, is it not?" said the other, "who knows the impracticable nature of the times and yet will be doing in them."[157]

Ch'ang-chü and Chieh-ni were at work in the field together, when Conufcius passed by them, and sent Tzŭ-lu to inquire for the ford.

Ch'ang-chü said, "Who is he that holds the reins in the carriage there?" Tzŭ-lu told him, "It is K'ung Ch'iu." "Is it not K'ung Ch'iu of Lu?" asked he. "Yes," was the reply, to which the other rejoined, "He knows the ford."

Tzu-lŭ then inquired of Chieh-ni, who said to him, "Who are you, Sir?" He answered, "I am Chung Yu." "Are you not the disciple of K'ung Ch'iu of Lu?" asked the other. "I am," replied he, and then Chieh-ni said to him, "Disorder, like a swelling flood, spreads over the whole empire, and who is he that will change its state for you? Than follow one who merely withdraws from this one and that one, had you not better follow those who have withdrawn from the world altogether?" With this he fell to covering up the seed and proceeded with his work, without stopping.

Tzŭ-lu went and reported their remarks, when the Master observed with a sigh, "It is impossible to associate with birds and beasts as if they were the same with us. If I associate not with these people—with mankind—with whom shall I associate? If the Way prevailed through the empire, there would be no use for me to change its state."[158]

So it is that the superior man imposes requirements on himself, while the mean man imposes requirements on others. The best illustration of the superior man is in archery, where if his shooting is inaccurate, he does some soul-searching. In this sense, the superior man "does not murmur against Heaven or grumble against men" because he has the ability to search himself.

The Master said, "What the superior man seeks is in himself. What the mean man seeks is in others."[159]

The Master said, "In archery we have something like the way of the superior man. When the archer missess the center of the target, he turns around and seeks for the cause of his failure in himself."[160]

The Master said, "I do not murmur against Heaven. I do not grumble against men."[161]

It is not always a man's own fault that he is ridiculed. In

such instances, soul-searching is necessary to determine if one really has a fault. If a fault exists, it should be corrected; if not, further effort is required nevertheless. Both Confucius and King Wên, for example, were able to do this.

> Mê Chi said, "I have been subjected to great ridicule."
> Mencius observed, "There is no harm in that. Scholars are more liable to be criticized by others.
> "It is said in the *Book of Songs*,
> 'My heart is disquieted and grieved,
> I am hated by the crowd of mean creatures.'
> This might have been said by Confucius, and again,
> 'Though he did not remove their wrath,
> He did not let fall his own fame,'
> This was said of King Wên."[162]

Those who seek fame are fond of having a good name. Their belittlement of gain may not be genuine and may be a trick to deceive the world. This is a bad example to follow.

> Mencius said, "A man who loves fame may be able to decline a State of a thousand chariots; but if he is not really the man to do such a thing, it (greed) will appear in his countenance even in the matter of a dish of rice or a platter of soup."[163]

Self-requirement is aimed at self-establishment, self-enlargement and freedom from reliance on others so as to build a lofty character.

4. Watchfulness Over Oneself When Alone

In English grammar, when one refers to oneself, the first person is used. If one seeks to deceive the first person, there can be no question about the treatment of the second and third persons. Therefore, sincerity to oneself is an important lesson in personal cultivation, especially when one is alone. Therefore, watchfulness over oneself is not simply a test of self-control; rather, it is the first step toward self-restraint.

> What is meant by "making the thoughts sincere" is to avoid self-deception, as when we hate a bad smell and as when we love what is beautiful. This is called self-enjoyment. Therefore the superior man must be watchful over himself when he is alone."[164]
> ...On this account the superior man does not wait till he sees things to be cautious, nor till he hears things to be apprehensive. There is nothing more visible than what is concealed and nothing

more manifest than what is minute. Therefore the superior man is watchful over himself when he is alone.[165]

Every religious teacher attaches importance to watchfulness over oneself when alone. It is the beginning of the establishment of sincerity and the foundation for the perfection of virtue.

5. Self-Examination

Self-examination is a periodic exercise to determine if one has made any mistakes in past speech or action. If mistakes have been made, self-examination urges us to correct them. If no mistakes have been made, then self-examination suggests that further effort be exerted. It was the philosopher Tsêng's practice to engage in such self-examination daily on three points.

> The philosopher Tsêng said, "I daily examine myself on three points: whether, in transacting business for others, I may not have been faithful; whether, in intercourse with friends, I may not have been sincere; whether I may not have mastered and practiced the instructions of my teacher."[166]

When a person meets an evil man, he examines himself to make sure he does not have the faults of the evil one. However, when a person meets a good man, he hopes to follow his example.

> The Master said, "When we see men of worth, we should think of equalling them: when we see men of a contrary character, we should turn inwards and examine ourselves."[167]

Self-examination brings self-realization, and only with this awareness can we control ourselves and reduce our faults.

> The Master said, "The cautious seldom err."[168]

Prayer is a form of self-examination. Confucius himself prayed, and he advised his disciples to do so constantly, not only on specific occasions.

> The Master being very sick, Tzŭ-lu asked leave to pray for him. He said, "May such a thing be done?" Tzŭ-lu replied, "It may. In the 'Eulogies' it is said, 'Prayer has been made for thee to the spirits of the upper and lower worlds.'" The Master said, "My prayer has been for a long time."[169]

Anything contrary to divine principle should be corrected immediately. Prayer alone avails nothing.

> Wang-sun Chia asked, saying, "What is the meaning of the saying, 'It is better to pay court to the furnace than to the southwest corner (of the house)'?"
> The Master said, "Not so. He who offends against Heaven has none to whom he can pray."[170]

While it may be possible to escape calamities sent from Heaven, those which men bring upon themselves with their eyes open to the consequences cannot be excused.

> Confucius said, "...This is illustrated in the passage of the 'T'ai Chia,' 'When Heaven sends down calamities, it is still possible to escape them. When we occasion the calamities ourselves, it is not possible any longer to live.'"[171]

It is better to take precautions against faults than to repent after they have already been committed. Just as a periodically checked automobile will be involved in fewer accidents, so can a man who examines himself from time to time be free of faults.

6. Self-Inquiry

Self-inquiry is distinguished from self-examination in that it takes place only after something has come to pass. If something does not come up to our expectations, or if someone has treated us with insolence, we must determine the cause. We must attempt to find out if the fault is ours so that we may guard against future mistakes and have the courage to forge ahead.

Mencius gave detailed instructions regarding the method of self-inquiry.

> Mencius said, "That whereby the superior man is distinguished from other men is what he peserves in his heart; namely benevolence and propriety.
> "The benevolent man loves others. The man of propriety shows respect to others. He who loves others is constantly loved by them. He who respects others is constantly respected by them.
> "Here is a man who treats me in a perverse and unreasonable manner. The superior man in such a case will turn round upon himself—'I must have been wanting in benevolence; I must have been wanting in propriety; how should this have happened to me?'

"He examines himself and finds himself to be benevolent. He turns round upon himself to be observant of propriety. The perversity and unreasonableness of the other, however, are still the same. The superior man will again turn round on himself—'I must have been unfaithful.'

"He turns round upon himself and finds himself to be faithful, but still the perversity and unreasonableness of the other are repeated. On this the superior man says, 'This is a man utterly lost indeed! Since he conducts himself so, what is there to choose between him and a brute? Why should I go to contend with a brute?'

"Thus it is that the superior man has a life-long anxiety and not one day's calamity. As to what is matter of anxiety to him, that indeed he has. He says, 'Shun was a man, and I also am a man. But Shun became an example to all the empire, and his conduct was worthy to be handed down to after ages, while I am nothing better than a villager.' This indeed is the proper matter of anxiety to him. And in what way is he anxious about it? Just that he may be like Shun—then only will he stop. As to what the superior man would feel to be a calamity, there is no such thing. He does nothing which is not according to benevolence and propriety. If there should befall him one day's calamity, the superior man does not account it a calamity."[172]

Mencius said, "...Formerly the philosopher Tsêng said to Tzŭ-hsiang, "Do you love valor? I heard a case of great valor from the Master. It speaks thus: 'If, on self-examination, I find that I am not upright, shall I not be in fear even of a poor man in his loose garments of coarse cloth? If, on self-examination, I find that I am upright, I will go forward against thousands and tens of thousands.'..."[173]

When one engages in self-inquiry, one can refrain from blaming others by mistake (diverting one's anger) or repeating a mistake. Only through self-inquiry can we obtain what we seek in ourselves.

Mencius said, "If a man loves others and no responsive attachment is shown to him, let him turn inwards and examine his own benevolence. If he is trying to rule others and his government is unsuccessful, let him turn inwards and examine his wisdom. If he treats others politely and they do not return his politeness, let him turn inwards and examine his own feeling of respect.

"When we do not, by what we do, realize what we desire, we must turn inwards and examine ourselves in every point. When a man's person is correct, the whole empire will turn to him with recognition and submission.

"It is said in the *Book of Songs*,

'Be always studious to be in harmony with the ordinances of God,

And you will obtain much happiness.'"[174]

Self-inquiry is aimed at the search for knowledge from one's conduct and the understanding of one's own responsibility. It is a man's subjection of himself to self-trial, so as to avoid the disgrace of trial by others.

7. Self-Censure

If after self-examination and self-inquiry, a man still finds faults within himself, he should censure himself strictly without blaming others in order to fix the responsibility and invite criticism. This is expressed in the familiar proverb, "There should be heavy censure of oneself and light censure of others."

> The Master said, "He who censures himself strongly and others lightly will keep himself far away from resentment."[175]

Self-censure is self-punishment to guard against repeatieg a mistake. If a fault is repeated and the penalty is administered by others, the loss will be even greater.

8. Rectification of Faults

Since "to err is human," it is difficult for anyone to be free from fault. The reasons for error or fault will be more easily discovered, however, if constant self-examination and self-inquiry take place. Self-censure then is the determination of responsibility, but only rectification can guard against future mistakes. Therefore, if we wish to have as few faults as posssble, it is necessary to rectify previous mistakes. Whitewashing our faults is a deception, whereas their rectification is an enlightened act. Whitewashing may deceive others, but it also is a self-deception and indicates the difference between the superior and the mean man.

> Tzǔ-kung said "The faults of the superior man are like the eclipses of the sun and moon. He has his faults, and all men see them; he changes again, and all men look up to him."[176]

Tzŭ-hsia said, "The mean man is sure to gloss his faults."[177]

As soon as a fault is discovered, no matter how small, it should be rectified without delay.

> The Master said, "...When you have faults, do not fear to rectify them."[178]
>
> The Master said, "Hold loyalty and faithfulness as first principles. Have no friends not equal to yourself. When you have faults, do not fear to rectify them."[179]
>
> Tai Ying-chih said to Mencius, "I am not able at present and immediately to do with the levying of a tithe only and abolishing the duties charged at the passes and in the markets. I will ask permission, however, to lighten both the tax and the duties, until next year, and will then make an end of them. What do you think of such a course?"
>
> Mencius said, "Here is a man, who every day appropriates some of his neighbor's strayed fowls. Someone says to him, 'Such is not the way of a good man;' and he replies, 'With your leave I will diminish my appropriations and will only take one fowl a month, until next year, when I will make an end of the practice.'
>
> "If you know that the thing is unrighteous, then use all dispatch in putting an end to it; why wait till next year?"[180]

Here are some more examples:

Answering a question asked by the Minister of Crime of Ch'ên, Confucius hesitated to criticize the rule of his country in front of the official of another State. But later, when Confucius received the report of a subsequent interview between one of his disciples and the Minister, the Master immediately confessed that he had erred.

> The Minister of Crime of Ch'ên asked whether Duke Chao (of Lu) knew propriety, and Confucius said, "He knows propriety."
>
> Confucius having retired, the minister bowed to Wu-ma Ch'i to come forward and said, "I have heard that the superior man is not a partisan. May the superior man be a partisan also? The prince married a daughter of the house of Wu, of the same surname with himself, and called her 'the Elder Tzu of Wu.' If the prince knew propriety, who does not know it?"
>
> Wu-ma Ch'i reported these remarks, and the Master said, "I am fortunate! If I have any errors, people are sure to know them.[181]

It is better to be free from faults than to have few faults.

and it is better to have few faults than to have many. Men should be encouraged to strive to have few faults, thus reducing the number of occasions demanding rectification. The messenger of Ch'ü Po-yü, when telling Confucius that his master was trying to reduce the number of his faults, showed that he was touched by his master's virtue.

> Ch'ü Po-yü sent a messenger with friendly inquiries to Confucius. Confucius sat with him and questioned him. "What," said he, is your master engaged in?" The messenger replied, "My master is anxious to make his faults few, but he has not yet succeeded." He then went out, and the Master said, "A messenger indeed! A messenger indeed!"[182]

All men dislke beauty turned to ugliness, and all men admire evil changed to good. As a proverb so aptly puts it, "A person becomes a Buddha immediately after he lays down the butcher's knife." It is human to love good and hate evil. To open up a new road for self-renovation, each of us must not be afraid to rectify his faults.

> Mencius said, "If the lady Hsi had been covered with something unclean, all people would have stopped their noses in passing her. But though a man may be ugly, yet if he purifies his heart, fasts and bathes, he may sacrifice to God.[183]

The rectification of faults is a publicly self-administered penalty, and so there may frequently be hesitation in carrying it out, lest others find out and compromise one's good name. It is, however, the failure to correct errors that is more disgraceful. If the discovery of one's faults engenders self-reproach and the feeling of shame, one is bound to summon the courage to rectify them ("The knowledge of shame is near to courage") and thus win the respect of others ("he changes again, and all men look up to him").

> The Master said, "To have faults and not to reform them—this, indeeed, should be pronounced having faults."[184]
> The Master said, "It is all over! I have not yet seen one who could perceive his faults and inwardly accuse himself.[185]

It is good enough if a man corrects his mistakes after he discovers them. If, on the other hand, he does not know his faults and must be reminded of them by others, he should sincerely accept their advice and show willingness to correct them. After all, there are few indeed who are willing to call attention to our faults, and it is these few who are really concerned with us.

Shun, Yü and Tzŭ-lu were the best examples of men who were courageous enough to rectify their faults and who also helped others to do good.

> Mencius said, "When anyone told Tzŭ-lu that he had a fault, he rejoiced.
>
> "When Yü heard good words, he bowed to the speaker.
>
> "The great Shun had a still greater delight in what was good. He regarded virtue as the common property of himself and others, giving up his own way to follow that of others and delighting to learn from others to practice what was good.
>
> "From the time when he plowed and sowed, exercised the plotter's art and was a fisherman, to the time when he became the emperor, he was continually learning from others.
>
> "To take example from others to practice virtue is to help them in the same practice. Therefore there is no attribute of the superior man greater than his helping men to practice virtue."[186]

When others advise us of our faults, whether bluntly or diplomatically, we should consider their advice carefully, accept it cheerfully and carry it out courageously. If we simply assent verbally with no attempt to heed this advice, we manifest insincerity and "without sincerity there can be nothing." Even Confucius could not help the insincere.

> The Master said, "Can men refuse to assent to the words of strict admonition? But it is reforming the conduct because of them which is valuable. Can men refuse to be pleased with words of gentle advice? But it is unfolding their aim which is valuable. If a man is pleased with these words but does not unfold their aim, and assents to them but does not reform his conduct, I can really do nothing with him."[187]

In short, the value of rectification of faults lies in its promptness and the absence of delay or hesitancy. When others offer advice regarding the correction of our faults, we should accept it sincerely, examine it carefully and courageously carry it out. In this spirit, we can take pleasure in goodness without weariness and, at the same time, take a practical step toward the cultivation of the person.

9. Self-Exertion

When one is not equal to others, one must strive to surpass them. On the other hand, when one excels others, one must be humble about it. As the ancient teaching puts it: "Pride brings loss, and humility gain." If a man always has a feeling of discontent with the amount of his learning, awe and respect toward the laws of heaven and reverence for sages and holy men, he is engaged in self-exertion.

Confucius said, "Contemplating good and pursuing it, as if they could not reach it; contemplating evil and shrinking from it, as they would from thrusting the hand into boiling water—I have seen such men, as I have heard such words.

"Living in retirement to study their aims and practicing righteousness to carry out their principle—I have heard these words, but I have not seen such men."[188]

Confucius said, "There are three things of which the superior man stands in awe. He stands in awe of the ordinances of Heaven. He stands in awe of great men. He stands in awe of the words of sages."[189]

Although Confucius frequently practiced self-exertion, he remained always humble. He said there were many things he should have done which he did not succeed in doing.

The Master said, "Abroad, to serve the high ministers and nobles; at home, to serve one's father and elder brother; in all duties to the dead, not to dare not to exert oneself; and not to be overcome of wine—have I attained to these things?"[190]

Self-exertion toward goodness brings constant progress. On the other hand, a resignation to evil-doing and a willingness to remain depraved brings not only backwardness but also does damage to one's good name to the extent that one is identified with evil-doing. Thus, should one not be extremely cautious?

Tzŭ-kung said, "Chou's wickedness was not so great as that name implies. Therefore the superior man hates to dwell in a low-lying situation, where all the evil of the world will flow in upon him."[191]

In short, self-exertion is the most effective method to ensure progress and prevent backsliding.

10. Strengthening Oneself

Men differ in intelligence and strength, and deficiencies can be corrected only by unceasing effort; hence the saying:

> If another man succeeds by one effort, he will use a hundred efforts. If another man succeeds by ten efforts, he will use a thousand.[192]

While success is not easily achieved, failure can be expected at any time. Only unceasing effort can bring favorable results.

> The Master said, "There are cases in which the blade springs but the plant does not go on to flower! There are cases where it flowers but no fruit is subsequently produced!"[193]

Between success and failure there may be the difference of only one basketful of earth. It all depends on vigor.

> The Master said, "The prosecution of learning may be compared to what may happen in raising a mound. If only one basketful of earth is needed to complete the work, and I stop, the stopping is my own work. It may be compared to throwing down the earth on the level ground. Though but one basketful is thrown at a time, the advancing with it is my own going forward."[194]

While environment (Heaven) can help men achieve success, it can also cause them to fail. The determining factor is one's will.

> The Master said, "...Thus it is that Heaven, in the production of things, is sure to be bountiful to them according to their qualities. Hence the tree that flourishes, it nourishes, while that which is ready to fall, it overthrows."[195]

As the Western saying puts it: "God helps those who help themselves." This points out even more clearly the importance of strengthening oneself.

11. Self-Confidence

Man desires the perfection of himself and other things. He knows how to practice self-examination, self-inquiry, self-censure and self-exertion. He is capable of possessing the courage to rectify his faults, delighting in goodness and making an unceasing effort to strengthen himself. Thus, he should have the wisdom to know himself. Those who know themselves are sure to possess self-confidence. They can predict the success of their undertakings, and they are free from anxiety and fear.

The following passages indicate the self-confidence of Confucius:

> The Master said, "If there were any (of the princes) who would employ me, in the course of twelve months, I should have done something considerable. In three years, the government would be perfected."[196]

> The Master was put in fear of K'uang. He said, "After the death of King Wên, were not the cultural institutions lodged in me? If Heaven had wished to let these institutions perish, then I, a future mortal, should not have got such a relation to those institutions. While Heaven does not wish to let those institutions perish, what can the people of K'uang do to me?"[197]

> The Master said, "Heaven produced the virtue that is in me. Huan T'ui—what can he do to me?"[198]

"He whose goodness is part of himself is what is called an honest man." So, the man who goes to extremes or fails to go far enough cannot be self-confident because he does not possess a clear knowledge of himself. The man of excessive action does violence to himself, and the man who attaches too little importance to his actions wastes himself. Both extremes are equally injurious. Only by living benevolently and following the path of righteousness can one attain the Mean and possess self-confidence.

> Mencius said, "With those who do violence to themselves it is impossible to speak. With those who throw themselves away it is impossible to do anything. To disown in his conversation propriety and righteousness is what we mean by doing violence to oneself. To say, 'I am not able to dwell in benevolence or pursue the path of righteousness' is what we mean by throwing oneself away.

> "Benevolence is the tranquil habitation of man, and righteousness is his straight path. Alas for them, who leave the tranquil dwelling empty, and who abandon the right path and do not pursue it!"[199]

When Jan Ch'iu admitted that he did not have sufficient strength for learning and lacked self-confidence, Confucius exhorted him to guard against wasting himself.

> Jan Ch'iu said, "It is not that I do not delight in your Way,

but my strength is insufficient." The Master said, "Those whose strength is insufficient give over in the middle of the way, but now you limit yourself."[200]

Answering a question put by Wan Chang, Mencius denied a rumor which implied that Pai-li Hsi had sold himself out for worldly honors. Mencius said that, judging by his wisdom and accomplishments, Pai-li Hsi could not have done so.

> Wan Chang asked Mencius, "Some say that Pai-Li Hsi sold himself to a cattle-keeper of Ch'in for the skins of five rams and fed his oxen, in order to seek employment from Duke Mu of Ch'in; was this the case?" Mencius said, "No, it was not so. This story was invented by men fond of strange things.
>
> "Pai-li Hsi was a man of Yü. The people of Chin, by the inducement of a good piece of jade from Ch'ui-chi and four horses of the Ch'ü breed, borrowed a passage through Yü to attack Kuo. On that occasion Kung Chih-ch'i remonstrated against granting their request, and Pai-li Hsi did not remonstrate,
>
> "When he knew that the Duke of Yü was not to be remonstrated with, and, leaving that State, went to Ch'i, he had reached the age of seventy. If by that time he did not know that it would be a mean thing to seek employment from Duke Mu of Ch'in by feeding oxen, could he be called wise? But not remonstrating where it was of no use to remonstrate, could he be said not to be wise? Knowing that the Duke of Yü would be ruined and leaving him before that event, he cannot be said not to have been wise. Being then advanced in Ch'in he knew that Duke Mu was one with whom he would enjoy a field for action, and became prime minister to him; could he, acting thus, be said not to be wise? Having become chief minister of Ch'in, he made his prince distinguished throughout the empire and worthy of being handed down to future ages; could he have done this if he had not been a worthy man? As to selling himself in order to accomplish all the aims of his prince, even a villager who had regard for himself would not do such a thing; and shall we say that a worthy man did it?"[201]

In short, self-confidence is an accurate measure of the extent to which goodness forms a part of oneself. Where there is self-confidence, there is no excess or inadequacy. Additionally, it must be remembered that, sincerity and the Mean are indeed primary conditions for success.

12. Self-Gratification

There are a number of conditions for self-gratification. The qualities so required are: a mental preservation of benevolence and propriety; self-confidence and self-strength; full devotion to duty and a perfect state of goodness. Such a man "adds nothing to his virtue when his Way prevails and loses nothing when remaining in poverty." He pays no attention to gain or loss; he does not murmur against Heaven or complain about men, and so is completely self-gratified.

> The superior man does what is proper to the station in which he is; he does not desire to go beyond this.
>
> In a position of wealth and honor, he does what is proper to a position of wealth and honor. In a poor and low position, he does what is proper to a poor and low position. Situated among barbarous tribes, he does what is proper to a situation among barbarous tribes. In a position of sorrow and difficulty, he does what is proper to a position of sorrow and difficulty. The superior man can find himself in no situation in which he is not self-gratified.
>
> In a high situation he does not domineer over his inferiors. In a low situation he does not court the favors of his superiors. He rectifes himself and seeks for nothing from others so that he has no dissatisfactions. He does not murmur against Heaven, nor grumble against men.
>
> Thus it is that the superior man is quiet and calm, waiting for his destiny, while the mean man walks in dangerous paths expecting the uncertain chances of luck.
>
> The Master said, "In archery we have someting like the way of the superior man. When the archer misses the center of the target, he turns round and seeks for the cause of his failure in himself."[202]
>
> Mencius said, "The superior man deepens his advances by the proper course, wishing to acquire his learning by his own effort. Having acquired it by his own effort, he abides in it calmly and firmly. Abiding in it calmly and firmly, he reposes a deep reliance on it. Reposing a deep reliance on it, he seizes it on the left and right, meeting everywhere with it as a fountain from which things flow. It is on this account that the superior man wishes to acquire his learning by his own effort."[203]

Self-gratification is the source of internal happiness, bringing one unlimited and real delight, and evidencing clearly the prevalence of the Way. It is the highest state of human existence, and none but the wisest and most benevolent can reach it.

13. Self-Control

The "love of the people" is a heavy burden, hence the saying: "Benevolence is the burden which he (a scholar or official) considers it his responsibility to sustain—is it not heavy?" It is also a lifetime burden; thus it is said, "Only with death does his course stop—is it not long?" To undertake this heavy burden, one must harden oneself. "It (Heaven) first exercises his mind with suffering and his sinews and bones with toil. It exposes his body to hunger and subjects him to extreme poverty. It confounds his undertakings. By all these methods, it stimulates his mind, hardens his nature and supplies his incompetencies." In this way a person is enabled to undertake responsibility and stand firm in accordance with the saying, "to hold Heaven on top and stand on earth." This preparation and training are called self-control.

> Mencius said, "Shun rose from among the channeled fields. Fu Yüeh was called to office from the midst of his building frames; Chiao Ko from his fish and sale; Kuan Yi-wu from the hands of his gaoler; Sun-shu Ao from his hiding by the seashore; and Pai li Hsi from the marketplace.
>
> "Thus, when Heaven is about to confer a great office on any man, it first exercises his mind with suffering and his sinews and bones with toil. It exposes his body to hunger and subjects him to extreme poverty. It confounds his undertakngs. By all these methods it stimulates his mind, hardens his nature and supplies his incompetencies.
>
> "Men for the most part err, and are afterwards able to reform. They are distressed in mind and perplexed in their thoughts, and then they arise to vigorous reformation. When things have been evidenced in men's looks and set forth in their voices, then they understand them.
>
> "If a prince has not about his court families attached to the laws and worthy counselorse, and if abroad there are not hostile States or other external calamities, his kingdom will generally come to ruin.
>
> "From these things we see how life springs from sorrow and calamity and death from ease and pleasure."[204]

The real significance of self-control can best be understood by considering the training of an army. Why does an army require strict training at all times? It is because an army will display the greatest wisdom and courage on the battlefield if it has trained by enduring hardships like hunger and cold, worked hard, and not done what is improper. Thus, an army defeats its foe, producing the fruits of victory and defending its country with a view to achieving benevolence. These principles are explained in great detail by Dr. Sun Yatsen in his discourses on "The Spiritual Education of Military Men."

Scholars are capable of sacrificing their lives in time of danger and dying for benevolence and righteousness. How can this nobility of character be achieved without constant cultivation? Though the forms of self-control adopted by military men and civilians differ, the principle remains the same. For the military man, the training is collective and works from without to within. For the civilian, it is individual self-cultivation and works from within to without. Military men live in a constant state of peril and take great precautions against calamity. So do civilians who control themselves. Thus, military men can win their battles, and civilians are distinguished for their intelligence.

> Yen Yüan asked about benevolence. The Master said, "To subdue oneself and return to propriety is benevolence. If a man can for one day subdue himself and return to propriety, all under heaven will ascribe benevolence to him. Is the practice of benevolence from a man himself or is it from others?"
>
> Yen Yüan said, "I beg to ask the steps of that process." The Master replied, "Look not at what is contrary to propriety; listen not to what is contrary to propriety; speak not what is contrary to propriety; make no movement which is contrary to propriety." Yen Yüan then said, "Though I am deficient in intelligence, I will make it my business to practice this lesson."[205]
>
> Mencius said, "Men who are possessed of virtue, intelligence, tact and talent will generally be found to have been in distress. Only the friendless minister and concubine's son keep their hearts under a sense of peril and use deep precautions against calamity. On this account they become distinguished for their intelligence."[206]

Because they preserve benevolence in their minds and because they look, listen, speak and act in accordance with propriety, those who practice self-control always maintain an attitude of solemnity, act with elegance and speak truthfully.

The Master said, "...When his (a man's) wisdom is sufficient to attain and he has not virtue enough to hold fast, if he cannot govern with dignity, the people will not respect him.

"When his wisdom is sufficicient to attain and he has virtue enough to hold fast, when he governs also with dignity; yet if he tries to move the people contrary to the rules of propriety—full excellence is not reached."[207]

The Master said, "If the superior man is not grave, he will not call forth any veneration and his learning will not be solid. Hold loyalty and faithfulness as first principles. Have no friends not equal to yourself. When you have faults, do not fear to rectify them."[208]

The Master said, "The firm, the enduring, the simple and the modest are near to benevolence."[209]

Confucius, who was "mild and yet dignified, majestic and yet not fierce, respectful and yet easy," was an example of great self-control.

The Master was mild, and yet dignified; majecstic, and yet not fierce; respectful and yet easy.[210]

Those who practice self-control are sure to achieve diligence, endurance, frugality and simplicity.

In the *Book of History*, it is said, "Human livelihood depends on diligence." Han Yü, the great scholar of the T'ang dynasty, said, "Enterprise is perfected by diligence and wasted by playfulness." In ancient times the Chinese placed great emphasis on diligence since it involves the perpetual continuance of motion and the unceasing growth of life. Through the centuries, the whole world has admired the Chinese for their endurance and forbearance. These attributes have been regarded as surpassing qualities; so we must never lose this virtue of diligence.

The Master said, "The sage and the man of perfect virtue—how dare I rank myself with them? It may simply be said of me that I strive to become such without satiety and teach others without weariness." Kung-hsi Hua said, "This is just what your disciples cannot imitate you in."[211]

The sage has always regarded diligence as the foundation of success. To remain unsatiated and fresh has always been an indication of great perseverance. Confucius was humble enough to deny that he was a sage and possessed perfect virtue, but he admitted to his diligence and endurance. These qualities were not equaled by his disciples.

> The Master said, "Never flagging when I set forth anything to him—ah! that is Hui."[212]

Just as Confucius was diligent in teaching, so Yen Hui was diligent in learning. During a lecture, neither teacher nor pupil showed signs of weariness. As regards diligence in learning, Yen Hui was one of Confucius' most outstanding disciples.

> The Duke of Shêh asked Tzŭ-lu about Confucius, and Tzŭ-lu did not answer him.
> The Master said, "Why did you not say to him, 'He is simply a man, who in his eager pursuit (of knowledge) forgets his food, who in the joy of its attainment forgets his sorrows and who does not perceive that old age is coming on!?"[213]

When Confucius admitted that he could work hard and even forget to eat while in the pursuit of knowledge—something the average person could hardly do—Confucius was not boasting. He was simply urging his students to follow his example. Since life is short, a person can only compensate for this brevity with diligence. The self-confidence of youth, unfortunately, overestimates the length of life, and the young are liable to fail to make good use of the time available to them until it is too late. Then, when they are old, they will have regrets, but to no avail.

Diligence denotes two things: hard work and endurance. Hard work refers to the amount of work done, and endurance to the length of time spent on it. Both elements are of equal importance to the practice of self-control.

When "Yü separated the nine streams, cleared the courses of Chi and T'o and led them all to the sea; opened a vent for the Ju and Han and regulated the course of the Huai and Ssŭ so that they all flowed into the Chiang,"[214] he worked hard. When "Yü was eight years away from home, and though he thrice passed the door of it, he did not enter,"[215] he showed great endurance.

Confucius learned without becoming satiated and taught without becoming weary. His learning and teaching both involved hard work. These qualities of insatiety and unweariness were an indication of his endurance.

Thus, Yü succeeded in controlling the great flood and so contributed to the people's well-being. Confucius established the Way and became the teacher and example for all ages. Both men benefited greatly from their hard work and endurance, thereby indicating that success cannot be achieved without effort.

Human beings should regard labor as sacred because only through labor can there be life. Any person who does not labor is a poisonous element within a group of people. Therefore, all wholesome elements of society should labor according to their own natures and talents.

Mencius said, "Some labor with their minds, and some labor with their strength. Those who labor with their minds govern others; those who labor with their strength are governed by others."[216] This passage should not be interpreted to imply class distinctions. Since those who do mental labor plan and direct, they "govern others." Since those who do physical labor share the work with others and are subject to direction, they are "governed by others." Those who govern are not oppressors, however, and those who are governed are not oppressed. If we regard labor as service to society, those who labor are merely performing their duties to human life, no matter what their respective roles are.

Confucius once asked, "Can a man who is loved be exempted from labor?"[217] When the superior man loves others, he expects them to be virtuous. Not only does he perform his own labor, he also urges others to do the same. If, because of blind love, he permits them to remain idle, he destroys their future. The Master said, "The scholar who cherishes the love of comfort is not fit to be deemed a scholar."[218] The ancient scholar was the equivalent of the modern intellectual. With all his knowledge, if such a man allowed himself to become accustomed to comfort and idleness for his own enjoyment and even avoided work, he would be of no use to society, no matter how rich his knowledge. It has been said that such a man is "not fit to be deemed a scholar."

The virtue of frugality is closely connected with the cultivation of the person. The average person, however, may easily overlook frugality and consider it mere pennypinching. Such a person then is forgetting that frugality leads to propriety, builds up incorruptibility, reduces human want and simplifies life. Not only does frugality have an important bearing on the cultivation of the person, it can also produce a salutary effect on collective living.

> Mencius said, "The respectful do not despise others. The frugal do not plunder others."[219]

Extravagance is the antithesis of frugality. It is excessive expenditure for the satisfaction of individual desire, and, inevitably, results in the usurpation of the rights of others. The larger the appropriation by one side, the greater is the deprivation on the other side. In this way the inequalities in society are created. Confucius said,

> I have heard that rulers of States and chiefs of families are not troubled lest their people should be few, but are troubled lest there is no contented repose among them; that they are not troubled with fears of poverty, but are troubled lest their people do not share equally. For when the people share equally, there will be no poverty; when harmony prevails, there will be no scarcity of people; and when there is such a contented repose, there will be no rebellious upsettings[220]

In collective living, if the majority do not engage in productive work but indulge in excessive consumption, it would be inconsistent with the principles relating to the development of social economy. These principles have been aptly stated in the *Great Learning:* "Let the producers be many and consumers few. Let there be activity in the production and economy in the expenditure."[221] The inevitable result of the opposite state of affairs would be national weakness and poverty.

In stressing the virtue of frugality, we do not mean to reduce to the minimum the expenditures which must be made for clothing, food, housing, transportation, education and recreation. What we do mean is the avoidance of unnecessary waste in the fulfillment of these requirements of living. This is what is called the Mean. Thus, frugality has a greater bearing on the cultivation of virtue than on the conservation of material resources. It has greater influence on the livelihood of the masses than of individuals.

> The Master said, "Extravagance leads to insubordinaton and parsimony to simplicity. It is better to be simple than to be insubordinate."[222]

While insubordination is overstepping one's bounds, simplicity is keeping one's due. Too much simplicity might render a person somewhat inflexible, but by not giving or taking unduly, he does no harm to society. As a common saying puts it, "It is easy to turn extravagant from a state of frugality, but difficult to do the opposite." During the Spring and Autumn periods, when plunder was the order of the day, frugality was naturally preferable, for it tended to turn back the tide of pride, extravagance and depredation.

> Tzŭ-ch'in asked Tzŭ-kung, saying, When our Master comes to any country, he does not fail to learn all about its government. Does he ask his information? Or is it given to him?"
>
> Tzŭ-kung said, "Our Master is benign, upright, courteous, frugal and complaisant, and thus he gets his information. The master's mode of asking information—is it not different from that of other men?"[223]

Tzŭ-kung described Confucius as benign, upright, courteous, frugal and affable. This made him a man of perfect virtue. However, a careful analysis reveals that courtesy and frugality give rise to the other qualities. Furthermore, a man is courteous largely because he is frugal. The extravagant man is almost certain to be sensual and proud. Thus we can conclude that all these virtues are made possible by frugality.

The proud refuse to consider others, while the frugal restrain themselves. Refraining from treating others with scorn and taking things from them, the frugal are free from the jealousy of others. Others are happy to confide in such people; so information is given to them even before they ask. That is why Confucius was able to gather information about the government of any country, especially the State of Lu.

In one instance, "The disciple Jan, returning from the court, the Master said to him, 'How are you so late?' He replied, 'We had government business.' The Master said, 'It must have been family affairs. If there had been government business, though I am not now in office, I should have been consulted about it.' "[224] This is clear evidence of the effect of frugality. Courtesy and affability, produced by frugality, are always consistent with propriety. Pride and idleness, produced by extravagance, are always opposed to propriety and law.

The Master said, "Small indeed was the capacity of Kuan Chung!"

Someone said, "Was Kuan Chung frugal?" "Kuan," was the reply, "had the three Kuei, and his officials performed no double duties; how can he be considered frugal?"

"Then, did Kuan Chung know the rules of propriety?" The Master said, "The princes of States had a screen intercepting the view at their gates. Kuan had likewise a screen at his gate. The princes of States on any friendly meeting between two of them had a stand on which to place their inverted cups. Kuan had also such a stand. If Kuan knew the rules of propriety, who does not know them?"[225]

Kuei means tower. Having married three times, Kuan Chung built a tower for each of his three brides, indicating his extravagance in providing for habitation. When official business was scarce, one official could have been given the duties of two, but Kuan Chung failed to institute such a system, once again manifesting extravagance.

The proud and extravagant frequently fail to realize their violation of established custom. Thus, in having the aforementioned screen and stand, Kuan Chung violated the royal prerogative; so Confucius censured him for his lack of frngality and his failure to observe the rules of propriety.

The Master said, "Tsáng Wên-chung built a house to keep a large tortoise. On the capitals of its pillars he had hills carved, and on the small pillars above the beams he had duckweed painted. Of what sort was his wisdom.?"[226]

Tsang Wên-chung's extravagant acts were inconsistent with the virtue of frugality; so Confucius questioned his wisdom. The benevolent can often economize and extend their love to others, and the wise can often exercise control in the management of affairs. Waste and extravagance are always offenses against benevolence and wisdom.

People have attacked frugality because they mistook it for parsimony. The parsimonious refuse to give what ought to be given and refuse to spend what ought to be spent. They often think of benefiting themselves at the expense of others. The frugal, on the other hand, would rather exercise self-control than take advantage of others. The parsimonious want to take more than they give, while the frugal give what is due and refuse to take what they should not.

The parsimonious are stingy with themselves as well as with others. The frugal, however, meet the requirements of others as well as their own. They may lead a simple life without exceeding the limits of basic requirements, but they do not encourage excessive material shortage.

Confucius was frugal, but he did not choose to do without a chariot and walk when he held the office of Ta-fu. When Yüan Ssŭ was governor, Confucius gave him nine hundred bushels of grain. Such was the Mean practiced by the sage who was as frugal as he had to be.

Frugality—the virtue extolled by the ancients—contains the elements of simplicity and unpretentiousness. Simplicity implies adequacy, not wealth, while the absence of pretense connotes practical utility rather than ornamentation. For the individual, simplicity and the absence of pretense should be sought. For people as a whole however, both adequacy and wealth must be considered. In this sense, there is no contradiction between the two terms.

In short, self-control is the discipline given to oneself in preparation for the assumption of the heavy responsibilities he will bear in the future. From time immemorial, the saints worshiped in religion and all the sages reverenced in the realm of virtue have lived austerely. They manifested the greatest sincerity and fairness both in speech and action, and their altruism and unselfishness earned them the respect of all. Because of their personal example, they became the moral teachers of mankind. Thus, Mencius concluded that with regard to human life:

> "...From these things we see how life springs from sorrow and calamity and death from ease and pleasure."[227]

14. Self-Regulation

One should cultivate oneself not only in virtue, but also in physique. The care of the physique requires a well-regulated life and necessitates that attention be paid to one's physical condition so that disease can be prevented and a state of fitness be maintained. Since the mind is closely related to the body, when the body is not sound, the mind is also affected.

> The philosopher Tsêng being ill, he called to him the disciples of his school and said, "Uncover my feet, uncover my hands. It is said in the *Book of Songs*, 'We should be apprehensive and cautious, as if on the brink of a deep gulf, as if treading on thin ice.' Now and hereafter, I know my escape from all injury to my person, O ye, my little children."[228]

Of the three things which Confucius thought deserving of careful consideration, one was sickness.

> The things in reference to which the Master exercised the greatest caution were—fasting, war and sickness."[229]

Daily life comprises clothing, food, lodging and transportation. They should all be well-regulated, so that health may be preserved and the rules of propriety and righteousness observed. Let us now cite the teachings of Confucius with regard to living

(a) Food

Attention should be paid to the freshness and refinement of food, its cutting, its seasoning, its colors and flavors. Eating should not be in excess of capacity, and there should be no conversation while eating. Certain rules of propriety should be observed when gifts are received from superiors.

> He did not dislike to have his rice finely cleaned, nor to have his minced meat cut quite small.
> He did not eat rice which had been injured by heat or damp and turned sour, nor fish or meat which was gone. He did not eat what was discolored or what was of a bad flavor, nor anything which was ill-cooked or was not in season.
> He did not eat food which was not cut properly, nor what was served without its proper seacu.
> Though there might be a large quantity of meat, he would not allow what he took to exceed the due proportion for the rice. It was only in wine that he laid down no limit for himself, but he did not allow himself to be confused by it.
> He did not partake of wine and dried meat bought in the market.
> He was never without ginger when he ate.
> He did not eat much.

When he had been assisting at the prince's sacrifice, he did not keep the meat which he received overnight. The meat of his family sacrifice he did not keep over three days. If kept over three days, it was not eaten.

When eating, he did not converse. When in bed, he did not speak.

Although his food might be coarse rice and vegetable soup, he would offer a little of it in sacrifice with a grave respectful air.[230]

When he was at an entertainment where there was an abundance of provisions set before him, he would change countenance and rise up.[231]

When the prince sent him a gift of food, he would adjust his mat and taste it first. When the prince sent him a gift of undressed meat, he would have it cooked and offer it to the spirits of his ancestors. When the prince sent him a gift of a living animal, he would keep it alive. When he was in attendance on the prince and joining in the entertainment, the prince only sacrificed. He first tasted everything for the prince.[232]

(b) Clothing

Clothing keeps one warm, preserves health, gives a proper appearance and complies with the rules of propriety. It changes with the seasons and the weather. There are distinctions in its thickness, styles and colors. Attention should especially be paid to the fulfillment of the requirements of time and environment.

The superior man did not use a deep purple or a puce color in the ornaments of his dress.

Even in his undress he did not wear anything of a red or purple color.

In warm weather he had a single garment of coarse or fine texture, but he wore it displayed over an inner garment.

Over lamb's fur he wore a garment of black; over fawn's fur, one of white; and over fox's fur, one of yellow.

The fur robe of his undress was long, with the right sleeve short.

He required his sleeping dress to be half as long again as his body.

When staying at home, he used thick furs of the fox or the badger.

When he put off mourning, he wore all jade appendages.

His dress, except that for court audiences and sacrifices, was cut narrow above and wide below.

He did not wear lamb's fur or a black cap on a visit of condolence.

On the first day of the month he put on his court robes and presented himself at court.[233]

When he was ill and the prince came to visit him, he had his head to the east, made his court robes over him and drew his girdle across them.[234]

(c) Lodging

Lodging should be comfortable and pleasant. But attention should be paid to deportment, the rules of propriety and environment.

When the Master was unoccupied with business, his manner was easy and he looked pleased.[235]

If his mat was not straight, he did not sit on it.[236]

In bed, he did not lie like a corpse. At home, he did not put on any formal deportment...On a sudden clap of thunder or a violent wind, he would change countenance.[237]

(d) Transportation

In walking, riding or attending a meeting, not only was personal conduct important, but attention had to be given to the order of precedence and those attitudes compatible with the rules of propriety.

When the villagers were drinking together, on those who carried staffs (those over sixty years of age) going out, he went out immediately after. When the villagers were going through their ceremonies to drive away pestilential influences, he put on his court robes and stood on the eastern steps.[238]

Confucius, in his village, looked simple and sincere, and as if he were not able to speak. When he was in the prince's ancestral temple or in the court, he spoke minutely on every point, but cautiously.[239]

When he was waiting at court, in speaking with the great officials of the lower grade, he spoke freely, but in a straightforward manner; in speaking with those of the higher grade, he did so blandly, but precisely. When the ruler was present, his manner displayed respectful uneasiness; it was grave, but self-possessed.[240]

When the prince called him to employ him in the reception of a visitor, his countenance appeared to change and his legs to move forward with difficulty. He inclined himself to the other officials among whom he stood, moving his left or right arm as their position required, but keeping the skirts of his robe before and behind evenly adjusted. He hastened forward, with his arms like the wings of a bird. When the guest had retired, he would report to the prince, "The visitor is not turning round any more."[241]

When he entered the palace gate, he seemed to bend his body, as if it were not sufficient to admit him.

When he was standing, he did not occupy the middle of the gate-way; when he passed in or out, he did not tread upon the threshold.

When he was passing the vacant place of the prince, his countenance appeared to change and his legs to bend under him, and his words came as if he hardly had breath to utter them.

He ascended the reception hall, holding his robe with his hands, and his body bent: holding in his breath also, as if he dared not breathe.

When he came out from the audience, as soon as he had descended one step, he began to relax his countenance and had a pleasant look. When he had got to the bottom of the steps, he advanced rapidly to his place, with his arms like wings, and on occupying it, his manner still showed respectful uneasiness.[242]

When he was carrying the scepter of his ruler, he seemed to bend his body, as if he were not able to bear its weight. He did not hold it higher than the position of the hands in making a bow nor lower than their position in giving anything to another. His countenance seemed to change and look apprehensive, and he dragged his feet along as if they had to follow a certain track.

In presenting the presents with which he was charged, he wore a placid appearance.

At his private audience he looked highly pleased.[243]

When he was about to mount the carriage, he would stand straight, holding the cord. When he was in the carriage, he did not turn his head quite round, he did not talk loudly and quickly, he did not point with his hands.[244]

When he saw anyone in a mourning dress, though it might be a close acquaintance, he would change countenance; when he saw anyone wearing the cap of full dress or a blind person, though it might also be a close acquaintance, he would salute him in a ceremonious manner. To any person in mourning he bowed forward to the cross-bar of his carriage; he bowed in the same way to anyone bearing official charts and tables.[245]

When the prince's order called him, without waiting for his carriage to be yoked, he went at once.[246]

In addition to these rules of daily living—which complied with the rules of propriety—those who officiated at sacrifices were required to fast and bathe before the ceremonies so as to show their sincerity and reverence. Considering sacrifice to be one of the three important things, Confucius insisted on conducting them in person.

> When fasting, he thought it necessary to have his clothes brightly clean and made of linen cloth. When fasting, he thought it necessary to change his food and also to change the place where he commonly sat in the apartment.[247]
>
> He sacrificed to the spirits of ancestors as if they were present. He sacrificed to the spirits of gods as if they were present. The Master said, "I consider my not being present at the sacrifice as if I did not sacrifice."[248]

15. Integrity

The true value of a man isn't apparent in ordinary times. Only in crises and emergencies—especially when life and death are involved—is the true value of a man apparent. We find an example in the pines and cypresses, which lose their leaves only in cold weather.

> The Master said, "When the year becomes cold, then we know how the pine and cypress are the last to lose their leaves."[249]

Mencius said that human conduct depended upon what one would not do and did not want to have. This is exactly what integrity means.

> Mencius said, "Let a man not do what his sense of righteousness tells him not to do and let him not desire what his sense of righteousness tells him not to desire; to act thus is all he has to do.[250]
>
> Mencius said, "...To dwell in the wide house of the world, to stand in the correct seat of the world and to walk in the great path of the world; when he obtains his desire for office, to practice the Way for the good of the people; and when that desire is disappointed, to practice it alone; to be above the power of riches and honors to make dissipated, of poverty and mean condition to make swerve from principle and of prowess and force to make bend:—these characteristics constitute the great man."[251]

To dwell in the wide house of the world is benevolence, to stand in the correct seat of the world is propriety, and to walk in the great path of the world is righteousness. With these three virtues, one can cultivate one's all-pervading passion-nature and achieve righteousness and benevolence. It is impossible to speak of integrity without living in benevolence, treading the path of righteousness and upholding propriety.

The connotations of integrity are quite varied. One is incorruptibility, which includes thinking of righteousness when seeing the possibility of gain. Another connotation is chastity. We see this when a widow, rather than marrying again, sacrifices herself and discharges her duty toward her children. Such chastity can even lead to martyrdom; for instance, when the woman gives up her life resisting the violent lust of a man.

This clearly shows that a person's character is revealed in an emergency or crisis. During such times, a man insists on doing what he must and refuses to do what he should not, even to the extent of sacrificing his life rather than compromising his principles.

16. Keeping to One's Due

While integrity refers to the perfection of the personality, keeping to one's due means maintaining a balance between responsibility and propriety. Neither excess nor deficiency is correct.

To put it simply, a man must be consistent both in speech and conduct. He must comply with the rules of propriety and righteousness both in giving and taking. Only when he can avoid what he should not do can a man do what he should.

> The Master said, "He who is not in any particular office has nothing to do with plans for the administration of its duties.[252]
> The philosopher Tsêng said, "The superior man, in his thoughts, does not go out of his place."[253]
> The superior man does what is proper to the station in which he is; he does not desire to go beyond this.
> In a position of wealth and honor, he does what is proper to a position of wealth and honor. In a poor and low position, he does what is proper to a poor and low position. Situated among barbarous tribes, he does what is proper to a situation among barbarous tribes. In a position of sorrow and difficulty, he does what is proper to a position of sorrow and difficulty. The superior man can find himself in no situation in which he is not self-gratified.[254]

Mencius said, "...Confucius was once keeper of stores, and he then said, 'My calculations must be all right. That is all I hav to care about.' He was once in charge of the public fields, and he then said, 'The oxen and sheep must be fat and strong, and superior. That is all I have to care about.'

"When one is in a low situation, to speak of high matters is an offense. When a scholar stands in a prince's court and the Way is not carried into practice, it is a shame to him."[255]

Mencius said, "Men must be decided on what they will not do, and then they are able to act with vigor in what they ought to do.[256]

Mencius cited as an example the attitudes and actions of Shun, in retirement and at court, to prove that "what belongs by his nature to the superior man cannot be increased by the extensive prevalence of the Way nor diminished by his dwelling in poverty and retirement because it is determinately apportioned to him by Heaven."

Mencius said, "Shun's manner of eating his parched grain and herbs was as if he were to be doing so all his life. When he became sovereign and had the embroidered robes to wear, the lute to play and the two daughters of Yao to wait on him, he acted as if those things had belonged to him all his life."[257]

When Duke Ching of Ch'i called his forester contrary to the rules of propriety, the forester did not come, and the duke was going to kill him. Confucius praised the forester's refusal at the risk of losing his life, saying "The determined official never forgets that his end may be in a ditch or a stream; the brave official never forgets that he may lose his head." Confucius approved the forester's refusal when summoned inappropriately because, by so refusing, he adhered to his position, kept to his due, and, with great propriety, demonstrated his belittlement of gain. Mencius also cited the example of Wang Liang to show that the superior man kept to the proper path.

Ch'ên Tai said to Mencius, "In not going to wait upon any of the princes, you seem to me to be standing on a small point. If now you were once to wait upon them, the result might be so great that you would make one of them sovereign, or, if smaller, that you would make one of them chief of all the other princes. Moreover, the books say, 'By bending only one cubit, you make eight cubits straight.' It appears to me like a thing that might be done."

Mencius said, "Formerly Duke Ching of Ch'i, once when he was hunting, called his forester to him by a flag. The forester would not come, and the duke was going to kill him. With reference to this incident, Confucius said, 'The determined official never forgets that his end may be in a ditch or a stream; the brave official never forgets that he may lose his head.' What was it in the forester that Confucius thus approved? He approved his not going to the Duke, when summoned by the article which was not appropriate to him. If one goes to see the princes without waiting to be called, what can be thought of him?

"Moreover, that sentences 'By bending only one cubit, you make eight cubits straight,' is spoken with reference to the gain that may be got. If gain is the object, then, if it can be got by bending eight cubits to make one cubit straight, may we likewise do that?

"Formerly the official Chao Chien made Wang Liang act as charioteer for his favorite Hsi, when, in the course of a whole day, they did not get a single bird. The favorite Hsi reported this result, saying, 'He is the poorest charioteer in the world.' Someone told this to Wang Liang, who said, 'I beg leave to try again.' By dint of pressing, this was accorded to him, when in one morning they got ten birds. The favorite, reporting this result, said, 'He is the best charioteer in the world.' Chien said, 'I will make him always drive your chariot for you.' When he told Wang Liang so, however, Liang refused, saying, 'I drove for him, strictly observing the proper rules for driving, and in the whole day he did not get one bird. I drove for him so as deceitfully to intercept the birds, and in one morning he got ten. It is said in the *Book of Songs*, "If there is no failure in the driving of their horses, the arrows should be discharged surely." I am not accustomed to driving for a mean man. I beg leave to decline the office.'

"Thus this charioteer even was ashamed to bend improperly to the will of an archer. Though, by bending to it, they would have caught birds and animals sufficient to form a hill, he would not do so. If I were to bend my principles and follow those princes, of what kind would my conduct be? And you are wrong. Never has a man who has bent himself been able to make others straight."[258]

To give nothing and take nothing is incorruptibility or integrity. By doing thus, one keeps to his due without going beyond it. Therefore, "When it appears proper to take a thing, and afterwards not proper, to take it is contrary to moderation. When it appears proper to give a thing, and afterwards not proper, to give it is contrary to kindness." Mencius used this criterion to praise Hui of Liu-hsia for choosing to do good and tenaciously adhering to his principles. In the same respect, Mencius criticized Ch'ên Chung for stressing minor principles and overlooking the essentials.

Mencius said, "Hui of Liu-hsia would not for the three highest offices of state have changed his firm purpose of life."[259]

K'uang Chang said, "Is not Ch'ên Chung a man of true self-denying purity? He was living in Wu-ling and for three days was without food, till he could neither hear nor see. Over a wall there grew a plum tree, the fruit of which had been half eaten by worms. He crawled to it and tried to eat some of the fruit, when, after three swallowing mouthfuls, he recovered his sight and hearing."

Mencius replied, "Among the scholars of Ch'i, I must regard Chung as the thumb among the fingers. But still, where is the self-denying purity he pretends to? To carry out the principles which he holds to the full, one must become an earthworm, for so only can it be done.

"Now an earthworm eats the dry earth above and drinks the yellowspring below. Was the house in which Chung dwells built by a Po-i? Or was it built by a robber like Chih? Was the millet which he eats planted by a Po-i or was it planted by a robber like Chih? These are things which cannot be known."

"But," said Chang, "what does that matter? He himself weaves sandals of hemp, and his wife twists and dresses threads of hemp to sell or exchange them."

Mencius rejoined, "Chung belongs to an ancient and noble family of Ch'i. His elder brother Tai received from Ko a revenue of 10,000 *chung*, but he considered his brother's emolument to be unrighteous and would not eat of it, and in the same way he considered his brother's house to be unrighteous and would not dwell in it. Avoiding his brother and leaving his mother, he went and dwelt in Wu-ling. One day afterwards, he returned to their house, when it happened that someone sent his brother a present of a live goose. He, knitting his eyebrows, said, 'What are you going to use that cackling thing for?' By-and-by his mother killed the goose and gave him some of it to eat. Just then his brother came into the house and said, 'It is the flesh of that cackling thing,' upon which he went out and vomited it.

"Thus, what his mother gave him he would not eat, but what his wife gives him he eats. He will not dwell in his brother's house, but he dwells in Wu-ling. How can he, with such conduct, carry out his principles to the full? A man like Chung must be an earthworm, and then he can carry them out in full."[260]

Mencius said, "Supposing that the State of Ch'i were offered, contrary to righteousness, to Ch'ên Chung, he would not receive it, and all people would believe in his sincerity. But this is only the righteousness which declines a dish of rice or a plate of soup. A man can have no greater crimes than to disown his parents and relatives, and the relations between sovereign and minister, superiors and inferiors. How can it be allowed to give a man credit for the great excellences because he possesses a small one?"[261]

In view of the covetousness of those in high position, Confucius tried to show them the error of their ways by praising the contentment of Ching, a high official of the State of Wei.

The Master said of Ching, a scion of the ducal family of Wei, that he knew the economy of a family well. When he began to have means, he said, "Ha! here is a collection!" When they were a little increased, he said, "Ha! this is complete!" When he had become rich, he said, "Ha! this is admirable!"[262]

Keeping to one's due means not despising others spiritually and not plundering them materially. This can be accomplished only by being respectful and frugal. What is especially required is internal sincerity and reverence because it cannot be done with a show of external affability.

Mencius said, "The respectful do not despise others. The frugal do not plunder others. The prince who treats men with despite and plunders them is only afraid that they may not prove obedient to him—how can he be regarded as respectful or frugal? How can respectfulnes and frugality be made out of tones of the voice and a smiling manner?"[263]

Keeping to one's due is part of the process of rectification of the mind. The first step is to resist external temptations, the most alluring of which are wealth and honor. Everyone hopes for these things, but not everyone can succeed in in getting them. Therefore, the means of gaining wealth and honor and the way to preserve them are important considerations.

Whoever helps another gain wealth or honor receives that part of these things to which he is entitled. Otherwise such a person would lose his share even after receiving it. The thought of helping others gain wealth and honor is benevolence, and the action which translates it into practice is righteousness. To carry out the proper Way wholeheartedly is faithfulness. To have unswerving confidence in the face of difficulty is sincerity. To seek the state of perfect goodness constantly and unceasingly is unwearied delight in goodness.

> Mencius said, "There is a nobility of Heaven, and there is a nobility of man. Benevolence, righteousness, loyalty and faithfulness, with unwearied joy in goodness—these conititute the nobility of Heaven. To be a *kung*, a *ch'ing* or a *ta-fu*—this constitutes the nobility of man.
>
> "The men of antiquity cultivated their nobility of Heaven, and the nobility of man came to them in its train.
>
> "The men of the present day cultivate their nobility of Heaven in order to seek for the nobility of man, and when they have obtained that, they throw away the other; their delusion is extreme. The issue is simply this, that they must lose that nobility of man as well."[264]

The nobility of Heaven consists of the wealth and honor with which man is endowed by Heaven. The nobility of man is the wealth and honor conferred upon one man by another. The nobility of Heaven is sought internally and the nobility of man externally. The control over what is sought internally is exercised by oneself, and the control over what is sought externally is exercised by others. With regard to the nobility of Heaven, there need be no anxiety about the lack of the nobility of man. If the nobility of Heaven is used as a means and the nobility of man taken as an end, the inevitable result is failure. It is tantamount to the abandonment of the root and the pursuit of the branches. That is what is meant by the saying, "What can be reached by wisdom and cannot be held firm by benevolence is sure to be lost, even if it is obtained."

> Mencius said, "When we get by our seeking and lose by our neglecting, in that case seeking is of use to getting, and the things sought for are those which are in ourselves.
>
> "When the seeking is according to the proper course and the getting is only as appointed, in that case the seeking is of no use to getting, and the things sought are without ourselves."[265]
>
> Mencius said, "To desire to be honored is the common mind of man. And all men have in themselves that which is truly honorable. Only they do not think of it. The honor which men confer is not inherent honor. Those whom Chao the Great ennobles he can make

mean again. It is said in the *Book of Songs,*

> He has filled us with his wine,
> He has satiated us with his virtue.

'Satiated us with his virtue,' that is, satiated us with benevolence and righteousness and he who is so satiated, consequently, does not wish for the fat meat and fine millet of men. A good reputation and far-reaching praise fall to him, and he does not desire the elegant emboidered garments of men."[366]

Therefore it is said, "Wealth adorns the house, and virtue adorns the body." Virtue is real wealth, and the practice of the Way real honor. With both wealth and honor, there is joy. As a result, "what belongs by his nature to the superior man cannot be increased by the extensive prevalence of the Way nor diminished by his dwelling in poverty and retirement, because it is determinately apportioned to him by Heaven." In this way, a man fulfills the objectives of human life by seeking and obtaining benevolence, fulfilling his nature and practicing the Way.

> Mencius said, "Wide territory and a numerous people are desired by the superior man, but what he delights in is not here.
>
> "To stand in the center of the empire and tranquillize the people within the four seas—the superior man delights in this, but the highest enjoyment of his nature is not here.
>
> "What belongs by his nature to the superior man cannot be increased by the extensive prevalence of the Way nor diminished by his dwelling in poverty and retirement, because it is determinately apportioned to him by Heaven.
>
> "What belongs by his nature to the superior man are benevolence, righteousness, propriety and wisdom. These are rooted in his heart; their growth and manifestation are a mild harmony appearing in the countenance, a rich fullness in the back and the character imparted to the four limbs. Those limbs understand to arrange themselves, without being told."[267]

That is the reason why Confucius said that wealth could not be forcibly sought. To seek it forcibly is not keeping to one's due. Wealth must be gained by the proper course.

> The Master said, "If the search for riches is sure to be successful, though I should become a groom with whip in hand to get them, I will do so. As the search may not be successful, I will follow after that which I love."[268]

The Master said, "Riches and honors are what men desire. If it cannot be obtained in the proper way, they should not be held. Poverty and meanness are what men dislike. If it cannot be obtained in the proper way, they should not be avoided.

"If a superior man abandons benevolence, how can he achieve his good name?

"The superior man does not, even for the space of a single meal, act contrary to benevolence. In moments of haste he cleaves to it. In seasons of danger he cleaves to it."[269]

To search for riches and honors without the sense of shame is surely something to be deplored. Witness the story of the man from the State of Ch'i.

A man of Ch'i had a wife and a concubine and lived together with them in his house. When their husband went out, he would get himself well filled with wine and meat, and then return, and, on his wife's asking him with whom he ate and drank, they were sure to be all wealthy and honorable people. The wife informed the concubine, saying "When our husband goes out, he is sure to come back having partaken plentifully of wine and meat. I asked him with whom he ate and drank, and they are all, it seems, wealthy and honorable people. And yet no people of distinction ever come here. I will spy out where our husband goes." Accordingly, she got up early in the morning and privately followed wherever her husband went. Throughout the whole city, there was no one who stood or talked with him.

At last, he came to those who were sacrificing among the tombs beyond the outer wall on the east, and begged what they had over. Not being satisfied, he looked about and went to another party; and this was the way in which he got himself satiated.

His wife returned and informed the concubine, saying, "It was to our husband that we looked up in helpful contemplation, with whom our lot is cast for life; and now these are his ways!" On this, along with the concubine she reviled their husband and they wept together in the middle hall.

In the meantime the husband, knowing nothing of all this, came in with a jaunty air, carrying himself proudly to his wife and concubine.

In the view of a superior man, as to the ways by which men seek for riches, honors, gain and advancement, there are few of their wives and concubines who would not be ashamed and weep together on account of them."[270]

17. Repose in Poverty and Joy in the Way

Since wealth and honors are what men desire, is it not contrary to human nature to have repose in poverty? Although poverty is the usual lot of scholars, we do not necessarily expect them to be poor and yet have repose in their poverty. Hence Mencius said, "Only a scholar can have a fixed heart when he has no fixed livelihood." The intellectuals of today, who are the equivalent of the scholars of ancient times, have above-average intelligence, of course, and have a responsibility to place themselves at the disposal of society so as to promote the well-being of the people. If the people are happy, the Way is said to prevail. The intellectual, being of the people, is happy in turn and need have no anxiety.

It is easy to see that the intellectual, with this basic knowledge, is anxious about the prevalence of the Way rather than his own enjoyment. Therefore, to have repose in poverty and delight in the Way is the due of the intellectual. Not only is it favorable to the wealth and power of the nation, but it is conducive to it.

> The Master said, "A scholar, whose mind is set on the Way and who is ashamed of bad clothes and bad food, is not fit to be discoursed with."[271]
> The Master said, "The object of the superior man is the Way. Food is not his object. There is plowing; even in that there is sometimes want. So with learning; emolument may be found in it. The superior man is anxious lest he should not obtain the Way; he is not anxious lest poverty should come upon him."[272]

Both Confucius and Mencius lived in unfavorable times. The rulers of the various States were not unaware of their abilities, but they would not employ them for any length of time. As a result, both Confucius and Mencius suffered the fate of being unable to make their Way prevail, and they regretted it all their lives. The Master said, "Alas! How is it that the Way does not prevail!"[273]

> Mencius said, "From Yao and Shun down to T'ang were 500 years and more. As to Yü and Kao Yao, they saw those earliest sages, and so knew their doctrines, while T'ang heard their doctrines as transmitted, and so knew them.
> "From T'ang to King Wên were 500 years and more. Yi Yin and Lai Chu, they saw T'ang and knew his doctrines, while King Wên heard them as transmitted and so knew them. From King

Wên to Confucius were 500 years and more. As to Tai-kung Wang and San Yi-shêng, they saw King Wên, and so knew his doctrines. while Confucius heard them as transmitted, and so knew them.

"From Confucius downwards until now, there are only 100 years and somewhat more. The distance in time from the the the sage is so far from being remote, and so very near at hand was the sage's residence. Not only has there been none who saw him and knew his doctrines, but there has been none who heard them as transmitted, and so knew them."[274]

What the ancients called the Way is called doctrine today. The Way is a path, and righteousness is also a path. The practice of benevolent government is the prevalence of the Way, and the opposite is the absence of the Way.

A doctrine is more often applied to the art of politics. By promoting the well-being of the people, a doctrine receives their faith and support. Joy in the practice of the Way passes through the stages of possessing knowledge and being fond of it. With such joy, the superior man never does anything contrary to the Way, not even for the span of a single meal. He cleaves to it in moments of haste and times of danger; the love of the Way transcends even the love of one's own life. Since the superior man would sacrifice life itself for the Way, how can wealth and honor or poverty and meanness be on his mind? It is easy for such a man to let things follow their natural course and to emain at ease, even with poverty, if necessary.

Once the superior man succeeds in making the Way prevail, he can set the State in order, bring peace to the world and confer benefit cn all the people. On the other hand, if he fails, he does not seek the fulfillment of his aim by force, but rather cultivates his person further while biding his time. Hence, it is said that the superior man is inclined "when he obtains his desire for office to practice his principles for the good of his people, and when that desire is disappointed, to practice them alone."[275] It is also said, "If poor, they (men of antiquity) attended to their own virtue in solitude; if advanced to dignity, they made the whole empire virtuous as well."[276]

Since the intellectual holds himself responsible for practicing the Way, he does his best to shoulder this responsibility when he holds public office, without thinking of his own happiness. In this way, his viewpoint differs from that of the average man. Mencius expressed himself in detail on this point.

> Mencius said, "Those who give counsel to the great should despise them and not look at their pomp and display.
>
> "Halls several times eight cubits high, with beams projecting several cubits—these, if my wishes were to be realized, I would not have. Food spread before me over ten cubits square and attendants and concubines to the amount of hundreds—these, though my wishes were realized, I would not have. Pleasure and wine and the dash of hunting, with thousands of chariots following after me—these, though my wishes were realized, I would not have. What they esteem is what I would have nothing to do with; what I esteem are the rules of the ancients. Why should I stand in awe of them?"[277]

When a man cannot fulfill his desire for office and remains in retirement, he must not envy those who are rich and honorable. He should have no feeling of gain or loss. Rather, he should observe the rules of propriety, have repose and joy in poverty and feel happy and satisfied.

> Mencius said, "The reason why the superior man was reduced to straits between Ch'ên and Ts'ai was because neither the princes of the time nor their ministers sympathized or communicated with him."[278]
>
> The Master said, "There are those mean creatures! Is it possible along with them to serve one's ruler?
>
> "While they have not got their aims, their anxiety is how to get them. When they have got them, their anxiety is lest they should lose them.
>
> "When they are anxious lest such things should be lost, there is nothing to which they will not proceed."[279]
>
> Mencius said, "Add to a man the families of Han and Wei. If he then looks upon himself without being elated, he is far beyond the mass of men."[280]
>
> The Master said, "With coarse rice to eat, with water to drink, and my bended arm for a pillow—I still have joy in the midst of these things. Riches and honors acquired by unrighteousness are to me as a floating cloud."[281]

Having understood the above, we can see that only the superior man can speak of manifesting his will by being moderate. The mean man, who is not able to do this, is only attracted by gain, and so he cannot have repose in poverty. The Master said, "The superior man may indeed have to endure want, but the mean man, when he is in want, gives way to unbridled license."[282] Once he succeeds in realizing his desire for office, the mean man profits by his position to gain personal riches and honor. He does not choose the means to his end. He risks danger in the pursuit of luck, and he is anxious with regard to gain and loss. He will, in fact, do anything to attain his goals.

In addition to his own example in having repose in poverty and joy in the practice of the Way, Confucius made special mention of Yen Hui.

> The Master said, "Admirable indeed was the virtue of Hui! With a single bamboo dish of rice, a single ladleful of prink, and living in his mean narrow lane, while others could not have endured the distress, he did not allow his joy to be affected by it. Admirable indeed was the virtue of Hui!"[283]
> The Master said, "There is Hui! He has nearly attained to perfect virtue. He is often in want.
> "Tz'ŭ does not acquiesce in the appointments of Heaven, and he goes into business. Yet his judgments are often correct."[284]

Tzŭ-kung was in business to earn his living. Though he could not have repose in poverty, as Yen Hui could, Confucius praised his ability because his success in business was due him and could not be compared to ill-gotten riches obtained in public office. Since people in general could not be expected to remain at ease in poverty:

> Mencius said, "...They are only men of education who, without a certain livelihood, are able to maintain a fixed heart. As to the people, if they have not a certain livelihood, it follows that they will not have a fixed heart. And if they have not a fixed heart, there is nothing which they will not do, in the way of self-abandonment, of moral deflection, of depravity and of wild license."[285]

Without a livelihood, a man is poor. The possession of a fixed heart refers to joy in the practice of the Way, so far as the scholar is concerned. For the common people, it means joy in the practice of business. But only the scholar can have repose in poverty and joy in the practice of the Way.

18. Exercise of Care in Assumption of Office and Retirement, Differentiation between Quitting and Remaining in Office

The time for one's assumption of office and one's retirement, as well as the conditions for quitting and remaining in office, should be in accordance with the rules of propriety and righteousness. Otherwise, these acts would not redound to the benefit of either the individual or the public. The matter is so important that care should always be exercised. Mencius had the following to say with regard to the acceptance and leaving of office:

> The disciple Ch'ên said, "What were the principles on which superior men of old took office?" Mencius replied, "There were three cases in which they accepted office, and three in which they left.
>
> "If received with the utmost respect and all polite observances, and told that their words would be carried into practice, then they took office. Afterwards, although there might be no remission in the polite demeanor of the prince, if their words were not carried into practice, they would leave him.
>
> "The second case was that in which, though the prince could not be expected at once to carry their words into practice, yet being received by him with the utmost respect, they took office with him. But afterwards, if there was a remission in his polite demeanor, they would leave him.
>
> "The last case was that of the superior man who had nothing to eat, either morning or evening, was so famished that he could not move out of his door. If the prince, on hearing of his state, said, 'I have first of all failed to adopt his Way and also to follow his words, and I am ashamed to subject him to starvation in my country;' the relief offered in such a case might be received, but not beyond what was sufficient to avert death."[286]

Ancient men of morality who had lost their positions and had retired to private life were criticized by Confucius. As long as they complied with propriety and righteousness, he saw no reason why they insisted on their own preferences.

> The men who have retired to privacy from the world have been Po-i, Shu-ch'i, Yü-chung, Yi-i, Chu-chang, Hui of Liu-hsia and Shao-lien.

The Master said, "Refusing to surrender their wills or to submit to any taint in their persons; such, I think, were Po-i and Shu-ch'i.

"It may be said of Hui of Liu-hsia and of Shao-lien that they surrendered their wills and submitted to taint in their persons, but their words corresponded with reason and their actions were such as men are anxious to see. This is all that is to be remarked in them.

"It may be said of Yü-chung and Yi-i that, while thy hid themselves in their seclusion, they gave a license to their words; but, in their persons, they succeeded in preserving their purity, and, in their retirement, they acted according to the exigency of the times.

"I am different from all these. I have no course for which I am predetermined and no course against which I am predetermined."[387]

Mencius said, "...Confucius took office when he saw that the practice of his doctrines was likely; he took office when his reception was proper; he took office when he was supported by the State. In the case of his relation to Chi Huan, he took office, seeing that the practice of his doctrines was likely. With Duke Ling of Wei he took office, becase his reception was proper. With Duke Hsiao of Wei he took office, because he was maintatined by the State."[288]

Anxious to serve the world by putting his Way into practice, Mencius journeyed 1,000 *li* to the State of Ch'i. He was disappointed, but lingered before he left because he felt obliged to do so.

When Mencius had left Ch'i, Yin Shih spoke about him to others, saying, "If he did not know that the king could not be made a T'ang or a Wu, that showed his want of intelligence. If he knew that he could not be made such, and came notwithstanding, that shows he was seeking his own benefit. He came a thousand *li* to wait on the king; because he did not find in him a ruler to suit him, he took his leave, but how dilatory and lingering was his departure, stopping three nights before he quit Chou! I am dissatisfied on account of this."

The disciple Kao informed Mencius of these remarks. Mencius said, "How should Yin Shih know me! When I came a thousand *li* to wait on the king, it was what I desired to do. When I went away because I did not find in him a ruler to suit me, was that what I desired to do? I felt myself constrained to do it.

"When I stopped three nights before I quit Chou, in my own mind I still considered my departure speedy. I was hoping that the king would change. If the king had changed, he would certainly have recalled me.

"When I quit Chou and the king had not sent after me, then, and not till then, was my mind resolutely bent on returning to Tsou. But, notwithstanding that, how can it be said that I give up the king? The king, after all, is one who may be made to do good. If he were to use me, would it be for the happiness of the people of Ch'i only? It would be for the happiness of the people of the whole empire. I am hoping that the king will change. I am daily hoping for this.

"Am I like one of your little-minded people? They will remonstrate with their prince, and on their remonstrance not being accepted, they get angry; and with their passion displayed in their countenance, they take their leave and travel with all their strength for a whole day, before they will stop for the night."

When Yin Sh̄ih heard this explanation, he said, "I am indeed a small man.[289]

When he had left Ch'i, Mencius showed some displeasure. But when Ch'ung Yü questioned him, Mencius said that the time for his service to the empire had arrived, and he expressed confidence that he would succeed. When he was disappointed, he was forced to quit, but he had not expected this.

When Mencius left Ch'i,. Ch'ung Yü questioned him upon the way, saying, "Master, you look· like one who carries an air of dissatisfaction in his countenance. But formerly I heard you say, 'The superior man does not murmur against Heaven, nor grudge against men.' "

Mencius said, "That was one time, and this is another.

"It is a rule that a true royal sovereign should arise in the course of five hundred years, and that during that time there should be men illustrious in their generation.

"From the commencement of the Chou dynasty till now, more than seven hundred years have elapsed. Judging numerically, the time is past. Examining the character of the present time, we might expect the rise of such individuals in it.

"But Heaven does not yet wish that the empire should enjoy tranquillity and good order. If it wished this, who is there besides me to bring it about? How should I be dissatisfied?"[290]

Confucius believed that holding office had the prevalence of the Way as its object. He also felt that learning should be devoted to useful work, not to the search for riches or honors. He believed that when the environment permitted it, one should hold office in government, and that when nothing could be done, one should retire.

The Master said, "With sincere faith he (a man) unites the love of learning; holding firm to death, he is perfecting the Way.

"Such a person will not enter a tottering State, nor dwell in a disorganized one. When the Way prevails in the empire, he will show himself; when it does not, he will keep concealed.

When the Way prevails in a country, poverty and a mean condition are things to be ashamed of. When it does not prevail, riches and honors are things to be ashamed of."[291]

The Master said to Yen Yüan, "When called to office, to undertake its duties; when not so called, to lie retired—it is only I and you who have attained to this."[292]

The Master said, "...A superior man indeed is Ch'ü po-yü! When the Way prevails in his State, he is to be found in office. When it does not, he can roll his principles up and keep them in his breast."[293]

With learning, a man can hold office and make the Way prevail, but to keep up with the times, he continues to learn while he is in office.

Tzŭ-hsia said, "The accomplished official should devote himself to learning. The accomplished student should seek to be an official."[294]

Mencius explained that his departure from Ch'i had been due to failure to make the Way prevail, not to any sense of gain or loss. So, he quoted the words of Chi-sun to censure Tzŭ-shu Yi.

Mencius gave up his office and made arrangements for returning to his native State.

The king went to visit him and said, "Formerly I wished to see you, but in vain. Then I got the opportunity of being by your side, and all my court joyed exceedingly along with me. Now again you abandon me and are returning home. I do not know if hereafter I may expect to have another opportunity of seeing you." Mencius replied, "I dare not request permission to visit you at any particular time, but, indeed, it is what I desire"

Another day, the king said to the official Shih, "I wish to give Mencius a house, somewhere in the middle of the kingdom, and to support his disciples with an allowance of 10,000 *chung*, that all the officials and the people may have such an example to reverence and imitate. Had you not better tell him this for me?"

Shih took advantage to convey this message by means of the disciple Ch'ên, who reported his words to Mencius.

Mencius said, "Yes, but how should the official Shih know that the thing could not be? Suppose that I wanted to be rich, having formerly declined 100,000 *chung*, would my now accepting 10,000 be the conduct of one desiring riches?

"Chi-sun said, 'A strange man Tzǔ-shu Yi. He pushed himself into the service of government. His prince declining to employ him, he should have stopped, but he again schemed that his son or younger brother should be made a high official. Who indeed is there of men but wishes for riches and honors? But he only, among the seekers of these, tried to monopolize the conspicuous mound.

"'Of old time, the market dealers exchanged the articles which they had for others which they had not, and simply had certain officials to keep order among them. It happened that there was a mean fellow, who made it a point to look out for a conspicuous mound and get up upon it. Thence he looked right and left, to catch in his net the whole gain of the market. The people all thought his conduct mean, and therefore they proceeded to lay a tax upon his wares. The taxing of traders took its rise from this mean fellow.'"[295]

Holding office aims at neither riches nor honors, but it is not for the relief of poverty either. In extraordinary circumstances, however, it is justified to seek office for the relief of poverty. If so, one must decline an honorable position and occupy a low one and decline riches in favor of poverty to show that one is constrained to make the choice. Mencius cited the example of Confucius in accepting low positions on more than one occasion.

Mencius said, "Office is not sought on account of poverty, yet there are times when one seeks office on that accout. Marriage is not entered into for the sake of being attended to by the wife, yet there are times when one marries on that account.

"He who takes office on account of his poverty must decline an nonorable situation and occupy a low one; he must decline riches and prefer to be poor.

"What office will be in harmony with this declining an honorable situation and occupying a low one, this declining riches and preferring to be poor? Such an office as that of guarding the gates or beating the watchman's stick.

"Confucius was once keeper of stores, and he then said, 'My

calculations must be all right. That is all I have to care about.'
He was once in charge of the public fields, and he then said, 'The
oxen and sheep must be fat and strong, and superior. That is all
I have to care about.'

"When one is in a low situation, to speak of high matters is an
offense. When a scholar stands in a prince's court and the Way is
not carried into practice, it is a shame to him."[296]

Out of dire need one may take a low position temporarily
for the relief of poverty, but it is equally important to choose
the proper master to serve so as to ward off disdain.

Mencius, addressing the disciple Yüeh-chêng, said to him, "Your
coming here in the company of Tzŭ-ao was only because of the
food and the drink. I could not have thought that you, having
learned the doctrines of the ancients, would have acted with a view
to eating and drinkg."[297]

Mencius praised highly Yi Yin's sense of responsibility and,
denying a rumor about this great statesman, expressed the belief
that his conduct in accepting and declining offices was completely
in compliance with propriety and righteousness.

Wan Chang asked Mencius, saying, "People say that Yi Yin
sought an introduction to T'ang by his knowledge of cookery. Was
it so?"

Mencius replied, "No, it was not so. Yi Yin was a farmer in
the lands of the Prince of Hsin, delighting in the principles of Yao
and Shun. In any matter contrary to the righteousness which they
prescribed or contrary to their principles, though he had been offered
the throne, he would not have regarded it; though there had been
yoked for him a thousand teams of horses, he would not have looked
at them. In any matter contrary to the righteousness which they
prescribed or contrary to their principles, he would neither have
given nor taken a single straw.

"T'ang sent persons with presents of silk to entreat him to enter
his service. With an air of indifference and self-satisfaction he said,
'What can I do with those silks with which T'ang invites me? Is
it not best for me to abide in the channeled fields and so delight
myself with the principles of Yao ahd Shun?'

"T'ang thrice sent messengers to invite him. After this, with
the change of resolution displayed in his countenance, he spoke in
a different style, 'Instead of abiding in the channeled fields and
thereby delighting myself with the principles of Yao and Shun, had

I not better make this prince a prince like Yao and Shun and this people like the people of Yao and Shun? Had I not better in my own person see these things for myself?

" 'Heaven's plan in the production of mankind is this: that they who are first informed should instruct those who are later in being informed, and they who first apprehend the Way should instruct those who are slower to do so. I am one of Heaven's people who have first apprehended; and I will take this Way and instruct this people in it. If I do not instruct them, who will do so?'

"He thought that among all the people of the empire, even the private men and women, if there were any who did not enjoy such benefits as Yao and Shun conferred, it was as if he himself pushed them into a ditch. He took upon himself the heavy charge of the empire in this Way, and therefore he went to T'ang and pressed upon him the subject of attacking Hsia and saving the people.

"I have not heard of one who bent oneself and at the same time made others straight; how much less could one disgrace oneself and thereby rectify the whole empire? The actions of the sages have been different. Some have kept remote from court, and some have drawn near to it; some have left their offices, and some have not done so—that to which those difficult courses all agree is simply the keeping of their persons pure.

"I have heard that Yi Yin sought an introduction to T'ang by the doctrines of Yao and Shun. I have not heard that he did so by his knowledge of cookery.

"In the 'Instructions of Yi Yin' it is said, 'Heaven destroying Chieh commenced attacking him in the palace of Mu. I commenced in Po' "[298]

Since office-holding had as its object the prevalence of the Way, official position was the tool for this purpose, just as farming implements are essential to cultivation. Therefore, once a scholar lost his position, he was no different from a farmer who had lost his implements. Naturally, he was anxious and unhappy. But the search for office had to comply with the Way; otherwise, it would be like stealing the implements, something which would not benefit the farming.

Chou Hsiao asked Mencius, saying, "Did superior men of old take office?" Mencius replied, "They did. The Record says, 'If Confucius was three months without being employed by some ruler, he looked anxious and unhappy. When he passed from the boundary of a State, he was sure to carry with him his proper gift of introduction.' Kung-ming Yi said, 'Among the ancients, if an official was three months unemployed by a ruler, he was condoled with.'"

Hsiao said, "Did not this condoling, on being three months unemployed by a ruler, show a too great urgency?"

Mencius answered, "The loss of his place to an official is like the loss of his State to a prince. It is said in the *Book of Rites,* 'A prince plows himself and is assisted by the people, to supply the millet for sacrifice. His wife keeps silkworms and unwinds their cocoons, to make the garments for sacrifice. If the victims be not perfect, the millet not pure and the dress not complete, he does not presume to sacrifice. And the scholar who, out of office, has no holy field, in the same way, does not sacrifice.' The victims for slaughter, the vessels and the garments, not being all complete, he does not presume to sacrifice, and then neither may he dare to feel happy. Is there not here sufficient ground for condolence?"

Hsiao again asked, "What was the meaning of Confucius' always carrying his proper gift of introduction with him, when he passed over the boundaries of the State where he had been?"

"An official's being in office," was the reply, "is like the plowing of a husbandman. Does a husbandman part with his plow, because he goes from one State to another?"

Hsiao pursued, "The State of Chin is one, as well as others, of official employments, but I have not heard of anyone being thus earnest about being in office. If there should be this urgency, why does a superior man make any difficulty about taking it?" Mencius answered, "When a son is born, what is desired for him is that he may have a wife; when a daughter is born, what is desired for her is that she may have a husband. This feeling of the parents is possessed by all men. If the young people, without waiting for the orders of their parents and the arrangements of the go-betweens, shall bore holes to steal a sight of each other or get over the wall to be with each other, then their parents and all other people will despise them. The ancients did indeed always desire to be in office, but they also hated being so by any improper way. To seek office by an improper way is of a class with young people's boring holes."[299]

Therefore, whenever an opportunity for making the Way prevail presents itself, it should not be lightly missed. Like a beautiful gem, a superior man should not always remain hidden and unused.

Tzŭ-kung said, "There is a beautiful gem here. Should I try

to lay it up in a case and keep it? Or should I seek for a good price and sell it?" The Master said, "Sell it! Sell it! But I would wait for one to offer the price."[300]

For example, Chi was a powerful minister whom Confucius disliked. When a subordinate of Chi, a man named Kung-shan Fu-jao, revolted and invited Confucius to join him, the sage was favorably inclined. In his view, it was a golden opportunity to overthrow Chi, but Tzŭ-lu had his doubts.

> Kung-shan Fu-jao, when he was holding Pi, and in an attitude of rebellion, invited the Master to visit him, who was rather inclined to go.
>
> Tzŭ-lu was displeased and said, "If there is no place to go, let it be. Why must you think of going to see Kung-shan?"
>
> The Master said, "Can it be without some reason that he has invited me? If anyone employs me, may I not make an eastern Chou?[301]

Naturally, it was beneath Confucius' dignity to serve under a crafty politician, and even his disciple, Min Tzŭ-ch'ien, disapproved of it. When Yang Huo, Chi's subordinate, wished to see him, Confucius tried to evade him and used great tact in dealing with him. Mencius took the opportunity to explain why a scholar should not see a prince.

> The chief of the Chi family sent to ask Min Tzŭ-ch'ien to be Governor of Pi. Min Tzŭ-ch'ien said, "Decline the offer for me politely. If anyone comes again to me with a second invitation, I shall be obliged to go and live on the banks of the Wên."[302]
>
> Yang Huo wished to see Confucius, but Confucius would not go to see him. On this, he sent a present of a pig to Confucius, who, having chosen a time when Huo was not at home, went to pay his respects for the gift. He met him, however, on the way.
>
> He said to Confucius, "Come, let me speak with you." He then asked, "Can he be called benevolent who keeps his jewel in his bosom and leaves his country to confusion?" Confucius replied, "No." "Can he be called wise who is anxious to be engaged in public employment and yet is constantly losing the opportunity of being so?" Confucius again said, "No." "The days and months are passing away; the years do not wait for us." Confucius said, "Right; I will go into office."[303]
>
> Kung-sun Ch'ou asked Mencius, saying, "What is the meaning of not going to see the princes?" Mencius replied, "Among the

ancients, if one had not been a minister in a State, one did not go to see the sovereign.

"Tuan-kan Mu leaped over his wall to avoid the prince. Hsieh Liu shut his door and would not admit the prince. These two, however, went to excess. When a prince urgently seeks a meeting, it is not improper to see him.

"Yang Huo wished to get Confucius to go to see him but disliked doing so by any want of propriety. As it is the rule, therefore, that when a great official sends a gift to a scholar, if the latter is not at home to receive it, he must go to the official's to pay his respects, Yang Huo watched when Confucius was out, and sent him a roasted pig. Confucius, in his turn, watched when Huo was out, and went to pay his respects to him. At that time Yang Huo had taken the initiative; how could Confucius decline going to see him?

"Tsêng-tzŭ said, 'They who shrug up their shoulders and laugh in a flattering way toil harder than the summer laborer in the fields.' Tzŭ-lu said, 'There are those who talk with people with whom they have no great community of feeling. If you look at their countenance, they are full of blushes. I cannot understand such persons.' By considering these remarks, the spirit which the superior man nourishes may be known."[304]

Mencius also reprimanded his disciple, Yüeh-chêng, for holding office under a crafty minister.

> The disciple Yüeh-chêng went in the train of Tzŭ-ao to Ch'i. He came to see Mencius, who said to him, "Are you also come to see me?" Yüeh-chêng replied, "Master, why do you speak such words?" "How many days have you been here?" asked Mencius. "I came day before yesterday." "Day before yesterday! Is it not with reason then that I speak thus?" "My lodging-house was not arranged." "Have you heard that a scholar's lodging-house must be arranged before he visits his elder?" Yüeh-chêng said, "I have done wrong."[305]

Retirement can show one's will, and though a passive act, it produces a positive effect. When the Way does not prevail in the world, the superior man should retire, as the mean man gains ascendancy. It is time for the former to adopt the method of non-cooperation with the latter. Thereby he is sure to accelerate the failure of the mean man. If the superior man should associate freely with the mean man, he would be contaminated, and there would be no distinction between the pure and impure.

The Master said, "Some worthy men retire from the world. Some retire from particular States. Some retire because of disrespectful looks. Some retire because of contradictory language."[306]

Jan Yu said, "Is our Master for the ruler of Wei?" Tzŭ-kung said, "Oh! I will ask him."

He went in accordingly, and said, "What sort of men were Po-i and Shu-ch'i?" "They were ancient worthies," said the Master. "Did they have any repinings?" The Master again replied, "They sought to act virtuously, and they succeeded in doing so; what was there for them to repine about?" On this, Tzŭ-kung went out and said, "Our Master is not for him."[307]

On one occasion, when Tzŭ-lu was looking for Confucius, he met an old man and questioned him. The old man was courteous to Tzŭ-lu, but he sharply criticized Confucius. After Tzŭ-lu told this to Confucius next day, the Master decided that the old man was a recluse whom he would like to meet. The Master missed meeting him, but Tzŭ-lu explained to the old man's people the principles upheld by the Master in accepting and declining office. The Master, he said, regarded retirement as a passive act, but saw holding office as a positive one. The implication was that it was only under unavoidable circumstances that a person should retire.

Tzŭ-lu, following the Master, happened to fall behind, when he met an old man, carrying across his shoulder on a staff a basket for weeds. Tzŭ-lu said to him, "Have you seen my Master, Sir?" The old man replied, "Your four limbs are unaccustomed to toil; you cannot distinguish the five kinds of grain; who is your Master?" With this, he planted his staff in the ground and proceeded to weed.

Tzŭ-lu joined his hands across his breast and stood before him.

The old man kept Tzŭ-lu to pass the night in his house, killed a fowl, prepared millet and feasted him. He also introduced to him his two sons.

Next day, Tzŭ-lu went on his way and reported his adventure. The Master said, "He is a recluse," and sent Tzŭ-lu back to see him again, but when he got to the place, the old man was gone.

Tzŭ-lu then said to the family, "Not to take office is not righteous. If the relations between old and young may not be neglected, how is it that he sets aside the duties that should be observed between sovereign and minister? Wishing to maintain his personal purity, he allows that great relation to come to confusion. A superior man takes office and performs the righteous duties belonging to it. It has of course long been known that the Way does not prevail"[308]

Since the aim of holding office was to make the Way prevail and to assume the responsibility of "making the whole empire virtuous at the same time," the decision as to wheher office should be accepted or rejected depended on whether the Way could prevail. If the the ruler acted against benevolence and the Way, did not intend to do good or refused to accept remonstrances, it was proper to seek speeedy retirement.   Let us cite the following examples:

(a)   Retirement in case of the ruler's fondness of lust

The people of Ch'i sent to Lu a present of female musicians, which Chi Huan received, and for three days no court was held. Confucius took his departure.[309]

(b)   Retirement in case of the ruler's fondness of war

Duke Ling of Wei asked Confucius about tactics. Confucius replied, "I have heard all about sacrificial vessels, but I have not learned military matters."   On this, he took his departure the next day.

When he was in Ch'ên, their provisions were exhausted, and his followers became so ill that they were unable to rise.

Tzŭ-lu, with evident dissatisfaction, said, "Has the superior man likewise to endure want?"   The Master said, "The superior man may indeed have to endure want, but the mean man, when he is in want, gives way to unbridled license."[310]

(c)   Retirement in case of the ruler's fondness of killing

Mencius said, "When scholars are put to death without any crime, the great officials may leave the country.   When the people are slaughtered without any crime, the scholars may move."[311]

(d)   Retirement in case of the ruler's lack of sincerity

Duke Ching of Ch'i, with reference to the manner in which he should treat Confucius, said, "I cannot treat him as I would the chief of the Chi family.   I will treat him in a manner between that accorded to the chief of the Chi and that given to the chief of the Mêng family."   He also said, "I am old; I cannot use him." Confucius took his departure.[312]

(e) An official retired when he could not discharge his official functions

(f) He who had the responsibility of speaking (a Censor) retired when his remonstrances were not accepted.

> Mencius said to Ch'ih Wa, "There seemed to be reason in your declining the governorship of Ling-ch'iu and requesting to be appointed chief criminal judge, because the latter office would afford you the opportunity of speaking your views. Now several months have elapsed, and have you yet found nothing of which you might speak?"
>
> On this, Ch'ih Wa remonstrated on some matter with the king, and, his counsel not being taken, resigned his office and went away.
>
> The people of Ch'i said, "In the course which he marked out for Ch'ih Wa he did well, but we do not know as to the course which he pursues for himself."
>
> His disciple Kung-tu told him these remarks.
>
> Mencius said, "I have heard that he who is in charge of an office, when he is prevented from fulfilling his duties, ought to take his departure, and that when he on whom is the responsibility of giving his opinion, when he finds his words unattended to, ought to do the same. But I am in charge of no office; on me devolves no duty of speaking out my opinion. May not I therefore act freely and without any constraint, either in going forward or in retiring?"[313]

When any condition for retirement exists the determination to quit should ensue. No matter how hard the ruler tries to retain the party concerned, he should refuse to stay, because it would not help matters if he acceded to a request contrary to principle.

> Mencius, having taken his leave of Ch'i, was passing the night in Chou.
>
> A person who wished to detain him on behalf of the king came and sat down, and began to speak to him. Mencius gave him no answer, but leant upon his table and slept.
>
> The visitor was displeased and said, "I passed the night in careful vigil, before I would venture to speak to you, and you, Master, sleep and do not listen to me. Allow me to request that I may not again presume to see you." Mencius replied, "Sit down, and I will explain the case clearly to you. Formerly, if Duke Mu had not kept a person by the side of Tzŭ-ssŭ, he could not have induced Tsŭ-ssŭ to remain with him. If Hsieh Liu and Shên

Hsiang had not had a remembrancer by the side of Duke Mu, he would not have been able to make them feel at home and remain with him.

"You anxiously form plans with reference to me, but you do not treat me as Tsŭ-ssŭ was treated. Is it you, Sir, who cut me? Or is it I who cut you?"[314]

Once it was decided to take leave, there was no room for hesitation. If, after quitting, the party returned, he would indeed be subjected to ridicule and would be no different from Fêng Fu, whose story was told by Mencius.

> When Ch'i was suffering from famine, Ch'ên Chên said to Mencius, "The people are all thinking that you, Master, will again ask that the granary of T'ang be opened for them. I apprehend you will not do so a second time."
>
> Mencius said, "To do it would be to act like Fêng Fu. There was a man of that name in Chin, famous for his skill in seizing tigers. Afterwards he became a scholar of reputation, and going once out to the wild country, he found the people all in pursuit of a tiger. The tiger took refuge in a corner of a hill, where no one dared to attack him, but when they saw Fêng Fu, they ran and met him. Fêng Fu immediately bared his arms and descended from the carriage. The multitude was pleased with him, but those who were scholars laughed at him."[315]

Sometimes an exception to the rule was unavoidable. For example, when Confucius went to see Nan-tzŭ, Tzŭ-lu, a straightforward man, showed his displeasure. But Confucius vowed to him that he would not have a change of heart.

> The Master having visited Nan-tzŭ, Tzŭ-lu was displeased, on which the Master swore, saying, "Wherein I have done improperly, may Heaven reject me! may Heaven reject me!"[316]

To leave one's own country on finding the Way did not prevail was certainly a great agony. It engendered a feeling totally different from that which one felt on depature from a foreign country. Therefore, the trip was often delayed.

> Mencius said, "When Confucius was leaving Lu, he said, 'I will set out by-and-by;'—this was the way in which to leave the State of his parents. When he was leaving Ch'i, he strained

off with his hand the water in which his rice was being rinsed, took the rice and went away;—this was the way in which to leave a strange State."[317]

In short, whether accepting or declining office, whether remaining behind or leaving a country, the object should be n to enrich or to honor oneself, but to seek the well-being ot mankind. The decision reached should be in accordance with the rules of righteousness and propriety; otherwise, it would be impossible to show one's will or to make the Way prevail. Therefore, a careful choice should be made of the sovereign to serve and the time to serve him. If it is clearly established that it is impossible for the Way to prevail, retirement or departure is preferable to dishonorable collaboration and fruitless endeavor. As has been well said, one should "appear where the Way prevails and retire where it does not." But, in accepting office, there is always a preference for the "State of one's parents;" i.e., one's native country, which should not be left for little or no reason.

19. Care in Social Intercourse and in Taking and Giving

In human dealings, mutual aid, both spiritual and material, is unavoidable. At times, it involves an exchange between "haves" and "have-nots," an interchange of respect and, occasionally, even a bribe looking toward the fulfillment of selfish desire. A careful investigation is called for, to determine whether the taking or giving in each instance is in accordance withe righteousness and the rules of propriety.

> Tzŭ-chang said, "The scholar, trained for public duty, seeing threatening danger, is prepared to sacrifiice his life. When the opportunity of gain is presented to him, he thinks of righteousness. In sacrificing, his thoughts are reverential. In mourning, his thoughts are about the grief which he should feel. Such a man commands our approbation indeed."[318]

To take what should not be taken is contrary to moderation, and to give what should not be given is contrary to kindness.

> Mencius said, "...The imparting by a man to others of his wealth is called 'kindness.'"[319]
>
> Mencius said, "When it appears proper to take a thing, and afterwards not proper, to take it is contrary to moderation. When

it appears proper to give a thing and afterwards not proper, to give it is contrary to kindness."[320]

While it is easy to decide whether to accept something from relatives or friends, a difficulty may arise when the gift is from an elder or sovereign. Mencius comments on this in great detail.

Wan Chang asked Mencius, saying. "I venture to ask what feeling of the mind is expressed in the presents of friendship?" Mencius replied, "The feeling of respect."

"How is it," pursued Chang, "that the declining of a present is accounted disrespectful?" The answer was, "When one of honorable rank presents a gift, to say in the mind, 'Was the way in which he got this righteous or not? I must know this before I can receive it;'—this is deemed disrespectful, and therefore presents are not declined."

Wan Chang asked again, "When one does not take on him in so many express words to refuse the gift, but having declined it in his heart, saying, 'It was taken by him unrighteously from the people,' and then assigns some other reason for not receiving it; is not this a proper course?" Mencius said, "When the donor offers it on a ground of reason and his manner of doing so is according to propriety; in such a case Confucius would have received it."

Wan Chang said, "Here now is one who stops and robs people outside the gates of the city. He offers his gift on a ground of reason and does so in a manner according to propriety; would the reception of it so acquired by robbery be proper?" Mencius replied, "It would not be proper. In 'The Announcement to K'ang' it is said, 'When men kill others and roll over their bodies to take their property, being reckless and fearless of death, among all the people there are none but detest them:'—thus, such characters are to be put to death without waiting to give them warning. Yin received this rule from Hsia, and Chou received it from Yin. It cannot be questioned, and today it is even better acknowaledged. How can the gift of a robber be received?"

Wan Chang said, "The princes of the present day take from their people just as a robber despoils his victim. Yet if they put a good face of propriety on their gifts, then the superior man receives them. I venture to ask how you explain this." Mencius answered, "Do you think that, if there should arise a truly royal sovereign, he would collect the princes of the present day and put them all to death? Or would he admonish them, and then, on their not changing their ways, put them to death? Indeed, to call everyone who takes what does not properly belong to him a robber is pushing a point of resemblance to the utmost and insisting on the most refined idea of righteousness. When Confucius was in office in Lu, the people struggled together for the game taken in hunting, and he also did the same. If that struggling for the captured game was proper, how much more may the gifts from the princes be received?"

Chang urged, "Then are we to suppose that when Confucius held office, it was not with the view to carrying his doctrines into practice?" "It was with that view," Mencius replied, and Chang rejoined, "If the practice of his doctrines was his business, what had he to do with that struggling for the captured game?" Mencius said, "Confucius first rectified his vessels of sacrifice according to the registers, and did not fill them so rectified with food gathered from every quarter." "But why did he not go away?" "He wished to make a trial of carrying his doctrines into practice. When that trial was sufficient to show that they could be practiced and they were still not practiced, then he went away, and thus it was that he never completed in any State a residence of three years.

"Confucius took office when he saw that the practice of his doctrines was likely; he took office when his reception was proper; he took office when he was supported by the State. In the case of his relation to Chi Huan, he took office, seeing that the practice of his doctrines was likely. With Duke Ling of Wei, he took office because his reception was proper. With Duke Hsiao of Wei, he took office because he was maintained by the State."[321]

The value of social intercourse lies in the exchange of civilities rather than gifts, which may not necessarily represent the expression of sincerity. Therefore, when Mencius received gifts from ruling princes, the measure of his thanks depended upon whether the offer was an expression of sincerity.

When Mencius was residing in Tsou, Chi Jên, the younger brother of the Chief of Jên, who was guardian of Jên at the time, paid his respects to him with a present of silks, which Mencius received, but did not acknowledge. When he was sojourning in P'ing-lu, Ch'u, who was prime minister of the State, sent him a similar gift, which he received in the same way.

Subsequently, going from Tsou to Jên, he visited the guardian; but when he went from P'ing-lu to the capital of Ch'i, he did not visit the minister Ch'u. The disciple Wu-lu was glad and said, "I have got an opportunity to obtain some instruction."

He asked accordingly, "Master, when you went to Jên, you visited the chief's brother; and when you went to Ch'i you did not visit Ch'u. Was it because he is only the prime minister?"

Mencius replied, "No. It is said in the *Book of History*, 'In presenting an offering to a superior, most depends on the demonstrations of respect. If those demonstrations are not equal to the things offered, we say there is no offering, that is, there is no act of the will in presenting the offering.'

"This is because the things so offered do not constitute an offering."

Wu-lu was pleased, and when someone asked him what Mencius meant, he said, "Chi could not go to Tsou, but Ch'u might have gone to P'ing-lu."[322]

Ch'ên Chên asked Mencius, saying, "Formerly, when you were in Ch'i, the king sent you a present of 2,400 taels of fine silver, and you refused to accept it. When you were in Sung, 1680 taels were sent to you, which you accepted; and when you were in Hsüeh, 1,200 taels were sent, which you likewise accepted. If your declining to accept the gift in the first case was right, your accepting it in the latter cases was wrong· If your accepting it in the latter cases was right, your declining to do so in the first case was wrong. You must accept, Master, one of these alternatives."

Mencius said, "I did right in all the cases.

"When I was in Sung, I was about to take a long journey. Travelers must be provided with what is necessary for their expenses. The prince's message was, 'A present against traveling expenses.' Why should I have declined the gift?

"When I was in Hsüeh, I was apprehensive of my safety and taking measures for my protection. The message was, 'I have heard that you are taking measures to protect yourself, and send this to help you in procuring arms.' Why should I have declined the gift?

"But when I was in Ch'i, I had no occasion for money. To send a man a gift when he has no occasion for it is to bribe him. How is it possible that a superior man should be presented with a bribe?"[323]

When a friend was entrusted with a message to someone far away, it was customary to bow to the messenger as a sign of respect. When medicine was sent as a gift from another person, it was permissible to receive it with a bow, but not to take it in case of doubt.

When he (Confucius) was sending complimentary inquiries to anyone in another State, he bowed twice as he escorted the messenger away.

Chi K'ang having sent him a present of physic, he bowed and

received it, saying "I do not know it. I dare not taste it."[324]

In short, both taking and giving must be in accordance with propriety and righteousness, appropriate and timely. If the recipient has more than enough, he can also share the surplus with others, but he should help those who do not have enough rather than help to make the rich richer.

> Tzŭ-hua being employed on a mission to Ch'i, the disciple Jan requested grain for his mother. The Master said, "Give her a *fu*." Jan requested more. "Give her a *yü* (in addition)," said the Master. Jan gave her five *ping*.
> The Master said, "When Ch'ih was proceeding to Ch'i, he had fat horses to his carriage and wore light furs. I have heard that a superior man helps the distressed, but does not add to the wealth of the rich."
> Yüan Ssŭ being made governor of his town by the Master, he gave him nine hundred measures of grain, but Ssŭ declined them.
> The Master said, "Do not decline them. May you not give them away in the neighborhoods, hamlets, towns, and villages?"[325]

It is indeed a good thing to help others materially, but it is even better to help them morally.

> Mencius said, "A bad year cannot prove the cause of death to him whose stores of grain are large; an age of corruption cannot confound him whose equipment of virtue is complete."[326]

20. Selection and Transformation of Environment

Just as man can transform his environment, so can environment influence the condition of man. It follows that care must be exercised in the selection of one's environment. A wise choice is to live in a virtuous neighborhood.

> The Master said, "It is virtuous manners which constitute the excellence of a neighborhood. If a man in selecting a residence does not fix on one where such manners prevail, how can he be wise?"[327]

One's character can be changed by one's environment and situation. As it is said, "One's position alters the air, just as the nurture affects the body." If the body is affected, the mind is affected so much more. If one progresses so far as to live in benevolence and tread the path of righteousness, the inevitable result is the improvement of one's personality.

> Mencius, going from Fan to Ch'i, saw the King of Ch'i's son at a distance and said with a deep sigh, "One's position alters the air, just as the nurture affects the body. Great is the influence of position! But is he not just like the sons of all men?
>
> "The residence, the carriages and horses, and the dress of the king's son are mostly the same as those of other men. That he looks so is occasioned by his position. How much more should a peculiar air distinguish him whose position is in the wide house of the world?
>
> "When the prince of Lu went to Sung, he called out at the Tieh-tsê gate, and the keeper said, 'This is not our prince. How is it that his voice is so like that of our prince?' This was occasioned by nothing but correspondence of their positions.' "[328]

In paying attention to environment, a careful watch should first be kept over those who are near to you, for it is they whose words and acts most easily influence you. Hence, it is said, "... there are few men in the world who love and at the same time know the bad qualities of their love, or who hate and yet know the excellences of the object of their hatred."[329] The following passage contains the answer given by Confucius to Tzŭ-chang's question on what constituted intelligence and how a person could be free from delusion.

> Tzŭ-chang asked what constituted intelligence. The Master said, "He with whom neither slander that gradually soaks into the mind nor statements that startle like a wound in the flesh are successful may be called intelligent indeed. Yea, he with whom neither soaking slander nor startling statements are successful may be called far-seeing."[330]

While the influence of envirnoment on ordinary men is very strong, it is much less so on those who have faith, virtue and wisdom.

> The Master was wishing to go and live among the nine wild tribes of the east.
>
> Someone said, "It is a rude locality. How can you do such a thing?" The Master said, "If a superior man dwelt there, what rudeness would there be?"[331]

The influence of environment is least on two types of persons: the wisest and the most stupid.

> The Master said, "There are only the wise of the highest class and the stupid of the lowest class who cannot be changed."[332]

When careful selection of one's environment is not made, one is open to misunderstanding, criticism and rebuke. In answering a question put to him by Wan Chang, Mencius took occasion to clear up some misunderstanding about Confucius.

> Wan Chang asked Mencius, saying, "Some say that Confucius, when he was in Wei, lived with the ulcer-doctor, and when he was in Ch'i, with the attendant Chi Huan; was it so?" Mencius replied, "No, it was not so. Those are inventions of men fond of strange things.
>
> "When he was in Wei, he lived with Yen Ch'ou-yü. The wives of the official Mi and Tzŭ-lu were sisters, and Mi told Tzŭ-lu, 'If Confucius will lodge with me, he may attain to the dignity of a high noble of Wei.' Tzŭ-lu informed Confucius of this, and he said, 'That is as ordered by Heaven.' Confucius went into office according to propriety and retired from it according to righteousness. In regard to his obtaining office or not obtaining it, he said, 'That is as ordered.' But if he had lodged with the ulcer-doctor and the attendant Chi Huan, that would neither have been according to righteousness nor any ordering of Heaven.
>
> "When Confucius, being dissatisfied in Lu and Wei, had left those States, he met with the attempt of Huan, Minister of War of Sung, to intercept and kill him. He assumed, however, the dress of a common man and passed by Sung. At that time, though Confucius was in circumstances of distress, he lodged with the city-master Chêng, who was then a minister of Chou, Marquis of Ch'ên.
>
> "I have heard that the characters of ministers about court may be discerned from those whom they entertain, and those of more remote officials, from those with whom they lodge. If Confucius had lodged with the ulcer-doctor and with the attendant Chi Huan, how could he have been Confucius?"[333]

Confucius never let pass an opportunity to make the Way prevail because he was confident that he could transform his environment and be free of its control.

> Pi Hsi inviting him to visit him, the Master was inclined to go.

Tzǔ-lu said, "Master, formerly I have heard you say, 'When a man in his own person is guilty of doing evil, a superior man will not associate with him Pi Hsi is in rebellion, holding possession of Chung-mou; if you go to him, what shall be said?"

The Master said, "Yes, I did use these words. But is it not said that, if a thing be really hard, it may be ground without being made thin? Is it not said that, if a thing be really white, it may be steeped in a dark fluid without being made black?

"Am I a bitter gourd? How can I be hung up out of the way of being eaten?"[334]

To meet the exigencies of environment is popularly described as compliance with convention, and it is often quite necessary. But one should refrain from going out of the way to be accommodating, so as not to damage righteousness and run counter to propriety.

The Master said, "The linen cap is that prescribed by the rules of ceremony, but now a silk one is worn. It is economical, and I follow the common practice.

The rules of ceremony prescribe the bowing below the hall, but now the practice is to bow only after ascending it. That is arrogant. I continue to bow below the hall, though I go against the common practice."[335]

21. Creation of and Wait for Circumstances

Time and circumstances are two important factors influencing success or failure. Circumstances can be created or they can be awaited, depending on one's own wisdom or judgment. No reliance should be placed on others for the decision.

Mencius said, "The mass of men wait for a King Wên, and then they will receive a rousing impulse. Scholars distinguished from the mass, even without a King Wên, rouse themselves."[336]

Mencius said, "...The people of Ch'i have a saying—'A man may have wisdom and discernment, but that is not like embracing the favorable opportunity. A man may have instruments of husbandry, but that is not like waiting for the farming seasons."[337]

In timeliness and the ability to take advantage of opportunity lies the secret of success. Hence, it is said:

Seeing the countenance, it instantly rises. It flies round, and by and by settles.

The Master said, "There is the hen-pheasant on the hill bridge. How timely! How timely!" Tzŭ-lu got hold of it. Thrice it fluttered its wings and then rose.[388]

22. Selection of Skills, Arts and Habits

Skills and arts have a great deal to do with the choice of one's profession, and so they influence one's psychological condition. When these are practiced for a long time, they unwittingly tend to change one's moral conceptions. As a common saying puts it, "Habits become second nature." Since this can be very dangerous, it behooves one to choose his skills and arts very carefully.

Mencius said, "Is the arrow-maker less benevolent than the maker of armor of defence? And yet, the arrow-maker's only fear is lest man should not be hurt, and the armor-maker's only fear is lest men should be hurt. So it is with the priest and the coffin-maker. The choice of a profession, therefore, is a thing in which great caution is required.

"Confucius said, 'It is virtuous manners which constitute the excellence of a neighborhood. If a man, in selecting a residence, does not fix on one where such manners prevail, how can he be wise?' Now, benevolence is the most honorable dignity conferred by Heaven and the quiet home in which man should dwell. Since no one can hinder us from being so, if yet we are not benevolent, this is being not wise.

"From the want of benevolence and the want of wisdom will ensue the entire absence of propriety and righteousness; he who is in such a case must be the servant of other men. To be the servant of men and yet ashamed of such servitude is like a bow-maker's being ashamed to make bows or an arrow-maker's being ashamed to make arrows.

"If he be ashamed of his case, his best course is to practice benevolence.

"The man who would be benevolent is like the archer. The archer adjusts himself and then shoots. If he misses, he does not murmur against those who surpass him. He simply turns round and seeks the cause of his failure in himself."[389]

Would it not be a corollary from the above that no one would care to be a coffin-maker or arrow-maker? As a matter of fact, both are required—one for the armament of a country, the other for fulfilling a need in times of peace. The supply of each is needed to meet a specific demand. Confucius' real intention was to call attention to the greater importance of virtue when compared to skill, which should not be permitted to overshadow virtue. In this way, he admonished arrow-makers and coffin-makers to be constantly on their guard.

A man cannot do without the things in which he takes special delight. Such things provide him with interest in human life and increase his vitality. But he must not become addicted to them to the extent that they become bad habits. Therefore, only delight in those things which are beneficial to mind and body and the exercise of moderation can give real pleasure and stimulate interest.

> Confucius said, "There ere three things men find enjoyment in which are advantageous, and three things they find enjoyment in which are injurious. To find enjoyment in the discriminating study of ceremonies and music; to find enjoyment in speaking of the goodness of others; to find enjoyment in having many worthy friends; these are advantageous. To find enjoyment in extravagant pleasures; to find enjoyment in idleness and sauntering; to find enjoyment in the pleasures of feasting; these are injurious."[310]

Confucius set no limit on drinking, but "he did not allow himself to be confused by it."[341] He was humble enough to say, "What if I am not distressed by drinking?" The point he was driving at was that while it is difficult to exercise moderation in this instance, it is necessary to do so.

23. Prudence in Speech

Speech must be truthful and practicable. It should not be excessive; indeed it is sufficient if it conveys the meaning, for it can produce its effect only when its time, weight and objects are just right. These points are illustrated by the following passages:

> (a) The Master said, "I do not know how a man without truthfulness is to get on. How can a large carriage be made to go without the cross-bar for yoking the oxen to, or a small carriage without the arrangements for yoking the horses?"[342]
>
> (b) Tzŭ-kung said, "For one word a man is often deemed to be wise, and for one word he is often deemed to be foolish. We ought to be careful indeed in what we say."[343]

(c) The Master said, "In language it is simply required that it convey the meaning..."[341]

(d) The Master asked Kung-ming Chia about Kung-shu Wên, saying, "Is it true that your master speaks not, laughs not and takes not?"

Kung-ming Chia replied, "This has arisen from the reporters going beyond the truth. My master speaks when it is time to speak, and so men do not get tired of his speaking. He laughs when there is occasion to be joyful, and so men do not get tired of his laughing. He takes when it is consistent with righteousness to do so, and so men do not get tired of his taking." The Master said, "So! But is it so with him?"[345]

(e) The Master said, "The reason why the ancients did not readily give utterance to their words was that they feared their actions should not come up to them."[346]

(f) The Master said, "To those whose talents are above mediocrity the highest subjects may be announced. To those who are below mediocirty the highest subjects may not be announced."[347]

(g) The Master said, "When a man may be spoken with, not to speak to him is to err in reference to the man. When a man may not be spoken with, to speak to him is to err in reference to our words. The wise err neither in regard to their man nor their words."[348]

Confucius advised against saying much about anything that had happened and that could not be remedied.

Duke Ai asked Tsai Wo about the altars of the spirits of the land. Tsai Wo replied, "The Hsia sovereign planted the pine tree about them; the men of the Yin planted the cypress; and the men of the Chou planted the chestnut tree, meaning thereby to cause the people to be in awe."

When the Master heard it, he said, "Things that are done, it is needless to speak about; things that have had their course, it is needless to remonstrate about; things that are past, it is needless to blame."[349]

It is often difficult to do anything about what has been said or done erroneously or contrary to reason. Moreover, in such instances, unreasonable replies are frequently elicited. Therefore, one should take care to be prudent in speech.

Nan Jung was frequently repeating the lines about a piece of white jade (which describe the difficulty of removing the stain caused by erroneous speech). Confucius gave him the daughter of his elder brother to wife.[350]

And hence, the ruler's words going forth contrary to right will come back to him in the same way.[351]

A man speaks as he pleases if he has never received a rebuke from others, for this tends to make him careless.

> Mencius said, "Men's being ready with their tongues arises simply from their not having been reproved."[352]

Things are often said which a speaker cannot avoid saying in a given situation. When forced to do so, both Confucius and Mencius on occasion expressed their anxiety about the prevailing situation.

> Wei-shêng Mou said to Confucius, "Ch'iu, how is it that you keep roosting about? Is it not that you are an insinuating talker?"
>
> Confucius said, "I do not dare to play the part of such a talker, but I hate obstinacy."[353]
>
> The disciple Kung-tu said to Mencius, "The people beyond our school all speak of you as being fond of disputing. I venture to ask why." Mencius said, "Am I fond of disputing? I am compelled to do it.
>
> "A long time has elapsed since this world of men received its being, and there has been along its history now a period of good order, and now a period of confusion.
>
> "In the time of Yao, the waters, flowing out of their channels, inundated the Middle Kingdom. Snakes and dragons occupied it, and the people had no place where they could settle themselves. In the low grounds they made nests for themselves, and in the high grounds they made caves. It is said in the *Book of History*, 'The waters in their wild course warned me.' Those 'waters in their wild course' were the waters of great inundation.
>
> "Shun employed Yü to reduce the waters to order. Yü dug open their obstructed channels and conducted them to the sea. He drove away the snakes and dragons and forced them into the grassy marches. On this, the waters pursued their course through the country, even the Chiang, the Huai, the Ho and the Han, and the dangers and obstructions which they had occasioned were removed. The birds and beasts which had injured the people also disappeared, and after this men found the plains available for them and occupied them.
>
> "After the death of Yao and Shun, the Way of the sages fell into decay. Oppressive sovereigns arose one after another, who

pulled down houses to make ponds and lakes, so that the people knew not where they could rest in quiet; they threw fields out of cultivation to form gardens and parks, so that the people could not get clothes and food. Afterwards, corrupt speakings and oppressive deeds became more rife; gardens and parks, ponds and lakes, thickets and marshes became more numerous, and birds and beasts swarmed. By the time of the tyrant Chou, the empire was again in a state of great confusion.

"The Duke of Chou assisted King Wu and destroyed .Chou. He smote Yen and after three years put its sovereign to death. He drove Fei-lien to a corner by the sea and slew him. The States which he extinguished amounted to fifty. He drove far away also the tigers, leopards, rhinoceroses and elephants; and all the people were greatly delighted. It is said in the *Book of History*, 'Great and splendid were the plans of King Wên! Great was the succession of King Wu and glorious his deeds! They are for the assistance and instruction of us who are of an after day. They are all in principle correct and deficient in nothing.'

"Again the world fell into decay and the Way faded away. Perverse speakings and oppressive deeds waxed rife again. There were instances of ministers who murdered their sovereigns, and of sons who murdered their fathers.

Confucius was afraid and made the *Spring and Autumn Annals*. What the *Spring and Autumn Annals* contains are matters proper to the sovereign. On this account Confucius said, 'Yes! It is the *Spring and Autumn Annals* which will make men know me, and it is the *Spring and Autumn Annals* which will make men condemn me.'

"Once more, sage sovereigns cease to arise, and the princes of the States give the reins to their lusts. Unemployed scholars indulge in unreasonable discussions. The words of Yang Chu and Mo Ti fill the country. If you listen to people's discourses throughout it, you will find that they have adopted the views either of Yang or of Mo. Now, Yang's principle is: 'each one for himself,' which does not acknowledge the claims of the sovereign. Mo's principle is: 'to love all equally,' which does not acknowledge the peculiar affection due to a father. But to acknowledge neither father nor king is to be in the state of a beast. Kung-ming Yi said, 'In their kitchens there is fat meat. In their stables there are fat horses. But their people have the look of hunger, and on the wilds there are those who have died of famine. This is leading on beasts to devour men.' If the principles of Yang and Mo be not stopped and the Way of Confucius not set forth, then those perverse speakings will delude the people and stop up the path of benevolence and righteousness. When benevolence and righteousness are stopped up, beasts will be led on to devour men, and men will devour one another.

"I am alarmed by these things and address myself to the defense of the Way of the former sages and to oppose Yang and Mo. I drive away their licentious expressions, so that such perverse speakers my not be able to show themselves. Their delusions spring up in men's minds and do injury to their practice of affairs. Shown in their practice of affairs, they are pernicious to their government. When sages shall rise up again, they will not change my words.

"In former times, Yü repressed the waters of the inundation, and the country was reduced to order. The Duke of Chou's achievements extented even to the barbarous tribes of the east and north, and he drove away all ferocious animals, and the people enjoyed repose. Confucius completed the *Spring and Autumn Annals,* and rebellious ministers and villainous sons were struck with terror.

"It is said, in the *Book of Songs,*

'He smote the barbarians of the west and the north;
He punished Ching and Shu;
And no one dared to resist us.'

These father-deniers and king-deniers would have been smitten by the Duke of Chou.

"I also wish to rectify men's hearts and to put an end to those perverse doctrines, to oppose their one-sided actions and banish away their licentious expressions; and thus to carry on the work of the three sages. Do I do so because I am fond of disputing? I am compelled to do it.

"Whoever is able to oppose Yang and Mo is a disciple of the sages."[354]

When the Way prevails in a country, it is harmless to have much to say. On the other hand, when the Way does not prevail, it is best to remain silent.

When the Way prevails in a country, he (who occupies a high position) is sure to cause its rise by his words; and when the Way does not prevail, he is sure to preserve himself by his silence.[355]

The Master said, "When the Way prevails in a country, language and actions may be lofty and bold. When it does not prevail, the actions may be lofty and bold, but the language may be with some reserve."[356]

To a mean man, one should say as little as possible to avoid trouble.

Mencius, occupying the position of a high dingnitary in Ch'i, went on a mission of condolence to T'êng. The King also sent Wang Huan, the governor of Ko, as assistant commissioner. Wang Huan, morning and evening, waited upon Mencius, who, during all the Way to T'êng and back, never spoke to him about the business of their mission.

Kung-sun Ch'ou said to Mencius, "The position of a high dignitary of Ch'i is not a small one; the road from Ch'i to T'êng is not short. How was it that during all the way there and back, you never spoke to Huan about the matters of your mission?" Mencius replied, "There were the proper officials to attend to them. What occasion had I to speak to him about them?"[357]

There are three mistakes which can be committed in speech. Attention should be given to them at all times.

Confucius said, "There are three errors to which they who stand in the presence of a man of virtue and station are liable. They may speak when it does not come to them to speak; this is called rashness. They may not speak when it comes to them to speak; this is called concealment. They may speak without looking at the countenance of their superior; this is called blindness."[358]

In short, speaking has as its object the conveying of one's meaning and the production of the anticipated effect. If there is a possibility of causing misunderstanding without producing the anticipated result, it is better not to speak. Failure to put into practice what is said is untruthfulness. To say something which goes beyond the facts shows a lack of sincerity. Ill-timed speech is empty talk, and speech which loses sight of its object is unwise. Therefore, care should be exercised in speech.

24. Prudence in Conduct

Conduct must be earnest and respectful. In other words, it must be truthful and serious, winning confidence with facts, which is far superior to doing so with mere words. The answer Confucius gave Tzŭ-chang on this point was most explicit.

Tzŭ-chang asked how a man should conduct himself.
The Master said, "Let his words be sincere and truthful and his actions earnest and respectful; such conduct may be effective even among the rude tribes of the South or the North. If his words be not sincere and truthful and his actions not earnest and respectful,

will he, with such conduct, be appreciated even in his neighborhood?

"When he is standing, let him see those two things, as it were, fronting him. When he is in a carriage, let him see them attached to the yoke. Then may he get along well everywhere."

Tzŭ-chang wrote these counsels on the end of his sash.[359]

When a man can practice what he says and when his conduct is near to righteousness and propriety, he lays the foundation for confidence in his subsequent conduct. Therefore it is most important to be cautious at the beginning.

The philosopher Yu said, "When agreements are made according to what is right, what is spoken can be made good. When respect is shown according to what is proper, one keeps far from shame and disgrace. When the parties upon whom a man leans are proper persons to be intimate with, he can make them his guides and masters."[360]

When words and actions are consistent, credibility is established. Then, one can solve others' problems even after hearing only one side in a dispute. Straightforward and sincere, Tzŭ-lu was praised by Confucius as capable of settling litigations after hearing only one side. Confucius also praised him for never sleeping over a promise.

The Master said, "Ah! It is Yu who could, after hearing only one side, settle litigations."

Tzŭ-lu never slept over a promise.[361]

One should plan before embarking on anything. Nothing should be attempted in haste.

The Master said, "...In all things success depends on previous preparation, and without such previous preparation there is sure to be failure. If what is to be spoken is previously determied, there will be no stumbling. If affairs are previously determined, there will be no difficulty with them. If one's actions have been previously determined, there will be no regret. If principles of conduct have been previously determined, the practice of them will be smooth."[362]

To act hasitly and without sufficient prior consideration is to be careless in one's conduct. Nothing can be done with a person guilty of such conduct.

The Master said, "When a man is not in the habit of saying: 'What shall I think of this?' What shall I think of this?' I can indeed do nothing with him."[363]

In short, to engage in learning, there must be "earnest conduct"; to achieve virtue, there must be "vigorous action"; to succeed in one's performance, there must be "cautious behavior." The most accurate observation and distinction of men is from their actions, hence the importance of prudent conduct.

25. Respect for Teachers

Since benevolence is the fundamental principle governing human conduct, it should be easy to understand that the love and assistance of men is one's duty, and whenever there is an opportunity to do right, there should be the courage to do so. However, it does not follow that others will regard the love and assistance of oneself as their duty. Although the result of the practice of benevolence is mutual aid, the concept of equality of rights and obligations should not enter into the picture. Of course, when favors are received, they should be reciprocated, or at least they should not be forgotten. When the first opportunity to return them occurs, it should be taken.

The relations of childern to their parents, students to their teachers, friends to friends and other human relations are guided by the following principle: "Never forget the root; never forget favors received." The teacher deserves not only the lifelong respect of the student, but the esteem of all the members of his family as well. In our country, respect for teachers is regarded as an extremely important virtue because this respect symbolizes the importance of the Way. It shows the origin of all knowledge and virtue and is the foundation for the cultivation of the person. Such a concept is not held in any other country in the world.

For several thousand years, our people have never ceased to pay homage to one teacher, i.e., Confucius, who is known as the "Most Accomplished and Highest Ancient Teacher." Today, though, with the development of individualism, reverence for the teacher has declined. The situation has deteriorated to such an extent that schools are regarded as mere markets, teachers as storekeepers, and learning as a business transaction. Only by means of vigorous effort can this unwholesome tide be stemmed.

As stated in the *Doctrine of the Mean*, instruction is the cultivation of the Way. From this it is clear that respect for the teacher symbolizes the importance attached to the Way. The teacher must follow the Way, uphold propriety and set a personal example in giving instruction in order to win the respect of his pupils. In turn, respect shown to superiors engenders their love of inferiors and of the next generation. Thus they can naturally pass on their knowledge and talents to them. This indeed is not merely a lifetime delight.

> Mencius said, "...That he (the superior man) can get from the whole world the most talented individuals and educate them; this is the third delight."[364]

It is also one of a man's important responsibilities in his lifetime.

> Mencius said, "...Yi Yin...said, 'Heaven's plan in the production of mankind is this: that they who are first informed should instruct those who are later in being informed, and they who first apprehend the Way should instruct those who are slower to do so. I am one of Heaven's people who have first apprehended; I will take this Way and instruct this people in it."[365]

The teacher is respected because of his instruction to men on proper conduct. Knowledge and skills are only of secondary importance. If this condition is reversed, serious injury will result.

> P'ang Mêng learned archery of Yi. When he had acquired all the art of Yi, he thought that in all the empire only Yi was superior to himself, and so he slew him. Mencius said, "In this case Yi was also to blame. Kung-ming Yi indeed said, 'It would appear as if he were not to be blamed,' but he thereby only meant that his blame was slight. How can he be held without any blame?"[366]

One way of observing the character of a man is to find out what his teacher and good friends are like. If they are superior men, then he must be a superior man and his pupils and good friends must likewise be superior men.

> "The people of Chêng sent Tzŭ-cho Ju to make an attack on Wei, which sent Yü-kung Ssŭ to pursue him. Tzŭ-cho Ju said,

"Today I feel unwell, so that I cannot hold my bow. I am a dead man!' At the same time he asked his driver, 'Who is it that is pursuing me?' The driver said, 'It is Yü-kung Ssŭ,' on which he exclaimed, 'I shall live.' The driver said, 'Yü-kung Ssŭ is the best archer of Wei, what do you mean by saying "I shall live"?' Ju replied, 'Yü-kung Ssŭ learned archery from Yin-kung T'o, who again learned it from me. Now, Yin-kung T'o is an upright man, and the friends of his selection must be upright also.' When Yü-kung Ssŭ came up, he said, 'Master, why are you not holding your bow?' Ju answered, 'Today I am feeling unwell and cannot hold my bow.' On this Ssŭ said, 'I learned archery from Yin-kung T'o, who again learned it from you. I cannot bear to injure you with your own art. The business of today, however, is the prince's business, which I dare not neglect.' He then took his arrows, knocked off their steel points against the carriage wheel, discharged four of them and returned."[367]

Respect for the teacher is also an indication of the love of learning. With the love of learning, one can find everything to be worth learning and everyone to be a good teacher.

The Master said, "When three of us walk along, one or both of the others can surely serve as my teachers. I will select their good qualities and follow them, their bad qualities and avoid them.[368]

A general human weakness is frequent self-complacency with one's learning and one's capacity to teach.

Mencius said, "The evil of men is that they like to be teachers of others."[369]

Naturally, the relationship between teacher and pupil is a warm one. It is comparable to that between father and son. While the teacher is alive, the pupil serves him in accordance with propriety. When the teacher dies, the pupil buries him in accordance with propriety. Mencius explains in the following passage how Confucius' disciples were pleased with him and how they submitted to him.

Mencius said, "...When one by force subdues men, they do not submit to him in heart. They submit, because their strength is not adequate to resist. When one subdues men by virtue, in their hearts' core they are pleased, and sincerely submit, as in the case of the seventy disciples in their submission to Confucius."[370]

Here is the testimony of Yen Yüan, Tzŭ-kung and Tsai Yü regarding their reverence for and submission to their Master.

Yen Yüan, in admiration of the Master's doctrines, sighed and said, "I looked up to them, and they seemed to become more high; I tried to penetrate them, and they seemed to become more firm; I looked at them before me, and suddenly they seemed to be behind.

"The Master by orderly method skillfully leads men on. He enlarged my mind with learning and taught me the restraints of propriety.

"When I wish to give over the study of his doctrines, I cannot do so, and having exerted all my ability, there seems something to stand right up before me; but though I wish to follow and lay hold of it, I really find no way to do so."[371]

Shu-sun Wu-shu having spoken revilingly of Chung-ni, Tzŭ-kung said, "It is of no use doing so. Chung-ni cannot be reviled. The talents and virtue of other men are hillocks and mounds, which may be stepped over. Chung-ni is the sun or moon, which it is impossible to step over. Although a man may wish to cut himself off from the sage, what harm can he do to the sun or moon? He only shows that he does not know his own capacity."[372]

Shu-sun Wu-shu observed to the great officials in the court, saying, "Tzŭ-kung is superior to Chung-ni."

Tzŭ-fu Ching-po reported the observation to Tzŭ-kung, who said, "Let me use the comparison of a house and its encompassing wall. My wall only reaches to the shoulders. One may peep over it and see whatever is valuable in the apartments. The wall of my Master is several fathoms high. If one does not find the door and enter by it, he cannot see the ancestral temple with its beauties nor all the officials in their rich array. But I assume that they are few who find the door. Was not the observation of the chief only what might have been expected?"[373]

Ch'ên Tzŭ-ch'in, addressing Tzŭ-kung, said, "You are just being polite. How can Chung-ni be said to be superior to you?"

Tzŭ-kung said, "For one word a man is often deemed to be wise, and for one word he is often deemed to be foolish. We ought to be careful indeed in what we say.

"Our Master cannot be attained to, just in the same way as the heavens cannot be gone up to by the steps of a stair.

"Were our Master in the position of the ruler of a State, he would plant the people and forthwith they would be established; he would lead them on and forthwith they would follow him; he would make them happy and forthwith multitudes would resort to his dominions; he would stimulate them and forthwith they would be harmonious. While he lives, he is glorious. When he dies, he will be bitterly lamented. How is it possible for him to be attained to?"[374]

Mencius said, "···Tsai Wo said, 'According to my view of our Master, he is far superior to Yao and Shun.'

"Tzǔ-kung said, 'By viewing the ceremonial ordinances of a prince, we know the character of his government. By hearing his music, we know the character of his virtue. After the lapse of a hundred ages I can arrange, according to their merits, the kings of a hundred ages; not one of them can escape me. From the birth of mankind till now, there has never been another like our Master.'

"Yo Jo said, 'Is it only among men that it is so? There is the unicorn among quadrupeds, the phoenix among birds, the T'ai mountain among mounds and ant-hills, and rivers and seas among rain-pools. Though different in degree, they are the same in kind. So the sages among mankind are also the same in kind. But they stand out from their fellows and rise above the level, and from the birth of mankind till now, there never has been one so glorious as Confucius."[375]

On his part, Confucius could not have been more kind or more solicitous toward his disciples.

Po-niu being ill, the Master went to make an inquiry. He took hold of his hand through the window and said, "It is killing him. It is destiny, alas! That such a man should have such a sickness! That such a man should have such a sickness!"[376]

The Master was put in fear in K'uang and Yen Yüan fell behind. The Master, on his rejoining him, said, "I thought you had died." Hui replied, "While you are alive, how dare I die?"[377]

When Confucius died, his disciples lamented bitterly as if they had lost their father. Tzǔ-kung was so grief-stricken that he built a house at the gravesite and remained there for an additional three years.

Mencius said, "...Formerly when Confucius died, after three years had elapsed, his disciples collected their baggage and prepared to return to their several homes. But on entering to take their leave of Tzǔ-kung, as they looked towards one another, they wailed till they all lost their voice. After this they returned to their homes, but Tzǔ-kung went back and built a house for himself on the gravesite, where he lived alone for another three years, before he returned home..."[378]

To repeat, respect for the teacher shows the importance of the Way. Of course, a pupil should follow his teacher by learning from him. He should also yield to him and be humble and respectful toward him. There is but one exception: in the performance of virtue, one does not yield even to one's teacher.

> The Master said, "In the performance of virtue a man may not yield even to his teacher."[379]

26. Faithfulness to Friends

The relationship between friends is, according to Confucianism, one of the five human relationships. In addition to the public relationship between the ruler and his subjects and the private relationships between father and son, brother and brother, and husband and wife, there is the social relationship between friends. It is easy to understand how important this relationship is. For this reason, it is imperative to consult and comprehend the teachings of ancient philosophers regarding (1) the objectives of the formation of friendships, (2) the attitudes and responsibilities toward friends, (3) how to make friends, and (4) what friends should be sought and which should be avoided.

Friendships are founded on faithfulness. Only when there is mutual faith can friendships be maintained; hence the statement, "Friends should be faithful."

The object of forming friendships is to help practice virtue. In other words, it is necessary to have friends in order to be mutually helpful in making possible virtuous conduct. The method is to "meet with friends on grounds of culture."

> The philosopher Tsêng said, "The superior man on grounds of culture meets with his friends, and by their friendship helps his virtue."[380]

For this reason, one should seek out as friends those who excel in virtue and learning. As Confucius said, "...Have no friends not equal to yourself."[381]

It is advantageous to associate with friends who are upright, sincere and observant. On the other hand, it is obviously not to one's advantage to associate with friends who are specious, insinuating or glib-tongued, since "fine words and insinuating appearance are seldom associated with true virtue."[382] Such persons are unable to "help in the performance of virtue." Only the first three described types of friends can assist one in cultivating virtue and learning.

> Confucius said, "There are three friendships which are advantageous, and three which are injurious. Friendship with the upright; friendship with the sincere; and friendship with the man of much observation—these are advantageous. Friendship with the man of specious airs; friendship with the insinuatingly soft; and friendship with the glib-tongued—these are injurious."[383]

Those who are like-minded naturally go together. That is why we can often judge from the virtue of a friend the character of men with whom he associates.

> The Master said of Tzŭ-chien, "Of superior virtue indeed is such a man! If there were not virtuous men in Lu, how could this man have acquired this character?"[384]

To form advantageous friendships, one must first be good oneself, otherwise those whom one would like to take as one's friends might not react the same way. Only the superior man can tolerate those not equal to him, and this is why he is so rare and highly prized.

> The disciples of Tzŭ-hsia asked Tzŭ-chang about the principles that should characterize mutual intercourse. Tzŭ-chang asked, "What does Tzŭ-hsia say on the subject?" They replied, "Tzŭ-hsia says: 'Associate with those who can benefit you. Reject those who cannot do so.'" Tzŭ-chang observed, "This is different from what I have learned. The superior man honors the worthy and bears with all. He praises the good and pities the incompetent. Am I possessed of great talents and virtue? Who is there among men whom I will not bear with? Am I devoid of talents and virtue?—men will reject me. What have I to do with the rejection of others?"[385]

Respect should be maintained between friends, and familiarity should not be permitted to beget contempt.

> The Master said, "Yen P'ing-chung knew well how to maintain friendly intercourse. Even after a long acquaintance he showed the same respect."[386]

When a friend has a fault, he should be advised in a proper but gentle manner to rectify it.

Mencius said, "...To urge one another to what is good by reproofs is the way of friends."[387]

If a friend's advice is accepted and complied with superficially, but the fault is not rectified, it shows a lack of sincerity in the performance of good. In this case even a sage can do nothing.

The Master said, "Can men refuse to assent to the words of strict admonition? But it is reforming the conduct because of them which is valuable. Can men refuse to be pleased with words of gentle advice? But it is unfolding their aim which is valuable. If a man is pleased with these words but does not unfold their aim, and assents to them but does not reform his conduct, I can really do nothing with him."[388]

After sincere advice is offered but not accepted, there is nothing further to be done.

Tzŭ-kung asked about friendship. The Master said, "Faithfully admonish your friend and skillfully lead him on. If you find him impracticable, stop. Do not disgrace yourself."[389]

Friendly advice cannot be given too frequently, however, or estrangement will ensue.

Tzŭ-yu said, "In serving a prince, frequent remonstrances lead to disgrace. Between friends, frequent reproofs make the friendship distant."[390]

If another man's fundamental faith is different from one's own, one should not go out of one's way to make plans with him.

The Master said, "Those whose courses are different cannot lay plans for one another."[391]

When friends get together and, instead of discussing what is right, practice petty shrewdness, it is contrary to the meaning of friendship.

The Master said, "When a number of people are together, for a whole day, without their conversation turning on righteousness, and when they are fond of carrying out the suggestions of a small shrewdness—theirs is indeed a hard case."[392]

Friendship is not limited by time or space. When a man

does good, he makes friends with those who do the same all over the world. If he is still not contented, he can befriend the ancients, read their books and poems and try to know them.

> Mencius said to Wan Chang, "The scholar whose virtue is most distinguished in a village shall make friends of all the virtuous scholars in the village. The scholar whose virtue is most distinguished throughout a State shall make friends of all the virtuous scholars of that State. The scholar whose virtue is most distinguished throughout the empire shall make friends of all the virtuous scholars of the empire.
>
> When a scholar feels that his friendship with all the virtuous scholars of the empire is not sufficient to satisfy him, he proceeds to ascend to consider the men of antiquity. He reads their poems and books. But would it be right not to know what they were as men? To ascertain this, therefore, he considers their history. This is to ascend and make friends of the men of antiquity."[393]

Friends from afar bring new knowledge and can be of assistance to one both intellectually and morally. This provides great delight in human life. Not surprisingly, it is one of the first things mentioned in the *Analects*.

> The Master said, "...Is it not delightful to have friends coming from distant quarters?"[394]

We must ask ourselves what we can do for our friends before we can expect them to do anything for us. Friendship implies mutual assistance. For this reason, Confucius humbly admitted that he had failed to behave toward his friend as he expected him to behave toward him.

> The Master said, "...In the way of the superior man there are four things, to not one of which have I as yet attained;...be first to behave to a friend, as I would require him to behave to me—to this I have not attained..."[395]

A faithful friend should take care of the burial of one who dies without means. When gifts are received from friends, one should bow only in case of meat for sacrificial purposes.

> When any of his (Confucius') friends died, if he had no relations who could be depended on for the necessary offices, he would say, "I will bury him."

When a friend sent him a present, though it might be a carriage and horses, he did not bow. The only present for which he bowed was that of the meat of sacrifice.[396]

What is most harmful to friendship is presumption, such as presumption on the grounds of age, station or the circumstances of one's relatives. Anyone who is merely interested in the use which can be made of a friendship is not a true friend. A Son of Heaven could make friends with a lowly commoner and thus show respect for the worthy with no presumption of station.

Wan Chang asked Mencius, "I venture to ask the principles of friendship." Mencius replied, "Friendship should be maintained without any presumption on the ground of one's superior age or station or the circumstances of his relatives. Friendship with a man is friendship with his virtue and does not admit of assumptions of superiority.

There was Mêng Hsien, chief of a family of a hundred chariots. He had five friends, namely, Yüeh-chêng Ch'iu, Mu Chung and three others whose names I have forgotten. With these five men Hsien maintained a friendship, because they thought nothing about his family. If they had thought about his family, he would not have maintained his friendship with them.

"Not only has the chief of a family of a hundred chariots acted thus. The same thing was exemplified by the sovereign of a small State. Duke Hui of Pi said, 'I treat Tzŭ-ssŭ as my teacher and Yen Pan as my friend. As to Wang Shun and Ch'ang Hsi, they serve me.'

"Not only has the sovereign of a small State acted thus. The same thing has been exemplified by the sovereign of a large State. There was Duke P'ing of Chin with Hai T'ang: when T'ang told him to enter his house, he entered; when he told him to be seated, he sat; when he told him to eat, he ate. There might only be coarse rice and soup of vegetables, but he always ate his fill, not daring to do otherwise. Here, however, he stopped and went no farther. He did not call him to share any of Heaven's palaces, or to govern any of Heaven's offices, or to partake of any of Heaven's emoluments. His conduct was but a scholar's honoring virtue and talents, not the honoring them proper to a king or a duke.

"Shun went to court and saw the sovereign who lodged him as his son-in-law in the second palace. The sovereign also enjoyed there Shun's hospitality. Alternately they acted as host and guest. Here was the sovereign maintaining friendship with a private man.

"Respect shown by inferiors to superiors is called giving to the noble the observance due to rank. Respect shown by superiors to inferiors is called giving honor to talents and virtue. In each case the significance is the same."[397]

27. Loyalty and Reciprocity

In Confucianism there are five human relationships. Although there are differences among men in age, superiority and inferiority, these relationships concern the intercourse between man and man. However, what one man desires may not be the same as what another man wishes. When applied to the other man, it may or may not be proper at all times. Especially when forcibly applied, it may harm rather than help the human relationship. Most of all, this is true of the extension of principles cherished by one country in regard to another. Only by not doing to others what one would not have them do to oneself can the greatest good and the least harm result. This is so because once one knows what to avoid, one can easily know what should be done. One word which Confucius regarded as practicable for one's entire life is "reciprocity."

> Tzǔ-kung asked, saying, "Is there one word which may serve as a rule of practice for all one's life?" The Master said, "Is not 'reciprocity' such a word? What you do not want done to yourself, do not do to others."[398]

This principle is very clear; the difficulty is in applying it. Therefore, Confucius set an example for his disciples by putting this principle into practice.

> Tzǔ-kung said, "What I do not wish men to do to me, I also wish not to do to men." The Master said, "Tz'ǔ, this is not what you can attain."[399]

In everything one should exhaust his capabilities. This is loyalty or faithfulness; it is also reciprocity. Hence, it is said, "The exhaustion of what one can do is called faithfulness," and "teaching others what is good is called faithfulness."[400]

If a man does not wish to do his full duty and be a good man, but wishes others to do their duty and be good men, he is unfaithful to himself and lacks understanding of others. Such a man cannot begin to speak of any principle. Only the philosopher Tsêng could understand Confucius' consistent principle, from which he drew this conclusion:

The Master said, "Shên, my Way is all based on a connected principle. The disciple Tsêng replied, "Yes."

The Master went out, and the other disciples asked, saying, "What do his words mean?" Tsêng said, "The Way of our Master is based only on loyalty and reciprocity."[401]

On this account, the ruler must himself be possessed of the good qualities, and then he may require them in the people. He must not have the bad qualities in himself, and then he may require that they shall not be in the people. Never has there been a man, who, not having reference to his own character and wishes in dealing with others, was able effectually to instruct them.[402]

The most effective way of determining what not to do to others is to ask oneself whether one would approve of this action or quality in another person. For example, if a person does not wish others to show inordinate pride toward him, he should refrain from showing such pride himself. If he does not wish others to be jealous of him, he should refrain from being jealous of others. All of this should be constantly subjected to scrutiny and rectification. This principle and method are in the category known as "regulation of conduct."

What a man dislikes in his superiors, let him not display in the treatment of his inferiors; what he dislikes in his inferiors, let him not display in the service of his superiors; what he hates in those who are before him, let him not therewith precede those who are behind him; what he hates in those who are behind him, let him not therewith follow those who are before him: what he hates to receive on the right, let him not bestow on the left; what he hates to receive on the left, let him not bestow on the right—this is what is called "the principle with which, as with a measuring-square, to regulate one's conduct."[403]

Let us enumerate those things which a man does not wish others to do to him and which, for this reason, he should not do to others

(a) Pride and Insubordination

He (the superior man) reviews his old knowledge and thus continually acquires new. He exerts an honest, generous earnestness in the esteem and practice of all propriety.

Thus, when occupying a high situation, he is not proud, and in a low situation, he is not insubordinate.[404]

(b) Injury and Covetousness

The Master said, "Dressed himself in a tattered robe quilted with hemp, yet standing by the side of men dressed in furs and not ashamed—ah! it is Yu who is equal to this!

" 'He injures none, he covets nothing; what can he do but what is good?' "

"Tzŭ-lu kept continually repeating these words of the ode when the Master said, "This is only one way, but those things are by no means sufficient to constitute (perfect) excellence."[405]

Mencius said, "Words which are not true are inauspicious, and the words which are truly inauspicious are those which throw worthy men into the shade."[406]

(c) Suspicion

The Master said, "He who does not anticipate attempts to deceive him, nor think beforehand of his not being believed, and yet apprehends these things readily (when they occur)—is he not a man of superior worth?"[407]

(d) Niggardliness

The Master said, "Though a man has abilites as admirable as those of the Duke of Chou, yet if he is proud and niggardly, those other things are really not worth being looked at."[408]

(e) Boasting

The Master said, "Mêng Chih-fan does not boast of his merit. Being in the rear on an occasion of flight, when they were about to enter the gate, he whipped up his horse, saying, "It is not that I dare to be last. My horse would not advance."[409]

(f) Criticism of Others

The Master said, "...He (the superior man) hates those who proclaim the evil of others. He hates the man who, being in a low position, slanders his superiors..."[410]

The Master said, "In my dealings with men, whose evil do I blame, whose goodness do I praise? If I do sometimes praise a person, I must have tried him out. This people are the same as those who were taught to practice righteousness in the three dynasties."[411]

Mencius said, "What future trouble have they and ought they to endure, who talk of what is not good in others?"[412]

Tzŭ-kung was in the habit of criticizing others. The Master said, "Is Tz'ŭ really worthy? As to me, I have not leisure for this."[413]

(g) Not Letting Bygones Be Bygones

It was difficult to talk with the people of Hu-hsiang, and a lad of that place having had an interview with the Master, the disciples doubted.

The Master said, "If someone purifies himself to come forward to me, I approve of his purification without looking into his past conduct. I approve of his coming forward, and not his going backward. Why should I be so severe?"[114]

(h) Remembrance of Old Wickedness

The Master said, "Po-i and Shu-ch'i did not keep the former wickedness of men in mind, and so the resentments directed towards them were few."[415]

(i) Strong Reproach of Others

The Master said, "He who reproaches himself strongly and others lightly will keep himself far away from resentment."[416]

(j) Going to the Extreme

Mencius said, "Chung-ni never went to the extreme."[417]

Mencius said, "Those who are fleeing from the errors of Mo naturally turn to Yang, and those who are fleeing from the errors of Yang naturally turn to Confucianism. When they so turn, they should at once and simply be received.

"Those who now dispute with the followers of Yang and Mo do so as if they were pursuing a stray pig, the leg of which, after they have got it to enter the pen, they proceed to tie."[418]

(k) Return of Injury for Injury

Someone said, "What do you say concerning the principle that injury should be recompensed with kindness?"

The Master said, "With what then will you recompense kindness?

"Recompense injury with justice and recompense kindness with kindness."[419]

These are examples of what one does not wish others to do to oneself and what one should not do to others. But, positively, what does one desire and expect from others? Here are the answers:

(a) When a man is in distress, what he needs most is sympathy—benevolence, the feeling of commiseration.

(b) When a man is wronged ar incapable of meeting a situation, what he needs most is justice and support—righteousness, the feeling of shame and dislike.

(c) When a man has a conflict of interest with others and cannot settle the dispute, what he needs most is the respect of others' interests and mutual concession—propriety, the feeling of respect and the feeling of modesty and concession.

(d) When a man has an insoluble problem, what he needs most is full justification for himself and fairness for others—wisdom, the feeling of right and wrong.

Benevolence, righteousness, propriety and wisdom are inherent in the nature of everyone; thus it is unnecessary for men to seek them externally. Rather, they can obtain them by seeking inwardly.

> Mencius said, "...He is not a man who is without the feeling of commiseration, the feeling of dislike and shame, the feeling of modesty and concession, and the feeling of right and wrong.
>
> "The feeling of commiseration is the beginning of benevolence, the feeling of shame and dislike the beginning of righteousness, the feeling of modesty and concession the beginning of propriety, and the feeling of right and wrong the beginning of wisdom.
>
> "Men have these four beginnings, just as they have their four limbs. When men, having these four beginnings, yet say of themselves as being incapable of them, they inflict injury on themselves."[420]

When men have these four beginnings and extend them further, they can dwell in a tranquil habitation (benevolence); when they rest, they can take the straight path (righteousness); when they move, they can have the proper standards (propriety) for their conduct and be well-oriented (wisdom) in their movements. They are likely to do what they should do and avoid what they should not do. Everywhere they can comply with the principles of loyalty and reciprocity.

Now let us consider one by one the feelings of commiseration, shame and dislike, modesty and concession, and right and wrong.

(a) The feeling of commiseration is what Mencius called the "mind which cannot bear to see the sufferings of others," and is the same as what is called "sympathy" today. Whenever others meet with difficulty, danger or distress, when such a sense of responsibility is produced in one that action follows to fulfill it, this is the beginning of benevolence. The extension of this beginning becomes universal love, which, when developed to the utmost, leads to the sacrifice of the small self for the sake of the greater self. This is the consummation of benevolence and signifies the achievement of the whole essence and great utility of benevolence.

He who is without sympathy is liable to be selfish and unkind. The unkind lose their good nature and take delight in others' distress. Mencius said, "How is it possible to speak with those princes who are not benevolent? Their perils they count safety, their calamities they count profitable, and they have pleasure in the things by which they perish."[421]

Sympathy is expressed in daily life. Here are some examples:

When the Master was eating by the side of a mourner, he never ate to the full.

He did not sing on the same day in which he had been weeping for the dead.[422]

The Music-master, Mien, having called upon him, when they came to the steps, the Master said, "Here are the steps." When they came to the mat for the guest to sit upon, he said, "Here is the seat." When all were seated, the Master informed him, saying, "So and so is here; so and so is here."

The Music-master, Mien, having gone out, Tzŭ-chang asked, saying, "Is it the rule to tell those things to the Music-master?"

The Master said, "Yes. This is certainly the rule for those who lead the blind."[423]

When the Master saw a person in a mourning dress, or anyone with the cap and upper and lower garments of full dress, or a blind person, on observing them approaching, though they were younger than himself, he would rise up, and if he had to pass by them, he would do so hastily.[424]

The Master angled, but did not use a net. He shot, but not at birds perching.[425]

The object of sympathy may be small or large. It may be as small as an individual and as large as the whole of mankind.

The extension of sympathy may start from the feeling of commiseration as a beginning to the regulation of a family, the ordering of a country and the world. For example, "When someone was drowned in the empire, Yü thought that he was responsible for drowning him; and when someone was hungry in the world, Chi thought he was responsible for giving him hunger." These were sages who "were ahead of all the people under heaven in bearing sorrow and behind them all in the enjoyment of pleasure." This was indeed the expression of the greatest sympathy.

(b) The feeling of shame and dislike is what is called the sense of justice today. Where there is shame, there are certain things which one does not do; and where there is dislike, there are certain things which one does not desire. With the exclusion of those things which are not done and desired, all that remains is what should be done and desired, which is righteousness. "Righteousness is what is appropriate," i. e., the straight path open to a man. When a man courageously does what he perceives to be righteous, when he is admired because of the performance of good, when he takes untiring delight in goodness, then he has the nobility of Heaven.

The Master said, "Only the superior man can love and hate others..." So, in answering a question put by Tzǔ-kung, Coufucius said the superior man "has his hatreds."

Tzǔ-kung said, "Has the superior man his hatreds also?" The Master said, "He has his hatreds. He hates those who proclaim the evil of others. He hates the man who, being in a low position, slanders his superiors. He hates those who have valor merely and are unobservant of propriety. He hates those who are forward and determined and, at the same time, of contracted understanding."

The Master then inquired, "Tz'ǔ, have you also your hatreds?" Tzǔ-kung replied, "I hate those who pry out matters and ascribe the knowledge to their wisdom. I hate those who are only not modest and think that they are valorous. I hate those who make known secrets and think that they are straightforward."[426]

Mencius said, "Let a man not do what his sense of righteousness tells him not to do, and let him not desire what his sense of righteousness tells him not to desire—to act thus is all he has to do."[427]

(c)   The feeling of respect (modesty and concession) is the expression of respect or esteem to a superior or worthy person. As has been stated before, the distinction between the respect shown to relatives and to worthy men is the basis of propriety. Hence it is said, "The feeling of modesty and concession is the beginning 'of propriety," and "the feeling of respect is common to all men...it is propriety." This is because "those who respect others are always respected." Where there is mutual respect, both individuals involved are prone to advance morally day by day, and the order of society is naturally maintained. When a man respects others, he has no dispute with them. This is personal humility and propriety toward others. In short, whether spiritually or materially, if concessions are made wherever personal interests are involved, there can be nothing inconsistent with propriety.

Though sage and wise, Confucius was always humble. Here are a few examples:

(i)   He did not dare to rank himself with the sage and virtuous.

> The Master said, "The sage and the man of perfect virtue—how dare I rank myself with them? It may simply be said of me that I strive to become such without satiety and teach others without weariness." Kung-hsi Hua said, "This is just what your disciples cannot imitate you in."[428]

(ii)   He made the humble admission that he did not have various abilities.

> A high official asked Tzŭ-kung, saying, "May we not say that your Master is a sage? How various his ability is!"
> Tzŭ-kung said, "Certainly Heaven has endowed him unlimitedly to be a great sage. And, moreover, his ability is various."
> The Master heard of the conversation and said, "Does the high official know me? When I was young, my condition was low, and therefore I acquired my ability in many things, but they were mean matters. Does the superior man think much of such variety of ability? No, he does not."
> Lao said, "The Master said, 'Having no official employment, I acquired many arts.'"[429]

(iii)   He made the humble admission that he had not practiced the Way of the superior man.

The Master said, "The way of the superior man is threefold, but I am not equal to it. Benevolent, he is free from anxieties; wise, he is free from perplexities; courageous, he is free from fear."
Tzŭ-kung said, "Our Master was speaking of himself here."[430]

(iv) He made the humble admission that he had not made any contribution to learning.

The Master said, "A transmitter and not a maker, believing in and loving ancient studies, I venture to compare myself with our old P'eng."[431]

(v) He made the humble admission that it might only be said of him that he strove to be a sage and man of virtue without satiety and taught others without weariness.

The Master said, "...It may simply be said of me that I strive to become such (a sage and man of prefect virtue) without satiety and teach others without weariness."[432]

(vi) He made the humble admission that his learning was not really profound, but that he only did what he could to enlighten others.

The Master said, "Am I indeed possessed of knowledge? No, but if an uneducated person asks anything of me with sincerity, I set it forth from one end to the other and exhaust it."[433]

Humility confers benefit, while respect does away with insolence. In addition to setting a personal example, Confucius invariably encouraged his disciples to be humble. He praised the modesty of T'ai-po as the "highest point of virtuous action."

The Master was wishing Ch'i-tiao K'ai to enter on official employment. He replied, "I am not yet able to rest in the assurance of this." The master was pleased.[434]
The Master said, "T'ai-po may be said to have reached the highest point of virtuous action. Thrice he declined the empire, and the people in ignorance of his motives could not express their approbation of his conduct."[435]

Confucius criticized his old friend Yüan Jang severely and even struck him with his staff for failure to observe propriety. He also taught the youth of the village of Ch'üeh how to work and learn the rules of propriety.

Yüan Jang was squatting on his heels, and so waited the approach of the Master, who said to him, "In youth, you were not humble as befits a junior; in manhood, doing nothing worthy of being handed down; and even then, you are not dying in old age which makes you a pest." With this he hit him on the shank with his staff.[436]

A youth of the village of Ch'üeh was employed by Confucius to carry the messages between him and his visitors. Someone asked about him, saying, "Has he made great progress?"

The Master said, "I observe that he is fond of occupying the seat of a full-grown man; I observe that he walks shoulder to shoulder with his elders. He is not one who is seeking to make progress in learning. He wishes quickly to complete his work."[437]

Though in letter propriety has its differentiations, in spirit its rules are equally applicable. Goodness and profit are shared with others. Here the virtue of modesty and concession is involved, and herein lies the basic spirit of propriety.

When the Master was in company with a person who was singing, if he sang well, he would make him repeat the song, while he accompanied it with his own voice.[438]

(d) The feeling of right and wrong is the basis of sincerity of thoughts. The object of the investigation of things and the extension of knowledge is the sincerity of thoughts. But whether thoughts can be sincere depends first of all on the determination of good and evil. Only when right and wrong, good and evil are determined can there be fondness for goodness and dislike of evil. Hence it is said, "If a man does not understand what is good, he will not attain sincerity in himself."[439] Therefore, only when there is the ability to determine right and wrong and discriminate between good and evil can the wisdom thus manifested be significant and valuable.

But sincerity and intelligence are conducive to each other and have a mutual relationship of cause and effect. When a man's naturally endowed wisdom is applied to his conduct toward others, it cannot be separated from the determination of right and wrong. This is why the feeling of right and wrong is the beginning of wisdom. Since the subject of wisdom has already been discussed in detail in the chapters on "The Investigation of Things" and the "The Extension of Knowledge" as well as at the beginning of the present chapter, there is no need for repetition.

If a man can apply his inherent benevolence to others as well as his righteousness, propriety and wisdom, and if the other side can also reciprocate, then these virtues are echoed and the great Way between man and man will be traveled without obstruction. So, the "accordance with...nature is called the Way." One who cultivates his person does so to bring tranquillity to others and advances to the state of establishing himself as well as others in virtue and enlarging himself as well as others. Hence it is said, "The person is cultivated by means of the Way." Loyalty and reciprocity signify the extension of oneself to others and the treatment of others like oneself. It is also said, "Loyalty and reciprocity are not far from the Way," and "The Way of our Master is based only on loyalty and reciprocity."

From the above, it can be seen that the preparations for self-restraint are the setting of the will, fondness for goodness, self-requirement, prudence while alone, self-examination, self-inquiry, self-censure, rectification of faults, self-exertion, self-strength, self-confidence and self-gratification. Likewise, the "restoration of propriety" in practice calls for self-regulation, integrity, keeping to one's due, rest in poverty and delight in the Way, care in accepting and declining office, determination of departure and remaining behind, prudence in social intercourse and in taking and giving, the selection and transformation of environment, the creation of and the wait for circumstances, selection of arts, skills and habits, care in speech and action, respect of teachers, faith in friends and loyalty and reciprocity. Self-restraint and the restoration of propriety aim at the performance of belevolence and the perfection of things.

It should be added, of course, that in all the above respects both wisdom and courage are required. Where wisdom and courage exist, coupled with earnest practice, one can seek benevolence and obtain it. This is called the cultivation of the person.

Footnotes for Chapter VI

1. *Great Learning.* Text. *Vide supra,* p. 7.
2. *Doctrine of the Mean,* Ch. XX.
3. *Ibid.*
4. *Ibid.*

5. *Ibid. Vide supra,* on this page
6. *Analects,* Bk. I, Ch. XIV.
7. *Ibid.,* Bk. VIII, Ch. XVII.
8. *Ibid.,* Bk. I, Ch. I. *Vide supra,* p. 20.
9. *Analects,* Bk. XIX, Ch. V. *Vide supra,* p. 21.
10. *Analects,* Bk. II, Ch. IV.
11. *Ibid.,* Bk. VII, Ch. XVI. *Vide supra,* p. 67.
12. *Works of Mencius,* Bk. II, Pt. I, Ch. II. *Vide supra,* p. 212.
13. *Analects,* Bk. VII, Ch. XIX, *Vide supra,* p. 23.
14. *Analects,* Bk. V, Ch. XXVII.
15. *Ibid.,* Bk. VII, Ch. I. *Vide supra,* p. 26.
16. *Analects,* Bk. VII, Ch. XVIII.
17. *Ibid.,* Bk. VI, Ch. II.
18. *Ibid.,* Bk. XI, Ch. VI.
19. *Ibid.,* Bk. IX, Ch. XIX.
20. *Ibid.,* Ch. XX.
21. *Ibid.,* Bk. II, Ch. IX. *Vide supra,* p. 126.
22. *Analects,* Bk. XI, Ch. VIII.
23. *Ibid.,* Ch. IX.
24. *Works of Mencius,* Bk. VI, Pt. I, Ch. IX.
25. *Analects,* Bk. VIII, Ch. XII.
26. *Ibid.,* Bk. XVII, Ch. VIII.
27. *Ibid.,* Bk. I, Ch. III. *Vide supra,* p. 111.
28. *Analects,* Bk. XVII, Ch. XVII.
29. *Ibid.,* Bk. XIII, Ch. XXVII. *Vide supra,* p. 111.
30. *Analects,* Bk. XIX, Ch. VI. *Vide supra,* p. 111.
31. *Analects,* Bk. VI, Ch. XXVIII.
32. *Ibid.,* Bk. I, Ch. VII.
33. *Ibid.,* Bk. V, Ch. XVII.
34. *Ibid.,* Bk. XVIII, Ch. I.
35. *Ibid.,* Bk. XIX, Ch. VII. *Vide supra,* pp. 102.
36. *Analects,* Bk. XVII, Ch. IV.
37. *Ibid.,* Bk., XIV, Ch. XXV. *Vide supra,* p. 169.
38. *Works of Mencius* Bk. IV, Pt. I, Ch. X. *Vide supra,* p. 73.
39. *Works of Mencius,* Bk. VI, Pt. I, Ch. XIX.
40. *Ibid.* Bk. VII, Pt. II, Ch. XXXI.
41. *Op. cit.,* Ch. XX.
42. *Analects,* Bk. XV, Ch. XVII.
43. *Works of Mencius,* Bk. V, Pt. II, Ch. VII.
44. *Ibid.,* Bk. VI, Pt. I, Ch. XI.
45. *Ibid.,* Bk. IV, Pt. I, Ch. X.
46. *Ibid.,* Bk. VII, Pt. I, Ch. XXXIII.
47. *Ibid.,* Pt. II, Ch. XXXI.
48. *Ibid.,* Bk. IV, Pt. II, Ch. VIII.
49. *Ibid.,* Bk. VII, Pt. I, Ch. XXXIII.
50. *Ibid.,* Bk. II, Pt. I, Ch. VI.
51. *Doctrine of the Mean,* Ch. XXV.
52. *Works of Mencius,* Bk. VI, Pt. I, Ch. X. *Vide supra,* p. 74.
53. *Analects,* Bk. II, Ch. III.

54. *Works of Mencius*, Bk. VII, Pt. I, Ch. VII.
55. *Analects*, Bk. VII, Ch. III.
56. *Works of Mencius*, Bk. VII, Pt. I, Ch. VII.
57. *Analects*, Bk. XIV, Ch. I,
58. *Ibid.*, Bk. VIII, Ch. XIII.
59. *Ibid.*, Bk. V, Ch. XXIV.
60. *Ibid.*, Bk. VI, Ch. XIV.
61. *Ibid.*, Bk. XIV, Ch. XXIX. *Vide supra*, p. 46.
62. *Analects*, Bk. IV, Ch. IX.
63. *Ibid.*, Bk. IX, Ch. XXVI.
64. *Works of Mencius*, Bk. VII, Pt. I, Ch. XXI.
65. *Analects*, Bk. VII, Ch. XXV.
66. *Works of Mencius*, Bk. VI, Pt. I, Ch. XV. *Vide supra*, p. 144.
67. *Works of Mencius*, Bk. IV, Pt. I, Ch. II.
68. *Doctrine of the Mean*, Ch. XXIX.
69. *Works of Mencius*, Bk. VII, Pt. II, Ch. XV.
70. *Ibid.*, Bk. VII, Pt. II, Ch. XXV.
71. *Doctrine of the Mean*, Ch. XXVII. *Vide supra*, p. 218.
72. *Works of Mencius*, Bk. V, Pt. II, Ch. I. The first part of Legge's rendering of the description of Confucius' culmination in sagehood was scarcely adequate.
73. *Doctrine of the Mean*, Ch. XXXI.
74. *Analects*, Bk. XIX, Ch. XXII. *Vide supra*. p. 25.
75. *Analects*, Bk. XIV, Ch. XXXI.
76. *Ibid.*, Ch. XXXIII.
77. *Works of Mencius*, Bk. VII, Pt. II, Ch. XX.
78. *Analects*, Bk. XIV, Ch. XXXIX.
79. *Works of Mencius*, Bk. VII, Pt. I, Ch. XXXI.
80. *Analects*, Bk. I, Ch. XIV.
81. *Ibid.*, Bk. XV, Ch. XXXI.
82. *Ibid.*, Bk., I, Ch. I.
83. *Ibid.*, Bk. XV, Ch. XVIII. *Vide supra*, p. 159.
84. *Analects*, Bk. XV, Ch. XIX.
85. *Doctrine of the Mean*, Ch. XIII. *Vide supra*, p. 84.
86. *Analects*, Bk. I, Ch. II. *Vide supra*, p. 87.
87. *Analects*, Bk. I, Ch. VIII; Bk. IX, Ch. XXIV.
88. *Ibid.*, Bk. XIX, Ch. XXI.
89. *Ibid.*, Bk. VI, Ch. XVI. *Vide supra*, p. 92.
90. *Analects*, Bk. II, Ch. XII.
91. *Ibid.*, Bk. XIV, Ch. XXIX. *Vide supra*, p. 46.
92. *Analects*, Bk. V, Ch. XXIV. *Vide supra*, p. 46.
93. *Analects*, Bk. IV, Ch. X.
94. *Ibid.*, Bk. XV, Ch. XXXVI.
95. *Ibid.*
96. *Works of Mencius*, Bk. VI, Pt. II, Ch. XII. *Vide supra*, p. 197.
97. *Analects*, Bk. XV, Ch. XXI.
98. *Ibid.*, Bk. III, Ch. VII.
99. *Ibid.*, Bk. XV. Ch. XXI.
100. *Ibid.*, Bk. XIV, Ch. V.

101. *Ibid.*, Bk. IV, Ch. V. *Vide supra*, p. 104.
102. *Analects*. Bk. XIV, Ch. XXX. The last remark by Tzǔ-kung was mistranslated by Legge.
103. *Ibid.*, Bk. XX, Ch. V.
104. *Ibid.*, Bk. XVI, Ch. VII.
105. *Ibid.*, Bk. XIX, Ch. IX.
106. *Ibid.*, Bk. VII, Ch. XXXVII.
107. *Ibid.*, Bk. XVI, Ch. X. *Vide supra*, p. 34.
108. *Works of Mencius*. Bk. VII, Pt. I, Ch. XX.
109. *Ibid.*, Ch. XXI.
110. *Ibid.*, Ch. XIII.
111. *Analects*. Bk. XIV, Ch. XLV.
112. *Ibid.*, Bk. XIV, Ch. XIII.
113. *Ibid.*, Bk. XI, Ch. XIX.
114. *Works of Mencius*. Bk. VII, Pt. II, Ch. XXV.
115. *Analects*, Bk. XIII, Ch. XXIX.
116. *Ibid.*, Ch. XI.
117. *Ibid.*, Ch. XXII.
118. *Ibid.*, Bk. IX, Ch. XVIII.
119. *Works of Mencius*, Bk. VII, Pt. I, Ch. XXIX.
120. *Analects*, Bk. VII, Ch. XXV. *Vide supra*, p. 250.
121. *Doctrine of the Mean*, Ch. XXVI. *Vide supra*, p. 22.
122. *Great Learning*, Text. *Vide supra*, p. 188.
123. *Analects*, Bk. XV, Ch. XI. *Vide supra*, p. 167.
124. *Analects*, Bk. II, Ch. IV. *Vide supra*, p. 235.
125. *Analects*, Bk. XVII, Ch. XXVI.
126. *Ibid.*, Bk. IX, Ch. XXII.
127. *Ibid.*, Bk. XVII, Ch. IX.
128. *Ibid.*, Bk. VIII, Ch. VIII.
129. *Ibid.*, Bk. XVII, Ch. X.
130. *Ibid.*, Bk. II, Ch. II.
131. *Ibid.*, Bk. III, Ch. XX.
132. *Works of Mencius*, Bk. II, Pt. I, Ch. II. *Vide supra*, pp. 117, 211.
133. *Analects*, Bk. IX, Ch. XXV.
134. *Ibid.*, Bk. V, Ch. XXV.
135. *Ibid.*, Bk. XI, Ch. XXV.
136. *Works of Mencius*. Bk. VI, Pt. I, Ch. XVI. *Vide supra*, p. 72.
137. *Works of Mencius*, Bk. VII, Pt. I, Ch. XXV.
138. *Ibid.*, Ch. XVI.
139. *Ibid.*, Bk. II, Pt. I, Ch. VII.
140. *Great Learning*, Com., Ch. X.
141. *Works of Mencius*, Bk. VI, Pt. II, Ch. XIII.
142. *Great Learning*, Com., Ch. IX.
143. *Works of Mencius*, Bk. VII, Pt. II, Ch. XXV. *Vide supra*, p. 263.
144. *Analects*. Bk. IV, Ch. XIV.
145. *Ibid.*, Bk. XIV, Ch. XXXII.
146. *Ibid.*, Bk. XIV, Ch. XXV.
147. *Ibid.*, Bk. V, Ch. XXI.
148. *Ibid.*, Bk. III, Ch. XIV.

149. *Ibid.*, Bk. VI, Ch. XXIII.
150. *Ibid.*, Bk. XIV, Ch. X.
151. *Ibid.*, Bk. XIII, Ch. VII.
152. *Ibid.* Bk. XV, Ch. XXV.
153. *Ibid.*, Bk. IX, Ch. VIII.
154. *Ibid.*, Bk. III, Ch. XXIV.
155. *Ibid.*, Bk. XVIII, Ch. V.
156. *Ibid.*, Bk. XIV, Ch. XLII. *Vide supra*, p. 168.
157. *Analects*, Bk. XIV, Ch. XLI.
158. *Ibid.*, Bk. XVIII, Ch. VI.
159. *Ibid.*, Bk. XV, Ch. XX. *Vide supra*, p. 138.
160. *Doctrine of the Mean*, Ch. XIV.
161. *Analects*, Bk. XIV, Ch. XXXVII.
162. *Works, of Mencius*, Bk. VII, Pt. II, Ch. XIX.
163. *Ibid.*, Ch. XIX.
164. *Great Learning*, Com., Ch. VI.
165. *Doctrine of the Mean*, Ch. I. *Vide supra*, pp. 84.
166. *Analects*, Bk. I, Ch. IV.
167. *Ibid.*, Bk. IV, Ch. XVII.
168. *Ibid.*, Ch. XXIII.
169. *Ibid.*, Bk. VII, Ch. XXXIV.
170. *Ibid.*, Bk. III, Ch. XIII. *Vide supra*, p. 63.
171. *Works of Mencius*, Bk. IV, Pt. I, Ch. VIII. *Vide surpa*, p. 59.
172. *Works of Mencius*, Bk. IV, Pt. II, Ch. XXVIII.
173. *Ibid.*, Bk. II, Pt. I, Ch. II. *Vide supra*, p. 117.
174. *Works of Mencius*, Bk. IV, Pt. I, Ch. IV.
175. *Analects*, Bk. XV, Ch. XIV.
176. *Ibid.*, Bk. XIX, Ch. XXI. *Vide supra*, 257.
177. *Analects*, Bk. XIX, Ch. VIII. *Vide supra*, p. 129.
178. *Analects*, Bk. I, Ch. VIII.
179. *Ibid.*, Bk. IX, Ch. XXIV. *Vide supra*, p. 257.
180. *Works of Mencius*, Bk. III, Pt. II, Ch. VIII.
181. *Analects*, Bk. VII, Ch. XXX.
182. *Ibid.*, Bk. XIV, Ch. XXVI.
183. *Works of Mencius*, Bk. IV, Pt. II, Ch. XXV. *Vide supra*, p. 57.
184. *Analects*, Bk. XV, Ch. XXIX.
185. *Ibid.*, Bk. V, Ch. XXVI.
186. *Works of Mencius*, Bk. II, Pt. I, Ch. VIII. *Vide supra*, p. 271.
187. *Analects*, Bk. IX, Ch. XXIII.
188. *Ibid.*, Bk. XVI, Ch. XI.
189. *Ibid.*, Ch. VIII. *Vide supra*, p. 64.
190. *Analects*, Bk. IX, Ch. XV.
191. *Ibid.*, Bk. XIX, Ch. XX.
192. *Doctrine of the Mean*, Ch. XX. *Vide supar*, p. 18.
193. *Analects*, Bk. IX, Ch. XXI.
194. *Ibid.*, Ch. XVIII. *Vide supra*, p. 264.
195. *Doctrine of the Mean*, Ch. XVII.
196. *Analects*, Bk. XIII, Ch. X.
197. *Ibid.*, Bk. IX, Ch. V.

198. *Ibid.*, Bk. VII, Ch. XXII. *Vide supra*, p. 62.
199. *Works of Mencius*, Bk. IV, Pt. I, Ch. X.
200. *Analects* Bk. VI, Ch. X.
201. *Works of Mencius*, Bk. V, Pt. I, Ch. IX.
202. *Doctrine of the Mean*, Ch. XIV, *Vide supra*, pp. 65. 275.
203. *Works of Mencius*, Bk. IV, Pt. II, Ch. XIV.
204. *Ibid.*, Bk. VI, Pt. II, Ch. XV.
205. *Analects*, Bk. XII, Ch. I. *Vide supra*, p. 104.
206. *Works of Mencius*, Bk. VII. Pt. I, Ch. XVIII.
207. *Analects*. Bk. XV, Ch. XXXII. *Vide supra*. p. 152.
208. *Analects*, Bk. I, Ch. VIII. *Vide supra*, p. 257.
209. *Analects*, Bk. XIII, Ch. XXVII. *Vide supra*, pp. 111, 239.
210. *Analects*. Bk. VII, Ch. XXXVII.
211. *Ibid.*, Ch. XXXIII.
212. *Ibid.*, Bk. VII. Ch. IX. Ch. XIX. *Vide supra*, p. 237.
213. *Analects*, Bk. VII, ch. XVIII. *Vide supra*, pp. 237.
214. *Works of Mencius*. Bk. III, Pt. I, Ch. IV.
215. *Ibid.*
216. *Ibid.*
217. *Analects*, Bk. XIV, Ch. VIII.
218. *Ibid.*, Ch. III.
219. *Works of Mencius*, Bk. IV, Pt. I, Ch. XVI.
220. *Analects*, Bk. XVI, Ch. I.
221. *Great Learning*, Com., Ch. X.
222. *Analects*, Bk. VII, Ch. XXXV.
223. *Ibid.*, Bk. I, Ch. X.
224. *Ibid.*, Bk. XIII, Ch. XIV.
225. *Ibid.*, Bk. III, Ch. XXII.
226. *Ibid.*, Bk. V, Ch. XVII. *Vide supra*, p. 240,
227. *Works of Mencius*. Bk. VI, Pt. II, Ch. XV.
228. *Analects*. Bk. VIII, Ch. III.
229. *Ibid.*, Bk. VII, Ch. XII.
230. *Ibid.*, Bk. X, Ch. VIII.
231. *Ibid.*, Ch. XVI.
232. *Ibid.*, Ch. XIII
233. *Ibid.*, Ch. VI.
234. *Ibid.*, Ch. XIII.
235. *Ibid.*. Bk. VII, Ch. IV.
236. *Ibid*, Bk. X, Ch. IX.
237. *Ibid.*, Ch. XVI.
238. *Ibid.*, Ch. X.
239. *Ibid.*, Ch. I.
240. *Ibid.*, Ch. II.
241. *Ibid.*, Ch. III.
242. *Ibid.*, Ch. IV.
243. *Ibid.*, Ch. V.
244. *Ibid.*, Ch. XVI.
245. *Ibid.*, Ch. XVII.
246. *Ibid.*. Ch. XIII.

247. *Ibid.*, Ch. VII.
248. *Ibid.*, Bk. III, Ch. XII.
249. *Ibid.*, Bk. IX, Ch. XXVII.
250. *Works of Mencius*, Bk. VII, Pt. I, Ch. XVII.
251. *Ibid.*, Bk. III, Pt. I, Ch. II. *Vide supra*, p. 214.
252. *Analects*, Bk. VIII, Ch. XIV; Bk. XIV, Ch. XXVII.
253. *Ibid.* Ch. XXVIII.
254. *Doctrine of the Mean*, Ch. XIV. *Vide snpra.* p. 288.
255. *Works of Mencius*, Bk. V, Pt. II, Ch. V.
256. *Ibid.*, Bk. IV, Pt. II, Ch. VIII.
257. *Ibid.*, Bk. VII, Pt. II, Ch. VI.
258. *Ibid.*, Bk. III, Pt. II, Ch. I.
259. *Ibid.*, Bk. VII, Pt. I, Ck. XXVIII,
260. *Ibid.*, Bk. III, Pt. II, Ch. X.
261. *Ibid.*, Bk. VII, Pt. I, Ch. XXXIV.
262. *Analects*, Bk. XIII, Ch. VIII.
263. *Works of Mencius*, Bk. IV, Pt. I, Ch. XVI. *Vide supra*, p. 294.
264. *Works of Mencius*, Bk. VI, Pt. I, Ch. XVI. *Vide supra*, pp. 72, 270.
265. *Works of Mencius*, Bk. VII, Pt. I, Ch. III.
266. *Ibid.*, Bk. VI, Pt. I, Ch. XVII. *Vide supra*, p. 157.
267. *Works of Mencius*, Bk. VII, Pt. I, Ch. XX. *Vide supra*, p. 261.
268. *Analects*, Bk. VII, Ch. XI,
269. *Ibid.*, Bk. IV, Ch. V.
270. *Works of Mencius*, Bk. IV, Pt. II, Ch. XXXIII.
271. *Analects*, Bk. IV, Ch. VIII.
272. *Ibid.*, Bk. XV, Ch. XXXI. *Vide supra*, p. 256.
273. *Doctrine of the Mean.* Ch. V.
274. *Works of Mencius*, Bk. VII, Pt. II, Ch. XXXVIII.
275. *Ibid.*, Bk. VII, Pt. II, Ch. II.
276. *Ibid.*, Bk. VII, Pt. I, Ch. IX.
277. *Ibid.*, Pt. II, Ch. XXXIV.
278. *Ibid.*, Ch. XVIII,
279. *Analects*, Bk. XVII, Ch. XV. *Vide supra*, p. 151.
280. *Works of Mencius*, Bk. VII, Pt. I, Ch. XI.
281. *Analects*, Bk. VII, Ch. XV.
282. *Ibid.*, Bk. XV, Ch. I.
283. *Ibid.*, Bk. VI, Ch. IX.
284. *Ibid.*, Bk. XI, Ch. XVIII.
285. *Works of Mencius*, Bk. I, Pt. I, Ch. VII.
286. *Ibid.*, Bk. VI, Pt. II, Ch. XIV. *Vide supra*, p. 165.
287. *Analects*, Bk. XVIII, Ch. VIII.
288. *Works of Mencius*, Bk. V, Pt. II, Ch. IV.
289. *Ibid.*, Bk. II, Pt. II, Ch. XII.
290. *Ibid.*, Ch. XIII.
291. *Analects*, Bk. VIII, Ch. XIII. *Vide supra*, p. 247.
292. *Analects*, Bk. VII. Ch. X. *Vide supra.* p. 114
293. *Analects*, Bk. XV. Ch. VI.
294. *Ibid.*, Bk. XIX, Ch. XIII.

295. *Works of Mencius*, Bk. II, Pt. II, Ch. X.

296. *Ibid.*, Bk. V, Pt. II, Ch. V.

297. *Ibid.*, Bk. IV, Pt. I, Ch. XX.

298. *Ibid.*, Bk. V, Pt. I, Ch. VII. *Vide supra*, p. 63.

299. *Works of Mencius*, Bk. III, Pt. II, Ch. X.

300. *Analects*, Bk. IX, Ch. XII.

301. *Ibid.*, Bk. XVII, Ch. V.

302. *Ibid.*, Bk. VI, Ch. VII.

303. *Ibid.*, Bk. XVII, Ch. I.

304. *Works of Mencius*, Bk. III, Pt. II, Ch. VII. What was translated by Legge as "the point of righteousness" accually means "meaning."

305. *Ibid.*, Bk. IV, Pt. I, Ch. XXIV.

306. *Analects*, Bk. XIV, Ch. XXXIX. *Vide supra*. p. 255.

307. *Analects*, Bk. VII, Ch. XIV. *Vide supra*, p. 74.

308. *Analects*, Bk. XVIII, Ch. VII.

309. *Ibid.*, Ch. IV. *Vide supra*, p. 96.

310. *Analects*. Bk. XV, Ch. I. *Vide supra*, p. 138.

311. *Works of Mencius*, Bk. IV, Pt. II, Ch. IV.

312. *Analects*, Bk. XVIII. Ch. III.

313. *Works of Mencius*, Bk. II, Pt. II, Ch. V.

314. *Ibid.*, Ch. XI.

315. *Ibid.*, Bk. VII, Pt. II, Ch. XXIII.

316. *Analects*. Bk. VI, Ch. XXVI.

317. *Works of Mencius*, Bk. VII, Pt. II, Ch. XVII.

318. *Analects*, Bk. XIX, Ch. I.

319. *Works of Mencius*, Bk. III, Pt. I, Ch. IV.

320. *Ibid.*, Bk. IV, Pt. II, Ch. XVIII. *Vide supra*, pp. 221.

321. *Works of Mencius*, Bk. V, Pt. II, Ch. IV.

322. *Ibid.*, Bk. VI, Pt. II, Ch. V.

323. *Ibid.*, Bk. II, Pt. II, Ch. III.

324. *Analects*, Bk. X, Ch. XI.

325. *Ibid.*, Bk. VI, Ch. III.

326. *Works of Mencius*, Bk. VII, Pt. II, Ch. X.

327. *Analects*, Bk. IV, Ch. I.

328. *Works of Mencius*, Bk. VII, Pt. I, Ch. XXXVI.

329. *Great Learning*, Com., Ch. VIII.

330. *Analects*, Bk. XII, Ch. VI. *Vide supra*. p. 39.

331. *Analects*, Bk. IX, Ch. XIII.

332. *Ibid.*, Bk. XVII, Ch. III. *Vide supra*, p. 192.

333. *Works of Mencius*, Bk. V, Pt I, Ch. VIII. Toward the end of the second paragraph, Legge left out the words "the ulcer-doctor and" before "the attendant Chi Huan." In the third paragraph, the title of Huan was erroneously translated as "Master of the Horse".

334. *Analects*, Bk. XVII, Ch. VII.

335. *Ibid.*, Bk. IX, Ch. III.

336. *Works of Mencius*, Bk. VII, Pt. I, Ch. X.

337. *Ibid.*, Bk. II, Pt. I, Ch. I.

338. *Analects*, Bk. X, Ch. XVIII. The word "smelt" was a mistranslation by Legge.

339. *Works of Mencius,* Bk. II, Pt. I, Ch. VII.
340. *Analects,* Bk. XVI, Ch. V. *Vide supra,* pp. 154
341. *Analects,* Bk. X, Ch. VIII.
342. *Ibid.,* Bk. I, Ch. XXII. *Vide supra,* p. 133.
343. *Analects.* Bk. XIX, Ch. XXV.
344. *Ibid.,* Bk. XV, Ch. XL.
345. *Ibid.,* Bk. XIV, Ch. XIV.
346. *Ibid..* Bk. IV, Ch. XXII. *Vide supra,* p. 46.
347. *Analects,* Bk. VI, Ch. XIX.
348. *Ibid.* Bk. XV, Ch. VII.
349. *Ibid..* Bk. III, Ch. XXI.
350. *Ibid..* Bk. XI, Ch. V.
351. *Great Learning.* Com., Ch. X. *Vide supra,* pp. 16, 140.
352. *Works of Mencius,* Bk. IV, Pt. I, Ch. XXII.
353. *Analects,* Bk. XIV, Ch. XXXIV.
354. *Works of Mencius.* Bk. III, Pt. II. Ch. IX. *Vide supra,* pp. 58, 218, 222.
355. *Doctrine of the Mean.* Ch. XXVII.
356. *Analects.* Bk. XIV, Ch. IV.
357. *Works of Mencius.* Bk. II, Pt. II, Ch. VI.
358. *Analects,* Bk. XVI, Ch. VI.
359. *Ibid.,* Bk. XV, Ch. V.
360. *Ibid.,* Bk. I, Ch. XIII.
361. *Ibid..* Bk. XII, Ch. XII.
362. *Doctrine of the Mean,* Ch. XX.
363. *Analects.* Bk. XV, Ch. XV. *Vide supra,* p. 35.
364. *Works of Mencius.* Bk. VII, Pt. I, Ch. XX. *Vide supra,* p. 260.
365. *Works of Mencius,* Bk. V, Pt. II, Ch. I. *Vide supra,* p. 125.
366. *Works of Mencius,* Bk. IV, Pt. II, Ch. XXIV. *Vide supra,* p. 127.
367. *Works of Mencius,* Bk. IV, Pt. II, Ch. XXIV. *Vide supra,* pp. 127.
368. *Analects.* Bk. VII, Ch. XXI. *Vide supra,* p. 26.
369. *Works of Mencius,* Bk. IV, Pt. I, Ch. XXIII.
370. *Ibid.,* Bk. II, Pt. I, Ch. III.
371. *Analects,* Bk. IX, Ch. X.
372. *Ibid.,* Bk. XIX, Ch. XXIV.
373. *Ibid..* Ch. XXIII.
374. *Ibid..* Ch. XXV.
375. *Works of Mencius,* Bk. II, Pt. I, Ch. II. *Vide supraa,* p. 213.
376. *Analects,* Bk. VI, Ch. VIII. *Vide supra,* p. 66.
377. *Analects,* Bk. XI, Ch. XXII.
378. *Works of Mencius,* Bk. III, Pt. I, Ch. IV.
379. *Analects,* Bk. XV, Ch· XXXV.
380. *Analects.* Bk. XII, Ch. XXIV, *Vide supra,* p. 26.
381. *Analects.* Bk. I, Ch. VIII. *Vide supra,* pp. 257. 281, 291.
382. *Analects.* Bk. I, Ch. III.
383. *Ibid..* Bk. XVI, Ch. IV. *Vide supra,* p. 154.
384. *Analects,* Bk. V, Ch. II.
385. *Ibid.,* Bk. XIX, Ch. III.
386. *Ibid..* Bk. V, Ch. XVI.

387. *Works. of Mencius*, Bk. IV, Pt. II, Ch. XXX.
388. *Analects*, Bk. IX, Ch. XXIII. *Vide supra*. p. 283.
389. *Analects*. Bk. XII, Ch. XXIII.
390. *Ibid.*, Bk. IV, Ch. XXVI.
391. *Ibid.*, Bk. XV, Ch. XXXIX.
392. *Ibid.*. Ch. XVI.
393. *Works of Mencius*, Bk. V, Pt. II, Ch. VIII.
394. *Analects*, Bk. I, Ch. I.
395. *Doctrine of the Mean*, Ch. XIII. *Vide supra*. pp. 84, 257.
396. *Analects*, Bk. X, Ch. XV.
397. *Works of Mencius*. Bk. V, Pt. II, Ch. III.
398. *Analects*, Bk. XV, Ch. XXIII.
399. *Ibid.*, Bk. V, Ch. XI.
400. *Works of Mencius*, Bk. III, Pt. I, Ch. IV.
401. *Analects*, Bk. IV, Ch. XV. *Vide supra*, p. 2.
402. *Great Learning*, Com., Ch. IX. *Vide supra*, p. 272.
403. *Great Learning*, Com., Ch. X. *Vide supra*, p. 85.
404. *Doctrine of the Mean*, Ch. XXVII.
405. *Analects*, Bk. IX, Ch. XXVI. *Vide supra*, p. 249.
406. *Works of Mencius*, Bk. IV, Pt. II, Ch. XVII.
407. *Analects*, Bk. XIV. Ch. XXXIII.
408. *Ibid.*, Bk. VIII, Ch. XI.
409. *Ibid.*, Bk. VI, Ch. XIII.
410. *Ibid.*. Bk. XVII, Ch. XXIV. *Vide supra*, p. 113.
411. *Analects*, Bk. XV, Ch. XXIV.
412. *Works of Mencius*, Bk. IV. Pt. II, Ch. IX.
413. *Analects*, Bk. XIV, Ch. XXVI. *Vide supra*, p. 254.
414. *Analects*, Bk. VII, Ch. XXVIII.
415. *Ibid.*, Bk. V, Ch. XXII.
416. *Ibid.*. Bk. XV, Ch. XIV. *Vide supra*, p. 280. Legge's rendering of the first part was wrong.
417. *Works of Mencius*, Bk. IV, Pt. II, Ch, X. Legge's rendering was erroneous.
418. *Ibid.*, Bk. VII, Pt. II, Ch. XXVII.
419. *Analects*, Bk. XIV, Ch. XXXVI.
420. *Works of Mencius*, Bk. II, Pt. I, Ch. VI.
421. *Ibid.*, Bk. IV, Pt. I, Ch. VIII.
422. *Analects*. Bk. VII, Ch. IX.
423. *Ibid.*. Bk. XV, Ch. XLI.
424. *Ibid.*, Bk. IX, Ch. IX.
425. *Ibid.*, Bk. VII, Ch. XXVI.
426. *Ibid.*, Bk. XVII, Ch. XXIV. *Vide supra*, pp. 113, 357.
427. *Works of Mencius*, Bk. VII, Pt. I, Ch. XVII. *Vide supra*, p. 302.
428. *Analects*. Bk. VII, Ch. XXXIII. *Vide supra*, p. 291.
429. *Analects*. Bk. IX, Ch. VI. *Vide supra*. p. 20.
430. *Analects*. Bk. XIV, Ch. XXX. *Vide supra*, p. 259.
431. *Analects*, Bk. VII, Ch. I. *Vide supra*, p. 23.
432. *Analects*, Bk. VII, Ch. XXXIII. *Vide supra*. p. 291.

433. *Analects*, Bk. IX, Ch. VII. Legge's Rendering of *K'ung K'ung* as "empty-like" was a mistake.
434. *Ibid.*, Bk. V, Ch. V.
435. *Ibid.*, Bk. VIII, Ch. I.
436. *Ibid.*, Bk. XIV, Ch. XIVI.
437. *Ibid.*, Ch. XLVII.
438. *Ibid.*, Bk. VII, Ch. XXXI.
439. *Doctrine of the Mean*, Ch. XX.

CHAPTER VII

The Regulation of the Family

The continuation of life is one of the instincts with which man is endowed by Heaven, and so sex and the search for the mate do not have to be learned. Confucius said, "I have not seen one who loves virtue as he loves sex."[1]

In consequence, without the strict regulation of the relations between men and women it is difficult to maintain social order. As a rule, the strong stop at nothing to satisfy their wants, while the weak cannot even obtain their due. Because of the open and covert conflict going on at all times, society is often fraught with serious dangers—including homicide. At the same time, sexually unsatisfied men and women abound, and they are a menace to social peace and tranquillity. For this reason, an important function of government and education, as well as religion, is to regulate human relationships.

> Mencius said, "...That male and female should dwell together is the greatest of human relations."[2]
>
> Mencius said, "...The Minister of Agriculture taught the people to sow and reap, cultivating the five kinds of grain. When the five kinds of grain were brought to maturity, the people all obtained a subsistence. But men possess a moral nature; and if they are well fed, warmly clad and comfortably lodged, without being taught at the same time, they become almost like the beasts. This was a subject of anxious solicitude to the sage Shun, and he appointed Hsueh to be the Minister of Instruction, to teach the relations of

humanity: how, between father and son there should be affection; between sovereign and minister, righteousness; between husband and wife, attention to their separate functions; between old and young, a proper order; and between friends, fidelity."[3]

Mencius said, "...But it is now the Middle Kingdom that we live in. To banish the relationships of men and have no superior men—how can such a state of things be thought of?"[4]

In an age in which human relationships were not yet well-defined, children knew only who their mothers were; they did not know their fathers. Owing to the confusion of blood relationships, the ties between brothers and sisters were even less clear. As long as relations between husband and wife remained undefined, those between father and son and between brothers could not be established even basically. Under these circumstances, the relations between man and man would be based on desire, not on love, and the continuation of life would depend on force, not virtue. While desire and force were factors which sustained the age of barbarity, love and virtue have been responsible for the production of human civilization. If the civilized world of today were not to stress human relationships, it would revert to the age of barbarity. This is what concerns us most.

> The Way of the superior man begins with the relations between husband and wife; but at its utmost, it reaches as far as heaven and earth."[5]

Since the Way involves the highest principles of the common existence of mankind, the husband and wife must live together and assume the responsibility for maintaining and continuing life. So, the husband-wife relationship reflects the beginnings of the Way. With the establishment of this relationship and the stabilization of the family, the foundation is laid for the continuation of human life, and the affection and love between man and man yields its results. So, at its utmost, the Way reaches as far as heaven and earth.

The importance of the relations between husband and wife cannot be overestimated, since they are the beginning of all human relationships. For this reason, it is essential for them to exercise care from beginning to end and maintain a long period of harmony, so that they may obtain their family bliss.

> The Way of the superior man may be compared to what takes place on traveling, when to go to a distance we must first traverse the space that is near, and in ascending a height, when we must begin from the lower ground.

> It is said in the *Book of Songs,* "Happy union with wife and children is like the music of lutes and harps. When there is concord among brothers, the harmony is delightful. Thus may you regulate your family and enjoy the pleasure of your wife and children."

> The Master said, "In such a state of things are the parents not complacent?"[6]

When relations between husband and wife are harmonious and like the music of lutes and harps, the children are brought up in an atmosphere of affection and happiness, which naturally engenders respect and love among brothers and sisters. When children are treated kindly by their parents, their reaction is to be filial and obedient. Thus, in an organization in which there is mutual love and affection between those above (fathers) and below (sons), in front (elder brothers) and behind (younger brothers), left (husbands) and right (wives), there is bound to be abundant unity, propriety, righteousness and good order. Hence a family like this is called "regulated." If all the families in a country are regulated, the country must be strong and cannot be despised.

> Mencius said, "...A man must first despise himself, and then others will despise him. A family must first destory itself, and then others will destroy it. A State must first smite itself, and then others will smite it."[7]

> From the loving example of one family a whole State becomes loving, and from its courtesies the whole State becomes courteous, while, from the ambition and perverseness of the one man, the whole State may be led to rebellious disorder; such is the nature of the influence. This verifies the saying, "Affairs may be ruined by a single sentence; a kingdom may be settled by its one man."[8]

Another meaning of the word *ch'i* is "equality." Since a family is composed basically of a husband and wife, its affairs, unlike those of other organizations, cannot be determined by one person, and a division of labor must be applied. As a rule, the internal affairs of a family are decided by the wife, while its external affairs are decided by the husband. As far as the children are concerned, the father is generally strict and the mother kind. Strictness tends to lead to wisdom, while kindness consolidates affection; the two together tend to build a rising generation which is both wise and affectionate. Thus, though two persons are in control, a single result is produced. Just like the lute and the harp—which are two distinct instruments but which make harmonious music and cannot be differentiated—the husband and wife are merged into each other in such a way that they cannot be clearly differentiated.

What does it mean when we say that the first prerequisite of the regulation of a family is filial piety?

The affection of a man within the family can be divided into three stages:

> Mencius said, "...The desire of the child is towards his father and mother. When he becomes conscious of the attractions of sex, his desire is towards young and beautiful women. When he comes to have a wife and children, his desire is towards them."[9]

When one is in office, a change is wrought in one's affection again.

> "...When he obtains office, his desire is towards his sovereign; if he cannot get the regard of his sovereign, he burns within. But the man of great filial piety, to the end of his life, has his desire towards his parents. In the great Shun I see the case of one whose desire even at fifty years was towards them."[10]

Only a man who never forgets his origin, even in the later stages of life, and continues to love and be concerned about his parents can be called a man of great filial piety. The best example was the great Shun, whom both Confucius and Mencius eulogized.

> The Master said, "Was not Shun a man of great filial piety? His virtue was that of a sage; his dignity was the throne; his riches were all within the four seas. After his death his spirit was sacrificed to in the ancestral temple, and his descendants preserved the sacrifices to him for long generations.
>
> "Therefore, having such great virtue, it could not but be that he should obtain the throne, that he should obtain those riches, that he should obtain his fame, that he should attain to his long life.
>
> "Thus it is that Heaven, in the production of things, is sure to be bountiful to them, according to their qualities. Hence the tree

that is flourishing, it nourishes, while that which is ready to fall, it overthrows.

"In the *Book of Songs* it is said, 'The admirable, amiable prince displayed conspicuously his excelling virtue. He was suited to rule over his people. Therefore, he received from Heaven the emoluments of dignity. It protected him, blessed him and decreed him the throne, sending from Heaven these favors repeatedly.'

"We must say therefore that he who has great virtue will be sure to receive the appointment of Heaven."[11]

Mencius said, "Suppose the case of the whole empire turning in great delight to an individual to submit to him. To regard the whole empire thus turning to him in great delight but as a bundle of grass—only Shun was capable of this. He considered that if a man could not get the hearts of his parents he could not be considered a man, and that if he could not get to an entire accord with his parents, he could not be considered a son.

"By Shun's completely fulfilling everything by which a parent could be served, Ku-sou was delighted. When Ku-sou was brought to find that delight, the whole empire was transformed. When Ku-sou was brought to find that delight, the duties of all fathers and sons in the empire were established. This is called great filial piety."[12]

Kung-sun Ch'ou asked, saying, "The scholar Kao observed, 'The "Hsiao-p'an" is the ode of a little man.'" Mencius asked, "Why did he say so?" "Because of the murmuring which it expresses," was the reply.

Mencius answered, "How stupid that old Kao was in dealing with the ode! There is a man here, and a native of Yüeh bends his bow to shoot him. I will advise him not to do so, but speaking calmly and smilingly—for no other reason but that he is not related to me. But if my own brother is bending his bow to shoot the man, then I will advise him not to do so, while I weep and cry—for no other reason than that he is related to me. The dissatisfaction expressed in the 'Hsiao-p'an' is due to love of one's parent, and this love shows benevolence. Stupid indeed was old Kao's criticism on the ode."

Ch'ou then said, "How is it that there is no dissatisfaction expressed in the K'ai-fêng?"

Mencius replied, "The parent's fault referred to in the 'K'ai-fêng' is small; that referred to in the 'Hsiao-p'an' is great. Where the parent's fault was great, not to have murmured on account of it would have increased the want of natural affection. Where the parent's fault was small, to have murmured on account of it would have been to act like water which frets and foams about a stone that interrupts its course. To increase the want of natural affection would have been unfilial, and to fret and foam in such a manner would also have been unfilial.

"Confucius said, 'Shun was indeed perfectly filial! Even when he was fifty, he was full of longing desire about his parents.' "[13]

Wan Chang asked Mencius, saying, "When Shun went into the fields, he cried out and wept towards the pitying heavens. Why did he cry and weep?" Mencius replied, "He was dissatisfied and full of earnest desire."

Wan Chang said, "When his parents love him, a son rejoices and forgets them not. When his parents hate him, he works hard but does not murmur. Was Shun then murmuring against his parents?" Mencius answered, "Ch'ang Hsi asked Kung-ming Kao, 'As to Shun's going into the fields, I have received your instructions, but I do not know about his weeping and crying out to the pitying heavens and to his parents.' Kung-ming Kao answered him, 'You do not understand that matter.' Now, Kung-ming Kao supposed that the heart of the filial son could not be so free of sorrow. Shun would say, 'I exert my strength to cultivate the fields, but I am thereby only discharging my office as a son. What can there be in me that my parents do not love me?'

"The Emperor caused his own children, nine sons and two daughters, the various officials, oxen and sheep, storehouses and granaries, all to be prepared, to serve Shun amid the channeled fields. Of the scholars of the empire there were multitudes who flocked to him. The sovereign designed that the empire should be handed over to him. But because his parents were not in accord with him, he felt like a poor man who has nowhere to turn to.

"To be delighted in by all the scholars of the empire is what men desire, but it was not sufficient to remove the sorrow of Shun.

"The possession of beauty is what men desire, and Shun had for his wives the two daughters of the sovereign, but this was not sufficient to remove his sorrow. Riches are what men desire, and the empire was the rich property of Shun, but this was not sufficient to remove his sorrow. Honors are what men desire, and Shun had the dignity of being sovereign, but this was not sufficient to remove his sorrow. The reason why being the object of men's delight, with the possession of beauty, riches and honors was not sufficient to remove his sorrow was that it could be removed only by getting his parents to be in accord with him.

"The desire of the child is towards his father and mother. When he becomes conscious of the attractions of sex, his desire is towards young and beautiful women. When he comes to have wife and children, his desire is towards them. When he obtains office, his desire is towards his sovereign; if he cannot get the regard of his sovereign, he burns within. But the man of great filial piety, to the end of his life, has his desire towards his parents. In the great Shun I see the case of one whose desire even at fifty years was towards them."[14]

"It is not until a child is three years old that it leaves the arms of its parents," and so it is naturally closest to its parents morning and night. It is nurtured, educated and supported by its parents as it grows up. During all of this period, it is so attached to them that its filial love is a matter of course.

When a son eventually learns about sex, it is human nature for him to turn his thoughts to young and beautiful women. At this time, the parents are likely to be in the prime of their lives. While they do not love their son any the less, they do not have to expect too much from him in the way of care and support.

During the third stage, when his parents are advanced in age and may have reached the point of retirement, the son himself is likely to have entered middle age, with his own family burden and professional obligations to occupy him. If he can still attend to his filial duties, he can be regarded as a man of virtue at heart and of reverence in his action. He it is who has not lost the heart of a child and who is indeed a filial son. He deserves to be called a man of great filial piety. But since his parents have reached the autumn of their lives at that point, there is little time left for the practice of filial piety. Consequently, whenever he thinks of this, he cannot help feeling both happy and apprehensive—happy because his parents are living, apprehensive because he is not sure how much longer they will live.

> The Master said, "The ages of parents may by no means not be unknown, as an occasion at once for joy and for fear."[15]

To relieve his parents of anxiety, a son should keep himself at their side at all possible times and try his best to refrain from distant travels.

> The Master said, "While his parents are alive, the son may not go abroad to a distance. If he does go abroad, he must have a fixed place to which he goes."[16]

In an agricultural society, the people are settled on the soil and clans cluster together, This naturally leads to the establishment of the large family system.   Sometimes as many as three generations live under the same roof, and since all are occupied with farming, generation after generation may continue to live together.   For this reason, it is essential to consolidate the relations between one generation and another.   Thus, filial piety and kindness take on great importance.

Since land scarcely changes and is impossible to move, it would be a serious problem to have no one of the coming generation to inherit it.   Owing to this economic requirement, the traditional thought arose which viewed the lack of posterity as the greatest unfiliality.   At the same time, the concept of valuing male children more than females evolved.   For example, the relations of humanity make reference to only father and not to mother and daughter.   This resulted because, after a daughter grows up, she is married off to another family, and the family property cannot be handed down to her.   So, the failure to have a son was seen in the same light as the total lack of offspring. When a man was without offspring, he could not assume his responsibility in the continuation of life; moreover he also cut off his own family lineage, and this constituted an even more important reason for his being regarded as unfilial.

> Mencius said, "There are three things which are unfilial, and to have no posterity is the greatest of them. Shun married without informing his parents because of this—lest he should have no posterity. Superior men consider that his doing so was the same as if he had informed them."[17]

One of the attributes of filial piety was the ability to carry on earlier cultural attainments and pave the way for further future development.

> The Master said, "How far-extending the filial piety of King Wu and the Duke of Chou was!
>
> "Now filial piety is seen in the skillful carrying out of the wishes of our forefathers and the skillful carrying forward of their undertakings.
>
> "In spring and autumn, they repaired and beautified the temple-halls of their forefathers, set forth their ancestral vessels, displayed their various robes and presented the offerings of the several seasons.
>
> "By means of the ceremonies of the ancestral temple, they distinguished the royal kindred according to their order of descent. By ordering the parties according to their rank, they distinguished

the more noble and the less. By the arrangement of the services, they made a distinction of talents and worth. In the ceremony of general pledging, the inferiors presented their cups to their superiors, and thus something was given the lowest to do. At the concluding feast, places were given according to the color of the hair, and thus was made the distinction of years.

"They occupied the places of their forefathers, practiced their ceremonies and performed their music. They reverenced those whom they honored and loved those whom they regarded with affection. Thus they served the dead as they would have served them alive; they served the departed as they would have served them had they been continued among them. This was the highest exemplification of filial piety.

"By the caremonies of the sacrifices to Heaven and Earth they served God, and by the ceremonies of the ancestral temple they sacrificed to their ancestors. He who understands the ceremonies of the sacrifices to Heaven and Earth and the meaning of the several sacrifices to ancestors would find the government of a State as easy as to look into his palm!"[18]

The Master said' "While a man's father is alive, look at the bent of his will; when his father is dead, look at his conduct. If for three years he does not alter from the way of his father, he may be called filial."[19]

The Master said, "If the son for three years does not alter from the way of his father, he may be called filial."[20]

The philosopher Tsêng said, "I have heard this from our Master: 'The filial piety of Mêng Chuang, in other matters, was what other men are competent to, but, as seen in his not changing the ministers of his father nor his father's mode of government, it is difficult to be attained to.' "[21]

The above four passages concern the life's work of a man. While his life is limited, his work is not. If a son can continue with the unfinished work of his parents, their efforts are not wasted and their achievements can be further developed. If everyone can carry this out, the national culture of the country concerned will not only be handed down naturally without interruption, but will be built upon and improved.

The scholars of the world have often wondered why of all the world cultures the Chinese has stood the test of time best and has continued to flourish with the longest history. They have overlooked the fact that the real reason lies in the virtue of "filial piety." I believe that the ability to "carry on the past and pave the way for the future" is the most appropriate definition of filial piety. It does not follow, however, that personal love and reverence for one's parents is enough. There must also be the assumption of one's responsibility for continuing the national life and culture of one's country.

However, in an industrial and commercial society, the situation is different. There the professions of father and son may be totally different, and their interests may not be the same. The property of the father consists mainly of corporate securities and land and house deeds. These can be carried easily on the person, and no question of their transmission exists. Thus, whether one has a son or not is not significant.

Just as the conservation of water is vital to agriculture, means of communication are prerequisites for the development of commerce and industry. As a result, men are in a state of continual flux, and it is next to impossible to maintain the old system of several generations living together, or even to keep one's immediate family together. Moreover, not only are father and son economically independent of each other, but womenfolk as well leave their homes and maintain their economic independence by means of their own work. Of course, it is a good thing for each man and woman to have this spirit of independence, but it has its disadvantages as well. For one thing, individualism (which may also stand for selfishness) and materialism (which may also stand for self-interest) are universally developed. For another, owing to their frequent contacts, the relations between men and women become increasingly complicated, and the word "chastity" is not as highly regarded as it was before. Though marriage is still solemnized before God and his priest or in the presence of a judge, its maintenance has at times become problematic because of the rise of human depravity. As Shun said to Yü, "The mundane mind is perilous, and the moral mind delicate."

Large metropolitan areas, where industry and commerce are centered, have become not only economic but also cultural centers where morality has deteriorated and the family system broken down. Gradually, this tendency has invaded the countryside as well, and, consequently, the virtue of filial piety has been on the decline. After a child is born, the necessity for the mother's working away from home has resulted in a virtual shifting of the care of the child to a stranger. As the child grows older, he goes to nursery school, kindergarten, elementary school, high school and college. Thus, his contacts with persons outside the family and the time he spends with them far exceeds the time and contact he has with his parents, and the parent-child intimacy is greatly diluted. After marriage, he leaves his parents for good, a regrettable development which is specifically referred to evenin the Christian Bible.

> Mencius replied, "There are five things which are pronounced in the common usage to be unfilial...The third is being fond of goods and money and unselfishly attached to his wife and children, without attending to the nourishment of his parents..."[22]

While the Chinese regarded and still consider such things unfilial, they are not uncommon or improper in a Western community where the tragic fate of the aged can be witnessed everywhere; reference is even made to "heaven for the young and hell for the aged." But is it not unreasonable that heaven and hell should exist together? Since children cannot take care of their parents, the government has had to devise the system of Social Security to reduce the anxieties of the aged in their remaining years. But this can only solve the material problem, while the spiritual problem remains.

Our ancestors profoundly understood that the problem of existence depends on attention to the spiritual as well as the material for its solution. They also saw that the past and future are merely relative terms and that without loving the past there can be no future. Therefore, they could not separate the prevalence of the great Way from filial piety and kindness, which in their view should be further extended.

> Therefore people did not love their own parents only, nor treat as children only their own sons.[23]

Only in this way would the following be achieved:

> Provision was made for the aged till their death, the adult rendered serviceable, and the young capable of growth.[24]

In describing his wishes, Confucius said, "They are, in regard to the aged, to give them rest; in regard to friends, to show them

sincerity, and in regard to the young, to treat them tenderly."[25]
But how can the aged be given their rest? In addition to the
material comfort conferred on them when "men of fifty can wear
silk and men of seventy can eat meat," the principal requirements
are those of reverence and love. These two virtues—reverence and
love—make it possible for the aged to be taken care of both while
they live and after they die.

> They reverenced those whom they honored and loved those
> whom they regarded with affection. Thus they served the dead as
> they would have served them alive; they served the departed as they
> would have served them had they been continued among them.[26]
>
> Mêng Yi asked about filial piety. The Master said, "It is not
> being disobedient."
>
> Soon after, as Fan Ch'ih was driving him, the Master told him,
> "Mêng-sun asked me about filial piety, and I answered him, 'not
> being disobedient.' "
>
> Fan Ch'ih said, "What did you mean?" The Master replied,
> "That parents, when alive, should be served according to propriety;
> that, when dead, they should be buried according to propriety; and
> that they should be sacrificed to according to propriety."[27]

Filial piety includes reverence and love. The filial piety of
children is never sought by their parents; it is the expression of
natural instinct. It does not involve the existence of any conception
of right and obligation; rather it is the beginning of the search
for benevolence and its attainment. Hence, "affection to one's
parents, benevolence to the people and love to all things." Also:

> Filial piety and fraternal submission! are they not the root of
> benevolent actions?[28]

One received one's earliest education from one's parents. What
one learns from childhood frequently has an influence on one's
later life. So, the family system cannot be maintained without
family education. The sages and worthy men of our country have
adopted filial piety, parental kindness and fraternal love as the
main principles for the regulation of the family.

> As a son, he (King Wên) rested in filial piety. As a father, he
> rested in kindness.[29]

Though filial piety, parental kindness and fraternal love form
the center of family education, their objective is not merely the

regulation of the family, but the government of the State. It is true that benevolence to the people and love for all things begin with affection for parents; however, the answer to the question of how to serve the sovereign and elders is the extension of filial piety, parental kindness and fraternal love.

What is meant by "In order rightly to govern the State, it is necessary first to regulate the family" is this: It is not possible for one to teach others, while he cannot teach his own family. Therefore the ruler, without going beyond his family, completes the lessons for the State. There is filial piety; therewith the sovereign should be served. There is fraternal submission; therewith elders and superiors should be served. There is parental kindness; therewith the multitude should be treated.

In the "Announcement to K'ang" it is said, "Act as if you were watching over an infant." If (a mother) is really anxious about it, though she may not hit exactly the wants of her infant, she will not be far from doing so. There never had been a girl who learned to bring up a child, that she might afterwards marry.

From the loving example of one family a whole State becomes loving, and from its courtesies the whole State becomes courteous, while, from the ambition and perverseness of the One man, the whole State may be led to rebellious disorder; such is the nature of the influence. This verifies the saying "Affairs may be ruined by a single sentence; a kingdom may be settled by its One man."[30]

But how should a son serve his parents before he can be called filial? According to Confucius, mere material support, without the expression of reverence and affection, could not be called filial piety.

Tzŭ-yu asked about filial piety. The Master said, "The filial piety of nowadays means the support of one's parents. But dogs and horses likewise are able to do something in the way of support; without reverence, what is there to distinguish the one support given from the other?"[31]

Tzŭ-hsia asked about filial piety. The Master said, "The difficulty is with the countenance. If, when their elders have anything to attend to, the young take the toil of them, and if, when the young have wine and food, they set them before their elders, is this to be considered filial piety?"[32]

Mencius also said that the mere material support of one's

parents without spiritual consolation could not be called filial piety.

> Mencius said, "Of services, which is the greatest? The service of parents is the greatest. Of charges, which is the greatest? The charge of oneself is the greatest. That those who do not fail to keep themselves are able to serve their parents is what I have heard. But I have never heard of any, who, having failed to keep themselves, were able notwithstanding to serve their parents.
>
> "There are many services, but the service of parents is the root of all others. There are many charges, but the charge of oneself is the root of all others.
>
> "The philosopher Tsêng, in nourishing Tsêng Hsi, was always sure to have wine and meat provided. And when they were being removed, he would ask respectfully to whom he should give what was left. If his father asked whether there was anything left, he was sure to say, 'There is.' After the death of Tsêng Hsi, when Tsêng Yüan came to nourish Tsêng-tzŭ, he was always sure to have wine and meat provided. But when the things were being removed, he did not ask to whom he should give what was left, and if his father asked whether there was anything left, he would answer, 'No,'—intending to bring them in again. This was what is called 'nourishing the mouth and body.' We may call Tsêng-tzŭ's practice 'nourishing the will.'
>
> To serve one's parents as Tsêng-tzŭ served his, may be accepted as filial piety."[33]

Is invariable obedience filial piety? The answer is no. The habits and viewpoints of the aged and the young are frequently different. Of course, it is necessary for children to accommodate their parents at times, and in this way they can be said to be obedient and filial. But this is improper when their parents are in the wrong, and the children do not make any remonstrances. In making such remonstrances, however, they should adopt a gentle and respectful attitude, so as to influence their parents in such a way that the advice may be accepted.

> The Master said, "In serving his parents, a son may remonstrate with them, but gently; when he sees that they do not incline to follow his advice, he continues to show his reverence without countering them; and he feels sorry without murmuring."[34]

When the parents are at fault, children also have their responsibilities; so it is the duty of children to seek the rectification of their parents' mistakes. From the standpoint of the single whole formed by father and son, either side should not take up the position of a third party. It is never right for children to expose the faults of their parents publicly, just as it is always wrong for parents to do nothing but reproach their children for their mistakes. This would be neither filial piety on the one side nor parental kindness on the other.

> The Duke of Shêh informed Confucius, saying, "Among us here there are those who may be styled upright in their conduct and who, when their father has stolen a sheep, they will bear witness to the fact."
>
> Confucius said, "Among us, in our part of the country, those who are upright are different from this. The father conceals the misconduct of the son, and the son conceals the misconduct of the father. Uprightness is to be found in this."[35]
>
> Kun-sun Ch'ou said, "Why is it that the superior man does not himself teach his son?"
>
> Mencius replied, "The circumstances of the case forbid its being done. The teacher must inculcate what is correct. When he inculcates what is correct and his lessons are not practiced, he follows them up with being angry. When he follows them up with being angry, then, contrary to what should be, he offends his son. At the same time, the pupil says, 'My master inculcates on me what is correct, and he himself does not proceed in a correct path.' The result of this is that father and son are offended with each other. When father and son come to be offended with each other, the case is evil.
>
> "The ancients exchanged sons, and one taught the son of another.
>
> "Between father and son there should be no reproving admonitions to what is good. Such reproofs lead to alienation, and there is nothing more inauspicious than alienation."[36]

It is because the feeling between father and son should not be injured that a father should not serve as his son's formal teacher. A teacher can frequently reprove a pupil angrily, but this is inappropriate for a father.

On the other hand, if a son's education is neglected because of the anxiety to maintain the bond between father and son, it will not be to the son's benefit. Therefore, the exchange of sons for instruction is the best method.

Instruction in the mode of living and conduct, however, is a responsibility which the father should not shirk. In this type of education, his virtuous example is more important than verbal instruction. Frequently, one word uttered by a father or mother, or one act performed by either of them, constitutes an intangible influence which may profoundly affect a son all his life. This is why it is valuable for children to have worthy parents and elder brothers.

> Mencius said, "Those who keep the Mean train up those who do not, and those who have abilities train up those who do not, and hence men rejoice in having worthy fathers and elder brothers. If those who keep the Mean spurn those who do not and those who have abilities spurn those who do not, then the space between them— those so gifted and the ungifted—will not admit an inch."[37]

Confucius praised Min Tzŭ-Ch'ien for filial piety. His parents and brothers concurred, and others shared the same view. This indisputable fact was no mere accident.

> The Master said, "Filial indeed is Min Tzŭ-ch'ien! Other people say nothing different from the comments of his parents and brothers."[38]

Parents are concerned about their children; they love and protect them in every respect. What gives them the greatest anxiety is their children's health. Therefore, it is part of filial piety to pay attention to one's health and relieve parents somewhat of this anxiety.

> Mêng Wu asked about filial piety. The Master said, "Parents are anxious lest their children should be sick."[39]

Among the historic personages in our country's past, there was no man who could practice filial piety and fraternal love under more unfavorable circumstances than Shun, who did so despite the great unkindness of his parents and the most unusual lack of fraternal love in his younger brother. Because of this, Shun has always been viewed as a model of great filial piety. In answering questions put to him by his disciples T'ao Ying and Wan Chang, Mencius described in full the consideration Shun gave his father and younger brother after he became sovereign.

> T'ao Ying asked, saying, "Shun being sovereign and Kao Yao chief minister of justice, if Ku-sou had murdered a man, what would have been done in the case?"

Mencius said, "Kao Yao would simply have apprehended him.'

"But would not Shun have forbidden such a thing?"

"Indeed, how could Shun have forbidden it? Kao Yao had received the appointment from the proper source."

"In that case what would Shun have done?"

"Shun would have regarded abandoning the empire as throwing away a pair of worn-out sandals. He would privately have taken his father on his back and retired into concealment, living somewhere along the sea-coast. There he would have been all his life, cheerful and happy, forgetting the empire."[10]

If the father of a sovereign had committed murder, he would have been punished in the same way as a common man. So, Mencius thought that if Shun could not have met both his public and private obligations, the best course open to him would have been to retire and continue to do his filial duty.

Wan Chang said, "Hsiang made it his daily businese to slay Shun. When Shun was made sovereign, how was it that he only banished him?" Mencius said, "He raised him to be a prince. Some supposed that it was banishing him."

Wan-Chang said, "Shun banished the superintedent of works to Yu-chou; he sent away Huan-tou to the mountain Ch'ung; he slew the prince of San-miao in San-wei; and he killed Kun on the mountain Yü. When the crimes of those four were thus punished, the whole empire acquiesced; it was a cutting off of men who were destitute of benevolence. But Hsiang was of all men the most destitute of benevolence, and Shun raised him to be the prince of Yu-pi; of what crimes had the people of Yu-pi been guilty? Does a benevolent man really act thus? In the case of other men, he cut them off; in the case of his brother, he raised him to be a prince." Mencius replied, "A benevolent man does not lay up anger, nor cherish resentment against his brother, but only regards him with affection and love. Regarding him with affection, he wishes him to be honorable; regarding him with love, he wishes him to be rich. The appointment of Hsiang to be the prince of Yu-pi was to enrich and ennoble him. If while Shun was himself sovereign, his brother had been a common man, could he have been said to regard him with affection and love? "

Wan Chang said, "I venture to ask what you mean by saying that some supposed that it was a banishing of Hsiang?" Mencius replied, "Hsiang could do nothing in the State. The Son of Heaven appointed an officer to administer its government and to pay over its revenues to him. This treatment of him led to its being said that he was banished. How indeed could he be allowed the means of oppressing the people? Nevertheless Shun wished to be continually seeing him, and by this arrangement, he came incessantly to court, as is signified in that expression, 'He did not wait for the rendering of tribute to receive the prince of Yu-pi on the affairs of government.' "[41]

Thus, without harboring any resentment against Hsiang for his design to assassinate him, Shun raised his brother to nobility in a distant State. At the same time, he made arrangements for the country to be administered by another competent official who was instructed to remit to Hsiang all the revenues. In this way, not only were his brother's requirements completely met, but his brother had no opportunity to oppress the people. Such was the careful consideration Shun gave to this matter, and such was the reasonable way he treated his brother under the most distressing circumstances.

Wan Chang asked Mencius, saying, "it is said in the *Book of Songs*,

'In marrying a wife, how ought a man to proceed?
He must inform his parents.'

If the rule be indeed as here expressed, no man ought to have illustrated it so well as Shun. How was it that Shun's marriage took place without his informing his parents?" Mencius replied, "If he had informed them, he would not have been able to marry. That male and female should dwell together is the greatest of human relations. If Shun had informed his parents, he must have made void this greatest of human relations, thereby incurring their resentment. On this account he did not inform them."

Wan Chang said, "As to Shun's marrying without informing his parents, I have heard your instructions; but how was it that Emperor Yao gave his daughters as wives without informing Shun's parents?" Mencius said, "The emperor also knew that if he had informed them, he could not have married his daughters to him."

Wan Chang said, "His parents set Shun to repair a granary, to which, the ladder having been removed, Ku-sou set fire. They also made him dig a well. He got out, but they, not knowing that, proceeded to cover it up. Hsiang said, 'Of the scheme to cover up the capital-forming prince, the merit is all mine. Let my parents have his oxen and sheep. Let them have his storehouses and granaries. His shield and spear shall be mine. His lute shall be mine. His bow shall be mine. His two wives I shall make attend for me to my bed.'

Hsiang then went away into Shun's palace, and there was Shun on his couch playing on his lute. Hsiang said, 'I am come simply because I was thinking anxiously about you.' At the same time he blushed deeply. Shun said to him, 'There are all my officials:—do you undertake the government of them for me.' I do not know whether Shun was ignorant of Hsiang's wishing to kill him." Mencius answered, "How could he be ignorant of that? But when Hsiang was sorrowful, he was also sorrowful; when Hsiang was joyful, he was also joyful."

Chang said, "In that case, then, did not Shun rejoice hypocritically?" Mencius replied, "No. Formerly someone sent a present of a live fish to Tzŭ-ch'an of Chêng. Tzŭ-ch'an ordered his pond-keeper to keep it in the pond, but that officer cooked it and reported the execution of his commission, saying, 'When I first let it go, it appeared distressed. In a little while it seemed to be somewhat at ease, and then it swam away joyfully.' Tzŭ-ch'an said, 'It had got into its element! It had got into its element!' The pond-keeper then went out and said, 'Who calls Tzŭ-ch'an a wise man? After I had cooked and eaten the fish, he says, "It had got into its element! It had got into its element!," Thus a superior man may be imposed on by what seems to be as it ought to be, but he cannot be entrapped by what is contrary to the right principle. Hsiang came in the way in which the love of his elder brother would have made him come; therefore Shun sincerely believed him and rejoiced. What hypocrisy was there?"[42]

Ordinarily, when the father is kind, the son is filial; and when the elder brother is fraternal, the younger brother is respectful. But there are exceptions to the rule. For example, Shun was extremely filial when his father was extremely unkind, and he was extremely fraternal when his younger brother was extremely disrespectful. Another example was given by Confucius, namely that of Chung-kung, who was a worthy man though his father was an evil-doer.

> The Master, speaking of Chung-kung, said, "If the calf of a brindled cow be red and horned, although men may not wish to use it, would the spirits of the mountains and rivers put it aside?"[43]

The meaning as well as examples of filial piety are found throughout the *Four Books*. The full essence and extensive usefulness of this virtue are further stated in the *Book of Filial Piety*. With regard to what is unfilial, Mencius made it abundantly clear in his answer to a question raised by Kung-tu about K'uang

Chang, who was alleged to be unfilial, but whom Mencius defended. From this discussion, we can easily infer what filial piety is.

> The disciple Kung-tu said, "Throughout the whole empire everybody pronounces K'uang Chang unfilial. But you, Master, keep company with him, and moreover treat him with politeness. I venture to ask why you do so."
>
> Mencius replied, "There are five things which are pronounced in the common usage of the age to be unfilial. The first is laxness in the use of a man's four limbs, without attending to the nourishment of his parents. The second is gambling and chess-playing and being fond of wine, without attending to the nourishment of his parents. The third is being fond of goods and money and selfishly attached to his wife and children, without attending to the nourisment of his parents. The fourth is following the desires of his ears and eyes, so as to bring his parents to disgrace. The fifth is being fond of bravery, fighting and quarreling so as to endanger his parents. Is Chang guilty of any one of these things?
>
> "Now between Chang and his father there arose disagreement, he, the son, reproving his father, to urge him to what was good.
>
> "To urge one another to what is good by reproofs is the way of friends. But such urging between father and son is the greatest injury to the kindness, which should prevail between them.
>
> "Moreover, did not Chang wish to have in his family the relationships of husband and wife, child and mother? But because he had offended his father and was not permitted to approach him, he sent away his wife and drove forth his son, and all his life receives no cherishing attention from them. He settled it in his mind that if he did not act in this way, his would be one of the greatest of crimes. Such and nothing more is the case of Chang."[44]

Of the five things which are regarded as unfilial, as stated above, only the fifth, "being fond of bravery, fighting and quarreling so as to endanger his parents," needs further elucidation. When a man is prone to fight with others, he is liable to injure himself and even get killed, thus depriving his parents of the benefit of his sustenance which is unfilial in the first instance. Then, if he should kill another person, it is natural that the bereaved children would take revenge by killing his parents in return. Thus, the lives of his parents might be endangered. If they should be killed because of their son's combativeness, it would be tantamount to the slaughter of his own parents. How unfilial this would be!

Mencius said, "From this time forth I know the heavy consequences of killing a man's near relations. When a man kills another's father, the other will kill his father; when a man kills another's elder brother, that other will kill his elder brother. So he does not himself indeed do the act, but there is only an interval between him and it."[15]

In his reply to a query of Fan Ch'ih, Confucius made the same observation as Mencius. Since the wise are free from perplexities, he who has delusions is unwise.

Fan Ch'ih, rambling with the Master under the trees about the rain altars, said, "I venture to ask how to exalt virtue, to correct cherished evil and to discover delusions.

The Master said, "Truly a good question!...For a day's anger to disregard one's own life and involve that of his parents; is not this a case of delusion?"[16]

In short, filial piety toward one's parents while they are living should include (1) not only love, but also reverence; (2) not only material support, but spiritual consolation; (3) the elimination of all bad habits, so as not to affect one's parents as a result of one's own humiliation or injury; (4) care of one's own health, so as not to cause one's parents any anxiety; and (5) remonstrances to parents with gentleness if there is disagreement with them.

After the death of one's parents, what should be considered filial piety?

Mencius said, "...The philospher Tsêng said, 'When parents are alive, they should be served according to propriety; when they are dead, they should be buried according to propriety; and they should be sacrificed to according to propriety—this may be called filial piety.' "[17]

The Master said, "...Thus they served the dead as they would have served them alive; they served the departed as they would have served them had they been continued among them. This was the highest form of filial piety."[18]

Tsêng Hsi, Tsêng-tzǔ's father, was fond of sheep-dates, a sweet and precious fruit. When he was alive, Tsêng-tzǔ often offered this fruit to him. After his death, Tsêng-tzǔ could not bear to eat the fruit, because he was reminded of his father whenever he saw it. This unlimited affection for his father was a genuine expression of filial piety. In the Western industrial and commercial society where only materialsm and realism are stressed and there is less regard for human sentiments, it may be difficult to make this last passage well understood.

> Tsêng Hsi was fond of sheep-dates, and his son, the philosopher Tsêng, could not bear to eat sheep-dates.
>
> Kung-sun Ch'ou asked, saying, "Which is best, minced meat and broiled meat or sheep-dates?" Mencius said, "Minced and broiled meat, to be sure." Kung-sun Ch'ou went on, "Then why did the philosopher Tsêng eat minced and broiled meat and would not eat sheep-dates?" Mencius answered, "For minced and broiled meat there is a common liking, while that for sheep-dates was peculiar. We avoid the name, but do not avoid the surname. The surname is common; the name is peculiar."[49]

The importance attached to burial and sacrifices is based on the same principle: it is a reminder that one should not forget one's origins or the favors one has received and that affection does not live and die with the body, for it is eternal and inexhaustible. That is what Tsêng-tzŭ meant in the following passage:

> The philosopher Tsêng said, "Let there be a careful attention to perform the funeral rites to parents, and let there be sacrifices to ancestors long after their death—then the virtue of the people will tend to be pure."[50]

The death of parents marks the end of the son's service to them while alive and the beginning of his service to them after their lives have ended. It is not uncommon for children to feel the inadequacies in their service to their parents during their lifetime should be made up, if possible, by service to them after their deaths. That is why the performance of funeral rites is called "the great thing."

> Mencius said, "The nourishment of parents when living is not sufficient to be accounted the great thing. It is only in the performance of obsequies when dead that we have what can be considered the great thing."[51]
>
> Mencius said, "...In discharging the funeral duties to parents, men indeed are constrained to do their utmost."[52]
>
> The philosopher Tsêng said, "I heard this from our Master:

'Men do not show what is in them to the full, unless it is in mourning for their parents.' "[53]

Tzŭ-yu said, "Mourning, having been carried to the utmost degree of grief, should stop with that."[54]

Formerly, the period of mourning for parents was set at three years. This rule dated back to the three ancient dynasties of Hsia, Shang and Chou, and it applied to all people from the sovereign on down. The origin of the rule was probably the statement that "it is not till a child is three yeors old that it leaves the arms of its parents." It was perhaps to show some appreciation of parental kindness that the rule was adopted. On this subject, Confucius made the following explanations:

Tzŭ-chang said, "In the *Book of History* it is said, 'Kao-tsung, while observing the usual imperial mourning, was for three years without speaking!' What does this mean?"

The Master said, "Why must Kao-tsung be referred to as an example of this? The ancients all did so. When the sovereign died, the officials all attended to their several duties, taking instructions from the prime minister for three years."[55]

Tsai Wo asked about the three years' mourning for parents, saying, "One year is long enough. If the superior man abstains for three years from the observances of propriety, those observances will be quite lost. If for three years he abstains from music, music will be ruined.

"Within a year the old grain is exhausted and the new grain has sprung up, and, in procuring fire by friction, we go through all the changes of wood for that purpose. After a complete year the mourning may stop."

The Master said, "If you were, after a year, to eat good rice and wear embroidered clothes, would you feel at ease?" "I should," replied Wo.

The Master said, "If you can feel at ease, do it. But a superior man, during the whole period of mourning, does not enjoy pleasant food which he may eat, nor derive pleasure from music which he may hear. He also does not feel at ease, if he is comfortably lodged. Therefore he does not do what you propose. But now you feel at ease and may do it."

Tsai Wo then went out, and the Master said, "This shows Yü's want of virtue. It is not till a child is three years old that it leaves the arms of its parents. And the three years' mourning is universally observed throughout the empire. Has Yü got three years' love for his parents?"[55]

The Master said, "Was King Wên not the only man who had no cause for grief? His father was King Chi and his son was King Wu. His father laid the foundations of his dignity, and his son transmitted it.

"King Wu continued the enterprise of King T'ai, King Chi and King Wên. Once he buckled on his armor, he got possession of the empire. He did not lose the distinguished personal reputation which he had throughout the empire. His dignity was the imperial throne. His riches were the possession of all within the four seas. After his death his spirit was sacrificed to in the temple, and his descendants maintained the sacrifice to him.

"It was in his old age that King Wu received the appointment to the throne, and the Duke of Chou completed the virtuous course of Kings Wên and Wu. He carried up the title of king to T'ai and Chi and sacrificed to all the former dukes above them with the imperial ceremonies. And this rule he extended to the princes of the empire, the great officials, the scholars and the common people. If the father were a great official and the son a scholar, then the burial was that due to a great official and the sacrifices that due to a scholar. If the father were a scholar and the son a great official then the burial was that due to a scholar and the sacrifice that due to a great official. The one year's mourning was made to extend only to the great officials, but the three years' mourning extended to the Son of Heaven. In the mourning for a father or mother, he allowed no difference between the noble and the mean."[57]

When Duke Ting of T'êng died, the crown prince sent Jan Yu to Tsou to ask Mencius about the funeral ceremonies. Mencius replied that the three years' mourning should be applied. Ruling out all objections, the crown prince observed this period of mourning and won praise from all sides. The crown prince said, "It is so. The matter does indeed depend on me," an illustration of the statement, "In discharging the funeral duties to parents, men indeed are constrained to do their utmost."

When Duke Ting of T'êng died, the (crown) prince said to Jan Yu, "Formerly Mencius spoke with me in Sung, and in my mind I have never forgotten his words. Now, alas! this great duty to my father devolves upon me; I wish to send you to ask the advice of Mencius, and then to proceed to its various services."

Jan Yu accordingly proceeded to Tsou and consulted Mencius. Mencius said, "Is this not good? In discharging the funeral duties to parents, men indeed are constrained to do their utmost. The philosopher Tsêng said, 'When parents are alive, they should be served according to propriety; when they are dead, they should be buried according to propriety; and they should be sacrificed to according to propriety—this may be called filial piety.' The ceremonies to be observed by the princes I have not learned, but I have heard these points: that the three years' mourning, the garment of coarse cloth with its lower edge even, and the eating of congee were equally prescribed by the three dynasties and binding on all, from the sovereign to the mass of the people."

Jan Yu reported the execution of his mission, and the prince determined that the three years' mourning should be observed. His aged relatives and the body of the officials did not wish that it should be so, and said, "The former princes of Lu. that State which has also descended from the same family with ours, have, none of them, observed this practice, neither have any of our own former princes observed it. For you to act contrary to their example is not proper. Mereover, the books say 'In the observances of mourning and sacrifice, ancestors are to be followed.' " The prince said, "We have received some fresh advice." He said again to Jan Yu, "Hitherto I have not given myself to the pursuit of learning, but have found my pleasure in horsemanship and sword-exercise, and now I don't come up to the wishes of my aged relatives and the officials. I am afraid I may not be able to discharge my duty in the great business that I have entered on; do you again consult Mencius for me."

On this, Jan Yu went again to Tsou and consulted Mencius. Mencius said, "It is so, but he may not seek a remedy in others, but only in himself. Confucius said, 'When a prince dies, his successor entrusts the administration to the prime minister. He sips the congee. His face is of deep black. He approaches the place of mourning and weeps. Of all the officials and inferior ministers there is not one who will presume not to join in the lamentation, he setting them this example. What the superior loves, his inferiors will be found surely to exceed it. The relation between supeirors and inferiors is like that between the wind and grass. The grass must bend when the wind blows npon it. The business depends on the prince."

Jan Yu returned with this answer to his commission, and the prince said, "It is so. The matter does indeed depend on me." So, for five months he dwelt in the shed, without issuing an order or a caution. All the officials and his relatives said, "He may be said to understand the ceremonies." When the time of interment arrived, they came from all quarters of the State to witness it. Those who had come to condole with him were greatly pleased with the deep dejection of his countenance and the mournfulness of his wailing and weeping.[58]

When King Hsüan of Ch'i wished to curtail the period of mourning, Mencius observed that the three-year period was one in which the filial son could do the utmost to show his grief; it was not an opportunity to show off to others. He thought that longer or shorter periods represented the depth of one's affection, a matter which should be decided by oneself without interference. However, in the case of a ruler, it would have been improper for him to alter the ancient system, for in that case, "what the superior loves, the inferiors will surely be found to exceed it." In the end, the shorter period of mourning might have deteriorated to no mourning at all, thus lessening the purity of social morality.

> King Hsüan of Ch'i wanted to shorten the period of mourning. Kung-sun Ch'ou said, "To have one whole year's mourning is better than doing away with it altogether."
> Mencius said, "That is just as if there were someone twisting the arm of his elder brother and you were merely to say to him, 'Gently, gently, if you please.' Your only course should be to teach such a man filial piety and fraternal duty."
> At that time, the mother of one of the king's sons had died, and his tutor asked for him that he might be allowed to observe a few months' mourning. Kung-sun Ch'ou asked, "What do you say of this?"
> Mencius replied, "This is a case where the party wishes to complete the whole period, but finds it impossible to do so. The addition of even a single day is better than not mourning at all. I spoke of the case where there was no hindrance and the party neglected the thing itself."[59]

The origin of the use of both the inner and outer coffins for burial was discussed in detail by Mencius. The primary aim was to prevent the body of a dead parent from being eaten by birds and animals and from being bitten by gnats and flies. It was an attempt by the son to do his utmost in such matters. It was also in compliance with the principle contained in the statement regarding the service of the departed as if they were still among us.

> Mencius said, "...And, in the most ancient times, there were some who did not inter their parents. When their parents died,

they took them up and threw them into some water-channel. Afterwards, when passing by them, they saw foxes and wildcats devouring them and flies and gnats biting at them. The perspiration started out upon their foreheads, and they looked away, unable to bear the sight. It was not on account of other people that this perspiration flowed. The emotions of their hearts affected their faces and eyes, and instantly they went home, and came back with baskets and spades and covered the bodies. If the covering was thus indeed right, you may see that the filial son and virtuous man, in interring in a decent manner their parents, acts according to a proper rule."[60]

Later, when the system of propriety was more complete, the thickness of the inner and outer coffins and the quality of the wood used came under more detailed regulation. In replying to a question put by Ch'ung Yü, Mencius said that the choice of inner and outer coffins should not be for the sake of beauty, but for the expression of affection, due consideration always being given to the law and the cost, with the ultimate objective of preventing the contamination of the body by the earth and assuring the offspring of their peace of mind. Of course, it is expected that every son will unstintingly do whatever his finances permit in burying his parents. And it is not uncommon for the friends of needy persons to take care of their burials. "When any of his (Confucius') friends died, if he had no relatives who could be depended on for the necessary offices, he would say, 'I will bury him.' "[61] How much more should be expected from a son when his parent dies? Hence, "the superior man will not for all the world be niggardly to his parents."

Mencius went from Ch'i to Lu to bury his mother. On his return to Ch'i he stopped at Ying, where Ch'ung Yü begged to put a question to him and said, "Formerly, in ignorance of my incompetency, you employed me to superintend the making of the coffin. As you were then pressed by the urgency of the business, I did not venture to put any question to you. Now, however, I wish to take the liberty to submit the matter. The wood of the coffin, it appeared to me, was too good."

Mencius replied. "Anciently, there was no rule for the size of either the inner or the outer coffin. In middle antiquity, the inner coffin was made seven inches thick, and the outer one in proportion to it. This was done by all, from the sovereign to the common people, and not simply for the beauty of the appearance, but because they thus satisfied the natural feelings of their hearts.

"If prevented by statutory regulations from making their coffins in this way, men cannot have the feeling of pleasure. If they have not the money to make them in this way, they cannot have the feeling of pleasure. When they were not prevented and had the money the ancients all used this style. Why should I alone not do so?

"And, moreover, is there no satisfaction to the natural feelings of a man in preventing the earth from getting near to the bodies of his dead?

"I have heard that the superior man will not for all the world be niggardly to his parents."[62]

With regard to the burial of his parents, Mencius, in his conversation with the Mohist, Yi Chih, criticized Mohism for its theory of universal love and the equality of all men, irrespective of age or relation. Mencius regarded this theory as impractical and contrary to human relationships.

The Mohist, Yi Chih, sought through Hsü P'i to see Mencius. Mencius said, "I indeed wish to see him, but at present I am still unwell. When I am well, I will myself go and see him. He need not come here again."

Next day, Yi Chih again sought to see Mencius. Mencius said, "Today I am able to see him. But if I do not correct his errors, the true principles will not be fully evident. Let me first correct him. I have heard that Yi is a Mohist. Now Mo considers that in the regulation of funeral matters a spare simplicity should be the rule. Yi thinks with Mo's doctrines to change the customs of the empire: is it not because he regards anything contrary as not honorable? Notwithstanding his views, Yi buried his parents in a sumptuous manner, and so he served them in the way which his doctrines discountenance."

The disciple Hsü informed Yi of these remarks. Yi said, "Even according to the Confucianists, the ancients acted towards the people 'as if they were watching over an infant.' What does this expression mean? To me it sounds that we are to love all without difference of degree: but the manifestation of love must begin with our parents." Hsü reported this reply to Mencius, who said, "Now, does Yi really think that a man's affection for the child of his brother is merely like his affection for the infant of a neighbor? He does not realize that the above expression has its special meaning: that if an infant crawling about is about to fall into a wall, it is no crime in the infant. Moreover, Heaven gives birth to creatures in such a way that they have one root, and Yi makes them to have two roots. This is the cause of his error.

"And, in the most ancient times, there were some who did not inter their parents. When their parents died, they took them up and threw them into some water-channel. Afterwards, when passing by them, they saw foxes and wildcats devouring them and flies and gnats biting at them. The perspiration started out upon their foreheads, and they looked away, unable to bear the sight. It was not on account of other people that this perspiration flowed. The emotions of their hearts affected their faces and eyes, and instantly they went home, and came back with baskets and spades and covered the bodies. If the covering them thus was indeed right, you may see that the filial son and virtuous man, in interring in a decent manner their parents, act according to a proper rule."

The disciple Hsü informed Yi of what Mencius had said. Yi was thoughtful for a short time, and then said, "He has instructed me."[33]

Sacrifices are aimed at the remembrance of those who are loved and reverenced. They take place on anniversaries of the birth and death of the deceased. The rites performed belong to the realm of emotion and faith and should not be subjected to rational criticism. When Western missionaries first arrived in China, they did not understand the depth of Chinese culture and did everything possible to attack ancestor worship as a form of superstition. They claimed, though, that prayer was not a form of superstition. The only result was that obstacles were placed in the way of preaching religion. More than half a century later, thanks to the wisdom of Pope Pius XII, permission was given to Chinese Christians on December 8, 1939, to participate in sacrifices and bow before the deceased or their tablets. Thereafter this hindrance to the preaching of the Christian religion was finally removed. The importance attached to sacrifices by Confucius can be seen in the following passages:

He sacrificed to the spirits of ancestors, as if they were present. He sacrificed to the spirits of gods, as if they were present. The Master said, "I consider my not being present at the sacrifice as if I did not sacrifice."[34]

The Master said, "...By the ceremonies of the sacrifices to Heaven and Earth they (King Wu and the Duke of Chou) served God, and by the ceremonies of the ancestral temple they sacrificed to their ancestors. He who understands the ceremonies of the sacrifices to Heaven and Earth and the meaning of the several sacrifices to ancestors would find the government of a kingdom as easy as to look into his palm!"[35]

Confucius seldom referred to ghosts and spirits, but the following passage is found in the *Doctrine of the Mean:*

> The Master said, "How abundantly spiritual beings display the powers that belong to them!
>
> "We look for them, but do not see them; we listen to, but do not hear them; yet they enter into things, and there is nothing without them.
>
> "They cause all the people in the empire to fast and purify themselves and array themselves in their richest dresses, in order to attend at their sacrifices. Then, like overflowing water, they seem to be over the heads, and on the right and left, of their worshipers.
>
> "It is said in the *Book of Songs,* 'The approaches of the spirits, you cannot surmise—and can you treat them with indifference?'
>
> "Such is the manifestation of what is minute! Such is the impossibility of repressing the outgoings of sincerity!"[66]

Confucius never spoke to his disciples about extraordinary things, feats of strength, disorder or spiritual beings. When he was asked about sacrifices, he replied that he did not know. These were subjects that he found difficult indeed.

> The subjcts on which the Master did not talk were: extraordinary things, feats of strength, disorder and spiritual beings.[67]
>
> Someone asked the meaning of the great sacrifice. The Master said, "I do not know. He who knows its meaning would find it as eary to govern the empire as to look on this"—pointing to his palm.[68]

Things which cannot be seen or heard cannot be easily known. Since there is no real knowledge of them, it is not easy to talk about them. To regard what is unknown as known is pretense, the result being deception of oneself as well as others. So what Confucius said in the following passage represents not only the wisest attitude possible, but is also in compliance with the scientific spirit.

> The Master said, "Yu, shall I teach you what knowledge is? When you know a thing, to hold that you know it; and when you

do not know a thing, to allow that you do not know it—this is knowledge."[69]

Sacrifices are intended to express devotion to the memory of the dead and the inexhaustible feeling toward them. Whether the deceased are spiritual beings is another question. If a son did not serve his parents according to propriety while they were alive, and if he tries to make up for it by offering sacrifices according to propriety after their deaths, it is an empty, formal gesture without substance. It is no remedy for the neglect of filial piety.

> Chi Lu asked about serving the spirits of the dead. The Master said, "While you are not able to serve men, how can you serve their spirits?" Chi Lu added, "I venture to ask about death." He was answered, "While you do not know life, how can you know about death?"[70]

Mencius defined the "spirit-man" as follows when he discussed the different classes of men:

> Hao-shêng Pu-hai asked, saying, "What sort of man is Yüeh-chêng?" Mencius replied, "He is a good man, a truthful man."
>
> "What do you mean by 'a good man,' 'a truthful man?'"
>
> The reply was, "A man who commands our liking is what is called a good man. He whose goodness is part of himself is what is called a truthful man. He whose goodness has been filled up is what is called a beautiful man. He whose completed goodness is brightly displayed is what is called a great man. When this great man exercises a transforming influence, he is what is called a sage. When the sage is beyond our knowledge, he is what is called a spirit-man.
>
> "Yüeh-chêng is between the two first categories and below the four last."[71]

In other words, though a sage is great and exercises a transforming influence, he is still knowable, and his character can be inferred. But if a sage becomes so inestimable that he assumes the character of a spirit-man, he is outside the pale of knowledge. And many of those things whose principles we can explain today by means of our scientific knowledge and method were once regarded as spiritual. This was implied by Dr. Sun Yatsen when he said, "The scope of the universe is the scope of wisdom."

So, what is outside the pale of wisdom has been regarded as

pertaining to the universe, the sphere of the spirit. That sphere is unlimited, and although the scope of wisdom is widening all the time and absorbing the sphere of the spirit, the progress made has been limited (because $8 - x$ is still 8). The distance to be traveled is still immense, and, being inexhaustible, it will always be there. To show our respect for true knowledge, which is still unattainable, we must not be indifferent. Hence in answering Fan Ch'ih's question, Confucius said:

> "...while respecting spiritual beings, to keep aloof from them may be called wisdom."[72]

Not to disdain what is unknown, not to reach arbitrary decisions, but to strive incessantly to pursue knowledge is exactly what the scientific spirit is.

The correct attitude toward things, men and learning is not to forget the past nor to be indifferent to the future. The same thing is true of the attitude of children toward their deceased parents. It is said, "When parents are alive, they should be served according to propriety; when they are dead, they should be buried according to propriety, and they should be sacrificed to according to propriety. This may be called filial piety."[73]

To serve the aged who have died as if they are still alive is a consolation to the aged who are still living. Because of this, the aged love and protect the young all the more. As a result, "Provision was made for the aged till their death...and the young (rendered) capable of growth," and the continuation of human life is more effectively safeguarded. For everything in the world is relative, and each act contains its educational meaning. If a man is unfilial to his own parents but expects his children to be filial, he can never succeed because it is contrary to the principle that "one must be possessed of the good qualities, and then one may require them in others." Also, "one must not have the bad qualities in oneself, and then one may require that they shall not be in others."

A man who can be filial has reverence and love in his heart. He can make sacrifices, render service willingly, speak truthfully and act earnestly and reverently. He can practice his Way even in a barbarous country. Towards his brothers and sisters he can, of course, maintain the relations of fraternity and respectfulness.

Likewise, he can extend to his whole family and even to the government of his country the same principles he has applied in his dealings with different individuals,

> Someone addressed Confucius, saying, "Sir, why are you not engaged in the government?
> The Master said, "This is what the *Book of History* says about filial piety: 'Be filial, discharge your brotherly duties.' When these qualities are applied to government, this also constitutes the exercise of government. Why must one be in office?"[74]

If men can extend their fraternal love to all, then all are brothers within the four seas.

> Ssŭ-ma Niu, full of anxiety, said, "Other men all have their brothers, I only have not."
> Tzŭ-hsia said to him, "There is the following saying which I have heard: 'Death and life have their determined destiny; riches and honors depend upon Heaven.'
> "Let the superior man never fail reverentially to order his own conduct and let him be respectful to others and observant of propriety—then all within the four seas will be his brothers. Why should the superior man be distressed because he has no brothers?"[75]

A man must be filial and fraternal; only thus is the root firmly established. Otherwise, he would not be able to walk in the right path nor would his wife and children do the same. And in that case, how could he rectify others? So, the first requisite for the regulation of the family is emphasis on filial piety and fraternal love.

> Mencius said, "If a man himself does not walk in the right path, it will not be walked in even by his wife and children. If he orders men according to what is not the right way, he will not be able to get the obedience of even his wife and children."[76]

In a Western family, love between husband and wife is of first importance. On the other hand, while a husband and wife may stay together, they can also be divided and the love between them is something which can fluctuate. Especially in an industrial and commercial society where equality of rights and obligations is emphasized and individualism is highly developed, a married couple are like friends. Thus, their family ties can be dissolved at any time. If we use this kind of family relationship as the foundation of love and affection, it is no different from the construction of a house on a sandbank which is in constant danger of collapse. Surely, the love between husband and wife offers no comparison to filial piety, an affection which endures and which can be developed *ad infinitum.*

Moreover, a man can be without brothers and sisters and may not marry, but he must have parents. So, filial piety is the most stable foundation of all love. Our ancient sages have taught us that to order well our country, we must first regulate our families, and in order to regulate our families, we must first attend to filial piety and fraternal love because these are fundamental principles which should never be overlooked.

As far as the country is concerned, what is the influence of this basic virtue, filial piety? Let us give some examples:

(1) Relation to Population Policy. When there is filial piety, no one is willing to be without posterity. In this way, the population of a country will, naturally, increase in appropriate numbers at all times.

(2) Relation to Cultural Policy. When there is filial piety, everyone will seek to carry on past tradition, and since there is no danger of interrupting the unfinished work, continuity of a country's culture is a foregone conclusion.

(3) Relation to Educational Policy. Since the cultivation of the Way is instruction, the root of the Way lies in benevolence, and benevolence is rooted in filial piety and fraternal love; filial piety is indeed the foundation of education. Though religious faith, in name, is not involved, it is ever-present in fact.

(4) Relation to Social Policy. The requirements of society are order, law-abiding conduct and mutual assistance. With filial piety, families are regulated, and with the regulation of all families, society is sure to be stabilized. Hence, "wishing to order well their States, they (the ancients) first regulated their families."

Footnotes for Chapter VII

1. *Analecs,* Bk. IX, Ch. XVII.
2. *Works of Mencius,* Bk. V, Pt. I, Ch. II.
3. *Idib.,* Bk. III, Pt. I, Ch. IV.
4. *Ibid.,* Bk. VI, Pt. II, Ch. X.
5. *Doctrine of the Mean,* Ch. XII. *Vide supra,* p 229.

6. *Doctrine of the Mean*, Ch. XV.
7. *Works of Mencius*, Bk. IV, Pt. I, Ch. VIII.
8. *Great Learning*, Com., Ch. IX.
9. *Works of Mencius*, Bk. V, Pt. I, Ch. I.
10. *Ibid.*
11. *Doctrine of the Mean*, Ch. XVII. *Vide supra*, p. 62.
12. *Works of Mencius*, Bk. IV, pt. I, Ch. XXVIII.
13 .*Ibid.*, Bk. VI, Pt. II, Ch. III.
14. *Ibid.*, Bk. V, Pt. I, Ch. I. *Vide supra*, pp. 379.
15. *Analects*, Bk. IV, Ch. XXI.
16. *Ibid.*, Ch. XIX.
17. *Works of Mencius*, Bk. IV, Pt. I, Ch. XXVI.
18. *Doctrine of the Mean*, Ch. XIX.
19. *Analects*, Bk. I, Ch. XI.
20. *Ibid.*, Bk. IV, Ch. XX.
21. *Ibid.*, Bk. XIX, Ch. XVIII.
22. *Works of Mencius*, Bk. IV, Pt. II, Ch. XXX.
23. Chapter on "Li Yün," *Li Chi*. Chai, *The Humanist Way in Ancient China*, p. 338; Lin, *Wisdom of Confucius*, p. 227; Legge, *Sacred Books of China*, Vol. III, p. 365.
24. *Ibid.*,
25. *Analects*, Bk. V, Ch. XXV.
26. *Doctrine of the Mean*, Ch. XIX. *Vide supra*, p. 384.
27. *Analects*, Bk. II, Ch. V.
28. *Ibid.*, Bk. I, Ch. II. *Vide supra*, p. 87.
29. *Great Learning*, Com., Ch. III.
30. Ibid., Ch. IX. *Vide supra*, p. 378.
31. *Analects*, Bk. II, Ch. VII.
32. *Ibid.*, Ch. VIII.
33. *Works of Mencius*, Bk. IV. Pt. I, Ch. XIX.
34. *Analects*, Bk. IV, Ch. XVIII.
35. *Ibid.*, Bk. XIII, Ch. XVIII.
36. *Works of Mencius*, Bk. IV, Pt. I, Ch. XVIII.
37. *Ibid.*, Bk. IV, Pt. II, Ch. VII.
38. *Analects*, Bk. XI, Ch. IV.
39. *Ibid.*, Bk. II, Ch. VI.
40. *Works of Mencius*, Bk. VII, Pt. I, Ch. XXXV.
41. *Ibid.*, Bk. V, Pt. I, Ch. III.
42. *Ibid.*, Ch. II.
43. *Analects*, Bk. VI, Ch. IV.
44. *Works of Mencius*, Bk. IV, Pt. II. Ch. XXX. *Vide supra*, p. 386.
45. *Works of Mencius*, Bk. VIII, Pt. II, Ch. VII.
46. *Analects*, Bk. XIII, Ch.XXI. *Vide supra*, p. 29.
47. *Works of Mencius*, Bk. III, Pt. I, Ch. II.
48. *Doctrine of the Mean*, Ch. XIX. *Vide supra*, pp. 384, 387.
49. *Works of Mencius*, Bk. VII, Pt. II, Ch. XXXVI.
50. *Analects*, Bk. I, Ch.IX.
51. *Works of Mencius*, Bk. IV, Pt. II, Ch. XIII.

52. *Ibid.*, Bk. III, Pt. I, Ch. II.
53. *Analects*, Bk. XIX, Ch. XVII.
54. *Ibid.*, Ch. XIV.
55. *Ibid.*, Bk. XIV, Ch. XLIII.
56. *Ibid.*, Bk. XVII, Ch. XXI.
57. *Doctrine of the Mean*, Ch. XVIII.
58. *Works of Mencius*, Bk. III, Pt. I, Ch. II.
59. *Ibid.*, Bk. VII, Pt. I, Ch. XXXIX.
60. *Ibid.*, Bk. III, Pt I, Ch. V.
61. *Analects*, Bk. X, Ch. XV.
62. *Works of Mencius*, Bk. II, pt. II, Ch. VII.
63. *Ibid.*, Bk. III, Pt. I, Ch. V. *Vide supra*, pp. 401-402.
64. *Analects*, Bk. III, Ch. XIII. *Vide supra*, P. 302.
65. *Doctrine of the Mean*, Bk. XIX. *Vide supra*, p. 384.
66. *Doctrine of the Mean*, Ch. XVI.
67. *Analects*, Bk. VII, Ch. XX.
68. *Ibid.*, Bk. II, Ch. XVII.
69. *Ibid.*, Bk. III, Ch. XI.
70. *Ibid.*, Bk. XI, Ch. XI. *Vide supra*, p. 161.
71. *Works of Mencius*, Bk. VII, Pt. II, Ch. XXV. *Vide supra*. p. 263.
72. *Analects*, Bk. VI, Ch. XX.
73. *Works of Mencius*, Bk. III, Pt. I, Ch. II. *Vide supra*, p. 396.
74. *Analects*, Bk II, Ch. XXI.
75. *Ibid.*, Bk. XII, Ch. V. *Vide supra*, p. 61.
76. *Works of Mencius*, Bk. VII, Pt. II, Ch. IX.

CHAPTER VIII

The Government of the State

A. A Preliminary Word

It is said in the *Great Learning*, "The ancients who wished to illustrate illustrious virtue throughout the empire first ordered well their own States." Again, "One's State being rightly governed, the whole world is pacified." The State is to the empire as the individual is to the family. If its component parts are perfect, the whole cannot be other than perfect. This is called "giving attention to what is radical (derived from the root)."

> Mencius said, "People have this common saying: 'The empire, the State, the family.' The root of the empire is in the State. The root of the State is in the family. The root of the family is in the person.' "

Only by enlarging and illustrating virtue can the person be cultivated, the family regulated and the State well-ordered. The well-ordered state is the foundation of peace in the empire and in the world. For morality is the principle that governs the common existence and evolution of mankind, and all these entities—the world, the empire, the State, the family—are composed basically of individual persons. Before the happiness of mankind and the peace of the world can be attained, all persons must be able to (1) "illustrate illustrious virtue," (2) engage in daily personal renewal, (3) take delight in goodness without wearying of it, and (4) jointly advance toward the objective of perfection.

The government of a State is a complex matter, so it is important to grasp the main principles involved. This outline may be helpful:

B. The Nine Standard Rules for the Government of a State

The Master said, "...All who have the government of the empire with its States to attend to have nine standard rules to follow; viz., the cultivation of their own persons; the honoring of worthy men; affection towards their relatives; respect towards the great ministers; kind and considerate treatment of the whole body of officials; dealing with the mass of the people as children; encouraging the resort of all classes of artisans; indulgent treatment of men from a distance; and the kindly cherishing of the princes of the States.

"By the ruler's cultivation of his own person, the Way is established. By honoring worthy men, he is preserved from errors of judgment. By showing affection to his relatives, there is no grumbling nor resentment among his uncles and brethren. By respecting the great ministers, he is kept from errors in the practice of government. By kind and considerate treatment of the whole body of officials, they are led to make the most grateful return for his courtesies. By dealing with the mass of the people as his children, they are led to exhort one another to what is good. By encouraging the resort of all classes of artisans, his resources for expenditure are rendered ample. By indulgent treatment of men from a distance, they are brought to resort to him from all quarters. And by kindly cherishing the princes of the States, the whole empire is brought to revere him.

"Self-adjustment and purification, with careful regulation of his dress, and the not making a movement contrary to the rules of propriety—this is the way for a ruler to cultivate his person. Discarding slanderers and keeping himself from the seductions of beauty; making light of riches and giving honor to virtue—this is the way for him to encourage worthy men. Giving them places of honor and large emolument and sharing with them in their likes and dislikes—this is the way for him to encourage his relatives to love him. Giving them numerous officials to discharge their orders and commissions—this is the way for him to encourage the great ministers. According to them a generous confidence and making their emoluments large—this is the way for him to encourage the body of officials.

Employing them only at the proper times and making the imposts light—this is the way to encourage the people. By daily examinations and monthly trials and by making their rations in accordance with their labors—this is the way to encourage the classes of artisans. To escort them on their departure and meet them on their coming; to commend the good among them and show compassion to the incompetent—this is the way to treat diligently men from a distance. To restore families whose line of succession has been broken and to revive States that have been extinguished; to reduce to order States that are in confusion and support those which are in peril; to have fixed times for their own reception at court and the reception of their envoys; to send them away with liberal gifts and welcome their coming with small contributions—this is the way to cherish the princes of the States.

"All who have to attend to the government of the empire with its States have the above nine standard rules. And there is only one means by which they are carried into practice."[2]

1. The Cultivation of the Person

With the cultivation of the person, the Way is established. And the person is cultivated by self-adjustment and purification, with careful regulation of one's dress.

Since all laws and orders in a monarchy emanate from the rules of a country, it goes without saying that the ruler must possess surpassing wisdom and courage; more, he must be a man of exemplary virtue so that he can merit the respect and confidence of the whole nation. When the ruler has these attributes, it can truly be said of him: "When he is looked at, there is not one among the people who does not respect him; when he speaks, there is not one among the people who does not believe him; and when he acts, there is not one among the people who is not delighted with him."

Since the sovereign is the symbol of virtue, he must adjust and purify himself as if he were fasting. He must regulate his dress carefully to show his dignity and respect. He must not make any move contrary to the rules of propriety. It is said, "If a man can for one day subdue himself and return to propriety, all under heaven will ascribe perfect virtue to him."[3]

The sovereign should rule his people with love (benevolence). If he loves his people without winning their love in return, if he rules them without gaining the objective of good government, if he treats them with politeness without seeing the compliment returned—then he should realize something is wrong. He should examine himself inwardly to see if he has failed in his practice of benevolence, wisdom and respect. For when a sovereign's person is correct, the people are easily ruled and the whole country will turn to him with recognition and submission.

> Mencius said, "If a man loves others and no responsive attachment is shown to him, let him turn inwards and examine his own benevolence. If he is trying to rule others and his government is unsuccessful, let him turn inwards and examine his wisdom. If he treats others politely and they do not return his politeness, let him turn inwards and examine his own feeling of respect.
>
> "When we do not, by what we do, realize what we desire, we must turn inwards and examine ourselves in every point. When a man's person is correct, the whole empire will turn to him with recognition and submission.
>
> "It is said in the *Book of Songs,*
>> 'Be always studious to be in harmony with the ordinances of God,
>> And you will obtain much happiness.' "[4]
>
> The Master said, "When rulers love to observe the rules of propriety, the people respond readily to the calls on them for service."[5]
>
> The Master said, "...If a superior loves propriety, the people will not dare not to be reverent. If he loves righteousness, the people will not dare not to submit to his example. If he loves good faith, the people will not dare not to be sincere."[3]

Why is it that when the sovereign's person is correct, the people will have confidence in him and submit to him? Quite simply, because virtue is best taught by example; only when a man has the good qualities in himself can he require them of others.

> Chi K'ang asked Confucius about government. Confucius replied, "To govern means to rectify. If you lead on the people with correctness, who will dare not to be correct?"[7]
>
> The Master said, "When a prince's personal conduct is correct, his government is effective without the issuing of orders. If his personal conduct is not correct, he may issue orders, but they will not be followed."[8]
>
> The Master said, "If a minister makes his own conduct correct, what difficulty will he have in assisting in government? If he cannot rectify himself, what has he to do with rectifying others?"[9]

> Mencius said, "...Let the prince be benevolent, and all his acts will be benevolent. Let the prince be righteous, and all his acts will be righteous."[10]

It goes without saying that during the age of monarchism the sovereign's words and actions were of the utmost importance. Yet today, when a president is elected by the people, the best (most virtuous) man does not always win. However, if he does win, he will lose his people's confidence quickly if he acts improperly. Obviously, on all levels the officials in his administration should be able to (1) perfect themselves morally and set a good example, (2) provide the people with meaningful leadership, (3) endure the hardships of stinging criticism and misunderstanding, (4) put in long hours of strenuous, diligent work, and (5) be incorruptible as well as dedicated to public service. If an administration conducts itself in this way, the people will readily trust it; at the same time thievery and disorder will not arise.

> Tzŭ-lu asked about government. The Master said, "Go before the people with your example, and be laborious in their affairs."
> He requested further instruction, and was answered, "Be not weary (in these things)."[11]
> Chi K'ang, distressed about the number of thieves in the State, inquired of Confucius how to do away with them. Confucius said, "If you, sir, were not covetous, although you should reward them to do it, they would not steal."[12]

Hence it is said, "With the cultivation of the person, the Way is established." Once the Way is established, the people will open their hearts to their ruler.

> ...by gaining the people, the kingdom is gained, and, by losing the people, the kingdom is lost.[13]
> In the "Announcement to K'ang" it is said, "The decree indeed may not always rest on us;" that is, goodness obtains the decree, and the want of confidence loses it.[14]

This indicates how important the cultivation of the person is to the government of a country. How can one be too careful? Hence it is said:

> From the Son of Heaven to the masses of the people, all must consider the cultivation of the person the root of everything besides.

It cannot be, when the root is neglected, that what should spring from it will be well ordered. It never has been the case that what was of great importance has been slightly cared for, and, at same time, that what was of slight importance has been greatly cared for.[15]

2. The Honoring of the Worthy

The ruler can avoid errors of judgment by honoring worthy men. By discarding slanderers, by guarding himself against the seductions of beauty, by making light of riches and giving honor to virtue—this is how he can encourage worthy men to help him make his administration a success.

The condition of a government depends not only on the wisdom of the sovereign, but also and especially on the loyalty and worthiness of his ministers. Therefore the ruler's first important task is to draw to him men of talent. For "...the administration of government lies in getting proper men," and "Let there be the men and the government will flourish; but without the men, their government decays and ceases." If the sovereign knows men and can place them properly so that "the worthy have their places and the capable exercise their functions," he can administer his government with ease.

However, a ruler cannot obtain worthy men just for the asking. Then what must he do? For one thing, he must be anxious to have their services. He must sincerely respect them for their worthiness and virtue. At the same time he must be broad-minded enough to accept their advice. Then when evil influences have been completely removed from the government—and only then—will worthy men come to the sovereign; in fact, they will come to him even from afar.

In the "Declaration of (the Duke of) Ch'in" it is said, "Let me have but one minister, plain and sincere, not pretending to other abilities, but with a simple, upright mind and great tolerance. When others have talent, he feels as if he had it himself; and, where he finds accomplished and perspicacious men, he loves them in heart and regards their words as if coming out of his own mouth, really showing himself able to bear and employ them—such a minister will be able to preserve my sons and grandsons and black-haired people, and benefits likewise to the kingdom may well be looked for from him. But if it be his character, when he finds men of ability, to be jealous and hate them; and, when he finds accomplished and perspicacious men, to oppose them and not allow their advancement, showing himself really not able to bear them— such a minister will not be able to protect my sons and grandsons and black-haired people; and may he not also be pronounced dangerous to the State?"

It is only the truly virtuous man who can send away such a man and banish him, driving him out among the barbarous tribes around, determined not to dwell along with him in the Middle Kingdom. This is in accordance with the saying, "It is only the truly virtuous man who can love or who can hate others."

To see men of worth and not be able to raise them to office; to raise them to office, but not to do so quickly—this is disrespectful. To see bad men and not be able to remove them; to remove them, but not to do so to a distance—this is a mistake.[16]

Mencius said, "If a ruler gives honor to worthy men and employs the able, so that offices shall all be filled by individuals of distinction and mark, then all the scholars of the empire will be pleased and wish to stand in his court."[17]

Otherwise the court would be devoid of good men, and even if the sovereign intended to provide good government, it would be impossible.

Mencius said, "If men of virtue and ability are not confided in, a State will become empty and void.

"Without the rules of propriety and distinctions of right, the high and low will be thrown into confusion.

"Without the great principles of government and their various business, there will not be wealth sufficient for the expenditure."[18]

How can a ruler show sincere respect to men of worth and talent? (a) By loving virtue and not flaunting his power. (b) By treating these men as friends—indeed, as teachers.

(a) Mencius said, "The virtuous monarchs of antiquity loved virtue and forgot their power. And shall an exception be made of the virtuous scholars of antiquity, that they did not do the same? They delighted in their own principles and were oblivious of the power of princes. Therefore, if kings and dukes did not show the utmost respect and observe all forms of ceremony, they were not permitted frequently to see them. If they thus could not even see them frequently, how much less could they get to employ them as ministers?"[19]

(b) Wan Chang said, "I venture to ask what it means not to see the princes." Mencius replied, "A scholar residing in the city is called 'a minister of the market-place and well,' and one residing in the country is called 'a minister of grass and plants.'" In both cases he is a common man, and it is the rule of propriety that common men who have not presented the introductory present and become ministers should not presume to have interviews with the prince."

Wan Chang said, "If a common man is called to perform any service, he goes and performs it; how is it that a scholar, when the prince, wishing to see him, calls him to his presence, refuses to go?" Mencius replied, "It is right to go and perform the service; it would not be right to go and see the prince."

"And," added Mencius, "on what account is it that the prince wishes to see the scholar?" "Because of his extensive information, or because of his worthiness," was the reply. "If because of his extensive information," said Mencius, "such a person is a teacher, and the sovereign would not call a teacher; how much less may any of the princes do so? If because of his worthiness, then I have not heard of anyone wishing to see a worthy person and calling him to his presence.

"During the frequent interviews of Duke Mu with Tzŭ-ssŭ, he one day said to him, 'Anciently, princes of a thousand chariots have yet been on terms of friendship with scholars; what do you think of such an intercourse?' Tzŭ-ssŭ was displeased and said, 'The ancients have said, "The scholar should be served; how should he merely be made a friend of?"' When Tzŭ-ssŭ was thus displeased, did he not say within himself, 'With regard to our stations, you are sovereign and I am subject. How can I presume to be on terms of friendship with my sovereign? With regard to our virtue, you ought to serve me. How can you be on terms of friendihip with me?' Thus, when a ruler of a thousand chariots sought to be on terms of friendship with a scholar, he could not obtain his wish; how much less could he call him to his presence?

"Duke Ching of Ch'i, once, when he was hunting, called his forester to him by a flag topped with feathers. The forester would not come, and the duke was going to kill him. With reference to this incident, Confucius said, 'The determined official never forgets that his end may be in a ditch or a stream; the brave official never forgets that he may lose his head.' What was in the forester that Confucius thus approved? He approved his not going to the duke, when summoned by the article which was not appropriate to him."

Chang said , "May I ask with what a forester should be summoned?" Mencius replied, "With a skin cap. A common man should be summoned with a plain banner; a scholar who has taken office, with one having dragons embroidered on it; and a Great Official, with one with feathers suspended from the top of the staff.

"When the forester was summoned with the article appropriate to the summoning of a Great Official, he would have died rather than presume to go. If a common man were summoned with the article appropriate to the summoning of a scholar, how could he presume to go? How much more may we expect this refusal to go, when a worthy man is summoned in a way which is inappropriate to his character?

"When a prince wishes to see a worthy man and does not take the proper course to get his wish, it is as if he wished him to enter and shut the door against him. Now, righteousness is the way, and propriety is the door, but it is only the superior man who can follow this way and go out and in by this door. It is said in the *Book of Songs*,

> 'The way to Chou is level like a whetstone,
> And straight as an arrow.
> The officials tread it,
> And the lower people see it.'"

Wan Chang said, "When Confucius received the prince's message calling him, he went without waiting for his carriage. Doing so, did Confucius do wrong?" Mencius replied, "Confucius was in office and had to observe its appropriate duties. And moreover, he was summoned on the business of his office."[20]

As Mencius was about to go to court to see the king, the king sent a person to him with this message, "I was wishing to come and see you. But I have got a cold and may not expose myself to the wind. In the morning I will hold my court. I do not know whether you will give me the opportunity of seeing you then. Mencius replied, "Unfortunately I am unwell and not able to go to the court."

Next day, he went out to pay a visit of condolence to someone of the Tung-kuo family, when Kung-sun Ch'ou said to him, "Yesterday you declined going to the court on the ground of being unwell, and today you are going to pay a visit of condolence. May this not be regarded as improper?" "Yesterday," said Mencius, "I was unwell; today I have recovered—why should I not pay this visit?"

In the meantime the king sent a messenger to inquire about his sickness, and also a physician. Mêng Chung replied to them, "Yesterday, when the king's order came, he was feeling a little unwell and could not go to the court. Today he was a little better and hastened to go to court. I do not know whether he can have reached it by this time or not." Having said this, he sent several men to look for Mencius on the way and say to him, "I beg that you must not return home and that you go to the court."

On this, Mencius felt himself compelled to go to Ching Ch'ou's and there stop for the night. Mr. Ching said to him, "In the family there is the relation of father and son; abroad there is the relation of prince and minister. They are the two great relations among men. Between father and son the ruling principle is kindness. Between prince and minister the ruling principle is respect. I have seen the respect of the king to you, Sir, but I have not seen in what way you show respect to him." Mencius replied, "Oh! what words are these? Among the people of Ch'i there is no one who speaks to the king about benevolence and righteousness. Are they thus silent because they do not think that benevolence and righteousness are not admirable? No, but in their hearts they say, 'This man is not fit to be spoken with about benevolence and righteousness.' Thus they manifest a disrespect than which there can be none greater. I do not dare to set forth before the king any but the Ways of Yao and Shun. There is therefore no man of Ch'i who respects the king so much as I do."

Mr. Ching said, "Not so. That was not what I meant. In the *Book of Rites* it is said, 'When a father calls, the answer must be without a moment's hesitation. When the prince's order calls, the carriage must not be waited for.' You were certainly going to the court, but when you heard the king's order, then you did not carry your purpose out. This does seem as if it were not in accordance with that rule of propriety."

Mencius answered him, "How can you give that meaning to my conduct? The philosopher Tsêng said, 'The wealth of Chin and Ch'u cannot be equaled. Let their rulers have their wealth; I have my benevolence. Let them have their nobility; I have my righteousness. What do I have to regret?' Now shall we say that these sentiments are not right? Seeing that the philosopher Tsêng spoke them, there is in them, I apprehend, a real principle. In the empire there are three things universally acknowledged to be honorable. Nobility is one of them, age is one of them; virtue is one of them. In courts, nobility holds the first place of the three; in villages, age holds the first place; and for helping one's generation and presiding over the people, the other two are not equal to virtue. How can the possession of only one of them be presumed on to despise one who possesses the other two?

"Therefore a prince who is to accomplish great deeds will certainly have ministers whom he does not call to go to him. When he wishes to consult with him, he goes to him. The prince who does not honor the virtuous and delight in their ways of doing to this extent is not worth having to do with.

"Accordingly, there was the behavior of T'ang to Yi Yin: he first learned of him and then employed him as his minister; and so without difficulty he became sovereign. There was the behavior of Duke Huan to Kuan Chung: he first learned of him and then employed him as his minister; and so without difficulty he became chief of all the princes.

"Now throughout the empire the territories of the princes are of equal extent, and in their virtues they are on a level. Not one of them is able to exceed the others. This is from no other reason but that they love to make ministers of those whom they teach and do not love to make ministers of those by whom they might be taught.

"So did T'ang behave to Yi Yin and Duke Huan to Kuan Chung that they would not venture to call them to go to them. If Kuan Chung might not be called to him by his prince, how much less may he be called who would not play the part of Kuan Chung?" [21]

Let us now consider some answers to this question: How can the factors contributing to the evil-doing of a ruler be removed from his surroundings?

(a) By removing mean men and forestalling slanders. Since mean men are bent solely on gain, they seek the good will of others by flattery. They tend to aggravate the evil-doing of their sovereign; at the same time they are jealous of the good and loyal. On the other hand, superior men feel they must, above all, retain their purity and self-respect. When their remonstrances are rejected by the sovereign, they have no recourse but to retire from office. When the evil way of the mean men gets the better of the virtuous way of the superior men, the latter yield to the former, for they can never exist together. So history tells us that the principal reason for the prevalence of bad government is the presence, the proximity, of mean men.

Mencius said to Tai Pu-shêng, "Do you desire your king to be virtuous? Let me tell you plainly how he may be made so. Suppose that there is a great official of Ch'u here, who wishes his son to learn the speech of Ch'i. Will he in that case employ a man of Ch'i as his tutor, or a man of Ch'u?" "He will employ a man of Ch'i to teach him," said Pu-shêng. Mencius went on, "If but one man of Ch'i is teaching him, and there are a multitude of men of Ch'u continually shouting out about him, although his father beats him every day, wishing him to learn the speech of Ch'i, it will be impossible for him to do so. But in the same way, if he were to be taken and placed for several years in Chuang or Yüeh, though his father should beat him, wishing him to speak the language of Ch'u, it would be impossible for him to do so.

"You supposed that Hsüeh Chü-chou was a scholar of virtue, and you have got him placed in attendance on the king. Suppose that all in attendance on the king, old and young, high and low, were Hsüeh Chü-chou, whom would the king have to do evil with? But what can one Hsüeh Chü-chou do for the king of Sung?" [22]

This puts into context Confucius' reply (given below) to Yen Hui's question on the administration of the government of a country. His advice: "Banish the songs of Chêng and keep far from specious talkers."

Yen Yüan asked how the government of a country should be administered.

The Master said, "Follow the seasons of Hsia. Ride in the state carriage of Yin. Wear the ceremonial cap of Chou. Let the music be the Shao with its dances. Banish the songs of Chêng and keep far from specious talkers. The songs of Chêng are licentious; specious talkers are dangerous." [23]

(b) By avoiding sex with a view to preventing degeneration. The inherent reason for political corruption has always had something to do with sex. The worst that can happen to a ruler is for him to become a victim of extreme sexual indulgence, for then he ceases to attend to the affairs of state, which gradually slip into the hands of mean men. Since it is not in the makeup of superior men to compete with others for intimacy with the sovereign, the last resort of the ruler's best men usually is to retire. A rare exception indeed was Pi-kan, one of the uncles of King Chou of the Shang dynasty, who committed suicide after fruitless remonstrances. This explains why Confucius spoke with such indignation about women and servants:

The Master said, "Of all people, girls and servants are the most difficult to behave to. If you are familiar with them, they lose their humility. If you maintain a reserve towards them, they are discontented." [24]

The people of Ch'i sent to Lu a present of female musicians, which Chi Huan received, and for three days no court was held. Confucius took his departure. [25]

The Viscount of Wei withdrew from the court. The Viscount of Chi became a slave to Chou. Pi-kan remonstrated with him and died. Confucius said, "The Yin dynasty possessed three men of virtue."[26]

(c) By belittling goods and money so as to show the absence of covetousness. The wealth of a country belongs to the people as a whole; the State takes some of this wealth and uses it for the benefit of the people. While those in government have the authority to exercise control over these resources and make use of them according to law, they do not have the power to make the State's wealth their own. The remuneration they receive from the State for their services is regulated by law and should never be in excess of what is legally provided for them.

However, in the age of monarchism the State coffers were regarded as the property of the sovereign, although even in those days the State's monies were not considered *privately* owned by him. This led to excesses. Where the superiors were fond of wealth, their inferiors were sure to comply with their wishes. The result? Corruption ran wild and the mean men gained additional power.

> When he who presides over a State makes his revenues his chief business, it must have started with mean men, who are capable in this respect. When such men are employed in the administration of a State, calamities and injuries will befall it together, and, though good men may take their place, they will not be able to remedy the evil. This illustrates again the saying, "In a State, gain is not to be considered prosperity, but its prosperity will be found in righteousness." [27]

Therefore, the things a ruler should value are his territory, his people and his government. There is nothing else he should regard as more precious. Mencius put it this way: "The precious things of a prince are three: the territory, the people and the government and its business. If one values as most precious pearls and jade, calamity is sure to befall him."[28]

When King Hsüan of Ch'i confided to Mencius, "I have an infirmity. I am fond of wealth," Mencius replied: "If Your Majesty loves wealth, share it with the people, and what difficulty will there be in your attaining the royal sway?"[29] What Mencius had in mind, of course, was to dissuade the king from indulging his love of wealth to the exclusion of all others, specifically his own subjects.

(d) By valuing virtuous conduct in order to show delight in the Way. All enlightened rulers of ancient times honored virtue and took delight in the Way. And when the superiors valued virtue, those under them copied their good example. "The virtue of the superior man is like wind, and the virtue of the mean man like grass. Grass is sure to bend when blown by wind." In other words, when the Way of the superior man is in the ascendancy, the way of the mean man is on the decline. If both those above and those below are fond of what is good, there is no question but that good government will prevail.

> Never has there been a case of the sovereign loving benevolence and the people not loving righteousness. Never has there been a case where the people have loved righteousness and the affairs of the sovereign have not been carried to completion. [39]
>
> Mencius said, "...Let the prince be benevolent, and all his acts will be benevolent. Let the prince be righteous, and all his acts will be righteous." [31]

Thus, in an environment upholding virtue and loving goodness, the sovereign constantly takes delight in what is good. In case of doubt, he seeks the advice of the worthy and the wise, who have no perplexities. In such an environment all laws and orders have the willing support and obedience of all the people; there is no suspicion between them and the government. In such circumstances the wise can indeed be said to be without perplexities.

If the sovereign respects the worthy, his ministers are sure to recommend such men for public service. If they can be placed in their proper positions, well and good. At the very least, they should be honored, supported, befriended, and even treated as teachers.

In regard to recommending worthy men, Confucius realized the ruler and his chief minister did not know enough such men to fill all governmental positions. But he maintained that if the minister recommended those he knew, these men in turn would find other worthy men whom the minister did not know personally.

Chung-kung, being chief minister to the Head of the Chi family, asked about government. The Master said, "Employ first the services of your various officials, pardon small faults and raise to office men of virtue and talents."

Chung-kung said, "How shall I know the men of virtue and talents, so that I may raise them to office?" He was answered, "Raise to office those whom you know. As to those whom you do not know, will others neglect them?" [32]

Confucius praised Kung-shu Wên for wisely recommending worthy men. At the same time he criticized Tsang Wên-chung for his inability to make similar recommendations.

The great official, Hsien, who had been family-minister to Kung-shu Wên, asceded to the prince's court in company with Wên.

The Master, having heard of it, said, "He deserved to be considered Wên (the accomplished)." [33]

The Master said, "Was not Tsang Wên-chung like one who had stolen his situation? He knew the virtue and talents of Hui of Liu-hsia, and yet did not procure that he should stand with him in court." [34]

Fan Ch'ih asked about benevolence. The Master said, "It is to love all men." He asked about wisdom. The Master said, "It is to know all men."

Fan Ch'ih did not immediately understand these answers. The Master said, "Employ the upright and put aside the crooked; in this way the crooked can be made to be upright."

Fan Ch'ih retired, and, seeing Tzŭ-hsia, he said to him, "A little while ago, I had an interview with our Master and asked him about wisdom. He said, 'Employ the upright and put aside the crooked; in this way, the crooked will be made to be upright.' What did he mean?"

Tzŭ-hsia said, "Truly rich is his saying! Shun, being in possession of the empire, selected from among all the people and employed Kao Yao, on which all who were devoid of virtue became virtuous as if the unvirtuous had gone far away. T'ang, being in possession of the empire, selected from among all the people and employed Yi Yin, and all who were devoid of virtue became virtuous, as if the unvirtuous had gone far away." [35]

This last passage notes that when worthy men are employed, mean men will keep their distance. However, the recommendation and employment of the worthy must be carried out with care. Even if someone is regarded by all as worthy, a thorough investigation should be made. The same should be done in the case of one who is regarded by all as unworthy.

> Mencius, having an interview with King Hsüan of Ch'i, said to him, "When men speak of 'an ancient kingdom,' it is not meant thereby that it has lofty trees in it, but that it has ministers sprung from families which have been noted in it for generations. Your Majesty has no intimate ministers even. Those whom you advanced yesterday are gone today, and you do not know it."
>
> The king said, "How shall I know that they have not ability and so avoid employing them at all?"
>
> The reply was, "The ruler of a State advances to office worthy men only as a matter of necessity. Since he will thereby cause the low to overstep the honorable and the distant to overstep his near relatives, ought he not to do so with caution?
>
> "When all those about you say, 'This is a worthy man,' you may not therefore believe it. When your great officials all say, 'This is a worthy man,' neither may you for that believe it. When all the people say, 'This is a worthy man,' then examine into the case, and when you find that the man is such, employ him. When all those about you say, 'This man won't do,' don't listen to them. When all your great officials say, 'This man won't do,' don't listen to them. When the people all say, 'This man won't do,' then examine into the case, and when you find that the man won't do, send him away.
>
> "When all those about you say, 'This man deserves death,' don't listen to them. When all your great officials say, 'This man deserves death,' don't listen to them. When the people all say, 'This man deserves death,' then inquire into the case, and when you see that the man deserves death, put him to death. In accordance with this we have the saying, 'The people killed him.'
>
> "You must act in this way in order to be the parent of the people."[36]

Mencius regarded Shun-yü K'un's method of recognizing virtue and worth as improper. He sought to correct it:

> Shun-yü K'un said, "He who makes fame and meritorious services his first objects acts with a regard to others. He who makes them only secondary objects acts with a regard to himself. You, Master, were ranked among the three chief ministers of the State, but before your fame and services have reached either to the prince or the people, you have left your place. Is this indeed the way of the virtuous?"

Mencius replied, "There was Po-i—he held an inferior situation and would not, with his worthiness, serve a degenerate prince. There was Yi Yin—he five times went to T'ang and five times went to Chieh. There was Hui of Liu-hsia—he did not disdain to serve a vile prince, nor did he decline a small office. The courses pursued by those three worthies were different, but their aim was one. And what was their one aim? We must answer, 'To be perfectly virtuous.' And so it is simply after this that superior men strive. Why must they pursue the same course?"

K'un pursued, "In the time of Duke Mu of Lu, the government was in the hands of Kung-i, while Tzŭ-liu and Tzŭ-ssŭ were ministers. And yet the dismemberment of Lu then increased exceedingly. Such was the case, a specimen of how your men of virtue are of no advantage to a country!"

Mencius said, "The prince of Yü did not use Pai-li Hsi and thereby lost his State. Duke Mu of Ch'in used him and became chief of all the princes. Ruin is the consequence of not employing worthy men; how can it rest with dismemberment merely?"

K'un urged again, "Formerly, when Wang Pao dwelt on the Ch'i, the people on the west of the Yellow River all became skillful in singing in his abrupt manner. When Mien Chü lived in Kao-t'ang, the people in the parts of Ch'i on the west became skillful at singing in his prolonged manner. The wives of Hua Chou and Ch'i Liang bewailed their husbands so skillfully that they changed the manners of the State. When there is the gift within, it manifests itself without. I have never seen the man who could do the deeds of a worthy and did not realize the work of one. Therefore there are now no worthy men. If there were, I should know them."

Mencius answered, "When Confucius was chief Minister of Justice in Lu, the prince came not to follow his counsels. Soon after there was the solstical sacrifice, and when a part of the meat presented in sacrifice was not sent to him, he went away even without taking off his cap of ceremony. Those who did not know him supposed that it was on account of the meat. Those who knew him supposed that it was on account of the neglect of the usual ceremony. The fact was that Confucius wanted to go away on occasion of some small offense, not wishing to do so without some apparent cause. All men cannot be expected to understand the conduct of a superior man."[37]

It stands to reason that when worthy men are respected, men of virtue and many talents will be appointed to office. But once they are in office, it is necessary to make good use of them and their fine qualities. Forming a government without men of virtue and talent is like building a large mansion in a desert sans landscaping and ornamentation; it is like trying to cut and polish a precious gem, ignoring the services of a skilled jeweler. Moreover, the employment of worthy men should not be limited by their backgrounds. Some ancient sages and worthy men sprang from humble origins, as Mencius pointed out a number of times.

> Mencius, having an interview with King Hsüan of Ch'i, said to him, "If you are going to build a large mansion, you will surely cause the Master of the workmen to look out for large trees, and when he has found such large trees, you will be glad, thinking that they will answer for the intended object. Should the workmen hew them so as to make them too small, Your Majesty will be angry, thinking that they will not answer for the purpose. Now, a man spends his youth in learning, and, being grown up to vigor, he wishes to put it in practice; if Your Majesty says to him, 'For the present put aside what you have learned and follow me,' what shall we say?
>
> "Here now you have a gem unwrought, in the stone. Although it may be worth 240,000 taels, you will surely employ a lapidary to cut and polish it. But when you come to the government of a State, then you say, 'For the present put aside what you have learned and follow me.' Why such a difference from your conduct in calling in the lapidary to cut the gem?"[38]
>
> Mencius said, "...T'ang held fast the Mean and employed worthy men without regard to their qualifications."[39]
>
> Mencius said, "Shun rose from among the channeled fields; Fu Yüeh was called to office from the midst of his building frames; Chiao Ko from his fish and salt; Kuan Yi-wu from the hands of his gaoler; Sun-shu Ao from his hiding by the seashore; and Pai-li Hsi from the market-place."[40]

Each administration has its own personnel system. But the number of top-rank positions (titles of nobility) is limited. This means an important position cannot be given to every man of worth. To keep these men in reserve, so to speak, it is necessary to confer on them the highest possible positions (titles) and provide them with the backing they need. This is called the support of scholars and worthy men. In this effort it is especially important to observe the rules of propriety to the full; otherwise men of their type cannot be retained for any length of time.

Wan Chang said, "What is the reason that a scholar does not accept a stated support from a prince?" Mencius replied, "He does not presume to do so. When a prince loses his State and then accepts a stated support from another prince, this is in accordance with propriety. But for a scholar to accept such support from any of the princes is not in accordance with propriety."

Wan Chang said, "If the prince sends him a present of grain, for instance, does he accept it?" "He accepts it," answered Mencius. "What is the meaning of this acceptance?" "Why—the prince ought to assist the people in their necessities."

Chang pursued, "Why is it that the scholar will thus accept the prince's help but will not accept his gift?" The answer was, "He does not presume to do so." "I venture to ask why he does not presume to do so." "Even the keepers of the gates, with their watchmen's sticks, have their regular offices for which they can take their support from the prince. He who without a regular office should receive the gift of the prince must be deemed disrespectful."

Chang asked, "If the prince sends a scholar a present, he accepts it; I do not know whether this present may be constantly repeated." Mencius answered, "There was the conduct of Duke Mu to Tzŭ-ssŭ. He made frequent inquiries after Tzŭ-ssŭ's health and sent him frequent presents of cooked meat. Tzŭ-ssŭ was displeased; and finally, having motioned to the messenger to go outside the gate, he bowed his head to the ground with his face to the north, did obeisance twice and declined the gift, saying, 'From this time forth I shall know that the prince supports me as a dog or a horse.' And so from that time a servant was not sent with the presents. When a prince professes to be pleased with a worthy man and can neither promote him to office nor support him in the proper way, can he be said to be pleased with him?"

Chang said, "I venture to ask how the sovereign of a State, when he wishes to support a superior man, must proceed, that he may be said to do so in the proper way." Mencius answered, "At first, the present must be offered with the prince's commission, and the scholar, making obeisance twice with his head bowed to the ground, will receive it. But after this the storekeeper will continue to send grain and the master of the kitchen to send meat, presenting it as if without the prince's express commission. Tzŭ-ssŭ considered that the meat from the prince's caldron, giving him the annoyance of constantly doing obeisance, was not the way to support a superior man.

"There was Yao's conduct to Shun: He caused his nine sons to serve him and gave his two daughters in marriage; he caused the various officials, oxen and sheep, storehouses and granaries, all to be prepared to support Shun amid the channeled fields, and then he raised him to the most exalted situation. From this we have the expression, 'This was the example of a king or duke honoring a worthy.'"[41]

It is fitting and proper that each nation have a reserve force of scholars. But it is questionable whether a scholar should receive remuneration without earning it through concrete service. In answering questions put by P'êng Kêng and Kung-sun Ch'ou, Mencius observed that one who taught men the Way was just as important as one who supplied the necessities of life and that both should be rewarded for their services. But Mencius also felt it was improper to receive state remuneration merely to satisfy one's wants.

> P'êng Kêng asked Mencius, saying, "Is it not an extravagant procedure to go from one prince to another and live upon them, followed by several tens of carriages and attended by several hundred men?" Mencius replied, "If there is not a proper ground for taking it, a single bamboo-cup of rice may not be received from a man. If there is such a proper ground, then Shun's receiving the empire from Yao is not to be considered excessive. Do you think it was excessive?"
>
> Kêng said, "No. But for a scholar performing no service to receive his support notwithstanding is improper."
>
> Mencius answered, "If you do not have an intercommunication of the productions of labor and an interchange of men's services, so that one from his overplus may supply the deficiency of another, then husbandmen will have a superfluity of grain and women will have a superfluity of cloth. If you have such an interchange, carpenters and carriage-wrights may all get their food from you. Here now is a man, who, at home, is filial, and abroad, respectful to his elders; who watches over the principles of the ancient kings, awaiting the rise of future learners—and yet you will refuse to support him. How is it that you give honor to the carpenter and carriage-wright and slight him who practices benevolence and righteousness?"
>
> P'êng Kêng said, "The aim of the carpenter and carriage-wright is by their trades to seek for a living. Is it also the aim of the superior man in his practice of principles thereby to seek for a living?" "What have you to do," returned Mencius, "with his purpose? He is of service to you. He deserves to be supported,

and should be supported. And let me ask, do you remunerate a man's intention or do you remunerate his service?" To this Kêng replied, "I remunerate his intention."

Mencius said, "There is a man here, who breaks your tiles and draws unsightly figures on your walls; his purpose may be thereby to seek for his living, but will you indeed remunerate him?" "No." said Kêng; and Mencius then concluded, "That being the case, it is not the purpose which you remunerate, but the work done."[42]

Kung-sun Ch'ou said, "It is said in the Book of Songs,

'He will not eat the bread of idleness!'

How is it that we see superior men eating without laboring?" Mencius replied, "When a superior man resides in a country, if its sovereign employs his counsels, he comes to tranquillity, wealth, honor and glory. If the young in it follow his instructions, they become filial, obedient to their elders, loyal and truthful. What greater example can there be than this of not eating the bread of idleness?"[43]

The remuneration of a scholar should be on the basis of the ruler's voluntary intention to honor the worthy and support the scholarly. But if a scholar stoops to the level of begging for advancement in office, or if he on his own initiative seeks the prince's support, then remuneration would not be permitted by propriety.

Wan Chang said, "What is the reason that a scholar does not accept a stated support from a prince?" Mencius replied, "He does not presume to do so. When a prince loses his State and then accepts a stated support from another prince, this is in accordance with propriety. But for a scholar to accept such support from any of the princes is not in accordance with propriety."[44]

This clarifies the passage: "By discarding slanderers, by guarding himself against the seductions of beauty; by making light of riches and giving honor to virtue—this is how he can encourage worthy men."

3. Affection to Relatives

When a ruler shows his affection to relatives, there is neither grumbling nor resentment from his uncles and brethren. Giving them places of honor, seeing that they get large emoluments, sharing their likes and dislikes—these are the ways a ruler encourages his relatives to love him.

The essential function of government is to rectify human relationships, just as the main function of education is to define these relationships. The most important elements in these relationships are filial piety and fraternal love; in other words, affection for relatives. Only when there is affection for relatives is there benevolence toward men, and only when there is benevolence toward men is there love for all things. Benevolence toward men and love for all things are the foundation of good government.

Since the root of a country is in its families, which are regulated by filial piety and fraternal love, those in control of government should set personal examples in practicing these virtues; otherwise, they will lose the respect of the people and be subjected to disgrace.

> What is meant by "The pacifying of the whole empire depends on the government of his State," is this: When the sovereign behaves to his aged, as the aged should be behaved to, the people become filial; when the sovereign behaves to his elders, as the elders should be behaved to, the people learn fraternal submission; when the sovereign treats compassionately the orphaned, the people will do the same. Thus the ruler has a principle with which, as with a measuring-square, he may regulate his conduct...

> In the *Book of Songs* it is said, "Lofty is that southern hill, with its rugged masses of rocks! Greatly distinguished are you, O grand-teacher Yin, the people all look up to you." Rulers of States may not neglect to be careful. If they deviate to a mean selfishness, they will be a disgrace in the empire.[45]

> Duke Wên's uncle, Fan, said, "The fugitive has nothing precious. What he considers precious is benevolence and affection."[46]

The practice of filial piety and fraternal love result in more than just exemplary conduct. It creates within the family an environment of affection and harmony. When a ruler practices these virtues, he will hear no grumbling from his grateful relatives (1) if at the same time he sees to it that good men, properly remunerated, are assigned to positions which fit their talents, and (2) if the ruler attempts to share with these men their likes and dislikes. If he fails to do these things, these men will be hard put to carry out their official duties; more, they will not set a good example for the people and thus will not exert a salutary influence on society as a whole. Thus, it is essential to give them places of honor and generous emoluments while sharing their likes and dislikes.

> What is meant by "In order to govern rightly the State, it is necessary first to regulate the family" is this: It is not·possible for one to teach others, while he cannot teach his own family.[47]
>
> The Master said, "...When those who are in high stations perform well all their duties to their relations, the people are aroused to virtue. When old friends are not neglected by them, the people are preserved from meanness."[48]
>
> Mencius said, "The Way lies in what is near, and men seek for it in what is remote. The work lies in what is easy, and men seek for it in what is difficult. If each man would love his parents and respect his elders, the whole world would enjoy peace."[49]

In the age of monarchism, the parents and brothers of the ruler were all members of the nobility and their emoluments were duly provided. This was done so that (1) there might be no grumbling, and (2) internal pacification might be achieved. In a republic, however, a father cannot share his official prominence with his son, nor can the son share it with his younger brother. Official posts are obtained through a personnel or civil service examination system. The aim of such systems is to do away with the evil practice of nepotisn and encourage the spirit of independent advancement.

However, despite the change of times, the principle of showing affection to one's relatives has remained. Relatives of persons holding official positions can ruin the reputations of all concerned if they resort to evil ways. It follows that relatives can play a considerable role by setting a personal example for others by showing affection to their own.

4. Respect toward the Great Ministers

A ruler can avoid errors in governing his people by respecting his key ministers. Respect includes encouragement, and he can encourage his great ministers by giving them numerous officials to discharge well their orders and commissions.

Stated simply, the ruler relies on his key ministers for planning and working out major state projects. What the chief of state does is to make the final decisions. Respect toward such great ministers implies confidence in them, in addition to reverential treatment of state affairs with a view to good government.

> The Master said, "To rule a country of a thousand chariots, there must be reverent attention to business and sincerity; economy in expenditure and love for men; and the employment of the people at the proper seasons."[50]

"Those who respect others are always respected by them also." If the ruler can respect his great ministers, they will respect him and carry out the assignments givem them. "As a minister, he (King Wên) rested in reverence."[51]

Because the great ministers occupy such high positions, they must have the confidence of the ruler; otherwise they would lose the trust of those working under them and the nation would not enjoy good government. "The Master said, '...When those in inferior situations do not possess the confidence of their superiors, they cannot succeed in governing the people.' "[52]

In the history of our country we have had unprincipled rulers who bungled in their administration of the government. But they had the knack of knowing their men and employing their services tactfully. It was this knack that saved the country from ruin. Duke Ling of Wei, for example:

> The Master was speaking about the unprincipled course of Duke Ling of Wei, when Chi K'ang said, "Since he is of such a character, how is it he does not lose his State?"
> Confucius said, "Chung-shu Yü has the superintendence of his guests and strangers; the litanist, T'o, has the management of his ancestral temple; and Wang-sun Chia has the direction of the army and forces—with such officials as these, how should he lose his State?"[53]

To give the great ministers numerous officials to discharge their orders and commissions means to get to know men, place them in their proper positions, make use of their talents, and bestow on them the rewards or penalties they deserve. In this way law and order can be maintained in a well-organized manner. Hence, it is said, "By respecting the great ministers, he (the ruler) is kept from errors in the practice of governmeut." When these great ministers are respected and they attend to their official duties reverently, the fruit of good government is reaped. Hence, "He can encourage his great ministers by giving them numerous officials to discharge well their orders and commissions."

5. Kind and Considerate Treatment of the Whole Body of Officials

Kindness and consideration prompt officials to make a most grateful return for these courtesies. According to them, a generous amount of confidence and large emoluments are the key elements in encouraging them in their work.

The whole body of officials was the equivalent of today's force of civil servants. Irrespective of rank, they bear an important relationship to the enforcement of law and order in the country. Therefore superiors must be considerate in their relations with them. This considerrtion should be both spiritual and material. According to them spiritual consideration is shown by bestowing great confidence in them, and material consideration is shown by making their remuneration large.

The scales of nobility and emoluments in the Chou dynasty contained the following provisions:

Pei-kung Yi asked Mencius, saying, "What was the arrangement of dignities and emolument determined by the House of Chou?"

Mencius replied, "The particulars of that arrangement cannot be learned, for the princes, disliking them as injurious to themselves, have destroyed all the records. Still I have learned the general outline of them.

"The Son of Heaven constituted one dignity: the Duke one; the Marquis one; the Earl one; and the Viscount and the Baron each one of equal rank—altogether making five degrees of rank. The ruler again constituted one dignity; the Chief Minister one; the Great Officials one; the Scholars of the First Class one; those of the Middle Class one; and those of the Lowest Class one—altogether making six degress of rank.

"To the Son of Heaven there was allotted a territory of a thousand *li* square. A Duke and a Marquis had each a hundred *li* square. An Earl had seventy *li*, and a Viscount and a Baron had each fifty *li*. The assignments altogether were of four amounts. Where the territory did not amount to fifty *li*, the chief could not have access himself to the Son of Heaven. His land was attached to some feudal lord, and was called a Vassal State.

"The Chief Ministers of the Son of Heaven received an amount of territory equal to that of a Marquis; a Great Official received as much as an Earl; and a Scholar of the First Class as much as a Viscount or a Baron.

"In a great State, where the territory was a hundred *li* equare, the ruler had ten times as much income as his Chief Ministers; a Chief Minister four times as much as a Great Official; a Great Official twice as much as a Scholar of the First Class; a Scholar of the First Class twice as much as one of the Middle; a Scholar of the Middle Class twice as much as one of the Lowest; the Scholars of the Lowest Class had the same emoluments as such of the common people as were employed about the government offices, who received as much as they would have made by tilling the fields.

"In a State of the next grade, where the territory was seventy *li* square, the ruler had ten times as much revenue as his Chief Minister; a Chief Minister three times as much as a Great Official; a Great Official twice as much as a Scholar of the First Class; a Scholar of the First Class twice as much as one of the Middle; a Scholar of the Middle Class twice as much as one of the Lowest; the Scholars of the Lowest Class had the same emoluments as such of the common people as were employed about the government offices, who received as much as they would have made by tilling the fields.

"In a small State, where the territory was fifty *li* square, the ruler had ten times as much revenue as his Chief Minister; a Chief Minister had twice as much as a Great Official; a Great Official twice as much as a Scholar of the First Class; a Scholar of the First Class twice as much as one of the Middle; a Scholar of the Middle Class twice as much as one of the Lowest; Scholars of the Lowest Class had the same emoluments as such of the common people as were employed about the government offices, who received as much as they would have made by tilling the fields.

"As to those who tilled the fields, each husbandman received a hundred *mou*. When those *mou* were manured, the best husbandman of the highest class supported eight. The best husbandmen of the second class supported seven individuals, and those ranking next to them supported six, while husbandmen of the lowest class only supported five. The salaries of the common people who were employed about the government offices differed according to this schedule.[54]

Since scholars were intellectuals, their knowledge was necessarily superior to that of the common people; also, their responsibility toward society was commensurably heavier, and their conduct had a greater influence on the masses. In other words, each act performed by a scholar and each word uttered by him should set a pattern for the people at large. For this reason, a scholar should subject himself to the strictest examination. The following passages show how Confucius dealt with the questions of Tzǔ-kung and Tzǔ-lu on the behavior of scholars:

> Tzǔ-kung asked, saying, "What qualities must a man possess to entitle him to be called a scholar?" The Master said, "He who in his conduct of himself maintains a sense of shame and when sent to any quarter will not disgrace his prince's commission, deserves to be called a scholar."
>
> Tzǔ-kung pursued, "I venture to ask who may be placed in the next lower rank," and he was told, "He whom the circle of his relatives pronounce to be filial, whom his fellow-villagers and neighbors pronounce to be fraternal."
>
> Again the disciple asked, "I venture to ask about the class still next in order." The Master said, "They are determined to be sincere in what they say and to carry out what they do. They are obstinate little men. Yet perhaps they may make the next class."
>
> Tzǔ-kung finally inquired, "Of what sort are those of the present day who engage in government?" The Master said, "Alas! They are so many pecks and hampers, not worth being taken into account."[55]
>
> Tzǔ-lu asked, saying, "What qualities must a man possess to entitle him to be called a scholar?" The Master said, "He must be thus earnest, urgent and bland—among his friends, earnest and urgent; among his brothers, bland."[56]

To sum up, we can see from the above passages that a scholar should be earnest and bland, have a sense of shame, do his duty, show filial piety to his parents and fraternal love to his brothers, speak sincerely and act with determination. Only thus can he set an example for others.

Confucius maintained that a scholar should not seek merely personal comfort. "The scholar who cherishes the love of comfort is not fit to be deemed a scholar."[57]

The philosopher Tsêng and Tzǔ-chang had even higher requirements for the scholar.

> The philosopher Tsêng said, "The scholar may not be without breadth of mind and vigorous endurance. His burden is heavy and his course is long.

"Perfect virtue is the burden which he considers it is his to sustain; is it not heavy? Only with death does his course stop; is it not long?"[58]

Tzŭ-chang said, "The scholar, trained for public duty, seeing threatening danger, is prepared to sacrifice his life. When the opportunity of gain is presented to him, he thinks of righteousness. In sacrificing, his thoughts are reverential. In mourning, his thoughts are about the grief he should feel. Such a man commands our approbation indeed."[59]

According to these two men, a scholar should be broad-minded and vigorous, regard perfect virtue as his responsibility, be willing to sacrifice his life when the country is in danger, and think of righteousness when the opportunity of gain presents itself, of reverence in sacrificing and of grief in mourning. In this way he can exhibit his great personality.

According to Mencius, a scholar must have lofty ambition, dwell in benevolence, practice righteousness, attend to his own virtue in solitude when poor, and do what he can to make the whole empire virtuous when he is advanced in dignity.

The King's son, Tien, asked Mencius, saying, "What is the business of the scholar?"

Mencius replied, "To exalt his aim."

Tien asked again, "What do you mean by exalting the aim?" The answer was, "Setting it on benevolence and righteousness. He thinks how to put a single innocent person to death is contrary to benevolence; how to take what one has not a right to is contrary to righteousness; that one's dwelling should be benevolence; and one's path should be righteousness. Where else should he dwell? What other path should he pursue? When he dwells in benevolence and practices righteousness, the businese of a great man is complete."[60]

Mencius said to Sung Kou-chien, "Are you fond, Sir, of traveling to the different courts? I will tell you about such traveling.

"If others acknowledge you, be perfectly satisfied. If no one does so, be the same."

Kou-chion said, "What is to be done to secure this satisfaction?" Mencius replied, "Honor virtue and delight in righteousness, and so you may always be perfectly satisfied.

"Therefore a scholar, though poor, does not let go his righteousness; though prosperous, he does not leave the Way.

"Poor and not letting righteousness go; it is thus that the scholar holds possession of himself. Prosperous and not leaving the Way; it is thus that the people's expectations of him are not disappointed.

> "When the men of antiquity realized their wishes, benefits were conferred by them on the people. If they did not realize their wishes, they cultivated their personal character and became illustrious in the world. If poor, they attended to their virtue in solitude; if advanced to dignity, they made the whole empire virtuous as well."[61]

In short, the scholar is a man of perfect personality, a man who possesses all the conditions necessary for holding office. Since he maintains contact with officials at court, he is familiar with the political situation. If the ruler has confidence in his ministers, if he is not overbearing toward them, and if he can ungrudgingly give them large remunerations, then scholars already in office will be more than just grateful. They will render faithful service in the common effort to bring about a peaceful rule. Even those in various sections of the country who are not part of the administration will "all be pleased and willing to hold office at court."

> Thus we see that the sovereign has a great Way to pursue. He must show loyalty and faithfulness to attain it, and by pride and extravagance he will lose it."[62]

Hence it is said, "Kindness and consideration prompt officials to make most grateful return for these courtesies," and "According to them a generous amount of confidence and large emoluments are the key elements in encouraging them in their work."

6. Treatment of the People as Children

By dealing with the mass of the people as his (the ruler's) children, he can lead them to exhort one another to what is good; employing them only at the proper times and making the imposts light—this is the way to encourage the people.

In an agricultural country based on the family system, it is natural to draw all illustrations from those things which are habitually encountered. For example, the ruler is often referred to as "parent of the people," and the people as "juniors" or "children." The service of the ruler is regarded as an extension of filial piety: "There is filial piety—therewith the sovereign should be served."[63] Love of the people is considered an extension of kindness to children: "There is kindness—therewith the multitude should be treated."[64] Hence the "dealing with the mass of the people as his children."

In the *Book of Songs* it is said, "How much to be rejoiced in are these princes, the parents of the people!" When a prince loves what the people love, and hates what the people hate, then is he what is called the parent of the people.,"[35]

In the "Announcement to K'ang" it is said, "Act as if you were watching over an infant." If (a mother) is really anxious about it, though she may not hit exactly the wants of her infant, she will not be far from doing so."[36]

Mencius said, "...From the first birth of mankind till now, never has anyone led children to attack their parent and succeeded in his design."[37]

Since there is no parent who does not love his children, how can a ruler do otherwise than love his people? Since a parent's love for his children is unbounded and he is willing to sacrifice everything for them, how can a ruler be different from a parent? While the great Yü was personally very frugal, he did his best to fulfill the wants of his people. He forgot himself in his devotion to the public, and he forgot his family for the sake of the country. Confucius eulogized him as the example of a ruler who really loved his people:

The Master said, "I can find no flaw in the character of Yü. He used himself coarse food and drink, but displayed the utmost filial piety towards the spirits. His ordinary garments were poor, but he displayed the utmost elegance in his sacrificial cap and apron. He lived in a low mean house, but expended all his strength on the ditches and water-channels. I can find nothing like a flaw in Yü."[38]

Confucius once said that "parents are anxious only about their (children's) sicknesses." The same is true of a worthy ruler's thoughts regarding his people. "King Wên," Mencius said, "looked on the people as if they had been wounded..."[39]

Parents must do everything possible to nourish, protect, control and educate their children. In like manner, he who has the responsibility of ruling the country is expected to carry out his duties with regard to the people's nourishment, protection, control and education.

Mencius said, "...Yao said (to Hsüeh), 'Urge them to be diligent, rectify them, help and instruct them, so as to make them preserve their inherently good nature. Then follow this up by giving them relief and conferring benefits on them.' When the sages were exercising their solicitude for the people in this way, had they leisure to cultivate the ground?..."[70]

When the Duke of Chou served as Prime Minister of King Ch'êng, his nephew, he was so solicitous about the people and affairs of state that he often interrupted his meal, sometimes as many as three times at a single sitting. He was anxious day and night, and the welfare of the people was forever in his mind. Once he thought of a solution, he sat up till dawn considering it.

> Mencius said, "...The Duke of Chou desired to unite in himself the virtues of those kings, those founders of the three dynasties, that he might display in his practice the four things which they did. If he saw anything in them not suited to his time, he looked up and thought about it, from daytime into the night, and when he was fortunate enough to master the difficulty, he sat waiting for the morning."[71]

The Duke of Chou was a genius and a man of perfect virtue. He possessed unsurpassable knowledge of both civilian and military affairs. An altruistic servant of the people, he worked unceasingly and sincerely for their interests. During his administration the rules of propriety were adopted, the pattern of national music was set, militarism was suppressed and culture was further enriched. He laid the earliest foundation for the unity and prosperity of the Chinese nation. Indeed, the Duke of Chou was the greatest statesman ever produced in China.

The first essential of a good reign is to win the people's hearts. The importance of this precept is that the gain and loss of political power is directly linked to winning or losing the people's hearts. The way to win them can be summarized thus: "to collect for them what they like and not to lay on them what they dislike" (See the passage below). The principle involved is: "Do not do unto others what you would not have them do to you."

> Mencius said, "Chieh and Chou's losing the throne arose from their losing the people, and to lose the people means to lose their hearts. There is a way to get the empire: get the people, and the empiere is got. There is a way to get the people: get their hearts, and the people are got. There is a way to get their hearts: it is

simply to collect for them what they like and not to lay on them what they dislike.

"The people turn to a benevolent rule as water flows downwards and as wild beasts fly to the wilderness.

"Accordingly, as the otter aids the deep waters, driving the fish into them, and the hawk aids the thickets, driving the little birds to them, so Chieh and Chou aided T'ang and Wu, driving the people to them.

"If among the present rulers of the empire there were one who loved benevolence, all the other princes would aid him by driving the people to him. Although he wished not to become sovereign, he could not avoid becoming so.

"The case of the present princes wishing to become sovereign is like having to seek for mugwort three years old, to cure a seven years' sickness. If it has not been kept in store, the patient may all his life not get it. If the princes do not set their wills on benevolence, all their days will be in sorrow and disgrace, and they will be plunged into death.

"This is illustrated by what is said in the *Book of Songs*.

'Who can do good?
All will be plunged into confusion and ruin.' "[72]

The people contribute their money and services to the State for its use. If these are taken properly, they do not occasion resentment. It is only by assuming their obligations that the people can enjoy their rights. But there are two things which they hate: (1) conflict in the time needed for public and private services, and (2) excess of contributions over the legally prescribed amount of taxation. These violate the principles embodied in "employing them only at the proper seasons and making the imposts light."

Farmers are subject to the influence of climate. Their labor is seasonal, and the leisure available to them varies considerably during the year. Therefore, in an agricultural state, the requisition of the people's services must not be detrimental to farming and cause a reduction of production. Also, it is most important to make an appropriate dispostion of the available time. Hence it is said, "The services of the people should be employed at the proper time."

Mencius replied, "...Let there not be taken away the time that is proper for the cultivation of the farm with its hundred *mou*, and the family of several mouths that is supported by it shall not suffer from hunger."[73]

If the nation's movers only exploited the people, without encouraging and helping them to increase production, they would be killing the goose for its golden eggs. Such exploitation would inflict incalculable sufferings on the people. In fact, it would be equivalent to spiritually strangling them. Confucius hated it so much that he said in the *Great Learning:* "Than to have such a minister (as looks out for imposts that he may lay them on the people), it were better for that house to have one who should rob it of its revenues."[74] The inference is that the agony of the one robbery would be less than the combined sufferings of the daily exploitations.

Confucius regarded such exploiters as mean men and called them the "unbenevolent."

> When he who presides over a State makes his revenues his chief business, it must have started with mean men who are capable in this respect. When such men are employed in the administration of a State, calamities and injuries will befall it together, and, though good men may take their place, they will not be able to remedy the evil. This illustrates again the saying, "In a State gain is not to be considered prosperity, but its prosperity will be found in righteousness."[75]
>
> The benevolent ruler, by means of his wealth, makes himself more distinguished. The unbenevolent ruler accumulates wealth at the expense of his life.[76]

While exploitation can never be permitted, irregular levies in addition to lawful requisitions of services and grain are even more inappropriate. If tolerated, they, too, will impoverish the people.

> Mencius said, "There are the exactions of hempen-cloth and silk, of grain and of personal service. The prince requires but one of these at once, deferring the other two. If he requires two of them at once, then the people die of hunger. If he requires the three at once, then fathers and sons are separated."[77]

It was because of such exploitation that Confucius called on his disciples to attack Jan Yu, who, far from being a tax expert, knew only how to be an exorbitant tax-collector.

The head of the Chi family was richer than the Duke of Chou had been, and yet Ch'iu collected his imposts for him and increased his wealth. The Master said, "He is no disciple of mine. My little children, beat the drum and assail him."[78]

Confucius regarded "reverent attention to business and sincerity, economy in expenditure and love for men, and the employment of the people at the proper seasons"[79] as essentials for ruling a country of a thousand chariots. Economy in expenditure corresponds to "making the imposts light," and "the employment of the people at the proper seasons" is the same as "employing them only at the proper times." Hence, "Employing them only at the proper times and making the imposts light—this is the way to encourage the people."

7. Encouragement of the Resort of All Classes of Artisans

A ruler can gain ample monies for expenditure by encouraging the resourcefulness of all classes of artisans. By daily examinations and monthly trials and by making their rations accord with their labors—this is the way to encourage the classes of artisans.

In ancient times, besides agriculture the people engaged in the production of only the simple articles they needed for food, clothihg, lodging, transportation, education and recreation. There was no large-scale machine manufacturing. In the "Record of Works," *Chou Li* (Ritual of Chou), it is stated: "The business of all classes of artisans was the work of the sages. The melting of metal into cutters, the condensation of earth into utensils, the construction of carriages for land and of vessels for water transport —these were all carried out by sages."

Artisans are required in handicraft work as well as in industry. The "Record of Works" was not the only ancient tract which considered the business of all classes of artisans as important. The *Doctrine of the Mean* also included the "resort of all classes of artisans" as one of the nine standard rules essential for the administration of a State, saying, "By encouraging the resort of all classes of artisans, his resources for expenditure are rendered ample." In modern parlance, this means a country can be enriched only by encouraging and developing industry.

As to method, it is said, "By daily examinations and monthly trials and by making their rations in accordance with their labors —this is the way to encourage the classes of artisans." In modern parlance, this means that industrial products must be examined daily, experiments must be performed on them monthly, remuneration should be brought in line with technique and skill— and only then can progress be encouraged. This is in complete accord with modern industry's stress on the development of research and improved treatment of technical personnel. It shows that while the times have changed, the principles to be followed remain the same.

Though Confucius was born in an agricultural society, he was the first to suggest the "investigation of things." He even went so far as to say, "He who can complete the nature of men can complete the nature of things." He went on to say, "By encouraging the resort of all classes of artisans, his resources for expenditure are rendered ample." This farsightedness indeed entitled him to be the teacher of countless ages.

It is regrettable, however, that the great scholars down through the ages have emphasized only the completion of the nature of men, while neglecting the completion of the nature of things. As a result, our country has remained in a state of poverty and weakness, and our science and industry have continued in a backward condition. But for this Confucius was certainly not to blame, and Mencius was right when he called Confucius the "timeous" (timely) sage, for the adjective is most fitting and proper for him.

It is not too late even today for us to catch up. But we still have to take to heart the pertinent teachings of Confucius that "by encouraging the resort of all classes of artisans, his resources for expenditure are rendered ample," and "by daily examinations and monthly trials and by making their rations in accordance with their labors—this is the way to encourage the classes of artisans."

8. Indulgent Treatment of Men from a Distance

By indulgent treatment of men from a distance, they are drawn to the ruler from all quarters. To escort them on their departure and meet them on their arrival, to commend the good among them and show compassion to the incompetent—this is the way to treat indulgently men from a distance.

These men include those who have retired to remote regions as well as visitors from foreign countries. Their decision to examine closely an administration with which they are not fully familiar is rooted in either admiration or a special motive. Naturally they should be cordially treated on their arrival and departure; in between they should be informed of conditions within the State. In order that all the visitors may leave the capital with a feeling of accomplishment, the good among them should be commended, and the incompetent forgiven and helped. In this way, as the good goverment of a country becomes known in distant regions, (1) those who have retired will be pleased to cooperate with it, (2) scholars of neighboring countries will be eager to visit it and perhaps even stand in its court, (3) farmers will be willing to cultivate its soil, merchants to trade in its markets, travelers to tour it, and (4) men who resent their ruler will be inclined to appeal to its benevolence.

Hence it is said, "To escort them on their departure and meet them on their arrival; to commend the good among them and show compassion to the incompetent—this is the way to treat indulgently men from a distance." Also, "Good government obtains, when those who are near are made happy and those who are far off are attracted."[80]

In this connection, Mencius cited a number of examples to illustrate the point.

> Mencius said, "Po-i, that he might avoid Chou, was dwelling on the coast of the northern sea. When he heard of the rise of King Wên, he roused himself and said, 'Why should I not go and follow him? I have heard that the chief of the West knows well how to nourish the old.' T'ai-kung, that he might avoid Chou, was dwelling on the coast of the eastern sea. When he heard of the rise of King Wên, he roused himself and said, 'Why should I not go and follow him? I have heard that the chief of the West knows well how to nourish the old.'
>
> "Those two old men were the greatest old men of the empire. When they came to follow King Wên, it was the fathers of the empire coming to follow him. When the fathers of the empire joined him, how could the sons go to any other?
>
> "Were any of the princes to practice the government of King Wên, within seven years he would be sure to assume the government

of the empire."[81]

Mencius said, "If a ruler gives honor to worthy men and employs the able, so that offices shall all be filled by individuals of distinction and mark: then all the scholars of the empire will be pleased and wish to stand in his court.

"If, in the market-place of his capital, he levies a ground-rent on the shops but does not tax the goods, or enforces the proper regulations without levying a ground-rent, then all the traders of the empire will be pleased and wish to store their goods in his market-place.

"If, at his frontier-passes, there is an inspection of persons, but no taxes charged, then all the travelers of the empire will be pleased and wish to make their tours on his roads.

"If he requires that the husbandmen give their mutual aid to cultivate the public field, and exacts no other taxes from them, then all the husbandmen of the empire will be pleased and wish to plough in his fields.

"If from the occupiers of the shops in his market-place he does not exact the fine of the individual idler or of the hamlet's quota of cloth, then all the people of the empire will be pleased and wish to come and be his people.

"If a ruler can truly practice these five things, then the people in the neighboring countries will look up to him as a parent. From the first birth of mankind till now, never has anyone led children to attack their parent and succeeded in his design. Thus, such a ruler will not have an enemy in all the empire, and he who has no enemy in the empire is the minister of Heaven. Never has there been a ruler in such a case who did not attain to the royal dignity."[82]

Hence it is said, "By indulgent treatment of men from a distance, they are drawn to him from all quarters."

9. Cherishing of the Princes of the States

The whole empire will revere a ruler who cherishes the princes of States. To restore families whose line of succession has been broken and to revive States that have been extinguished; to bring order to States that are in confusion and support those which are in peril; to have fixed times for their own reception at court and the reception of their envoys; to send them away with liberal gifts and welcome their coming with small contributions—this is the way to cherish the princes of States.

The first eight standard rules are the essentials for the government of a country. The last—cherishing the princes of States—envisages a step toward kingly government. All the measures enumerated here are destined to win the reverence of the princes and lay the foundation for the Kingly Way, the success of the administration under the Son of Heaven.

Hence it is said, "The whole empire will revere a ruler who cherishes the princes of the States."

Of the nine standard rules, the first involves their demonstration, the second through the seventh deal with encouragement, the eighth concerns the cultivation of virtue, and the ninth embodies the conferring of grace. They show that in the government of a country, example is a better means of instruction than mere words. Also, encouragement is better than punishment, the cultivation of virtue is more effective than reliance on force, and the conferring of grace preferable to the consolidation of power. These nine standard rules permeate the Kingly Way.

C. The Kingly Way or Way of Right vs. the Way of Might

Planning on a long-term basis is a highly desirable practice for an individual. For a nation it is even more so. That is why it is said, "It is only the individual possessed of the most entire sincerity that can exist under heaven, who can adjust the great invariable relations of mankind, establish the fundamental virtues of humanity..." Rulers can lay a permanent and firm foundation for national growth if with complete sincerity they use farsighted judgment and apply those principles which aim at the prolongation and duration of human life. They will find that the people will respond to benevolence and virtue; indeed, they will rally to such rulers from all quarters.

Our sages and worthy men in their teachings have set the pacification of the world as the ultimate objective of government. They discovered that the Way is essential to ensure the common existence of mankind; also, that benevolence is the prerequisite for cultivation of the Way. It follows that whoever can govern with benevolence can follow the Way and win the hearts of the people. With the people behind him, a ruler can guide his nation, and indeed the world, along the road of progress. This means that the secret of governing a country lies in stressing virtue, not force; in gaining the people's love and respect rather than their territory. In brief, this is the theoretical basis of what is called the rule of virtue and propriety.

The Master said, "He who exercises government by means of his virtue may be compared to the north polar star, which keeps its place and towards which all the stars turn." [83]

The Master said, "If the people are led by laws and uniformity is sought to be given them by punishments, they will try to avoid the punishments, but have no sense of shame.

"If they are led by virtue and uniformity is sought to be given them by rules of propriety, they will have the sense of shame and moreover will become good." [84]

The Master said, "Is a prince able to govern his country with the complaisance proper to the rules of propriety? If so, what difficulty will he have? If he cannot govern it with that complaisanc, what has he to do with the rules of propriety?" [85]

Why is the rule of virtue and propriety called the Kingly Way? The three horizontal strokes in the character *Wang* 王 represent heaven, earth and man; the vertical stroke represents the connecting link for the Ways of heaven, earth and man. The explanation given in the book Shuo-wen Chieh-tzŭ (On Etymology and the Explanation of Characters) on the character *wang* is that *wang* is he to whom the whole empire flocks. Tung Chung-shu[86] explained it this way: "The ancients who coined words called the character with three horizontal strokes connected by one vertical stroke *wang*. The three respresent heaven, earth and man, and the king is the one who links them up." Confucius said, "The king is one who links up the three."

In short, he who appreciates the Way of Heaven and Earth in their love of life, he who governs with a view to common existence—he is an advocate of the Kingly Way, of benevolent government. (See Chapters II and III on "The Investigation of Things" and "The Extension of Knowledge" for a discussion of the Way of Heaven and Earth.) The difference between the Kingly Way of Right and Way of Might is simply this: The Way of Right uses virtue and practices benevolence, while the Way of Might uses force and makes only a pretence to benevolence.

Mencius said, "He who, using force, makes a pretence to benevolence, is the leader of the princes. A leader of the princes requires a large kingdom. He who, using virtue, practices benevolence is the sovereign of the empire. To become the sovereign of the empire, a prince need not wait for a large kingdom. T'ang did it with only seventy *li*, and King Wên with only a hundred.

"When a man subdues others by force, they do not submit to him in heart. They submit, because their strength is not adequate to resist. When one subdues them by virtue, in their hearts' core they are pleased and sincerely submit, as was the case with the seventy disciples in their submission to Confucius. What is said in the *Book of Songs.*

'From the west, from the east,
From the south, form the north,
There was not one who thought of refusing submission.'
is an illustration of this."[87]

When a ruler pretends benevolence while actually using force to subdue his subjects, the people do not really submit to him in their deepest heart; rather, they submit superficially because they do not have enough strength to resist. On the other hand, when a virtuous ruler practices benevolence, he deeply pleases his people, and they willingly and sincerely submit to his rule. The former condition, based on physical force, gains only a passive obedience in most instances. No sooner does the pressure of force diminish than strong opposition becomes evident. Once the hearts of the people are lost, they become resentful even to the point of open rebellion. They accept the risk of losing their lives and if their strength surpasses that of the ruling authority, they succeed in overthrowing the government in power.

The history of our country shows that the Way of Might and tyrannical rule has never survived more than thirty years.

At the other end of the spectrum is the virtuous sovereign who rules with tranquil benevolence. In what seems an almost chemical change, he transforms the people with his perfect sincerity and great virtue, and the people obey the law almost entirety on their own initiative. This is the meaning of the statements, "The people turn to a benevolent rule as water flows downwards and as wild beasts fly to the wilderness," and "From day to day they (the people) move towards what is good without knowing who makes them do so."

When a ruler practices the Way, his people obey the law. When he observes the rules of propriety, his people live righteous lives. And this splendid ruler-people cooperation contributes to a rule of peace. Of course, whether the Way of Right or the Way of Might can endure depends on the sentiments of the people.

> Mencius said, "Under a chief, leading all the princes, the people look brisk and cheerful. Under a true sovereign, they have an air of deep contentment. Though he slays them, they do not murmur. When he benefits them, they do not think of his merit. From day to day they move towards what is good, without knowing who makes them do so.
>
> Wherever the superior man passes through, transformation follows; wherever he abides, his influence is of a spiritual nature. It flows abroad, above and beneath, like that of Heaven and Earth. How can it be said that he mends society but in a small way?" [88]
>
> Mencius said, "Benevolence and righteousness were natural to Yao and Shun. T'ang and Wu made them their own. The five chiefs of the princes feigned them. Having borrowed them long and not returned them, how could it be known that they did not own them?" [89]

Perhaps the Way of Might can achieve partial success. But since it is not the Heavenly Way destined to meet the wishes of the people, it easily loses a country after gaining it, and so it can never last long.

> Mencius said, "There are instances of individuals without benevolence who have got possession of a single State, but there has been no instance of the empire's being got by one without benevolence." [90]

Why? Because what is gained by wisdom is lost when it cannot be held by one's virtue.

> The Master said, "When a man's wisdom is sufficient to attain, and his virtue is not sufficient to enable him to hold, whatever he may have gained, he will lose again.
>
> "When his wisdom is sufficient to attain and he has virtue enough to hold fast, if he cannot govern with dignity, the people will not respect him.
>
> "When his wisdom is sufficient to attain and he has virtue enough to hold fast; when he governs also with dignity, yet if he tries to move the people contrary to the rules of propriety—full excellence is not reached." [91]

A ruler who practices the Way of Might is not overly concerned with what is good. Even when he goes contrary to his nature and does good, it does not work out. For he seeks to subdue rather than nourish the people with the good he does. The result is that he takes on goodness without conferring the benefit of goodness on others and this is inconsistent with the basic conditions of good government.

> Mencius said, "Never has he who would by his excellence subdue men been able to subdue them. Let a prince seek by his excellence to nourish men, and he will be able to subdue the whole empire. It is impossible that anyone should become ruler of the people when they have not yielded to him the subjection of the heart."[92]

The Way of Right can start with a small country. If the example of King Wên were copied, good government could be brought about in seven years. Unlike a tyrant, who would require a big country, T'ang could start with a territory of only seventy li and King Wên with one of a hundred *li*. Once virtue is used to practice benevolence, "the lesser virtues are like river currents; the greater virtues are seen in mighty transformations," and "the flowing progress of virtue is more rapid than the transmission of royal orders by stages and couriers." Again, "Within the four seas all raise their heads and look up to him (one who practices the Way of Right) as their sovereign." Even recluses and the aged would be roused—and pleased—to flock to such a ruler.

> Mencius said, "Po-i, that he might avoid Chou, was dwelling on the coast of the northern sea. When he heard of the rise of King Wên, he roused himself and said, 'Why should I not go and follow him? I have heard that the chief of the West knows well how to nourish the old.' T'ai-kung, that he might avoid Chou, was dwelling on the coast of the eastern sea. When he heard of the rise of King Wên, he roused himself and said, 'Why should I not go and follow him? I have heard that the chief of the West knows well how to nourish the old.'
>
> "Those two old men were the greatest old men of the empire. When they came to follow King Wên, it was the fathers of the empire coming to follow him. When the fathers of the empire joined him, how could the sons go to any other?
>
> "Were any of the princes to practice the government of King

Wên, within seven years he would be sure to assume the government of the empire."[93]

When a ruler who practiced the Way of Right was constrained to resort to arms, "when he struck in the east, the rude tribes in the west murmured. So did those on the north, when he was engaged in the south. Their cry was: 'Why does he make us last?' Thus, the people's longing for him was like their longing for rain in time of great drought. The frequenters of the markets stopped not. Those engaged in weeding in the fields made no change in their operations."[94]

"He who obtains the Way has many to assist him. He who loses the Way has few to assist him. When this—the being assisted by few—reaches its extreme point, his own relations revolt from the prince. When the being assisted by many reaches its highest point, the whole empire becomes obedient to the prince. When one to whom the whole empire is prepared to be obedient attacks those from whom their own relations revolt, what must be the result? Therefore the true ruler may not fight, but if he does fight, he must overcome." For the object was to "save the people from the midst of fire and water, seizing only their oppressors and destroying them."

The word "struck" referred to a punitive expedition dispatched by superiors against inferiors. Only when such expeditions proceeded from the Son of Heaven did the Way prevail. It is also said, "When the ruler is fond of benevolence, he has no enemy in the world."

Confucius said, "When the Way prevails in the empire, ceremonies, music and punitive military expeditions proceed from the Son of Heaven. When the Way does not prevail in the empire, ceremonies, music and punitive military expeditions proceed from the princes. When these things proceed from the princes, as a rule, the cases will be few in which they do not lose their power in ten generations. When they proceed from the Great Officials of the princes, the cases will be few in which they do not lose their power in five generations. When the subsidiary ministers of the Great Officials hold in their grasp the orders of the State, as a rule, the cases will be few in which they do not lose their power in three generations.

"When the Way prevails in the empire, government will not be in the hands of the Great Officials.

"When the Way prevails in the empire, there will be no discussions among the common people."[35]

Mencius said, "In the 'Spring and Autumn' there are no righteous wars. Instances indeed there are of one war better than others.

" 'Striking' is when the supreme authority punishes its subjects by force of arms. Hostile States do not strike at one another."[96]

Mencius said, "When the Way prevails in the empire, princes of little virtue are submissive to those of great, and those of little worth to those of great. When the Way does not prevail in the empire, princes of small power are submissive to those of great and the weak to the stong. Both these cases are the rule of Heaven. They who accord with Heaven are preserved, and they who rebel against Heaven perish.

"Duke Ching of Ch'i said, 'Not to be able to command others and at the same time to refuse to receive their commands is to cut oneself off from all intercourse with others.' His tears flowed forth while he gave his daughter to be married to the prince of Wu.

"Now the small States imitate the large, and yet are ashamed to receive their commands. This is like a scholar's being ashamed to receive the commands of his master.

"For a prince who is ashamed of this, the best plan is to imitate King Wên. Let him imitate King Wên, in five years, if his State be large, or in seven years, if it be small, he will be sure to assume the government of the empire.

"It is said in the *Book of Songs*,

'The descendants of the sovereigns of the Shang dynasty,
Are in number more than hundreds of thousands,
But, God having passed His decree,
They are all submissive to Chou.
They are submissive to Chou,
Because the decree of Heaven is not unchanging.
The officials of Yin, admirable and alèrt,
Pour out the libations and assist in the capital of Chou.'

Confucius said, 'As against so benevolent a sovereign, they could not be deemed a multitude.' Thus, if the prince of a State loves benevolence, he will have no opponent in all the empire.

"Now they wish to have no opponent in all the empire, but they do not seek to attain this by being benevolent. This is like a man laying hold of a heated substance and not having first dipped it in water. It is said in the *Book of Songs*,

'Who can take up a heated substance
Without first dipping it (in water)?' "[97]

Wan Chang asked Mencius, saying, "Sung is a small State. Its ruler is now setting about to practice the true royal government, and Ch'i and Ch'u hate and attack him. What in this case is to be done?"

Mencius replied, "When T'ang dwelt in Po, he adjoined to the State of Ko, the chief of which was living in a dissolute state and neglecting his proper sacrifices. T'ang sent messengers to inquire why he did not sacrifice. He replied, 'I have no means of supplying the necessary victims.' On this, T'ang caused oxen and sheep to be sent to him, but he ate them and still continued not to sacrifice. T'ang again sent messengers to ask him the same question as before, when he replied, 'I have no means of obtaining the necessary millet.' On this, T'ang sent the mass of the people of Po to go and till the ground for him, while the old and feeble carried their food to him. The chief of Ko led his people to intercept those who were thus charged with wine, cooked rice, millet and paddy, and took their stores from them, while they killed those who refused to give them up. There was a boy who had some millet and meat for the laborers, who was thus slain and robbed. What is said in the *Book of History*, 'The chief of Ko behaved as an enemy to the provision-carriers,' has reference to this.

"Because of his murder of this boy, T'ang proceeded to punish him. All within the four seas said, 'It is not because he desires the riches of the empire, but to avenge a common man and woman.'

When T'ang began his work of executing justice, he commenced with Ko, and though he made eleven punitive expeditions, he had not an enemy in the empire. When he struck in the east, the rude tribes in the west murmured. So did those on the north, when he was engaged in the south. Their cry was, 'Why does he make us last?' Thus the people's longing for him was like their longing for rain in a time of great drought. The frequenters of the markets stopped not. Those engaged in weeding in the fields made no change in their operations. While he put their ruler to death, he consoled the people. His progress was like the falling of opportune rain, and the people were delighted. It is said in the *Book of History*, 'We have waited for our prince. When our prince comes, we may escape from the punishments under which we suffer.'

"There being some who would not become the subjects of Chou, King Wu proceeded to punish them on the east. He gave tranquillity to their people, who welcomed him with baskets full of their black and yellow silks, asying, 'From henceforth we shall serve the sovereign of our dynasty of Chou, that we may be made happy by him.' So they joined themselves, as subjects, to the great city of Chou. Thus the man of station of Shang took baskets full of black and yellow silks to meet the men of station of Chou, and the lower classes of the one met those of the other with baskets of rice and vessels of congee. Wu saved the people from the midst of fire and water, seizing only their oppressor and destroying him.

"In the 'Great Declaration' it is said, 'My power shall be put forth, and invading the territories of Shang, I will seize the oppressor. I will put him to death to punish him; so shall the greatness of my work add luster to T'ang.'

"Sung is not, as you say, practicing true royal government. If it were practicing royal government, all within the four seas would be lifting up their heads, ank looking for its prince, wishing to have him for their sovereign. Great as Ch'i and Ch'u are, what would there be to fear from them?"[98]

Why was it that by practicing the Way of Right a ruler could internally gain the hearts of the people and externally have no opposition in the empire? Mencius analyzed this point minutely and came to the conclusion that such a ruler was "minister of heaven" who practiced the Way of Heaven.

Mencius said, "If a ruler gives honor to worthy men and employs the able, so that the offices shall be filled by individuals of distinction and mark—then all the scholars of the empire will be pleased and wish to stand in his court.

"If in the market-place of his capital, he levies a ground-rent on the shops but does not tax the goods, or enforces the proper regulations without levying a ground-rent—then all the traders of the empire will be pleased and wish to store their goods in his market-place.

"If, at his frontier-passes, there is an inspection of persons but no taxes charged, then all the travelers of the empire will be pleased and wish to make their tours on his roads.

"If he requires that the husbandmen give their mutual aid to cultivate the public field and exacts no other taxes from them—then all the husbandmen of the empire will be pleased and wish to plough in his fields.

"If from the occupiers of the shops in his market-place he does not exact the fine of the individual idler or of the hamlet's quota of cloth, then all the people of the empire will be pleased and wish to come and be his people.

"If a ruler can truly practice these five things, then the people in the neighboring countries will look up to him as a parent. From the first birth of mankind till now, never has anyone led children to attack their parent and succeeded in his design. Thus, such a ruler will not have an enemy in all the empire and he who has no enemy in the empire is the minister of Heaven. Never has there been a ruler in such a case who did not attain to the royal dignity."[99]

After discussing the Kingly Way practiced by Yao, Shun, Yü, T'ang, Wên and Wu, Confucius reduced the essentials of their administrations to generosity, sincerity, earnest activity and justice.

Yao said, "Oh! you, Shun, the Heaven-determined order of succession now rests in your person. Sincerely hold fast the due Mean. If there shall be distress and want within the four seas, the Heavenly revenue will come to a perpetual end."

Shun also used the same language in giving charge to Yü.

T'ang said, "I, the child Lü, presume to use a dark-colored victim and presume to announce to thee, O most great and sovereign God, that the sinner I dare not pardon, and they ministers, O God, I do not keep in obscurity. The examination of them is by thy mind, O God! If, in my person, I commit offenses, they are not to be attributed to the people of the myriad regions. If these people in the myriad regions commit offenses, these offenses must rest on my person."

Chou conferred great gifts, and the good were enriched.

"Although he has his near relatives, they are not equal to my virtuous men. When the people have faults, the blame is on me alone."

He carefully attended to the weights and measures, examined the body of the laws, restored the discarded officials, and the good government of the empire took its course.

He revived States that had been extinguished, restored families whose line of succession had been broken and called to office those who had retired into obscurity, so that throughout the empire the hearts of the people turned towards him.

What he attached chief importance to were the food of the people, the duties of mourning and sacrifices.

"By his generosity, he won all. By his sincerity, he made the people repose trust in him. By his earnest activity, his achievements were great. By his justice, all were delighted."[100]

Mencius constantly met warlike rulers, for he was born in the Warring States period and by the time he died warfare had become the order of the day. As a result, Mencius detested the Way of Might. He branded the warlike as unbenevolent. He described those who sought the expansion of their territory at the expense of their people's lives as "beginning with what they do not care for and proceeding to what they care for."

Mencius said, "The opposite indeed of benevolent was King Hui of Liang. The benevolent, beginning with what they care for, proceed to what they do not care for. Those who are the opposite of benevolent, beginning with what they do not care for, proceed to what they care for.

Kung-sun Ch'ou said, "What do you mean?" Mencius answered, "King Hui of Liang, for the matter of territory, tore and destroyed his people, leading them to battle. Sustaining a great defeat, he would engage again, and afraid lest they should not be able to secure the victory, urged the youths whom he loved till he sacrificed them altogether. This is what I call 'beginning with what they do not care for and proceeding to what they care for.' "[101]

Mencius could see nothing worthwhile in the Way of Might. For this reason he refused to compare himself to Kuan Chung, who "raised his prince to be the leader of all the other princes, and Yen-tzŭ, who "made his prince illustrious." He was even reluctant to refer to the achievements of Duke Huan of Ch'i and Duke Wên of Chin. Rather, he concentrated his effort on extolling the practice of the Way of Right.

Kung-sun Ch'ou asked Mencius, saying, "Master, if you were to obtain the ordering of the government in Ch'i, could you promise yourself to accomplish anew such results as those realized by Kuan Chung and Yen-tzŭ?"

Mencius said, "You are indeed a man of Ch'i. You know about Kuan Chung and Yen-tzŭ, and nothing more.

"Someone asked Tsêng Hsi, saying, 'Sir, to which do you give the superiority—to yourself or to Tsŭ-lu?' Tsêng Hsi looked uneasy and said, 'He was an object of veneration to my late grandfather.' 'Then,' pursued the other, 'Do you give the superiority to yourself or to Kuan Chung?' Tsêng Hsi, flushed with anger and displeased, said, 'How dare you compare me with Kuan Chung? Considering how entirely Kuan Chung possessed the confidence of his prince, how long he enjoyed the direction of the government of the State, and how low, after all, was what he accomplished—how is it that you liken me to him?'

"Thus," concluded Mencius, "Tsêng Hsi would not play Kuan Chung, and is it what you desire for me that I should do so?"

Kung-sun Ch'ou said, "Kuan Chung raised his prince to be the leader of all the other princes and Yen-tzŭ made his prince illustrious, and do you still think it would not be enough for you to do what they did?"

Mencius answered, "To raise Ch'i to the royal dignity would be as easy as it is to turn round the hand."

"So!" returned the other. "The perplexity of your disciple is hereby very much increased. There was King Wên, moreover, with all the virtue that belonged to him; and who did not die till he had reached a hundred years—and till his influence had not penetrated throughout the empire. It required King Wu and the Duke of Chou to continue his course, before that influence greatly prevailed. Now you say that the royal dignity might be so easily obtained—is King Wên then not a sufficient object for imitation?"

Mencius said, "How can King Wên be matched? From T'ang to Wu-ting there had appeared six or seven worthy and sage sovereigns. The empire had been attached to Yin for a long time, and this length of time made a change difficult. Wu-ting had all the princes coming to his court and possessed the empire as if it had been a thing which he moved round in his palm. Then Chou was removed from Wu-ting by no great interval of time. There were still remaining some of the ancient families and of the old manners, of the influence also which had emanated from the earlier sovereigns, and of their good government. Moreover, there were the Viscount of Wei and his second son (or brother), their Royal Highnesses Pi-kan and Viscount of Chi, and Chiao Ko, all men of ability and virtue, who gave their joint assistance to Chou in his government. In consequence of these things, it took a long time for him to lose the throne. There was not a foot of ground which he did not possess. There was not one of all the people who was not his subject. But King Wên at his beginning had only a territory of one hundred square *li*. On all these accounts it was difficult for him immediately to attain to the royal dignity.

"The people of Ch'i have a saying—"A man may have wisdom and discernment, but that is not like embracing the favorable opportunity. A man may have instruments of husbandry, but that is not like waiting for the farming seasons.' The present time is one in which the royal dignity may be easily attained.

In the flourishing periods of the Hsia, Yin and Chou dynasties, the royal domain did not exceed a thousand *li*, and Ch'i embraces so much territory. Cocks crow and dogs bark to one another, all the way to the four borders of the State—so Ch'i possesses the people. No change is needed for the enlarging of its territory: no change is needed for the collecting of a population. If its ruler will put in practice a benevolent government, no power will be able to prevent his becoming sovereign.

"Moveover, never was there a time farther removed than the present from the rise of a true sovereign: never was there a time when the sufferings of the people from tyrannical government were more intense than the present. The hungry readily partake of any food, and the thirsty of any drink.

"Confucius said, 'The flowing progress of virtue is more rapid than the transmission of royal orders by stages and couriers.'

"At the present time, in a country of ten thousand chariots, let benevolent government be put in practice, and the people will be delighted with it, as if they were relieved from hanging by the heels. With half the effort of the ancients, double their achievement is sure to be realized. It is only at this time that such could be the case."[102]

King Hsüan of Ch'i asked, saying, "May I be informed by you of the transactions cf Huan of Ch'i and Wên of Chin?"

Mencius replied, "There were none of the disciples of Chung-ni who spoke about the affairs of Huan and Wên, and therefore they have not been transmitted to these after-ages—your servant has not heard them. If you will have me speak, let it be about royal government."

The King said, "What virtue must there be in order to attain to royal sway?" Mencius answered, 'The love and protection of the people; with this there is no power which can prevent a ruler from attaining to it."[103]

Mencius regarded the five chiefs of the princes (in the passage below) as sinners against the three kings, and the other princes of the time as sinners against the five chiefs. As for the great officials of the time, Mencius regarded them as sinners against the princes because they aided and abetted the princes' pursuits of war, thus conniving with them in their evil-doing.

However, though the five chiefs abandoned the Way of Right, they did succeed in doing certain things that were beneficial to the people. It was the other princes of the time who violated the five prohibitions impossed by the chiefs; they stopped at nothing to exploit and harm the people. That was why Mencius deprecated the Way of Might and exalted the Way of Right on all his visits and in all his pleas to the reigning princes. What he sought very hard was an opportunity to serve them, to bring about good government, to save the people from "water and fire."

Mencius said, "The five chiefs of the princes were sinners against the three kings. The princes of the present day are sinners against the five chiefs. The Great Officials of the present day are sinners against the princes.

"The sovereign visited the princes, which was called 'a Tour of Inspection.' The princes attended at the court of the sovereign, which was called 'Giving a report of office.' It was a custom in the spring to examine the ploughing and supply any deficiency of seed, and in autumn to examine the reaping and assist where there was a deficiency of the crop. When the sovereign entered the boundaries of State, if the new ground was being reclaimed and the old fields well cultivated; if the old were nourished and the worthy honored; and if men of distinguished talents were placed in office: then the prince was rewarded—rewarded with an addition to his territory. On the other hand, if, on entering a State, the ground was found left wild or overrun with weeds; if the old were neglected and the worthy abandoned; and if the offices were filled with hard tax-gatherers: then the prince was reprimanded. If a prince once omitted his attendance at court, he was punished by degradation of rank; if he did so a second time, he was deprived of a portion of his territory; if he did so a third time, the royal forces were set in motion and he was removed from his government. Thus the sovereign commanded the punishment, but did not himself inflict it, while the princes inflicted the punishment, but did not command it. The five chiefs, however, dragged the princes to punish other princes, and hence I say that they were sinners against the three kings.

"Of the five chiefs the most powerful was Duke Huan. At the assembly of the princes in K'uei-ch'iu, he bound the victim and placed the writing upon it but did not slay it to smear their mouths with the blood. The first injunction in their agreement was, 'Slay the unfilial; change not the son who has been appointed heir; exalt not a concubine to be the wife.' The second was, 'Honor the worthy and maintain the talented, to give distinction to the virtuous.' The third was, 'Respect the old and be kind to the young. Be not forgetful of strangers and travelers.' The fourth was, 'Let not offices be hereditary, nor let officials be pluralists. In the selection of officials let the object be to get the proper man. Let not a ruler take it on himself to put to death a Great Official.' The fifth was, 'Follow no crooked policy in making embankments. Impose no restrictions on the sale of grain. Let there be no promotions without first announcing them to the sovereign.' It was then said, 'All we who have united in this agreement shall hereafter maintain amicable relations.' The princes of the present day all violate these five prohibitions, and therefore I say that the princes of the present day are sinners against the five chiefs.

"The crime of him who connives at, and aids, the wickedness of his prince is small, but the crime of him who anticipates and excites that wickedness is great. The Great Officials of the present day all go to meet their sovereigns' wickedness, and so I say that the Great Officials of the present day are sinners against the princes."[104]

Mencius said, "There are men who say, 'I am skillful in marshalling troops, I am skillful at conducting a battle.' They are great criminals.

"If the ruler of a State loves benevolence, he will have no enemy in the empire.

"When T'ang struck in the south, the rude tribes on the north murmured. When he was doing so in the east, the rude tribes on the west murmured. Their cry was, 'Why does he make us last?'

"When King Wu punished Yin, he had only three hundred chariots of war and three thousand life-guards.

"The king said, 'Do not fear. I come to pacify you. I am no enemy to the people.' On this, they bowed their heads to the earth, like falling mountains.

"Striking is but another form of the word 'rectification.' Each State wishing itself to be rectified, what need is there for fighting?"[105]

Confucius never advocated "strength." This was one of the four things he never discussed. ("The subjects on which the Master did not talk were: extraordinary things, feats of strength, disorder and spiritual beings." [106] He was of course even more staunchly opposed to war. But in his criticism of Kuan Chung he recognized Kuan's strength, as shown in his services to the country. Nevertheless, he said Kuan was not frugal, nor knew he propriety.

Tzŭ-lu said, "Duke Huan caused his brother Chiu to be killed, when Chao-Hu died with his master, but Kuan Chung did not die. May not I say that Kuan Chung was wanting in benevolence?"

The Master said, "Duke Huan assembled all the princes together, and that not with weapons of war and chariots—it was all through the influence of Kuan Chung. It was his benevolence. It was his benevolence."[107]

Tsŭ-kung said, "Was Kuan Chung not wanting in benevolence? When Duke Huan caused his brother Chiu to be killed, Kuan Chung was not able to die with him. Moreover, he became prime minister to Huan."

The Master said, "Kuan Chung served as Prime Minister to Duke Huan, made him leader of all the princes and united and rectified the whole empire. Down to the present day, the people enjoy the gifts which he conferred. But for Kuan Chung, we should now be wearing our hair unbound and the lappets of our coats buttoning on the left side.

"Will you require from him the small fidelity of common men and common women, who would commit suicide in a stream or ditch, no one knowing anything about them?" [108]

Someone asked about Tzŭ-ch'an. The Master said, "He was a kind man."

He asked about Tzŭ-hsi. The Master said, "That man! That man!"

He asked again about Kuan Chung. "For him," said the Master, "the city of P'ien with three hundred families was taken from the chief of the Po family, who did not utter a murmuring word, though, to the end of his life, he had only coarse rice to eat." [109]

Kuan Chung was the first to initiate international organization in China, He assembled the princes and unified the country by agreement (treaty) rather than war. However, since this association of States relied on the Way of Might, it could not and did not last long.

As the author of the *Spring and Autumn Annals,* Confucius of course could not omit mentioning the deeds of Duke Huan of Ch'i and Duke Wên of Chin. He commented: "Duke Wên of Chin was crafty and not upright. Duke Huan of Ch'i was upright and not crafty." [110]

Both Confucius and Mencius had tremendous self-confidence in their ability to bring about the restoration of the Kingly Way. They felt that, given an opportunity to run any government, they could accomplish the task in a short time. According to Confucius, "In three years the government would be perfected." Mencius said, "...in five years, if his (a prince's) State be large, or in seven years, if it be small, he will be sure to assume the government of the empire."

The Master said, "...If anyone employs me, may I not make an eastern Chou?" [111]

The Master said, "If there were any (of the princes) who would employ me, in the course of twelve months, I should have done something considerable. In three years, the government would be perfected." [112]

Mencius said, "...Now the small States imitate the large, and yet are ashamed to receive their commands. This is like a scholar's being ashamed to receive the commands of his master.

"For a prince who is ashamed of this, the best plan is to imitate King Wên. Let him imitate King Wên, and in five years, if his State be large, or in seven years, if it be small, he will be sure to assume the government of the empire." [113]

Confucius maintained that any change in the political system of a country would take time. But he regarded change from the Way of Might to the Way of Right as compatible with the evolution of political institutions. In other words, such a change was in line with the will of Heaven and the wishes of men, and therefore it should pose no great difficulty.

The Master said, "If a truly royal ruler were to arise, it would still require a generation, and then virtue would prevail." [114]

The Master said, "Ch'i, by one change, would come to the State of Lu. Lu, by one change, would come to a State where the Way prevailed." [115]

In order to convince the reigning princes that the practice of the Way of Right would not be difficult, Mencius in simple language showed that the starting point of the Kingly Way is the "mind which cannot bear to see the sufferings of others." This is the feeling of commiseration, which is the beginning of benevolence. It is inherent in every human being. If a ruler can include the practice of benevolence in his administration, he is well on the Way of Right.

Mencius said, "All men have a mind which cannot bear to see the sufferings of others.

"The ancient kings had this commiserating mind, and they, as a matter of course, had likewise a commiserating government. When with a commiserating mind was practiced a commiserating government, to rule the empire was as easy a matter as to make anything go round in the palm.

"When I say that all men have a mind which cannot bear to see the sufferings of others, my meaning may be illustrated thus: even nowadays, if men suddenly see a child about to fall into a well, they will without exception experience a feeling of alarm and distress. They will feel so, not as a ground on which they may befriend the child's parents, nor as a ground on which they may seek the praise of their neighbors and friends, nor from a dislike of the cry made by the child.

"From this case we may perceive that he who does not have the feeling of commiseration is not a man, that he who does not have the feeling of shame and dislike is not a man, that he who does not have the feeling of modesty and concession is not a man, and that he who does not have the feeling of right and wrong is not a man.

"The feeling of commiseration is the beginning of benevolence. The feeling of shame and dislike is the beginning of righteousness. The feeling of modesty and concession is the beginning of propriety. The feeling of right and wrong is the beginning of wisdom.

"Men have these four beginnings just as they have their four limbs. When men, having these four beginnings, yet say of themselves that they cannot have them, they play the thief with themselves, and he who says of his prince that he cannot have them plays the thief with his prince.

"Since all men have these four beginnings in themselves, let them know to give them all their development and completion, and the issue will be like that of fire which has begun to burn or that of a spring which has begun to find vent. Let them have their complete development, and they will suffice to love and protect all within the four seas. Let them be denied that development, and they will not suffice for a man to serve his parents with." [116]

Mencius encouraged King Hsüan of Ch'i by telling him that when the king could not bear to kill an ox, it was due to his feeling of benevolence. If the king could extend that feeling to the treatment of his subjects, Mencius said, he would be "practicing a commiserating government with a commiserating mind." And this would be the beginning of the Way of Right. Mencius emphasized this was something the King *did* not do, not what he *could* not do. Since at that time the State of Ch'i embraced a territory equal to 90 per cent of the whole empire, the practice of the Kingly Way would have been easier than at the time of T'ang and King Wên.

Mencius' plea so touched King Hsüan that the king responded: "When you, Master, spoke those words, the movements of compassion began to work in my mind." He added: "Although I am deficient in intelligence and vigor, I will try to carry your instructions into effect." And so Mencius spoke to the king in detail about the enrichment and education of the people in accordance with the Kingly Way.

King Hsüan of Ch'i asked, saying, "May I be informed by you of the transactions of Huan of Ch'i and Wên of Chin?"

Mencius replied, "There were none of the disciples of Chung-ni who spoke about the affairs of Huan and Wên, and therefore they have not been transmitted to these after-ages; your servant has not heard of them. If you will have me speak, let it be about royal government.

The king said, "What virtue must there be in order to attain to royal sway?" Mencius answered, "the love and protection of the people; with this there is no power which can prevent a ruler from attaining to it."

The king asked again, "Is such a man as I competent to love and protect the people?" Mencius said, "Yes." "How do you know that I am competent for that?" "I heard the following incident from Hu Ho: 'The king,' said he, 'was sitting aloft in the hall, when a man appeared, leading an ox past the lower part of it. The king saw him and asked, "Where is the ox going?" The man replied, "We are going to consecrate a bell with its blood." The king said, "Let it go. I cannot bear its frightened appearance, as if it were innocent and going to the place of death." The man answered, "Shall we then omit the consecration of the bell?" The king said, "How can that be omitted? Change it for a sheep." ' I do not know whether this incident really occurred."

The king replied, "It did," and then Mencius said, "The heart seen in this is sufficient to carry you to the royal sway. The people all supposed that Your Majesty grudged the animal, but your servant knows surely that it was Your Majesty's not being able to bear the sight which made you do as you did."

The king said, "You are right. And yet there really were people who thought the way they did. But though Ch'i is a small and narrow State, how should I grudge one ox? Indeed it was because I could not bear its frightened appearance, as if it were innocent and going to the place of death, that therefore I changed it for a sheep."

Mencius pursued, "Let not Your Majesty deem it strange that the people should think you were grudging the animal. When you changed a large one for a small, how should they know the true reason? If you felt pained by its being led without guilt to the place of death, what was there to choose between an ox and a sheep? The king laughed and said, "What really was my mind in the matter? I did not grudge the expense of it and changed it for a sheep. There was reason in the people's saying that I grudged it."

"There is no harm in their saying so," said Mencius. "Your conduct was an artifice of benevolence. You saw the ox and had not seen the sheep. So is the superior man affected towards animals, that, having seen them alive, he cannot bear to see them die; having heard their dying cries, he cannot bear to eat their flesh. Therefore he keeps away from his kitchen."

The king was pleased and said, "It is said in the *Book of Songs*, 'The minds of others, I am able to conjecture;' this is verified, my Master, in your discovery of my motive. I indeed did the thing, but when I turned my thoughts inward and examined into it, I could not discover my own mind. When you, Master, spoke those words, they moved my heart. How is it that this heart has in it what is equal to the royal sway?"

Mencius replied, "Suppose a man were to make this statement to Your Majesty, 'My strength is sufficient to lift three thousand catties, but it is not sufficient to lift one feather; my eyesight is sharp enough to examine the point of an autumn hair, but I do not see a wagon-load of faggots;' would Your Majesty believe what he said?" "No," was the answer, on which Mencius proceeded, "Now here is kindness sufficient to reach animals, but no benefits are extended from it to the people. How is this? Is an exception to be made here? The truth is, the feather is not lifted, because strength is not used; the wagon-load of firewood is not seen, because the eyesight is not used; and the people are not loved and protected, because kindness is not employed. Therefore Your Majesty's not exercising the royal sway is because you do not do it, not because you are not able to do it."

The king asked, "How may the difference between the not doing a thing and the not being able to do it be represented?" Mencius replied, "In such a thing as taking the T'ai mountain under your arm and leaping over the north sea over it, if you say to people— 'I am not able to it,' that is a real case of not being able. In such a matter as breaking off a branch from a tree at the order of a superior, if you say to people 'I am not able to do it,' that is a case of not doing it; it is not a case of not being able to do it. Therefore Your Majesty's not exercising the royal sway is not such a case as that of taking the T'ai mountain under your arm and leaping over the north sea with it. Your Majesty's not exercising the royal sway is a case like that of breaking off a branch from a tree.

"Treat with the reverence due to age the elders in your own family, so that the elders in the families of others shall be similarly treated; treat with the kindness due to youth the young in your own family, so that the young in the families of others shall be similarly treated—do this, and the empire may be made to go round in your palm. It is said in the *Book of Songs*, 'His example affected his wife. It reached to his brothers, and was put into practice in the family and country.' The language shows how

King Wên took his kindly heart and exercised it towards those parties. Therefore a prince's carrying out his kindly heart will suffice for the love and protection of all within the four seas, and if he does not carry it out, he will not be able to protect his wife and children. The way in which the ancients came greatly to surpass other men was no other but this: simply that they knew how to carry out, so as to affect others, what they themselves did. Now your kindness is sufficient to reach to animals, but no benefits are extended from it to reach the people. How is this? Is an exception to be made here?

"By weighing, we know what things are light and what heavy. By measuring, we know what things are long and what short. The relations of all things may be thus determined, and it is especially true of the mind. I beg Your Majesty to measure it.

"You collect your equipments of war, endanger your soldiers and officers and excite the resentment of the other princes; do these things cause you pleasure in your mind?"

The king replied, "No. How should I derive pleasure from these things? My object in them is to seek for what I greatly desire."

Mencius said, "May I hear from you what it is that you greatly desire?" The king laughed and did not speak. Mencius resumed, "Are you led to desire it, because you have not enough of rich and sweet food for your mouth? Or because you have not enough of light and warm clothing for your body? Or because you have not enough of beautifully colored objects to delight your eyes? Or because you have not voices and tones enough to please your ears? Or because you have not enough attendants and favorites to stand before you and receive your orders? Your Majesty's officials are sufficient to supply you with those things. How can Your Majesty be led to entertain a desire for such things?"   "No" said the king; "my desire is not for them." Mencius added, "Then, what Your Majesty greatly desires may be known. You wish to enlarge your territory, to have Ch'in and Ch'u wait at your court, to rule the Middle Kingdom and pacify the barbarous tribes that surround it. But doing what you do to seek for what you desire is like climbing a tree to seek for fish."

The king said, "Is it so bad as that?" "It is even worse," was the reply. "If you climb a tree to seek for fish, although you do not get the fish, you will not suffer any subsequent calamity. But doing what you do to seek for what you desire, doing it moreover with all your heart, you will assuredly afterwards meet with calamities." The king asked, "May I hear from you all about it?" Mencius said, "If the people of Tsou should fight with the people

of Ch'u, which of them does Your Majesty think would conquer?"
"The people of Ch'u would conquer." "And so it is certain that a
small country cannot contend with a great, that few cannot contend
with many, that the weak cannot contend with the strong. The
territory within the four seas embraces nine divisions, each of a
thousand *li* square. All Ch'i together is but one of them. If with
one part you try to subdue the other eight, what is the difference
between that and Tsou's contending with Ch'u? Perhaps you should
go back to the root of the matter.

"Now, if Your Majesty will institute a government whose action
shall be benevolent, this will cause all the officials in the empire to
stand in Your Majesty's court, all the farmers to wish to plough in
Your Majesty's fields, all the merchants to wish to store their goods
in Your Majesty's market-places, all travelers to make their tours
on Your Majesty's roads, and all throughout the empire who feel
aggrieved by their rulers to wish to come and complain to Your
Majesty. And when they are so bent, who will be able to keep
them back?"

The king said, "I am stupid and not able to advance to this. I
wish you, my Master, to assist my intentions. Teach me clearly;
although I am deficient in intelligence and vigor, I will try to carry
your instructions into effect."

Mencius replied, "They are only men of education who, without
a certain livelihood, are able to maintain a fixed heart. As to the
people, if they have not a certain livelihood, it follows that they
will not have a fixed heart. And if they have not a fixed heart,
there is nothing which they will not do, in the way of self-
abandonment, of moral deflection, of depravity and of wild license.
When they are thus involved in crime, to follow them up and punish
them—this is to entrap the people. How can such a thing as
entrapping a people be done under the rule of a benevolent man?

"Therefore an intelligent ruler will regulate the livelihood of
the people, so as to make sure that, above, they shall have sufficient
wherewith to serve their parents and, below, sufficient wherewith to
support their wives and children; that in good years they shall
always be abundantly satisfied, and that in bad years they shall
escape the danger of perishing. After this he may urge them to
what is good, for in this case the people will follow after it with ease.

"Now, the livelihood of the people is so regulated that, above,
they have not sufficient wherewith to serve their parents and, below,
they have not sufficient wherewith to support their wives and
children. Notwithstanding good years, their lives are continually
distressing and, in bad years, they do not escape perishing. In such
circumstances they do not even find it possible to save themselves

from death. What leisure have they to cultivate propriety and righteousness?

"If Your Majesty wishes to effect this regulation of the livelihood of the people, why not turn to the root of the matter?

"Let mulberry-trees be planted about the homesteads with their five *mou*, and persons of fifty years may be clothed with silk. In keeping fowls, pigs, dogs and swine, let not their times of breeding be neglected, and persons of seventy years may eat meat. Let there not be taken away the time that is proper for the cultivation of the farm with its hundred *mou*, and the family of eight mouths that is supported by it shall not suffer from hunger. Let careful attention be paid to education in schools, the inculcation in it especially of the filial and fraternal duties, and gray-haired men will not be seen upon the roads, carrying burdens on their backs or on their heads. It never has been that the ruler of a State where such results were seen—the old wearing silk and eating meat and the black-haired people suffering neither from hunger nor cold—did not attain to the royal dignity."[117]

King Hsüan of Ch'i confessed to Mencius that he had the "infirmities" of being "fond of sex" and "fond of wealth," which might prevent him from practicing the Kingly Way. Mencius replied that if he could provide the people with what they should have in the way of "sex" and "wealth," he would not incur their displeasure by giving himself somewhat more than they enjoyed. In short, "When a prince loves what the people love and hates what the people hate, then is he what is called the parent of the people." Thus there is no conflict with the Kingly Way.

King Hsüan of Ch'i said, "People all tell me to destroy the Hall of Distinction. Shall I do so?"

Mencius replied, "The Hall of Distinction is appropriate to the sovereigns. If Your Majesty wishes to practice the true royal government, then do not destroy it."

The King said, "May I hear from you what the true royal government is?" "Formerly," was the reply, "King Wên's government of Ch'i was as follows: The husbandmen cultivated for the government one-ninth of the land; the descendants of officials were salaried; at the passes and in the markets, strangers were inspected, but goods were not taxed; there were no prohibitions respecting the ponds and weirs; the wives and children of criminals were not involved in their guilt. There were the old and wifeless, or widowers; the old and husbandless, or widows; the old and childless, or solitaries; the young and fatherless, or orphans—those four classes are the most destitute of the people and have none to whom they can tell their wants, and King Wên, in the institution of his government with its benevolent action, made them the first objects of his regard, as it is said in the *Book of Songs*,

'The rich may get through life well;

But alas; for the miserable and solitary!' "

The king said, "O excellent words!" Mencius said, "Since Your Majesty deems them excellent, why do you not practice them?" The reply was, "Formerly Kung-liu was fond of wealth. It is said in the *Book of Songs*,

'He reared his ricks and filled his granaries,

He tied up dried provisions and grain,

In bottomless bags and sacks,

That he might gather his people together and glorify his State.

With bows and arrows all displayed,

With shields and spears and battle-axes, large and small,

He commenced his march.'

In this way those who remained in their old seat had their ricks and granaries, and those who marched had their bags of provisions. It was not till after this that he thought he could begin his march. If Your Majesty loves wealth, share it with the people, and what difficulty will there be in your attaining the royal sway?"

The king said, "I have an infirmity; I am fond of sex." The reply was, "Formerly King T'ai was fond of sex and loved his wife. It is said in the *Book of Songs*,

'Ku-kung T'an-fu

Was departing next morning on horseback.

By the banks of the western waters,

As far as the foot of Ch'i hill,

Along with the Lady of Chiang,

He came, and together chose the site for their settlement.'

At that time, in the seclusion of the house, there were no dissatisfied women, and abroad, there were no unmarried men. If Your Majesty loves sex, share the same gratification with the people, and what difficulty will there be in your attaining the royal sway?"[118]

The Kingly Way did not mean anarchy. The law still had its proper role to play. But when benevolent government prevailed, the people had enough to wear and eat. They enjoyed peace and prosperity, upheld propriety and cultivated virtue. They had neither apprehensions nor disputes; rather, they moved constantly toward what was good and lawful. Hence Confucius said. "In hearing litigations, I am like any other body. What is necessary, however, is to cause the people to have no litigations."[119]

"With adequate clothing and food, there is knowledge of propriety and righteousness; and with full granaries, there is knowledge of honor and disgrace." In other words, when the root is well-ordered, the branches are equally well-ordered. On the other hand, where the Way of Might prevails, so do strict laws and severe punishments to force obedience on the people. The difference between the rule of propriety and the rule of law depends on which one receives the most emphasis. When stress is laid on propriety, government and education go hand in hand, the ruler sets a personal example, the people pursue what is good as water flows downward, and though there is law, there is little occasion for its application. However, when stress is laid on law, force enters in; the people must obey the law rather than perform good on their own initiative. "Virtue alone is not sufficient for the exercise of government; laws alone cannot carry themselves into practice."[120]

Law originates from propriety; propriety from virtue; and virtue from the Way. Law is man-made. At times it can be misinterpreted, toyed with or circumvented. While propriety and virtue are not as concrete as law, nor as clearly delineated, yet they are understood by all men. This is so because all men share the same reasoning about the law and cannot easily evade it. To talk about law in the absence of virtue is to dispense with the root and pursue the branches. The reason our ancient sages upheld the Kingly Way (the Way of Right) and condemned the Way of Might was to impress on their offspring the importance of the root. Then they could establish the great standard rules of conduct, make progress toward perfection and highest excellence, and lay the foundation for the eternal existence of the Chinese nation.

Like individuals, States with a glorious history are fond of recalling their past. For one thing, by reviewing past accomplishments, they can better assess what the future may bring and be more certain that their nation's success will extend into the oncoming ages. In the several thousand years of China's history countless dynasties have changed hands. The reasons for their rise and fall are clear. That is the meaning of the saying.

"An unforgotten past is a teacher for the future."

Today the conclusions we deduce from thousands of experiments are called scientific principles, formulas and standards. In like manner, are not the political principles, systems and measures worked out by the people through several thousand years of practical experience valuable to their descendants and worthy of emulation? Hence it is said, "To raise a thing high, we must begin from the top of a mound or a hill; to dig to a great depth, we must commence in the low ground of a stream or a marsh. Can he be pronounced wise, who, in the exercise of government, does not proceed according to the Ways of the former kings?" For only in this way can the pitfalls of earlier rulers be avoided. And not only can a great deal of time be saved, but quick results can be produced.

Benevolent government is of supreme importance in the administration of a country and in the pacification of the world. Mencius compared it to the importance of the compass and square in the formation of circles and squares. Again, he saw it as just as important as pitch-tubes were to the determination of the five notes. What he counseled against most was the condition depicted in this passage: "Let a man who is ignorant be fond of using his own judgment; let a man without rank be fond of assuming a directing power to himself; let a man who is living in the present age go back to the ways of antiquity—on the persons of all who act thus calamities will be sure to come."[121]

Mencius said, "The power of vision of Li Lou and skill of hand of Kung-shu, without the compass and square, could not form squares and circles. The acute ear of the music-master K'uang, without the pitch-tubes, could not determine correctly the five notes. The Ways of Yao and Shun, without a benevolent government, could not pacify and govern the empire.

"There are now princes who have benovolent hearts and a reputation for benevolence, while yet the people do not receive any benefits from them, nor will they leave any example to future ages—all because they do not put into practice the Ways of the ancient kings.

"Hence we have the saying: 'Virtue alone is not sufficient for the exercise of government; laws alone cannot carry themselves into practice.'

"It is said in the *Book of Songs*,

> 'Without transgression, without forgetfulness,
> Follow the ancient statutes.'

Never has anyone fallen into error who followed the laws of the ancient kings.

"When the sages had used the vigor of their eyes, they called in to their aid the compass, the square, the level and the line, to make things round, square, level and straight—the use of the instruments is inexhaustible. When they had used their power of hearing to the utmost, they called in the pitch-tubes to their aid to determine the five notes—the use of those tubes is inexhaustible. When they had extended to the utmost the thoughts of their hearts, they called in to their aid a government that could not endure to witness the sufferings of men—and their benevolence overspread the empire.

"Hence we have the saying: 'To raise a thing high, we must begin from the top of a mound or a hill; to dig to a great depth, we must commence in the low ground of a stream or a marsh.' Can he be pronounced wise who, in the exercise of government, does not proceed according to the Ways of the former kings?

"Therefore only the benevolent ought to be in high stations. When a man destitute of benevolence is in a high station, he thereby disseminates his wickedness among all below him.

"When the prince has no principles by which he examines his administration and his ministers have no laws by which they keep themselves in the discharge of their duties, then in the court obedience is not paid to principle and in the office obedience is not paid to rule. Superiors violate the laws of righteousness and inferiors violate the penal laws. It is only by a fortunate chance that a State in such a case is preserved.

"Therefore it is said, 'It is not the exterior and interior walls being incomplete and the supply of weapons offensive and defensive not being large, which constitutes the calamity of a country. It is not the cultivable area not being extended and stores and wealth not being accumulated which occasions the ruin of a State.' When superiors do not observe the rules of propriety and inferiors do not learn, then seditious people spring up and that State will perish in no time.

"It is said in the *Book of Songs*,

> 'When such an overthrow of Chou is being produced by Heaven,
> Be not ye so much at your ease!'

" 'At your ease'—that is, dilatory. And so dilatory may these officials be deemed who serve their prince without righteousness, who take office and retire from it without regard to propriety and who in their words disown the Ways of the ancient kings.

"Therefore it is said, 'To urge one's sovereign to difficult achievements may be called showing respect for him. To set before him what is good and repress his perversities may be called showing reverence for him. He who does not do these things, saying to himself, "My sovereign is incompetent to this," may be said to play the thief with him.' "[122]

Mencius said, "It was by benevolence that the three dynasties gained the throne, and by not being benevolent that they lost it.

"It is by the same means that the decaying and flourishing, the preservation and perishing, of States are determined.

"If the sovereign is not benevolent, he cannot preserve his territory within the four seas. If the Head of a State is not benevolent, he cannot preserve his rule. If a high noble or great official is not benevolent, he cannot preserve his ancestral temple. If a scholar or common man is not benevolent, he cannot preserve his four limbs..."[123]

The practice of benevolent government, it is true, depends on the implementation of ancient principles. But the human factor likewise cannot be ignored. Hence, "only the benevolent ought to be in high stations. When a man destitute of benevolence is in a high station, he thereby disseminates his wickedness among all below him." Why is it that such a man can do this? Because "the fondness of a superior for anything is sure to be exceeded by that of his inferiors." In addition to Yao and Shun, there were also Yü, T'ang, Wên, Wu and the Duke of Chou who enjoyed successful kingly administrations. All were devoted to their government. They treated their people as if they had been injured, practiced what was good with delight and without weariness, and employed the worthy without regard to their qualifications. Their benevolence became a lofty example for later ages.

Mencius said, "Yü hated the pleasant wine and loved good words. T'ang held fast the Mean and employed worthy men without regard to their qualifications. King Wên looked on the people as he would on a man who was wounded, and he looked towards the Way as if he could not see it. King Wu did not slight the near and did not forget the distant. The Duke of Chou desired to unite in himself the virtues of those kings, those founders of the three dynasties, that he might display in his practice the four things which they did. If he saw anything in them not suited to his time, he looked up and thought about it, from daytime into the night, and when he was fortunate enough to master the difficulty, he sat waiting for the morning."[124]

In short, although morality is intangible, its strength is nevertheless unfathomable. The reason is rather obvious. Since morality embraces the principle governing the common existence and evolution of mankind and its application, it is of vital importance to every one of us. In the mind and vision of everyone there is a definite moral standard which all are willing to maintain. As a result everyone has the ability and is qualified to judge. No matter what a man's past conduct has been, when he dies, a final judgment is passed. This is due to the fact that a reliable public opinion is always in existence in society. A man may have done a hundred good deeds, but once he commits an evil one it can cancel out all the good he has done. The strictness of this judgment shows what moral strength it possesses.

Intangible strength prevails over tangible strength—and so morality prevails over force and the Kingly Way of Right, over the Way of Might.

For this reason Confucius was even inclined to praise a horse —not for its strength, but for its other good qualities—thus pointing the way to future generations in the shaping of their conduct. "The Master said, 'A horse is called a *chi*, not because of its strength, but because of its other good qualities.' "[125]

D. Principles Governing Order and Confusion, Rise and Fall

The rise and fall of a country are generally attributable to certain causes which have not been present for merely a day or two. These causes are not traceable to external factors even in one out of ten cases. In general, those who merely enjoy their existence and are blind to the possibility of their ruin are doomed to extinction. On the other hand, those who realize their approaching ruin and strive to avoid the catastrophe are likely to succeed. Hence, it is said:

> ...When a nation is about to flourish, there are sure to be happy
> omens; and when it is about to perish, there are sure to be unlucky
> omens. Such events are seen in the milfoil and tortoise and affect
> the movements of the four limbs. When calamity or happiness is
> about to come, the good shall certainly be foreknown by him (who
> has the most entire sincerity), and the evil also...[126]

Since the people are the foundation of a nation, a country
can enjoy peace and tranquillity only when they are consolidated.
Therefore, gaining the hearts of the people not only has a bearing
on the peace and order of a country but vitally affects its rise
and fall.

> Mencius said, "Chieh and Chou's losing the throne arose from
> their losing the people, and to lose the people means to lose their
> hearts. There is a way to get the empire: get the people, and the
> empire is got. There is a way to get the people: get their hearts,
> and the people are got. There is a way to get their hearts: it is
> simply to collect for them what they like and not to lay on them
> what they dislike.
> "The people turn to a benevolent rule as water flows downwards.
> and as wild animals fly to the wilderness."[127]

How can the hearts of the people be gained?. By any one of
the nine standard rules stated above. When these rules are applied,
the ruler is said to have a good omen. to have obtained the Way
and to have acted in accord with Heaven, achieving a well-ordered
and flourishing State. On the other hand, when the rules are not
applied, the ruler is said to have a bad or unlucky omen, to have
lost the Way and rebelled against Heaven, bringing disorder and
possibly ruin to his State.

> Mencius said, "...He who obtains the Way has many to assist
> him. He who loses the Way has few to assist him. When this—
> being assisted by few—reaches its extreme point, his relations revolt
> from the prince. When being assisted by many reaches its highest
> point, the whole empire becomes obedient to the prince..."[128]
> ...This shows that, by gaining the people, the kingdom is gained,
> and, by losing the people, the kingdom is lost...[129]
> In the "Announcement to K'ang" it is said, "The decree indeed
> may not always rest on us; that is, goodness obtains the decree, and
> the want of goodness loses it."[130]
> Mencius said, "...They who accord with Heaven are preserved,
> and they who rebel against Heaven perish."[131]

The nine standard rules are conducive to gaining the people's hearts because they are consistent with the Way, hinge on benevolence, accord with Heaven and respond to the requirements of men. First, the cultivation of the person upholds propriety and stresses reverence. Secondly, the honoring of worthy men means the respect of virtue and delight in the Way. Third, affection towards relatives is the basis of benevolence. Fourth, respect towards the great ministers involves reverent attendance to duty and sincerity. Fifth, the kind and considerate treatment of the whole body of officials brings loyalty and truthfulness to the fore. Sixth, dealing with the mass of people as children means the widespread extension of benevolence and love. Seventh, the encouragement of all classes of artisans results in the enrichment of the people and the strengthening of the country. Eighth, the indulgent treatment of men who live far off shows a love of goodness and politeness. Ninth, the kindly cherishing of the princes of the States gives rise to the diffusion of benevolence throughout the empire.

Although there are nine rules to be applied, the crux lies in the first, which deals with the cultivation of personal character as an example to all the people. Hence, it is said, "When the person is cultivated, the Way is established," and when the Way is followed by the upper classes, the laws will be obeyed by the others, obedience will be paid to the Way in court and office, superior men will follow the rules of righteousness and common men will avoid the violation of penal laws. In a word, there would be benevolent government. Under these circumstances, could anything other than a well-established and flourishing State exist?

> Mencius said, "When the prince has no principles by which he examines his administration and his ministers have no laws by which they keep themselves in the discharge of their duties, then in the court obedience is not paid to principle and in the office obedience is not paid to rule. Superiors violate the laws of righteousness and inferiors violate the penal laws. It is only by a fortunate chance that a State in such a case is preserved.
>
> "Therefore it is said, 'It is not the exterior and interior walls being incomplete and the supply of weapons offensive and defensive not being large, which constitutes the calamity of a country. It is not the cultivable area not being extended and stores and wealth not being accumulated, which occasions the ruin of a State.' When

superiors do not observe the rules of propriety and inferiors do not
learn, then seditious people spring up and that State will perish in
no time."[132]

All this emphasizes how important it is to establish the Way
and achieve benevolent government. But we must reiterate that
"government depends on men." The practice of benevolent
government cannot be accomplished without men of benevolence,
especially those who occupy high positions in the administration.
Hence it is said, "It (the Way of the ancient sages) waits for the
proper man, and then it is trodden."[133]

> Mencius said, "...Therefore only the benevolent ought to be in
> high stations. When a man destitute of benevolence is in a high
> station, he thereby disseminates his wickedness among all below
> him."[134]

If a non-benevolent man in a high office can have a bad
influence on those below him, can a benevolent man in a similar
situation have a good influence on those below him? The answer
is "Yes."

> Never has there been a case of the sovereign loving benevolence
> and the people not loving righteousness. Never has there been a
> case where the people have loved righteousness and the affairs of
> the sovereign have not been carried to completion.[135]
> The Master said, "...If a superior loves propriety, the people
> will not dare not to be reverent. If he loves righteousness, the
> people will not dare not to be sincere.[136]

When benevolent government is practiced, worthy and able
men are in their rightful places, and the country is free of
irritating tensions and troubles. At such a time, if the ruler can
gain—and work with—a clear insight into the principles of
government and its legal sanctions, even great States will stand in
awe of him.

> Mencius said, "Benevolence brings glory to a prince, and the
> opposite of it brings disgrace. For the princes of the present day
> to hate disgrace and yet to live complacently doing what is not
> benevolent is like hating moisture and yet living in a low situation.
> "If a prince hates disgrace, the best course for him to pursue
> is to esteem virtue and honor virtuous scholars, giving the worthiest
> among them places of dignity and the able offices of trust. When

throughout the kingdom there is leisure and rest from external troubles, let him, taking advantage of such a season, clearly digest the principles of his government with its legal sanctions, and then even great kingdoms will be constrained to stand in awe of him.

"It is said in the *Book of Songs*,

'Before the heavens were dark with rain,
I gathered the bark from the roots of the mulberry trees,
And wove it closely to form the window and door of my nest;
Now, I thought, ye people below,
Perhaps ye will not dare to insult me.'

Confucius said, 'Did not he who made the ode understand the Way?' If a prince is able rightly to govern his kingdom, who will dare to insult him?

"But now the princes take advantage of the time when throughout their kingdoms there is leisure and rest from external troubles, to abandon themselves to pleasure and indolent indifference; they in fact seek for calamities for themselves.

"Calamity and happiness in all cases are men's own seeking. This is illustrated in what is said in the *Book of Songs*,

'Be always studious to be in harmony with the ordinances of God,
So you will certainly get for yourself much happiness.'

and by the passage of the "T'ai Chia," 'When Heaven sends down calamities, it is still possible to escape from them; when we occasion the calamities ourselves, it is not possible any longer to live.' "[137]

By not practicing benevolent government and by engaging in warfare for territorial expansion, a ruler merely digs his own grave.

The people of Ch'i, having smitten Yen, took possession of it, and upon this, the princes of the various States deliberated together and resolved to deliver Yen from their power. King Hsüan said to Mencius, "Most of the princes have plotted to attack me—how shall I prepare myself for them?" Mencius replied, "I have heard of one who with seventy *li* exercised all the functions of governmet throughout the empire. That was T'ang. I have never heard of a prince with a thousand *li* standing in fear of others.

"It is said in the *Book of History*, 'T'ang first struck Ko. The whole empire had confidence in him. When he struck in the east, the rude tribes on the west murmured. So did those on the north when he was engaged in the south. Their cry was, "Why does he make us last?" Thus the people looked to him as we look in time of great drought to the clouds and rainbows. The frequenters of the markets stopped not. The husbandmen made no change in their operations. While he put to death their rulers, he consoled the people. His progress was like the falling of the opportune rain and the people were delighted. It is said again in the *Book of History*, 'We have waited for our prince; the prince's coming will be our reviving.'

"Now the ruler of Yen was tyrannizing over his people, and Your Majesty went and punished him. The people supposed that you were going to deliver them out of the water and the fire, and brought baskets of rice and vessels of congee, to meet Your Majesty's host. But you have slain their fathers and elder brothers and put their sons and younger brothers in confinemet. You have pulled down the ancestral temple of the State and are removing to Ch'i its precious vessels. How can such a course be deemed proper? The rest of the empire is indeed jealously afraid of the strength of Ch'i; and now, when with a doubled territory you do not put in practice a benevolent government; it is this which sets the arms of the empire in motion.

"If Your Majesty will make haste to issue an ordinance, restoring your captives, old and young, stopping the removal of the precious vessels, and saying that, after consulting with the people of Yen, you will appoint them a ruler and withdraw from the country; in this way you may still be able to stop the threatened attack." [138]

When a ruler does not love benevolence, he disregards the sufferings of the people. He then thinks nothing of exploiting the labor of the people and enriching himself. As a result, the people are impoverished, and inhumane treatment becomes the order of the day. In their desperation, the people have no alternative but to resort to violence and sedition.

The Master said, "The man who is fond of daring and is dissatisfied with poverty will proceed to insubordination. So will the man who is not virtuous, when you carry your dislike of him to an extreme." [139]

The rise of a country depends on the unity of its people. In this condition all of the people are more or less of one mind. Only when such harmony prevails can internal production be increased and external aggression be withheld. It is much more important than advantages that accrue from climate and soil and from military and economic strength.

Mencius said, "Opportunities of time vouchsafed by Heaven are not equal to advantages of situation afforded by the Earth, and advantages of situation afforded by the Earth are not equal to the union arising from the accord of men.

"There is a city, with an inner wall three *li* in circumference and an outer wall of seven. The enemy surround and attack it, but they are not able to take it. Now, to surround and attack it, there must have been vouchsafed to them by Heaven the opportunity of time, and in such case their not taking it is because opportuntities of time vouchsafed by Heaven are not equal to advantages of situation afforded by the Earth.

"There ·is a city whose walls are distinguished for their height and whose moats are distinguished for their depth, where the arms of its defenders, offensive and defensive, are distinguished for their strength and sharpness and the stores of rice and other grain are very large. Yet it is obliged to be given up and abandoned. This is because advantages of situation afforded by the Earth are not equal to the union arising from the accord of men.

"In accordance with these principles, it is said, 'A people is bounded in, not by the limits of dykes and borders; a State is secured, not by the strengths of mountains and rivers; the empire is overawed, not by the sharpness and strenghth of arms.' He who obtains the Way has many to assist him. He who loses the Way has few to assist him. When this—being assisted by few—reaches its extreme point, his own relations revolt from the prince. When being assisted by many reaches its highest point, the whole empire becomes obedient to the prince.

"When one to whom the whole empire is prepared to be obedient attacks those from whom their own relations revolt, what must be the result? Therefore the true ruler may not fight; but if he does fight, he must overcome."[140]

As has been stated above, the extinction of States has been attributable to external factors only in rare instances. But it cannot be overlooked that States have come to ruin because of the absence of hostile neighbors or other external forces. Wherever such a condition prevails, the ruler and his ministers are indolent and generally run a lax administration. Thus, no official sees fit to make frank remonstrances, and preparedness against external agression is neglected. As a result, once an attack is threatened from abroad, there is usually no time for adequate preparation and effective resistance. Thus the fate of such a State is often sealed.

Mencius said, "...If a prince has not about his court families attached to the laws and worthy counsellors, and if abroad there are not hostile States or other external calamities, his country will generally come to ruin."[141]

When smaller countries are situated between larger neighbors determined to expand their territories, the only course open to them is to copy the example of their predecessors. This means practicing benevolence and carrying on a struggle for existence through self-exertion. In his answers to the questions of Duke Wên of T'êng, Mencius made most pertinent observations in this regard.

Duke Wên of T'êng asked Mencius, saying, "T'eng is a small country and lies between Ch'i and Ch'u. Shall I serve Ch'i? Or shall I serve Ch'u?"

Mencius replied, "This plan which you propose is beyond me. If you will have me counsel you, there is one thing I can suggest. Dig deeper your moats; build higher your walls; guard them with your people. In case of attack, be prepared to die in your defense, and have the people so that they will not leave you; this is a proper course."[142]

Duke Wên of T'êng asked Mencius, saying, "The people of Ch'i are going to fortify Hsüeh. The movement occasions me great alarm. What is the proper course for me to take in the case?"

Mencius replied, "Formerly, when King T'ai dwelt in Pin, the barbarians of the north were continually making incursions upon it. He therefore left it, went to the foot of Mount Ch'i and there took up his residence. He did not take that situation as having selected it. It was a matter of necessity with him.

"If you do good, among your descendants, in after generations, there shall be one who will attain to the royal dignity. A prince lays the foundation of the inheritance and hands down the beginning he has made, doing what may be continued by his successors. As to the accomplishment of the great result, that is with heaven. What can you do to deal with Ch'i? Only by doing good to the best of your ability."[143]

When the prince, afterwards Duke Wên of T'êng, had to go to Ch'u, he went by way of Sung and visited Mencius.

Mencius spoke to him on how the nature of man is good, and when speaking, always made laudatory reference to Yao and Shun.

When the prince was returning from Ch'u, he again visited Mencius. Mencius said to him, "Prince, do you doubt my words? The Way is one, and only one.

"Ch'ên Chien said to Duke Ching of Ch'i, 'They were men. I am a man. Why should I stand in awe of them?' Yen Yüan said, 'What kind of man was Shun? What kind of man am I? He who exerts himself will also become such as he was.' Kung-ming Yi said, 'King Wên is my teacher. How should the Duke of Chou deceive me by those words?'

"Now T'êng, taking its length with its breadth, will amount, I suppose, to fifty *li*. It is small, but still sufficient to make a good State. It is said in the *Book of History*, 'If medicine does not make a commotion in the patient, his disease will not be cured at all.'"[144]

Lack of benevolence generally starts with the lust and covetousness of the ruler, who usually also exhibits a love for travel and daring deeds. Gradually the superior men stand aloof and mean men gain favor. The popular will is left undone. The people's hearts are lost; their interests are neglected, and they become impoverished and indigent. In the end, their labor is exploited without regard to the time of its employment, and wealth is accumulated unrelentingly by those in high positions. With the rise of popular resentment, forcible measures are adopted by the government which stops at nothing to deceive and persecute the people. A man must first despise himself, and then others will despise him. Doubtless, the destruction of either a family or a State is caused by the family or State itself. The main reason is the lack of benevolence. That is why it is said in "T'ai Chia," "When Heaven sends down calamities, it is still possible to escape them; when we occasion the calamities ourselves, it is not possible any longer to live."

Mencius said, "How is it possible to speak with those princes who are not benevolent? Their perils they count safety, their calamities they count profitable, and they have pleasure in the things by which they perish. If it were possible to talk with them who so violate benevolence, how could we have such destruction of States and ruin of families?

"There was a boy singing,
    'When the water of Ts'ang-lang is clear,
    It does to wash the strings of my cap;
    When the water of the Ts'ang-lang is muddy,
    It does to wash my feet.'
Confucius said, 'Hear what he sings, my children. When clear, then he will wash his cap-strings; and when muddy, he will wash

his feet with it. This different application is brought by the water on itself.'

"A man must first despise himself, and then others will despise him. A family must first destroy itself, and then others will destroy it. A State must first smite itself, and then others will smite it.

"This is illustrated in the passage of the 'T'ai' Chia,' 'When Heaven sends down calamities, it is still possible to escape them; when we occasion the calamities ourselves, it is not possible any longer to live.' "[145]

In short, when benevolent government is practiced by a ruler who is benevolent, the country is destined to be well-ordered and flourishing; when the opposite happens, the country will fall prey to disorder and ruin. Without any distinction whatsoever in space or time, history has provided us with many outstanding examples. Both Confucius and Mencius drew the same conclusions.

Mencius said, "Shun was born in Chu-feng, removed to Fu-hsia and died in Ming-t'iao—a man near the wild tribes on the east.

"King Wên was born in Chou by Mount Ch'i and died in Pi-ying—a man near the wild tribes on the west.

"Those regions were distant from each other more than a thousand *li*, and the age of the one sage was posterior to that of the other more than a thousand years. But when they got their wish and carried their principles into practice throughout the Middle Kingdom, it was like uniting the two halves of a seal.

"When we examine those sages, both the earlier and the later, their principles are found to be the same."[146]

Mencius said, "It was by benevolence that the three dynasties gained the throne and by not being benevolent that they lost it.

"It is by the same means that the decaying and flourishing, the preservation and perishing, of States are determined

"If the sovereign is not benevolent, he cannot preserve his territory within the four seas. If the Head of a State is not benevolent, he cannot preserve his rule. If a high noble or great official is not benevolent, he cannot preserve his ancestral temple. If a scholar or common man is not benevolent, he cannot preserve his four limbs.

"Now they hate death and ruin and yet delight in being not benevolent; this is like hating to be drunk and yet forcing oneself to drink wine."[147]

Mencius said, "...Confucius said, 'There are but two courses which can be pursued, that of virtue and its opposite.

"A ruler who carries the oppression of his people to the highest pitch will himself be slain and his State will perish. If he stops short of the highest pitch, his life will notwithstanding be in danger and his State will be weakened. He will be styled 'The Dark' or 'The Cruel,' and though he may have filial sons and affectionate grandsons, they will not be able in a hundred generations to change the designation.

"This is what is intended in the words of the *Book of Songs*,

"The beacon of Yin is not remote,

It is in the time of the (last) sovereign of Hsia.' "[148]

E. Proper Conduct between Sovereign and Minister

A country has to attend to the affairs of state which affect people's welfare. The machinery which takes care of such affairs is called government. Interestingly, the definition set down by Dr. Sun Yatsen for "politics" is "the administration of the affairs of the multitude."

The so-called sovereign represents the people of the whole country externally and assumes control over all its affairs internally. Formerly, in the empire the title "Son of Heaven" was conferred on the sovereign and in one of the States under him he was designated as a prince. However, the generic title is "ruler" or "sovereign." Today, the head of state is called "president" in many countries.

Those who directly assisted the ruler were known as "ministers." They included nobles and great officials. Today these men are designated as prime ministers, council presidents or ministers—but all can be grouped under the name "political appointees."

Both the ruler and the ministers must possess the wisdom and ability to administer the affairs of the people and the virtue to set a personal example for them. It is of prime importance for them to grasp their mutual relations and behavior. Otherwise, if the administrative machinery acted improperly and rendered itself incompetent, it would not be able to carry out its functions. It is only when the affairs of the people are administered in an orderly manner that the country can be said to be well-ordered. Then also it can be said that the Way holds sway and benevolent government prevails. On the other hand, if the opposite state of affairs occurs, the country is in disarry, the Way is lost, and tyrannical or despotic government prevails.

From time immemorial, our country always has given first importance to the people and their affairs in the realm of government, second importance to the spirits of the land and grain, and least importance to the ruler.

> Mencius said, "The people are the most important element in a nation; the spirits of the land and grain are the next; the sovereign is the lightest."[149]
>
> Duke Wên of T'êng asked Mencius about the proper way of governing a kingdom. Mencius said, "The business of the people may not be remissly attended to."[150]

Though it is said, "the precious things of a prince are three: the territory, the people and the government,"[151] the territory no longer belongs to the ruler once the people are disobedient to his government. As a corollary, there will be no affairs of state to administer if both the people and the territory are not amenable to the government which exists then in name only.

Therefore, these things deserve detailed study: (1) the relations between sovereign and minister, (2) the art of being a ruler, and (3) ways of serving as a minister.

1. Relations between Sovereign and Minister

Why is it that one man and not another can serve as a ruler? Why is it that the people have confidence in him and in no other and are willing to subject themselves to his rule? Surely it must be because the virtue of this man can serve as an example for all the people. Surely he must be the man described in the *Doctrine of the Mean*, where it is said, "He is seen and the people all reverence him; he speaks and the people all believe him; he acts and the people all are pleased with him."[152]

He is a man whose complete trust is in the love of his people and whose sacred mission is to serve their interests. Like King Wên: "As a sovereign, he(King Wên) rested in benevolence."[153] All his measures were never far from benevolence. Nor were they against the Way. And so they indeed laid the foundation for benevolent government.

Since the minister is the ruler's assistant, he should be reverential to his sovereign and discharge well all his responsibilities and functions. "To exhaust what one can do is loyalty." and loyalty is nothing more than the full discharge of one's responsibilities and functions—in the case of a minister, without disappointing the trust which is placed in him by his sovereign. The full discharge of one's responsibilities and functions is also called "reverence to one's duties." A minister should be reverential to both his sovereign and his duties. Hence it is said: "As a minister, he rested in reverence."[154]

With this understood, we may proceed to consider what a ruler's attitude should be toward his ministers, and vice versa.

> Duke Ting asked how a prince should employ his ministers and how ministers should serve their prince. Confucius replied, "A prince should employ his ministers according to the rules of propriety; ministers should serve their prince with loyalty."[155]

If a ruler is devoid of propriety toward his ministers, they are not obliged to be loyal. Their option is to retire. They are, moreover, under no obligation to mourn for their prince when he dies.

> Mencius said to King Hsüan of Ch'i, "When the prince regards his ministers as his hands and feet, his ministers regard their prince as their belly and heart; when he regards them as his dogs and horses, they regard him as any other man; when he regards them as the ground or as grass, they regard him as a robber and an enemy."
>
> The king said, "According to the rules of propriety, a minister wears mourning when he has left the service of a prince. How must a prince behave that his old ministers may thus go into mourning?"
>
> Mencius replied, "The admonitions of a minister having been followed and his advice listened to, so that blessings have descended on the people, if for some cause he leaves the country, the prince sends an escort to conduct him beyond the boundaries. He also anticipates with recommendatory intimations his arrival in the country to which he is proceeding. When he has been gone three years and does not return, only then at length does he take back his fields and residence. This treatment is what is called a 'thrice-repeated display of consideration.' When a prince acts thus, mourning will be worn on leaving his service.

"Nowadays the remonstrances of a minister are not followed and his advice is not listened to, so that no blessings descend on the people. When for any cause he leaves the country, the prince tries to seize him and hold him a prisoner. He also pushes him to extremity in the country to which he has gone, and on the very day of his departure, takes back his fields and residence. This treatment shows him to be what we call 'a robber and an enemy.' What mourning can be worn for a robber and an enemy?"[156]

Since antiquity, no ruler has equaled Yao and Shun in maintaining proper relationships between sovereign and minister and in setting a personal example for later ages.

Mencius said, "The compass and square produce perfect circles and squares. By the sages, the human relations are perfectly exhibited.

"He who as a sovereign would perfectly discharge the duties of a sovereign, and he who as a minister would perfectly discharge the duties of a minister, have only to imitate—the one Yao, and the other Shun. He who does not serve his sovereign as Shun served Yao does not respect his sovereign; and he who does not rule his people as Yao ruled his injures his people.

"Confucius said, 'There are but two courses which can be pursued, that of virtue and its opposite.'

"A ruler who carries the oppression of his people to the highest pitch will himself be slain and his State will perish. If he stops short of the highest pitch, his life will nothwithstanding be in danger, and his State will be weakened. He will be styled 'The Dark' or 'The Cruel,' and though he may have filial sons and affectionate grandsons, they will not be able in a hundred generations to change the designation. This is what is intended in the words of the *Book of Songs*,

'The beacon of Yin is not remote,
It is in the time of the (last) sovereign of Hsia.' "[157]

Why were Yao and Shun good examples for all later ages? Because they were public-spirited and unselfish. They led the world with their benevolence and, foregoing their share in the benefits of the empire, they did not regard the throne as a source of wealth, honor, exaltation and glory. Rather, they considered the search for the happiness of their people as their duty. Thus, they exalted virtue and respected men of worth; they tried to find and employ men beneficial to the empire. ("Finding a man who shall benefit the world is called 'benevolence'" (see below).

> Yao and Shun led on the empire with benevolence and the people followed them."[158]
>
> The Master said, "Great indeed was Yao as a sovereign! How majestic he was! It is only Heaven that is great, and only Yao corresponded to it. How vast his virtue was! The people could find no name for it.
>
> "How majestic he was in the works which he accomplished! How glorious in the elegant regulations which he instituted!"[159]
>
> The Master said, "How majestic was the manner in which Shun and Yü held possession of the empire, as if they had no part in it!"[160]
>
> Mencius said, "...What Yao felt giving him anxiety was the inability to get Shun. What Shun felt giving him anxiety was the inability to get Yü and Kao Yao.
>
> "...Finding a man who shall benefit the empire is called 'benevolence.' Hence to give the throne to another man would be easy; to find a man who shall benefit the empire is difficult.
>
> "Confucius said, 'Great indeed was Yao as a sovereign. It is only Heaven that is great, and only Yao corresponded to it. How vast his virtue was! The people could find no name for it. Princely indeed was Shun! How majestic he was, having possession of the empire, and yet seeming as if he had no part in it!'"[161]

To show their perfect devotion to the public, both Yao and Shun abdicated, not in favor of their sons but in favor of worthy men. Mencius has made detailed observations on Yao's abdication and corrected certain misconceptions about the relations between Shun and his father, Ku-sou, to show the proper attitude of a minister toward his sovereign and of a son toward his father.

> Hsien-ch'iu Mêng asked Mencius, saying, "There is the saying, 'A scholar of complete virtue may not be employed as a minister by his sovereign, nor treated as a son by his father.' Shun stood with his face to the south, and Yao, at the head of all his princes, appeared before him at court with his face to the north. Ku-sou also did the same· When Shun saw Ku-sou, his countenance became discomposed. Confucius said, 'At this time, in what a perilous condition the empire was! Its state was indeed unsettled.' I do not know whether what is here said really took place."
>
> Mencius replied, "No. These are not the words of a superior man. They are the sayings of an uncultivated person of the east

of Ch'i. When Yao was old, Shun was associated with him in the government. It is said in the 'Canon of Yao,' 'After twenty and eight years Yao deceased. The people acted as if they were mourning for father or mother for three years, and up to the borders of the four seas every sound of music was hushed.' Confucius said, 'There are not two suns in the sky, nor two sovereigns over the people.' Shun having been sovereign and, moreover, leading all the princes in the empire to observe the three years' mourning for Yao, there would have been in this case two sovereigns'"

Hsien-ch'iu Mêng said, "On the point of Shun's not treating Yao as a minister, I have received your instructions. But it is said in the *Book of Songs*,

> 'Under the whole heaven,
> Every spot is the sovereign's ground;
> To the borders of the sovereign's land,
> Every individual is the sovereign's subject,'

and Shun had become sovereign. I venture to ask how it was that Ku-sou was not one of his subjebts."

Mencius answered, "That ode is not to be understood in that way—it speaks of being laboriously engaged in the sovereign's business, so as not to be able to nourish one's parents, as if another said, 'This is all the sovereign's business, and how is it that I alone am supposed to be worth and made to toil in it?' Therefore those who explain the odes may not insist on one term so as to do violence to one sentence, nor on a sentence so as to do violence to the general scope. They must try with their thoughts to meet that scope, and then we shall apprehend it. If we simply take single sentences, there is that in the ode called 'The Milky Way,'

> 'Of the black-haired people of the remnant of Chou,
> There is not a single one left.'

if it had really been as thus expressed, then not an individual of the people of Chou was left.

"Of all which a filial son can attain to, there is nothing greater than honoring his parents. And of what can be attained to in the honoring of one's parents, there is nothing greater than nourishing them with the whole empire. Ku-sou was the father of the sovereign—this was the height of honor. Shun nourished him with the whole empire—this was the height of nourishing. In this was verified the sentiment in the *Book of Songs*,

> 'Ever cherishing filial thoughts,
> Those filial thoughts became an example to after ages.'

"It is said in the *Book of History*, 'Reverently performing his duties, he waited on Ku-sou, and he was full of veneration and awe. Ku-sou also believed him and conformed to virtue'—This is the true case of the scholar of complete virtue not being treated as a son by his father."[162]

True, when the sovereign and his ministers are virtuous and talented and proper relations are maintained between them, the inevitable result is this: they are united and the people are pleased with them. But however gratifying and important this is, it is not enough. If the sovereign and his ministers can take further and unceasing delight in what is good, then political progress will increase day by day, and "all within the four seas will count one thousand *li* but a small distance and will come and lay their good thonghts before him." By reaping the "good thoughts" of the people, the sovereign and his ministers can join their efforts with those of others in doing what is good.

Mencius said, "...When Yü heard good words, he bowed to the speaker.

"The great Shun had a still greater delight in what was good. He regarded virtue as the common property of himself and others, giving up his own way to follow that of others and delighting to learn from others to practice what was good.

"From the time when he plowed and sowed, exercised the potter's art and was a fisherman, to the time when he became emperor, he was continually learning from others.

"To take example from others to practice virtue is to help them in the same practice. Therefore there is no attribute of the superior man greater than his helping men to practice virtue."[163]

In the Book of Ch'u it is said, "Nothing is valued in the State of Ch'u except the practice of goodness."[164]

The prince of Lu wanting to commit the administration of his government to the disciple Yüeh-chêng, Mencius said, "When I heard of it, I was so glad that I could not sleep."

Kung-sun Ch'ou said, "Is Yüeh-chêng a man of vigor?" and was answered, "No." "Is he wise in council?" "No." "Is he possessed of much information?" "No."

"What then made you so glad that you could not sleep?"

"He is a man who loves what is good."

"Is the love of what is good sufficient?"

"The love of what is good is more than a sufficient qualification for the government of the empire—how much more is it so for the State of Lu?

"If a minister loves what is good, all within the four seas will count 1,000 *li* but a small distance and will come and lay their good thoughts before him.

"If he does not love what is good, men will say, 'How self-conceited he looks. He is saying to himself, I know it.' The language and looks of that self-conceit will keep men off at a distance of 1,000 *li*. When good men stop 1,000 *li* off, calumniators, flatterers and sycophants will make their appearance. When a minister lives among calumniators, flatterers and sycophants, though he may wish the State to be well governed, is it possible for it to be so?"[165]

Mencius told the King of Ch'i and his minister, K'ung Chü-hsin, about the responsibilities of the sovereign and his ministers— the love and nourishment of the people—saying that if those in power were unable to assume these responsibilities they should return the government to the people. Both the king and K'ung admitted their deficiency, thus showing they were lovers of what was good.

Mencius, having gone to P'ing-lu, addressed the governor of it, saying, "If one of your spearmen should lose his place in the ranks three times in one day, would you, Sir, remove him or not?" "I would not wait for three times to do so," was the reply.

Mencius said, "Well, then, you, Sir, have likewise lost your place in the ranks many times. In calamitous years and years of famine, the old and feeble of your people, who have been found lying in the ditches and water-channels, and the able-bodied, who have been scattered about to the four quarters, have amounted to several thousand." The governor replied, "That is a state of things which it does not belong to me, Chü-hsin, to act."

"Here," said Mencius, "is a man who receives charge of the cattle and sheep of another and undertakes to feed them for him; of course he must search for pasture-ground and grass for them. If after searching for those, he cannot find them, will he return his charge to the owner? Or will he stand by and see them die?" "Herein," said the official, "I am guilty."

Another day, Mencius had an audience of the king and said to him, "Of the governors of Your Majesty's cities I am acquainted with five, but the only one who knows his faults is K'ung Chü-hsin." He then repeated the conversation to the King, who said, "In this matter I am the guilty one."[166]

In an environment in which both the sovereign and his

ministers are fond of what is good, superior men are chosen as counselors. Calumniators, flatterers and sycophants do not appear. The sovereign and his ministers work in unison for the well-being of the people. Thus, proper relations are maintained between the sovereign and his subjects.

> Duke Ching of Ch'i asked Confucius about government. Confucius replied, "There is government, when the prince is prince and the minister is minister; when the father is father and the son is son."
>
> "Good," said the duke, "if, indeed, the prince is not prince, the minister not minister, the father not father and son not son, although I have the grain, can I eat it?"[167]

The country is sure to flourish (1) if the sovereign realizes the difficulty of his high station and practices self-restraint and propriety in fulfilling his role, and (2) if all his ministers appreciate their difficulties, attend to the affairs of state reverently, are loyal to their functions and practice sincerity. Confucius gave this answer to Duke Ting of Lu with regard to the "single sentence which can make a country prosperous."

> Duke Ting asked, "Is there a single sentence which can make a country prosperous?" Confucius replied, "Such an effect cannot be expected from one sentence.
>
> "There is a saying, however, which people have—'To be a prince is difficult; to be a minister is not easy.'
>
> "If a ruler knows this—the difficulty of being a prince—may it not be expected from this one sentence the prosperity of a country?"
>
> The duke then said, "Is there a single sentence which can ruin a country?" Confucius replied, "Such an effect as that cannot be expected from one sentence. There is, however, the saying which people have—'I have no pleasure in being a prince, but only in that no one can offer any opposition to what I say.'
>
> "If a ruler's words are good and no one opposes them, is it not good? But if they are not good and no one opposes them, may there not be expected from this one sentence the ruin of his country?"[168]

2. The Way of Being a Ruler

In judging rulers, Confucius made the great Yü his first choice because (1) he was public-spirited and unselfish; (2) he put his country first, even before his home; (3) he practiced strict frugality and sought the greatest abundance for his people; and (4) he conducted himself with unparalleled and clearly visible sincerity.

> The Master said, "I can find no flaw in the character of Yü. He used himself coarse food and drink, but displayed the utmost filial piety towards the spirits. His ordinary garments were poor, but he displayed the utmost elegance in his sacrificial cap and apron. He lived in a low mean house, but extended all his strength on the ditches and water-channels. I can find nothing like a flaw in Yü."[109]

The affairs of state cannot be dealt with by the ruler alone. He must have worthy and able men in key positions so that the country can attain the stage of so-called "leisure" (orderly government). Therefore, it is of primary importance that a ruler carefully choose his ministers. Shun secured five men and achieved good government. King Wu selected ten men and did the same. Of the ten, one was a woman, showing that women served in the government as early as the Chou era.

> Shun had five ministers, and the empire was well-governed.
>
> King Wu said, "I have ten able ministers."
>
> Confucius said, "Is not the saying true that talents are difficult to find? Only when the dynasties of T'ang and Yü met were they more abundant than in this of Chou, yet there was a woman among them. The able ministers were no more than nine men.
>
> "King Wên possessed two of the three parts of the empire, and with those he served the dynasty of Yin. The virtue of the house of Chou may be said to have reached the highest point indeed."[170]

Talented men are indeed difficult to obtain. Without searching for them with sincerity and treating them with great propriety, it is not easy to secure them. And even if they are hired, it is hard to retain them for any length of time.

> Mencius said, "To feed a scholar and not love him is to treat him as a pig. To love him and not respect him is to keep him as a domestic animal.
>
> "Honoring and respecting are what exist before any offering of gifts. If there are honoring and respecting without the reality of them, a superior man may not be retained by such empty demonstration."[171]

This section has delved into two of the nine standard rules—those relating to the cultivation of the person and to honoring worthy men. The remaining seven—those relating to affection towards relatives, respect towards great ministers, considerate treatment of all officials, dealing with the mass of people as children, encouraging the initiative of all classes of artisans, the indulgent treatment of men in far-off areas and the cherishing of princes of States—are all traceable to benevolence. Hence it is said, "As a soverign, he (King Wên) rested in benevolence." Since we discussed this in the first section above, we need not repeat it here.

We have seen that the ruler assumes the responsibility of leading the entire populace. But if the country is badly governed and the people hungry and starving, he should admit his failure by surrendering the reins of power.

> Mencius said to King Hsüan of Ch'i, "Suppose that one of Your Majesty's ministers were to entrust his wife and children to the care of his friend, while he himself went into Ch'u to travel, and that, on his return, he should find that the friend had let his wife and children suffer from cold and hunger—how ought he to deal with him?" The king said, "He should cast him off."
> Mencius proceeded, "Suppose that the chief criminal judge could not regulate the officials under him, how would you deal with him?" The king said, "Dismiss him."
> Mencius again said, "If within the four borders of your kingdom there is not good government, what is to be done?" The king looked to the right and left and spoke of other matters.[172]

Therefore sage and worthy rulers, whenever a flood, drought or other natural calamity occurred, always issued decrees of self-reprimand and refrained from putting the blame on others. This is seen in the following instances:

> Yao said, "Oh! you, Shun, the Heaven-determined order of succession now rests in your person. Sincerely hold fast the due Mean. If there shall be distress and want within the four seas, the Heavenly revenue will come to a perpetual end."
> Shun also used the same language in giving charge to Yü.
> T'ang said, "I, the child Lü, presume to use a dark-colored victim and presume to announce to thee, O most great and sovereign God, that the sinner I dare not pardon, and thy ministers, O God,

I do not keep in obscurity. The examination of them is by thy mind, O God. If, in my person, I commit offenses, they are not to be attributed to the people of the myriad regions. If the people in the myriad regions commit offenses, these offenses must rest on my person."[173]

In short, a ruler should not give himself credit for any meritorious service, nor should he shift the blame to others for any of his faults. He should be benevolent to his people and love all things so that he can perfect himself and his contribution to the country. This in a ruler is virtue.

3. The Way of Being a Minister

With their differing characters, men have various motives for becoming ministers. Briefly, there are four kinds of motives:

Mencius said, "There are persons who serve the, prince; they serve the prince, that is, for the sake of his countenance and favor.

"There are ministers who seek the tranquillity of the State and find their pleasure in securing that tranquillity.

"There are those who are the people of Heaven. They, judging that, if they were in office, they could carry out their principles throughout the empire, proceed so to carry them out.

"There are those who are great men. They rectify themselves, and others are rectified."[174]

There are three examples which show extraordinary character as regards being a minister.

Mencius said, "...Not to serve a prince whom he did not esteem, nor command a people whom he did not approve; in a time of good government, to take office, and on the occurrence of confusion, to retire—this was Po-i. To say, 'Whom may I not serve as my ruler? Whom may I not command as my people?' In a time of good government, to take office, and when disorder prevailed, also to take office—this was Yi Yin. When it was proper to go into office, then to go into it; when it was proper to keep retired from office, then to keep retired from it; when it was proper to continue in it long, then to continue in it long; when it was proper to withdraw from it quickly, then to withdraw quickly—this was Confucius."[175]

In speaking of ways of being ministers, Confucius praised Tzŭ-ch'an of Chêng and Ning Wu of Wei.

The Master said of Tzŭ-ch'an that he had four of the characteristics of a superior man: in his conduct of himself he was humble; in serving his superiors he was respectful; in nourishing the people he was kind; in ordering the people he was just."[176]

The Master said, "When the Way prevailed in his country, Ning Wu acted the part of a wise man. When the Way did not prevail, he acted the part of a stupid man. Others may equal his wisdom, but they cannot equal his stupidity."[177]

Respect and loyalty do not mean unquestioning obedience. Since it is the duty of a minister to assist his sovereign, he should do his best to help his sovereign do what he should do. He must help him in applying the nine standard rules of conduct. He should remonstrate against and, if possible, stop what should not be done, for example, actions evolving from lust, covetousness and close association with evil men. He should also speak out against the accumulation of wealth and the untimely employment of the people. Knowing full well that a minister should rest in respect, Mencius defined the word as follows:

Mencius said, "...To urge one's sovereign to difficult achievements may be called showing respect for him. To set before him what is good and repress his perversities may be called showing reverence for him. He who does not do these things, saying to himself, 'My sovereign is incompetent to this,' may be said to play the thief with him."[178]

Confucius also said that loyalty required straightforward remonstrances on the part of the sovereign's ministers, even to the extent of opposing him to his face.

The Master said, "Can there be love without urging laboriousness on its object? Can there be loyalty without instructing its object"[179]

Tzŭ-lu asked how a ruler should be served. The Master said, "Do not deceive him (by pretending to obey him), and, moreover, withstand him to his face."[180]

Taking advantage of a question put by Chi Tzŭ-jan, Confucius explained the difference between great and ordinary ministers. A great minister, he said, is one who serves his sovereign according to the Way, while an ordinary minister, except in a parricide or regicide, merely obeys his sovereign.

Chi Tzŭ-jan asked whether Chung Yu and Jan Ch'iu could be called great ministers.

The Master said, "I thought you would ask about something else, and you only ask about Yu and Ch'iu!

"What is called a great minister is one who serves his prince according to the Way, and when he cannot find he does so, retires.

"Now, as to Yu and Ch'iu, they may be called ordinary ministers."

Tzŭ-jan said, "Then they will always follow their chief—will they?"

The Master said, "In an act of parricide or regicide, they would not follow him."[181]

When a minister makes his remonstrances, he should confine them to important matters and they should be within his province. If his personal character is upright and he bases his counsel on important principles of righteousness, he is likely to be heard with approval. If, on the other hand, he persists in making inconsequential protestations, he is sure to invite disgrace.

Mencius said, "It is not worthwhile to remonstrate with a sovereign on account of the mal-employment of ministers, nor to blame errors of government. It is only the great man who can rectify what is wrong in the sovereign's mind. Let the prince be benevolent, and all his acts will be benevolent. Let the prince be righteous, and all his acts will be righteous. Let the prince be correct, and everything will be correct. Once rectify the ruler, and the country will be firmly settled."[182]

Mencius said, "...When one is in a low situation, to speak of high matters is an offense. When a scholar stands in a prince's court and the Way is not carried into practice, it is a shame to him."[183]

Tzŭ-yu said, "In serving a prince, frequent remonstrances lead to disgrace. Between friends, frequent reproofs make the friendship distant."[184]

In serving a ruler, a minister can be satisfied if he does not overstep the due bounds of propriety, and he can ignore the criticisms leveled at him.

The Master said, "The full observance of the rules of propriety in serving one's prince is accounted by people to be flattery."[185]

Without winning the confidence of his sovereign, a minister cannot govern. If he makes remonstrances under such circumstances, he may be misunderstood. The sovereign may think he is engaging in slander, and instead of helping matters remonstrances may aggravate them. Therefore, it behooves the minister to be cautious.

> The Master said, "...When those in inferior situations do not obtain the confidence of the sovereign, they cannot succeed in governing the people."[186]
>
> Tzŭ-hsia said, "The superior man, having obtained their confidence, may then impose labors on his people. If he has not gained their confidence, they will think that he is oppressing them. Having obtained the confidence of his prince, he may then remonstrate with him. If he has not gained his confidence, the prince will think that he is vilifying him."[187]

Whenever important principles of righteousness are involved, a minister should offer his counsel to the sovereign on his own initiative. He also should see that the plots of crafty ministers do not materialize.

> Ch'ên Ch'êng murdered Duke Chien of Ch'i. Confucius bathed, went to court and informed Duke Ai, saying, "Ch'ên Hêng has slain his sovereign. I beg that you will undertake to punish him."
>
> The duke said, "Inform the chiefs of the three families of it."
>
> Confucius retired and said, "Following in the rear of the great officials, I did not dare not to represent such a matter, and my prince says, 'Inform the chiefs of the three families of it.'"
>
> He went to the chiefs and informed them, but they would not act. Confucius then said, "Following in the rear of the great officials, I did not dare not to represent such a matter.[188]
>
> The head of the Chi family was going to attack Chuan-yü. Jan Yu and Chi Lu had an interview with Confucius and said, "Our chief, Chi, is going to commence operations against Chuan-yü."
>
> Confucius said, "Ch'iu, is it not you who are in fault here? Now, in regard to Chuan-yü, long ago, a former king appointed its ruler to preside over the sacrifices to the eastern Mêng; moreover, it is in the midst of the territory of our State; and its ruler is a minister in direct connection with the sovereign—What has your chief to do with attacking it?"
>
> Jan Yu said, "Our master wishes the thing; neither of us two ministers wishes it."
>
> Confucius said, "Ch'iu, there are the words of Chou Jên, 'When he can put forth his ability, he takes his place in the ranks of office; when he finds himself unable to do so, he retires from it.'

How can he be used as a guide to a blind man, who does not support him when tottering, nor raise him up when fallen?

"And further you speak wrongly. When a tiger or rhinoceros escapes from his cage; when a tortoise or piece of jade is injured in its repository—whose is the fault?"

Jan Yu said, "But at present Chuan-yü is strong and near to Pi; if our chief does not now take it, it will hereafter be a sorrow to his descendants."

Confucius said, "Ch'iu, the superior man hates not saying, 'I want such and such a thing,'" and framing explantions for the conduct.

"I have heard that rulers of States and chiefs of families are not troubled with fears of poverty, but are troubled lest their people should not keep their several places; that they are not troubled lest their people should be few, but are troubled with a want of contented repose among the people in their several places. For when the people keep their several places, there will be no poverty; when harmony prevails, there will be no scarcity of people; and when there is such a contented repose, there will be no rebellious upsettings.

"Therefore, if remoter people are not submissive, all the influences of civil culture and virtue are to be cultivated to attract them to come over; and when they do come over, they must be made contented and tranquil.

"Now, here you are, Yu and Ch'iu, assisting your chief. Remoter people are not submissive and, with your help, he cannot attract them to come over. In his own territory there are divisions and downfalls, leavings and separations, and, with your help, he cannot preserve it.

"And yet he is planning these hostile movements within the State. I am afraid that the sorrow of the Chi-sun family will not be on account of Chuan-yü, but will be found within the screen of their own court."[189]

When a ruler has faults and a minister cannot remonstrate against them, he has failed in the discharge of his duties. The failure is even worse if he tries to whitewash the faults of the sovereign.

The people of Yen having rebelled, the king of Ch'i said, "I feel very much ashamed when I think of Mencius."

Ch'ên Chia said to him, "Let Your Majesty not be grieved. Does Your Majesty consider yourself or the Duke of Chou the more benevolent and wise?" The king said, "Oh! what words are those?"

"The Duke of Chou," said Chia, "appointed Kuan-shu to oversee the heir of Yin, but Kuan-shu with the power of the State of Yin rebelled. If knowing that this would happen, he appointed Kuan-shu, he was deficient in benevolence. If he appointed him, not knowing that it would happen, he was deficient in wisdom. If the Duke of Chou was not completely benevolent and wise, how much less can Your Majesty be expected to be so! I beg to go and see Mencius and relieve Your Majesty from that feeling."

Ch'ên Chia accordingly saw Mencius and asked him, saying, "What kind of man was the Duke of Chou?" "An ancient sage," was the reply. "Is it the fact that he appointed Kuan-shu to oversee the heir of Yin and that Kuan-shu with the State of Yin rebelled?" "It is." "Did the Duke of Chou know that he would rebel and purposely appointed him to that office?" Mencius said, "He did not know." "Then, though a sage, he still fell into error?" "The Duke of Chou," answered Mencius, "was the younger brother. Kuan-shu was his elder brother. Was not the error of the Duke of Chou to be expected?

"Moreover, when the superior men of old had errors, they corrected them. The superior men of the present time, when they have errors, persist in them. The errors of the superior men of old were like eclipses of the sun and moon. All the people witnessed them, and when they had corrected them, all the people looked up to them with their former admiration. But do the superior men of the present day only persist in their errors? They go on to apologize for them likewise."[190]

A minister does wrong by covering over his sovereign's faults. But he commits a greater wrong if he not only cooperates with the wickedness of his prince but anticipates and excites it. This is inexcusable.

Mencius said, "...The crime of him who connives at, and aids the wickedness of his prince is small, but the crime of him who anticipates and excites that wickedness is great. The Great Officials of the present day all go to meet their sovereigns' wickedness, and so I say that the Great Officials of the present day are sinners against the princes."[191]

Kung-sun Yen and Chang Yi, with their skillful pleas to reigning princes during their travels, could persuade them to mobilize their forces and engage in punitive expeditions. For this reason Ching Ch'un regarded them as great men. Mencius, however, felt they were as wicked as their sovereigns. In Mencius' view, this was not the way ministers should act, nor was it what great men should do.

> Ching Ch'un said to Mencius, "Are not Kung-sun Yen and Chang Yi really great men? Let them once be angry, and all the princes are afraid. Let them live quietly, and the flames of trouble are extinguished throughout the empire."
>
> Mencius said, "How can such men be great men? Have you not read the Ritual Usages? 'At the capping of a young man, his father admonishes him. At the marrying away of a young woman, her mother admonishes her, accompanying her to the door on her leaving and cautioning her with these words, "You are going to your home. You must be respectful; you must be careful. Do not disobey your husband." Thus, to look upon compliance as their correct course is the rule for women.
>
> "To dwell in the wide house of the world, to stand in the correct seat of the world and to practice the great Way of the world; when he obtains his desire for office, to practice the Way for the people; and when the desire is disappointed, to practice it alone; to be above the power of riches and honors to make dissipated, of poverty and mean condition to make swerve from principle, and of power and force to make bend—these characteristics constitute the great man."[192]

The serious examples of a minister collaborating with the wickedness of his soveign are those in which (1) militarism is encouraged with a view to territorial expansion and (2) accumulation of wealth is urged to fill the coffers of the State. To Mencius, the first type tended to destroy the people and the latter to rob them. Both are contrary to benevolence and injurious to the sovereign. Neither can be regarded as correct conduct for a minister.

> The prince of Lu wanted to make Minister Shên commander of his army. Mencius said, "To employ an uninstructed people in war may be said to be destroying them. A destroyer of the people would not have been tolerated in the times of Yao and Shun. Though by a single battle you should subdue Ch'i and get possession of Nan-yang, it is not the right thing to do."
>
> Shên changed countenance and said in displeasure, "This is what I, Ku-li, do not understand."
>
> Mencius said, "I will lay the case plainly before you. The territory appropriated to the sovereign is now 1,000 li square. Without a thousand li he would not have sufficient for his

entertainment of the princes. The territory appropriated to a prince is 100 *li* square. Without 100 *li* he would not have sufficient wherewith to observe the statutes kept in his ancestral temple.

"When the Duke of Chou was invested with the principality of Lu, it was a hundred *li* square. The territory was indeed not insufficient, but it was not more than 100 *li*. When T'ai-kung was invested with the principality of Ch'i, it was also 100 *li* square. The territory was indeed not insufficient, but it was not more than 100 *li*.

"Now Lu is five times 100 *li*. If a true royal ruler were to arise, do you think that Lu would be diminished or increased by him?

"If it were merely taking the place from one State to give it to the other, a benevolent man would not do it; how much less will he do so, when the end is to be sought by the slaughter of men?

"The way in which a superior man serves his prince contemplates simply by leading him in the right path and directing his mind to benevolence."[193]

Mencius said, "Ch'iu acted as chief official to the head of the Chi family, whose evil ways he was unable to change, while he exacted from the people double the grain formerly paid. Confucius said, 'Ch'iu is no disciple of mine. Children, beat the drum and assail him.!

"Looking at the subject from this case, we percieve that when a prince was not practicing benevolent government, all his ministers who enriched him were rejected by Confucius—how much more would he have rejected those who are vehement to fight for their prince? When contentions about territory are the ground on which they fight, they slaughter men till the fields are filled with them. When some struggle for a city is the ground on which they fight, they slaughter men till the city is filled with them. This is what is called 'leading on the land to devour human flesh.!' Death is not enough for such a crime.

"Therefore those who are skillful to fight should suffer the highest punishment. Next to them should be punished those who unite some princes in leagues against others; and next to them, those who take in grassy commons, imposing the cultivation of the ground on the people."[194]

Mencius said, "Those who nowadays serve their sovereigns say, 'We can for our sovereign enlarge the limits of the cultivated ground and fill his treasuries and granaries.' Such persons are nowadays called 'Good ministers,' but anciently they were called 'Robbers of the people.' If a sovereign follows not the right way, nor has his mind bent on benevolence, to seek to enrich him is to enrich a Chieh.

"Or they will say, 'We can for our sovereign form alliances with other States, so that our battles must be successful.! Such persons are nowadays called 'Good ministers,' but anciently they were called 'Robbers of the people.' If a sovereign follows not the right way, nor has mind directed to benevolence, to seek to help him engage in violence and war is to assist a Chieh.

"Although a prince, pursuing the path of the present day and not changing its practices, were the throne given to him, he could not retain it for a single day."[195]

Those who collaborate with their sovereign's wickedness and those who anticipate and excite it at least bear their sovereign fully in mind, but ministers who impose on their sovereign—those who are arrogant and usurp power—are disrespectful and act contrary to propriety. Completely deviating from their roles as ministers, they should be summarily dismissed. Hence it is said, "When the Way prevails in the empire, government will not be in the hands of the great officials."[196]

The Master said, "Tsang Wu-chung, keeping possession of Fang, asked of the duke of Lu to appoint a successor to him in his family. If it be said that he was not using force with his sovereign, I would not believe it."[197]

Confucius said, "Official emoluments have not come from the ducal House now for five generations. The government has been in the hands of the Great Officials for four generations. On this account, the descendants of the three Huan are on the decline."[198]

The chief of the Chi family was about to sacrifice to the T'ai mountain. The Master said to Jan Yu, "Can you not save him from this?" He answered, "I cannot." Confucius said, "Alas! will you say that the T'ai mountain is not so discerning as Lin Fang?"[199]

In view of the disorder prevailing among the princes of his time, Confucius could not help expressing his regrets.

The Master said, "Even the rude tribes of the east and north showed due respect to their chiefs. They are not like the States of our great land which disregard their soverigns:"[200]

When a young prince fails to govern properly and does not pay heed to the remonstrances of his ministers, who cannot retire, is it proper to banish him? Though Mencius cited an example from ancient history, he set a condition for banishment.

Kung-sun Ch'ou said, "Yi Yin said, 'I cannot be near and see him so disobedient to reason,' and therewith he banished T'ai-chia to T'ung. The people were much pleased. When T'ai-chia became virtuous, he brought him back, and the people were again much pleased.

"When worthies are ministers, may they indeed banish their sovereigns in this way when they are not virtuous?"

Mencius replied, "If they have the same purpose as Yi Yin, they may. If they have not the same purpose, it would be usurpation."[201]

When there are high ministers belonging to the ruling household, they may dethrone rulers who have committed serious faults and pay no heed to repeated remonstrances. If these ministers do not belong to the ruling household, they should retire after their counsel has been rejected. Though Yi Yin was a high minister who was not from the royal family, because of his prolonged service under T'ang he had the reputation among the people of being worthy and virtuous and completely free from selfish motives. Mencius called him the "responsible sage," due to his unequaled sense of responsibility and vigorous spirit.

King Hsüan of Ch'i asked about the office of high ministers. Mencius said, "Which high ministers is Your Majesty asking about?" "Are there differences among them?" inquired the king. "There are," was the reply. "There are the high ministers who are noble and relatives of the prince, and there are those who are of a different surname." The king said, "I beg to ask about the high ministers who are noble and relatives of the prince." Mencius answered, "If the prince has great faults, they ought to remonstrate with him, and if he does not listen to them after they have done so again and again, they ought to dethrone him."

The king on this looked moved and changed countenance. Mencius said, "Let Your Majesty not be offended. You asked me, and I dare not answer but according to truth."

The king's countenance became composed, and then begged to ask about high ministers who were of a different surname from the prince. Mencius said, "When the prince has faults, they ought to remonstrate with him; and if he does not listen to them after they have done this again and again, they ought to quit."[202]

True, the banishment of a sovereign required the purpose of a Yi Yin, but the actual dethronement had to come from a high minister belonging to a ruling household. If a sovereign was tyrannical and deviated from the Way, would it be in order for a minister to kill him to save the people? In Mencius' view, if a sovereign became such a ruffian and a robber that he was no better than a "mere fellow," it would not be wrong for a minister to kill him. He reasoned that the basic condition of a sovereign was to "rest in benevolence"; once this condition was not fulfilled, the sovereign really was no longer a sovereign.

> King Hsüan of Ch'i asked, saying, "Was it so, that T'ang banished Chieh and that King Wu smote Chou?" Mencius replied, "It is so in the records."
> The king said, "May a minister then put his sovereign to death?"
> Mencius said, "He who outrages the benevolence proper to his nature is called a robber; he who outrages righteousness is called a ruffian. The robber and ruffian we call a mere fellow. I have heard of the cutting off of the fellow Chou, but I have not heard of the putting a sovereign to death, in his case."[303]

In addition to reverence and loyalty—qualities which must be possessed by him—a minister must have the ability to be trusted with the care of a young sovereign before he reaches his majority. In such an emergency, a minister must be of lofty character and determined to see the crisis through.

> The philosopher Tsêng said, "Suppose that there is an individual who can be entrusted with the charge of a young orphan prince and can be commissioned with authority over a State of a hundred *li*, and whom no emergency however great can drive from his principles—is such a man a superior man? He is a superior man indeed."[204]

When a minister cannot win the confidence of his sovereign, it is impossible for him to govern. Under such circumstances, he should make a self-examination. More often than not he will come to realize that his flaw is a lack of sincerity.

> The Master said, "...When those in inferior situations do not obtain the confidence of the sovereign, they cannot succeed in governing the people. There is a way to obtain the confidence of the sovereign; if a man is not trusted by his friends, he will not get the confidence of his sovereign. There is a way to being trusted

by a man's friends; if he is not obedient to his parents, he will not be true to his friends. There is a way to being obedient to a man's parents; if he, on turning his thoughts in upon himself, finds a want of sincerity, he will not be obedient to his parents. There is a way to the attainment of sincerity in oneself; if a man does not understand what is good, he will not attain sincerity in himself."[205]

Mencius said, "When those occupying inferior situations do not obtain the confidence of the sovereign, they cannot succeed in governing the people. There is a way to obtain the confidence of the sovereign: if a man is not trusted by his friends, he will not obtain the confidence of his sovereign. There is a way of being trusted by a man's friends: if he does not serve his parents so as to make them pleased, he will not be trusted by his friends. There is a way to make a man's parents pleased: if he, on turning his thoughts inwards, finds a want of sincerity, he will not give pleasure to his parents. There is a way to the attainment of sincerity in oneself: if a man does not understand what is good, he will not attain sincerity in himself.

"Therefore sincerity is the Way of Heaven. To think how to be sincere is the Way of man.

"Never has there been one possessed of complete sincerity who did not move others. Never has there been one who had not sincerity who was able to move others."[206]

While it is vital for a minister to turn his thoughts inward and attain sincerity in order to obtain the confidence of his sovereign, it is even more important for him to be well enough informed to act in compliance with the people's best interests. A minister also must be cautious in speech and action to lessen the possibility of regrettable consequences.

Tzŭ-chang was learning how to seek official emolument. The Master said, "Hear much and put aside the points of which you stand in doubt, while you speak cautiously at the same time of the others—then you will find few occasions for regret. See much and put aside the things which seem perilous, while you are cautious at the same time in carrying the others into practice—then you will have few occasions for repentance. When one gives few occasions for blame in one's words and few occasions for repentance in one's conduct, one is in the way to get emolument."[207]

Because there are myriad types of circumstances and functions, ones's conduct must be different according to each specific case.

When the philosopher Tsêng dwelt in Wu-ch'êng, there came a band from Yüeh to plunder it. Someone said to him, "The plunderers are coming—why not leave?" Tsêng on this left the city, saying to the man in charge of the house, "Do not lodge any person in my house, lest they break and injure the plants and trees." When the plunderers withdrew he sent word to him, saying, "Repair the walls of my house. I am about to return." When the plunderers retired, the philosopher Tsêng returned accordingly. His disciples said, "Since our Master was treated with so much sincerity and respect, for him to go away on the arrival of the plunderers, so as to be looked upon by the people as an example; and then to return on their retiring, appears to us to be improper." Shên-yu Hsing said, "You do not understand this matter. Formerly, when the Shên-yus were exposed to the outbreak of the rebel Fu-tz'u, there were seventy disciples in our Master's following, and none of them were injured."

When Tzŭ-ssŭ was living in Wei, there came a band from Ch'i to plunder. Someone said to him, "The plunderers are coming; why not leave?" Tzŭ-ssŭ said, "If I go away, whom will the prince have to guard the State with?"

Mencius said, "The philosopher Tsêng and Tzŭ-ssŭ agreed in the principle of their conduct. Tsêng was a teacher; in the place of a father or elder brother. Tzŭ-ssŭ was a minister; in a meaner place. If the philosopher Tsêng and Tzŭ-ssŭ had exchanged places, the one would have done what the other did."[208]

Yü and Chi, in an age when the world was being brought back to order, thrice passed their doors without entering them. Confucius praised them.

The disciple Yen, in an age of disorder, dwelt in a mean narrow lane, having his single bamboo-cup of rice and his single ladleful of water; other men could not have endured the distress, but he did not allow his joy to be affected by it. Confucius praised him.

Mencius said, "Yü, Chi and Yen Hui agreed in the principle of their conduct.

"Yü thought that if anyone in the empire were drowned, it was as if he drowned him. Chi thought if anyone in the empire suffered hunger, it was as if he famished him. It was on this account that they were so anxious and in such haste.

"If Yü, Chi and Yen-tsŭ had exchanged places, each would have done what the other did.

"Here now in the same apartment with you are people fighting; you ought to part them. Though you part them with your cap simply tied over your unbound hair, your conduct will be allowable. If the fighting is only in the village or neighborhood, if you go to put an end to it with your cap tied over your hair unbound, you will be in error. Although you should shut your door in such a case, your conduct will be allowable."[209]

While in office, a minister ordinarily receives remuneration. If, however, he intends to retire but is constrained to continue in service a bit longer, he may then continue in office but he should accept no remuneration. In this way he can retain his freedom of movement.

> When Mencius left Ch'i, he dwelt in Hsiu. There Kung-sun Ch'ou asked him, saying, "Was it the way of the ancients to hold office without receiving salary?"
> Mencius replied, "No; when I first saw the king in Ch'ung, it was my intention, on retiring from the interview, to go away. Because I did not wish to change this intention, I declined to receive any salary.
> "Immediately after, there came orders for the collection of troops, when it would have been improper for me to beg permission to leave. But to remain so long in Ch'i was not my purpose."[210]

To sum up, the cultivation of the person (the first standard rule for the government of a country) and affection toward relatives (the third rule) are indispensable conditions which should be held in common by the sovereign and his ministers. The remaining seven rules—relating to the exaltation of propriety, devotion to reverence and the practice of benevolence—while indispensable to a sovereign, should be enforced by him with the assistance of his ministers. It is remarkable that even in an age of monarchy Mencius was bold enough to advocate the theory that "the people are the most important element in a nation; the spirits of the land and grain, the next; and the sovereign the lightest."[211] He even went so far as to express the view that under certain conditions the sovereign might be removed, banished and even put to death by his ministers. He also maintained that "those who give counsel to the great should despise them, and not look at them with pomp and display."[212]

Confucius cited the example of King Wên to show that a sovereign should rest in benevolence and a minister in respect. Later generations could then know that a sovereign who is not benevolent is not fit to be called one, and that a minister who is not respectful is not fit to be called one. Those who are unfit to be sovereigns and ministers should, therefore, be open to attack by everyone under their jurisdiction.

The First Emperor of Ch'in resorted to such extreme measures as the burning of books and the burying of scholars alive. As a result, his dynasty did not last beyond the second generation. Thereafter, the rulers of China have consistently upheld the lofty teachings of our sages as the standard rules for their government. For this reason, the Way of Might and tyrannical rule have never been able to endure in China.

Thus the spirit of the philosophy of Confucius and Mencius is truly no different from that of the Western theory of democracy. With this as a background, we need have no anxiety about the continuing growth of democracy in our country.

F. Important Tasks of Government

Government is the administration of the affairs of the multitude. It cannot be separated from the rules or laws relating to it. Yet, not only the governed, but the governors, too, are persons. Therefore, the human factor involved in government is extremely important. This point was stressed by Confucius in his reply to Duke Ai of Lu on the subject.

> Duke Ai asked about government. The Master said, "The government of King Wên and Wu is displayed in the records, the tablets of wood and bamboo. Let there be the men and the government will flourish; but without the men their government ceases.
>
> "With the right men the growth of government is rapid, just as the vegetation is rapid in the earth; and moreover their government might be called an easily-growing rush.
>
> "Therefore the administration of government lies in getting proper men."[213]

Every one of the nine standard rules has to do with men. They envisage a method which shows (1) how to cultivate the person as an example for others, (2) how to select worthy and able men, (3) how to exhort what is good, (4) how to comfort and attract those who have preferred to live away from the capital, (5) how to employ people at the proper time, (6) how to treat indulgently men from a distance, and (7) how to cherish

the princes of States. In a word, the crux of the matter is men.
With the right men, if the people are behind the ruler, a country
can be well governed and prosperous; without the right men,
especially if the people refuse to support the ruler, a country
will be in disorder and perhaps even come to ruin.

> The Duke of Shêh asked about government. The Master said,
> "Good government obtains, when those who are near are made
> happy and those who are far off are attracted."[214]
> Duke Ai asked, saying, "What should be done in order to
> secure the submission of the people?" Confucius replied, "Advance
> the upright and set aside the crooked, then the people will submit.
> Advance the crooked and set aside the upright, the people will not
> submit."[215]

Next comes administration. A good administration depends
on the knowledge of properly employed men. They should have
distinct duties and functions so that their work can be regulated
at every level. The ideal is to have these men cooperate perfectly,
proceed at an even pace and assume responsibility for everything
at all times and in all places. They should work like a perfectly
functioning machine which, once it is set in motion, operates
automatically without care. We can call this a government
administered "without exertion." It does not mean that nothing
is done by the government; rather, everything is accomplished
effortlessly. This, of course, is the highest stage which
administration can reach. Only the great wisdom of Shun could
have made it possible, and only an exalted sage like Confucius
and a cultivated philosopher like Lao-tzŭ could have envisaged it.

> The master said, "May not Shun be instanced as having
> governed efficiently without exertion? What did he do? He did
> nothing but gravely and reverently occupy his royal seat."[216]

Mencius said that with worthy men in places of dignity and
able men in offices of trust, there is leisure and freedom from
external trouble throughout the country. This "leisure" refers to
the state of a government administered without exertion.

With the employment of worthy and able men in their proper
places, the first step toward political stability is achieved. Next,
all political activities must have long-term goals and be devoted
to solving the most important problems. Then all the people

will benefit. Another key point: Do not seek quick results.

> Tzŭ-hsia, being governor of Chü-fu, asked about government.
> The Master said, "Do not be desirous to have things done quickly;
> do not look at small advantages. Desire to have things done
> quickly prevents their being done thoroughly. Looking at small
> advantages prevents great affairs from being accomplished."[217]

Government does not consist in conferring small favors on a
minority or on a few individuals. It also does not demand that
a ruler give his personal attention to everything. Tzŭ-ch'an of
Chêng offered his own carriage for carrying people across the
river, and Mencius commented, "It was kind, but showed that he
did not understand the practice of government." Confucius also
said of him merely, "He was a kind man."[218]

> When Tzŭ-ch'an was chief minister of the State of Chêng, he
> would convey people across the Chên and Wei in his own carriage.
> Mencius said, "It was kind, but showed that he did not
> understand the practice of government.
> "When in the eleventh month of the year the foot-bridges are
> completed. and the carriage bridges in the twelfth month, the
> people have not the trouble of wading.
> "Let a governor conduct his rule on principles of equal justice,
> and when he goes abroad, he may cause people to be removed out
> of his path. But how can he convey everybody across the rivers?
> "It follows that if a governor will try to please everybody, he
> will find the days not sufficient for his work."[219]

Specialization is required for cultivating the technique and
art of such things as agriculture, industry and commerce. Those
who govern should have a general knowledge of their respective
fields, but they need not be specialists. The object of government
is to secure the submission of the people by virtuous conduct.
As long as all the offices are occupied by qualified personnel,
there is no need to give personal attention to everything. Moreover,
it is impossible for any one man to attend to all the matters of
government, and it is reasonable to leave specialized knowledge
and technique to the experts in each field. Let us quote Confucius'
reply to Fan Ch'ih.

> Fan Ch'ih requested to be taught husbandry. The Master said,
> "I am not so good for that as an old husbandman." He requested

also to be taught gardening, and was answered, "I am not so good
for that as an old gardener."

Fan Ch'ih having gone out, the Master said, "A small man,
indeed, is Fan Hsü!

"If a superior loves propriety, the people will not dare not to
be reverent. If he loves righteousness, the people will not dare not
to submit to his example. If he loves good faith, the people will
not dare not to be sincere. Now, when these things obtain, the
people from all quarters will come to him, bearing their children
on their backs; what need has he of a knowledge of husbandry?"[220]

The most urgent affairs of the multitude—those which call
for preparation and thorough planning—can be listed as the
"business of the people." Topping this list in ancient China was,
of course, agriculture.

> Duke Wên of T'êng asked Mencius about the proper way of
> governing a country. Mencius said, "The business of the people
> may not be remissly attended to. It is said in the *Book of Songs*,
>
> 'In the daylight go and gather the grass,
> And at night twist your ropes;
> Then get up quickly on the roofs;—
> Soon must we begin sowing again the grain.' "[221]

There is great variety in the affairs that can be catalogued
under the "business of the people." Moreover, with their varying
levels of education, the people cannot be expected to comprehend
all the measures taken by their government. But as long as these
measures are simple, easily understood and based on the people's
general welfare, they can produce satisfactory results.

> Mencius said, "To act without understanding and to do so
> habitually without examination, pursuing the proper path all the
> life without knowing its nature; this is the way of multitudes."[222]
>
> The Master said, "The people may be made to follow a path
> of action, but they may not be made to understand it."[223]
>
> The Master said, "There is Yung! He might occupy the place
> of a prince.
>
> Chung-Kung asked about Tzŭ-sang Po-tzŭ. The Master said,
> "He may pass. He does not mind small matters."
>
> Chung-Kung said, "If a man cherishes in himself a reverential
> feeling of the necessity of attention to business, though he may be
> easy in small matters in his government of the people, that may
> be allowed. But if he cherishes in himself that easy feeling and

also carries it out in practice, is not such an easy mode of procedure excessive?"

The Master said, "Yung's words are right."[324]

The practice of government should not set its aims too high. Nor should it be one-sided. Rather, it must be rational (according to the Mean) and easily carried out. Above all, it must meet the requirements of the people. Therefore, the practical application of a measure should be preceded by a many-sided investigation so that all aspects and implications of the measure are examined in a thorough hearing.

> The Master said, "Was Shun not a great intellect? Shun had a natural curiosity of mind and he loved to inquire into ordinary conversation. He ignored the bad in others and broadcast the good. Taking two extreme counsels, he held the mean between them and applied it in his dealings with the people. Was it by this that he was Shun?"[225]

The above principles of government are of great importance. An attempt must be made to determine how basically sound every administrative measure is. Along with this, a judgment must be made as to its urgency and priority. The following are some of the key problems that must be handled.

1. Stress of Morality and Determination of Human Relations

A nation is a conglomeration of human beings. If these human beings live together without being able to enjoy the happiness of their common existence, is it not a great tragedy? And this can happen, for the uneven distribution of material goods can bring on strife and slaughter. It follows that wealth without virtue is a source of contention and homicide. On the other hand, wealth with virtue is the road to common existence. This is why it is said that virtue is the root and wealth the branch.

> On this account, the ruler will first take pains about his own virtue. Possessing virtue will give him the people. Possessing the people will give him the territory. Possessing the territory will give him its wealth. Possessing the wealth, he will have resources for expenditure.

Virtue is the root; wealth is the result.

If he makes the root his secondary object and the result his primary, he will only contend with his people and teach them rapine.

Hence the accumulation of wealth is the way to scatter the people; and the letting it be scattered is the way to collect the people. And hence the ruler's words going forth contrary to right will come back to him in the same way, and wealth, gotten by improper ways, will take its departure by the same.[226]

Wealth is required for the administration of government. But the production of wealth in an agricultural society depends entirely on the coordination of human labor and the yield of the soil. Hence, "Possessing the people will give him the territory. Possessing the territory will give him its wealth. Possessing the wealth, he will have the resources for expenditure." If the people lack public spirit and are selfish, the nation will come to grief. How can its territory then be preserved? Virtue is an important condition for harmony, and it possesses a very strong adhesive power. A people without virtue is like a plate of loose sand; it is devoid of the strength needed for unity. This type of nation is fortunate if it can maintain its existence; and, of course, it cannot be called well-ordered.

Confucius said, "Duke Ching of Ch'i had a thousand teams, each of four horses, but on the day of his death, the people did not praise him for a single virtue. Po-i and Shu-ch'i died of hunger at the foot of the Shou-yang Mountain, and the people, down to the present time, praise them."

Is this not illustrated in the saying, "Wealth is not the reason for praise, which is only due to extraordinary conduct?[227]

In the *Great Learning* it is said, "This is in accordance with the saying: 'In a State pecuniary gain is not to be considered to be prosperity, but its prosperity will be found in righteousness.' "[228] Mencius also made a distinction between righteousness and profit:

Mencius went to see King Hui of Liang. The king said, "Venerable Sir, since you have not counted it far to come here, a distance of a thousand *li*, may I presume that you are provided with counsels to profit my kingdom?"

Mencius replied, "Why must Your Majesty use that word 'profit?' It will suffice to have benevolence and righteousness.

"If Your Majesty says, 'What is to be done to profit my kingdom?' the great officials will say, 'What is to be done to profit our families?' and the inferior officials and the common people will say, 'What is to be done to profit our persons?' Superiors and inferiors will try to snatch this profit the one from the other, and in the kingdom of ten thousand chariots, the murderer of his sovereign shall be the chief of a family of a thousand chariots. In a country of a thousand chariots, the murderer of his prince shall be the chief of a family of a hundred chariots. To have a thousand in ten thousand and a hundred in a thousand cannot be said not to be a large allotment, but if righteousness be put last, and profit be put first, they will not be satisfied without snatching all.

"There never has been a benevolent man who neglected his parents. There never has been a righteous man who made his sovereign an after consideration.

"Let Your Majesty say, 'Benevolence and righteousness' only. Why must you use that word—'profit?'[229]

When it comes to emphasizing morality, priority must go to the determination of human relations. Also, those in high positions must set the example. Next in importance comes the one who demonstrates respect for human relations—the superior man. Finally, great weight should be attached to the teaching of propriety and music, which are expressions of morality in our daily life.

Duke Ching of Ch'i asked Confucius about government. Confucius replied, "There is government, when the prince is prince and the minister is minister; when the father is father and the son is son."

"Good," said the Duke, "If, indeed, the prince is not prince, the minister not minister, the father not father and the son not son, although I have my grain, can I eat it?"[230]

Mencius said, "...The Minister of Agriculture taught the people to sow and reap, cultivating the five kinds of grain. When the five kinds of grain were brought to maturity, the people all obtained a subsistence. But men possess a moral nature; and if they are well fed, warmly clad, comfortably lodged, without being taught at the same time, they become almost like the beasts. This was a subject of anxious solicitude to the sage Shun, and he appointed Hsüeh to be the Minister of Instruction, to teach the relations of humanity—how, between father and son, there should be affection; between husband and wife, attention to their separate functions; between old and young, the proper order; and between friends, fidelity."[231]

Mencius said, "...But now it is the Middle Kingdom that we

live in. To banish the relationships of men and have no superior men; how can such a state of things be thought of?

"With but few potters a kingdom cannot subsist; how much less can it subsist without men of a higher rank than others?"[232]

Mencius said, "...Tzŭ-kung said, 'By viewing the ceremonial ordinances of a prince, we know the character of his government. By hearing his music, we know the character of his virtue.' "[233]

The inculcation of virtue depends less on verbal instruction than on personal example. Therefore the practice of government does not require many words. However, once the words are spoken, they must be carried out. If they are not and if actions do not correspond to them, the confidence of the people cannot be gained and they will not follow whoever is in the lead. This is why Confucius put such a high priority on gaining the people's confidence. He regarded it more important than "sufficiency of food and sufficiency of military equipment."

Yao and Shun led on the empire with benevolence, and the people followed them. Chieh and Chou led on the empire with violence, and the people followed them. If the orders which these issued had been contrary to the practices which they loved, the people would not have followed them."[234]

The philosopher Tsêng being ill, Mêng Ching went to ask how he was. Tsêng said to him, "When a bird is about to die, its notes are mournful; when a man is about to die, his words are kind.

"There are three principles of conduct which the man of high rank should consider specially important: that if his deportment and manner are regulated by propriety, he can keep from violence and heedlessness; that if he can rectify his countenance according to propriety, he can keep near to sincerity; and that if he can utter words and tones according to propriety, he can keep far from lowness and irrationality. As to such matters as attending to the sacrificial vessels, there are competent officials for them."[235]

Tzŭ-kung asked about government. The Master said, "The requisites of government are that there be sufficiency of food and sufficiency of military equipment, with which the confidence of the people will be gained."

Tzŭ-kung said, "If it cannot be helped, and one of these must be dispensed with, which of the three should be foregone first?" "The military equipment," said the Master.

Tzŭ-kung again asked, "If it cannot be helped, and one of the remaining two must be dispensed with, which of them should be foregone?" "The Master answered, "Part with the food. From of old, death has been the lot of all men; but if the people have no faith in their rulers, there is no standing for the State."[236]

Rulers who have gained the confidence of the people can expect a peaceful adminstration. For one thing, the people will not doubt the orders of their government. Also, although they may have to work hard, they will not complain.

> Tzŭ-hsia said, "The superior man, having obtained their confidence, may then impose labors on his people. If he has not gained their confidence, they will think that he is oppressing them. Having obtained the confidence of his prince, he may then remonstrate with him. If he has not gained his confidence, the prince will think that he is vilifying him."[237]

To put it another way, if a person is in darkness himself, it is impossible for him to enlighten others, let alone gain their confidence. As Mencius said, "Anciently worthy men by means of their own enlightenment made others enlightened. Nowadays it is tried, while they are themselves in darkness, and by means of that darkness, to make others enlightened."[238]

Personal example is required to establish not only confidence but also the virtues of industry, economy, reverence and faithfulness. Let us cite the relevant passages:

> Tzŭ-chang asked about government. The Master said, "The art of governing is to keep its affairs before the mind without weariness and to practice them with undeviating consistency."[239]

> The Master said, "To rule a country of a thousand chariots, there must be reverent attention to business and sincerity; economy in expenditure and love for men; and the employment of the people at the proper seasons."[240]

> Chi K'ang asked how to cause the people to reverence their ruler, to be faithful to him and to go on to nerve themselves to virtue. The Master said, "Let him preside over them with gravity; then they will reverence him. Let him be filial and kind; then they will be faithful to him. Let him advance the good and teach the incompetent; then they will eagerly seek to be virtuous."[241]

When the people stress virtue, they have human harmony, and this is more important than the timeliness of heaven and the benefit of earth. When the sovereign stresses virtue, he gains the people's confidence, and this is more important than sufficient food and military equipment.

Of all our former rulers, Confucius regarded the great Yü and the Duke of Chou as the ones who set the best examples for their people. Yü was away from home for eight years while he devoted himself to harnessing the turbulent rivers and waterways; though he passed his own door three times, he did not enter. In his personal life he was content with shabby clothes and a humble house. He always tried to make the most of his time, he bowed to the speaker of good words, he was reverent to his duties and faithful to all. The Duke of Chou was so wholeheartedly occupied by and devoted to the affairs of state that he often interrupted his meals and baths—three times on one occasion—to attend to them.

Of the great Yü, Confucius said, "I can find no flaw in him," and even in his dreams he could not forget the Duke of Chou. The Master once said, "Extreme is my decay. For a long time I have not dreamed, as I was wont to do, that I saw the Duke of Chou."[242]

Confucius summarized the conduct of government as the "honoring" of the "five excellent things" and the "banishment" of the "four bad things." To put his thought in a nutshell, when benevolence is loved and its opposite is discarded, then the people will believe, submit to, love and rally around the ruler. It is an immutable truth that "possessing virtue will give him the people."

> Tzǔ-chang asked Confucius, saying, "In what way should a person in authority act in order that he may conduct government properly?" The Master replied, "Let him honor the five excellent, and banish away the four bad, things; then may he conduct government properly."
>
> Tzǔ-chang said, "What are meant by the five excellent things?" The Master said, "When the person in authority is beneficent without great expenditure; when he lays tasks on the people without their repining; when he pursues what he desires without being covetous; when he maintains a dignified ease without being proud; when he is majestic without being fierce."
>
> Tzǔ-chang said, "What is meant by being beneficent without great expenditure?" The Master replied, "When the person in authority makes more beneficial to the people the things from which they naturally derive benefit—is not this being beneficent without great expense? When he chooses the labors which are proper and makes them labor on them, who will repine? When his desires are set on benevolent government and he secures it, who will accuse him of covetousness? Whether he has to do with many people or few or with men great or small, he does not dare to indicate any

disrespect—is not this to maintain a dignified ease without any pride? He adjusts his clothes and cap and throws a dignity into his looks, he is looked at with awe—is not this to be majestic without being fierce?"

Tzŭ-chang then said, "What are meant by the four bad things?" The Master said, "To put the people to death without having instructed them—this is called cruelty. To require from them, suddenly, the full tale of work, without having given them warning —this is called oppression. To issue orders as if without urgency and, when the time comes, to insist on them with severity—this is called injury. And, generally, in giving pay and rewards to men, to do it in a stingy way—this is called acting the part of a mere official."[243]

There are several other points which seem inconsequential. But they are of great importance, and attention should be paid to them. They are: (a) not to confuse public and private capacities, (b) not to overlook the views of social leaders, (c) not to disregard those relatives and old subordinates who are good (see the third rule above), (d) not to cause great ministers to feel they are not honored (see the fourth standard rule) and (e) not to be fond of killing people.

(a) The disciple Jan returning from the court, the Master said to him, "How are you so late?" He replied, "We had government business." The Master said, "It must have been family affairs. If there had been government business, though I am not now in office, I should have been consulted about it."[244]

(b) Mencius said, "The administration of government is not difficult; it lies in not offending the great families. He whom the great families affect will be affected by the whole State; and he whom any one State affects will be affected by the whole empire. When this is the case, such a man's virtue and teachings will spread all within the four seas like the rush of water."[245]

(c) and (d) The Duke of Chou addressed his son, the Duke of Lu, saying, "The virtuous prince does not neglect his relations. He does not cause the great ministers to repine at his not employing them. Without some great cause, he does not dismiss from their offices old ministers. He does not seek in one man talents for every employment."[246]

(e) Mencius went to see King Hsiang of Liang. On coming out from the interview, he said to some persons, "When I looked at him from a distance, he did not appear like a sovereign; when

I drew near to him, I saw nothing venerable about him. Abruptly he asked me, 'How can the empire be settled?' I replied, 'It will be settled by being united under one sway.'

" 'Who can so unite it?'

"I replied, 'He who has no pleasure in killing men can so unite it.'

" 'Who can give it to him?'

"I replied, 'All the people of the nation will unanimously give it to him. Does Your Majesty understand the way of the growing grain? During the seventh and eighth months, when drought prevails, the plants become dry. Then the clouds collect densely in the heavens, they send down torrents of rain, and the grain erects itself, as if by a shoot. When it does so, who can keep it back? Now among the shepherds of men throughout the nation, there is not one who does not find pleasure in killing men. If there were one who did not find pleasure in killing men, all the people in the nation would look towards him with outstretched necks. Such being indeed the case, the people would flock to him, as water flows downwards with a rush, which no one can repress.[247]

Capital punishment is the most severe of all penalties. Only when there are compelling circumstances is it used. The existence of one man must be a menace to the existence of many persons before he can be put to death according to law. This is called using death to preserve life.

> Mencius said, "Let the people be employed in the way which is intended to secure their ease, and though they are toiled, they will not murmur. Let them be put to death in the way which is intended to preserve their lives, and though they die, they will not murmur at him who puts them to death."[248]

The killing of an innocent person may well lose the people's hearts; it may even lead to war. So it must be examined carefully. The final decision on punishments by death must rest with the people. Even then a detailed investigation must be carried out before the decision is reached. Only then can it be said to be based on the people's wishes, only then will there be no complaint.

> Mencius said, "...When all those about you say, 'This man deserves death,' don't listen to them. When all your great officials say, 'This man deserves death,' don't listen to them. When the people all say, 'This man deserves death,' then inquire into the case, and when you see that the man deserves death, put him to death,

In accordance with this we have the saying, 'The people killed him.'

"You must act in this way in order to be the parent of the people."[249]

The deterrent effect of capital punishment is not always in evidence. If good government does not prevail, the people—who are oppressed and not in any way afraid of death—cannot be frightened with it. By taking delight in killing men, a ruler simply commits suicide. If he desires to unify his country, all the more should he not take delight in killing men (see passage quoted in (e) above).

Chi K'ang asked Confucius about government, saying, "What do you say to killing the unprincipled for the principled?" Confucius replied, "Sire, in carrying on your government, why should you use killing at all? Let your evinced desires be for what is good, and the people will be good. The relation between superiors and inferiors is like that between the wind and the grass. The grass must bend, when the wind blows across it."[250]

2. Rectification of Names and Adoption of Weights and Measures

The affairs of the multitude are different from those of an individual. Each title and position must have its clear-cut functions and powers. Each vessel and each thing must be gauged by common weights and measures. When all titles and positions are well-defined, the language accords with the truth of things. When they are not, there will be self-justification on all sides, and the lack of commonly accepted standards will cause infinite strife and dispute. And this is surely not the way to conduct the business of government.

It is said, "Government is rectification," which denotes justice, porpriety and accuracy. It follows that when titles and positions are well-defined, a ruler will know how to be a ruler, and a minister how to be a minister. Each will keep to his own sphere without trespassing on the province of the other. When weights are adopted, the vessels and things used in daily life will not be a source of dispute with regard to their weight, length and quantity. Even if disputes arise. there are criteria that can be used to distinguish between good and evil, right and wrong, and thus the disputes can be dissipated.

> Tzǔ-lu said, "The ruler of Wei has been waiting for you, in order with you to administer the government. What will you consider the first thing to be done?"
>
> The Master replied, "What is necessary is to rectify names."
>
> "So, indeed!" said Tzǔ-lu. "You are wide of the mark! Why must there be such rectificaton?"
>
> The Master said, "How uncultivated you are, Yu! A superior man, in regard to what he does not know, shows a cautious reserve.
>
> "If names are not correct, language is not in accordance with the truth of things, affairs cannot be carried on to success. If affairs cannot be carried on to success, proprieties and music will not flourish. When proprieties and music do not flourish, punishments will not be properly awarded. When punishments are not properly awarded, the people do not know how to move hand or foot.
>
> "Therefore a superior man considers it necessary that the names he uses may be spoken appropriately, and that what he speaks may be carried out appropriately. What the superior man requires is just that in his words there may be nothing incorrect."[251]
>
> He (King Wu) carefully attended to the weights and measures, examined the body of the laws, restored the discarded officials, and the good government of the empire took its course.[252]

In compiling the *Spring and Autumn Annals*, Confucius aimed mainly at the rectification of names. That is why Chuang-tzǔ said, "The *Spring and Autumn Annals* is to define names." (See chapter, "All Under Heaven," in the Book of Chuang-tzǔ.) When names are rectified, good and evil are distinguished, right and wrong determined, and rewards and punishments properly awarded. So, Mencius said, "Confucius completed the *Spring and Autumn Annals*, and rebellious ministers and villainous sons were struck with terror."[253]

The rectification of names is shown in the following passages. The first two have to do with ministers who were not ministers, and the third with the correct title of a prince's wife.

> Confucius said of the head of the Chi family, who had eight rows of pantomimes in his ancestral temple, "If he can bear to do this (usurpation of an imperial prerogative), what may he not bear to do?"[254]

The three families used the Yung ode, while the vessels were being removed, at the conclusion of the sacrifice. The Master said, " 'Assisting are the princes; the son of heaven looks profound and grave'—what application can these words have in the hall of the three families?"[255]

The wife of the prince of a State is called by him *fu-jên*. She calls herself *hsiao-t'ung*. The people of the State call her *chün-fu-jên*, and to the people of other States, she calls herself *kua-hsiao-chün*. The people of other States also call her *chün-fu-jên*[256]

The importance of weights and measures lies in their application to things, much as the significance of names lies in their application to persons. Today, as social relationships become increasingly complex and the varieties of things more and more numerous, the demand for necessary standards is markedly urgent. At the same time, while the importance of names used to be to make a distinction between sovereign and minister, today personnel in every walk of life must measure up to certain standards. These standards are determined by examinations or personnel regulations.

As for engineers, lawyers, physicians, accountants and other technical personnel, they must first fulfill certain standard requirements before they can use professional titles. At the same time they are not permitted to usurp these titles or fall short of their requirements. Certain prescribed standards also are essential for many of our daily necessities not covered by weights and measures. For example, conductors of light, sound, electricity and heat must meet certain specifications, as must industrial products, commodities and raw materials. This is necessary to insure progress.

3. Employment of the Worthy and Able, Emphasis on Public Opinion

The importance of recommending, supporting and employing worthy men has been dealt with in a preceding section in connection with the standard rule on this point. To summarize briefly, when a large number of talented men can be placed in suitable governmental positions, the country is likely to be well-governed. If this is not or cannot be done, the country is destined for disorder and possibly ruin. For example, the prosperity of the Chou dynasty was ascribable to the abundance of talented men.

"To Chou belonged the eight officials, Po-ta, Po-kua, Chung-t'u, Chung-hu, Shu-yêh, Shu-hsia, Chi-sui and Chi-kua."[257]

The man who can make good use of talent is he who has a sure knowledge of men. He can perceive the merits of each person and place him accordingly.

> Tzŭ-yu being governor of Wu-ch'eng, the Master said to him, "Have you got good men there?" He answered, "There is T'an-t'ai Mieh-ming, who never in walking takes a short cut, and never comes to my office except on public business."[258]
>
> Chi K'ang asked, saying, "Is Chung-yu fit to be employed as a government official?" The Master said, "Yu is a man of decision; what difficulty would he find in being a government official?" K'ang asked, "Is Tz'ŭ fit to be employed as a government official?" and was answered, "Tz'ŭ is a man of intelligence; what difficulty would he find in being a government official?" And to the same question about Ch'iu the Master gave the same reply, saying "Ch'iu is a man of various ability."[259]

In the absence of talent, virtue is also a qualification for employment.

> The Master said, "Mêng Kung-ch'o is more than fit to be chief official of the families of Chao and Wei, but he is not fit to be great official to either the State of T'êng or Hsüeh."[260]

The measures of worthy and able officials are sure to further the happiness and interests of the people. It is true that the three key elements of a State are its territory, people and government. But by far the most important of the three is the people. For, without people, a territory is barren of production. Without people there can be no government to speak of and, of course, no necessity for creating and filling functional offices, including those of the sovereign and his chief officials. Accordingly:

> Mencius said, "The people are the most important element in a nation; the spirits of the land and grain are the next; the sovereign is the lightest.
>
> "Therefore to gain the peasantry is the way to become sovereign; to gain the sovereign is the way to become a prince of a State; to gain the prince of a State is the way to become a great official.
>
> "When a prince endangers the altars of the spirits of the land and grain, he is changed and another appointed in his place.
>
> "When the sacrificial victims have been perfect, the millet in

its vessel all pure and the sacrifices offered at their proper seasons, if yet there ensues drought or the waters overflow, the spirits of the land and grain are changed and others appointed in their place."[261]

This means that while a prince and the spirits of the land and grain may be subject to change and replacement, there can be no change in the people. In short, the people can never be replaced. Therefore government today is said to be "of the people," and the sovereign is there "for the people."

To extend this thought further, all the affairs of state must revolve around the wishes of the people. "Love what the people love, and hate what the people hate." "Collect for them what they like, and do not lay on them what they dislike."

Coming from the farms, Shun knew that only when the wishes of the people were transmitted upward to the ruler could the decrees of the government be consistent with the facts. When Yü left home for eight years to harness the river's turbulence, he penetrated into the midst of the people and became well acquainted with their inner feelings. "Shun loved to question others and study their words, though they might be shallow." "When Yü heard good words, he bowed to the speaker."

It was not easy for such rulers as Shun and Yü to seek out the wishes of the people. They must have had a sincere desire to know the inner feelings of their subjects. On the other hand, if the people were rebellious and expressed some discontent, the ruler would never have found out their deepest wishes. In the most aggravated cases this would have led to the ruin of the country. The answers of Confucius to the questions of Duke Ting are relevant here.

> Duke Ting asked, "Is there a single sentence which can make a country prosperous?" Confucius replied, "Such an effect cannot be expected from one sentence.
>
> "There is a saying, however, which people have, 'To be a prince is difficult; to be a minister is not easy.'
>
> "If a ruler knows this—the difficulty of being a prince—may there not be expected from this one sentence the prosperity of his country?"
>
> The duke then said, "Is there a single sentence which can ruin a country?" Confucius replied, "Such an effect as that cannot be expected from one sentence. There is, however, the saying which

people have—'I have no pleasure in being a prince, but only in that no one can offer any opposition to what I say!'

"If a ruler's words are good, and no one opposes them, is it not good? But if they are not good and no one opposes them, may there not be expected from this one sentence the ruin of his country?"[362]

What happens when the wishes of the people are disregarded or, even worse, when public opinion is subject to restriction? Laws and orders will not reflect the popular will; in fact they will probably digress from it even more. Compliance or non-compliance with the interests of the people is no longer considered, and their hearts are gradually lost. As this neglect of the people's interests increases, the affections and loyalty of the people themselves are lost.

Both Yao and Shun abdicated and left the throne to worthy men, but Yü did not follow their example. In commenting on past history, Mencius said the question of whether the throne should be handed down to a worthy man or to one's own son should be decided by public opinion. Mencius felt that the sovereign had no right to give the throne to anyone else.

An interesting case in point is the banishment of T'ai-chia and his later restoration after he had reformed. Public spirit was behind both these actions of Yi Yin; he had the courage to defer to public opinion. "Yi Yin said, 'I cannot be near and see him so disobedient to reason,' and therewith he banished T'ai-chia to T'ung. The people were much pleased. When T'ai-chia became virtuous, he brought him back; and the people were again much pleased."

Wan Chang said, "Was it the case that Yao gave the throne to Shun?" Mencius said, "No. The sovereign cannot give the throne to another.

"Yes—but Shun had the throne. Who gave it to him?" "Heaven gave it to him," was the answer.

"'Heaven gave it to him'—did Heaven confer its appointment on him with specific injunctions?"

Mencius replied, "No. Heaven does not speak. It simply showed its will by his personal conduct and his conduct of affairs."

"'It showed its will by his personal conduct and his conduct of affairs'—how was this?" Mencius' answer was, "The sovereign can present a man to Heaven, but he cannot make Heaven give that man the throne. A prince can present a man to the sovereign, but he cannot cause the sovereign to make the man a prince. A great official can present a man to his prince, but he cannot cause the prince to make that man a great official. Yao presented Shun to Heaven, and Heaven accepted him. He presented him to the people, and the people accepted him. Therefore I say, 'Heaven does not speak. It simply indicated its will by his personal conduct and his conduct of affairs.' "

Chang said, "I presume to ask how it was that Yao presented Shun to Heaven, and Heaven accepted him; and that he exhibited him to the people, and the people accepted him." Mencius replied, "He caused him to preside over the sacrifices, and all the spirits accepted the offerings with pleasure; thus Heaven accepted him. He caused him to preside over the conduct of affairs, and affairs were well administered, so that the people reposed under him; thus the people accepted him. Heaven gave the throne to him. The people gave it to him. Therefore I said, 'The sovereign cannot give the throne to another.'

"Shun assisted Yao in the government for twenty and eight years; this was more than man could have done, and was from Heaven. After the death of Yao, when the three years' mourning was completed, Shun withdrew from the son of Yao to the south of South river. The princes of the empire, however, repairing to court, went not to the son of Yao, but they went to Shun. Litigants went not to the son of Yao, but they went to Shun. Singers sang not to the son of Yao, but they sang Shun. Therefore I said, 'Heaven gave him the throne.' It was after these things that he went to the Middle Kingdom and occupied the seat of the Son of Heaven. If he had, before these things, taken up his residence in the palace of Yao and had applied pressure to the son of Yao, it would have been an act of usurpation, and not the gift of Heaven.

"This sentiment is expressed in the words of the 'Great Declaration'—'Heaven sees as my people see; Heaven hears as my people hear.' "[63]

Wan Chang asked Mencius, saying, "People say, 'When the disposal of the empire came to Yü, his virtue was inferior to that of Yao and Shun, and he transmitted it not to the worthiest but to his son.' Was this so?" Mencius replied, "No; it was not so. When Heaven gave the empire to the worthiest, it was given to the worthiest. When Heaven gave it to the son of the preceding sovereign, it was given to him. Shun presented Yü to Heaven. Seventeen years elapsed, and Shun died. When the three years' mourning expired, Yü withdrew from the son of Shun to Yang-ch'êng. The people of the empire followed him just as after the death of Yao, instead of following his son, they had followed Shun.

"Yü presented Yi to Heaven. Seven years elapsed, and Yü died. When the three years' mourning expired, Yi withdrew from the son of Yü to the north of mount Ch'i. The princes, repairing to court, went not to Yi, but they went to Ch'i. Litigants did not go to Yi, but they went to Ch'i, saying, 'He is the son of our sovereign;' the singers did not sing Yi, but they sang Ch'i, saying, 'He is the son of our sovereign.'

"That Tan-chu was not equal to his father and Shun's son not equal to his; that Shun assisted Yao and Yü assisted Shun, for many years, conferring benefits on the people for a long time; that Ch'i was able, as a worthy man, reverently to pursue the same course as Yü; that Yi assisted Yü only for a few years and had not long conferred benefits on the people; that the periods of service of Shun, Yü and Yi were so different; and that the sons were one superior and the other not superior—all this was from Heaven and what could not be brought about by man. That which is done without man's doing is from Heaven. That which happens without man's causing is from the ordinance of Heaven.

"In the case of a private individual obtaining the throne, there must be in him virtue equal to that of Shun and Yü; and moreover there must be the presenting of him to Heaven by the preceding sovereign. It was on this account that Confucius did not obtain the throne.

"When the empire is possessed by natural succession, the sovereign who is displaced by Heaven must be like Chieh or Chou. It was on this account that Yi, Yi Yin and the Duke of Chou did not obtain the throne.

Yi Yin assisted T'ang so that he became sovereign over the empire. After the demise of T'ang, T'ai-ting having died before he could be appointed sovereign, Wai-ping reigned two years and Chung-jên four. T'ai-chia was then turning upside down the statutes of T'ang, when Yi Yin banished him to T'ung for three years. There T'ai-chia repented of his errors, was contrite and reformed himself. In T'ung he came to dwell in benevolence and change to righteousness during those three years, listening to the lessons given to him by Yi Yin. Then Yi Yin again returned with him to Po.

"The Duke of Chou's not getting the throne was like the case of Yi and the throne of Hsia or like that of Yi Yin and the throne of Yin.

"Confucius said, 'T'ang and Yü abdicated the throne to their worthy ministers. The sovereign of Hsia and those of Yin and Chou transmitted it to their sons. The meaning was the same in all the cases."[264]

As it is said above, "Yao presented Shun to Heaven, and Heaven accepted him; he presented him to the people, and the people accepted him." Also, "Heaven sees as my people see; Heaven hears as my people hear." It is clear that the people's wishes are the same as Heaven's wishes. Hence it is said that the arrangement was "obedient to Heaven and responsive to man."

Since the position of sovereign must be decided by the popular will, how can his laws and orders not give their weight to this same popular will?

The crucial test of public opinion comes when there is external aggression. It is then that public opinion decides which course of action to choose—a stubborn defense or withdrawal. If the people are willing to be "prepared to die for" the country, the choice is a stubborn defense. If the people are willing to follow their sovereign to another country "like crowds hastening to market," a temporary withdrawal is harmless. But if it is the wish of the people neither to defend their country nor to withdraw, then the land is in fact no longer theirs.

Duke Wên of T'êng asked Mencius, saying, "T'êng is a small State. Though I do my best to serve those large kingdoms on either side of it, we cannot escape suffering from them. What course shall I take that we may do so?"

Mencius replied, "Formerly, when King T'ai dwelt in Pin, the barbarians of the north were constantly making incursions upon it. He served them with skins and silks, and still he suffered from them. He served them with dogs and horses, and still he suffered from them. He served them with pearls and gems, and still he suffered from them. Seeing this, he assembled the old men and announced to them, saying, 'What the barbarians want is my territory. I have heard this—that a ruler does not injure his people with that wherewith he nourishes them. My children, why should you be troubled about having no prince? I will leave.' Accordingly he left Pin, crossed the mountain Liang, built a town at the foot of Mount Ch'i and dwelt there. The people of Pin said, 'He is a benevolent man. We must not lose him.' Those who followed him looked like crowds hastening to market.

"On the other hand some say, 'The kingdom is a thing to be kept from generation to generation. One individual cannot undertake to dispose of it in his person. Let him be prepared to die for it. Let him not quit it.'

"I ask you, prince, to make your election between these two courses."[265]

It can happen that in normal times a ruler cares only about his own enjoyment, disregarding the sufferings of his people. In such a case, he cannot possibly expect his people to give their blood for the defense of their country when it is invaded. This is especially so when the ruler of the invading country governs benevolently and rallies his people under the high motive of removing a foreign tyrant and saving his people. The invasion is seen by those suffering under the oppressive regime as an opportunity for revenge and salvation. In the midst of their deep agonies, they can even go so far as to help the invader bring about the downfall of their own despot. True, this is a course of action that the people of the invaded country will embark upon only in extraodinary circumstances. But it is also a vital test of public opinion.

There had been a brush between Tsou and Lu when Duke Mu asked Mencius, saying, "Of my officials there were killed thirty-three men, and none of the people would die in their defense. If I sentence them to death for their conduct, it is impossible to put such a multitude to death. If I do not put them to death, then there is the crime unpunished of their looking angrily on at the death of their officials and not saving them. How is the exigency of the case to be met?"

Mencius replied, "In calamitous years and years of famine, the old and weak of your people, who have been found lying in the ditches and water-channels, and the able-bodied who have been scattered to the four quarters, have amounted to several thousands. All the while, your granaries, O prince, have been stored with grain and your treasuries have been full, and not one of your officials has told you of the distress. Thus negligent have the superiors in your State been and cruel to their inferiors. The philosopher Tsêng said, 'Beware, beware. What proceeds from you will return to you again.' Now at length the people have paid back the conduct of their officials to them. How can you blame them?

"If you will put in practice a benevolent government the people will love you and all above them and will die for their officials."[266]

When the Way prevails in a country, the people are obedient and live in harmony. On the other hand, when the Way does not prevail, the people vacillate. If a crime is committed and truth is established, the trial judge should have compassion and sympathize with the guilty rather than pride himself on his keen judgment.

> The chief of the Mêng family having appointed Yang Fu to be chief criminal judge, the latter consulted the philosopher Tsêng. Tsêng said, "The rulers have failed in their duties, and the people consequently have been disorganized for a long time. When you have found out the truth of any accusation, be grieved for and pity them and do not feel joy at your own ability."[267]

In answering a question of King Hsüan of Ch'i, Mencius underlined the importance of public opinion. He said the question of whether or not the State of Yen should be taken ought to be decided according to public opinion—not by the king himself considering only his military strength. To back up his opinion, Mencius cited the examples of Kings Wên and Wu.

> The people of Ch'i attacked Yen and conquered it. King Hsüan asked, saying, "Some tell me not to take possession of it, and some tell me to take possession of it. For a kingdom of ten thousand chariots, attacking another of ten thousand chariots, to complete the conquest of it in fifty days is an achievement beyond mere human strength. If I do not take possession of it, calamities from Heaven will surely come upon me. What do you say to my taking possession of it?"
>
> Mencius replied, "If the people of Yen will be pleased with your taking possession of it, then do so. Among the ancients there was one who acted on this principle, namely, King Wu. If the people of Yen will not be pleassed with your taking possession of it, then do not do so. Among the ancients there was one who acted on this principle, namely, King Wên.
>
> "When, with all the strength of your country of ten thousand chariots, you attacked another of ten thousand chariots, and the people brought baskets of rice and vessels of congee, to meet Your Majesty's host, was there any other reason for this but that they hoped to escape out of fire and water? If you make the water more deep and the fire more fierce, they will have to seek their salvation from another quarter."[268]

· In short, if the government is in the hands of worthy and able men and if public opinion is given full play, all legislation is certain to be enforced without delay.

4. Promotion of Production and Enrichment of the People

The affairs of state may be grouped under two main divisions: those concerned with mental labor and those concerned with physical labor. The former is not applied to direct production, but the latter is. Those engaged in mental labor are supported by others. In this group are administrative workers (for management), educational workers (for instruction) and security workers. The second group (those engaged in physical work), who can support themselves and others, comprise farmers, laborers, and merchants.

> Mencius said, "...Hence there is the saying, 'Some labor with their minds, and some labor with their strength. Those who labor with their minds govern others; those who labor with their strength are governed by others. Those who are governed by others support them; those who govern others are supported by them.' This is a principle universally recognized.[269]

To Ch'ên Hsiang, Mencius explained why those who labored with their minds could not at the same time do physical work. Quite simply, it was due to the division of labor—and the professional people were not getting something for nothing. According to Mencius, there was no class distinction between the governing and the governed. However, those who governed were entrusted by those who were governed with the task of administering the joint affairs of the multitude. (Those who governed in those times were the equivalent of the public functionaries of today.) When they governed well, he felt, they would receive the confidence of the governed; when they did not, they should retire and return their charge to the governed. In this connection, Mencius told Chü-hsin, "Here is a man who receives charge of the cattle and sheep of another and undertakes to feed them for him; of course he must search for pasture-ground and grass for them. If after searching for those, he cannot find them, will he return his charge to the owner: Or will he stand by and see them die?" Mencius also criticized the following theories of Hsü Hsing as impractical.

> There came from Ch'u to T'êng one Hsü Hsing, who gave out that he acted according to the words of Shên-nung. Coming right to his gate, he addressed Duke Wên, saying, "A man of a distant region, I have heard that you, Prince, are practicing a benevolent

government, and I wish to receive a site for a house and to become one of your people." Duke Wên gave him a dwelling-place. His disciples, amounting to several tens, all wore clothes of haircloth, and made sandals of hemp and wove mats for a living.

At the same time, Ch'ên Hsiang, a disciple of Ch'ên Liang, and his younger brother, Hsin, with their plow-handles and shares on their backs, came from Sung to T'êng, saying, "We have heard that you, Prince, are putting into practice the government of the ancient sages, showing that you are likewise a sage. We wish to become the subjects of a sage."

When Ch'ên Hsiang saw Hsü Hsing, he was greatly pleased with him, and abandoning entirely whatever he had learned, became his disciple. Having an interview with Mencius, he related to him with approbation the words of Hsü Hsing to the following effect: "The prince of T'êng is indeed a worthy prince. He has not yet heard, however, the Way of the ancient sages. Now, worthy princes should cultivate the ground equally and together with their people, and eat the fruit of their labor. They should prepare their own meals, morning and evening, while at the same time they carry on their government. But now, the prince of T'êng has his granaries and treasuries, which is an oppressing of the people to nourish himself. How can he be deemed a real worthy prince?"

Mencius said, "Does Hsü Hsing have to sow grain and eat the produce?" "It is so," was the answer. "Does he have to weave cloth and wear his own manufacture?" 'No. Hsü wears clothes of haircloth." "Does he wear a cap?" "He wears a cap." "What kind of cap?" "A plain cap." "Is it woven by himself?" "No. He gets it in exchange for grain." "Why does Hsü not weave for himself?" "That would injure his husbandry." "Does Hsü cook his food in boilers and earthenware pans, and does he plow with an iron share?" "Yes." "Does he make those articles himself?" "No. He gets them in exchange for grain."

Mencius then said, "Getting those articles in exchange for grain is not oppressive to the potter and the founder, and the potter and founder in their turn, in exchanging their various articles for grain, are not oppressive to the husbandman. How should such things be supposed? And moreover, why does not Hsü act the potter and founder, supplying himself with the articles which he uses solely from his own establishment? Why does he go confusedly dealing and exchanging with the handicraftsmen? Why does he not spare himself so much trouble?" Ch'ên Hsiang replied, "The business of the handicraftsman can by no means be carried on along with the business of husbandry."

Mencius resumed, "Then is it the government of the empire

which alone can be carried on along with the practice of husbandry? Great men have their proper business, and little men have their proper business. Moreover, in case any single individual were to perform the business of all the handicraftsmen and if he must himself make everything he uses, this way of doing would keep all the people running about upon the roads. Hence, there is the saying, 'Some labor with their minds, and some labor with their strength. Those who labor with their minds govern others; those who labor with their strength are governed by others. Those who are governed by others support them; those who govern others are supported by them.' This is a principle universally recognized.

"In the time of Yao, when the world had not yet been perfectly reduced to order, the vast waters, flowing out of their channels, made a universal inundation. Vegetation was luxuriant, and birds and beasts swarmed. The various kinds of grain could not be grown. The birds and beasts pressed upon men. The paths marked by the feet of beasts and prints of birds crossed one another throughout the Middle Kingdom. To Yao alone this caused anxious sorrow. He raised Shun to office, and measures to regulate the disorder were set forth. Shun committed to Yi the direction of the fire to be employed, and Yi set fire to, and consumed, the forests and vegetation on the mountains and in the marshes, so that the birds and beasts fled away to hide themselves. Yü separated the nine streams, cleared the courses of the Chi and T'a and led them all to the sea. He opened a vent also for the Ju and Han and regulated the course of the Huai and Ssŭ, so that they all flowed into the Chiang. When this was done, it became possible for the people of the Middle Kingdom to cultivate the ground and get food for themselves. During that time, Yü was eight years away from home, and although he thrice passed the door of it, he did not enter. Even if he had wished to cultivate the ground, could he have done so?

"The Minister of Agriculture taught the people to sow and reap, cultivating the five kinds of grain. When the five kinds of grain were brought to maturity, the people all obtained a subsistence. But men possess a moral nature; and if they are well fed, warmly lodged, without being taught at the same time, they become almost like the beasts. This was a subject of anxious solicitude to the sage Shun, and he appointed Hsüeh to be the Minister of Instruction, to teach the relations of humanity: how, between father and son, there should be affection; between sovereign and minister, righteousness; between husband and wife, attention to their separate functions; between old and young, a proper order; and between friends, fidelity. Yao said to him, 'Urge them to be diligent, rectify them, help and instruct them, so as to make them preserve their inherently good nature. Then follow this up by giving them relief and conferring benefits on them.' When the sages were exercising their solicitude for the people in this way, had they leisure to cultivate the ground?

"What Yao felt giving him anxiety was the inablility to get Shun. What Shun felt giving him anxiety was the inability to get Yü and Kao Yao. But he whose anxiety is about his hundred *mou* not being properly cultivated is a mere husbandman.

"The imparting by a man to others of his wealth is called 'kindness.' The teaching others what is good is called 'the exercise of fidelity.' The finding a man who shall benefit the empire is called 'benevolence.' Hence to give the throne to another man would be easy; to find a man who shall benefit the empire is difficult.

"Confucius said, 'Great indeed was Yao as a sovereign. It is only Heaven that is great, and only Yao corresponded to it. How vast his virtue was! The people could find no name for it. Princely indeed was Shun. How majestic he was, having possession of the empire, and yet seeming as if he had no part in it! In their governing the empire, were there no subjects on which Yao and Shun employed their minds? There were subjects; only they did not employ their minds on the cultivation of the ground.

"I have heard of men using the doctrines of our great land to change barbarians, but I have never heard yet of any being changed by barbarians. Ch'ên Liang was a native of Ch'u. Pleased with the doctrines of the Duke of Chou and Chung-ni, he came northwards to the Middle Kingdom and studied them. Among the scholars of the northern regions there was probably no one who excelled him. He was what you call a scholar of high and distinguiseed qualities. You and your brother followed him some tens of years, and now that your master is dead, you forthwith turn away from him.

"Formerly, when Confucius died, after three years had elapsed, his disciples collected their baggage and prepared to return to their several homes. But on entering to take their leave of Tzǔ-kung, as they looked towards one another, they wailed till they all lost their voices. After this they returned to their homes, but Tzǔ-kung went back and built a house for himself on the grave-site, where he lived alone for another three years before he returned home. On another occasion, Tzǔ-hsia, Tzǔ-chang and Tzǔ-yu, thinking that Yu Jo resembled the sage, wished to render to him the same observances which they had rendered to Confucius. They tried to force the disciple Tsêng to join with them, but he said, 'This may not be done. What has been washed in the waters of the Chiang and Han and bleached in the autumn sun—how glistening it is! Nothing can be added to it.'

"Now here is the shrike-tongued barbarian of the south, whose doctrines are not those of the ancient kings. You turn away from your master and become his disciple. Your conduct is different indeed from that of the philosopher Tsêng.

"I have heard of birds leaving dark valleys to remove to lofty trees, but I have not heard of their descending from lofty trees to enter into dark valleys,

"In the Praise-songs of Lu it is said,

'He smote the barbarians of the west and the north,
He punished Ching and Shu.'

Thus the Duke of Chou would be sure to smite them, and you become their disciples again; it appears that your change is not good."

Ch'ên Hsiang said, "If Hsü's doctrines were followed, then there would not be two prices in the market, nor any deceit in the kingdom. If a boy of five cubits were sent to the market, no one would impose on him; linen and silk of the same length would be of the same price. So it would be with bundles of hemp and silk, being of the same weight; with the different kinds of grain, being the same in quantity; and with shoes which were of the same size."

Mencius replied, "It is the nature of things to be of unequal quality. Some are twice, some five times, some ten times, some a hundred times, some a thousand times, some ten thousand times as valuable as others. If you reduce them all to the same standard, that must throw the empire into confusion. If large shoes and small shoes were of the same price, who would make the large ones? For people to follow the doctrines of Hsü would be for them to lead one another on to practice deceit. How can they avail for the government of a State?"[270]

Those who govern others must have definite functions especially assigned to them, and their food must be raised by others. It is said, "The emoluments can suffice to take the place of the cultivation of land." The emoluments (equivalent to today's salaries) come from the revenue of the State. Therefore the revenue of the State is the payment by the people for the administration and services of the government (including education, defense, water conservation, communications, etc.) The greater the economic development of the country, the larger will be the amount of its revenue. It follows that "if the people have plenty, their prince will not be left to want alone. If the people are in want, their prince cannot enjoy plenty alone."[271]

From this it is evident that the first step to be taken in the finance and economy of a country is the enrichment of the people.

> When the Master went to Wei, Jan Yu acted as the driver of his carriage.
>
> The Master observed, "How numerous the people are!"
>
> Yu said, "Since they are thus numerous, what more shall be done for them?" "Enrich them," was the reply.
>
> "And when they are enriched, what more shall be done?" The Master said, "Teach them."[272]

Here are the ways of enriching the people:

(a) By providing them with definite livelihood "so as to make sure that, above, they shall have sufficient wherewith to serve their parents, and, below, sufficient wherewith to support their wives and children; that in good years they shall always be abundantly satisfied, and that in bad years they shall escape the danger of perishing."[273]

(b) By helping the people to increase their production. For example, in agriculture ancient kings "in the spring examined the plowing and supplied any deficiency of yield."[274] In industry there should be "daily examinations and monthly trials," and "their (the artisans') rations" should be made "in accordance with their labors."[275]

(c) By making the people's imposts light and employing them only at the proper times, so that their burdens are lightened and their agricultural labors are not hampered by undue interference.

(d) By giving attention to water conservation and communciations. This is necessary so that the productive capacity of the soil can be fully utilized and the circulation of commodities can be facilitated.

(e) By paying close attention to the accurate demarcation of land and the equalization of its ownership. The object here is to make certain that taxes are levied fairly and official corruption is eliminated.

(f) By adopting an emigration policy which will adjust the relationihip between the country's production capacity and its population.

Some comments on these points follow:

(a) Why is it necessary for the people to have a definite livelihood? Mencius said, "If they have a certain livelihood, they will have a fixed heart." What would be the result of a lack of a fixed heart? Mencius answered this question and discussed the ancient systems of taxation and land tenure in his reply to a query from Duke Wên of T'êng about the proper way to govern a country.

Mencius said, "...The way of the people is this: If they have a certain livelihood, they will have a fixed heart; if they have not a fixed heart, there is nothing which they will not do in the way of self-abandonment, of moral deflection, of depravity and of wild license. When they have thus been involved in crime, to follow them up and punish them: this is to entrap the people. How can such a thing as entrapping the people be done under the rule of a benevolent man?

"Therefore a ruler who is worthy will be greatly complaisant and economical, showing a respectful politeness to his ministers and taking from the people only in accordance with regulated limits.

"Yang Hu said, 'He who seeks to be rich will not be benevolent. He who wishes to be benevolent will not be rich.'

"The sovereign of the Hsia dynasty enacted the fifty *mou* allotment and the payment of a tax. The founder of the Yin enacted the seventy *mou* allotment and the system of mutual aid. The founder of the Chou enacted the hundred *mou* allotment and the share system. In reality, what was paid in all these was a tithe. The share system means mutual division. The aid system means dependence.

"Lung said, 'For regulating the lands there is no better system than that of mutual aid, and none which is not better than that of taxing. By the tax system, the regular amount was fixed by taking the average of several years. In good years, when the grain lies about in abundance, much might be taken without its being oppressive, and the actual exaction would be small. But in bad years, the produce being not sufficient to repay the manuring of the fields, this system still requires the taking of the full amount. When the parent of the people causes the people to wear the looks of distress, and, after the whole year's toil, yet not to be able to nourish their parents, so that they proceed to borrowing to increase their means, till the old people and children are found lying in the ditches and water-channels—where, in such a case, is his parental relation to the people?'

"As to the system of hereditary salaries, that is already observed in T'êng.

"It is said in the *Book of Songs*,

'May the rain come down on our public land,
And then upon our private lands!'

It is only in the system of mutual aid that there is a public field, and from this passage we perceive that even in the Chou dynasty this system has been recognized.

"Establish *hsiang, hsü, hsüeh,* and *hsiao*—all those educational institutions—for the instruction of the people. The name *hsiang* indicates nourishing as its object; *hsiao* indicates teaching; and *hsü* indicates archery. By the Hsia dynasty the name *hsiao* was used; by the Yin, that of *hsü*; and by the Chou, that of *hsiang.* As to the *hsüeh,* they belonged to all three dynasties, and by that name. The object of them all is to illustrate the human relations. When those are thus illustrated by superiors, kindly feeling will prevail among the inferior people below.

"Should a real sovereign arise, he will certainly come and take an example from you; and thus you will be the teacher of the true sovereign.

"It is said in the *Book of Songs,*
'Although Chou was an old country,
It received a new destiny.'
That is said with reference to King Wên. Do you practice those things with vigor, and you also will by them make new your State."

The duke afterwards sent Pi Chan to consult Mencius about the nine-square system of dividing the land. Mencius said to him. "Since your prince, wishing to put in practice a benevolent government, has made choice of you and put you into this employment, you must exert yourself to the utmost. Now the first thing towards a benevolent government must be to lay down the boundaries. If the boundaries are not defined correctly, the division of the land into squares will not be equal, and the produce available for salaries will not be evenly distributed. On this account, oppressive rulers and impure ministers are sure to neglect this defining of the boundaries. When the boundaries have been defined correctly, the division of the fields and the regulation of allowances may be determined by you, sitting at your ease.

"Although the territory of T'êng is narrow and small, yet there must be in it men of a superior grade and there must be in it countrymen. If there were not men of a superior grade, there would be none to rule the countrymen. If there were not countrymen, there would be none to support the men of superior grade.

"I would ask you, in the remoter districts, observing the nine-square divison, to reserve one division to be cultivated on the system of mutual aid, and in the more central parts of the State, to make the people pay for themselves a tenth part of their produce.

"From the highest officials to the lowest, each one must have his holy field, consisting of fitfty *mou*.

"Let the supernumerary males have their twenty-five *mou*.

"On occasions of death or removal from one dwelling to another, there will be no quitting the district. In the fields of a district, those who belong to the same nine squares render all friendly offices to one another in their going out and coming in, aid one another in keeping watch and ward, and sustain one another in sickness. Thus the people are brought to live in affection and harmony.

"A squares *li* covers nine squares of land, which nine squares contain nine hundred *mou*. The central square is the public field, and eight families, each having its private hundred *mou*, cultivate in common the public field. And not until the public work is finished may they presume to attend to their private affairs. This is the way by which the countrymen are distinguished from those of a superior grade.

"These are the great outlines of the system. Happily to modify and adapt it depends on the prince and you."[276]

Mencius also said that men of education, though without a certain livelihood, could maintain a fixed heart. So, with self-sufficiency as the objective, an ecomomic unit such as a family of eight could live well with one hundred *mou* of land.

Mencius said, "They are only men of education, who, without a certain livelihood, are able to maintain a fixed heart. As to the people, if they have not a certain livelihood, it follows that they will not have a fixed heart. And if they have not a fixed heart, there is nothing which they will not do, in the way of self-abandonment, of moral deflection, of depravity and of wild license. When they thus have been involved in crime, to follow them up and punish them—this is to entrap the people. How can such a thing as entrapping the people be done under the rule of a benevolent man?

"Therefore an intelligent ruler will regulate the livelihood of the people so as to make sure that, above, they shall have sufficient wherewith to serve their parents, and, below, sufficient wherewith to support their wives and children; that in good years they shall always be abundantly satisfied, and that in bad years they shall escape the danger of perishing. After this he may urge them, and they will proceed to what is good, for in this case the people will follow after it with ease.

"Now, the livelihood of the people is so regulated that, above, they have not sufficient wherewith to serve their parents and, below, they have not sufficient wherewith to support their wives and children. Notwithstanding good years, their lives are continually embittered and, in bad years, they do not escape perishing. In such circumstances they do not even find it possible to save themselves from death. What leisure have they to cultivate propriety and righteousness?

"If Your Majesty wishes to effect this regulation of the livelihood of the people, why not turn to that which is the root of the matter?

"Let mulberry-trees be planted about the homesteads with their five *mou*, and persons of fifty years my be clothed with silk. In keeping fowls, pigs, dogs and swines, let not their times of breeding be neglected, and persons of seventy years may eat meat. Let there not be taken away the time that is proper for the cultivation of the farm with its hundred *mou*, and the family of eight mouths that is supported by it shall not suffer from hunger. Let careful attention be paid to education in schools, the inculcation in it especially of the filial and fraternal duties, and grey-haired men will not be seen upon the roads, carrying burdens on their backs or on their heads. It never has been that the ruler of a State where such results were seen—the old wearing silk and eating meat and the black-haired people suffering neither from hunger nor cold—did not attain to the royal dignity."[277]

(b) In an agricultural society the economy centers, of course, on farming. The responsibility for solving the questions of agricultural guidance and farm credits should be assumed by the government. In answering a question of Duke Ching of Ch'i, Yen-tzŭ noted that the journeys of the sovereign were not for pleasure, but for the transaction of government business. In spring and autumn, for instance, the ruler made special trips to inspect the state of agricultural production, so that the practical requirements of rural areas could be determined and the policy of state aid mapped out.

Mencius said, "...Formerly, Duke Ching of Ch'i asked the minister Yen, saying, 'I wish to pay a visit of inspection to Chuan-fu and Ch'ao-wu, and then to bend my course southward along the shore, till I come to Lang-ya. What shall I do that my tour may be fit to be compared with the visits of inspection by the ancient sovereigns?'

"The minister Yen replied, 'An excellent inquiry! When the Son of Heaven visited the princes, it was called a tour of inspection, that is, he surveyed the States under their care. When the princes attended at the court of the Son of Heaven, it was called a report of office, that is, they reported their administration of their offices. Thus, neither of the proceedings was without a purpose. And moreover, in the spring they examined the plowing and supplied any deficiency of seed; in the autumn they examined the reaping and supplied any deficiency of yield. There is the saying of the Hsia dynasty, 'If our king does not take his ramble, what will become of our happiness? If our king does not have his pleasure, what will become of our help? That ramble and that pleasure were a pattern to the princes.[278]

But a grain policy is only one part of the overall administration of agriculture. Intervals for the breeding of fowls, pigs, dogs and swine should not be neglected. Also, fishing should be regulated so that close nets will not ravish pools and ponds. With the right regulations, animals and fish will continue plentiful and the result will be a sufficiency of food (the aged will always have meat to eat).

As for clothing, it was thought in those times that planting only hemp and cotton was not enough. Houses of five *mou* should be surrounded by mulberry trees so that the aged could wear silk, a light but warm fabric.

Finally there was the question of lodging, fuel and burial. To provide the wood required for homes, firewood and coffins, forests had to be protected by law. Outside of the prescribed times, the felling of trees, especially young ones, had to be prohibited so that the supply of timber would not be exhausted. In this way the requirements of both the living and the dead could be provided. Actually, this was regarded as the beginning of a government based on the Way of Right.

> Mencius said, "...If the seasons of husbandry are not interfered with, the grain will be more than can be eaten. If close nets are not allowed to enter the pools and ponds, the fishes and turtles will be more than can be consumed. If the axes and bills enter the hills and forests only at the proper time, the wood will be more than can be used. When the grain and turtles are more than can be eaten, and there is more wood than can be used, this enables the people to nourish their living and mourn for their dead, without any regrets. This condition, in which the people nourish their living and bury their dead without any regrets, is the first step of royal government.
>
> "Let mulberry-tres be planted about the homesteads with their

five *mou*, and persons of fifty years may be clothed with silk. In keeping fowls, pigs, dogs and swine, let not their times of breeding be neglected, and persons of seventy years may eat meat."[279]

In the area of industrial production, the policy of encouragement should be adopted. To assure continued progress, emphasis must be put on research and experimentation. The treatment of technical personnel should be liberal and correspond to their work. This point was stated as one of the standard rules for the government of a country; it concluded, "By encouraging the resort of all classes of artisans, his (the ruler's) resources for expenditures are rendered ample."

> By daily examinations and monthly trials, and by making their rations in accordance with their labors: this is the way to encourage the classes of artisans.[280]

There is a proverb which says, "To the people food is Heaven." A sufficiency of food has to be the first objective of production. The goal is to cause "pulse and grain to be as abundant as water and fire."

> Mencius said, "...The people cannot live without water and fire, yet if you knock at a man's door in the dusk of the evening and ask for water and fire, there is no man who will not give them, such is the abundance of these things. A sage governs the empire so as to cause pulse and grain to be as abundant as water and fire. When pulse and grain are as abundant as water and fire, how shall the people be other than virtuous?"[281]

There must be an abundance in the other areas of production, too, according to the plan of economic development and the premise of the financial policy. "There is a great course also for the production of wealth. Let the producers be many and the consumers few. Let there be activity in the production and economy in the expenditure. Then the wealth will always be sufficient."[282]

(c) The affairs of the people must be managed by a corps of trusted, specially designated personnel. And the people must pay the expenses of this select group. Likewise, construction of public facilities for the use and enjoyment of the people must be handled by another group of specialists, and again it is the people who must sign the checks. Two ways of meeting the expense involved are taxation and the requisition of labor. But if everything taken from the people is used for the people, there can be no complaint. On the other hand, if money taken from the people finds its way into the pockets of officials, the people are sure to murmur. Therefore, taxation must be as light as possible, and labor should be requisitioned only at the proper times. This point is stressed in the standard rule for the government of a country, "dealing with the people as children." It counsels "employing them at the proper times and making their imposts light."

The ruler must be economical in government spending, and unnecessary expenses should be avoided. Yet, whatever is necessary must be defrayed, no matter what the cost.

> Mencius said, "...Therefore a ruler who is worthy will be greatly complaisant and economical, showing a respectful politeness to his ministers and taking from the people only in accordance with regulated limits.
>
> "Yang Hu said, 'He who seeks to be rich will not be benevolent. He who wishes to be benevolent will not be rich."[283]
>
> The Master said, "To rule a country of a thousand chariots, there must be reverent attention to business and sincerity; economy in expenditure and love for men; and the employment of the people at the proper seasons."[284]
>
> Mencius said, "Let it be seen to that their fields are well cultivated and make the taxes on them light; so the people may be made rich.
>
> "Let it be seen to that the people use their resources of food seasonably and expend their wealth only on the prescribed ceremonies—so their wealth will be more than can be consumed."[285]

Each time Mencius answered the queries of reigning princes on the conduct of kingly government, he warned that the people should not be deprived of their working time. Before him Confucius had inveighed against the accumulation of wealth by the ruler; he called it an act of the mean man and saw it as a sure way of bringing injury and disaster to his nation. It can be seen from this how much the sages detested heavy taxation and unseasonal employment of the people.

In modern times reduction of taxes is often regarded as a means to greater economic prosperity. It is no mere coincidence that this farsighted financial policy complies with Mencius' counsel: "...make the tax on them light...so the people may be made rich."

But what exactly is a reasonable system of taxation? The tithe, one-tenth, or one-ninth, was the usual rate adopted in the past. Details of the ancient systems were described by Mencius as follows:

> Mencius said, "...The sovereign of the Hsia dynasty enacted the fifty *mou* allotment and the payment of a tax. The founder of the Yin enacted the seventy *mou* allotment and the system of mutual aid. The founder of the Chou enacted the hundred *mou* allotment and the share system. In reality, what was paid in all these was a tithe. The share system means mutual division. The aid system means dependence.
>
> "Lung said, 'For regulating the lands there is no better system than that of mutual aid, none which is not better than that of taxing. By the tax system, the regular amount was fixed by taking the average of several years. In good years, when the grain lies about in abundance, much might be taken without its being oppressive, and the actual exaction would be small. But in bad years, the produce being not sufficient to repay the manuring of the fields, this system still requires the taking of the full amount. When the parent of the people causes the people to wear the looks of distress, and, after the whole year's toil, yet not to be able to nourish their parents, so that they proceed to borrowing to increase their means, till the old people and children are found lying in the ditches and water—where, in such a case, is his parental relation to the people?
>
> "As to the system of hereditary salaries, that is already observed in T'êng.
>
> "It is said in the *Book of Songs*,
>
>> 'May the rain come down on our public land,
>> And then upon our private lands!'
>
> It is only in the system of mutual aid that there is a public field, and from this passage we perceive that even in the Chou dynasty this system has been recognized."[236]

> Mencius said, "...Although the territory of T'êng is narrow and small, yet there must be in it men of a superior grade and there must be in it countrymen. If there were not men of a superior grade, there would be none to rule the countrymen. If there were not countrymen, there would be none to support the men of superior grade.
>
> "I would ask you, in the remoter districts, observing the nine-square division, to reserve one division to be cultivated on the system of mutual aid, and in the more central parts of the State, to make the people pay for themselves a tenth part of their produce.
>
> "From the highest officials to the lowest, each one must have

his holy field, consisting of fifty *mou*.

"Let the supernumerary males have their twenty-five *mou*.

"On occassions of death or removal from one dwelling to another, there will be no quitting the district. In the fields of a district, those who belong to the same nine squares render all friendly offices to one another in their going out and coming in, aid one another in keeping watch and ward, and sustain one another in sickness. Thus the people are brought to live in affection and harmony.

"A square *li* covers nine squares of land, which nine squares contain nine hundred *mou*. The central square is the public field, and eight families, each having its private hundred *mou*, cultivate in common the public field. And not until the public work is finished may they presume to attend to their private affairs. This is the way by which the countrymen are distinguished from those of a superior grade.

"These are the great outlines of the system. Happily to modify and adapt it depends on the prince and you."[287]

The tithe was a comparatively reasonable rate. After it had been in force for a long time, it was unnecessary to raise or lower it. Two-tenths would have been too onerous for the people; and one-twentieth, insufficient to meet the expenses of the State. If attention had been paid only to revenue and economic development neglected, it would have been an example of the pursuit of the branches instead of the root.

Some parties in Lu were going to take down and rebuild the treasury Long. Min Tzu-ch'ien said, "Suppose it were to be repaired after its old style; why must it be altered and made anew?"

The Master said, "This man seldom speaks; when he does, he is sure to hit the point."[288]

Duke Ai inquired of Yu Jo, saying, "The year is one of scarcity, and the returns for expenditure are not sufficient; what is to be done?"

Yu Jo replied to him, "Why not simply tithe the people?"

"With two-tenths," said the duke, "I find them not enough; how could I do with that system of one-tenth?"

Yu Jo answered, "If the people have plenty, their prince will not be left to want alone. If the people are in want, their prince cannot enjoy plenty alone."[289]

Po Kuei said, "I wish to take a twentieth of the produce only as the tax. What do you think of it?"

Mencius said, "Your way would be that of Mo.

"In a country of ten thousand families, would it do to have only one potter?" Kuei replied, "No. The vessels would not be enough to use!"

Mencius went on, "In Mo all the five kinds of grain are not grown; it only produces the millet. There are no fortified cities, no edifices, no ancestral temples, no ceremonies of sacrifice; there are no princes requiring presents and entertainments; there is no system of officials with their various subordinates. On these accounts a tax of one-twentieth of the produce is sufficient there.

"But now it is the Middle Kingdom that we live in. To banish the relationships of men and have no superior men; how can such a state of things be thought of?

"With but few potters a country cannot subsist; how much less can it subsist without men of a higher rank than others?

"If we wish to make the taxation lighter than the system of Yao and Shun, we shall just have a great Mo and a small Mo. If we wish to make it heavier, we shall just have the great Chieh and the small Chieh."[290]

In ancient times, to insure unrestricted distribution, commodities were not taxed. Later, with the advent of monopolies, commodities were taxed.

Mencius said, "...Of old time, the market-dealers exchanged the articles which they had for others which they had not, and simply had certain officials to keep order among them. It happened that there was a mean fellow, who made it a point to look out for a conspicuous mound and get up upon it. Thence he looked right and left to catch in his net the whole gain of the market. The people all thought his conduct mean, and therefore they proceeded to lay a tax upon his wares. The taxing of traders took its rise from this mean fellow."[291]

Mencius said, "...If, in the market-place of his (a ruler's) capital, he levies a ground-rent on the shops but does not tax the goods, or enforces the proper regulations without levying a ground-rent— then all the traders of the empire will be pleased and wish to store their goods in his market-place.

"If, at his frontier-passes, there is an inspection of persons, but no taxes charged, then all the travelers of the empire will be pleased and wish to make their tours on his roads."[292]

(d) Water conservation is a prerequisite for agriculture, much as communications are for industry and commerce. "Benefiting the people where they can be benefited," the ruler and his officials must use common sense when it comes to water conservation. Whenever a flood innundates an area, they must be the first to engage in the work of salvage and relief. The greatest flood in our country's history occurred at the time of Yao and Shun, and it was brought under control only by the brilliant engineering feats of Yü. The story is told in Mencius' works:

> Mencius said, "...In the time of Yao, when the world had not yet been perfectly reduced to order, the vast waters, flowing out of their channels, made a universal inundation. Vegetation was luxuriant, and birds and beasts swarmed. The various kinds of grain could not be grown. The birds and beasts pressed upon men. The paths marked by the feet of beasts and prints of birds crossed one another throughout the Middle Kingdom. To Yao alone this caused anxious sorrow. He raised Shun to office, and measures to regulate the disorder were set forth. Shun committed to Yi the direction of the fire to be employed, and Yi set fire to, and consumed, the forests and vegetation on the mountains and in the marshes, so that the birds and beasts fled away to hide themselves. Yü separated the nine streams, cleared the courses of the Chi and T'a and led them all to the sea. He opened a vent also for the Ju and Han and regulated the course of the Huai and Ssŭ, so that they all flowed into the Chiang. When this was done, it became possible for the people of the Middle Kingdom to cultivate the ground and get food for themselves. During that time, Yü was eight years away from home, and though he thrice passed the door of it, he did not enter. Even if he had wished to cultivate the ground, could he have done so?"[293]

> Mencius said, "...In the time of Yao, the waters, flowing out of their channels, inundated the Middle Kingdom. Snakes and dragons occupied it, and the people had no place where they could settle themselves. In the low grounds they made nests for themselves, and in the high grounds they made caves. It is said in the Book of History, 'The waters in their wild course warned me.' Those 'waters in their wild course' were the waters of the great inundation.

> "Shun employed Yü to reduce the waters to order. Yü dug open their obstructed channels and conducted them to the sea. He drove away the snakes and dragons and forced them into the grassy marshes. On this, the waters pursued their courses through the country, even the Chiang, the Huai, the Ho and the Han, and the dangers and obstructions which they had occasioned were removed. The birds and beasts which had injured the people also disappeared.

and after this men found the plains available for them and occupied them.

"After the death of Yao and Shun, the Way of the sages fell into decay. Oppressive sovereigns arose one after another, who pulled down houses to make ponds and lakes, so that the people knew not where they could rest in quiet; they threw fields out of cultivation to form gardens and parks, so that the people could not get clothes and food. Afterwards, corrupt speakings and oppressive deeds became more rife; gardens and parks, ponds and lakes, thickets and marshes became more numerous, and birds and beasts swarmed. By the time of the tyrant Chou, the empire was again in a state of great confusion."[294]

This tragic experience taught such an unforgettable lesson that during the reign of every ruler down through the ages great attention was paid to water conservation. The great Yü has been looked upon as the model of successful flood control. A temple was erected to honor his memory in each of the key centers of water conservation projects, with sacrifices offered to him in the spring and autumn of each year. Confucius heaped high praise on the great sovereign by saying, "He lived in a low, mean house, but expended all his strength on the ditches and water-chanels. I can find nothing like a flaw in Yü."[295]

As water often flows through the territory of more than one State, it is imperative in the regulation of a waterway to pay heed to the interests of countries occupying a river's upper and lower reaches. If a neighboring country is used as a receptacle for surplus water, thereby causing injury, the waterway cannot be said to be properly regulated. In fact, such a situation could lead to war.

Po Kuei said, "My management of the waters is superior to that of Yü." Mencius replied, "You are wrong, Sir. Yü's regulation of the waters was according to the laws of water.

"He therefore made the four seas their receptacle, while you make the neighboring States their receptacle. Water flowing out of its channels is called an inundation, which is detested by a benevolent man. You are wrong, my good Sir."[296]

As a rule land and water communications facilities were built during the farmer's off-season. It was then that various projects were constructed to facilitate travel. As Mencius said, "...When in the eleventh month of the year the foot-bridges are completed, and the carriages in the twelfth month, the people have not the trouble of wading."[297]

In the interest of unimpeded travel through all the States, the distance between the two wheels of a carriage was carefully regulated. Hence it was said, "Now, over the empire, carriages have all wheels of the same size; all writing is with the same characters; and for conduct there are the same rules."[298]

(e) To restate, in an agricultural society the most important measure is to enable the people to have a definite livelihood—in other words, to own the land which they cultivate. The first step toward this goal is to work out equalization of land tenure, which tends to do away with distinctions between the rich and the poor. To equalize land ownership, it is necessary first to insure boundaries through accurate land surveys. Once the boundaries are fixed, the people's burden is equalized and the calculation of taxes is made easier. This will eliminate an opportunity for corruption by officials.

There are other important advantages too. In short, "rulers of States and chiefs of families are not troubled with fears of poverty, but are troubled lest their people should not keep their several places;...they are not troubled lest their people should be few, but are troubled with a want of contented repose among the people in their several places. For when the people keep their several places, there will be no poverty; when harmony prevails, there will be no scarcity of people; and when there is such a contented repose, there will be no rebellious upsettings."[299]

> Mencius said, "...Now, the first things toward a benevolent government must be to lay down the boundaries. If the boundaries are not defined correctly, the division of the land into squares will not be equal, and the produce available for salaries will not be evenly distributed. On this account, opporessive rulers and impure ministers are sure to neglect this defining of the boundaries. When the boundaries have been defined correctly, the division of the fields and the regulation of allowances may be determined by you, sitting at your ease."[300]

(f) The object of emigration is to regulate the economy in such a way that production and distribution will be proportionate to each other. However, King Hui of Liang did not carry it out effectively, because he did not engage in the development of the economy at the same time that he moved his people from one place to another. Mencius pointed out his mistake.

King Hui of Liang said, "In the government of my kingdom, I do indeed exert my mind to the utmost. If the year is bad on the inside of the river, I remove as many of the people as I can to the east of the river and convey grain to the country in the inside. When the year is bad on the east of the river, I act on the same plan. On examining the government of the neighboring countries, I do not find that there is any prince who exerts his mind as I do. And yet the people of the neighboring countries do not decrease, nor do my people increase. How is this?"

Mencius replied, "Your Majesty is fond of war; let me take an illustration from war. The soldiers move forward to the sound of drums; and after their weapons have been crossed, on one side they throw away their coats of mail, trail their arms behind them and run. Some run a hundred paces and stop; some run fifty paces and stop. What would you think if those who run fifty paces were to laugh at those who run a hundred paces?" The king said, "They should not do so. Though they did not run a hundred paces, yet they also ran away." "Since Your Majesty knows this," Mencius replied, "You need not hope that your people will become more numerous than those of the neighboring countries.

"If the seasons of husbandry are not interfered with, the grain will be more than can be eaten. If close nets are not allowed to enter the pools and ponds, the fishes and turtles will be more than can be consumed. If the axes and bills enter the hills and forests only at the proper time, the wood will be more than can be used. When the grain and fish and turtles are more than can be eaten, and there is more wood than can be used, this enables the people to nourish their living and mourn for their dead without any regrets. This condition, in which the people nourish their living and bury their dead without any regrets, is the first step of royal government.

"Let mulberry trees be planted about the homesteads with their fifty *mou*, and persons of fifty years may be clothed with silk. In keeping fowls, pigs, dogs and swine, let not their times of breeding be neglected, and persons of seventy years may eat meat. Let there not be taken away the time that is proper for the cultivation of the farm with its hundred *mou*, and the family of several mouths that is supported by it shall not suffer from hunger. Let careful attention be paid to education in schools, inculcating in it especially the filial and fraternal duties, and greyhaired men will not be seen upon the roads, carrying burdens on their backs or on their heads.

It never has been that the ruler of a State, where such results were seen—persons of seventy wearing silk and eating meat and the black-haired people suffering neither from hunger nor cold—did not attain to the royal dignity.

"Your dogs and swine eat the food of men, and you do not make any restrictive arrangements. There are people dying from famine on the roads, and you do not issue the stores of your granaries for them. When people die, you say, 'It is not owing to me; it is owing to the year.' In what does this differ from stabbing a man and killing him, and then saying, 'It was not I; it was the weapon'? Let Your Majesty cease to lay the blame on the year, and instantly from all the empire the people will come to you.[301]

To sum up the above, the successful promotion of production will result in all the people being peacefully settled and happily occupied. And if their wealth is increased, the revenue of the government will certainly rise. A nation can become strong only if it has wealth. The reverse is also true; no nation can ever become strong as long as its people are poor and its coffers empty. The government of King Wên was benevolent and set an example for later ages simply because, as a first fundamental step, it saved the people from hunger and cold; then it gradually built up the nation's wealth and strength. Here is what Mencius said.

Mencius said, "Po-i, that he might avoid Chou, was dwelling on the coast of the northern sea when he heard of the rise of King Wên. He roused himself and said, 'Why should I not go and follow him? I have heard that the chief of the West knows well how to nourish the old.'

"T'ai-kung, to avoid Chou, was dwelling on the coast of the eastern sea. When he heard of the rise of King Wên, he roused himself and said, 'Why should I not go and follow him? I have heard that the chief of the West knows well how to nourish the old.'

"If there were a prince in the empire who knew well how to nourish the old, all men of virtue would feel that he was the proper object for them to gather to.

"Around the homestead with its five *mou*, the space beneath the walls was planted with mulberry trees, with which the women nourished silkworms, and thus the old were able to have silk to wear. Each family had five brood hens and two brood sows, which were kept to their breeding seasons, and thus the old were able to have meat to eat. The hsubandmen cultivated their farms of 100 *mou*, and thus their families of eight mouths were secured against want.

"The expression, 'The chief of the West knows well how to nourish the old,' refers to his regulation of the fields and dwellings, his teaching them to plant the mulberry and nourish those animals and his instructing the wives and children, so as to make them nourish their aged. At fifty, warmth cannot be maintained without silks, and at seventy meat is necessary to satisfy the appetite. Persons not kept warm nor satisfied with food are said to be starved and famished, but among the people of King Wên there were no aged who were starved or famished. This is the meaning of the expression in question."[302]

After losing some of his territory in a luckless war, King Hui of Liang waited for the time when he could strike back and take revenge. But Mencius told him that benevolent government had to start with the promotion of production and an increase in the people's wealth. Moreover, Mencius maintained that adequate food supply was more important than military preparedness, that only the benevolent could be invincible. In other words, only when the people were assured of their wealth could the nation hope to gain in strength.

King Hui of Liang said, "There was not in the empire a stronger State than Chin, as you, venerable Sir, know. But since it descended to me, on the east we have been defeated by Ch'i, and then my eldest son perished; on the west we have lost seven hundred *li* to Ch'in; and on the south we have sustained disgrace at the hands of Ch'u. I have brought shame on my departed predecessors, and wish on their account to wipe it away once for all. What course is to be pursued to accomplish this?"

Mencius replied, "With a territory which is only a hundred *li* square, it is possible to attain to the royal dignity.

"If Your Majesty will indeed dispense a benevolent government to the people, being sparing in the use of punishments and fines and making the taxes and levies light, so causing that the fields shall be plowed deep and the weeding of them be carefully attended to, and that the strong-bodied, during their days of leisure, shall cultivate their filial piety, fraternal respectfulness, loyalty and faithfulness, serving thereby, at home, their fathers and elder brothers, and, abroad, their elders and superiors—you will then have a people who can be employed, with mere sticks which they have prepared, to oppose the strong mail and sharp weapons of the troops of Ch'in and Ch'u.

"The rulers of those States rob their people of their time, so that they cannot plow and weed their fields, in order to support their parents. Their parents suffer from cold and hunger. Brothers, wives and children are separated and scattered abroad.

"Those rulers, as it were, drive their people into pitfalls or drown them. Your Majesty will go to punish them. In such a case, who will oppose Your Majesty?

"In accordance with this is the saying, 'The benevolent has no enemy.' I beg Your Majesty not to doubt what I say."[303]

5. Alleviation of Suffering and Rejoicing with the People

When all parents love their children and all children are filial to their parents, the inevitable result is that provision can be made for the aged while the young respect their elders. And if there are others who need care, the government can well look after them, for their number is not likely to be large. Persons in this group fall into the categories listed here by Mencius:

Mencius said, "...There were the old and wifeless, or widowers; the old and husbandless, or widows; the old and childless, or solitaries; the young and fatherless, or orphans; these four classes are the most destitute of the people, and have none to whom they can tell their wants, and King Wên, in the institution of his government with its benevolent action, made them the first objects of his regard, as it is said in the *Book of Songs*,

'The rich may get through life well;
But alas! for the miserable and solitary!' "[304]

In addition to the poor mentioned above, those who have been disabled in the military service or in the course of their labor also should be supported by the government. This has been referred to in the chapter on "Li Yün" (Evolution of Ceremonies), *Li Chi* (Record of Rites).

Young men and women who have reached marriageable age but remain single should be encouraged by the government to get married. For "the continuation of human life is the responsibility of all mankind." At the same time society should be mindful that "the lack of offspring is one of the evidences of the want of filial piety." Therefore, public opinion should be guided in such a way that the unmarried have a place in the family group, so that "the male has his proper role and the female her home"[305] and "in the seclusion of the house there are no dissatisfied women and abroad, no unmarried men."[306]

Women who have reached marriageable age but remain single are frequently psychologically abnormal, and men of the same kind are often homeless and lead a transient life. These men and women are not only solitary and unhappy, but also a liability to social order and harmony.

One of the chief duties of the government is to see that the sufferings of the people are alleviated. These include unjust punishment, corruption by officials, oppression of the innocent by hoodlums, untimely employment of people by the government, accumulation of wealth by oppressive means, illegally enforced laws and orders. The people, though wronged, are usually reticent and this pent-up discontent acts against the government. Those in power should listen closely to complaints and remonstrances for two reasons; (1) to know the hidden feelings of the people and (2) to be able to take measures that will relieve the sufferings of the people.

Like the great Yü, every ruler should be the first man in the empire to be anxious about impending problems and the last to rejoice at their solution. His nation is more likely to flourish and less likely to become extinct.

It is rare indeed to see a ruler who can rejoice with his people. In the upper reaches of authority, he is prone to do whatever he pleases, and if he is not free from the influence of selfishness he can easily commit grave errors. Without men of integrity who can make straightforward remonstrances, he can become a completely self-centered person. Then, intent on his own pleasure, he will ignore the agonies of the people.

Mencius regarded himself as a minister who could not lightly be summoned by his sovereign. He therefore felt free to speak his mind whenever questions were put to him. He maintained that while a ruler did not have to avoid pleasures permitted by human nature, he should nevertheless share them with his people. Mencius also considered it more pleasant to enjoy music with others than by oneself or with only a chosen few.

> Chuang Pao, seeing Mencius, said to him, "I had an interview with the king. His Majesty told me that he loved music, and I was not prepared with anything to reply to him. What do you

pronounce about that love of music?" Mencius replied, "If the king's love of music were very great, the kingdom of Ch'i would be hopeful indeed."

Another day, Mencius, having an interview with the king, said, "Your Majesty, I have heard, told the official Chuang, that you love music; was it so?" The king changed color and said, "I am unable to love the music of the ancient sovereigns; I only love the music that suits the manners of the present age."

Mencius said, "If Your Majesty's love of music were very great, Ch'i would be hopeful indeed! The music of the present day is just like the music of antiquity."

The king said, "May I hear from you the proof of that?" Mencius asked, "Which is the more pleasant—to enjoy music by yourself alone or to enjoy it with others?" "To enjoy it with others," was the reply. "And which is the more pleasant—to enjoy music with a few or to enjoy it with many?" "To enjoy it with many."

Mencius proceeded, "Your servant begs to explain what he has said about music to Your Majesty.

"Now, Your Majesty is having music here. The people hear the noise of your bells and drums and the notes of your fifes and pipes, and they all, with aching heads and knitted brows, say to one another, 'That's how our king likes his music! But why does he reduce us to this extremity of distress? Fathers and sons cannot see one another. Elder brothers and younger brothers, wives, and children, are separated and scattered abroad.' Now, Your Majesty is hunting here. The people hear the noise of your carriages and horses and see the beauty of your plumes and streamers, and they all, with aching heads and knitted brows, say to one another, 'That's how our king likes his hunting! But why does he reduce us to this extremity of distress? Fathers and sons cannot see one another. Elder brothers and younger brothers, wives and children, are separated and scattered abroad.' Their feeling thus is from no other reason but that you do not share your pleasures with the people.

"Now, Your Majesty is having music here. The people hear the noise of your bells and drums and the notes of your fifes and pipes, and they all, delighted and with joyful looks, say to one another, 'That sounds as if our king were free from all sickness! If he were not, how could he enjoy this music?' Now, Your Majesty is hunting here. The people hear the noise of your carriages and horses and see the beauty of your plumes and streamers, and they all, delighted and with joyful looks, say to one another, 'That looks as if our king were free from all sickness! If he were not, how could he enjoy this hunting?' Their feeling thus is from no other reason but that you share your pleasures with the people.

"If Your Majesty will now share your pleasures with the people, the royal sway awaits you."[207]

The park of King Hsüan of Ch'i was forty square *li* in area. This was smaller than the park of King Wên of the Chou dynasty, which was seventy square *li*. Yet the people of Ch'i regarded King Hsüan's park as excessive in size, and the king asked Mencius about it. Mencius' reply was similar to the one on music quoted above. He stressed the point that the crux of the matter was not the size of the park. The important thing was that the ruler should share his pleasures with the people.

> King Hsüan of Ch'i asked, "Was it so, that the park of King Wên contained seventy square *li?*" Mencius replied, "It is so in the records."
> "Was it so large as that?" exclaimed the king. "The people," said Mencius, "still looked on it as small." The king added, "My park contains only forty square *li*, and the people still look on it as large. How is this?" "The park of King Wên," was the reply, "contained seventy square *li*, but the grass-cutters and fuel-gatherers had the privilege of entrance; so also had the catchers of pheasants and hares. He shared it with the people, and was it not with reason that they looked on it as small?
> "When I first arrived at the borders of your kingdom, I inquired about the great prohibitory regulations before I would venture to enter it; and I heard that inside the barrier-gates there was a park of forty square *li*, and that he who killed a deer in it was held guilty of the same crime as if he had killed a man. Thus those forty square *li* are a pitfall in the middle of the kingdom. Is it not with reason that the people look upon them as large?"[308]

Since King Wên shared his pleasures with the people, they were willing to build his park for him. However, when the people were anxious to see the early end of their sovereign, Chieh, he could not enjoy his pleasures alone for any length of time.

> Mencius saw King Hui of Liang. The king went and stood with him by a pond, and looking at the large round geese and deer, said, "Do the worthy also find pleasure in these things?"
> Mencius replied, "Only the worthy have pleasure in these things. In the case of the unworthy, though they have these things, they do not find pleasure.
> "It is said in the *Book of Songs*,
> 'He measured out and commenced his marvelous tower;

He measured it out and planned.
The people addressed themselves to it,
And in no time completed it.
When he measured and began it, he made no haste;
But the multitudes came as if they had been his children.
The king was in his marvelous park;
The does reposed about,
The does so sleek and far:
And the white birds shone glistening.
The king was by his marvelous pond;
How full was it of fishes leaping about!'

"King Wên used the strength of the people to make his tower and his pond, and yet the people rejoiced to do the work, calling the tower 'the marvelous tower,' calling the pond 'the marvelous pond,' and rejoicing that he had his large deer, his fishes and turtles. The ancients caused the people to have pleasure as well as themselves. and therefore they could enjoy it.

"In the 'Declaration of T'ang' it is said, 'O sun, when wilt thou expire? We will die together with thee.' The people wished for the death of Chieh, though they should die with him. Even if he had towers, ponds, birds and animals, how could he have had pleasure alone?"[309]

In making their tours of inspection and their reports of office, the ancient sovereigns and princes carried out their official functions. It would have been improper for them to "yield themselves to the current or urge their way against it" and be "wild" and "utterly lost"—all in disregard of the sufferings of the people. Under such circumstances, if the ruler did not share his pleasures with his people, Mencius warned, he would not be able to enjoy them, though he might have a Snow Palace.

King Hsüan of Ch'i had an interview with Mencius in the Snow Palace and said to him, "Do men of worth likewise find pleasure in these things?" Mencius replied, "They do; and if people generally are not able to enjoy themselves, they condemn their superiors. For them, when they cannot enjoy themselves, to condemn their superiors is wrong, but when the superiors of the people do not share their pleasures with the people, they also do wrong.

"When a ruler rejoices in the joy of his people, they also rejoice in his joy; when he grieves at the sorrow of his people, they also grieve at his sorrow. A sympathy of joy will pervade the empire; a sympathy of sorrow will do the same—in such a state of things, it cannot be but that the ruler will attain to the royal dignity.

"Formerly, Duke Ching of Ch'i asked the minister Yen, saying, 'I wish to pay a visit of inspection to Chuan-fu and Ch'ao-wu, and then to bend my course southward along the shore till I come to Lang-ya. What shall I do that my tour may be fit to be compared with the visits of inspection made by the ancient sovereigns?'

"The minister Yen replied, 'An excellent inquiry! When the Son of Heaven visited the princes, it was called a tour of inspection, that is, he surveyed the States under his care. When the princes attended at the court of the Son of Heaven, it was called a report of office, that is, they reported their administration of their offices. Thus neither of the proceedings was without a purpose. And moreover, in the spring they examined the plowing and supplied any deficienty of seed; in the autumn they examined the reaping and supplied any deficiency of yield. There is the saying of the Hsia dynasty, "If our king does not take his ramble, what will become of our happiness? If our king does not have his pleasure, what will become of our help? That ramble, and that pleasure, were a pattern to the princes."

" 'Now, the state of things is different. A host marches in attendance of the ruler and stores of provisions are consumed. The hungry are deprived of their food, and there is no rest for those who are called to toil. Maledictions are uttered by one to another, with eyes askance, and the people proceed to the commission of wickedness. Thus the royal ordinances are violated and the people are oppressed, and the supplies of food and drink flow away like water. The rulers yield themselves to the current or they urge their way against it; they are wild; they are utterly lost—these things proceed to the grief of the inferior princes.

" 'Descending along with the current and forgetting to return is what I call yielding to it. Pressing up against it and forgetting to return is what I call urging their way against it. Pursuing the chase without satiety is what I call being wild. Delighting in wine without satiety is what I call being lost.

" 'The ancient sovereigns had no pleasures to which they gave themselves as on the flowing stream; no doings which might be so characterized as wild and lost.

" 'It is for you, my prince, to pursue your course.' "

"Duke Ching was pleased. He issued a proclamation throughout his State, and went out and occupied a shed in the borders. From that time he began to open his granaries to supply the wants of the people, and calling the Grand music-master, he said to him, 'Make for me music to suit a prince and his minister pleased with each other.' And it was then that the Chih-shao and Chüeh-shao were made, in the words to which it was said, 'Is it a fault to restrain one's prince?' He who restrains his prince loves his prince."[210]

While it is improper for a ruler to indulge in lust and pleasure, it is equally serious for him—as serious as "leading on beasts to devour men"—to disregard the sufferings of his people. This holds true even if the ruler himself is no more than decently fed and clad. Such negligence is a tyrannical act which may lead to ruin.

> King Hui of Liang said, "I wish quietly to receive your instructions."
>
> Mencius replied, "Is there any difference between killing a man with a stick and with a sword?" The king said, "There is no difference."
>
> "Is there any difference between doing it with a sword and with the style of government?" "There is no difference," was the reply.
>
> Mencius then said, "In your kitchen there is fat meat; in your stable there are fat horses. But your people have the look of hunger, and on the wilds there are those who have died of famine. This is leading on beasts to devour men.
>
> "Beasts devour one another, and men hate them for doing so. When a prince, being the parent of his people, administers his government so as to be chargeable with leading on beasts to devour men, where is his parental relation to the people?
>
> "Chung-ni said, 'was he without posterity who first made wooden images to bury with the dead?' So he said, because that man made the semblances of men and used them for that purpose: what shall be thought of him who causes his people to die of hunger?"[211]

In short, the people cannot be satisfied with a government which injures them or which enables only a few favored persons to enjoy themselves. If a ruler cannot share his pleasures with the people and relieve them of their sufferings, he acts contrary to the aims of government—and the people will join forces to overthrow him.

6. Emphasis on Instruction and Security, Cultivation of Amity with Neighboring Countries

All governmental measures have their educational significance. The administration of government may be summed up as instruction, support and security. Instruction is education, support concerns the economy, and security has to do with military affairs. The content of education is the inculcation of the method of control, the techniques and skills of production, and the knowledge and ability to defend the nation.

(a) The method of control is no difficult to learn; the difficulty lies in acquiring the qualification for control. For only the virtuous are qualified to exercies control over others. It follows that the principal aim of education, as has been emphasized above, is the cultivation of the Way, the illustration of illustrious virtue and determination of the relationships of humanity.

> Mencius said, "...Establish *hsiang, hsü, hsüeh* and *hsiao*—all those educational institutions—for the instruction of the people. The name *hsiang* indicates nourishing as its object; *hsiao* indicates teaching; and *hsü* indicates archery. By the Hsia dynasty the name *hsiao* was used; by the Yin, that of *hsü;* and by the Chou, that of *hsiang.* As to the *hsüeh,* they belonged to all three dynasties, and by that name. The object of them all is to illustrate the human relations. When those are thus illustrated by superiors, kindly feeling will prevail among the inferior people below.
>
> "Should a real sovereign arise, he will certainly come and take an example from you; aud thus you will be the teacher of the true sovereign.
>
> "It is said in the *Book of Songs,*
> 'Although Chou was an old country,
> It received a new destiny.'
> That is said with reference to King Wên."[312]

Both control and instruction have their merits, but good instruction is destined to win the hearts of the people, which after all is the first step toward good government.

> Mencius said, "Kindly words do not enter so deeply into men as a reputation for kindness. Good government does not lay hold of the people so much as good instructions. Good government is feared by the people, while good instructions are loved by them. Good government gets the people's wealth, while good instructions get their hearts."[313]

(b) In an industrial society the techniques and skill of production are greatly stressed. However, the ancient agricultural society of China laid its principal emphasis on teaching the people soil cultivation and seeding. As to the techniques and skills for industrial production, they were transmitted from master to apprentice with the encouragement of the government. The seventh of the nine standard rules for a government was "encouragement of the resort of all classes of artisans."

There are various ways of encouraging the artisans' production; that is, how to "urge them to be diligent, rectify them, help and instruct them so as to make them preserve their inherently good nature and to follow this up by giving them relief and conferring benefits on them."[314] This subject has been discussed above in the section on increasing the people's wealth.

(c) Knowledge and ability in the area of national defense should be possessed by everyone. The six arts of ancient times included archery and charioteering. Bows and arrows as well as carriages and horses were used. Through the ages, of course, tremendous progress has been made in the development of weapons systems. However, the basic ideas on how, when and why defensive weapons should be used are still relevant.

It is true that to maintain its existence in the modern world, each nation must cultivate friendly relations with its neighbors. However, it is also true that the internal condition of another nation is always subject to change, and once a policy of war and territorial expansion is adopted by a "friendly" neighbor, the threat of aggression looms. Therefore, in time of peace every preparation should be made against the contingency of war. Military education and training should never be neglected, for as Confucius said, "To lead an uninstructed people to war is to throw them away."[315]

Moreover, when peace has reigned in a country for a long time, the defense establishment tends to get flabby. The people become accustomed to an easy life, and the government is liable to overlook the importance of preparedness. Such a nation runs the risk of defeat and extinction if it is suddenly attacked and invaded.

> Mencius said, "...If a prince has not about his court families attached to the laws and worthy counselors, and if abroad there are no hostile States or other external calamities, his country will generally come to ruin."[316]

However, the purpose of a national defense establishment is to oppose external aggression. Its object is not to spawn domestic evils and ride roughshod over the people. The Iron Curtain countries are a case in point.

> Mencius said, "Anciently, the establishment of frontier-gates was to guard against violence. Nowadays it is to exercise violence."[317]

It is often said either that "a weak country has no diplomcy to speak of" or that "diplomacy requires trickery." This is contrary to our ancient teachings. Actually, international relations can be viewed as an extension of social ties between individuals. The word "sincerity" describes the spirit and attitude which should govern the relationship both between one country and another, and between one individual and another.

But today with the decline of morality, men seem to know only how to benefit themselves at the expense of others. This accounts for the rise of imperialism and Communism. Both start from the wrong premises and cannot help but cause a great many mistakes. The so-called treaties their exponents sign and the so-called conferences which they attend are mere shams; they cannot yield any solution to their problems. Even in the same bloc, nations do not treat one another with sincerity, for often they resort to double-dealing. With this type of international relations, how can the nations of the world live in peace for any length of time? No wonder mankind is unwittingly marching toward its own destruction!

Mencius had this to say about international relations:

> King Hsüan of Ch'i asked, saying, "Is there any way to regulate the intercourse with neighboring countries?" Mencius replied, "There is. But it is only a perfectly virtuous prince who can, with a great country, serve a small one, as, for instance, T'ang served Ko and King Wên served the K'un barbarians. And it is only a wise prince who can, with a small country, serve a large one, as, for instance, King T'ai served the Hsün-yu and Kou-chien served Wu.

> "He who, with a great State, serves a small one delights in Heaven. He who, with a small State, serves a large one stands in awe of Heaven. He who delights in Heaven can preserve the whole empire. He who stands in awe of Heaven can preserve his own country.

> "It is said in the *Book of Songs*, 'I fear the Majesty of Heaven,

and thus I can protect my country.' "

The king said, "A great saying! But I have an infirmity—I love valor."

'"I beg Your Majesty," was the reply, "not to love small valor. If a man brandishes his sword, looks fiercely and says, 'How dare he withstand me?'—this is the valor of a common man, who can be the opponent only of a single individual. I beg Your Majesty to greaten it.

"It is said in the *Book of Songs*,

'The king blazed with anger,
And he marshaled his hosts,
To stop the march of Chü,
To consolidate the prosperity of Chou,
To meet the expectations of the nation'

This was the valor of King Wên. King Wên, in one burst of his anger, gave repose to all the people of the empire.

"In the *Book of History* it is said, 'Heaven, having produced the inferior people, made for them rulers and teachers, with the purpose that they should be assisting to God, and therefore distinguished them throughout the four quarters of the land. Whoever are offenders and whoever are innocent, here am I to deal with them. How dare any under heaven give indulgence to their refractory wills?' There was one man pursuing a violent and disorderly course in the empire, and King Wu was ashamed of it. This was the valor of King Wu. He also, by one display of his anger, gave repose to all the people of the empire.

"Let now Your Majesty also, in one burst of anger, give repose to all the people of the empire. The people are only afraid that Your Majesty does not love valor."[318]

In international relations, diplomatic correspondence is of the utmost importance. The strictest attention must be given to the use of each word and sentence so that no cause is given for future dispute.

The Master said, "In preparing the governmental notifications, P'i Shên first made the rough draft; Shi-shu examined and discussed its contents; Tzŭ-yü, the manager of foreign intercourse, then polished the style; and, finally, Tzŭ-ch'an of Tung-li gave it the proper elegance and finish."[319]

A ruler can "find the government of a country as easy as to look into his palm." But only if he does these several things: (1) observe the nine standard rules discussed at the beginning of this chapter, (2) follow the beaten path of the Kingly Way, (3) understand the causes of order and confusion, the rise and fall of dynasties, (4) adhere with his officials and people to the rules of propriety and righteousness, and (5) reverentially attend to the important affairs of state.

Footnotes for Chapter VIII

1. *Works of Mencius*, Bk. IV, Pt. I, Ch. V.
2. *Doctrine of the Mean*, Ch. XX.
3. *Analects*, Bk. XII, Ch. I.
4. *Works of Mencius*, Bk. IV, Pt. I, Ch. IV. *Vide supra*, p. 279
5. *Analects*, Bk. XIV, Ch. XLIV.
6. *Ibid.*, Bk. XIII, Ch. IV.
7. *Ibid.*, Bk. XII, Ch. XVII.
8. *Ibid.*, Bk. XIII, Ch. VI.
9. *Ibid.*, Ch. XIII.
10. *Works of Mencius*, Bk. IV, Pt. II, Ch. V.
11. *Analects*, Bk. XIII, Ch. I.
12. *Ibid.*, Bk. XII, Ch. XVIII.
13. *Great Learning*, Com., Ch. X. *Vide supra*, pp. 16, 150.
14. *Great Learning*, Com., Ch. X. *Vide supra*, p. 151.
15. *Great Learning*, Text. *Vide surpa*. pp. 7, 15.
16. *Great Learning*, Com., Ch. X.
17. *Works of Mencius*, Bk. II, Pt. I, Ch. V.
18. *Ibid.*, Bk. VII, Pt. II, Ch. XII.
19. *Ibid.*, Pt. I, Ch. VIII.
20. *Ibid.*, Bk. V. Pt. II, Ch. VII. In the first paragraph Legge's rendering of "what it means" as "what principle of righteousness is involved" was a mistake.
21. *Ibid.*, Bk. II, Pt. II, Ch. II.
22. *Ibid.*, Bk. III, Pt. II, Ch. VI.
23. *Analects*, Bk. XV, Ch. X.
24. *Ibid.*, Bk. XVII, Ch. XXV.
25. *Ibid.*, Bk. XVIII, Ch. IV. *Vide supra*, pp. 96, 326.
26. *Analects*, Bk. XVIII, Ch. I. *Vide supra*, p. 240.
27. *Great Learning*, Com., Ch. X. *Vide supra*, p. 173.
28. *Works of Mencius*, Bk. VII, Pt. II, Ch. XXVIII.
29. *Ibid.*, Bk. I, Pt II, Ch. V.
30. *Great Learning*, Com., Ch. X.
31. *Works of Mencius*, Bk. IV, Pt. II, Ch. V.
32. *Analects*, Bk. XIII, Ch. II.
33. *Ibid.*, Bk. XIV, Ch. XIX.
34. *Ibid.*, Bk. XV, Ch. XIII.
35. *Ibid.*, Bk. XII, Ch. XXII. *Vide supra*, p. 163.
36. *Works of Mencius*, Bk. I, Pt. II, Ch. VII.
37. *Ibid.*, Bk. VI, Pt. II, Ch. VI.
38. *Ibid.*, Bk. I, Pt. II, Ch. IX.

39. *Ibid.*, Bk. IV, Pt. II, Ch. XX.

40. *Ibid.*, Bk. VI, Pt. II, Ch. XV. *Vide supra*, p. 289.

41. *Works of Mencius*, Bk. V, Pt. II, Ch. VI. In the second paragraph the word "meaning" is the correct translation instead of Legge's rendering of "principle of righteousness."

42. *Ibid.*, Bk. III, Pt. II, Ch. IV.

43. *Ibid.*, Bk. VII, Pt. I, Ch. XXXII.

44. *Ibid.*, Bk. V, Pt. II, Ch. VI.

45. *Great Learning*, Com., Ch. X.

46. *Ibid.*

47. *Ibid.*, Ch. IX.

48. *Analects*, Bk. VIII, Ch. II. *Vide supra*, p. 94.

49. *Works of Mencius*, Bk. IV, Pt. I, Ch. XI. *Vide supra*, p. 84.

50. *Analects*, Bk. I, Ch. V.

51. *Great Learning*, Com., Ch. III.

52. *Doctrine of the Mean*, Ch. XX.

53. *Analects*, Bk. XIV, Ch. XX.

54. *Works of Mencius*, Bk. V, Pt. II, Ch. II.

55. *Analects*, Bk. XIII, Ch. XX.

56. *Ibid.*, Ch. XXVIII.

57. *Ibid.*, Bk. XIV, Ch. III.

58. *Ibid.*, Bk. VIII, Ch. VII. *Vide supra*, p. 111.

59. *Analects*, Bk. XIX, Ch. I. *Vide supra*, p. 329.

60. *Works of Mencius*, Bk. VII, Pt. I, Ch. XXIII.

61. *Ibid.*, Ch. IX, *Vide supra*, p. 157.

62. *Great Learning*, Com., Ch. X. *Vide supra*, pp. 16, 152.

63. *Great Learning*, Com., Ch. IX.

64. *Ibid.*

65. *Ibid.*, Ch. X. *Vide supra*, p. 163,

66. *Great Learning*, Com., Ch. IX. *Vide supra*, p. 388.

67. *Works of Mencius*, Bk. II, Pt. I, Ch. V.

68. *Analects*, Bk. VIII, Ch. XXI.

69. *Works of Mencius*, Bk. IV, Pt. II, Ch. XX.

70. *Ibid.*, Bk. III, Pt. I, Ch. IV.

71. *Ibid.*, Bk. IV, Pt. II, Ch. XX. *Vide supra*, p. 34.

72. *Works of Mencius*, Bk. IV, Pt. I, Ch. IX. *Vide supra*, p. 151.

73. *Works of Mencius*, Bk. I, Pt. I, Ch. III.

74. *Op. cit.*, Com., Ch. X.

75. *Ibid.*, Ch. X.

76. *Ibid.*

77. *Works of Mencius*, Bk. VII, Pt. II, Ch. XXVII.

78. *Analects*, Bk. XI, Ch. XVI.

79. *Ibid.*, Bk. I, Ch. V.

80. *Ibid.*, Bk. XIII, Ch. XVI.

81. *Works of Mencius*, Bk. IV, Pt. I, Ch. XIII.

82. *Ibid.*, Bk. II, Pt. I, Ch. V. *Vide supra*, p. 418.

83. *Analects*, Bk. II, Ch. I.

84. *Ibid.*, Ch. III. *Vide supra*, p. 246.

85. *Analects*, Bk. IV, Ch. XIII.
86. An erudite scholar of the Han dynasty.
87. *Works of Mencius*, Bk. II, Pt. I, Ch. III.
88. *Ibid.*, Bk. VII, Pt. I, Ch. XIII.
89. *Ibid.*, Ch. XXX.
90. *Ibid.*, Pt. II, Ch. XIV.
91. *Analects*, Bk. XV, Ch. XXXII.
92. *Works of Mencius*, Bk. IV, Pt. II, Ch. XVI.
93. *Ibid.*, Bk. IV, Pt. I, Ch. XIII.
94. *Ibid.*, Bk. III, Pt. II, Ch. V.
95. *Analects*, Bk. XVI, Ch. II.
96. *Works of Mencius*, Bk. VII, Pt. II, Ch. II.
97. *Ibid.*, Bk. IV, Pt. I, Ch. VII.
98. *Ibid.*, Bk. III, Pt. II, Ch. V.
99. *Ibid.*, Bk. II, Pt. I, Ch. V. *Vide supra*, pp. 418, 448.
100. *Analects*, Bk. XX, Ch. I.
101. *Works of Mencius*, Bk. VII, Pt. II, Ch. I.
102. *Ibid.*, Bk. II, Pt. I, Ch. I. *Vide supra* p. 336.
103. *Works of Mencius*, Bk. I Pt. I, Ch. VII.
104. *Ibid.*, Bk. VI, Pt. II, Ch. VII.
105. *Ibid.*, Bk. VII, Pt. II, Ch. IV. In the fifth paragraph the words "falling mountains" were erroneously rendered by Legge as "the horns of animals falling off."
106. *Analects*, Bk. VII, Ch. XX.
107. *Ibid.*, Bk. XIV, Ch. XVII. *Vide supra*, p. 107.
108. *Analects*, Bk. XIV, Ch. XVIII. *Vide supra*, p. 107.
109. *Analects*, Bk. XIV, Ch. X.
110. *Ibid.*, Ch. XVI.
111. *Ibid.*, Bk. XVII, Ch. V.
112. *Ibid.*, *Vide surpa*, p. 286.
113. *Works of Mencius*, Bk. IV, Pt. I, Ch. VII. *Vide supra*, p. 455.
114. *Analects*, Bk. XIII, Ch. XII.
115. *Ibid.*, Bk. VI, Ch. XXII.
116. *Works of Mencius*, Bk. II, Pt. I, Ch. VI. The last words of the third paragraph were erroneously rendered by Legge as "nor from a dislike of the reputation of being unmoved by such a thing."
117. *Ibid.*, Bk. I, Pt. I, Ch. VII. In the twelfth paragraph of this passage the words "was put into practice in the family and country" are the correct version, not Legge's rendering, "his family of the State was governed by it."
118. *Works of Mencius*, Bk. I, Pt. II, Ch. V.
119. *Analects*, Bk. XII, Ch. XIII. *Vide supra*, p. 16.
120. *Works of Mencius*, Bk. IV, Pt. I, Ch. I.
121. *Doctrine of the Mean*, Ch. XXVIII.
122. *Works of Mencius*, Bk. IV, Pt. I, Ch. I.
123. *Ibid.*, Ch. III.
124. *Ibid.*, Pt. II, Ch. XX. *Vide supra*, p. 34.
125. *Analects*, Bk. XIV, Ch. XXXV.

126. *Doctrine of the Mean*, Ch. XXIV. *Vide supra*, p. 197.

127. *Works of Mencius*, Bk. IV, Pt. I, Ch. IX. *Vide supra*, pp. 150, 442.

128. *Works of Mencius*, Bk. II, Pt. II, Ch. I.

129. *Great Learning*, Com., Ch. X. *Vide supra*, pp. 151, 416.

130. *Great Learning*, Com., Ch. X. *Vide Supra*, pp. 64, 151.

131. *Works of Mencius*, Bk. IV, Pt. I, Ch. VII. *Vide supra*, p. 152.

132. *Works of Mencius*, Bk. IV, Pt. I, Ch. I.

133. *Doctrine of the Mean*, Ch. XXVII.

134. *Works of Mencius*, Bk. IV, Pt. I, Ch. I.

135. *Great Learning*, Com., Ch. X. *Vide supra*, p. 425.

136. *Analects*, Bk. XIII, Ch. IV. *Vide supra*, p. 415.

137. *Works of Mencius*, Bk. II, Pt. I, Ch. IV. *Vide supra*, pp. 59, 156, 278.

138. *Works of Mencius*, Bk. I, Pt. II, Ch. XI. In the first paragraph, the rendering should be as set down here instead of Legge's version, "the princes have formed many plans to attack me".

139. *Analects*, Bk. VIII, Ch. X. *Vide supra*, p. 113.

140. *Works of Mencius*, Bk. II, Pt. II, Ch. I.

141. *Ibid.*, Ch. VI, Pt. II, Ch. XV. *Vide supra*, p. 169.

142. *Works of Mencius*, Bk. I, Pt. II, Ch. XIII.

143. *Ibid.*, Ch. XIV.

144. *Ibid.*, Bk. III, Pt. I, Ch. I.

145. *Ibid.*, Bk. IV, Pt. I, Ch. VIII. *Vide supra*, pp. 112, 148, 378.

146. *Works of Mencius*, Bk. IV, Pt. II, Ch. I.

147. *Ibid.*, Pt. I, Ch. III. Legge's version of "being strong" instead of "forcing oneself" is a mistake.

148. *Ibid.*, Bk. IV, Pt. I, Ch. II.

149. *Ibid.*, Bk. VII, Pt. II, Ch. XIV.

150. *Ibid.*, Bk. III, Pt. I, Ch. III.

151. *Ibid.*, Bk. VII, Pt. II, Ch. XXVIII.

152. *Op. cit.*, Ch. XXXI.

153. *Great Learning*, Com., Ch. III.

154. *Ibid.*

155. *Analects*, Bk. III, Ch. XIX.

156. *Works of Mencius*, Bk. IV, Pt. II, Ch. III.

157. *Ibid.*, Pt. I, Ch. II. *Vide supra*, p. 486.

158. *Great Learning*, Com., Ch. IX.

159. *Analects*, Bk. VIII, Ch. XIX.

160. *Ibid.*, Ch. XVIII.

161. *Works of Mencius*, Bk. III, Pt. I, Ch. IV.

162. *Ibid.*, Bk. V, Pt. I, Ch. IV.

163. *Ibid.*, Bk. II, Pt. I, Ch. VIII. *Vide supra*, pp. 271, 283.

164. *Great Learning*, Com., Ch. X. *Vide supra*, p. 271.

165. *Works of Mencius*, Bk. VI, Pt. II, Ch. XIII. *Vide supra*, p. 271.

166. *Works of Mencius*, Bk. II, Pt. II, Ch. IV.

167. *Analects*, Bk. XII, Ch. XI.

168. *Ibid.*, Bk. XIII, Ch. XV.

169. *Ibid.*, Bk. VIII, Ch. XXI. *Vide supra*, p. 441.

170. *Analects*, Bk. VIII, Ch. XX.

171. *Works of Mencius*, Bk. VII, Pt. I, Ch. XXXVII.
172. *Ibid.*, Bk. I, Pt. II, Ch. VI.
173. *Analects*, Bk. XX, Ch. I. *Vide supra*, p. 458.
174. *Works of Mencius*, Bk. VII, Pt. I, Ch. XIX.
175. *Ibid.*, Bk. II, Pt. I, Ch. II. *Vide supra*, p. 212.
176. *Analects*, Bk. V, Ch. XV.
177. *Ibid.*, Ch. XX.
178. *Works of Mencius*, Bk. IV, Pt. I, Ch. I. *Vide supra*, p. 476.
179. *Analects*, Bk. XIV, Ch. VIII.
180. *Ibid.*, Ch. XXIII.
181. *Ibid.*, Bk. XI, Ch. XXIII.
182. *Works of Mencius*, Bk. IV, Pt. I, Ch. XX. *Vide supra*, p. 416.
183. *Works of Mencius* Bk. V, Pt. II, Ch. V. *Vide supra*, pp. 304, 320.
184. *Analects*, Bk. IV, Ch. XXVI. *Vide supra*, p. 352.
185. *Analects*, Bk. III, Ch. XVIII.
186. *Doctrine of the Mean*, Ch. XX. *Vide supra*, p. 435.
187. *Great Learning*, Com., Ch. X.
188. *Analects*, Bk. XIV, Ch. XXII.
189. *Ibid.*, Bk. XVI, Ch. I.
190. *Works of Mencius*, Bk. II, Pt. II, Ch. IX.
191. *Ibid.*, Bk. VI, Pt. II, Ch. VII. *Vide supra*, p. 462.
192. *Works of Mencius*, Bk. III, Pt. II, Ch. II.
193. *Ibid.*, Bk. VI, Pt. II, Ch. IX.
194. *Ibid.*, Bk. IV, Pt. I, Ch. XIV.
195. *Ibid.*, Bk. VI. Pt. II, Ch. VIII. In the second paragraph, the last words were
    erroneously translated by Legge as "to seek to enrich him is to enrich Chieh".
196: *Analects*, Bk. XVI, Ch. II.
197. *Ibid.*, Bk. XIV, Ch. XV.
198. *Ibid.*, Bk. XVI, Ch. III.
199. *Ibid.*, Bk. III, Ch. VI.
200. *Ibid.*, Ch. V.
201. *Works of Mencius*, Bk. VII, Pt. I, Ch. XXXI. *Vide supra*, p. 255.
202. *Works of Mencius*, Bk. V, Pt. II, Ch. IX.
203. *Ibid.*, Bk. I, Pt. I, Ch. VIII.
204. *Analects*, Bk. VIII, Ch. VI.
205. *Doctrine of the Mean*, Ch. XX. *Vide supra*, pp. 435, 501.
206. *Works of Mencius*, Bk IV, Pt. I, Ch. XII.
207. *Analects*, Bk. II, Ch. XVIII.
208. *Works of Mencius*, Bk. IV, Pt. II, Ch. XXXI. In this passage. the name
    "Fu-tz'u" was erroneously translated by Legge as "the grass-carriers".
209. *Ibid.*, Ch. XXIX.
210. *Ibid.*, Bk. II, Pt. II, Ch. XIV.
211. *Vide supra*, p. 488.
212. *Works of Mencius*, Bk. VII, Pt. II, Ch. XXXIV.
213. *Doctrine of the Mean*, Ch. XX. *Vide supra*, p. 153.
214. *Analects*, Bk. XIII, Ch. XVI. *Vide supra*, p. 167.
215. *Analects*, Bk. II, Ch. XIX. *Vide supra*, p. 164.
216. *Analects*, Bk. XV, Ch. IV.

217. *Ibid.*, Bk. XIII, Ch. XVII. *Vide supra*, p. 143.

218. *Analects*, Bk. XIV, Ch. X.

219. *Works of Mencius*, Bk. IV, Pt. II, Ch. II.

220. *Analects*. Bk. XIII, Ch. IV. *Vide supra*, pp. 415, 480.

221. *Works of Mencius*, Bk. III, Pt. I, Ch. III. *Vida supra*, p. 488.

222. *Works of Mencius*, Bk. VII, Pt. I, Ch. V.

223. *Analects*, Bk. VIII, Ch. IX.

224. *Ibid.*, Bk. VI, Ch. I.

225. *Doctrine of the Mean*, Ch. VI. *Vide supra*, pp. 31, 103, 218.

226. *Great Learning*, Com., Ch. X. *Vide supra*, pp. 16, 140.

227. *Analects*, Bk. XVI, Ch. XII.

228. *Op. cit.*, Com., Ch. X.

229. *Works of Mencius*, Bk. I, Pt. I, Ch. I. *Vide supra*, p. 174.

230. *Analects*, Bk. XII, Ch. XI. *Vide supra*, pp. 488, 495.

231. *Works of Mencius*, Bk. VI, Pt. II, Ch. IV. *Vide supra*, p. 376.

232. *Works of Mencius*, Bk. VI, Pt. II, Ch. X. *Vide supra*, p. 377.

233. *Works of Mencius*, Bk. II, Pt. II, Ch. II. *Vide supra*, p. 96.

234. *Great Learning*, Com., Ch. IX. *Vide supra*, p. 491.

235. *Analects*, Bk. VIII, Ch. IV.

236. *Ibid.*, Bk. XII, Ch. VII.

237. *Ibid.*, Bk. XIX, Ch. X. *Vide supra*, pp. 135, 501.

238. *Works of Mencius*, Bk. VII, Pt. II, Ch. XX. *Vide supra*, p. 255.

239. *Analects*, Bk. XII, Ch. XIV.

240. *Ibid.*, Bk. I, Ch. V. *Vide supra*, p. 435.

241. *Analects*, Bk. II, Ch. XX.

242. *Ibid.*, Bk. VII, Ch. V.

243. *Ibid.*, Bk. XX, Ch. II.

244. *Ibid.*, Bk. XIII, Ch. XIV.

245. *Works of Mencius*, Bk. IV, Pt. I, Ch. VI.

246. *Analects*, Bk. XVIII, Ch. X.

247. *Works of Mencius*, Bk. I, Pt. I, Ch. I.

248. *Ibid.*, Bk. VII, Pt. I, Ch. XII.

249. *Ibid.*, Bk. I, Pt. II, Ch. VII. *Vide supra*, p. 427.

250. *Analects*, Bk. XII, Ch. XIX. *Vide supra*, p. 136.

251. *Analects*, Bk. XIII, Ch. III.

252. *Ibid.*, Bk. XX, Ch. I. *Vide supra*, p. 458.

253. *Works of Mencius*, Bk. III, Pt. II, Ch. IX.

254. *Analects*, Bk. III, Ch. I.

255. *Ibid.*, Ch. II.

256. *Ibid.*, Bk. XVI, Ch. XIV.

257. *Ibid.*, Bk. XVIII, Ch. XI.

258. *Ibid.*, Bk. VI, Ch. XII.

259. *Ibid.*, Ch. VI.

260. *Ibid.*, Bk. XIV, Ch. XII.

261. *Works of Mencius*, Bk. VII, Pt. II, Ch. XIV. *Vide supra*, pp. 488, 511.

262. *Analects*, Bk. XIII, Ch. XV. *Vide supra*, p. 495.

263. *Works of Mencius*, Bk. V, Pt. I, Ch. V.

264. *Ibid.*, Ch. VI. In the last sentence the word "meaning" was mistranslated by

Legge as "the principle of righteousness."

265. *Ibid.*, Bk. I, Pt. II, Ch. XV.
266. *Ibid.*, Ch. XII.
267. *Analects*, Bk. XIX, Ch. XIX.
268. *Works of Mencius*, Bk. I, Pt. II, Ch. X.
269. *Ibid.*, Bk. III, Pt. I, Ch. IV.
270. *Ibid.*, *Vide supra*, pp. 349, 376, 441, 491, 518.
271. *Analects*, Bk. XII, Ch. IX.
272. *Ibid.*, Bk. XIII, Ch. IX.
273. *Works of Mencius*, Bk. I, Pt. I, Ch. VII.
274. *Ibid.*, Pt. II, Ch. IV'
275. *Doctrine of the Mean*, Ch. XX.
276. *Works of Mencius*, Bk. III, Pt. I, Ch. III.
277. *Ibid.*, Bk. I, Pt. I, Ch. VII. *Vide supra*, p. 541.
278. *Works of Mencius*, Bk. I, Pt. II, Ch. IV. *Vide supra*, p. 462.
279. *Works of Mencius*, Bk. I, Pt. I, Ch. III. *Vide supra* p. 544.
280. *Doctrine of the Mean*, Ch. XX.
281. *Works of Mencius*, Bk. VII, Pt. I, Ch. XXIII.
282. *Great Learning*, Com., Ch. X.
283. *Works of Mencius*, Bk. III, Pt. I, Ch. III. *Vide supra*, p. 541.
284. *Analects*, Bk. I, Ch. V. *Vide supra*, pp. 435, 520.
285. *Works of Mencius*, Bk. VII, Pt. I, Ch. XXIII.
286. *Ibid.*, Bk. III, Pt. I, Ch. III. *Vide supra*, p. 533.
287. *Works of Mencius*, Bk. III, Pt. I, Ch. III. *Vida supra*, p. 542.
288. *Analects*. Bk. XI, Ch. XIII.
289. *Ibid.*, Bk. XII, Ch. IX.
290. *Works of Mencius*, Bk. VI, Pt. II, Ch. X.
291. *Works of Mencius*, Bk. II, Pt. II, Ch. X.
292. *Ibid.*, Bk. II, Pt. I, Ch. V. *Vide supra*, p. 457.
293. *Works of Mencius*, Bk. III, Pt. I, Ch. IV. *Vide supra*, p. 537.
294. *Works of Mencius*, Bk. III, Pt. II, Ch. IX. *Vide supra*, p. 340.
295. *Analects*, Bk. VIII, Ch. XXI.
296. *Works of Mencius*, Bk. VI, Pt. II, Ch. XI. *Vide supra*, p. 102.
297. *Works of Mencius*, Bk. IV, Pt. II, Ch. II. *Vide supra*, p, 514.
298. *Doctrine of the Mean*, Ch. XXVIII.
299. *Analects*, Bk. XVI, Ch. I. *Vide supra*, p. 502.
300. *Works of Mencius*, Bk. III. Pt. I, Ch. III. *Vide supra*, p. 542.
301. *Works of Mencius*, Bk. I, Pt. I, Ch. III. *Vide supra*, pp. 471, 544.
302. *Works of Mencius*, Bk. VII, Pt. I, Ch. XXII. *Vida supra*, p. 453.
303. *Works of Mencius*, Bk. I, Pt. I, Ch. V.
304. *Ibid.*, Pt. II, Ch. V. *Vide supra*, p. 471.
305. Chapter on "Li Yün," *Li Chi*. Chai, *op. cit.*, p. 338; Legge, *Sacred Books of China*, Vol. III, p. 365; Lin, *op. cit.*, p. 227. *Vide supra*, p. 577.
306. *Works of Mencius*, Bk. I, Pt. II, Ch. V.
307. *Ibid.*, Ch. I.
308. *Ibid.*, Ch. II.
309. *Ibid.*, Pt. I, Ch. II.
310. *Ibid.*, Pt. II, Ch. IV. *Vide supra*, pp. 462, 544.

311. *Works of Mencius*, Bk. I, Pt. I, Ch. IV.
312. *Ibid.*, Bk. III, Pt. I, Ch. III. *Vide supra*, p. 542.
313. *Works of Mencius*, Bk. VII, Pt. I, Ch. XIV.
314. *Ibid.*, Bk. III, Pt. I, Ch. IV. *Vide supra*, pp. 441, 537.
315. *Analects*, Bk. XIII, Ch. XXX.
316. *Works of Mencius*, Bk. VI, Pt. II, Ch. XV. *Vide supra*, p. 169.
317. *Works of Mencius*, Bk. VII, Pt. II, Ch. VIII.
318. *Ibid.*, Bk. I, Pt. II, Ch. III. *Vide supra*, p. 115.
319. *Analects*, Bk. XIV, Ch. IX.

CHAPTER IX

The Pacification of the World

From very early times the Chinese people have entertained the lofty thought of the "pacification of the world." In Chinese the word *p'ing* denotes equality, justice and peace. Every strife is traceable to the absence of *p'ing*. When equality or justice is absent, contention arises; when contention is ineffective, strife follows; and strife ends when the strongest prevails. But unfortunately the victory of the strongest does not bring true peace; for the vanquished are not submissive to the victor at heart; they bow to him only because of the inadequacy of their own use of force. Therefore, in the pursuit of real equality, the basic thrust must come from virtue, not strength.

It has been stated above that "he who, using force, makes a pretense to benevolence, is an exponent of the Way of Might; and he who, using virtue, practices benevolence, is an exponent of the Way of Right." Only the Way of Right is submissive to Heaven and responsive to the people. The practice of this Way is destined to bring about peace and order in the world.

The *Great Learning* regards the illustration of illustrious virtue as the first step to the ultimate objective: resting in what is good. The illustration of illustrious virtue means the prevalence of the Kingly Way in the world, and resting in what is good can be defined as the "pacification of the world."

The ancients, who wished to illustate illustrious virtue throughout the empire, first ordered well their own States. Wishing to order well their States, they first regulated their families. Wishing to regulate their families, they first cultivated their persons. Wishing to cultivate their persons, they first rectified their hearts. Wishing to rectify their hearts, they first sought to be sincere in their thoughts. Wishing to be sincere in their thoughts, they first extended to the utmost their knowledge. Such extension of knowledge lay in the investigation of things.

Things being investigated, knowledge becomes complete. Their knowledge being complete, their thoughts are sincere. Their thoughts being sincere, their hearts are rectified. Their hearts being rectified, their persons are cultivated. Their persons being cultivated, their families are regulated. Their families being regulated, their States are rightly governed. Their States being rightly governed, the whole world is pacified.[1]

In the chapter on "Li Yün" (Evolution of Rites), *Li Chi* (Record of Rites), it is said:

When the Great Way prevailed, the world community was equally shared by all. The worthy and able were chosen as office-holders. Mutual confidence was fostered and good neighborliness cultivated. Therefore people did not regard as parents only their own parents, nor did they treat as children only their own children. Provision was made for the aged till their death, the adult were given employment, and the young enabled to grow up. Old widows and widowers, the orphaned, the old and childless, as well as the sick and the disabled were all well taken care of. Men had their proper roles and women their homes. While they hated to see wealth lying about on the ground, they did not necessarily keep it for their own use. While they hated not to exert their effort, they did not necessarily devote it to their own ends. Thus evil schemings were repressed, and robbers, thieves and other lawless elements failed to arise, so that outer doors did not have to be shut. This was called the age of the Great Harmony.[2]

What is called the Great Way in this chapter is none other than the Kingly Way or Way of Right. Its fundamental spirit lies in the words "equally shared by all." Only when each nation rids itself of selfishness and becomes fair-minded can the Great Way prevail. The ultimate objective of the nine standard rules for the government of a country (see Chapter VIII above) is the pacification of the world. Each of the rules envisages the preparatory steps toward that goal. When each of these steps is consummated, peace is brought to the whole world.

Internally speaking, good government will prevail (1) if the ruler avoids nepotism and employs only those men who are worthy and able, (2) if these worthy and able men take the "service of thousands and thousands of people and the well-being of thousands and thousands of people" (Dr. Sun Yatsen's phrase) as their responsibility, and (3) if both the higher and lower intellectual classes of men are fair-minded. This is the meaning of the statement: "The worthy and able were chosen as office-holders."

Externally speaking, sincerity and courtesy will result, selfishness will disappear, and peace and harmony will prevail the world over when "mutual confidence" and "good neighborliness" become the only guiding principles in international relations. This is the meaning of the statement: "Mutual confidence was fostered and good neighborliness cultivated."

In education, the cultivation of the Way should be the root of everything. The determination of human relations should have priority, beginning with filial piety and kindness—and these apply not only to one's own aged and young folks but extend to the aged and young of others. This is the meaning of the statement: "Therefore people did not regard as parents only their own parents, nor did they treat as children only their own children." The inevitable result of this is that "provision was made for the aged till their death, the adult were given employment, and the young enabled to grow up."

Politically, all the people—male and female, old and young —should have their proper places, live a decent life and build their families. Those who cannot support themselves should be taken care of by the government. This is the meaning of the statements: "Provision was made for the aged till their death, the adult were given employment and the young enabled to grow up"; "Old widows and widowers, the orphaned, the old and childless, as well as the sick and the disabled, were all well taken care of"; "Men had their proper roles and women their homes." Justice was done in every case. Human talent was fully utilized. There was no occasion for regretting the "dislocation" of anyone.

Economically, the earth should be made to yield all its resources, all things should be made to contribute their utility, and the circulation of commodities should be extended to full development. All human and material resources should be devoted to the common enjoyment of all mankind; they should not be set aside for the personal use of any one party. With the public spirit prevalent everywhere, people could share their performance of good with others. This is the meaning of the statements: "While they hated to see wealth lying about on the ground, they did not necessarily keep it for their own use"; and "While they hated not to exert their effort, they did not necessarily devote it to their own ends."

As for security, when the Great Harmony prevailed, it was rendered practically needless by the successful results achieved in the fields of instruction, control and support as described above. The people were warmly clad and well fed. They lived in peace and happiness since (1) people could be affectionate toward their own relatives as well as everyone else, (2) they could respect and love one another, and (3) the upper classes were virtuous and the lower classes law-abiding. Moreover, with mutual confidence and good neighborliness established among nations, there was not only internal order but external peace. "Thus evil schemings were repressed, and robbers, thieves and other lawless elements failed to arise, so that outer doors did not have to be shut." Measures of security, while not neglected, were rendered unnecessary under these circumstances, for all the people had their self-respect and kept within their due bounds of propriety.

From all this we can see that in the era of the Great Harmony all governmental measures relating to control, instruction, support and security were aimed at the sharing of the world community by all and thus laying the foundation for the practice of the Great Way.

However, with their differing cultures and histories, the nations of today have their own peculiar traditional characteristics and it is impossible to equate them. Consequently we should all, with the greatest unselfishness and alltruism, cherish our similarities and respect our differences. Despite the latter, we shall march together toward a community of purpose. In this way we shall be able to usher in again what has been called the age of the "Great Harmony."

Footnotes for Chapter IX

1. *Great Learning*, Text. *Vide supra*, p. 6.
2. Chai, *Humanist Way in Ancient China*, p. 338, and *Li Chi*, Vol. I, p. 365;
   Legge, *Sacred Books of China*, Vol. III, p. 365, Lin, op. cit., p. 227. A serious
   mistake made by all these translators was their misreading of the character
   矜, which is the same as 鰥, as it appeared in the Classics. As a result,
   "widowers" was absent from all the translations.   Lin Yutang committed
   an even worse error by omitting the category of the "old and childless."

CHAPTER X

Conclusion

The purpose of this book is to make the *Four Books* a systematic reader. In summation, the following questions and answers are presented to bring out the essence of a concluding chapter.

Q. Was the Way of Confucius a connected way?

A. The Chinese nation has totaled 600 million people in one family and continued the development of its glorious history uninterruptedly for more than 5,000 years. This achievement is due to the fact that our ancestors discovered the principle of the common existence of mankind, which was handed down to every succeeding generation to be followed with unremitting tenacity. This principle is called the Way.

When applied to oneself, the Way is called sincerity.

When applied to others, the Way is called benevolence.

When applied to affairs, the Way is called the Mean.

When its application to oneself, to others and to affairs is integrated, the Way is called virtue.

When seen routinely in proper speech and conduct, the Way is called propriety.

Carrying on this great discovery of our ancestors, Confucius made adjustments in all its aspects and turned it into a set of systematic academic theories. The Way—its tenets are in the *Doctrine of the Mean;* its application is in the *Great Learning;* and its interpretation is in the *Analects.* Subsequently, Mencius further elucidated it in his *Works*.

As for the other classics, the *Book of Songs* gives vent to the human will, the *Book of History* records events, the *Book of Rites* regulates conduct, the *Book of Music* expresses harmony, the *Book of Changes* devotes itself to *yin* and *yang* (the negative and positive sides of things), the *Spring and Autumn Annals* distinguishes between right and wrong, and the *Book of Filial Piety* lays the foundation for the continuation of human species and embodies the sages' theory of the heavenly heart. All these books are intended to expand on the Way and illustrate virtue.

Since a man cannot maintain an isolated existence independently of other men, it is impossible to overlook the importance of harmonizing relations between man and man. The natural prerequisite for human conduct is to find how man can fit into his environment and fulfill the requirements of living, so as to make possible the common existence of mankind. Confucius' answer was to set down the cultivation of the person as the root of everything. From the cultivation of the person to the pacification of the world, all the necessary steps originate in justice. They start with complete sincerity, carry through with the search for benevolence, and are consummated in earnest practice.

The effect of all these steps depends on the rectification of hearts as a result of the application of the Mean and on the sincerity of thoughts as a result of intelligence. But the source of this rectification and sincerity is the completion of knowledge, the extension of which depends on the investigation of things. The things of the universe are investigated to generate wisdom, as good government and world peace are brought about to strengthen virtue. What is taken from the world is devoted to the benefit of that same world.

One is taught to dislike the strength which is not exerted by oneself. But this strength need not be employed for one's own good. The object is to serve all men and enhance their well-being, to seek and obtain benevolence, so as not to disgrace one's ancestors.

Could such a Way be other than connected?

Q. Why was Confucius canonized as the Ancient Teacher and Highest Sage?

A. The teachings of Confucius were answers to the various questions encountered in man's normal routine. They especially emphasize the difference between the root and the branches and between the beginning and the end. Hence, it is said in the *Great Learning:* "Things have their root and their branches. Affairs have their end and their beginning. To know what is first and what is last will lead man to the Way." In the *Analects* it is said: "The superior man bends his attention to what is radical. That being established, the Way is produced." The *Doctrine of the Mean* states: "It is only the individual possessed of the most entire sincerity that can...establish the great fundamental virtues of humanity..."

What is the root but the cultivation of the person? Hence, "From the Son of Heaven down to the mass of the people, all must consider the cultivation of the person the root of everything besides. It cannot be, when the root is neglected, that what should spring from it will be well ordered." Thus, it is also said, "The character is to be cultivated by his (the ruler's) treading in the ways of duty. And the treading those ways of duty is to be cultivated by the cherishing of benevolence," which is "the characteristic element of humanity."

Furthermore, the root of benevolence lies in filial piety and fraternal love ("Filial piety and fraternal submission! Are they not the root of all benevolent actions?") Since filial piety and fraternal love are the rudiments of all love, they are the foundation for the regulation of the family. For the component parts of every functional group in society—be it a family, a State or the world —invariably consist of human beings. Therefore, teachings for all men must form the basis for any exposition on one or another of these societal groupings.

As to the contents of these teachings for all human beings they focus on clarifying the normal relations between man and man. This is rational (*chung*) and simple (*yung*) and can easily be understood and practiced by everyone. In a word, these teachings are "consistent with human nature." When applied to the person, this Way cultivates him; when applied to the family, the Way regulates it; when applied to the State, the Way insures that it is well ordered; when applied to the world, the Way brings about peace. So it is said, "The Way is not far from man. When men seek the Way by going far away from man, this course cannot be considered the Way."

We have seen how the Way is interpreted as the principle of the common existence of mankind. Also, we have probed the cultivation of the person, the regulation of the family, the good government of a State and the pacification of the world, and we have found that they are ideals jointly pursued by mankind. It follows that the teachings of Confucius will last forever, or to put it another way they will last as long as this principle does not change and the ideals concerned are not lost. Therefore, since they are eternal, Confucius' teachings are not subject to the limitations of time and space. For this reason, the Way can be called "humanism" itself, and it is no exaggeration at all to refer to Confucius, who embodies this Way, as the Highest Sage and the Teacher of Myriad Ages.

Q. All of China's religions have come from abroad. Yet the only man who all through the ages has been reverenced in China —though never deified—is Confucius. Why is it that the moral standards of the Chinese people have always been equal—even higher than—those of professionally religious people?

A. The object of religion is to teach men how to rid themselves of selfishness, how to cultivate the sense of justice and how to sacrifice one's own interests and even one's own life to attain the goal of loving others and helping them. As for the theories of Heaven and Hell, they are employed to encourage good and deter evil. Although the rites of the various religions differ, their principles are the same.

Confucius has also mentioned heavenly destiny and God, but the effect of his teachings is altogether different. According to him, a man is a man because he is capable of guiding his natural endowment or instinct ("What Heaven has conferred is called the nature") to fit into the principle of the common existence of mankind—the Way ("an accordance with this nature is called the Way"), and of cultivating this Way (instruction) so well that it progresses without hindrance ("The cultivation of this Way is called instruction"). Only man can enlarge and cultivate the Way, copy the example of Heaven and be equal to it. A virtuous man does absolutely nothing to accomplish a purpose; rather, he does only what he should.

Confucius regarded "sincerity" as the motive power of morality. The *Doctrine of the Mean* in great detail clarifies the concept of sincerity, which is in every way compatible with the idea of God recognized in the Western world (see Chapter IV, "The Sincerity of Thoughts"). In the *Analects* the effect of benevolence is exhaustively examined. From the cultivation of the person to the pacification of the world, each step is inextricably involved with benevolence. And at its highest point, benevolence is sought through the sacrifice of life itself. This again coincides with the spirit of love and sacrifice taught by the religions of the world.

Although "holding to the Mean" was a treasured teaching handed down from Yao and Shun, Confucius was the first man to clarify this concept and call it the doctrine of the Mean. He realized that both excess and inadequacy are extremities and that only by understanding the Mean and holding to it could harmony be achieved. When this doctrine is applied to others, it involves the practice of faithfulness and reciprocity, in which a person is concerned not only with himself but with others. In this process a person establishes and enlarges others while seeking to establish and enlarge himself. He does not do unto others what he would not have them do unto himself.

When the Mean is applied to affairs, it prevents the possibility of paying attention to one side only while neglecting the other, of seeing the trees but not the wood. It thus lays the foundation for justice and equality. When this teaching is applied to reasoning, there is no excess or inadequacy, and contention between the part and the whole is avoided. It thus lays the foundation for peace. Also, in this doctrine lies the origin of the spirit of propriety as well as the basis of morality. This is how the Chinese emphasis on propriety and virtue arose.

Confucius never wished to appear knowledgeable about something when he was not. He therefore consistently avoided mention of the spirit, stopping short with the observation on "the highest sincerity, as in a spirit." It was Mencius who offered a definition of the word, "spirit," saying: "When the sage is beyond our knowledge, he is what is called a spirit-man."[1] This corresponds with what is said in the *Book of Changes:* "The spirit knows the future, and the wise store up the knowledge of the past." Since he refused to presume himself a sage, Confucius scrupulously avoided speaking about the spiritual world. But since the knowledge of the spiritual world was obscure to him, he did not dare to feel disrespectful. This sums up the attitude of Confucius toward divinity.

The teachings of Confucius thus had the reality of a religion, althoug it was not called a religion. In reverencing Confucius, the Chinese believe in his teachings, respect his personality and call him their teacher. Moreover, they strive to acquire his Way, which has no superstitious bias at all.

Q. The peoples of the West regard the affection of husband and wife as the basis of love. Why is it that the Chinese followers of Confucius veer from this concept and take filial piety as the basis of love?

A. Confucius lived in an agricultural country, where farmers settled down and lived together as clans. There was little movement of families, and the family system was an important factoɪ in maintaining social order. To perpetuate the family system, home education was needed. And from regulation of the family flowed the demand to teach first and foremost filial piety and fraternal love. At the same time this family training—involving the service of the father and the elder brother—extended to ties that bound the people to their sovereign and other superiors. Moreover, as the economic system required the transmission of property from one generation to another, special emphasis was laid on the father-son relationship. Indeed, this is an added reason why filial piety came to assume the key role it did.

Confucius' focal point, however, was the continuity of human life and so he took up first things first. To safeguard the common existence of mankind, it was vital to stress mutual interest, mutual assistance, the importance of not forgetting one's origins and of remembering favors received. As for the favors, what could be more important than the favors received by children from their parents? To relegate such favors to oblivion would result in failure to provide for the elderly and for the young in their formative years; this in turn would threaten the continuity of human life. For the sake of growth and durability, then, filial piety was viewed as the highest of all virtues.

Confucius also set great store by the love of husband and wife. Hence it is said, "The Way of the superior man begins with the relations of husband and wife."[2] It is also written in the *Book of Songs,* "Happy union with wife and children is like the music of lutes and harps."[3] · We all know, however, that the love of husband and wife, starting after a person comes of age, cannot compare with the love of parents for their children, which arises out of human nature and, eternally strong, endures from birth until death. If the foundation of love is permitted to rest merely on the easily fractured family ties of today, it is liable to totter at any time—and this is something which falls short of the expectations of the wise.

True, owing to the nature of work in modern industrial and commercial society, men move around much more than before. In this type of social environment even a small family is difficult to maintain, let alone larger family units. Filial piety, the foundation of love in the large family system, is bound to weaken. But this is a paradoxical observation. While the form of filial piety may change with time, the expression of real affection for mankind is nevertheless not subject to the limitations of time or space. Only when there is filial piety on the part of children can the kindness of parents be repaid—and if this happens on a universal scale, mankind will better endure. With this well understood, we can see that by teaching filial piety, Confucius aimed at widening and prolonging the growth of human life.

Q. Are the teachings of Confucius responsible for the backwardness of modern China's material civilization?

A. The teachings of Confucius emphasized both mind and matter. Confucius maintained the rectification of hearts should begin with the investigation of things. He said that only by fully developing his own nature could man give to the natures of things their full development, and thereby assist the transforming and nourishing powers of Heaven and Earth. In other words, Confucius regarded the humanities and natural sciences as equally important.

In the investigation of things, Confucius advocated "extensive study, accurate inquiry, careful reflection, clear discrimination and earnest practice." This coincides fully with today's scientific research and method. In regard to study, he said, "When you know a thing, to hold that you know it, this is knowledge." Obviously his attitude toward study is consistent with the scientific attitude of searching for the truth and for proof.

In discussing government, he said that the "enrichment" of the people should precede their "instruction." Though in an agricultural society, he went so far as to stress the importance of "all artisans," declaring that "by encouraging the resort of all classes of artisans, his (the ruler's) resources for expenditure are rendered ample." Referring to vessels and things, he said that—unlike men, who needed experience—they should be new. Hence it is said in the *Book of History*, "While only men who are old (familiar) should be sought, not old vessels, but new ones, should be sought." When it came to production, Confucius said, "Let the producers be many and the consumers few. Let there be activity in the production and economy in the expenditure. Then the wealth will always be sufficient."

All this was intended to show later generations that they should not overlook the importance of material life and the abundance and dispatch of material production.

China's contributions to the natural sciences in earlier times were by no means meager. However, after the Sung dynasty scholars inclined to stress the mind while neglecting matter. They did this because they lacked a clear understanding of the true significance of the principles inherent in the Doctrine of the Mean. The infiltration of Buddhism intensified this trend. Subsequently, remarkable progress was made by the West in the study of the natural sciences and in the promotion of industry. On her part, China was bogged down by bad government internally and foreign aggression externally. Scientifically backward, industrially incompetent and militarily weak, the country quickly degenerated into a sub-colony, and this was its status for almost a century. Now that we have awakened, not only do we exonerate ourselves from blame and feel no shame at all, but we hold Confucius responsible for what happened. Is this not a great wrong done to the Master?

Q. Do the teachings of Confucius run counter to modern democracy?

A. Since Confucius was born into an age of monarchy more than 2,500 years ago, we cannot very well charge him with not thinking in modern democratic terms. However, in his teachings, he invariably laid emphasis on the wishes of the people as the foundation of government.

As an example, we can cite the statement: "When a prince loves what the people love and hates what the people hate, then is he what is called the parent of the people." Furthermore, he frequently warned the reigning princes with this quotation from the *Book of History:* "The decree indeed may not always rest on us; that is, goodness obtains the decree, and the want of goodness loses it." He also said, "As a sovereign, he (King Wên) rested in benevolence." As one of the nine standard rules for the government of a country, he included "dealing with the mass of the people as children."

All this meant that a ruler could not really be called "ruler" if he did not love his people as his children and if he did not act in accordance with their wishes. It was all in perfect harmony with the spirit of democracy. The only difference was that the ruler was not elected by the people.

Mencius went even further than Confucius when he made the bold statement: "The people are the most important element in a nation; the spirits of the land and grain are the next; and the sovereign is the lightest." He also said (1) that high ministers of the royal house may dethrone a ruler, (2) that others not belonging to the royal house could banish him, as in the case of Yi Yin, (3) that a sovereign who acted like a robber and ruffian was called a "mere fellow" whom anyone could put to death, and (4) that a ruler who could not support the people should return his charge to them. All this was meant to exhort the reigning princes to remember that their role was to love and enrich their people.

Mencius even went a step further. Lest ministers hesitate to speak up when their sovereign was at fault, he defined the words "respect" and "reverence" as follows: "To urge one's sovereign to difficult achievements may be called showing respect. To set before him what is good and repress his perversities may be called showing reverence for him." His intent was twofold: (1) to enable ministers to discharge their functions completely and (2) to make certain that the wishes of the people would be heard at the higeest level of the government.

Both Confucius and Mencius respected the unique position of scholars. They felt that the sovereign should treat scholars as friends and teachers. For one thing, the ruler should himself visit scholars, rather than call them into his presence. This reverential high regard they had for worthy men was termed respect of virtue and delight in the Way.

Mencius was not personally instructed by Confucius. He was a pupil of Tzŭ-ssŭ, the grandson of Confucius, from whom he inherited indirectly the great Master's democratic thinking. It is obvious then that the concept of modern democracy was never new to the Chinese people. What remained to be achieved was the formal adoption of the democratic system and the technique necessary to bring it into play. This is why Dr. Sun Yatsen included his "First Steps of the People's Rights" as one of the practical requirements of social reconstruction.

Q. What is the content of China's original civilization? Is it worth salvaging from its roots? What are its possible contributions to the world? Can it catch up with Western civilization?

A. The greatest contributions made by Confucius were the editing of the *Book of Songs* and the *Book of History*, the compilation of the *Book of Rites* and the *Book of Music*, the annotation of the *Book of Changes* and the writing of the *Spring and Autumn Annals*. In carrying out these tasks, Confucius devoted his crowning effort to the collection of the ancient books of China, which have been designated by later generations as the Six Classics or Six Arts. As a culminating achievement, they can be said to embody the substantial content of China's original civilization.

Since Confucius, four attempts have been made at a similar collection of Chinese literary productions: (1) the "Chronicle of Arts and Literature" in the *Dynastic History of Han* (A. D. 22); (2) the "Chronicle of Arts and Literature" in the *Dynastic History of Sui* (A. D. 617); (3) the "Chronicle of Arts and Literature" in the *Dynastic History of Sung* (A. D. 1276); and (4) the *General Catalogue of the Complete Books of the Four Libraries* (A. D. 1782). But these efforts went little beyond the elucidation of the collection made by Confucius; the theories and principles propounded in the first collection did not undergo any substantial change.

A recent writer, Ma Yi-fu, maintained that the Six Arts integrated all the schools of philosophy, the four main divisions of learning and the studies introduced from the West. He went further, saying that the natural sciences were integrated in the *Book of Changes*, the social sciences or humanities in the *Spring and Autumn Annals*, literature and art in the *Book of Songs* and *Book of Music*, political science, law and economics in the *Book of History* and *Book of Rites*, religion in the *Book of Rites*. To him, philosophical thought approaches the *Book of Changes,* the *Book of Music* and *the Book of Rites.* The Chinese and Western civilizations can thus be joined.

However, our ancient books must be reorganized and reinterpreted to make them intelligible to the current generation. And herein lies the necessity for the scientific method.

It should not be forgotten, nonetheless, that there are fundamental differences between original Chinese civilization and its Western counterpart. First, the teachings of Confucius emphasized virtue rather than strength; hence the exaltation of the Kingly Way or the Way of Right and the rejection of the Way of Might.

Secondly, virtue was regarded as the root, and wealth as merely a branch. Hence, "Possessing virtue will give him (the ruler) the people. Possessing the people will give him the territory. Possessing the territory will give him its wealth. Possessing the wealth, he will have resources for expenditure. Virtue is the root; wealth is the result. If he makes the root his secondary object and the result his primary, he will only wrangle with his people and teach them rapine." In other words, the spiritual condition of human existence (virtue) should precede its material condition (wealth). With neither dispensable, the position of the root and branch should not be reversed nor their order of sequence confused.

Thirdly, virtue should have precedence over art. Hence, "Let the will be set on the Way. Let every attainment in what is good be firmly grasped. Let perfect virtue be accorded with. Let relaxation and enjoyment be found in the polite arts." To Confucius, teaching the arts without first teaching morality meant putting the branch over the root, an invitation to disaster.

Wealth and power—these are the things to which the people of our world attach the greatest importance. Strange, isn't it, that Confucius regarded them as less valuable than virtue? Today the two most sweeping tides of thought are capitalism and communism. Capitalsm focuses on wealth and military strength, while communism embraces force and materialsim. Modern educators emphasize technique and art at the expense of morality. Teaching morality, they feel, is the task of religion. As progress has been made in the natural sciences, religious faith has steadily dwindled in importance.

Since moral education is not stressed at all in the public schools, few pay any attention to it. In addition, society more and more comes to worship money and power; this, while the family system rapidly disintegrates. Neglect of the children's moral education has resulted in the unbridled growth of selfishness and human passion, with strife and violence the order of the day. Since the dawn of the atomic age, the brutality of the ambitious and aggressive has been immeasurably intensified, imperiling human civilization; indeed the destruction of civilization at any moment is a definite possibility. This is the result of stressing wealth and strength at the expense of virtue.

Only Confucius was farsighted enough to make these things clear: (1) that while wealth is indispensable, it cannot be regarded as the root; (2) that while strength cannot be ignored, it certainly cannot be relied upon as a long-term factor; (3) that while technique and art are essential to human life, true wisdom consists of knowing what virtue is and possessing the courage to practice it. The position of the root and the branch must be clearly understood, and their order of sequence carefully observed. Persons who bear this in mind and act accordingly are near to the Way.

The difference between the Chinese culture and its Western counterparts is this: China stresses ways to safeguard human life, while the West emphasizes ways to enrich human life. Both are important, but it is clear that China's approach is the essence; and the West's, the utility.

The Chinese people are proud of their spiritual civilization. But if they really try to understand the teachings of Confucius, they will come to realize that the *Book of Changes* long ago pointed out their misplaced pride. For solitary *yin* (female or negative factor) cannot lead to birth, nor can isolated *yang* (male or positive factor) lead to growth. The stress of spirit at the expense of matter, and vice versa, are both characteristic of lifeless civilizations which cannot long endure.

If this is understood, the merits of the Chinese people will not be lost. At the same time the Chinese will realize that it is time for them to forge ahead to catch up with the West in science and the study of matter, for in these areas they are still comparatively backward. On the other hand, the people of the West should learn from China what they have neglected—the fundamental importance of morality. If both peoples can complement each other, they can yet plan together prolongation and enrichment of human life.

Chinese youths who have studied in Western countries have generally done well in mathematics, chemistry and physics. Thus it should not be difficult for them to take up the serious study of the natural sciences. On the other hand, I regret to say that Western youths—because of their customary neglect of morality as they absorb themselves in science—will not find it easy to save themselves. This means that, comparatively, the Chinese have an advantage.

However, it is only with self-confidence that self-salvation can be accomplished; "God helps those who help themselves." Confucius said, "When we see men of worth, we should think of equaling them; when we see men of contrary character, we should turn inwards and examine ourselves." Again, "Have no friends not equal to yourself." Since these rules govern the relations between man and man, should there be any difference when it comes to the relations between sovereign nations? This is what Dr. Sun Yatsen was saying when he called on us to "save ourselves from the roots" and "forge ahead to catch up" with others.

Q. With her vast territory and huge population, once China is strong and prosperous, will she not be a menace to the world?

A. The Chinese people have been held together, not by brutal force, but by lofty virtue. This was thoroughly explained by Mencius in his discussion of the Kingly Way or the Way of Right. The Chinese people exalt the teachings of Confucius because they contain such high ideals for the world.

In connection with the "pacification of the world," we have seen that the word *p'ing* denotes equality, justice and peace. The Chinese people firmly believe that the happiness of mankind rests on *p'ing*. Virtue alone has the force to turn inequality into equality and injustice into justice—and this ideal condition cannot be attained by either money or military strength.

The Chinese conception of life is this: "So large and substantial, the individual possessing it is the co-equal of Earth. So high and brilliant, it makes him the co-equal of Heaven. So far-reaching and long-continuing, it makes him infinite." Only with "largeness" can there be capacity to contain matter. Only with "endurance" can there be the completion of matter. Only with the "Mean" can there be free sway to both the left and the right. Only with the "absence of change" can the long-term requirements of the great majority be met and can there be durability. This is the way to the widening and prolongation of human life which was stressed by Confucius. And it is still believed and upheld by our people. That is why our 600 million people have lived together as one family and have maintained without let-up a culture more than 5,000 years old. That is why they have possessed a very high power of assimilation and absorption.

Once this is clearly understood, Chinese culture can be comprehended by the people of the world and its benefit can be received by all mankind. Those Westerners who lack comprehension of Chinese culture imagine that when China becomes strong the "Yellow Peril" will emerge. This is due to either ignorance or faulty speculation. The fact is that the nationalism we uphold has as its object the equality of all the nationalities of the world. Our nationalism should not be misunderstood. Should China unfortunately abandon for good Dr. Sun Yatsen's *Three Principles of the People* and perpetuate instead the system of Communism, then indeed the menace would be inestimable—the menace posed by not only the so-called "Yellow Peril" but, what would be more realistic, the "Red Peril."

In the *Doctrine of the Mean* it is said, "...the way of the superior man seems concealed, but it daily becomes more illustrious, and the Way of the mean man seems to seek notoriety, but he daily goes more to ruin. The Way of the superior man is plain but not tiring, simple but polished, gentle but orderly. It knows the distant and the near, the main principles and the details, the minute and the manifest. Such a man can enter into virtue."[4] I wish to quote this passage as the conclusion of this book.

Footnotes for Chapter X

1. *Works of Mencius,* Bk. VII, Pt. II, Ch. XXV.
2. *Doctrine of the Mean,* Ch. XII.
3. *Ibid.,* Ch. XV.
4. *Ibid.,* Ch. XXXIII. *Vide supra,* p. 229.

GLOSSARY

"Announcement to K'ang"	One of the chapters in the *Book of History*
Ao	A strong man in the Hsia dynasty
"Canon of the Emperor (Yao)"	One of the chapters in the *Book of History*
Ch'ai, Kao	One of Confucius' disciples
Chang Yi	A politician in the State of Wei
Ch'ang Hsi	One of Kung-ming Kao's disciples
Chao Chien	A *ta-fu* of the State of Chin
Chao Hu	An official of the State of Ch'i
Chao Shuai	A *ta-fu* of the State of Chin
Chao of Sung	A son of the ruler of Sung
Chao the Great	The powerful aristocracy in the State of Chin
Chao-nan	One of the chapters in the *Book of Songs*
Ch'ên	One of the States under the Chou dynasty
Ch'ên (Ch'ên Chên)	One of Mencius' disciples
Ch'ên Chêng	A *ta-fu* of the State of Ch'i
Ch'ên Chia	A *ta-fu* of the State of Ch'i
Ch'ên Chung	A man from the State of Ch'i
Ch'ên Liang	A scholar in the State of Ch'u
Ch'ên Tai	One of Mencius' disciples
Ch'ên Wên	A *ta-fu* of the State of Ch'i
Chêng	One of the States under the Chou dynasty
Chi 稷	Minister of Agriculture under Emperor Shun
Chi 季	A powerful family in the State of Lu
Chi, the	A river in North China
Chi, Viscount	An uncle of the tyrant Chou of the Yin dynasty
Chi Huan 季桓	A *ta-fu* of the State of Lu
Chi Huan 瘠環	A eunuch at the court of Wei
Chi K'ang	A *ta-fu* of the State of Lu
Chi Sun	A *ta-fu* of the State of Lu
Chi Tzŭ-ch'êng	A *ta-fu* of the State of Wei
Chi Tzŭ-jan	A member of the powerful family of Chi in the State of Lu
Chi Wên	A *ta-fu* of the State of Lu
Ch'i 齊	One of the States under the Chou dynasty
Ch'i 杞	One of the States under the Chou dynasty
Ch'i Liang	A *ta-fu* of the State of Ch'i
Chi-jên	A brother of the ruler of Jên
Chi-lu	The courtesy name of Chung Yu, one of Confucius' disciples

Ch'i-tiao K'ai	One of Confucius' disciples
Chiang, the	The Yangtze River
Chiao Ko	A worthy of the Yin dynasty
Chiao of Ts'ao	A brother of the ruler of Ts'ao
Chieh	A tyrant of the Hsia dynasty
Chih	A notorious ancient robber
Ch'ih, Kung-hsi	One of Confucius' disciples
Ch'ih Wa	A ta-fu of the State of Ch'i
Chin	One of the States under the Chou dynasty
Ch'in	One of the States under the Chou dynasty
Ching	A ta-fu of the State of Wei
Ch'ing	Title of a high official ranking after kung
Ch'iu, Jan	One of Confucius' disciples
Ch'iu, K'ung	The name of Confucius
Chou	One of the ancient dynasties (1122-247 B. C.)
Chou Hsiao	A man from the State of Wei
Chou Jên	An ancient historiographer
Chou-nan	One of the chapters in the Book of Songs
Chu T'o	A ta-fu of the State of Wei
Ch'u 楚	One of the States under the Chou dynasty
Ch'u 儲子	A man from the State of Ch'i
Chu-chang	Supposed to denote the philosopher Hsün-tzŭ
Chü	One of the States under the Chou dynasty
Ch'ü Po-yü	One of Confucius' disciples and a ta-fu of the State of Wei
Chuan-yü	A small State under the Chou dynasty
Chuang	The name of a street in a town in the State of Ch'i
Chuang of Pien	A ta-fu of the State of Lu
Chuang Pao	A minister of the State of Ch'i
Chuang-tzŭ	A great philosopher of the Chou dynasty
Chung 鍾	An ancient measure of capacity
Chung 中	Equilibrium
Chung-jên	A brother of T'ai-ting
Chung-kung	Courtesy name of Jan Yung, one of Confucius' disciples
Chung-ni	Confucius' courtesy name
Chung Yu	The name of Tzŭ-lu, one of Confucius' disciples
Ch'ung Yü	One of Mencius' disciples
Chung Yung	The Doctrine of the Mean
"Counsels of Kao Yao"	One of the chapters in the Book of History
"Declaration of (the Duke of) Ch'in	One of the chapters in the Book of History

"Declaration of T'ang"	One of the chapters in the *Book of History*
Duke of Chou	The great prime minister of the Chou dynasty
Fan Ch'ih (Fan Hsü)	One of Confucius' disciples
Fu	An ancient measure of capacity
Fu Yüeh	The prime minister under Emperor Kao-tsung of the Yin dynasty
"Great Declaration"	One of the chapters in the *Book of History*
Hai T'ang	A recluse of the State of Chin
Han	One of the States under the Chou dynasty
Han, the	A river in Central China
Hao-shêng Pu-hai	A man from the State of Ch'i
Hsi	The courtesy name of Tsêng Tien, one of Confucius' disciples
Hsi, the lady	Hsi Shih 西施, a famed beauty in the Chou dynasty
Hsia	One of the ancient dynasties (2205-1767 B.C.)
Hsiang	The younger brother of Emperor Shun
"Hsiao-p'an"	One of the chapters in the *Book of Songs*
Hsieh Liu	A man from the State of Lu
Hsien, or Ssǔ, Yüan	One of Confucius' disciples
Hsien Ch'iu-mêng	One of Mencius' disciples
Hsü P'i (Hsü, the disciple)	One of Mencius' disciples
Hsüeh Chü-chou	A virtuous man in the State of Sung
Hsün-yu	A barbarian tribe, from which the Hsiung-nu descended
Hu Ho	A trusted minister of King Hsüan of Ch'i
Hua Chou	A *ta-fu* of the State of Ch'i
Huai, the	A river in Central China
Huan, Duke	A ruler of the State of Ch'i
Huan, Minister of War of Sung	Huan T'ui
Huan T'ui	A minister of war of the State of Sung
Hui, Yen	The name of Yen Yüan, one of Confucius' disciples
Hui of Liu-hsia	A gaoler of the State of Lu
Jan Niu, Jan Po-niu	One of Confucius' disciples
Jan Yu 冉有	One of Confucius' disciples
Jan Yu 然友	The teacher of the Crown Prince, later Duke Wên, of T'êng
Jên	One of the States under the Chou dynasty
Ju, the	A river in Honan Province
Ju Pei	A man from the State of Lu
"K'ai-fêng"	One of the chapters in the *Book of Songs*
Kao 告子	One of Mencius' disciples

Kao 高丁	One of Mencius' disciples
Kao Yao	A minister under Emperor Shun
Kao-tsung	King Wu-ting of the Yin dynasty
Kêng of T'êng	One of the brothers of Duke Wên of T'êng
Ko	One of the States under the Chou dynasty
Kou-chien	The king of Yüeh
Ku-kung T'an-fu	An ancestor of the royal household of Chou
Ku-sou	The father of Emperor Shun
Kuan-chü	One of the chapters in the *Book of Songs*
Kuan Chung	The courtesy name of Kuan Yi-wu
Kuan Yi-wu	A prime minister of the State of Ch'i
K'uang	The most accomplished music master in the State of Ch'i
K'uang Chang	A man from the State of Ch'ı
Kun	The father of Emperor Yü of the Hsia dynasty
K'un	One of the western barbarian tribes
Kung	A title of nobility
Kung Chih-ch'i	A *ta-fu* of the State of Yü
K'ung Ch'iu	The name of Confucius
Kung-ch'o, Mêng	A *ta-fu* of the State of Lu
K'ung Wên	A *ta-fu* of the State of Wei
Kung-hang	A *ta-fu* of the State of Ch'i
Kung-hsi Hua	Kung-hsi Ch'ih, one of Confucius' disciples
Kung-ming Chia	A man from the State of Wei
Kung-ming Kao	One of the philosopher Tsêng's disciples
Kung-ming Yi	A worthy of the State of Lu
Kung-po Liao	One of Confucius' disciples
Kung-shan Fu-jao	An official of the powerful Chi family in the State of Lu
Kung-shu	A mechanic of the State of Lu
Kung-shu Wên	A *ta-fu* of the State of Wei
Kung-sun Ch'ao	A *ta-fu* of the State of Wei
Kung-sun Ch'ou	One of Mencius' disciples
Kung-sun Yen	A politician in the State of Wei
Kung-tu	One of Mencius' disciples
Kung-yêh Ch'ang	One of Confucius' disciples
Kung-yi	A prime minister under Duke Mu of Lu
Kuo	One of the States under the Chou dynasty
Lai Chu	A worthy minister under Emperor T'ang of the Shang dynasty
Lady Chiang	A concubine of King T'ai, King Wên's grandfather
Lao, Ch'in	One of Confucius' disciples
Li	One of the tyrants of the Chou dynasty

Li, K'ung	The son of Confucius
Li Lou	An ancient with the sharpest sight
Lin Fang	A man from the State of Lu
Lu	One of the States under the Chou dynasty
Lung	An ancient worthy
Mêng	A powerful family in the State of Lu
Mêng Chih-fan	A *ta-fu* of the State of Lu
Mêng Ching	A *ta-fu* of the State of Lu
Mêng Chuang	A *ta-fu* of the State of Lu
Mêng Hsien	A worthy *ta-fu* of the State of Lu
Mêng K'o	The full name of Mencius
Mêng Kung-ch'o	A *ta-fu* of the State of Lu
Mêng Pên	A brave man in the Chou dynasty
Mêng Shih-shêh	A man's name
Mêng Wu-po	The son of Mêng Yi
Mêng Yi	A *ta-fu* of the State of Lu
Mi	Mi Tzŭ-hsia, a favorite minister of the ruler of Wei
Mien	A blind Music-master of the State of Lu
Min Tzŭ-ch'ien	One of Confucius' disciples
Mo Ti (Mo-tzŭ)	A philosopher of the Chou dynasty
Nan Jung, Nan Kung-kua	One of Confucius' disciples
Nan-tzŭ	Duchess of Wei
Ning Wu	A *ta-fu* of the State of Wu
Pai-li Hsi	A *Ta-fu* of the States of Yü and Chin
P'ang Mêng	A disciple of Yi, the archer in the Hsia dynasty
Pei-kung Yi	A man from the State of Wei
Pei-kung Yu	A man from the State of Ch'i
P'êng, Old	A worthy *ta-fu* of the Shang dynasty
P'êng Kêng	One of Mencius' disciples
Pi Chan	A minister under Duke Wên of T'êng
Pi Hsü	A family official of Chao Chien, a *ta-fu* of the State of Chin
Pi-kan	An uncle of the tyrant Chou of the Yin dynasty
Pin	The name of an ancient State
Ping	An ancient measure of capacity
Po Kuei	A man from the State of Chou
Po-niu, Jan	One of Confucius' disciples
Po-yi	A sage in the Yin dynasty
Po-yü	The courtesy name of K'ung Li, Confucius' son
San Yi-shêng	A worthy minister under King Wên of the Chou dynasty

Shang	One of the ancient dynasties (1766-1123 B.C.)
Shang, Pu	The name of Tzŭ-hsià, one of Confucius' disciples
Shao	The music of Emperor Shun
Shao-lien	A man from the district near the eastern barbarian tribe
Shêh, Duke of	A *ta-fu* of the State of Ch'u
Shên, Tsêng	The name of the philosopher Tsêng, one of Confucius' disciples
Shên Ch'ang	One of Confucius' disciples
Shên Hsiang	The son of Tzŭ-chang and a worthy in the State of Lu
Shên T'ung	A high official of the State of Ch'i
Shên-nung	Legendary emperor who taught agriculture, etc.
Shên-yu Hsing	One of the philospher Tsêng's disciples
Shêng	History of the State of Chin
Shih	A *ta-fu* of the State of Ch'i
Shih, Chuan-sun	One of Confucius' disciples
Shih-k'uang	A music-master in the service of Duke P'ing of Chin
Shih-shu	A *ta-fu* of the State of Chêng
Shu-ch'i	A worthy of the Yin dynasty
Shu-sun Wu-shu	A *ta-fu* of the State of Lu
Shun	The great emperor of the Yü dynasty (2255-2207 B.C.)
Shun-yü K'un	A man from the State of Ch'i, a contemporary of Mencius
Ssŭ, the	A river in Central China
Ssŭ, or Hsien, Yüan	One of Confucius' disciples
Ssŭ-ma Niu	One of Confucius' disciples
Sun-shu Ao	A prime minister of the State of Ch'u
Sung	One of the States under the Chou dynasty
T'a	A river in North China
Ta-fu	The title of an official ranking below *ch'ing;* a Great Official
Ta-hsiang	A village in the State of Lu
Tai Pu-sheng	A *ta-fu* of the State of Sung
Tai Ying-chih	A *ta-fu* of the State of Sung
T'ai, the	A mountain range in North China
T'ai-chia	An emperor of the Shang dynasty (1753-1721 B.C.), the grandson of Emperor T'ang
"T'ai-chia, the"	One of the chapters in the *Book of History*
T'ai, King (T'ai Wang)	The grandfather of King Wên of the Chou dynasty

T'ai-kung Wang	Lü Shang, the prime minister under King Wên of the Chou dynasty
T'ai-po	Uncle of King Wên of the Chou dynasty
T'ai-ting	Emperor T'ang's Crown Prince
Tan-chu	The son of Emperor Yao
T'an-t'ai Mieh-ming	One of Confucius' disciples
T'ang 唐	The name of an ancient dynasty (2357-2257 B.C.)
T'ang 湯	The name of the first emperor (1766-1760 B.C.) of the Shang dynasty
T'ao Ying	One of Mencius' disciples
T'ao-wu	The history of the State of Ch'u
T'êng	One of the States under the Chou dynasty
Three Dynasties, the	Hsia, Shang (Yin) and Chou
Tien, Tsêng	The name of Tsêng Hsi, father of the philosopher Tsêng and also one of Confucius' disciples
Tsang Wên-chung	A *ta-fu* of the State of Lu
Tsang Wu-chung	A *ta-fu* of the State of Lu
Tsêng Hsi 曾晳	The father of the philosopher Tsêng
Tsêng Hsi 曾西	The grandson of the philosopher Tsêng
Tsêng Yüan	The son of the philosopher Tsêng
Tso-ch'iu Ming	A scholar of the Chou dynasty
Tsou 郰	A district (home town of Confucius) in the State of Lu
Tsou 鄒	One of the States (home State of Mencius) under the Chou dynasty
Ts'ui	A *ta-fu* of the State of Ch'i
Tuan-kan Mu	A worthy of the State of Wei
T'ung	A tree, *Paulonia tomentosa*
Tung-kuo	A *ta-fu* of the State of Ch'i
Tzŭ	A tree, *Catalpa ovata*
Tzŭ-ao	The courtesy name of Wang Huan
Tzŭ-ch'an	A *ta-fu* of the State of Chêng
Tzŭ-chang	The courtesy name of Chuan-sun Shih, one of Confucius' disciples
Tzŭ-chien	The courtesy name of Fu Pu-ch'i, one of Confucius' disciples
Tzŭ-chih	The name of a prince of Yen
Tzŭ-ch'in	The courtesy name of Ch'ên K'ang, one of Confucius' disciples
Tzŭ-fan	A *ta-fu* of the State of Ch'u
Tzŭ-fu Ching-po	A *ta-fu* of the State of Lu
Tzŭ-hsia	The courtesy name of Pu Shang, one of Confucius' disciples

Tzŭ-hsiang	One of the philosopher Tsêng's disciples
Tzŭ-hua	The courtesy name of Kung-hsi Ch'ih, one of Confucius' disciples
Tzŭ-k'uai	The name of a prince of Yen, who abdicated to Tzŭ-chih
Tzŭ-kung	The courtesy name of Tuan-mu Tz'ü, one of Confucius' disciples
Tzŭ-liu	Liu Hsieh
Tzŭ-lu	The courtesy name of Chung Yu, one of Confucius' disciples
Tzŭ-ssŭ	The grandson of Confucius
Tzŭ-yu	The courtesy name of Yen Yen, one of Confucius' disciples
Tzŭ-yü	A ta-fu of the State of Chêng
Tz'ŭ, Tuan-mu	The name of Tzŭ-kung, one of Confucius' disciples
Tzŭ-hsi	A ta-fu of the State of Ch'u
Tzŭ-sang Po-tzŭ	A worthy of the State of Lu
Wai-ping	The brother of T'ai-ting
Wan Chang	One of Mencius' disciples
Wang Chi	The father of King Wên of the Chou dynasty
Wang Huan	A powerful minister in the State of Ch'i
Wang Pao	A man from the State of Wei
Wang-sun Chia	A ta-fu of the State of Wei
Wei 魏	One of the States under the Chou dynasty
Wei 衛	One of the States under the Chou dynasty
Wei, Viscount	A step-brother of the tyrant Chou of the Yin dynasty
Wei-shêng Kao	A man from the State of Lu
Wei-Shêng Mou	A recluse whom Confucius considered as his elder
Wên	The polished, the accomplished, the cultured.
Wên, Duke	A ruler of the State of Chin
Wên, King	The founder of the Chou dynasty
Wu 吳	One of the States under the Chou dynasty
Wu 武	The music of King Wu of the Chou dynasty
Wu, King	The first ruler of the Chou dynasty
Wu Huo	A strong man in ancient times
Wu-lu	One of Mencius' disciples
Wu-ma Ch'i	One of Confucius' disciples
Wu-ting	An emperor of the Yin dynasty
Yang Chu (Yang-tzŭ)	A philosopher of the Chou dynasty
Yang Fu	One of the philosopher Tsêng's disciples
Yang Hu	An official of the powerful Chi-sun family in the State of Lu

Yang Huo	An official of the powerful Chi family in the State of Lu
Yao	The great emperor of the T'ang dynasty (2357-2257 B.C.)
Yen 燕	One of the States under the Chou dynasty
Yen 奄	One of the States under the Chou dynasty
Yen Ch'ou-yu	A worthy *ta-fu* of the State of Wei
Yen P'ing-chung	A *ta-fu* of the State of Ch'i
Yen Yen	The name of Tzŭ-yu, one of Confucius' disciples
Yen Yüan	One of Confucius' disciples
Yen-tzŭ	Yen Yin, a *ta-fu* of the State of Ch'i
Yi 益	A minister under Emperor Shun
Yi 羿	A famous archer in the Hsia dynasty
Yi Yin	The great prime minister under Emperor T'ang of the Shang dynasty
Yi-ya	A famous chef in the service of Duke Huan of Ch'i
Yi-yi	The descendant of a barbarian
Yin	The new name of the Shang dynasty after 1401 B. C.
Yin Shih	A man from the State of Ch'i
Yu	One of the tyrants of the Chou dynasty
Yü 虞	One of the ancient dynasties (2205-2207 B.C.)
Yü 禹	The first emperor of the Hsia dynasty (2205-2198 B.C.)
Yü 庾	An ancient measure of capacity
Yu, Chung	The name of Tzŭ-lu, one of Confucius' disciples
Yu, the philosopher (Jan Yu, Jan Ch'iu)	One of Confucius' disciples
Yu Jo	One of Confucius' disciples
Yü-chung	Probably a descendant of Chung-yung, uncle of King Wên of the Chou dynasty
Yüan Jang	An old friend of Confucius from the State of Lu
Yüeh 越	One of the States under the Chou dynasty
Yüeh 嶽	The name of a street in a town in the State of Ch'i
Yüeh-chêng	One of Mencius' disciples
Yung, Jan	The name of Chung-kung, one of Confucius' disciples

BIBLIOGRAPHY

Chai, Ch'u and Winberg, *The Humanist Way in Ancient China: Essential Works of Confucianism*, edited and translated by. Toronto and London, Bantam Books, 1965.
Li. Chi. Two volumes. New Hyde Park, N. Y., University Books. 1967.

Couvreur, S., *Les Quatre Livres*, avec un commentaire abrégé en chinois, une double traduction en français et en latin, et un vocabulaire des lettres et des noms propres. Imprimerie de la Mission Catholique, Ho Kien fou, 2me edition, 1910.

Creel, H.G. (editor), *Literary Chinese* by the inductive method, Vol. II, Selections from the *Lun Yü*. Chicago, The. University of Chicago Press, 1939, 3rd impression, 1948.

Dobson, W.A.C., *Mencius*, a new translation arranged and annotated for the general reader by. 1963.

Ferguson, Thomas T.H., *Fragments of Confucian Lore;* a selection of short quotations, with the original text, by. Shanghai, North-China Daily News and Herald, Ltd., 1920.

Giles, Lionel, *The Sayings of Confucius*, a new translation of the greater part of the Confucian Analects, with introduction and notes. London, Wisdom of the East Series, 1907.
The Book of Mencius (abridged), translated from the Chinese by. London, J. Murray, 1942, reprinted 1949.

Hughes, E.R., *The Great Learning and the Mean-in-action*. London, Dent, 1942.

Jennings, William, *The Confucian Analects*, a translation with annotations and an introduction. London, George Routledge & Sons, n. d.

Legge, James, *The Chinese Classics,* with a translation, critical and exegetical notes, prolegomena and copious indexes. Five volumes. Hong Kong, Hong Kong University Press, 3rd edition, 1960.
The Sacred Books of China, the text of Confucianism, translated by. Four volumes. Oxford, the Clarendon Press, 1879-1885.

Lin, Yutang, *The Wisdom of Confucius*, edited and with an introduction by. New York, The Modern Library, 1938.

Lyall, Leonard A., *The Sayings of Confucius*. London, Longmans, Green 2nd edition, 1925.
Mencius, translated by. London, J. Murray, 1932.

Lyall, Leonard A., and King Chien-kün, *The Chung-Yung or The Centre, The Common*, translated by. London, Longmans, Green, 1927.

Pauthier, M.G., *Confucius et Mencius. Les Quatre Livres de Philosophie Morale et Politique de la Chine*, traduit du chinois par. Paris, G. Charpentier et Cie., 1890.

Pound, Ezra, *Confucian Analects,* reprinted by permission of the Hudson Review, New York, 1920.

Pyun Yung-tai, *Analects,* newly translated by, directly from the Chinese text. Seoul, Minjungsugwan, 1960.

Ssŭ-shu Tu-pên 四書讀本, edited by Shên Chih-fang 沈知方 and annotated by Chiang Po-ch'ien 蔣伯潛. Ch'i-ming Book Company, n. d.

Soothill, W.E., *The Analects;* or, The Coversations of Confucius with his disciples and certain others, as translated into English by. Edited by his daughter, Lady Hosie. London, Oxford University Press, H. Milford, 1937, reprinted 1951.

Upward, Allen, *Sayings of K'ung the Master,* selected, with an introduction, by. London, Wisdom of the East Series, The Orient Press, 1904.

Waley, Arthur, *The Analects of Confucius.* London, Allen and Unwin, 1938, reprinted by Vintage Books, New York, 1965.

Wilhelm, Richard, *Kung Futse, Gespräche* (Lun Yu). Jena, Eugen Diederichs, 1921; Weimar, Dietsch & Bruckner, 1945.

Wrede, Rudolf, *Worte des Konfuzius* (Aus dem Buch der Gespräche). München, Paul Hugendubel Verlag, 1942.

"Or they will say, 'We can for our sovereign form alliances with other States, so that our battles must be successful.! Such persons are nowadays called 'Good ministers,' but anciently they were called 'Robbers of the people.' If a sovereign follows not the right way, nor has mind directed to benevolence, to seek to help him engage in violence and war is to assist a Chieh.

"Although a prince, pursuing the path of the present day and not changing its practices, were the throne given to him, he could not retain it for a single day."[195]

Those who collaborate with their sovereign's wickedness and those who anticipate and excite it at least bear their sovereign fully in mind, but ministers who impose on their sovereign—those who are arrogant and usurp power—are disrespectful and act contrary to propriety. Completely deviating from their roles as ministers, they should be summarily dismissed. Hence it is said, "When the Way prevails in the empire, government will not be in the hands of the great officials."[196]

The Master said, "Tsang Wu-chung, keeping possession of Fang, asked of the duke of Lu to appoint a successor to him in his family. If it be said that he was not using force with his sovereign, I would not believe it."[197]

Confucius said, "Official emoluments have not come from the ducal House now for five generations. The government has been in the hands of the Great Officials for four generations. On this account, the descendants of the three Huan are on the decline."[198]

The chief of the Chi family was about to sacrifice to the T'ai mountain. The Master said to Jan Yu, "Can you not save him from this?" He answered, "I cannot." Confucius said, "Alas! will you say that the T'ai mountain is not so discerning as Lin Fang?"[199]

In view of the disorder prevailing among the princes of his time, Confucius could not help expressing his regrets.

The Master said, "Even the rude tribes of the east and north showed due respect to their chiefs. They are not like the States of our great land which disregard their soverigns:"[200]

When a young prince fails to govern properly and does not pay heed to the remonstrances of his ministers, who cannot retire, is it proper to banish him? Though Mencius cited an example from ancient history, he set a condition for banishment.

Kung-sun Ch'ou said, "Yi Yin said, 'I cannot be near and see him so disobedient to reason,' and therewith he banished T'ai-chia to T'ung. The people were much pleased. When T'ai-chia became virtuous, he brought him back, and the people were again much pleased.

"When worthies are ministers, may they indeed banish their sovereigns in this way when they are not virtuous?"

Mencius replied, "If they have the same purpose as Yi Yin, they may. If they have not the same purpose, it would be usurpation."[301]

When there are high ministers belonging to the ruling household, they may dethrone rulers who have committed serious faults and pay no heed to repeated remonstrances. If these ministers do not belong to the ruling household, they should retire after their counsel has been rejected. Though Yi Yin was a high minister who was not from the royal family, because of his prolonged service under T'ang he had the reputation among the people of being worthy and virtuous and completely free from selfish motives. Mencius called him the "responsible sage," due to his unequaled sense of responsibility and vigorous spirit.

King Hsüan of Ch'i asked about the office of high ministers. Mencius said, "Which high ministers is Your Majesty asking about?" "Are there differences among them?" inquired the king. "There are," was the reply. "There are the high ministers who are noble and relatives of the prince, and there are those who are of a different surname." The king said, "I beg to ask about the high ministers who are noble and relatives of the prince." Mencius answered, "If the prince has great faults, they ought to remonstrate with him, and if he does not listen to them after they have done so again and again, they ought to dethrone him."

The king on this looked moved and changed countenance. Mencius said, "Let Your Majesty not be offended. You asked me, and I dare not answer but according to truth."

The king's countenance became composed, and then begged to ask about high ministers who were of a different surname from the prince. Mencius said, "When the prince has faults, they ought to remonstrate with him; and if he does not listen to them after they have done this again and again, they ought to quit."[302]

True, the banishment of a sovereign required the purpose of a Yi Yin, but the actual dethronement had to come from a high